Rhetorical Star—the Rhetorical Star is a model used exclusively and throughout the text to provide a consistent, strategic framework for students to use in the writing process. >>

▶ **Activity**   Rhetorical Sta...

Choose an article or essay in a popular print o... or professional journal. Determine the five p... answering the following questions:

1. What is the subject?
2. Who is the primary audience? Is there a secondary audience? If so, who? What does the audience expect from the document?
3. What is the primary purpose? Does the author wish to inform, interpret, persuade, entertain, or express feelings? Has the author combined purposes? If so, which ones?
4. What strategy does the author use? Is the author narrating, describing, explaining a process, comparing or contrasting, explaining causes or effects, persuading, evaluating, or solving a problem? Is more than one strategy used? If so, what are they?
5. How is the article designed? Are headings, bullets, or visual aids included? How effective is the design?

Write Now uses a new approach and updated material to *engage the student* in a composition class. Processes are *easy to follow* and it is *clearly organized and well-designed*.

Kevin Kelly, *Andover College*

Graduate
SPOTLIGHT

Tawana Campbell, Occupational Therapy Assistant

Tawana Campbell earned a degree in occupational therapy assisting in 2008. She currently works as an occupational therapy assistant for a pediatric outpatient facility. Here's what Tawana has to say about the importance of writing in her career:

❝I take careful notes about each session I have with a patient and write a case study. I document everything that happens because the philosophy where I work is, 'If it isn't written down, it didn't happen.' When I meet with a patient, I write out an evaluation of his or her condition and needs, and I determine ways to get effective treatment. Written proof of my evaluation is necessary to persuade the insurance company that special adaptive equipment, such as a wheelchair, splint, or orthotic insert, is necessary.

Because I work with children, I have to be very creative with how I go about treatment. For example, one child had a deficiency in communication skills, so I showed him a movie and asked him to retell the plot. Another child was having problems with sensory motor skills, so I taught her to dance using her favorite songs from *High School Musical*. Also, I frequently use arts and crafts with children because something as simple as gluing a bead on a piece of construction paper is a useful task. These techniques work great for helping me to establish a good rapport with the children and evaluate their progress. They think we are just playing, but they are really working to overcome the challenges that they face. ❞

>> *Career-Based* DESCRIPTIVE WRITING

[preview] THE FOLLOWING is a description of exercise-induced asthma from **mayoclinic.com**. Have you had trouble breathing? What kinds of symptoms did you experience?

Exercise-Induced Asthma

Description
If you cough, wheeze, or feel out of breath during or after exercise, it may be more than exertion causing your symptoms. You might have exercise-induced asthma. As with asthma triggered by other things, exercise-induced asthma symptoms occur when your airways tighten and produce extra mucus.

Symptoms
Exercise-induced asthma symptoms can include:
• Coughing
• Wheezing
• Shortness of breath
• Chest tightness or pain
• Fatigue during exercise
• Poor athletic performance

Exercise-induced asthma symptoms may start a few minutes after you begin exercising. Some people have symptoms 10 to 15 minutes after finishing a workout. It's possible to have symptoms both during and after exercise.

Feeling a little short of breath or fatigued when you work out is normal, especially if you aren't in great shape. But with exercise-induced asthma, these symptoms can be more severe.

For many people, exercise is just one of a few asthma triggers. Others can include pollen, pet dander and other airborne allergens.

If you have exercise-induced asthma—also called exercise-induced bronchospasm (BRONG-ko-spaz-um)—physical exertion may be the only thing that triggers your symptoms. Or, exercise may be just one of several things that trigger your asthma. But having exercise-induced asthma doesn't mean you shouldn't exercise. Proper treatment and precautions can keep you active—whether you're strolling through the park or competing for Olympic gold.

Source: Mayo Clinic. www.mayoclinic.com/health/exercise-induced-asthma/DS01040/DSECTION=symptoms.

[QUESTIONS FOR REFLECTION]

1. What is the primary purpose of the article? Does the article achieve its purpose?
2. Which part of the article uses descriptive words? Does the article include strong sensory appeal? Explain.

3. Compare and contrast the design of this article to the design of a typical college essay. Which type of design is more effective for this type of writing? Why?
4. Why did the writer include headings? Are they useful? Why or why not?
5. What advice does the article give for people who suffer from asthma?

∧∧ **Graduate Spotlights**—testimonials of real college graduates emphasize the importance of writing in their careers.

<< **Career-Based writing examples**—each chapter in Part II has a section explaining how students will apply each writing strategy in school, in their careers, and in their personal lives. Each of these chapters includes at least one career-based writing example.

Write Now is an English composition book that does not compromise the important concepts of essay writing but *moves the material to new levels* by incorporating *career and life connections* to the writing process, *encouraging students* to see a composition course as *more than a general education requirement* but as a *necessary skill for the workforce*.

Karen Durand, *Miller-Motte College*

riteNow

efele

VICE PRESIDENT/DIRECTOR OF MARKETING **Alice Harra**

SPONSORING EDITOR **Barbara Owca**

DIRECTOR OF DEVELOPMENT **Sarah Wood**

DEVELOPMENTAL EDITOR **Kristin Bradley**

EXECUTIVE MARKETING MANAGER **Keari Green**

LEAD DIGITAL PRODUCT MANAGER **Damian Moshak**

DIGITAL DEVELOPMENT EDITOR **Kevin White**

DIRECTOR, EDITING/DESIGN/PRODUCTION **Jess Ann Kosic**

PROJECT MANAGER **Jean R. Starr**

BUYER II **Debra R. Sylvester**

SENIOR DESIGNER **Anna Kinigakis**

LEAD PHOTO RESEARCH COORDINATOR **Carrie K. Burger**

PHOTO RESEARCHER **Agate ProBooks**

MEDIA PROJECT MANAGER **Cathy L. Tepper**

OUTSIDE DEVELOPMENT HOUSE **Agate ProBooks**

COVER DESIGN **Alexa R. Viscius**

INTERIOR DESIGN **Kay Lieberherr**

TYPEFACE **11/13 Minion Pro**

COMPOSITOR **Agate ProBooks**

PRINTER **R. R. Donnelley**

CREDITS **The credits section for this book begins on page 433 and is considered an extension of the copyright page.**

WRITE NOW

Published by McGraw-Hill, a business unit of The McGraw-Hill Companies, Inc., 1221 Avenue of the Americas, New York, NY, 10020. Copyright © 2012 by The McGraw-Hill Companies, Inc. All rights reserved. No part of this publication may be reproduced or distributed in any form or by any means, or stored in a database or retrieval system, without the prior written consent of The McGraw-Hill Companies, Inc., including, but not limited to, in any network or other electronic storage or transmission, or broadcast for distance learning.

Some ancillaries, including electronic and print components, may not be available to customers outside the United States.

This book is printed on acid-free paper.

1 2 3 4 5 6 7 8 9 0 DOW/DOW 1 0 9 8 7 6 5 4 3 2 1

ISBN   978-0-07-339707-8
MHID   0-07-339707-5

Library of Congress Cataloging in Publication Data

Library of Congress Control Number: 2010939984

The Internet addresses listed in the text were accurate at the time of publication. The inclusion of a Web site does not indicate an endorsement by the authors or McGraw-Hill, and McGraw-Hill does not guarantee the accuracy of the information presented at these sites.

www.mhhe.com

ABOUT THE AUTHOR

Karin Russell is a college English teacher whose experience in helping students achieve success has spanned more than twenty years. Russell earned her undergraduate degree in Elementary Education at Stetson University and her master's degree in Reading and Language Arts Education at The Florida State University. She continued her education in the English field by earning thirty-six graduate credit hours beyond the master's degree. She has taught composition and literature courses for various Florida schools, including Brevard Community College, Nova Southeastern University, and several career colleges.

For more than fifteen years, Russell has been a full-time English instructor for Keiser University, where she is the University Department Chair for English, humanities, fine arts, and communications. She oversees curriculum development for a variety of writing, literature, and communication courses. She has been named an Instructor of Distinction four years in a row. She also serves as a member of the assessment committee and the Keiser Writes leadership team and as a faculty advisor to Phi Theta Kappa, a student leadership organization. Russell is especially interested in enabling students to develop their writing skills through a process-oriented approach and showing students how writing is applicable to their future careers. She passionately believes that nearly anyone can become a good writer with the right instruction and enough practice.

On a personal note, Karin Russell loves spending time with her loving husband, Todd, their amazing son, Cody, and their wonderful rescue dogs and cats. She also enjoys creating stained glass art pieces, riding her motorcycle and scooter, traveling about the U.S. in her family's RV, and reading multicultural novels. The author would like to extend a special thank you to Scott Clements and Sally Hudson for their insights.

KARIN L. RUSSELL

WriteNow

BRIEF TABLE OF CONTENTS

CH. 1
GETTING STARTED
WITH WRITING

∧ **CH. 13**
PLANNING AND
WRITING A
RESEARCH PAPER

< **CH. 6**
DESCRIBING:
MEDIA AND
POPULAR CULTURE

CH. 11 >
EVALUATING:
FILM AND THE
ARTS

Table of Contents

PART 1 INTRODUCTION TO WRITING

7 > Explaining a Process: Cultures and Traditions 138

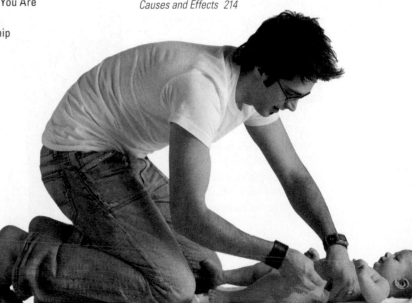

PART 4 EDITING GUIDE

Chapter 1

You will have an opportunity to create a writing environment that best suits your personality. You will also learn how to assess your rhetorical (or writing) situation.

Chapter 2

You will discover some strategies that work for you as you participate in the steps of the writing process to produce a final, polished document. You'll also see how a student writer went through the entire writing process.

Chapter 3

You will learn some methods for writing well-organized sentences, paragraphs, and essays.

Chapter 4

You will gain a better understanding of the connection between critical thinking, reading, and writing, and you will learn some strategies for applying critical thinking skills to analyze written and visual texts as well as Web sites.

PART 1

Introduction to Writing

Why Writing Is Important for Success

Writing effectively is an important skill, one that you can take with you and use for the rest of your life. To be successful in college, in your career, and in your life, you will need to be able to communicate effectively through writing. Whether you are composing a report for your boss, a paper for an instructor, or a letter to resolve a personal matter, being able to write well is essential. The good news is that you don't have to be naturally gifted to learn to become a strong writer. You can develop your writing skills by studying and practicing writing. Whether you are seventeen or seventy-seven, you have something worthwhile to say that others will be interested in reading. As you read *Write Now*, you will learn and practice many valuable techniques that will help you to become a better reader, critical thinker, and writer so that you are able to interpret and communicate messages in an effective manner. Those skills will help you to accomplish your educational, career, and personal goals.

CHAPTER 1

GETTING STARTED WITH WRITING

1.1 > Creating An Ideal Writing Environment

Even if you haven't had much success with writing in the past, you can become a good writer at school, on the job, and in your personal life. Your academic history doesn't define your future as a writer. Through this course, you will learn and apply many strategies that will strengthen your writing skills so you can say something worthwhile in a way that readers will find interesting. Instead of feeling overwhelmed by writing assignments, you will learn to break them into manageable tasks. Take a moment to visualize yourself writing a strong paper, one that you can proudly submit to your instructor or boss.

One way to help you achieve success is to create a comfortable writing atmosphere that contains everything you need to accomplish your task. Whether you are taking your class on campus or online, here are some steps to help you find your writing groove.

1. Find a Good Place to Write

Try writing in different places to discover where you experience the most success. Do you work better at home, in a library, in an empty classroom, outside, or in a café? Choose a place that won't be too distracting, whether at home or away from home. If you can't find a peaceful place, try listening to something soothing on your iPod to reduce outside interference.

2. Plan Your Time to Write

What time of day are you the sharpest? Do you like to compose first thing in the morning, or does your brain get fired up in the middle of the night? Try to structure your writing time when you are likely to develop your best work. If your busy life prevents you from writing at the opportune time, then learn to adapt your writing habits to your schedule. Though it may not be ideal, you can write a little bit at a time if necessary. For example, you might be able to write during your commute (if you're not driving) or even while waiting at the dentist's office. With the right attitude, you can be productive in nearly any environment at any time. Instead of making excuses for not having time to write, use the time that you do have wisely. Consider using a paper or digital planner to plan time to write. Look for gaps in your schedule. If it's in your planner, you are less likely to fill that time with other, less productive tasks such as hanging out with friends or watching television.

3. Select Your Materials

Before you begin writing, assemble the materials you will need. Some writers like to brainstorm ideas on paper. If that's your style, do you prefer a legal pad, spiral notebook, or fancy journal? Do you have a favorite pencil or pen? Also, have a dictionary and thesaurus nearby. Dictionary.com and Thesaurus.com are excellent Web-based resources.

Other writers are comfortable starting right in with a computer. Make sure you have enough battery strength or a power supply so you won't lose momentum by having to stop writing. Choose a font style, color, and size that make you comfortable during the composing process. You can always change them before you submit your work.

4. Establish a Method for Saving Your Work

Whether you are writing on paper or on a computer, you'll need a backup system. What happens if you lose the folder or notebook that has your assignment in it? Make a copy of written assignments. If you compose your assignment on a computer, then don't just trust your hard drive. Save a copy to a CD, flash drive, or other data-storage device. You can even e-mail your assignment to yourself as an extra precaution so that it is stored safely in cyberspace.

For an online class, compose your assignments in a word-processing program (such as Word or Pages). Then copy and paste them into the online course platform. That way if you lose your Internet connection, or if the course system goes down while you are trying to post your assignment, you won't lose your work.

5. Create an Inviting Atmosphere

Determine what kind of environment most inspires you to write. Do you prefer order or chaos? Do you like bright or soft lighting? Do you prefer complete silence, or does listening to music help you to think clearly? Are you most comfortable sitting at a desk, or are you more creative on the sofa? Try different scenarios to see what kind of ambience helps you produce your best work.

6. Minimize Distractions

If you live with other people, ask them to give you some time for writing without interruptions. If you have children, maybe someone else could watch them while you write. Also, you will probably benefit from turning off your TV and cell phone. Try to focus all of your energy on what you are writing so that you can concentrate and do your best work.

Sometimes you won't have an opportunity to choose your writing environment, such as when you're writing an in-class essay or when you're at work. If that's the case, do what you can to minimize distractions. Try to distance yourself from people with annoying habits, such as pen clicking or humming. Sit away from the door if noises from the hallway are likely to bother you. As you develop your writing skills, also work on learning to tune out distractions so that you are able to write in a variety of circumstances.

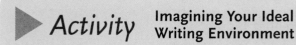
1.2 > Analyzing the Rhetorical Star: The Star Approach

FIGURE 1.1
The Rhetorical Star

The term *rhetoric* simply refers to the art of communicating effectively through writing or speaking. Whether you are writing an essay for school, a report for your boss, or an e-mail to your friend, your goal is to convey a message to the reader. You want to be sure that your reader understands the intent of your message. Therefore, every time you sit down to write, you need to consider five points of the rhetorical star: subject, audience, purpose, strategy, and design.

This is the "rhetorical star." Each point of the star is an essential component of your final written product. Using the rhetorical star will help to ensure that effective communication takes place.

Subject

You need to determine what topic to cover. What is the specific message that you want to convey to your readers? Choose an appropriate subject that fits within the parameters of your assignment. Make sure your topic is narrow enough that you can adequately cover it in your document. For example, you wouldn't be able to cover the entire subject of "staying fit" in a short paper, but you could adequately cover a few specific fitness techniques.

FIGURE 1.2   Subject

As you consider what you want to say and how much detail you want to include, keep your purpose and audience in mind. You might think about what your readers will already know about your subject and what they might want to learn. Also, consider whether research is necessary for you to adequately cover your topic.

Audience

Consider your readers. Are you writing for a particular *discourse community* (a group of people who share common interests, knowledge, and values related to a particular subject)? Each of us belongs to a number of discourse communities such as school clubs, social or religious groups, and professional organizations. Each group has its own vocabulary and conventions of communication, called *jargon*. For example, if you are writing a software review for members of the computer club, you can probably safely assume that they will understand terms that are specific to the computer world, such as *bits* and *bytes*. Similarly, if you are writing a letter to members of a certain professional field, such as health care or homeland security, you won't need to explain concepts related to that field.

FIGURE 1.3   Audience

Keep in mind the needs and interests of your primary audience, but realize that others (your secondary audience) might also read your document. Here are some audience characteristics to consider when you are writing:

Some audience characteristics will matter more than others depending on your subject and purpose. For example, if you are writing an article about a

TABLE 1.1

Audience Characteristics		
Age	Experience	Opinions
Beliefs	Gender	Political views
Cultural background	Interests	Reading ability
Education level	Knowledge of the subject	Religion
Ethnicity	Occupation	Socioeconomic status

work-related topic that will be published in your company's newsletter, your readers' interests and knowledge of the subject would be more important than their gender and cultural background. If most of the readers are employees, then you can use the vocabulary that is specific to your career field. If, on the other hand, the newsletter is geared more for your organization's clients, then you may need to explain specialized terms in more detail and consider other audience characteristics.

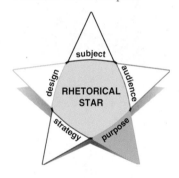

FIGURE 1.4   Purpose

Purpose

Determine your reason for writing. Why are you writing? What are you hoping to accomplish? What effect do you wish to have on your audience? Whether you are composing a class assignment, workplace document, or personal letter, your writing will meet at least one of five main purposes: inform, interpret, persuade, entertain, and express feelings.

1. Writing to Inform   Most writing is informative in some way. When you write to inform, your goal is to provide readers with useful information about your subject or teach them how to do something. For example, you might write an essay summarizing an article or a story you have read, a set of instructions explaining how to perform a workplace procedure, or a recipe for making your grandmother's special chili.

2. Writing to Interpret   Sometimes writing can help you or your audience better understand something. For example, you might write an essay interpreting (analyzing) a poem for a literature class, or you may write a comparison of two software packages that your boss is considering implementing. When you write interpretatively, you are giving your opinions about the subject rather than just reporting information. Sometimes your interpretation may include an evaluation of your subject. For instance, you might write an evaluation of an employee or a review of a movie you have seen.

>> *Netiquette*

You should always use proper *netiquette* (Internet etiquette) when communicating with your instructor via e-mail.

1. Use an appropriate screen name (e-mail address) that includes your name.
2. Write a clear subject heading.
3. Address your instructor professionally.
4. Write your message clearly and concisely. If you have questions, make them specific.
5. Use standard grammar, capitalization, and punctuation.
6. Avoid using all capital letters. This is considered shouting.
7. Maintain a professional tone.
8. End with a polite closing and your name.

Poor Netiquette

From: hotsexymamma@email.com
To: mwilliams@starsuniversity.edu
Subject: class

hey teach
i'm confuzed about the paper cuz i stayed up partying 2 late and blew off class what am i posed to do i can't afford to fail this class again HELP ME!!!!!!!!!!
BTW you better not bust me for turning it in late

Good Netiquette

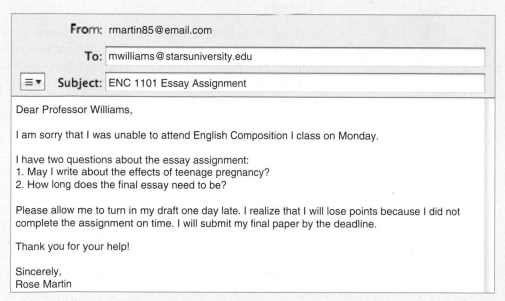

From: rmartin85@email.com
To: mwilliams@starsuniversity.edu
Subject: ENC 1101 Essay Assignment

Dear Professor Williams,

I am sorry that I was unable to attend English Composition I class on Monday.

I have two questions about the essay assignment:
1. May I write about the effects of teenage pregnancy?
2. How long does the final essay need to be?

Please allow me to turn in my draft one day late. I realize that I will lose points because I did not complete the assignment on time. I will submit my final paper by the deadline.

Thank you for your help!

Sincerely,
Rose Martin

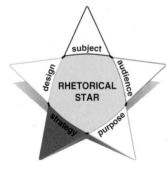

3. Writing to Persuade Although almost any type of writing needs to be convincing, sometimes your main purpose is to argue a point. For example, you might write an essay arguing for or against a proposed law, or you might submit a letter to your boss convincing him or her why you deserve a raise. Other times you may want to persuade your readers to actually do something. For instance, you might challenge your readers to do more than just recycle to help preserve the environment for future generations.

4. Writing to Entertain Some types of writing are primarily intended to entertain the readers. You might choose to write a creative story, poem, cartoon, or song lyrics to move your readers or make them laugh. Often you can entertain your readers at the same time that you address another purpose. You might want to use humor in an informative or persuasive paper to help engage your readers in the material being covered.

5. Writing to Express Feelings You can use personal expression in many ways. You might write a note to someone special, an essay about an exciting or scary event you experienced, a reaction to a magazine or newspaper article, or a letter to your landlord expressing your dissatisfaction with the length of time it is taking to get your leaky faucet repaired.

Combined Purposes The five purposes for writing are not mutually exclusive; they overlap. For instance, if you are writing an essay as part of an application for a scholarship, you may address three purposes by informing the readers about your background and situation, expressing your feelings about how much you need the scholarship and how grateful you would be to receive it, and persuading your readers that you are a worthy recipient of the scholarship.

Strategy

FIGURE 1.5 Strategy

You'll need to choose an approach that best serves your purpose and audience. In this textbook you will learn about eight major writing strategies: narrating, describing, explaining a process, comparing or contrasting, explaining causes or effects, persuading, solving a problem, and evaluating. On the opposite page is a quick overview of the different strategies.

Once you have determined your strategy, you'll also need to consider your tone and level of formality.

- **Tone:** *Tone* is the mood or feeling you are trying to create through your writing. Your tone can be businesslike (serious), academic, humorous, or opinionated. Choose a tone that is appropriate for your purpose and audience.

- **Level of formality:** Your writing style can be *formal* or *informal*. Formal writing tends to be more serious than informal writing. The use of contractions (such as *I'm* and *doesn't*) is usually limited. Spell out complete words and choose your words carefully. On the other hand, informal writing, such as the writing in this book, tends to be fairly casual. Contractions are acceptable and can help the writing to not sound too stuffy. You would likely use a more formal approach in a report for your boss than you would for an e-mail to a co-worker. In school, a research essay would be much more formal than a journal entry.

Design

FIGURE 1.6 Design

Finally, think about how you are going to design your document. Consider the design expectations of your instructor or boss and the discourse community for which you are writing. Determine the genre, format, length, appearance, and visual aids that are appropriate for your document.

TABLE 1.2

Writing Strategies	
Narrating	Tell a story about something that happened. Usually you will present the details of the event in chronological order, but occasionally a flashback can be useful. Be sure to cover *who, what, where, when, why, and how.*
Describing	Use words to paint a picture of an object, scene, or event for your audience using as many senses as are appropriate for your subject: sight, sound, taste, smell, touch. Include colorful adjectives to give your reader a clear impression of the subject.
Explaining a Process	Tell how something works or what something does. You may give step-by-step instructions so your reader can perform the task, or you can write an explanation so that your audience is able to understand your subject.
Comparing or Contrasting	Show how two people, places, or objects are similar and/or different. Be sure to make a worthwhile point while doing this.
Explaining Causes or Effects	Examine how one event or situation caused another to occur, or determine the effects of an event or situation. Be careful to apply sound logic as you analyze causes and effects.
Persuading	Take a stand about an important or controversial issue, and convince your reader that your position is valid. You may use personal experience or research to support your main idea.
Evaluating	Make a judgment about your subject by determining how well it meets specific criteria that you feel are important for that subject.
Solving a Problem	Explain a problem to your reader and offer several solutions. You may evaluate each possible solution before persuading your reader that one specific solution is best.

- **Genre:** What type of document do you need to write? Determine the genre that is most appropriate for your task: story, essay, research paper, letter, e-mail, memo, advertisement, flyer, Web site, blog, and so on. Most of the writing you do in college will be in essay form.

- **Format:** How should you structure your writing? Some instructors may allow you to turn in handwritten informal assignments, but others will require that you use a computer to write all assignments. Be sure to follow your instructor's guidelines very closely. Also, you may need to adhere to Modern Language Association (MLA) or American Psychological Association (APA) guidelines, especially if you are writing a paper based on research. See Chapters 13 and 14 for more information about writing and documenting research papers.

- **Length:** How long should your document be? Is there a word or page minimum (or limit)? If your instructor does not specify a length, then let the topic guide you. Be sure to fully develop each point that you want to make.

- **Appearance:** How should your document look? Find out if you need to single-space or double-space your papers. Typically, if you single-space a paper, you will begin each paragraph at the left margin. However, if you double-space a paper, you will need to indent each paragraph. Choose a font size, style, and color that are appropriate for your writing situation. Also, determine if you can use headings, bullets, columns, or boxes to emphasize your main points.

- **Visual aids:** Would adding visual aids enhance your paper? Often pictures, diagrams, charts, or graphs will help get your ideas across to your audience. For example, if you are including a variety of statistics in a research paper, then you may decide to include a chart or graph to help the reader visualize the impact of the concept you are portraying.

> article
"BE OUR GUEST. PLEASE."

Preview

"Be Our Guest. Please" appeared in the May 25, 2009 issue of *BusinessWeek*. As you read, notice the five points of the rhetorical star: subject, audience, purpose, strategy, and design. After you finish reading the article, look at the rhetorical star analysis that follows. You'll complete your own rhetorical star analysis with a different article afterward.

BE OUR GUEST. PLEASE

Pool passes for locals, contests for upgrades, free food, even rooms set aside for post-op patients. Hotel operators, desperate for business, are turning to all sorts of tricks. "Every guest has become important, every niche segment has become important," says hospitality researcher Bjorn Hanson at New York University.

U.S. hoteliers are suffering from the sharpest slide since the September 11, 2001, attacks. Industrywide, revenue per available room is down 20% from last spring–down 30% for luxury hotels, Hanson says. And occupancy rates are likely to slip to under 56% this year, from about 60% last year and 63% in 2007,

55.7%

Predicted 2009 occupancy rate for the U.S. hotel industry, down from 60% last year and 63% in 2007

Data PKF Hospital Research

according to Atlanta-based PKF Hospitality Research.

Thus the aggressive promotions. Dozens of Ritz-Carlton hotels are offering guests up to $200 worth of free food and spa services, depending on length of stay. The Four Seasons Hotel in Houston is appealing to locals, selling $20 weekend and holiday "daycation" passes to its outdoor pool, where attendants spritz patrons hourly with Evian water. Starwood Hotels & Resorts Worldwide, parent of the Westin and Sheraton brands, is charging guests based on their birth year for second and third night stays at some locations. (Customers born in 1960, for example, pay $60.) The Kimpton Hotel & Restaurant Group is advertising free room upgrades at check-in this summer for guests who can hulahoop for 20 seconds or win a game of rock, paper, scissors. And perhaps taking a cue from Los Angeles hotels that cater to plastic surgery patients, the Fairmont Chicago is offering post-operative recuperation rooms in partnership with the Neurologic & Orthopedic Hospital of Chicago. Post-surgical guests can bring their own nurses, physical therapists, and doctors to their rooms. The Fairmont's owner, Strategic Hotels & Resorts, has been publicizing a recent stay by Phyllis Coors, a member of the brewing family, who was a post-op guest for 10 days after traveling from Colorado for a double knee replacement. The company plans similar hospital partnerships in California—at its Loews Santa Monica, for instance. Industry experts say wooing such patients is risky, since hotel guests want to feel they're at a getaway, not a convalescent home. But Strategic Hotels CEO Laurence Geller isn't anticipating problems. "It's such a small but profitable population," he says. —*Joseph Weber and Christopher Palmeri*

MICHAEL WITTE

MAY 25, 2009 | **BUSINESSWEEK**

SOURCE: J. Weber and P. Christopher, "Be Our Guest. Please," *BusinessWeek*, May 25, 2009, p. 11.

Model Rhetorical Star Analysis of "Be Our Guest. Please"

Subject	Hotels are suffering financially, so they are experimenting with creative ways to draw in more guests.
Audience	The primary audience consists of people who are interested in current business trends and like to read *BusinessWeek*. A secondary audience includes readers who might be interested in staying in an upscale hotel for a good rate. The audience would expect to learn something about the status of the hotel industry.
Purpose	The main purpose is to inform readers about the unique strategies hotels are using to lure customers.
Strategy	The primary strategy is explaining cause and effect. The drop in revenue has caused hotels to find alternative methods of earning money. Additionally, the author compares and contrasts the strategies and prices of several different hotels.
Design	Nearly half of the article consists of a cartoon drawing that illustrates some of the concepts presented in the article, such as a customer being sprayed with Evian water and a patient receiving care while recuperating from surgery. The cartoon is colorful and detailed. The text is blocked into short, single-spaced, indented paragraphs. Columns are used to break up the text. One statistic is separated from the others in a box. A chart might have been useful to compare the other statistics, but isn't included. Overall, its design is very appealing.

> ▶ **Activity** **Rhetorical Star Analysis**

Choose an article or essay in a popular print or online newspaper, magazine, or professional journal. Determine the five points of the rhetorical star by answering the following questions:

1. What is the subject?

2. Who is the primary audience? Is there a secondary audience? If so, who? What does the audience expect from the document?

3. What is the primary purpose? Does the author wish to inform, interpret, persuade, entertain, or express feelings? Has the author combined purposes? If so, which ones?

4. What strategy does the author use? Is the author narrating, describing, explaining a process, comparing or contrasting, explaining causes or effects, persuading, evaluating, or solving a problem? Is more than one strategy used? If so, what are they?

5. How is the article designed? Are headings, bullets, or visual aids included? How effective is the design?

[CHAPTER SUMMARY]

1. Increase your chances for success by creating an ideal atmosphere for writing.

2. Every time you write, consider the five points of the rhetorical star: subject, audience, purpose, strategy, and design.

3. Choose an interesting and useful subject for your paper.

4. Consider your audience's needs and expectations as you write your document.

5. The five purposes for writing are to inform, interpret, persuade, entertain, and express feelings.

6. Choose a writing strategy that best suits your purpose and audience. Narrating, describing, explaining a process, comparing or contrasting, explaining causes or effects, persuading, solving a problem, and evaluating are all popular writing strategies.

7. Use an effective and appealing design for your document.

[WHAT I KNOW NOW]

Use this checklist to determine what you need to work on to feel comfortable with your understanding of the material in this chapter. Check off each item as you master it. Review the material for any unchecked items.

- ❏ **1.** I am ready to create my own **ideal writing environment**.
- ❏ **2.** I know the five points of the **rhetorical star**.
- ❏ **3.** I can choose an interesting and useful **subject**.
- ❏ **4.** I am aware of important **audience** characteristics to consider.
- ❏ **5.** I understand the five **purposes** for writing.
- ❏ **6.** I know what the eight **writing strategies** are.
- ❏ **7.** I know how to choose an effective document **design**.

[FURTHER READING ON THE WEB]

- ▪ Explore Writing: **www.explorewriting.co.uk/CreatingAWritingEnvironment.html**
- ▪ The Rhetorical Situation: **http://owl.english.purdue.edu/owl/resource/625/01/**
- ▪ Audience Analysis: **http://owl.english.purdue.edu/owl/resource/629/01/**
- ▪ Rhetorical Strategies for Essay Writing: **www.nvcc.edu/home/lshulman/rhetoric.htm**
- ▪ College Writing Info: **www.tc.umn.edu/~jewel001/CollegeWriting/home.htm**

2

THE WRITING
PROCESS

In this chapter you will learn techniques for the following:

2.1 Discovering ideas about a topic.

2.2: Planning and organizing a document.

2.3: Composing a document.

2.4: Getting appropriate feedback on a document.

2.5: Revising a document.

2.6: Editing a document.

2.7: Proofreading a document.

> # Following the Writing Process

After you have analyzed your rhetorical star (see Chapter 1), it's time to start writing. Just like you need to find your own ideal writing environment, you will need to find the writing process that works well for you. The seven steps to the writing process are (1) discovering, (2) planning, (3) composing, (4) getting feedback, (5) revising, (6) editing, and (7) proofreading. Learning to apply these seven steps will help you find the methods that work best for your writing process.

Writing can be a messy process, so you won't always follow all of the steps in sequence. Sometimes you might get to the composing step and decide you need more supporting points, which will take you back to the discovering step. Also, the steps are flexible. Some writers are comfortable beginning with the planning or even composing step while others prefer to try a number of discovering techniques before writing. Try different strategies to learn what works well for you. Continue working through the steps of the writing process until you are satisfied with your paper—or at least until your deadline arrives.

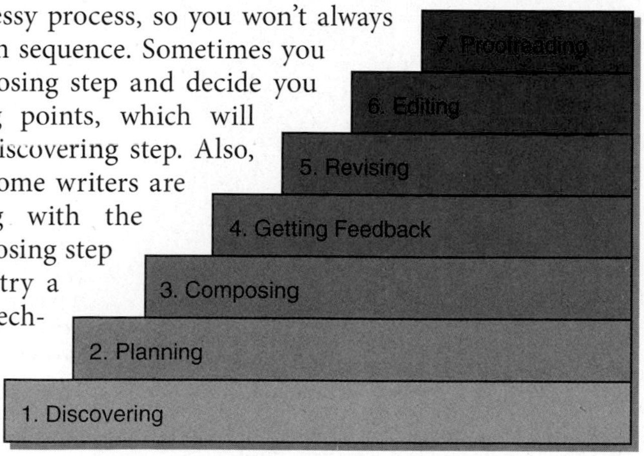

FIGURE 2.1 The Seven Steps of the Writing Process

7. Proofreading
6. Editing
5. Revising
4. Getting Feedback
3. Composing
2. Planning
1. Discovering

2.1 > Discovering

During this step you will explore your subject. You have several options for going about the discovery process. Your goal is to come up with a topic and generate ideas about it. Have you ever experienced writer's block? Try these suggestions to see what works to help you overcome that ominous blank piece of paper or computer screen.

Brainstorming Write whatever comes to mind about your topic. If you don't have a topic, then use this approach to generate one. You can write all over the page if you like. Use arrows, boxes, question marks, boxes, circles, doodles, or whatever you can think of to explore ideas. Don't worry about writing in complete sentences or organizing your ideas. Just let your creativity spill onto the page.

Amanda Laudato chose to write an essay for her English composition class about the influential musician Eminem. Here are her brainstorming notes:

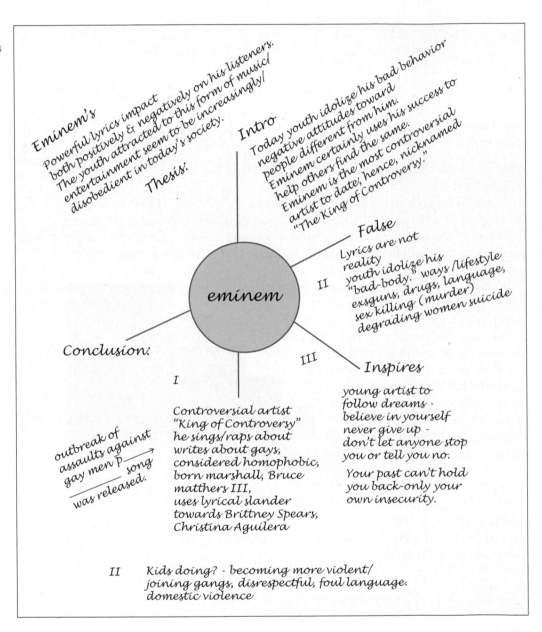

FIGURE 2.2
Brainstorming Notes

Listing List all the ideas that you can think of that relate to your subject. Listing is different from brainstorming because it's focused on a specific topic. There are no wrong ideas at this point. Keep writing for about 10 minutes. Then review your list to see which ideas you like and which you want to eliminate. Put an "X" next to items you think won't be useful, but don't cross them out because you may change your mind. You may find that some items on your list stand out as being main ideas and others would make good supporting points. If that's the case, your list will be helpful during the planning stage.

Here's a sample list on the subject of having a career rather than just a job:

greater financial reward	higher level of competence required
better attitude	long term instead of short term
higher interest level	larger contribution to the community
greater self-esteem	greater sense of satisfaction
better potential for development	using talents to do something well
learning experience	professionalism necessary
more required skills and training	higher education required
more advancement opportunities	status symbol

Freewriting Take 10 or 15 minutes to write everything that comes to mind about your topic. This discovery method is like brainstorming and listing except that you use complete sentences when you **freewrite**. Don't worry about grammar or punctuation; just keep writing. When finished, look at what you have written to see if you have stumbled upon any ideas that you would like to develop further. You might try a second freewriting session using one of the ideas you came up with during the first one.

> **Freewrite** Unstructured writing for a set amount of time.

Here's a sample freewriting exercise that Roberto Gonzales completed on his laptop computer in about 12 minutes during his English composition class:

Job vs Career
by Roberto Gonzales

A job is something you have to do. You need money to pay your bills and to eat and a job usually gets you there. A job is usually a way to get your foot in the door or to experiment with what you really like or don't like. Something might be fun for a few hours, but eight hours of such work might cause a change in your perspective.

A career is a ladder. You know where you want to be and you know you have to climb to get there. A career is more than a paycheck, but where you choose to make your contribution to society. In a career small things matter more… who you work for, what people think, are good are you doing compared to something else trying to climb that same ladder.

For most, their work experience starts with jobs. Not many people want to make food fast joint or supermarket a career. You make a little cash, meet people, and start learning to develop a work ethic. Once you're finished school and obtained an appropriate certification or degree, then the focus shifts unto a career. Some place you will end up working for a long time; that will provide you with the means to have a family and fund the American dream. A career is that security blanket that allows you to not worry so much about a job, but gives you the assurance that you're going places and that each step of that ladder equals a better life for you and your family.

Questioning Consider the journalist's questions as you try to discover ideas about your subject: Who? What? When? Where? Why? How? Write everything you can think of for each question. Afterward, you can decide which ideas seem relevant and you would like to investigate further. Use your answers as a starting point for your essay. This technique works especially well for informative pieces, narrative writing (storytelling), and problem solving.

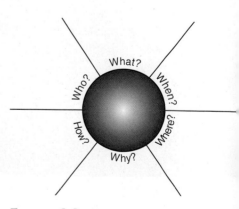

FIGURE 2.3
Journalist's Questions

Journaling Begin keeping a daily writer's journal (paper or electronic) where you jot down ideas that pop into your head. These ideas can be related to an assignment you are pondering or just general thoughts you have that you might like to explore later. You can use your journal to reflect on your feelings about yourself and your surroundings.

You might write about events from your past and consider how these events have affected you or others. You may even want to predict what could happen in the future. When journaling, don't worry about grammar or sentence structure; just let your ideas flow and see where they lead you. Reread your journal entries in search of ideas to expand on for your assignments.

Sketching Even if you don't have an artistic side, you may find that doodling or drawing will help you generate ideas about your topic, especially if you are a visual person. A simple stick figure sketch might help you visualize your subject and give you material you can write about later. You might write captions for your drawings so that when you review them later you'll remember what you had in mind when you were creating them.

Talking You may find it useful to bounce your ideas off classmates, friends, co-workers, or family members. Tell them about your assignment and the ideas you have about approaching the task. You may come up with a brilliant idea while you are talking about your assignment, or someone else may say something that sparks your interest. Either way, just hearing the ideas being spoken can stimulate your creativity. Additionally, you might seek out someone who is familiar with the subject of your paper. Ask the person questions to learn more about your subject. He or she might be able to help you focus your topic.

Reading Sometimes you may find it helpful to read what others have written about your topic. Printed or online books, magazines, newspapers, or professional journals can serve as great resources for an assignment. This is particularly true for a research essay. Seeing the approach that others have taken can enable you to formulate your own ideas. If you do decide to use someone else's words or ideas in your paper, be sure to cite your sources appropriately to avoid plagiarism. (See Part 3 to learn more about documenting sources).

Viewing Often you'll find that looking at a photograph, painting, advertisement, television show, film, or Web site will stir your emotions and inspire you to write. If you are having trouble coming up with a topic for a writing assignment, you might think about something you have seen recently that caught your attention. Or you could surf the Web to look for an intriguing subject. You might also watch the History Channel or Discovery Channel to get ideas for papers. As with printed sources, you will need to document visual sources if you use specific details from them in your writing (see Part 3).

What ideas come to mind when you look at this image?

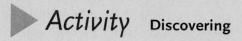

► Activity Discovering

Choose one of the following topics:

education	music	computers
health	movies	celebrities
pets	commercials	fashion
vacations	sports	musicians
crime	cuisine	medicine

Try one or more of the discovery techniques, such as brainstorming, listing, freewriting, questioning, or sketching, to see how many ideas you can come up with that relate to your topic in 5 to 10 minutes. Be prepared to share your findings.

2.2 > Planning

After you have discovered your topic and some supporting ideas, you will want to plan your essay. Having a plan will help you write a better finished product. Begin to organize what you came up with during the discovering stage. Also, remember to keep your rhetorical star (subject, audience, purpose, strategy, and design) in mind. Here are some planning techniques to try.

Narrowing Your Focus Often the ideas that writers generate during the discovery stage of the writing process are too broad to fully develop in a short paper. For example, "cooking" is too broad of a subject to write about in a short paper; however, you could focus an essay on "tips for healthy cooking." Have a tentative thesis in mind as you plan your essay. You can change your thesis later if you come up with a better concept.

► Activity Narrowing Your Focus

When you generate potential subjects for essays, you'll find that many are too broad to adequately cover in a short essay. When that happens, it's time to narrow your focus.

EXAMPLE
Broad Topic: Computers
Narrowed Topic: How computers influence the writing process

Narrow the focus of several of the following topics to make them suitable for a short essay:

careers	fitness
music	student organizations
entertainment	drugs
sports	business
natural disasters	terrorist events
laws	movies
college	children

Determining Main Points After your focus is clear, decide what main points you want to cover in your essay. You will need enough main points to fully support your thesis. While there is no "correct" number of main points, having three to five main points in an essay often works well. Choose your main points carefully. The next activity can help you determine your main points.

Clustering Write your topic in the center of the page and draw a circle around it. Draw several lines out from your topic. At the end of each line, write a main idea and circle it. Then draw lines radiating out from each main idea. At the end of each line, write supporting ideas that relate to the circled word it connects to and so on. One clustering exercise might lead to another. For instance, you may find that you have a lot to say about one of your main points and decide to shift your focus to just that main point. Then you may cluster again, this time putting the new idea in the center of the page. Clustering is a great way to begin to organize your ideas because it helps you to see the relationships among ideas. For example, if you are writing an essay about why your trip to the Bahamas was the best vacation you ever went on, your cluster might look like this:

FIGURE 2.4
Sample Cluster

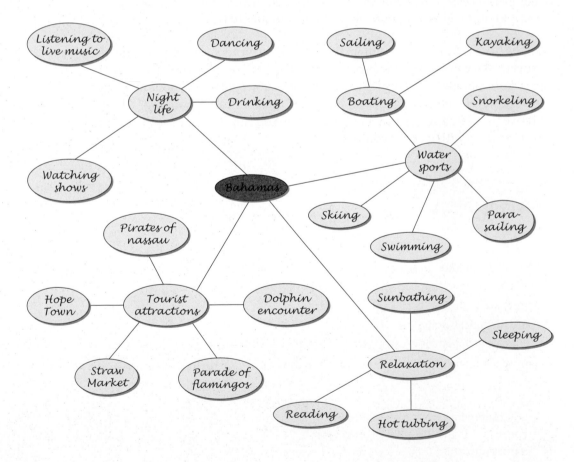

▶ *Activity* Clustering

Choose one of the following topics, or one that you used in a previous activity, and narrow it down to a smaller subtopic. For example, if you chose "exercise" as your topic, your subtopic might be "winter sports."

television shows	music artists
recreational activities	hobbies
exercise	magazines
MP3 players	video games
transportation	computers

Create a cluster diagram for your topic. Make sure that you have at least three or four headings radiating out from your main topic. If you find that you have a lot of ideas for one heading but not the others, you may want to begin again using that one as your main topic.

Creating a Graphic Organizer Developing graphic organizers can help you plan and organize your essays. They can enable you to see the relationships among your ideas so that you can put them into a logical order before composing your first draft.

Here are some examples of graphic organizers you can use for the various writing strategies covered in this textbook. You may modify them as needed to fit your specific writing assignments and preferences.

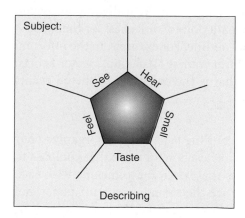

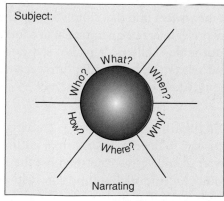

FIGURE 2.5 Sample Graphic Organizers

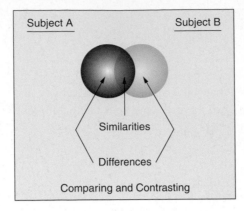

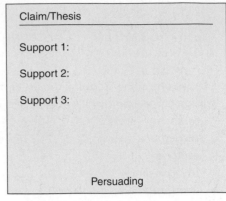

Subject:	
Criteria	Support
1.	
2.	
3.	
4.	
5.	

Evaluating

Problem:	
Solution 1	
Pros	Cons
Solution 2	
Pros	Cons
Solution 3	
Pros	Cons
Conclusion:	

Solving a Problem

Ordering Ideas After you've completed a cluster or rough graphic organizer, you'll need to decide how to arrange your main points logically in your paper. Some writers find that simply listing the main points works best for them. Others prefer to create an informal or a formal outline. For example, in the informal outline that follows, it makes sense to cover tourist attractions, water sports, and relaxation before nightlife because that is the order in which the events would likely occur.

Outlining One purpose for creating an outline is to help you organize your writing. To develop an informal outline, note each main point that you plan to cover in your essay, and then list the ideas that you want to include with each point. An informal outline can help you see the structure of your paper, but it is less detailed and cumbersome than a formal outline. Although you don't necessarily need to include the introduction or conclusion on your outline, you will need them for your final essay. (See Chapter 3 for more details about essay structure.)

Some writers prefer to use a formal outline, and some instructors require students to write one. A formal outline has more structure than an informal one. To develop a formal outline, assign each main point in your essay a Roman numeral, I, II, III, and so on. Then break down each idea into at least two parts (supporting points) and label those A, B, C, and so on.

Continue breaking down points as needed (see next page), but remember that you always have to have at least two points when you subdivide your ideas. In other words, an "A" must be followed by a "B," and a "1" must be followed by a "2." Capitalize the first word of each line and all proper nouns.

Sample Informal Outline

Attention-Getter: As soon as I stepped into my hotel room and looked out of the sliding glass doors that opened right onto the white sand beach and turquoise ocean, I knew this was going to be a trip to remember.

Thesis Statement: My vacation to the Bahamas was the best experience of my life.

Tourist Attractions
 Pirates of Nassau
 Hope Town
 Straw market
 Dolphin encounter
 Parade of flamingos
Water Sports
 Boating: sailing and kayaking
 Parasailing
 Swimming and snorkeling
 Skiing
Relaxation
 Reading books about local culture
 Sunbathing
 Sleeping
 Hot tubbing
Nightlife
 Listening to live music
 Watching shows
 Dancing

Basic Outline Structure

I. First main point
 A. First supporting point
  1. Major detail or example
   a. Minor detail or example
   b. Minor detail or example
  2. Major detail or example
  3. Major detail or example
 B. Second supporting point
  1. Major detail or example
  2. Major detail or example
II. Second main point (and so on)

Although you do not have to have the exact same number of supporting points under each heading, your outline should be somewhat balanced. If most of your ideas fit beneath one main point, then you may want to narrow your focus to just that point and break it down further.

Also, be sure to keep like ideas parallel. This means that you should state similar ideas in similar terms. (See Part 4 for more on parallel structure.)

Not Parallel: Parasailing, snorkeling, and to water ski are fun activities.
Parallel: <u>Parasailing</u>, <u>snorkeling</u>, and <u>skiing</u> are fun activities.
Discussion: The second sentence includes a series of words that end with "ing."
 Lists of nouns, verbs, adjectives, or adverbs should all be in the same form.

Sample Formal Outline

Attention-Getter: As soon as I stepped into my hotel room and looked out of the sliding glass doors that opened right onto the white sand beach and turquoise ocean, I knew this was going to be a trip to remember.

Thesis Statement: My vacation to the Bahamas was the best experience of my life.

I. Tourist Attractions
   A. Pirates of Nassau
      1. Brief history
      2. Museum
   B. Hope Town
   C. Straw market
      1. People
      2. Merchandise
   D. Dolphin encounter
   E. Parade of flamingos

II. Water Sports
   A. Boating
      1. Sailing
      2. Kayaking
   B. Parasailing
   C. Snorkeling
   D. Skiing

III. Relaxation
   A. Reading books about local culture
   B. Sunbathing
   C. Sitting in the hot tub

IV. Nightlife
   A. Listening to live island music
   B. Watching shows
   C. Dancing

▶ **Activity** Outlining

Based on the clustering activity that you completed, write a formal or informal outline. Be sure to organize your ideas logically. You may need to write a draft first and then rework it to make the ideas flow logically.

2.3 > Composing

Once you have narrowed your topic and have a plan for organizing your ideas, you are ready to begin composing your essay. Use the ideas that you generated during the discovering and planning stages to help you develop your rough draft. Let your cluster or outline serve as your guide. Also, be sure to focus on the first four points of the rhetorical star: subject, audience, purpose, and strategy. You can determine the design of your document later. As you begin to write, worry more about getting your ideas on paper (or on the computer screen) than on how you present your ideas. Go easy on yourself. You are not aiming for perfection, especially with the first draft.

You may want to write the easiest parts first to help build your confidence. In a short essay, you might write a paragraph about each main point. In a longer assignment, you might need several paragraphs to fully develop each main point. (See Chapter 3 for more details about thesis statements and essay development.)

Keep writing until you feel that you have covered all, or most, of the main points you had planned to address in your paper. Be sure to save your rough draft or put it in a safe place. Now take a well-deserved break! If you have time, let your ideas gel a bit before you continue to the next step of the writing process. If you give yourself a little time off, then you'll be able to review your work from a fresh perspective.

▶ *Activity* **Composing**

Write a paper based on the informal or formal outline you developed in the previous activity. Don't worry about grammar and punctuation for your first draft.

2.4 > Getting Feedback

After you have written your first draft, you'll want to get someone else's advice about your paper. Unless you are writing an essay for an in-class assignment, you should have an opportunity to get feedback from someone who can give you useful tips for revising your paper. Having a conference with your instructor, participating in a peer review activity with a classmate, or working with a campus-based or online writing tutor are all excellent ways to help you improve your writing.

Conferences One technique that you can use to get feedback on your assignment is to have a conference with your instructor, if possible. He or she should be able to provide you with excellent ideas for revision. If you're taking an online course, you may be able to e-mail your assignment to your instructor and wait for feedback. Many instructors are willing to provide students with general suggestions for improving their papers. However, don't expect your instructor to correct your paper for you. Your job is to learn how to revise and edit your own papers. You may also have a conference with a peer review partner or a writing lab tutor.

Peer Review Participating in a peer review exercise is a great way to improve your writing. Your instructor may give you an opportunity to complete a peer review activity in class. Usually this means that you pair up with another student (or a group of students) and provide each other with constructive criticism (ideas for improvement) about each other's drafts. You can also use this method in an online class via e-mail.

You'll receive valuable suggestions for revising your paper, and you will be able to offer your peer review partner helpful feedback as well. Additionally, you'll have an opportunity to see how someone else has approached the assignment. Even after you finish your writing course, you can continue to use these peer review strategies. In the real world, co-workers, family members, and friends often review each other's writing before it reaches its intended audience.

Tips for Peer Reviewers

- **Consider the writer's feelings.** Begin by pointing out something positive in the paper. What do you like best about the paper? Is there a particular part that you find especially interesting or insightful? What details and examples are most useful?

- **Provide constructive criticism.** Even if you are not the strongest writer, you know good writing when you see it. Are there specific areas that could be clearer or that need more explanation? Focus mostly on the larger issues, such as content, organization, and development. Avoid marking every error unless the writer has specifically asked you to do so. Be delicate with the comments you make, but don't just say you like everything if there are areas that need improvement.

  Additionally, be sure to give the writer concrete suggestions for how to improve the paper. For example, maybe the paper needs more specific examples to fully support the thesis statement, or perhaps some areas could be clearer.

Tips for Writers

- **Communicate with the reviewer.** Tell your peer review partner what you would like him or her to review. Depending on how rough your draft is, you might not be ready for help with grammar, punctuation, and mechanics. Maybe there are particular parts of your paper that you're not sure about or that seem awkward to you. Ask the reviewer to focus on those areas.

- **Take the suggestions in stride.** Remember that your peer review partner is trying to offer you constructive suggestions for making your paper better. Also, keep in mind that there are many ways (not just a right way and a wrong way) to approach a writing assignment. Thank the reviewer for the feedback, and then make your own decision about what to change…or not. In the end, you are the author, so the choices you make about your paper are up to you.

>> Sample Peer Review Questions

1. Which sentence states the main idea (thesis) of the essay? Is it clear? Is its placement appropriate? Why or why not?

2. Are there any additional details that could be included to help you better understand the essay? What is missing or unclear?

3. Are the details covered in a logical sequence? Which ones, if any, seem out of place?

4. What part of the essay is most memorable? Why?

5. Are transitions, such as "furthermore," "for example," and "next" used to help the ideas in the paper flow logically? If not, which ones would be useful?

6. Does the author provide the reader with a sense of completion at the end? If so, how?

7. What kinds of grammatical errors, if any, are evident in the essay?

8. What final suggestions do you have for the author?

Writing Centers and Online Writing Labs Some schools offer an avenue for getting feedback on your papers from a qualified professional through a writing center or online writing lab (OWL). These resources are designed for writers of all ability levels. If you have access to a writing center on campus, find out what kinds of services it provides and when it is open. At the writing center, you may have an opportunity to sit down with a person who can read your rough draft and provide suggestions for revising and editing. Additionally, writing centers often have a wide variety of print and computerized materials to help you with every aspect of the writing process.

If there isn't a writing center on campus, or if the timing doesn't work with your schedule, you might have an OWL you can utilize. When you use an OWL, you typically submit your draft electronically via e-mail and then receive feedback from a qualified professional, often within a day or two.

Tips for Working with Writing Tutors Regardless of whether you use a writing center or OWL, here are some tips that will help you make the most of it:

- **Have a rough draft ready.** If you haven't put any thought into your assignment, a writing tutor will have difficulty helping you. Even if your draft is extremely rough, you need to have something the writing tutor can read so that you can receive useful feedback.

- **Have your instructor's directions handy.** Often a writing tutor will ask you about the assignment's specifications. That way he or she can help determine if you have met your instructor's requirements or if you have gotten off track. Also, if your instructor provides you with grading criteria (such as through a rubric or grid), be sure to share that with your writing tutor.

- **Have specific questions in mind.** Asking a writing tutor to simply tell you what is wrong with your paper isn't the best approach. What specific areas would you like him or her to review? Are you concerned about the organization or development of your paper? Do you need help with any grammar issues? Also, don't expect to have your paper corrected for you. A writing tutor may point out a few errors so that you can see what kinds of issues you need to work on, but it is your responsibility to proofread and correct your paper.

- **Keep an open mind and a positive attitude.** Remember that the writing tutor, like a peer reviewer, wants to help you become a better writer by providing you with constructive criticism. Try not to be too sensitive about your work. Consider the feedback you receive, and make the changes you feel are necessary. Keep in mind that it is your paper. If you disagree with some of the feedback, or if you have additional questions, you can always get a second opinion. Ultimately, you have to decide what strategies work best for your paper.

2.5 > Revising

Many writers are tempted to take that first draft, correct the "mistakes," and then turn it in. If you do that, you will be skipping one of the most important steps. Good writers typically spend more time revising than working on any other step of the writing process. The term *revision* literally means to see again. You'll need to read back over your work and make improvements. Here are some higher order concerns to consider as you revise your paper:

Adding and Deleting Ideas

- Have you included all of the main points you had hoped to cover?
- Will including more ideas strengthen your essay?
- Are any of the points irrelevant?
- Are any points repetitious?
- Have you included any points that you could delete without weakening your paper?

Developing

- Have you included enough details and examples to support your main points?
- Can you expand on some points to provide greater clarity for your audience?

If you feel your paper needs more development, you can try additional discovery techniques to come up with more details and examples. You want to make sure to have enough support for your paper to convince your audience that the opinion in your thesis is accurate.

Arranging

- Does the order of your ideas make sense?
- Can you rearrange ideas to help your readers better understand the point you are making?

As you are revising your paper, move sentences and paragraphs around to see what flows better and makes more sense. If you are revising on a computer, the cutting and pasting features in your word processing program will simplify this procedure. Be sure to save different versions of your drafts so that you can go back to previous versions if you need to. If you are revising on paper, you can literally cut and paste (or tape or staple) sentences and paragraphs. You may want to make multiple copies of your draft before doing this so that you can remember how you originally wrote it. Continue cutting and pasting until you find the arrangement that best fits with your rhetorical star.

 Activity **Getting Feedback**

Have someone else (such as a classmate, writing tutor, friend, or family member) read the rough draft you composed in your last activity. Read the reviewer's feedback and decide which suggestions you want to accept, ignore, or modify. If you are working with another classmate, then you will need to provide him or her with constructive feedback as well.

2.6 > Editing

Once you are satisfied with the large-scale revisions you have made to your paper, you will want to examine it more closely. When you edit a paper, you are looking for lower order concerns, such as errors in words, sentence structure, grammar, punctuation, spelling, and mechanics. You can use your computer's spell checker as well as a print or digital thesaurus and dictionary to help you edit your paper. Read your paper aloud (to yourself or an audience). Listen to the flow of ideas. Consider the following questions as you edit your document and make changes accordingly. (See Part 4 for more details about editing.)

Word Choice (Diction)

- Have you chosen precise words that will create a specific picture in your readers' minds?

- Have you considered the different meanings of words that your readers might have?
- Are there any words that could be more interesting or lively?

Sentence Structure

- Do any sentences sound awkward?
- Do the sentences vary in length and style?
- Are any sentences too short and choppy?
- Are any sentences long enough to create confusion for the readers?

Grammar

- Are there any problems with subjects and verbs?
- Do all of the pronouns make sense?
- Are there enough adjectives to fully describe the nouns?
- Are all of the adverbs used correctly, such as *well* and *good*?
- Do all of the modifiers make sense?

Punctuation

- Do all sentences end with an appropriate punctuation mark?
- Are quotation marks used correctly?
- Are commas, semicolons, and colons used effectively?
- Do special punctuation marks, such as dashes and ellipses, fit with the writing?

Spelling

- Are there any words that the spell checker might overlook, such as *they're* and *their* or *you're* and *your*?
- Does the spelling of each word, such as *affect* or *effect*, reflect the intended meaning?

Mechanics

- Are the correct words capitalized?
- Are abbreviations appropriate, or do they need to be spelled out?
- Are numerals and spelled-out numbers used correctly?

2.7 > Proofreading

After you have finished revising and editing, be sure to proofread your final paper. As you read your paper this time, you are looking for the really nitpicky details, such as repeated words and typographical errors, that you may have overlooked previously. You might want to read your paper aloud again. Another strategy is to read your paper backward, from the last sentence to the first sentence. That way you can focus on every word. Most writers have difficulty finding all of the errors in their own papers. Therefore, you may want to have another person review your paper again. The more feedback you receive the better.

After you have proofread for the last time, be sure to submit your essay in the correct format. Is your paper supposed to be double-spaced? Are you expected to turn in a hard copy, an electronic version, or both? Have you followed all of the directions for the assignment? Following your instructor's guidelines is an important part of the assignment. Once you submit your final paper, you'll have the satisfaction of having completed an original piece of writing.

FIGURE 2.6 Editing Marks

Mark	Meaning	Mark	Meaning
ab	abbreviation	*logic*	not logical
ad	adjective problem	*mm*	misplaced modifier
adv	adverb problem	*nc*	not clear
agr	agreement problem	*nonst*	nonstandard language
ambig	ambiguous wording	*num*	numbers error
⋏	insert apostrophe	⌗	new paragraph
appr	inappropriate language	//	not parallel
awk	awkward expression	*omit*	omitted word
Cap ≡	capitalize	*pass*	passive voice
Case	case error	*pro ref*	pronoun reference
⅃⊏	center horizontal	" " ⋏ ⋏	insert quotation marks
⊔	center vertical	*rep*	too repetitive
◯	check this	*RO*	run-on sentence
Choppy	choppy style	*shift*	shift in tense or person
Coord	faulty coordination	⌒	close space
CS	comma splice	#	insert space
✗	delete	⟨Sp⟩	spelling
d	diction	*ss*	sentence structure
dev	develop idea more	*stet*	let it stand
dm	dangling modifier	*sub*	faulty subordination
d neg	double negative	*Support*	add more evidence
DS	double space	*t*	wrong verb tense
doc	documentation problem	*thesis*	thesis
frag	sentence fragment	*TS*	topic sentence
ger	be more specific	*trans*	weak transition
gram	grammatical error	*tr* ⊓⊔	transpose
inf	too informal	*vary*	add variety
irr	irregular verb error	*voice*	inconsistent voice
⋏	insert	*w*	wordy
ital ___	italicize or underline	*wc*	word choice
lc ═	use lower case	*wo*	word order

Use these editing marks to help you as you edit documents. Also, your instructor may use them when grading your papers.

> One Student's Journey through the Writing Process

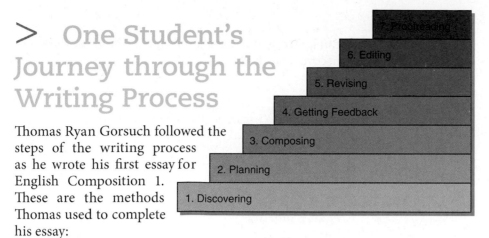

FIGURE 2.7   The Seven Steps of the Writing Process

7. Proofreading
6. Editing
5. Revising
4. Getting Feedback
3. Composing
2. Planning
1. Discovering

Thomas Ryan Gorsuch followed the steps of the writing process as he wrote his first essay for English Composition 1. These are the methods Thomas used to complete his essay:

FIGURE 2.8   Rhetorical Star Analysis Worksheet

Rhetorical Star Analysis Worksheet

Subject	Gaming media's influence of "Rock Band" and "Rock Band 2" How the gaming media has encouraged people to buy and play Rock Band.
Audience	People who might read this paper could range from young teens to late 40's. Might appeal to musicians and males or females.
Purpose	To inform the reader how the media has influenced people to think or feel that purchasing Rock Band they will have a more exciting healthy happy family life.
Strategy	Cause How were blinded by the truth about what the media has to say. appreciation for music Effects wanting to pursue musical arts, fun musicians Family togetherness, more fullfilling life
Design	APA format, 12 pt font, Times New Roman, Page # is in footer 5 or more paragraph essay, double spaced, indented paragraphs, Header and Title

1. Discovering

Thomas was fortunate and knew right away what his topic would be, so he was able to do much of his discovery work in his head.

2. Planning

Thomas created a cluster to begin to organize his ideas for his essay.

FIGURE 2.9 Thomas Gorsuch's Cluster

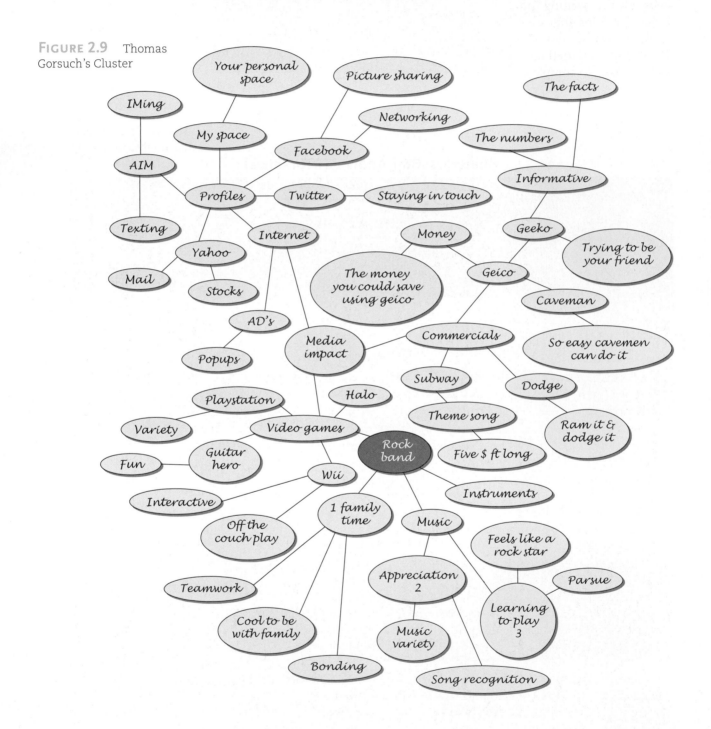

Informal Outline Thomas chose not to write a formal outline, but many students do benefit from creating one.

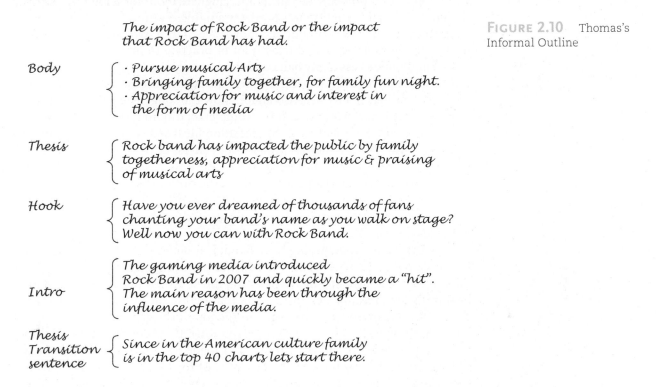

FIGURE 2.10 Thomas's Informal Outline

The impact of Rock Band or the impact that Rock Band has had.

Body
- Pursue musical Arts
- Bringing family together, for family fun night.
- Appreciation for music and interest in the form of media

Thesis
Rock band has impacted the public by family togetherness, appreciation for music & praising of musical arts

Hook
Have you ever dreamed of thousands of fans chanting your band's name as you walk on stage? Well now you can with Rock Band.

Intro
The gaming media introduced Rock Band in 2007 and quickly became a "hit". The main reason has been through the influence of the media.

Thesis Transition sentence
Since in the American culture family is in the top 40 charts lets start there.

3. Composing

Thomas Gorsuch's First Draft

Media Madness in the Music World

Have you ever dreamed of thousands of fans chanting your band name as you walk on stage? Well now you can live it, with Rock Band. The gaming media introduced Harmonix's Rock Band in 2007 and quickly became a "Hit". The main reason has been because of the influence of the media. Rock Band has impacted the public by encouraging family togetherness, teaching an appreciation for music, and pursuing of the musical arts. Since in American culture, family is rated "#1 on the top 40 charts," let's start there.

Family time, in this day in age, is rare to come by, so when it does come along I tend to hold on to and appreciate it. When I was younger I remember my family use to have a planned day that we called "family fun night". It was a night that we would all enjoy dinner together followed by a night of playing games. Sadly this is an activity that is rarely seen in family gatherings today. Through the media, this new game of Rock Band has made this picture more appealing and possible. Since this game reached stores everywhere I have heard many of my friends and family talk of how this game has brought them closer together. Since this game succeeds only when everyone works together, or in this case, plays together, this creates an attitude of team work and cooperation. Together, my family, friends and I each play a different instrument making up one Rock Band! Even if I'm not playing an instrument I feel included and involved by being part of the concert, cheering the band on, and becoming like one of the groupies. This new age of technology gaming has now replaced rolling dice on a flat game board to picking up an instrument or microphone, moving along as if really standing on stage. This get's my heart pumping, whether from trying to keep up with the beat, listening to cheering fans, or just from making a fool of myself. My family has so much fun, enjoying a wonderful experience that will bond us and probably be talked and laughed about for a long time. If you thought keeping the rhythm was hard, try singing on tune.

In this game, almost without my knowledge of it, it gave me an appreciation for music. Music is hard, and takes a lot of practice to perfect. When playing Rock Band the success of my band and the score shown is based on accuracy of hitting the right notes and the right time. This does not come naturally to everyone and definitely not to me. Although I know the song, listened to it in the car, or have scene it performed live, it is a completely different story to have to play it myself. Another point of music appreciation I learned is through the different styles of music. Rock Band has a variety of genres, of course starting out with Classic Rock turning to Alternative Rock, and now coming out with Country in July. When I play this game I learn about the different styles of music, how to play it, recognize it, and distinguish it apart from other styles. Suddenly I found that I had a new or renewed interest in music itself which lead to my interest in music lessons.

Now that I have been playing Rock Band, I, and many of my friends and family I have talked to, have wanted to learn to play an instrument for real. Rock Band gave me a taste of what performing music would be like and gave me a beginning level feel for each instrument that makes up a rock band. Thanks to the media, Rock Band slowly pushed to the top of the gaming list, making it a hit with everyone I know, including me. As Rock Band continues to add things making it even better and more difficult, it made me appreciate musicians and in turn, made me want to become one, at least for fun. I am not the only one, the media's influence in making Rock Band so popular has impacted the world in a way that many others have also taken up or started to pursue either a career or hobby in musical arts. I would say that the media has a pretty powerful influence.

As you can see, the media has influenced viewers like me, through TV, radio, and online advertisement that by purchasing Rock Band I will have a more exciting and fun life. It tells me that I will have fun with my family for a change, learn about music and its different genres, and also will help me to become a better musician, if I chose to pick up an instrument for real. So now let Rock Band bring you together, so you can have your own "family fun night!"

4. Getting Feedback

Peer Review Before making his revisions, Thomas submitted his paper to two classmates for peer review. Here is the feedback he received from Elizabeth Robson and Lana Darby.

FIGURE 2.11 Elizabeth's Peer Review

Author: Thomas Gorsuch
Reviewer: Elizabeth Robson

Peer Review Questions

1. Which sentence states the main idea (thesis) of the essay? Is it clear? Is its placement appropriate? Why or why not?

"Rock Band has impacted the public by encouraging family togetherness, teaching a appreciation..."

2. Are there any additional details that could be included to help you better understand the essay? What is missing or unclear?

Source for quote "#1 on top 40 charts"

3. Are the details covered in a logical sequence? Which ones, if any, seem out of place?

Yes, they are starting with family ending w/pursing of the musical arts.

4. What part of the essay is most memorable? Why?

"My family has so much fun...talked and laughed about for a long time."

5. Are transitions, such as "furthermore," "for example," and "next" used to help the ideas in the paper flow logically? If not, which ones would be useful?

Could use some transitions.
I only found couple, maybe use "As a Result" in 4 paragraph instead of "now that."

6. Does the author provide the reader with a sense of completion at the end? If so, how?

Yes, states thesis again and leaves me w/ a memorable statement.

7. What kinds of grammatical errors, if any, are evident in the essay?

A few or word should be replaced.
"now that" changed to since (4th paragraph)
takeout "it" out of sum sentence "... it, and many of ... family have ... ."

8. What final suggestions do you have for the author?

Use 3rd person point of view.

FIGURE 2.12   Lana's
Peer Review

Author: Thomas Gorsuch
Reviewer: Lana Darby

Peer Review Questions

1. Which sentence states the main idea (thesis) of the essay? Is it clear? Is its placement appropriate? Why or why not?

The 3rd sentence states the main idea. "The gaming media introduced Harmonic's Rock Band in 2007 and quickly became a "Hit." It is clear and is placed well following the opening attention getter" line.

2. Are there any additional details that could be included to help you better understand the essay? What is missing or unclear?

Explain gaming media. Explain to reader that this is a game that hooks up to XBox or Playstation. Therefore you and your family get interaction versus your son or daughter sitting in their room alone playing a war/or violent video game for hours while the parent watches it.

3. Are the details covered in a logical sequence? Which ones, if any, seem out of place?

Detail are O.K.

4. What part of the essay is most memorable? Why?

Parts that emphasize family time and once you spend time as a family you realize what you may have been missing.

5. Are transitions, such as "furthermore," "for example," and "next" used to help the ideas in the paper flow logically? If not, which ones would be useful?

"Since" is used a lot. Find different one.

6. Does the author provide the reader with a sense of completion at the end? If so, how?

Yes. The author recaps ideas in summary and ends with a positive suggestion.

7. What kinds of grammatical errors, if any, are evident in the essay?

Possible commas missing.

8. What final suggestions do you have for the author?

Detail more the options or features of the game. Also suggest that he hopes his children will remember the time as he remembered his family tradition.
Also, go in depth about how you can change levels in the singing and instrument. Start on easy move up to beginner then to harder levels. That makes you want to focus and try harder to achieve the goal. From personal experience, I know how hard it is to sing on key with the game.

Some schools provide students with online writing tutoring services through a third party, such as SmarThinking or NetTutor. Thomas was fortunate to have this opportunity. Here are the results from the NetTutor writing expert.

NetTutor Feedback

Paper Meta Information and Summary

FIGURE 2.13 NetTutor Sample

Your Name:	Thomas Gorsuch
Student ID:	XXXXXXXXXXXXXXX
Email:	XXXXXXXXXXXXXXX
Campus:	MELBOURNE
Course Title and #:	ENC1101 ENGLISH COMPOSITION I
Professor's Name:	RUSSELL, KARIN
Course Section:	Day
Due Date:	6-10-09
English as a second language?	No
Taken ENC 1101?	No
Describe Assignment:	The effect the media has on the public, in this case its the gaming media.
Required Length:	700 words
Two Areas for Feedback:	Grammar, Word Usage/Spelling

Proofing Summary:
Hi Thomas! Thank you for submitting your paper. I think you made the right choice of topic because this is something that you are familiar with and interested in. I really enjoyed reading about how a video game brought your family together where most people would guess that it would cause you to drift further apart. Your spelling was good for the most part but there are a couple instances where you have used the wrong word, but those are easily revised. Any other issues with the essay were small and sporadic. Look over your proofed paper for further feedback. Thanks again for your submission and good luck with your revisions!

5. Revising

Thomas made some revisions to his paper based on the NetTutor and peer review feedback he received. He focused mainly on adding, deleting, and rearranging ideas as he revised his first draft. For example, he switched the third and fourth paragraphs because he decided that it made more sense to discuss specific instruments before mentioning music appreciation in general. He also strengthened his topic sentences and added more transitions. (See Chapter 3 for more details about topic sentences and transitions.) All of Thomas's changes appear in brackets in red.

Thomas Gorsuch's Second Draft

Media Madness in the Music World

Have you ever dreamed of thousands of fans chanting your band name as you walk on stage? Well now you can live it, with <<*Rock Band or Rock Band II*>>. <<In 2007>> the gaming media introduced Harmonix's Rock Band, which quickly became a "Hit". The main reason has been because of the influence of the media. <<The *Rock* video games have been wildly popular among gamers of all ages throughout the United States.>> <<*Rock Band*>> has <<affected>> the public by encouraging family togetherness, <<influencing people to pursue>> the musical arts, and teaching an appreciation for music.

<<One way *Rock Band* has influenced families is by giving them an opportunity to spend time together. Today,>> family time is rare to come by, so families should hold on to and appreciate it. When I was younger I remember my family use to have a planned day that we called "family fun night". It was a night that we would all enjoy dinner together followed by a night of playing games. Sadly this is an activity that is rarely seen in family gatherings today. <<The new *Rock Band* game has>> made this picture more appealing and possible. Since this game reached stores everywhere I have heard many of my friends and family talk of how this game has brought them closer together. This new age of technology gaming has now replaced rolling dice on a flat game board to picking up an instrument or microphone, moving along as if really standing on stage. Since this game is successful only when everyone plays together, this creates an attitude of team work and cooperation. Together, my family, friends, and I play a different making up one Rock Band! Even if I'm not playing an instrument I feel included and involved by being part of the concert, cheering the band on like groupies. <<*Rock Band* get's the players' hearts>> pumping, whether from trying to keep up with the beat, listening to cheering fans, or just from making a fool of myself. My family has so much fun <<playing *Rock Band* and>> enjoying a wonderful experience that we will probably <<talk and laugh>> about for a long time. If you thought keeping the rhythm was hard, try singing on tune.

<<Another effect of the *Rock Band* game is that it has caused many players to want to play a real instrument. *Rock Band*>> gave me a taste of what performing music <<as a singer, guitar player or drummer>> would be like and a beginning level feel for each instrument that makes up a rock band. As <<players progress through Rock Band, the game>> continues to add <<new levels, songs, and venues, causing the game to be>> even better and more difficult. <<These advancements>> make me appreciate musicians and in turn, want to become one, at least for fun. The media's influence in making Rock Band so popular has <<affected>> the world in a way that <<has likely caused>> many <<people>> to pursue either a career or hobby in musical arts.

<<Furthermore, the Rock Band game has helped people to develop a stronger>> appreciation for music. Music <<can be difficult to perform>>, and takes a lot of practice to perfect. When playing Rock Band the success of <<the>> band and the score shown is based on accuracy of hitting the right notes and the right time. This does not come naturally to everyone. Although I know the song <<from listening>> to it in the car or <<hearing>> it performed live, it is a completely different story to have to play it myself. <<*Rock Band* also helps gamers to appreciate>> music is through <<introducing them to>> different styles of music. Rock Band has a variety of <<musical>> genres, <<such as>> Classic Rock, turning to Alternative Rock, and now coming out with Country in July. When I learn about the different styles of music, how to play it, recognize it, and distinguish it apart from other styles. Suddenly I found that I had a new or renewed interest in music itself which lead to my interest in music lessons.

As you can see, the media has influenced viewers like me, through TV, radio, and online advertisement that by purchasing <<*Rock Band* they>> will have a more exciting and fun life. <<Players>> will have fun with <<their families>> for a change, become <<better musicians, if they choose to pick up an instrument for real>>, and learn <<more>> about music and its different genres, So now let <<*Rock Band*>> bring you together <<with your family and friends>>, so you can have your own "family fun night!"

6. Editing

After Thomas, completed his second draft, he used the paper proof that he received from his NetTutor feedback to help him edit his paper. During this step, he focused mostly on correcting his grammar, punctuation, and sentence structure. Thomas knew not to rely completely on the paper proof, but he did find it useful for catching some areas of his paper that needed attention.

Additionally, he took his classmate's peer review suggestion and switched from the first-person to the third-person point of view, which uses *he, she*, and *they* instead of *I, me*, and *my*. All of his changes appear in brackets in red.

NetTutor Paper Proof Thomas received some proofreader suggestions in addition to the narrative explanation with suggestions from the writing tutor from NetTutor.

FIGURE 2.14 NetTutor Paper Proof

Thomas Gorsuch
English Comp 1
6/7/09

Media Madness in the Music World

Have you ever dreamed of thousands of fans chanting your *band's* name as you walk on stage? Well now you can live it, with Rock Band. The gaming media introduced Harmonix's Rock Band in 2007 and quickly became a *lc* Hit . The main reason has been because of the influence of the media. Rock Band has impacted the public by encouraging family togetherness, teaching an appreciation for music, and pursuing of the musical arts. Since in American culture, family is rated "#1 on the top 40 charts," let's start there.

Is this an actual quote? If it isn't, you don't need to put it in quotations.

Family time, in this day in age, is rare to come by *cap* so when it does come along I tend to hold on to and appreciate it. When I was younger, I remember my family use to have a planned day that we called "family fun night. It was a night that we would all enjoy dinner together, followed by a night of playing games. Sadly this is an activity that is rarely seen in family gatherings today¶ Through the media, this new game of Rock Band has made this picture more appealing and possible. Since this game reached stores everywhere, I have heard many of my friends and family talk of how this game has brought them closer together. Since this game succeeds only when everyone works together, or in this case, plays together, this creates an attitude of team work and cooperation. Together, my family, friends and I each play a different instrument making up one Rock Band! Even if I'm not playing an instrument I feel included and involved by being part of the concert, cheering the band on, and becoming like one of the *fans* groupies. This new age of technology gaming has now replaced rolling dice on a flat game board to picking up an instrument or microphone, *and* moving along as if really standing on stage. This get's my heart pumping, whether from trying to keep up with the beat, listening to cheering fans, or just from making a fool of myself. My family has so much fun, enjoying a wonderful experience that will bond us and probably be talked and laughed about for a long time. If you thought keeping the rhythm was hard, try singing on tune.

This doesn't fit here. If you want to include it, you should move it to the section that discusses the game.

In this game, almost without my knowledge of it, It gave me an appreciation for music. Music is hard, and takes a lot of practice to perfect. When playing Rock Band, the success of my band and the score shown is based on accuracy of hitting the right notes and the right time. This does not come naturally to everyone and definitely not to me. Althought I know the song, *have* listened to it in the car, or have *ww* scene it performed live, it is a completely different story to have to play it myself. Another point of music appreciation I learned is through the different styles of music. Rock Band has a variety of genres, of course starting out with Classic Rock turning to Alternative Rock, and now coming out with Country in July. When I play this game, I learn about the different styles of music, how to play it, recognize it, and distinguish it apart from other styles. Suddenly, I found that I had a new or renewed interest in music itself which *led* to my interest in music lessons.

Now that I have been playing Rock Band, I, and many of my friends and family I have talked to, have wanted to learn to play an *actual* instrument for real. Rock Band gave me a taste of what performing music would be like and gave me a beginning level feel for each instrument that makes up a rock band. Thanks to the media, Rock Band slowly pushed to the top of the gaming list, making it a hit with everyone I know, including me. As Rock Band continues to add things, making it even better and more difficult, it made me appreciate musicians and, in turn, made me want to become one, at least for fun. I am not the only one [cap] the media's influence in making Rock Band so popular has impacted the [awk] world in a way that many others have also taken up or started to pursue either a career or hobby in musical arts. I would say that the media has a pretty powerful influence.

As you can see, the media has influenced viewers like me, through TV, radio, and online [You may want to mention this in your opening paragraph. It doesn't fit here if you are mentioning it for the first time.] advertisement that by purchasing Rock Band I will have a more exciting and fun life. It tells me that I will have fun with my family for a change, learn about music and its different genres, and also will help me to become a better musician, if I chose to pickup an instrument for real. So now [cap] let Rock Band bring you together, so you can have your own "family fun night"

Thomas Gorsuch's Third Draft

Media Madness in the Music World

Have you ever dreamed of thousands of fans chanting your band name as you walk on stage? Well now you can live it, with *Rock Band* or *Rock Band II*. <<In 2007>> the gaming media introduced Harmonix's *Rock Band*, which quickly became a "Hit". <<The *Rock Band* video games have been wildly popular among gamers of all ages throughout the United States.>> *Rock Band* has <<affected>> the public by encouraging family togetherness, <<influencing people to pursue>> the musical arts, and teaching an appreciation for music.

<<One way *Rock Band* has influenced families is by giving them an opportunity to spend time together. Today,>> family time is rare to come by, so families should hold on to and appreciate it. <<In the past, some families uses to have planned nights when they>> would all enjoy dinner together followed by a night of playing games. Sadly this is an activity that is rarely seen in family gatherings today. <<The new *Rock Band* game has>> made this picture more appealing and possible. Since this game reached stores, it has brought <<families>> closer together. This new age of technology gaming has now replaced rolling dice on a flat game board to picking up an instrument or microphone, moving along as if really standing on stage. Since this game is successful only when everyone plays together, this creates an attitude of team work and cooperation. <<Each participant plays>> a different instrument making up one Rock Band! Even <<the people who are not>> playing an instrument feel included and involved by being part of the concert. <<They cheer>> the band on like groupies. <<*Rock Band* get's the players' hearts>> pumping, whether from trying to keep up with the beat, listening to cheering fans, or just from making a fool of <<themselves>>. <<Families have>> so much fun <<playing *Rock Band* and>> enjoying a wonderful experience that <<they>> probably <<will talk and laugh>> about for a long time. If you thought keeping the rhythm was hard, try singing on tune.

<<Another effect of the *Rock Band* game is that it has caused many players to want to play a real instrument.>> *Rock Band* <<gives players>> a taste of what performing music <<as a singer, guitar player or drummer>> would be like and a beginning level feel for each instrument that makes up a rock band. As <<players progress through Rock Band, the game>> continues to add <<new levels, songs, and venues, causing the game to be>> even better and more difficult. <<These advancements help players to>> appreciate musicians and in

turn, want to become one, at least for fun. The media's influence in making Rock Band so popular has <<affected>> the world in a way that <<has likely caused>> many <<people>> to pursue either a career or hobby in musical arts.

<<Furthermore, the *Rock Band* game has helped people to develop a stronger>> appreciation for music. Music <<can be difficult to perform>>, and takes a lot of practice to perfect. When playing *Rock Band* the success of <<the>> band and the score shown is based on accuracy of hitting the right notes and the right time. This does not come naturally to everyone. <<Even if players are familiar with a>> song <<from listening>> to it in the car or <<hearing>> it performed live, it is a completely different story to have to play it <<themselves>>. <<*Rock Band* also helps gamers to appreciate>> music is through <<introducing them to>> different styles of music. Rock Band has a variety of <<musical>> genres, <<such as>> Classic Rock, turning to Alternative Rock, and now coming out with Country in July. <<Players>> learn about the different styles of music, how to play it, recognize it, and distinguish it apart from other styles.

As you can see, the media has influenced viewers through TV, radio, and online advertisement that by purchasing Rock Band <<they>> will have a more exciting and fun life. <<Players>> will have fun with <<their families>> for a change, become <<better musicians, if they choose to pick up an instrument for real>>, and learn <<more>> about music and its different genres, So now let *Rock Band* bring you together <<with your family and friends>>, so you can have your own "family fun night!"

Rock Band Jam Session

7. Proofreading

Thomas read through his paper one more time, proofreading for errors, awkward sentences, and word choice. He also took out the word *media* in the title because his emphasis shifted from the media to just the Rock Band game. His final corrections appear in red brackets.

Thomas Gorsuch's Final Draft

Madness in the Music World

Have you ever dreamed of thousands of fans chanting your band<<'s>> name as you walk on stage? Well now you can live it, with *Rock Band* or *Rock Band II.*

In 2007 the gaming media introduced Harmonix's <<*Rock Band*>>, which quickly became a <<hit>>. <<Since then>> the *Rock Band* video games have been wildly popular among gamers of all ages throughout the United States. *Rock Band* has affected the public by encouraging family togetherness, influencing people to pursue the musical arts, and teaching an appreciation for music.

One way *Rock Band* has influenced families is by giving them an opportunity to spend time together <<and become closer.>> Today, family time is rare to come by, so families should appreciate <<the time they have together by doing something engaging>>. In the past, some families use<<d>> to have planned nights when they would all enjoy dinner together followed by a night of playing games. Sadly this is an activity that is rarely seen in family gatherings today. The new *Rock Band* game has made this picture more appealing and possible. This new age of technology gaming has now replaced rolling dice on a flat game board <<with>> picking up an instrument or microphone <<and playing songs>> as if <<the players are>> really <<performing>> on stage. Since this game is successful only when everyone plays together, <<it>> creates an attitude of <<teamwork>> and cooperation. Each participant plays a different instrument making up one <<r>>ock <<b>>and<<.>> *Rock Band* <<gets>> the players' hearts pumping, whether from trying to keep up with the beat, listening to cheering fans, or just making a fool of themselves. Even the people who are not playing an instrument feel included and involved by being part of the concert. <<The observers>> cheer the band on like groupies. Families have so much fun playing *Rock Band* and enjoying a wonderful experience that they probably will talk and laugh about <<it>> for a long time.

Another effect of the *Rock Band* game is that <<it encourages>> many players to want to play a real instrument. *Rock Band* gives players a taste of what performing music <<would be like>> as a singer, guitar player, or drummer and a beginning level feel for each instrument that makes up a rock band. As players progress through *Rock Band*, <<new levels, songs, and venues continue to open>>, causing the game to be even better and more <<challenging>>. These advancements help players to appreciate musicians and in turn, want to become <<like them>>, at least for fun. The media's influence in making *Rock Band* so popular has affected the world <<by influencing>> many people to pursue either a career or hobby in <<the>> musical arts.

Furthermore, the *Rock Band* game has helped people to develop a stronger appreciation for music. Music can be difficult to perform and takes a lot of practice to perfect. When playing *Rock Band*<<,>> the success of the band and the score shown <<are>> based on accuracy of hitting the right notes and the right time. This does not come naturally to everyone. Even if players are familiar with a song from listening to it in the car or hearing it performed live, <<they find it>> it completely different to have to play <<the song>> themselves. *Rock Band* also helps gamers to appreciate music through introducing them to different styles of music. *Rock Band* has a variety of musical genres, such as <<classic rock, alternative rock, and country.>> Players <<can>> learn about the different styles of music, how to play <<them>>, recognize <<them>>, and distinguish <<them>> from other styles.

<<*Rock Band* has revolutionized family fun time.>> Players will have <<a great time>> with their families for a change, become better musicians, if they choose to pick up an instrument for real, and learn more about music and its different genres<<.>> So now let *Rock Band* bring you <<and your family together,>> so you can have your own "family fun night!"

Madness in the Music World

Have you ever dreamed of thousands of fans chanting your band's name as you walk on stage? Well now you can live it, with *Rock Band* or *Rock Band II*. In 2007 the gaming media introduced Harmonix's *Rock Band*, which quickly became a hit. Since then the *Rock Band* video games have been wildly popular among gamers of all ages throughout the United States. *Rock Band* has affected the public by encouraging family togetherness, influencing people to pursue the musical arts, and teaching an appreciation for music.

One way *Rock Band* has influenced families is by giving them an opportunity to spend time together and become closer. Today, family time is rare to come by, so families should appreciate the time they have together by doing something engaging. In the past, some families used to have planned nights when they would all enjoy dinner together followed by a night of playing games. Sadly this is an activity that is rarely seen in family gatherings today. The new *Rock Band* game has made this picture more appealing and possible. This new age of technology gaming has now replaced rolling dice on a flat game board with picking up an instrument or microphone and playing songs as if the players are really performing on stage. Since this game is successful only when everyone plays together, it creates an attitude of teamwork and cooperation. Each participant plays a different instrument making up one rock band. *Rock Band* gets the players' hearts pumping, whether from trying to keep up with the beat, listening to cheering fans, or just making a fool of themselves. Even the people who are not playing an instrument feel included and involved by being part of the concert. The observers cheer the band on like groupies. Families have so much fun playing *Rock Band* and enjoying a wonderful experience that they probably will talk and laugh about it for a long time.

Another effect of the *Rock Band* game is that it encourages many players to want to play a real instrument. *Rock Band* gives players a taste of what performing music would be like as a singer, guitar player, or drummer and a beginning level feel for each instrument that makes up a rock band. As players progress through *Rock Band*, new levels, songs, and venues continue to open, causing the game to be even better and more challenging. These advancements help players to appreciate musicians and in turn, want to become like them, at least for fun. The media's influence in making *Rock Band* so popular has affected the world by influencing many people to pursue either a career or hobby in the musical arts.

Furthermore, the *Rock Band* game has helped people to develop a stronger appreciation for music. Music can be difficult to perform and takes a lot of practice to perfect. When playing *Rock Band*, the success of the band and the score shown are based on accuracy of hitting the right notes and the right time. This does not come naturally to everyone. Even if players are familiar with a song from listening to it in the car or hearing it performed live, they find it completely different to have to play the song themselves. *Rock Band* also helps gamers to appreciate music through introducing them to different styles of music. *Rock Band* has a variety of musical genres, such as classic rock, alternative rock, and country. Players can learn about the different styles of music, how to play them, recognize them, and distinguish them from other styles.

Rock Band has revolutionized family fun time. Players will have a great time with their families for a change, become better musicians, if they choose to pick up an instrument for real, and learn more about music and its different genres. So now let *Rock Band* bring you and your family together, so you can have your own "family fun night!"

[QUESTIONS FOR REFLECTION]

1. Read the first sentence. Does it capture your attention? Why or why not?
2. Based on the introduction, what do you expect from the rest of the essay?
3. Does the essay deliver what Thomas promised in the introduction? Explain.
4. Which supporting details seemed the most helpful? Why?
5. Would you want to play Rock Band based on this essay? Why or why not?

CHAPTER SUMMARY

1. Follow the seven stages of the **writing process** to write effective documents.

2. Use different **discovery** methods to help you choose and narrow your subject.

3. Create a cluster or outline to help you **plan** and organize your document.

4. **Compose** your rough draft without worrying too much about grammar and punctuation.

5. **Get feedback** on your paper from someone who can give you suggestions for revision.

6. When **revising** a document, you may add and delete ideas, further develop your concepts, or rearrange your points to make your writing more effective.

7. **Edit** your paper carefully for diction, sentence structure, grammar, punctuation, spelling, and mechanics.

8. **Proofread** your paper and make corrections before submitting your final draft.

WHAT I KNOW NOW

Use this checklist to determine what you need to work on to feel comfortable with your understanding of the material in this chapter. Check off each item as you master it. Review the material for any unchecked items.

❏ 1. I have found several **discovery methods** I can use to find and explore topics.

❏ 2. I am familiar with how to develop a cluster or outline to **plan** my paper.

❏ 3. I won't be too hard on myself as I **compose** my first draft.

❏ 4. I understand the importance of **getting feedback** from a classmate, tutor, or online writing service to help me improve my papers.

❏ 5. I am aware that I will need to **revise** my paper by adding, deleting, rearranging, and further developing my ideas.

❏ 6. I know that I need to carefully **edit** my papers for diction, sentence structure, grammar, punctuation, spelling, and mechanics.

❏ 7. I'll leave time to **proofread** my final paper before turning it in to my instructor.

FURTHER READING ON THE WEB

- Journaling Techniques: **http://journalingtechniques.info/how-to-find-journal-writing-topics-and-ideas/**
- Starting the Writing Process: **http://owl.english.purdue.edu/owl/resource/587/01/**
- Brainstorming Versus Outlining in Essay Writing: **http://educationalissues.suite101.com/article.cfm/ brainstorming_versus_outlining**
- The Writing Process: **www.csuohio.edu/academic/writingcenter/writproc.html**
- Editing and Proofreading: **www.bestessaytips.com/writing_steps_edit.php**

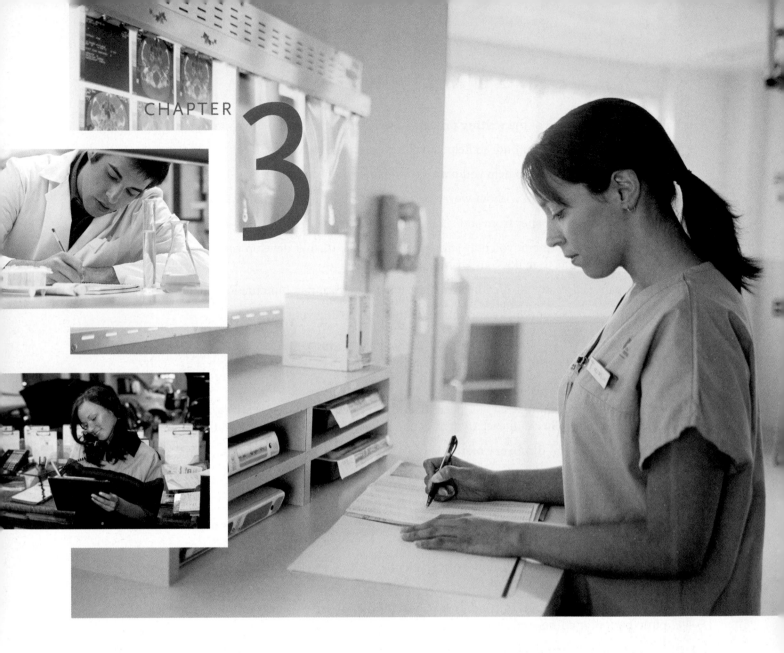

CHAPTER

3

WRITING SENTENCES, PARAGRAPHS, AND ESSAYS

LEARNING outcomes

> In this chapter you will learn techniques for the following:

3.1: Writing complete sentences, including topic sentences and thesis statements.

3.2: Writing and developing effective paragraphs using transitional words and phrases to create better flow.

3.3: Writing effective multi-paragraph essays that include an introduction, a body, and a conclusion.

3.1 > Writing a Sentence

Sentence Components

Writing an effective sentence requires careful thought. Basically, every sentence needs to have three elements. It needs to have a subject and a verb, and it needs to express a complete thought. The subject is the topic of your sentence; the verb is the action in the sentence; and the complete thought allows the sentence to stand on its own.

Incomplete sentence: While I was driving to work today.

Complete sentence: While I was driving to work today, I saw a bobcat near the road.

Discussion: The first sentence has a subject (I) and a verb (was driving), but the word *while* causes it to be incomplete.

 Activity Writing Complete Sentences

Revise each incomplete sentence below so that it contains a subject and a verb and expresses a complete thought:

1. While I was enrolling in college.
2. Some of the most popular college majors are.
3. Is the best instructor I have had so far.
4. Joining a social or professional organization.
5. The best way to achieve success in college.

Parts of Speech

Reviewing the eight *parts of speech* can help strengthen your sentence-writing skills. Basically, every word in a sentence serves a particular function. Although a complete sentence only needs to include a noun and a verb and express a complete thought, you may use other words, such as adjectives and prepositions, to provide more details for your readers.

TABLE 3.1

The Eight Parts of Speech		
Parts of Speech	**Descriptions**	**Examples**
Nouns	Name a person, place, or thing	Dr. Oz, New York, book
Pronouns	Replace a noun	Me, them, herself, it, that, who
Verbs	Show action or a state of being	Jump, surfed, has been running, will be swimming, is, was
Adjectives	Modify or describe a noun	Cute, sweetest, green, playful, funny, Asian
Adverbs	Modify or describe a verb, adjective, or other adverb	Slowly, carefully, completely, sooner
Prepositions	Link a noun to another word	To, before, on, over, with, beyond
Conjunctions	Join clauses, sentences, or words	For, and, nor, but, or, yet, so
Interjections	Express a strong feeling	Oh! Cool! Ouch!

▶ *Activity*   **Parts of Speech**

Identify the part of speech of each highlighted word in the sentences below:

1. The friends assembled food, drinks, and fishing gear for the outing.
2. It was a sunny day, and the water was perfectly calm.
3. Sophie said, "Wow! Look at the size of that fish."
4. She tried to get the fish into the boat, but it got away too quickly.
5. The boat rapidly approached the shore.

ESOL Tip >

When writing in standard American English, place an adjective before, not after, a noun. For example, Americans would write "the blue car" instead of "the car blue."

Sentence Variety

Whether you are writing a short paragraph or an entire essay, you'll need to vary your sentence length and style. If all of your sentences are similar, then your writing style will probably seem dull to your readers. A short simple sentence can help you to emphasize a key point, whereas a longer more complex sentence may enable you to illustrate the relationships among the ideas you are presenting. Varying your sentence lengths and patterns creates greater interest for the reader. Read the following passages:

▶ *Draft*

Some forms of body art have been around for centuries. Body art is growing in popularity. Many men and women are getting tattoos. Some people are also getting a variety of body piercings. Other people are getting implants to change their appearance. Many people who try body art want to make a bold statement.

Read the previous passage aloud. How does it sound? Is it exciting or boring? You probably noticed that the ideas are presented in a short, choppy manner and that some words are repeated unnecessarily. Basically, the sentences are similar in structure and lack variety.

▶ Revised for Better Sentence Variety

Although various forms of body art have been around for centuries, today it is growing in popularity. Many men and women are using tattoos, body piercings, and implants to change their appearance and make a bold statement.

The revised passage sounds much better when read aloud because the sentences vary in length and structure, and the ideas flow better together. Notice that some ideas were combined to create more variety in sentence structure and to eliminate repeated words such as *body art* and *people*.

▶ Activity   Sentence Variety

Revise the following paragraph by varying the structure of the sentences to make the ideas flow more smoothly. You may reword, reorganize, and combine sentences, but be sure to keep all of the ideas present in the original paragraph. To be effective, your final paragraph will need to have fewer sentences and words without losing any of the details.

Vacationing in Key West

Key West, Florida is a fun-filled vacation destination. It is an island situated at the southernmost point of the United States. First of all, there are many activities to enjoy in Key West. Some people enjoy water sports in Key West. The fishing is first-class. The dolphin encounters are wonderful for nature lovers. Diving and snorkeling are popular sports in Key West. Additionally, the nightlife in Key West is exceptional and makes it a fun place to visit. Duval Street has great bars. There are numerous bars with live music. Sloppy Joe's is a famous bar. Ernest Hemingway loved to go to Sloppy Joe's. Hog's Breath Saloon is a popular nightspot. Two Friends Bar is a popular evening destination. There is karaoke at Two Friends Bar. Key West provides tourists with opportunities for several other activities as well. There are quaint shops to visit. Visitors can see a live performance at the Tennessee Williams Theatre.

Key West, Florida

Travelers can tour Ernest Hemingway's house. There is so much to do in Key West. As a result, many people enjoy traveling to Key West every year.

3.2 > Writing a Paragraph

A paragraph is a group of sentences that all relate to one idea. Sometimes a paragraph can stand on its own, and other times a paragraph is part of a larger essay or document. Typically, a stand-alone paragraph consists of three main parts: a topic sentence, several main points with supporting sentences, and a concluding sentence.

FIGURE 3.1 Basic Paragraph Structure

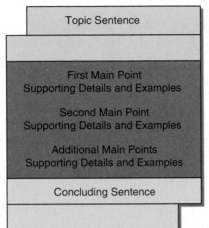

Topic Sentence

First Main Point
Supporting Details and Examples

Second Main Point
Supporting Details and Examples

Additional Main Points
Supporting Details and Examples

Concluding Sentence

Topic Sentence

A good topic sentence has two main components—a topic and an opinion about the topic. It also has to be a complete sentence. Remember, a complete sentence contains a subject and a verb and expresses a complete thought. For example, the following includes all of the necessary components of a good topic sentence: "Even though working and going to school full time can be challenging at times, the advantages far outweigh the disadvantages."

Poor topic sentence: Reasons to learn to write.

Revised topic sentence: Learning to become a better writer can help you to be more successful in achieving your educational, career, and personal goals.

Discussion: The poor sentence would not serve as an adequate topic sentence because there is no verb, opinion, or complete thought. The revised sentence has all of the required components.

▶ *Activity* **Writing Topic Sentences**

Brainstorm a list of at least five topics to which most college students could relate. The topics can be about music, television, movies, current events, school, careers, or other areas of interest. From that list, choose the two that you like best. Write a topic sentence for each topic you choose. Be sure each topic sentence includes the topic and opinion and is a complete sentence.

Supporting Sentences

The body of your paragraph will include specific main points with details and examples that support the opinion in your topic sentence. While there is no magic number of supporting sentences, you will usually need at least three to five sentences to support your main idea in an academic paper. You will want to have enough sentences to fully develop your main topic. Keep in mind that college writers are more likely to have too few supporting sentences than too many. Also, make sure that your paragraph is **unified**. In other words, every idea you include must help support the opinion in your topic sentence.

▶ *Activity*   **Writing Supporting Sentences**

Choose one of the topic sentences that you created in the "Writing Topic Sentences" activity. Write four to five supporting sentences to go along with your topic. Be sure that all sentences clearly relate to the opinion expressed in the topic sentence.

Transitions

Use transitional words and phrases throughout your paragraphs to help signal your reader when you are changing direction or moving to a new point. Transitions will help your writing to be more coherent for the audience because they serve to bridge ideas. Without transitions, your readers might not understand the connection you are trying to make between two ideas.

TABLE 3.2

Transitions	
Types of Transitions	**Examples**
To give examples	For example, for instance, such as, that is
To show time or order	About, after, afterward, as soon as, at, before, beforehand, during, finally, first, immediately, in the meantime, later, meanwhile, next, presently, second, soon, subsequently, then, third, today, tomorrow, until, when, without delay, yesterday
To show location	Above, across, against, along, alongside, among, around, away from, behind, below, beneath, beside, between, beyond, by, down, in back of, in front of, inside, into, near, nearby, off, on top of, onto, outside, over, throughout, to the left, under, underneath
To compare (show similarities)	Also, as, as though, in the same way, like, likewise, neither, both, similarly
To contrast (show differences)	Although, but, even though, however, in contrast, in spite of, on the other hand, otherwise, still, yet
To show a cause	Another reason, because, one reason, since
To show an effect	As a result, consequently, hence, therefore, thus
To add information	Additionally, again, along with, also, and, another, as well, besides, equally important, finally, furthermore, in addition, moreover, next
To show emphasis or repetition	Again, even, certainly, emphatically, in other words, in particular, in fact, in the same way, more importantly, more specifically, obviously, of course, to emphasize, truly
To conclude or summarize	All in all, as a result, consequently, finally, for this reason, hence, last, to conclude, to summarize

▶ Activity Narrowing Your Focus

Using the words below, fill in the blanks in the following paragraph by adding transitional words or phrases. Be sure that your transitions show the logical relationships among the ideas in the paragraph.

for example	all in all	first of all	also
in addition	another reason	as well	secondly

See You at the Movies

Going to see a movie at a theater is far superior to viewing one at home. _____, the technology is much better at the theater. _____, the screen is many times larger than home televisions. This causes the characters and events to appear much larger than in real life. The sound system is better _____. The Dolby surround sound and booming volume help viewers to feel as if they are actually on location with the actors. _____, sharing the experience with a large audience adds to the excitement of the movie. Audience members can laugh, gasp, or cheer together when important scenes occur. _____ why the theater is more enjoyable is the vast selection of snacks at the concession stand. _____ to the standard popcorn, chocolate, and cola products, most movie theaters _____

offer nachos with cheese, personal pizza, cinnamon-glazed nuts and a variety of other options to satisfy the audience's hunger. _____ watching a movie at the theater beats viewing one at home every time.

Concluding Sentence

If you are writing a stand-alone paragraph, the last sentence should serve as your conclusion. Restate the main idea and opinion you introduced in your topic sentence. Be sure to use different words than you did the first time.

> **Topic sentence:** Learning to become a better writer can help you to be more successful in achieving your educational, career, and personal goals.

> **Reworded concluding sentence:** Strengthening your writing skills will enable you to become more accomplished in school, on the job, and in your personal life.

Depending on the length of your paragraph, you may want to add one more sentence after your reworded thesis. If you choose to do that, you'll want to include something that is memorable for the reader. See the example in the model paragraph on the next page. Notice that the transitional words are highlighted.

▶ Activity Concluding Sentences

Write a concluding sentence for the topic sentence and supporting sentences you created in the activities on pages 50 and 51. Be sure your concluding sentence uses different words to remind your readers of the opinion in the topic sentence.

Model Paragraph

Internships

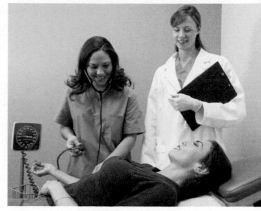

Topic Sentence ——— <u>Working as an intern for a local medical facility is an excellent way to begin your career in the allied health field.</u>

First Main Point ——— First of all, as an intern you will learn valuable skills that you may not learn in college. For example, you will have an

Supporting Details ⟨ opportunity to work with real patients and learn how to meet their needs while they are in the office. Also, you will gain a greater understanding of what doctors and other health professionals will expect from you while you are on the job.

Second Main Point ——— Another benefit to taking on an internship is that you will have a chance to prove that you are capable of handling the duties that you will be responsible for when you are on the job. For

Supporting Details ⟨ instance, you can demonstrate your competence in performing crucial administrative and clinical tasks. Finally, the greatest

Third Main Point ⟨ benefit to serving as an intern is that the experience may very well lead to a permanent position. If you work hard, know your

Supporting Details ⟨ stuff, and get along well with others, then you are likely to land a job at the intern site. <u>Consequently, the skills, real-world</u>

Concluding Sentence ⟨ <u>experience, and job opportunities that an internship provides are extremely advantageous to your career in the allied health field.</u>

Memorable Statement ——— Even though internships are usually not paid positions, they are well worth their time for the benefits you will receive.

3.3 > Writing an Essay

An **essay** (also known as a *composition*) is a group of paragraphs related to a particular subject or theme. Essays are usually designed to meet one of the five purposes for writing: inform, interpret, persuade, entertain, and express feelings (see Chapter 1 for more details). Having a clear organizational structure to your essay will help your readers to better understand what you are trying to say. Virtually every type of document that you write needs to have a beginning, a middle, and an ending (introduction, body, and conclusion).

[**Essay** A group of paragraphs related to a particular subject.

Introductory Paragraph

Your introduction should accomplish three tasks: capture the audience's attention, state your thesis, and provide an overview of the main points you will cover in the body of the essay. Avoid beginning a paper with dull statements such as, "This essay is going to be about…" or "I'm going to explain…." Instead, start with something that will capture your audience's interest.

Attention-Getters The first sentence is one of the most important sentences in your entire essay. This is your one chance to convince the audience that your paper is worth reading. You will need to make the most of this opportunity. Whatever type of lead-in you choose to get your audience's attention, you will want to ensure that it effectively introduces your thesis statement. The idea is to entice your audience to continue reading your paper.

FIGURE 3.2 Basic Essay Structure

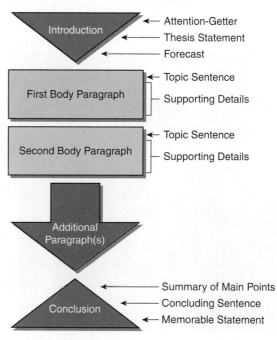

Introduction ← Attention-Getter
← Thesis Statement
← Forecast

First Body Paragraph ← Topic Sentence
⊢ Supporting Details

Second Body Paragraph ← Topic Sentence
⊢ Supporting Details

Additional Paragraph(s)

Conclusion ← Summary of Main Points
← Concluding Sentence
← Memorable Statement

TABLE 3.3

Sample Attention-Getters	
Brief description or story	Two trains were headed toward each other. One was traveling 70 mph, the other 45 mph. The trains collided, causing a loss of 14 lives and injuries to over 100 others. What the passengers didn't know when they boarded the train that fateful day was that one of the engineers had been smoking marijuana before work.
Comparison or contrast	Just as a tiger stalks its prey, serial killers often follow their victims before attacking them.
Dialogue	When Senator Joe Somebody was a young boy, his father said to him, "If you work hard, you're going to have a successful career someday." At the time Little Joey, as he was called then, had no idea of how true his father's words were.
Inspiring or intriguing quote	Samuel Johnson once stated, "Great works are performed, not by strength, but by perseverance."
List of relevant examples	Many public figures have used their celebrity status to help promote a worthy cause. Bono, the lead singer for the band U2, was nominated for the Nobel Peace Prize for his global humanitarian efforts. Talk show host Oprah Winfrey has inspired hundreds of thousands of people to read classic novels. Actress Angelina Jolie has encouraged people to consider the plight of children in Third World countries. Cancer survivor Lance Armstrong, who won the Tour de France seven times, created a foundation to help others struggling with cancer.
Relevant statistic	According to the United States Department of Labor, women made up 46 percent of the total labor force in 2007.
Short summary	On September 12, 2008, Hurricane Ike ripped through Galveston and then moved on to Houston, causing massive damage. It flooded streets, destroyed buildings, and left millions of people stranded without electricity.
Surprising statement	I looked into the woods beyond the rocky path and couldn't believe the grotesque creature I saw!
Thought-provoking question	Have you ever been in a situation that you knew would change your life forever?

Thesis Statement After you have gained your audience's attention, you'll need to state your **thesis**. Your thesis identifies the main idea of your essay for your audience. Typically, the thesis should appear early in the essay, in the first or second paragraph, depending on the length of the attention-getter and the length of the essay. A thesis statement is just like a topic sentence except that it serves an entire essay instead of just one paragraph. A thesis has the same two components as a topic sentence: the topic and your opinion. A thesis, like any complete sentence, needs to have a subject and a verb and express a complete thought.

Poor thesis: Many people earn a college education.

Poor thesis: The benefits of a college education.

Revised thesis: Earning a college education has several benefits.

TABLE 3.4

Sample Thesis Statements	
Strategy	**Example**
Narrating	What began as a casual camping trip to the Great Smoky Mountains turned into a near-tragic event for everyone involved.
Describing	Venice, Italy, is one of the most spectacular cities in the world.
Process writing	Landing the perfect job can be easy if you follow five simple steps.
Comparing and contrasting	Providing for the needs of a child is similar to maintaining a vehicle.
Analyzing causes and effects	Americans can help make the planet a greener place by changing a few simple habits at home, at work, and out in the community.
Persuading	The age at which adults can drink alcoholic beverages should be lowered to 18 throughout the United States.
Evaluating	The *Twilight* series by Stephenie Meyer is an excellent read for teens and adults.
Solving a problem	The best solution for finding a job in a tough economy is to earn a degree in a rapidly growing career field.

Discussion: The first "poor thesis" example simply states a fact about the subject without offering an opinion. The second "poor thesis" example has a subject and an opinion, but it lacks a verb and doesn't express a complete thought. The revised thesis is a complete sentence with a subject and an opinion.

Overview of Main Points Another function of an introduction is to give the reader an overview of the supporting ideas you will cover in the body of the paragraph. This is called a **forecast**. Similar to a forecast that predicts the weather, a forecast in an essay helps the reader to predict what the main points will be.

Thesis with forecast: Earning a college education is beneficial because it can lead to greater self-esteem, a higher-paying job, and a better style of living.

Discussion: This thesis statement suggests that the body paragraphs of the essay will explain each of the benefits mentioned: greater self-esteem, a higher-paying job, and a better style of living.

If the thesis does not contain an overview of the main points you will cover in the essay, then you can include another sentence, or a series of sentences, to give the reader an indication of what to expect. Remember, your forecast should not sound mechanical. You do not necessarily need to include a list of your main points; however, you owe it to your readers to give them some idea of what to expect in the body of the essay.

Body Paragraphs

Body paragraphs are similar to stand-alone paragraphs except that they are part of a larger essay. Often they begin with a topic sentence and include several supporting sentences. Be sure to include enough details and examples to fully support your topic sentence. You may develop your ideas by using one or more of the writing strategies covered in this text: narrating, describing, explaining a process, comparing and contrasting, analyzing causes and effects, persuading, evaluating, or solving a problem. Also, use transitions within the paragraph to help your ideas flow smoothly and at the end of the paragraph to lead the reader into the next body paragraph. To maintain **unity** in your essay, make sure every idea relates to the overall thesis of the essay.

Thesis Identifies the main idea of an essay.

Forecast Helps the reader predict the main points.

Unity Ensures every idea relates to the overall thesis of the essay.

Identify the sentences that do not support the opinion in the topic sentence of the following paragraph. Explain why those sentences should not be included in the paragraph.

Getting around on Two Wheels

Using a scooter for transportation has many benefits. First of all, riding a scooter saves gasoline. Scooters get anywhere from about 60-125 miles per gallon depending on the size of the motor. Riders can feel good about consuming less fuel and enjoy the reward of spending less money at the gas pump. Secondly, scooters are easy to park. They take up less space, giving riders more parking options. Some scooters have a center stand to use when parked that is difficult to operate. Also, many parking lots have spaces set aside for motorcycles and scooters. This can be extremely convenient, especially at places where parking lots tend to fill up. Finally, riding a scooter is fun. Commuting to work or school doesn't seem like a chore when riding a scooter. On a beautiful day riders can enjoy a great breeze and the soothing warmth of the sunshine. Riding in the rain is a whole different story. There's nothing worse than arriving at your destination soaked or muddy, which is why many scooter riders also own a car.

Concluding Paragraph

The last paragraph of your essay should wrap up the entire document. Similar to the introduction, the conclusion should accomplish three tasks: reword your thesis statement, summarize your main points, and end with a memorable thought.

> **Thesis statement in introduction:** Earning a college degree has several benefits.

> **Reworded thesis in conclusion:** Once you have completed your college education, you will enjoy the rewards for the rest of your life.

Avoid introducing new ideas, changing your focus, or upsetting your readers in your conclusion. Also, even though you might be tempted to end with a cliché, such as "and that's the way the cookie crumbles," please resist. Instead, end with a powerful idea that will make a lasting impression on the readers. You may use techniques that are similar to attention-getters, such as quotes, surprising statements, or thought-provoking questions.

Model Essay

"The Art of Eating Spaghetti" from *Growing Up* by Russell Baker

Introduction ⌐

Attention-Getter ⌐

The only thing that truly interested me was writing, and I knew that sixteen-year-olds did not come out of high school and become writers. I thought of writing as something to be done only by the rich. It was so obviously not real work, not a job at which you could earn a living. Still, I had begun to think of myself as a writer. It was the only thing for which I seemed to have the smallest talent, and, silly though it sounded when I told people I'd like to be a writer, it gave me a way of thinking about myself which satisfied my need to have an identity.

Thesis Statement — The notion of becoming a writer had flickered off and on in my head since the Belleville days, but it wasn't until my third year in high school that the possibility took hold. Until then I'd been bored by everything associated with English courses. I found English grammar dull and baffling. I hated the assignments to turn out "compositions," and went at them like heavy labor, turning out leaden, lackluster paragraphs that were agonies for teachers to read and for me to write. The classics thrust on me to read seemed as deadening as chloroform.

First Main Point — When our class was assigned to Mr. Fleagle for third-year English I anticipated another grim year in that dreariest of subjects. Mr. Fleagle was notorious among City students for dullness and inability to inspire. He was said to be stuffy, dull, and hopelessly out of date. To me he looked to be sixty or seventy and prim to a fault. He wore primly severe eyeglasses, his wavy hair was primly cut and primly combed. He wore prim vested suits with neckties blocked primly against the collar buttons of his primly starched white shirts. He had a primly pointed jaw, a primly straight nose, and a prim manner of speaking that was so correct, so gentlemanly, that he seemed a comic antique.

Supporting Details — I anticipated a listless, unfruitful year with Mr. Fleagle and for a long time was not disappointed. We read *Macbeth*. Mr. Fleagle loved *Macbeth* and wanted us to love it too, but he lacked the gift of infecting others with his own passion. He tried to convey the murderous ferocity of Lady Macbeth one day by reading aloud the passage that concludes.

… I have given suck, and know
How tender 'tis to love the babe that milks me.
I would, while it was smiling in my face,
Have plucked my nipple from his boneless gums…

The idea of prim Mr. Fleagle plucking his nipple from boneless gums was too much for the class. We burst into gasps of irrepressible snickering. Mr. Fleagle stopped.

"There is nothing funny, boys, about giving suck to a babe. It is the—the very essence of motherhood, don't you see."

He constantly sprinkled his sentences with "don't you see." It wasn't a question but an exclamation of mild surprise at our ignorance. "Your pronoun needs an antecedent, don't you see," he would say, very primly. "The purpose of the Porter's scene, boys, is to provide comic relief from the horror, don't you see."

Second Main Point — Late in the year we tackled the informal essay. "The essay, don't you see, is the…" My mind went numb. Of all forms of writing, none seemed so boring as the essay. Naturally we would have to write informal essays. Mr. Fleagle distributed a homework sheet offering us a choice of topics. None was quite so simple-minded as "What I Did on My Summer Vacation," but most seemed to be almost as dull. I took the list home and dawdled until the night before the essay was due. Sprawled on the sofa, I finally faced up to the grim task, took the list out of my notebook, and scanned it. The topic on which my eye stopped was "The Art of Eating Spaghetti."

Third Main Point — This title produced an extraordinary sequence of mental images. Surging up out of the depths of memory came a vivid recollection of a night in Belleville when all of us were seated around the supper table—Uncle Allen, my mother, Uncle Charlie, Doris, Uncle Hal—and Aunt Pat served spaghetti for supper. Spaghetti was an exotic treat in those days. Neither Doris nor I had ever eaten spaghetti, and none of the adults had enough experience to be good at it. All the good humor of Uncle Allen's house reawoke in my mind as I recalled the laughing arguments we had that night about the socially respectable method for moving spaghetti from plate to mouth.

Fourth Main Point — Suddenly I wanted to write about that, about the warmth and good feeling of it, but I wanted to put it down simply for my own joy, not for Mr. Fleagle. It was a moment I wanted to recapture and hold for myself. I wanted to relive the pleasure of an evening at New Street. To write it as I wanted, however, would violate all the rules of formal composition I'd learned in school, and Mr. Fleagle would surely give it a failing grade. Never mind, I would write something else for Mr. Fleagle after I had written this thing for myself.

When I finished it the night was half gone and there was no time left to compose a proper, respectable essay for Mr. Fleagle. There was no choice next morning but to turn in my private reminiscence of Belleville. Two days passed before Mr. Fleagle returned the graded papers, and he **Supporting Details** — returned everyone's but mine. I was bracing myself for a command to report to Mr. Fleagle immediately after school for discipline when I saw him lift my paper from his desk and rap for the class's attention.

"Now, boys," he said, "I want to read you an essay. This is titled 'The Art of Eating Spaghetti.'"

And he started to read. My words! He was reading *my words* out loud to the entire class. What's more, the entire class was listening. Listening attentively. Then somebody laughed, then the entire class was laughing, and not in contempt and ridicule, but with openhearted enjoyment. Even Mr. Fleagle stopped two or three times to repress a small prim smile.

Supporting Details —

I did my best to avoid showing pleasure, but what I was feeling was pure ecstasy at this startling demonstration that my words had the power to make people laugh. In the eleventh grade, at the eleventh hour as it were, I had discovered a calling. It was the happiest moment of my entire school career. When Mr. Fleagle finished he put the final seal on my happiness by saying, "Now that, boys, is an essay, don't you see. It's—don't you see—it's of the very essence of the essay, don't you see. Congratulations, Mr. Baker."

Conclusion —
Reworded Thesis —
Memorable Statement —

For the first time, light shone on a possibility. It wasn't a very heartening possibility, to be sure. Writing couldn't lead to a job after high school, and it was hardly honest work, but Mr. Fleagle had opened a door for me. After that I ranked Mr. Fleagle among the finest teachers in the school.

SOURCE: Russell Baker, "The Art of Eating Spaghetti" from pp. 186–189 of *Growing Up* by Russell Baker. Copyright © 1982 by Russell Baker. Published by Congdon and Weed/Contemporary Publishing. Reprinted by permission of Don Congdon Associates, Inc.

Activity Labeling an Article

Choose an interesting article from a printed or online magazine or professional journal. Make a copy of the article or print it out so that you can write on it. Label the essay parts or note any areas that are missing. Being aware of how professional writers organize their essays can help you to become a better writer.

Introduction: Attention-getter, thesis statement, overview of main points.

Body paragraphs: Topic sentences, supporting points, transitions.

Conclusion: Reworded thesis, summary of main points, memorable statement.

After you have labeled the document, determine the effectiveness, or lack thereof, of the article and its organization:

- How effective is the thesis?
- Does the conclusion seem sufficient? Why or why not?
- Are the supporting details sufficient?
- What, if anything, would make the article better?

Note: As an alternative the instructor may choose an article for the class to review individually or together or post it online for students to review in a threaded discussion.

> Writing Attitude Survey

How do you feel about writing? Do you find it to be painful, as Russell Baker once did? Or do you get excited about the prospect of creating a new written work? Take this attitude survey to explore your thoughts on writing. There are no right or wrong answers, but you may learn something about yourself as a writer when you review your answers.

1. How do you feel about writing in general?
2. What are characteristics of good writing?
3. Why is effective writing important?
4. How confident are you in your writing abilities?
5. What are your strengths and weaknesses with writing?
6. What kinds of writing do you enjoy?

7. What kinds of writing do you dislike?

8. How much time do you spend writing each week for work, school, and yourself?

9. What joys or challenges have you faced as a writer?

FIGURE 3.3 Student Example of a Writing Attitude Survey

Matthew Ruffell

Writing Attitude Survey

How do you feel about writing? Do you find it to be painful, as Russell Baker once did? Or do get excited about the prospect of creating a new written work? Take this attitude survey to explore your thoughts on writing. There are no right or wrong answers, but you may learn something about yourself as a writer when you review your answers.

1. How do you feel about writing in general?

    I feel that I spend too much
    time on wording my writing.
    I also put a lot of effort into
    writing, making it entertaining

2. What are characteristics of good writing?

    Good characteristics in writing:
    * *Organization:* Thoughts, not random babbling
    * *Flow:* Is it easy to read, no reading twice
    * *Drummar:* Is it written well, does it sound good reed out loud

3. Why is effective writing important?

    Effective writing is important to:
    * *Convey information of topic*
    * *To catch the reader's interest*

4. How confident are you in your writing abilities?

    I'm not as confident as did like to be.
    I haven't written a paper since 10th grade
    of high school. I'm challanged when it
    comes to choosing my words, using a better
    choice per say.

FIGURE 3.3 Student Example of a Writing Attitude Survey

USE SOME OF THE IDEAS from your responses to the writing attitude survey to write an essay about how you perceive yourself as a writer. Your thesis statement should state your overall view of how you see yourself as a writer. To support your main idea, be sure to include specific details about your past writing experiences.

For example, if writing is one of your favorite activities, you might include details about how you have always kept a journal or how you have received recognition for your excellent writing abilities. You may also choose to include what you like about writing and why it is important to you. If your feelings about writing aren't favorable, you might write about some of the experiences you have had that have led to your discomfort with or dislike for writing. You might also explore what it would take for you to become more confident in your writing abilities.

Another option is to focus on a pivotal experience that changed your perception of yourself as a writer (as Russell Baker did in his essay). Maybe you always hated (or loved) to write until you encountered a particular teacher, boss, or assignment. Exploring your perceptions of yourself as a writer will help you to make the most out of your composition class.

Matthew Ruffell completed a writing attitude survey (see previous page) as part of his discovery process. The following is Matthew's final essay about how he perceives himself as a writer.

A Literary Genius I Am Not
by Matthew Ruffell

When it comes to writing, I'm about as dumb as a bag of hammers. In other words, English composition is not my strongest course of study. I have always dreaded tackling anything that had to do with demonstrating my writing skills. The reason for this is that there are a number of challenges I face when it comes to writing.

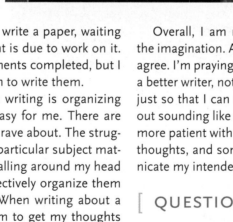

The first challenge I face when writing is having the patience to actually sit down and do the assignment. I don't typically write for any other purpose than an assignment for school or work. The truth is, I have never really had an interest in writing. I guess I have always thought of it as boring, just not for me. By nature, I'm more of a visual person. I prefer pictures and movies to written words. As a result, I always procrastinate when I have to write a paper, waiting until the day before the assignment is due to work on it. I always manage to get my assignments completed, but I find it difficult to be patient enough to write them.

The next challenge I face when writing is organizing my thoughts. Finding a topic is easy for me. There are plenty of things that I can rant and rave about. The struggle is collecting my thoughts on a particular subject matter. I have so many thoughts pin-balling around my head at any one given moment. To collectively organize them would take a lifetime to achieve. When writing about a particular subject, I just can't seem to get my thoughts out on paper. They tend to be choppy and not flow well together. I find myself spending much of my time writing and rewriting my thoughts. I spend much of my time trying to get the wording right and making sure I don't go off on a tangent about something unrelated to the topic. The last thing I want to do is confuse the reader by having an unorganized train of thought. In the end, I will eventually end up with a nicely organized and flowing paper that makes sense to the reader although I nearly beat myself blind doing so.

Another obstacle I face when writing is choosing the right words to emphasize my thoughts on a particular topic. I tend to think that much of my writing is boring, not very exciting to read. One reason for this is I don't have a very large vocabulary. I spend so much time searching for words that will add a little pizzazz to my work, which can be somewhat challenging. I often find myself asking questions such as, "Does that sound right?" "Will the readers understand what I mean?" I want to keep the readers interested and not lull them off to sleep. Using the right word combinations and substitutions in order to emphasize the key points and cut down wordiness is essential. There is almost nothing worse than reading a wordy and boring piece of writing.

Overall, I am not a literary genius by any stretch of the imagination. After reading this essay, you'll be sure to agree. I'm praying that by taking this course I will become a better writer, not so that I can go on to write novels, but just so that I can actually write a paragraph or two without sounding like an idiot. To do this, I'll need to become more patient with my writing, get better at organizing my thoughts, and somehow find the right words to communicate my intended message to my audience.

[QUESTIONS FOR REFLECTION]

1. Which sentence or sentences best state Matthew's main idea?

2. What three main points does Matthew make to support his main idea?

3. Are his supporting details effective? Why or why not?

4. Is Matthew as bad of a writer as he thinks he is? Why or why not?

5. How do your writing experiences compare with Matthew's?

CHAPTER SUMMARY

1. An effective sentence has a subject and a verb and expresses a complete thought.

2. Vary sentence length and structure to add interest to your writing style.

3. A good paragraph contains a topic sentence, supporting sentences, transitions, and a concluding sentence.

4. An effective essay includes an introduction, body, and conclusion.

5. A good introduction captures your audience's attention, states your thesis, and lets the reader know what to expect from the rest of the essay.

6. Well-developed body paragraphs provide enough details and examples to fully support the opinion in your thesis.

7. A solid concluding paragraph restates the thesis in different words, summarizes the main points in the essay, and ends with a memorable thought.

WHAT I KNOW NOW

Use this checklist to determine what you need to work on to feel comfortable with your understanding of the material in this chapter. Check off each item as you master it. Review the material for any unchecked items.

❏ 1. I understand the three requirements for a **complete sentence**.

❏ 2. I am able to **vary the structure** of my sentences.

❏ 3. I can write a suitable **topic sentence** and **concluding sentence** for a paragraph.

❏ 4. I understand how to develop a **paragraph** using specific **supporting details** and examples.

❏ 5. I know the three parts of an **essay**.

❏ 6. I understand how to write an **introductory paragraph** with a **clear thesis**.

❏ 7. I know how to develop **body paragraphs** in an essay.

❏ 8. I can write a solid **concluding paragraph** for an essay.

FURTHER READING ON THE WEB

- Paragraph Development and Topic Sentences:
  http://grammar.ccc.commnet.edu/grammar/paragraphs.htm
- Creating a Thesis Statement: **http://owl.english.purdue.edu/owl/resource/545/01/**
- How to Write an Essay: **http://howtowriteanessay.com**
- Organization of an Essay: **http://writing.colostate.edu/guides/processes/peerreview/organization.cfm**
- Essay Structure: **www.fas.harvard.edu/~wricntr/documents/structure.html**

4

THE CRITICAL THINKING, READING, AND WRITING CONNECTION

LEARNING outcomes

> **In this chapter you will learn techniques for the following:**

4.1 Interpreting written texts.

4.2 Participating in class discussions about readings.

4.3 Interpreting visual texts, including photographs, graphs, advertisements, and Web sites.

4.4 Identifying logical fallacies.

> Thinking Critically

You are surrounded by written and visual texts on a daily basis. Whether watching television, surfing the Web, reading an article, viewing a clip on YouTube.com, instant messaging with a friend, or studying a textbook, you are being bombarded by different kinds of messages and images. The messages that you encounter are often misleading or contradictory. Therefore, you have to be able to think critically about them to determine what ideas to accept or reject.

Critical thinking is similar to detective work. When you think critically, you interpret (analyze) ideas and reflect on them. You are going beyond the written or visual text to uncover the hidden meanings within. To do that you have to evaluate the credibility of the sources and the logic presented through them to determine if you agree or disagree with the information you are receiving. Being able to think critically will help you to become a better reader, writer, and decision maker. One way to strengthen your critical thinking skills is by learning how to read and interpret written and visual texts.

Critical thinking Interpreting ideas and reflecting on them.

4.1 > Reading and Interpreting Written Texts

Reading is one of the best ways to get inspiration for writing. In addition to providing stimulating ideas to respond to, reading helps you strengthen your vocabulary and see how others have approached writing tasks. Becoming a good analytical reader can help you become a good critical thinker and writer. These skills will help you to be successful in school, in your career, and in other areas of your life.

Reading critically is different from reading for pleasure. When you read with a critical eye, you are searching for clues, analyzing details, and making inferences to form your own opinions about the work. Different readers will likely have unique responses to a written text based on their knowledge, experiences, interests, and so on. While there may not be one "right" way to interpret a particular text, some interpretations are more informed than others. Use this three-step process for a close, critical reading: (1) pre-read and anticipate; (2) read and analyze; (3) reread and annotate.

1. Pre-read and Anticipate

Before reading, look at the work to get an idea of what to expect when you read it.

- **Publication information:** Where and when was the article originally published? Is the content relevant today, or does it provide a glimpse into the past?
- **Biographical information:** If you have access to it, consider the author's biographical information. What is the writer's occupation and education? Does he or she appear to be qualified to discuss the topic at hand? Does the writer seem to have any particular bias about the subject?
- **Title:** Contemplate the title. What do you expect from the work based on the title? Does the title entice you to want to read the material?
- **Overview:** Skim through the text. Look at headings, visual images, and overall organization to help prepare you for a more careful reading. Read the introductory paragraph and the topic sentence in each supporting paragraph so you have an idea of what you will learn from the material.
- **Predictions:** Based on your preview, identify what you already know about the subject, and make predictions about what you will learn from the text. Keep in mind that your predictions may or may not be accurate.

2. Read and Analyze

After you have skimmed through the text and thought about what you know about the subject and hope to find out, then it's time to read the text carefully and analyze it. The term *analyze* means to break something down into its parts. You can examine the parts of an essay to understand it better.

- **Main idea:** As you begin reading, find the author's thesis. What point is the author trying to convey to the reader? Is the thesis stated clearly and effectively?
- **Supporting points:** What specific details and examples does the author use to substantiate his or her thesis? How does the supporting material serve to extend or clarify the author's main point? Is the support sufficient and accurate?

FIGURE 4.1
The Rhetorical Star

- **Rhetorical star:** Determine the five points of the author's rhetorical star. What is the *subject*? What *audience* is the author trying to reach? What was the author's *purpose* in writing (to inform, persuade, analyze, express feelings, or entertain)? What writing *strategy* (or strategies) does the author use to achieve his or her purpose. Is the author narrating, describing, explaining a process, comparing and contrasting, explaining causes and effects, persuading, evaluating, or solving a problem? What is the *design* of the text? How is it organized? Are visuals included? (See Chapter 1 for more details about the rhetorical star.)

3. Reread and Annotate

After you have carefully read the text, you should read it again to highlight key ideas, make notes in the margins, and record your thoughts about what you're reading. Completing these tasks will help you to process what you have read so that you can use the information later for a test, discussion, or writing assignment.

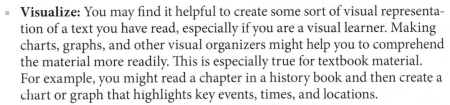

- **Define:** Note any words you come across that are unfamiliar to you. While you don't have to look up every new word you read, sometimes you may encounter a word that is critical to your understanding of the work. Determine if you need to look up the meanings of those words or if you can figure them out well enough in context.

- **Summarize:** One of the best ways to understand and remember something that you have read is to summarize it in your own words. When you write a summary, you focus on the main point and supporting details. Be sure to place any exact wording you borrow from the original text in quotation marks so that you can distinguish your words from the author's when you read your summary later.

- **Visualize:** You may find it helpful to create some sort of visual representation of a text you have read, especially if you are a visual learner. Making charts, graphs, and other visual organizers might help you to comprehend the material more readily. This is especially true for textbook material. For example, you might read a chapter in a history book and then create a chart or graph that highlights key events, times, and locations.

- **Synthesize:** The term *synthesize* means to put together. After you have read and broken down the material, then you want to put the ideas together in a meaningful way. When you synthesize, you connect the ideas you are reading to what you already know about the subject based on other texts and personal experience. When you connect the new material to prior knowledge, you'll be better able to comprehend and recall the new material.

- **Question and evaluate:** After you have carefully read and reread the text, critique it by asking a variety of questions:

  » What is the author's tone? Is it straightforward, sarcastic, or pretentious?

  » Is the thesis fully supported?

  » Are the details and examples relevant?

  » Does the author seem biased? If so, how?

  » Which details are based on verifiable facts, opinionated statements, or personal values?

  » Has the author used any logical fallacies?

  » Is the text convincing and effective? Why or why not?

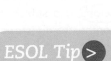

ESOL Tip >

Use contextual clues to determine the meaning of words instead of relying too heavily on dictionary definitions.

> annotated essay

"ANIMATING A BLOCKBUSTER: INSIDE PIXAR'S CREATIVE MAGIC"
BY JONAH LEHRER

Preview

Jonah Lehrer, a graduate of Columbia University, is the author of two books, *Proust Was a Neuroscientist* (2008) and *How We Decide* (2010). He has written articles for a number of periodicals, including *The New Yorker, The Washington Post*, and *The Boston Globe*. Currently he is a contributing editor for *Scientific American Mind* and *Wired* magazine, where the following article about Pixar's creative process was originally appeared. Go to Pixar. com for a complete list of movies and a more detailed explanation of how Pixar makes films. Have you ever seen a Pixar film, such as *Up* (2009) or Toy Story 3 (2010)? Did you enjoy it? Did you ever wonder how Pixar created its movies?

attention getter

Screenwriter William Goldman once famously declared that the most important fact of life in Hollywood is that "nobody knows anything." It was his way of describing a reality that continues to haunt the movie business: Studio executives have no idea which pictures will make money.

bold quote

Unless, of course, those pictures are made by Pixar Animation Studios. Since 1995, when the first *Toy Story* was released, Pixar has made nine films, and every one has been a smashing success.

main idea →

Pixar's secret? Its unusual creative process. Most of the time, a studio assembles a cast of freelance professionals to work on a single project and cuts them lose when the picture is done. At Pixar, a staff of writers, directors, animators, and technicians move from project to project. As a result, the studio has built a team of moviemakers who know and trust one another in ways unimaginable on most sets.

This explains Pixar's Creative Process.

Which explains how they can handle constant critiques that are at the heart of Pixar's relentless process. Animation days at the studio all begin the same way: The animators and director gather in a small screening room filled with comfy couches. They eat Cap'n Crunch and drink coffee. Then the team begins analyzing the few seconds of film animated the day before, as they ruthlessly "shred" each frame. Even the most junior staffers are encouraged to join in.

Do the sugar and caffeine help with creativity?

rank or level of authority

The upper echelons also subject themselves to megadoses of healthy criticism. Every few months, the director of each Pixar film meets with the brain trust, a group of senior creative staff. The purpose of the meeting is to offer comments on the work in progress, and that can lead to some major rivisions. "It's important that nobody gets mad at you for screwing up," says Lee Unkrich, director of *Toy Story 3*. "We know screwups are an essential part of making something good. That's why our goal is to screw up as fast as possible."

interesting term

Nice idea— "screw ups" are a welcome part of the creative process.

*ow! That's a
: of cash!*

The proof is in the product. The average international gross per Pixar film is more than ($550 million,) and the cartoons are critical darlings—the studio has collected 24 academy awards. Nobody in Hollywood knows anything. Pixar seems to know *everything* ← *italicized for emphasis*

This brainstorming process works for medical teams, business leaders, and more

SOURCE: Jonah Lehrer. "Animating a Blockbuster: Inside Pixar's Creative Magic" from the June 2010 issue of *Wired*, p. 141.

▶ *Activity*   **Interpreting an Essay**

Choose an interesting article from a newspaper, magazine, or online source that relates to your major or a particular interest or hobby.

Pre-read and anticipate: Preview the article and make predictions about what it will cover.

Read and analyze: Read through the text and determine the main points, supports, and rhetorical star.

Reread and annotate: Go through the text more thoroughly, and annotate it with your comments. You might circle vocabulary words, write questions, summarize material, create a visual organizer, and so on.

Note: You may want to choose a reading selection from later in this textbook or a chapter from a textbook for another class.

4.2 > Participating in Class Discussions about Readings

Whether you are taking your composition course on campus or online, your instructor will likely have you discuss some of the readings for the course. Here are some tips to follow for live or virtual class discussions:

1. Read the selection carefully, and have your notes and annotations handy during the discussion.

2. Skim through the questions at the end of the selection in case your instructor asks you to discuss some of them in class or in a threaded discussion.

3. Listen to (or read) your classmates' comments with an open mind.

4. Share your opinions about the work, even if they contradict another classmate's opinion. However, be tactful with your responses. Also, you'll need to back up your opinions with specific details and examples from the text.

5. Feel free to ask questions about areas of the text that are confusing or ambiguous (having more than one interpretation). If you have a question about a text, you are probably not the only one in the class who does.

6. Take notes during the discussion. You never know what might show up later on a test or writing assignment.

4.3 > Reading and Interpreting Visual Texts

Visual texts surround you on a daily basis. Sometimes visual texts accompany written texts, and other times they appear alone. You find them in e-mail messages, Web sites, magazines, television shows, films, billboards, textbooks, newspapers, and so on. Similar to written texts, visual texts are designed to serve a particular purpose and convey a message to the reader. As a result, you need to be visually literate to help make sense of them.

Visual literacy The ability to read and interpret a variety of visual texts.

Visual literacy refers to the idea of being able to read and interpret a variety of visual texts. While visual texts may seem easier to understand than written texts, often they are not. Sometimes the message is a little more challenging to discern. Understanding the hidden meanings in visual texts requires many of the critical thinking strategies that you use for written texts. Here are some ideas to consider when analyzing different images, such as photographs and paintings, charts and graphs, and advertisements:

Visual texts surround us every day. They are designed to serve a particular purpose and convey a specific message.

Reading and Interpreting Visual Texts

1. **Subject:** Does the image focus on people, objects, numbers, a setting, or an event? How is the subject matter portrayed? What kind of action is taking place (if any)?

2. **Purpose:** Is the goal to evoke emotions, persuade the viewer to do something, provide an example of a concept, or visually represent ideas presented in a written text? What message is being conveyed?

3. **Audience:** Who is targeted by the image? Is it geared toward the general public or people who represent a particular education level, age group, background, ethnicity, attitude, religious affiliation, hobby, or other group?

4. **Writing:** If written text is included, how does it integrate with the visual image? Does the text consist of just a caption, or are more details included? Do the written text and visual image complement each other, or are they contradictory? Does the written or visual text stand out more?

5. **Logic:** Is the image misleading in any way, or does it fairly and accurately represent the subject?

6. **Effectiveness:** Does the image or advertisement accomplish its purpose? Is it convincing? Why or why not?

> annotated photograph

Fish Pedicures: Carp Rid Human Feet of Scaly Skin

Ready for the latest in spa pampering? Prepare to dunk your tootsies in a tank of water and let tiny carp nibble away.

Fish pedicures are creating something of a splash in the D.C. area, where a northern Virginia spa has been offering them for the past four months. John Ho, who runs the Yvonne Hair and Nails salon with his wife, Yvonne Le, said 5,000 people have taken the plunge so far.

"This is a good treatment for everyone who likes to have nice feet," Ho said.

He said he wanted to come up with something unique while finding a replacement for pedicures that use razors to scrape off dead skin. The razors have fallen out of favor with state regulators because of concerns about whether they're sanitary.

Ho was skeptical at first about the fish, which are called garra rufa but typically known as doctor fish. They were first used in Turkey and have become popular in some Asian countries.

But Ho doubted they would thrive in the warm water needed for a comfortable footbath. And he didn't know if customers would like the idea.

"I know people were a little intimidated at first," Ho said. "But I just said, 'Let's give it a shot.'"

Customers were quickly hooked.

Tracy Roberts, 33, of Rockville, Md., heard about it on a local radio show. She said it was "the best pedicure I ever had" and has spread the word to friends and co-workers.

"I'd been an athlete all my life, so I've always had calluses on my feet. This was the first time somebody got rid of my calluses completely," she said.

First time customer KaNin Reese, 32, of Washington, described the tingling sensation created by the toothless fish: "It kind of feels like your foot's asleep," she said.

SOURCE: "Fish pedicures: Carp rid human feet of scaly skin," The Associated Press, July 21, 2008.

TABLE 4.1

Photograph Interpretation Notes	
Subject	Fish that give pedicures: The large photo is of a foot with red painted toenails that are submerged in water with fish that appear to be sucking on the toes. The small picture shows three women at a spa with their feet immersed in water that is filled with toe-sucking fish. From the looks on their faces, they seem to be intrigued by the fish.
Purpose	To illustrate a new trend that is beginning at spas.
Audience	Women primarily, and possibly men too, who go to spas and might be interested in a natural pedicure experience.
Writing	The title is very catchy. While the pictures stand out the most, the text does provide useful additional information, such as the costs for the spa owner and patrons interested in the fish pedicure experience. The written text also explains that the fish don't bite, which would be impossible to tell just from the photo. The photos and writing complement each other well, and both are essential to the audience's understanding of the subject.
Logic	The story is presented clearly and effectively. There are no tricks or apparent flaws in logic.
Effectiveness	The article is very effective for anyone interested in the subject. The close-up photograph of the fish makes the viewer wonder what it would be like to have a fish pedicure, even if the viewer doesn't regularly frequent spas.

> annotated graphs

NUMBERS

Yes, The Health-Care Business Is Recession-Proof

By Tara Kalwarski/Charts by David Foster

Health-care companies in the Standard & Poor's 500-stock index held up better than the overall market during the crash. In fact, many industry execs think the recession helped them. No wonder: Profit margins mostly rose, and the earnings outlook is good.

SOURCE: "Numbers: Yes, The Health-Care Business Is Recession-Proof," Bloomberg Businessweek, February, 2010, p.9.

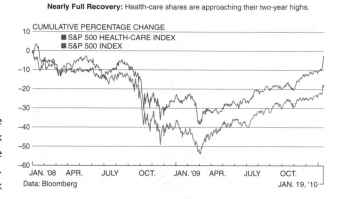

Nearly Full Recovery: Health-care shares are approaching their two-year highs.

CUMULATIVE PERCENTAGE CHANGE
- ■ S&P 500 HEALTH-CARE INDEX
- ■ S&P 500 INDEX

Data: Bloomberg

JAN. '08   APR.   JULY   OCT.   JAN. '09   APR.   JULY   OCT.   JAN. 19, '10

2010 FORECAST FOR LARGE U.S. HEALTH-CARE COMPANIES

	EARNINGS GROWTH	PROFIT MARGIN
Pfizer	11%	31%
Merck	6%	31%
Abbott Laboratories	12%	22%
Amgen	2%	36%
Medtronic	10%	26%

Data: Bloomberg

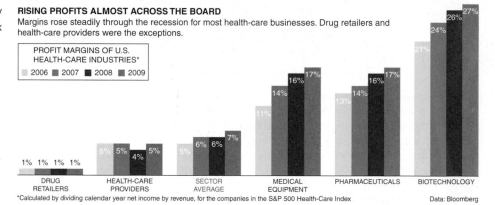

RISING PROFITS ALMOST ACROSS THE BOARD

Margins rose steadily through the recession for most health-care businesses. Drug retailers and health-care providers were the exceptions.

PROFIT MARGINS OF U.S. HEALTH-CARE INDUSTRIES*
■ 2006 ■ 2007 ■ 2008 ■ 2009

DRUG RETAILERS	HEALTH-CARE PROVIDERS	SECTOR AVERAGE	MEDICAL EQUIPMENT	PHARMACEUTICALS	BIOTECHNOLOGY
1% 1% 1% 1%	5% 5% 4% 5%	5% 6% 6% 7%	11% 14% 16% 17%	13% 14% 16% 17%	21% 24% 26% 27%

*Calculated by dividing calendar year net income by revenue, for the companies in the S&P 500 Health-Care Index

Data: Bloomberg

TABLE 4.2

	Graph Interpretation Notes
Subject	Health care: The graphs display various statistics related to the health care industry. The line graph illustrates that health care shares made a rebound in 2009. The chart at the top shows the earnings growth and profit margins for several companies. The bar graph at the bottom clearly indicates that rising profits were nearly universal in the heath care industry, with a couple of exceptions.
Purpose	The main purpose of the graphs is to inform the readers that the health care industry still thrives during a recession. A second purpose is to persuade the audience of the accuracy of the claim by including a variety of charts and graphs to help the audience visualize the positive growth.
Audience	The audience is the readership of *Bloomberg Businessweek*, which is probably a fairly educated group. Readers might include business owners, college students, people working in the health care industry, and people who are considering going into the health care field.
Writing	The title of the article is simply "Numbers," which may cause the readers to look more closely to find out what kinds of numbers are being discussed. The sentences at the beginning introduce the graphs and make the claim that the health care industry is recession-proof. Additionally, each chart or graph has a descriptive title to catch the audience's attention as well as a few clear labels and brief explanations.
Logic	The logic of the graph seems fine, and the numbers do not appear to be skewed or misrepresented in any way. The statistics illustrated in the charts and graphs come from reputable sources.
Effectiveness	The graph seems to depict the findings accurately; however, only five large health care companies are included in the findings. Additional research might be necessary to determine if those numbers hold true for other, smaller companies. Overall, the article appears to be effective.

> annotated ad

SOURCE: Advertisement from *Discover*, October 2008, p. 89.

TABLE 4.3

Advertisement Interpretation Notes	
Subject	Sanyo eneloop batteries: The ad contains a photograph of a professional man with five hands holding a mouse, computer, CDs, coffee, and the world. In the outlet is a set of four batteries charging.
Purpose	To persuade the readers that Sanyo eneloop batteries will help them to be successful in their careers by keeping their mouse, computer, and other electronics charged.
Audience	Busy, career-oriented men and women who use products that require batteries.
Writing	The written text at the top of the ad states, "eneloop is your life: encommand." The misspelling of *in command* is done intentionally to emphasize the "eneloop" product name. The text at the bottom of the ad clarifies the image by explaining that people have "deals to make, data to download…" so they "don't have time to worry about batteries." The writing enhances the image without overshadowing it.
Logic	The man has five hands and the world is in one of them, but the audience is not expected to take the image literally. The ad accurately illustrates the concept that some consumers feel overwhelmed by all of the tasks required of them. Many people feel that they need five hands (and coffee) to get everything accomplished.
Effectiveness	The ad is effective because many readers will relate to the concepts portrayed in the ad. Most people use batteries for a number of small electronic products, and many have had the frustrating experience of having dead batteries without convenient replacements handy. The ad leaves the impression that eneloop battery users will be in command of the world.

Choose a photograph, chart, or advertisement in a printed or online textbook, magazine, or newspaper. Interpret the image based on its subject, purpose, audience, writing, logic, and effectiveness. You may want to share your chart with another classmate or group.

> Reading and Interpreting Web Sites

Critical thinking skills are especially important when it comes to analyzing Web sites. Unlike books, magazines, television shows, and movies, some Web sites do not go through a review process. That means anyone with limited computer skills can post something on the Web, no matter how inaccurate it may be. While the Internet is an extremely valuable tool for gaining information, you want to be sure that the ideas and images presented are trustworthy. Use professional Web sites from reputable organizations. Here are some tips for making sure that the Web sites you use are useful and credible:

1. **Source:** Notice who posted the information on the Web. Is the author an expert in the field with the appropriate credentials? Is the organization reputable? If you have doubts about the author or organization, then you may want to investigate by searching for a biography of the author or the history of the organization. Also, check the uniform resource locator (URL). Look for clues that tell you about the identity of the Web site. For example, commercial sites end in "com," government sites end in "gov," educational sites end in "edu," and nonprofit organization sites end in "org."

2. **Date:** Check to see when the information was posted. In many cases you'll want to have the most up-to-date information. If the information seems too old, then find a more current source.

3. **Logic:** If the claims seem too good to be true or highly improbable, then you'll want to verify the information from another source.

4. **References:** Notice if the Web site documents its sources. Most reputable sites will include a bibliography to back up the information they presents. If there is a list of sources, look to see if they seem appropriate. If no sources are cited, then you may want to be wary of the information, unless an expert with good credentials provides the ideas.

5. **Visual images:** Use the strategies you read about earlier in the text to analyze the visual material included in the Web site. If you can hardly believe what you're looking at, then it's possible that a photograph has been altered and is intentionally misleading.

6. **Links:** See if the links work and if they lead to useful information. If they don't work or seem inappropriate, then you'll want to try another Web site.

7. **Effectiveness:** How useful is the content? Is it relevant? Is it presented clearly and logically? Does the material seem accurate? If a Web site you are viewing seems to be inaccurate, then you can always go to an *anti-hoax site* to check its validity. Two popular anti-hoax sites are www.nonprofit.net/hoax and www.scambusters.org. If the Web site you are viewing is listed, then find a new source.

> annotated web site

SOURCE: news.nationalgeographic.com/news/2008/09/photogalleries/animal-photosweek10/ index.html.

TABLE 4.4

Web Site Interpretation Notes	
Source	National Geographic: The URL ends in "com," but that's no guarantee of authenticity. National Geographic has a reputable magazine. John Roach is a regular writer for National Geographic and appears to be a credible author.
Date	The article was posted eight days after the event, so the material was current when it was posted.
Logic	The Web site presents factual information in a clear and effective manner. The title is intentionally misleading, but supported by the photograph of the pig "flying."
References	References are not included, but they are not necessary for this particular topic. The Web site is just reporting the event that took place in Melbourne, Australia.
Visual images	The "flying" pig photograph tells more than the words do. The picture really captures the essence of the event.
Links	All of the links work, and they lead to useful information from reputable sources.
Effectiveness	The Web site is quite effective. In addition to the pig story in the screen shot, the Web site covers a wide variety of other plant and animal subjects. This would be a useful Web source for a research project related to plants or animals.

Go to **www.malepregnancy.com**, or choose another Web site that interests you. You might consider a source on a topic that you might like to investigate further. Complete a chart, like the one above, giving your interpretation of the Web site. You may want to share your chart with another classmate or group.

4.6 >   Logical Fallacies

Logical fallacies Occur when someone draws a conclusion not based on sound reasoning.

Logical reasoning uses sound judgment. **Logical fallacies**, on the other hand, occur when someone draws a conclusion without using sound reasoning. To identify logical fallacies, or flaws in reasoning, you have to think critically about the written and visual texts you read. Sometimes writers purposely employ logical fallacies to try to mislead the reader into seeing things a particular way. For instance, politicians and advertisers may use logical fallacies to try to fool their audiences into believing they are the best candidate or have the best product. This is not an ethical approach for swaying the reader. Other times writers use logical fallacies inadvertently as they try to prove a point because they are not aware of the flawed reasoning they are presenting.

As you read written and visual texts, you need to be familiar with logical fallacies so that you can recognize them and interpret the texts accurately. You'll also want to avoid using flawed logic in your own writing. Here are a few of the most common types of logical fallacies.

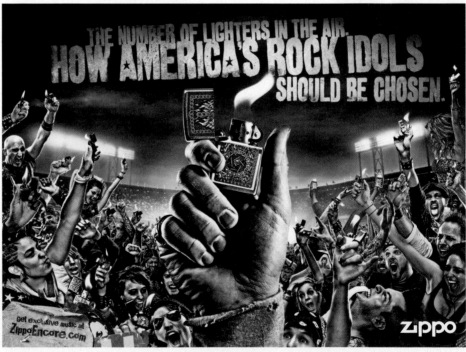

Band Wagon Fallacy: Everyone has a Zippo, so you should get one too.

SOURCE: Advertisement from *Rolling Stone*, June 11, 2009, p. 53.

TABLE 4.5

Logical Fallacies			
Type	**Definition**	**Example**	**Explanation**
Band Wagon	Implying that an idea must be accurate if it is popular. Join the crowd.	Everyone knows that holistic medicine is better than traditional medicine.	Even if many people believe it, that doesn't provide scientific proof for the argument.
Card Stacking	Providing evidence for only one side of a case or deliberately omitting essential information that would change the reader's opinion.	Sunni should get a promotion because she has never missed a day at work.	Supervisors consider many factors when deciding whom to promote. Maybe Sunni often arrives late or does poor work.
Character Attack or Ad Hominem	Attacking a person rather than an issue.	Candidate X should not become the next company president because he divorced his wife.	His divorce has nothing to do with whether or not he would make a good company president.
Circular Reasoning or Begging the Question	Attempting to support a position by simply restating it in a different way.	Dr. Brilliant is a good instructor because he teaches his students well.	The idea is merely being repeated without offering any specific evidence as to what makes Dr. Brilliant an effective instructor.
Either/Or Reasoning	Suggesting there are only two possible solutions to a problem (one right and one wrong) when, in reality, there could be many potential options for resolving the issue.	Either the government needs to subsidize gas costs or our economy is going to collapse.	First of all, does the entire economy depend on the price of gas? Also, there are several ways to cut down on fuel costs other than having the government help to offset the price.
False Analogy	Comparing things that are not similar in the most important respects.	The governor scored a touchdown with the new property tax increase proposal.	The governor is not a football player, so the analogy doesn't make sense.
False Authority or Testimonial	Mentioning an authority figure or celebrity as support for arguing a point.	Eric Zane, who plays Dr. Mark Gnome on *Haye's Anatomy*, recommends taking "Cure it All" pills, so they must be effective.	He is a television character, not a real doctor, so he is not qualified to recommend a specific type of treatment.
False Cause or Post Hoc	Suggesting that because one thing happened after another, the first event caused the second one.	I ate chocolate and my sore throat disappeared.	The sore throat could have gone away for another reason unrelated to the chocolate.
Glittering Generality	Using emotionally charged words, such as *love, truth, honor, democracy,* and *justice,* to gain the audience's approval.	If you are truly patriotic, you need to do the honorable thing and vote to increase your local sales tax.	The implication is that voting a particular way will determine if someone is (or is not) patriotic and honorable.
Hasty Generalization	Drawing a conclusion without having sufficient evidence.	A child comes home from school without homework, so the parent assumes that the teacher did not assign any.	The child may have forgotten to bring home the work or may be intentionally misleading the parent.
Non Sequitur	The conclusion does not logically follow the evidence that is provided.	Guns are legal in the United States. No wonder the crime rate is so high.	Many factors contribute to the crime rate in the United States. One can't assume that there is only one cause or that guns are the cause for crime.
Red Herring	Diverting the reader's attention away from the main issue by introducing something irrelevant. It comes from the practice of dragging a stinky fish across the ground to distract tracking dogs away from a scent.	The idea of gay marriages is an important issue, but do gay people really want to deal with all of the pressures associated with marriage?	The second part is irrelevant because it has nothing to do with whether gay marriages should be legal or not.

—continued

—*Table 4.5 continued*

Logical Fallacies			
Type	**Definition**	**Example**	**Explanation**
Slippery Slope	Suggesting that if one change occurs, then other, unwanted, changes will inevitably occur as well. The analogy is that once someone starts sliding down a "slippery slope," then he or she won't be able to stop.	If we allow dogs on the beach, then the next thing you know dogs will be sitting at tables in fine restaurants.	The two events are unrelated, so there's no reason to assume that one event will lead to the other.
Stereotyping	Attaching a trait to people who belong to a particular religious, ethnic, racial, age, or other group.	Old people make terrible drivers, so they shouldn't be allowed to drive.	This is an unfair claim because many senior citizens are fine drivers.
Tradition	If something has always been done a certain way, then it must be the correct way.	Our company has always bought cigars and champagne for our clients during the holidays. We don't need to change to something else.	Just because the tradition is long-standing doesn't mean that it's a good one. Some clients may not like cigars, and some might not be able to tolerate alcohol. Another gift might be more appropriate.

▶ *Activity* **Identifying Logical Fallacies**

A. Identify and explain the fallacies in these statements. Note that some statements contain more than one fallacy:

1. Amalie Dubois speaks English as a second language, so she will never be a good writer.
2. People who ride motorcycles are all rebellious outlaws who should be locked up in prison.
3. Dean Meanzie is incompetent because he doesn't know what he is doing.
4. We should nominate Susie Saucer for president of the Student Government Association because she gets good grades in math class.
5. Either the college will have to allow students to retake classes for free, or the enrollment is going to seriously decrease.
6. Everyone eats at Princess Pizza after the game, so that restaurant must have the best pizza in town.

B. Choose five types of logical fallacies and write original examples for them. If possible, trade lists with another classmate or group. Identify the fallacies in each other's examples and explain why the reasoning is flawed.

What logical fallacy appears in the M&M advertisement above?

SOURCE: Advertisement from *Rolling Stone*, June 11, 2009, p. 42.

Stacie Ross wrote the following essay in response to an advertisement for milk sponsored by America's Milk Processors that she came across in *Women's Health* magazine.

The Body of an Olympian
by Stacie Ross

Would you like to have a lean, sculpted, and healthy body? Drinking milk could help you develop the body of an Olympian. Well, that is the message implied in the milk advertisement that appeared in the June 2009 issue of *Women's Health* magazine. It's summer, that time of year when people will wear fewer clothes and want to look their best doing it. Subscribers are reading this magazine in hopes of learning new ways to achieve a healthier lifestyle. The "got milk?" ad is convincing because the images and words inspire readers to want to add nutritious milk to their diets so they can experience the healthful benefits.

The purpose of the ad is to convince readers that they too should drink milk after exercising to obtain the same wellness as an Olympic swimmer. The ad never makes any claims that anyone who drinks milk three times a day can look as good as Dara Torres, yet viewers cannot help but wonder if their bodies would look like that. Nor does that ad imply that drinking milk gives Dara the stamina to train hard and achieve picture perfect results. However, when consumers see this ad, they might want to knock back a big cool glass of low-fat or fat-free milk.

Additionally, the images in the ad are quite appealing and serve to make the ad more persuasive. There is an ocean of calm, blue water that seems to go on forever. It just about makes the readers want to jump in and go for a swim. Then there are the huge, fluffy, milky white clouds that let the reader almost feel the cool, gentle wind. There stands forty-six-year-old, five-times Olympic swimmer, Dara "Dairy" Torres with all her rippling muscles, wearing a tiny bikini, and sporting a thick, milk mustache. On a warm summer day, after a long, exhausting workout, athletes would want a cold, revitalizing drink to help them cool down.

Finally, Dara Torres's words in the "got milk?" advertisement add to its credibility. Dara states, "I'm a natural in water. But after a workout, my natural choice is milk." She also gives the readers a few facts about milk: "The protein helps build muscle, plus its unique mix of nutrients helps me refuel. Three glasses of lowfat or fat free milk a day. Lap it up." Her statements might convince the readers that milk is the logical choice of beverage they need to be strong and healthy. Many of the readers of *Women's Health* magazine are aware that the National Institute of Health has been advising consumers to drink more milk for years. Furthermore, women have become more aware of the fact that they need to con-

Dairy Torres.
I'm a natural in water. But after a workout, my natural choice is milk. It's a strong starting block for wellness. The protein helps build muscle, plus its unique mix of nutrients helps me refuel. Three glasses of lowfat or fat free milk a day. Lap it up.

Drink well. Live well.
got milk?

SOURCE: Advertisement from *Women's Health*, June 2009.

sume enough calcium daily to promote bone health and prevent osteoporosis. Savvy readers will react positively to the ad when they are reminded of these facts.

Most readers realize they will never attain the physique of Dara Torres. However, after viewing the "got milk?" advertisement in *Women's Health* magazine, many might just be persuaded to add a glass or two with their daily meals or after a workout. Why not drink milk if it could possibly help one to obtain the body of an Olympian?

[QUESTIONS FOR REFLECTION]

1. What kind of attention-getter does Stacie use? Is it effective? Why or why not?

2. Identify Stacie's thesis. What is her overall opinion of the "got milk?" advertisement? Do you agree or disagree with her position? Why?

3. What are the main points in the essay? Are the body paragraphs in the essay organized effectively? Why or why not?

4. Find examples of transitions in the essay. Are they helpful? Are there enough transitions for Stacie's essay to flow smoothly? Explain.

5. The advertisement uses the testimonial of a famous Olympian to help encourage consumers to buy milk. Is it logical for Dara Torres to sell milk? Is she a credible authority figure for this product? Why or why not?

Write NOW!

USE THE CRITICAL THINKING SKILLS you have learned in this chapter to write a response to the M&M advertisement or another visual image, Web site, or written text. If you haven't done so already, you may want to complete an interpretation chart on the subject before attempting your essay. Use the criteria provided in the chapter for the type of subject you choose.

[CHAPTER SUMMARY]

1. Strengthening your critical thinking skills will help you to become a better reader, writer, and decision maker.

2. Learning to read written texts, visual texts, and Web sites with a critical eye will help you to strengthen your reading and writing skills.

3. Applying your critical thinking skills during a live or online class discussion will help you to strengthen your reading and writing skills.

4. Learning to recognize logical fallacies will help you to strengthen your critical thinking, reading, and writing skills.

[WHAT I KNOW NOW]

Use this checklist to determine what you need to work on in order to feel comfortable with your understanding of the material in this chapter. Check off each item as you master it. Review the material for any unchecked items.

❏ 1. I know what **critical thinking** means.

❏ 2. I am familiar with the **three-step reading process**.

❏ 3. I know how to use an **interpretation chart** to evaluate a written text, image, or Web site.

❏ 4. I am aware of strategies I can use to communicate in **class discussions**.

❏ 5. I know how to recognize several different types of **logical fallacies**.

[FURTHER READING ON THE WEB]

- The Critical Thinking Community: **www.criticalthinking.org**
- Critical Thinking on the Web: **www.austhink.org/critical**
- SQ3R Reading Strategy: **www.studygs.net/texred2.htm**
- Picture This—Visual Literacy Activities: **http://museumca.org/picturethis/visual.html**
- Logical Fallacies: **www.logicalfallacies.info**

> OVERVIEW of Part 2

PART 2

Writing Strategies

Why Writing Strategies Can Be Combined

Each chapter in Part 2 is based on a writing strategy and a theme, so the readings and images are connected. The writing strategies are addressed one at a time so that you can master the specific skills that each type of writing requires. You may want to practice the strategies individually at first to become proficient with them. As you become more comfortable with each technique, then you may want to begin combining writing strategies as needed.

In the real world, writing methods are often combined, depending on the circumstances of the writing task. For example, someone writing an article about yoga might begin by describing what yoga is. Then the author may explain the physical and metal benefits (effects) of participating in yoga to convince (persuade) the reader that learning to do yoga is worthwhile. Finally, the writer might explain the steps in the process so that the reader understands what to do. You'll notice that many of the readings in this text reflect the common practice of mixing writing strategies. As you go about your writing assignments in Part 2, you'll want to choose the writing methods that best suit your rhetorical star.

NARRATING:
MEMORIES

LEARNING outcomes

> In this chapter you will learn techniques for the following:

5.1 Identifying real-world applications for writing a narrative.

5.2 Understanding the steps for writing a narrative.

5.3 Interpreting images and narrative readings about memories.

5.4 Analyzing the rhetorical star for narrating.

5.5 Applying the steps for writing a narrative.

> Writing Strategy Focus: Narrating

Narration is the art of storytelling. When we narrate a story, we document the facts to retell what happened, based on our memories, so that someone who wasn't there has a good idea of what happened. Although narratives can be fiction, this chapter focuses mostly on real, nonfiction narratives. While fictitious stories are fabricated, nonfiction narratives need to be based on events that really occurred.

We are constantly surrounded by stories in the news, documentaries, movies, television programs, commercials, and even e-mail messages. We find others' stories engaging because they allow us to peek into someone else's world. Sometimes we relate to the experiences of the storyteller, and other times we are surprised by the unique situations that others have faced. In this chapter you will have an opportunity to read about others' memories and to write about your own. Storytelling, however, is not limited to your personal life; you can also use narrative writing in college and in the workplace.

5.1 > Real-World Applications for Narrating

Writing Narratives in School

You will have many opportunities to write narratives in college. You might need to retell what happened during an important historical event. Your humanities instructor may ask you to attend a cultural event, such as a concert or play, and write about the experience. If doing fieldwork is a requirement for your major, your instructor may ask that you keep a narrative journal to document what you observe and do while in the field.

Writing Narratives in Your Daily Life

Writing narratives can also be an important part of your personal life. You may choose to keep a travel journal to document some of the places you visit. You might want to write stories about special occasions and events on your MySpace or Facebook page. If you have children, you may decide to keep a baby book where you record the details of their most memorable experiences so they can read about them when they're older. Additionally, if you have any special interests or hobbies, you may decide to participate in online forums and contribute to Weblogs (blogs) to retell your related stories with others who share your interests.

Writing Narratives in Your Career

Being able to write a good narrative can be critical to your career. Before interviewing for a job, you can benefit from writing a cover letter telling about some of your relevant work experiences to supplement your résumé. If you're applying for a promotion, you might write a report for your superiors, telling them about your past accomplishments and illustrating why you are a worthy candidate for the position. If you notice a problem with a procedure or employee in your workplace, you may need to write a narrative retelling the exact details of what occurred so that the problem can be resolved. Including accurate details in a narrative can be crucial because a poorly written narrative can cost a company money, lead to a lawsuit, or cause injury or even death. Here are a few specific applications for writing narratives on the job:

Health care: patient history, patient care report, accident report, medical narratives.

Law: deposition, court report, letter explaining an event to a client or opposing party, police report.

Education: report card narratives, observations of students or other teachers.

Homeland security: recollection of a terrorist event, details about past or current safety plans.

Business: history of financial activities for the IRS, story about a grand opening, explanation of findings for an audit report.

Graduate
SPOTLIGHT

Doug Tolliver, Ultrasound Technologist

Doug Tolliver has a degree in diagnostic medical sonography. He works as an ultrasound technologist in a hospital. Here's what Tolliver has to say about the importance of written communication to his career:

❝ Writing is really important to my work at the hospital. When a patient's image comes up on the screen, I have to annotate the image for the doctors. After that, I have to write a narrative explaining how I read each scan. For example, if I see a cancerous mass, an aneurysm, or a degenerative fetal condition, I must explain that in my notes. I also have to document in the patient's chart exactly what procedure I performed with the date and time. All of this documentation is important because the doctor will use the information I write to give a diagnosis to the patient. Therefore, writing an accurate narrative is critical to the patient's health and safety. **❞**

Culinary arts: regional history for a menu, story of how your restaurant got started for a newspaper or a magazine article.

Computers: story to accompany a video game being designed, history of how a computer company or program was developed, explanation documenting how you created a particular program.

> ► *Activity* **Real World Narrative Writing**

On your own, in pairs, or in small groups, brainstorm uses for writing narratives at school, in your daily life, and on the job. You may want to choose your own career field or the prospective career field(s) of the participants in your group. Be prepared to share your results.

5.2 > Steps for Writing a Narrative

Before reading professional or student examples of narrative writing, you'll need to understand the steps involved. Look for these steps when you read the selected essays in this chapter, and follow these steps when you write your own narrative essays.

1. Begin with an Engaging Introduction

Create a title for your narrative that will entice your readers. It can be fairly precise, such as "Backpacking on the Appalachian Trail" or a little more vague, such as "The Night When Terror Struck My Family's Home." Your introductory paragraph should include some kind of attention-getter to engage your readers in your narrative. For instance, you could begin your essay with an intriguing statement, such as, "As I stood at the edge of the hazy woods at dusk, I had the distinct sensation that I was not alone."

When writing a narrative, typically you'll want to state your thesis early so readers know what to expect as they continue reading. For example, your thesis might be, "Surviving Hurricane Ike helped me to fully appreciate how precious my family is to me." Occasionally, you might save your thesis for the ending of your narrative, as a lesson or moral to your story. This technique is particularly effective when you're trying to surprise your audience. In most types of essays, however, the thesis must appear in the introduction.

Note: Even though your title and introduction will come first in your final essay, many writers find success in writing them later. If you use that technique, be sure to have a thesis in mind as you write the body of your essay.

2. Establish the Time and Place

Somewhere in the early part of your narrative you'll need to mention when and where the event occurred. If you are writing about a really important event in your life, you may be able to give an exact date and time as well as a precise location of where the action took place. Keep in mind that an essay shouldn't read like a list of diary entries.

- **Time:** If you don't want to date yourself, you might just mention that the event occurred on the eve of your ninth birthday. Mentioning the time of year may also be relevant to your story. For example, hiking in the mountains in December is quite different from doing so in spring or summer.
- **Place:** Telling where the event took place will help readers better understand your story. Provide the readers with physical descriptions of the setting, including the natural environment, building, room, décor—whatever is necessary for your audience to visualize the events in your story.

3. Keep a Consistent Point of View

Although it is not appropriate in all types of academic and workplace writing, when you write about yourself it is typically best to use the first person point of view. Be careful not to begin too many sentences with *I*. Vary your sentence structure and approach. Also, generally it is better not to shift to the second person point of view; however, sometimes authors do that intentionally to make the readers feel as if they are right there in the story. If you do shift points of view, make sure you are doing so for a reason. You don't want to say something such as, "*I* was so scared because *you* didn't know what was going to happen next." If you are writing a narrative about someone else, then you should write in the third person point of view, using pronouns such as *he, she,* and *they.*

 Activity Shifting Viewpoints

Write a one-paragraph narrative about yourself in the first person point of view. Revise your narrative using the third person point of view. For example, your first version might start off as follows: "When I was in 10th grade, I...." Your second version might start this way: "When Danielle was in 10th grade, she...." Be prepared to share your writings and discuss how each version might affect the audience.

4. Keep the Verb Tense Consistent

Keep a consistent past or present verb tense throughout your narrative. You'll probably want to retell your story in the past tense to show that the event happened previously. For example, you might say, "I went to the edge of the murky river to get a better view and was alarmed when an alligator burst out of the water and looked me straight in the eyes." However, you may prefer to keep the action in the present tense. In that case, you might write, "As I am standing at the edge of the water to get a better view, I am alarmed when an alligator bursts out of the water and looks me straight in the eye." You don't want to shift verb tenses and write, "While I *stood* at the edge of the murky river an alligator *looks* me straight in the eyes." Whichever tense you choose, you'll be fine as long as you are consistent.

5. Include Plenty of Details and Sensory Appeal

When you're writing a story, be sure to consider all of the journalist's questions: who, what, where, when, why, and how. Also, include ample sensory details to fully engage your readers. What did you see, hear, feel, smell, and taste? You'll need to include enough concrete sensory details so that your reader fully grasps what it was like for you during the experience. You want your readers to feel something when they read your essay.

For example, if you are writing a story about family reunion, let the readers *hear* the loud music playing and the children gleefully laughing in the background; help them *see* the multigenerational family members gathered around picnic tables adorned with colorful arrays of homemade delicacies; make them *feel* the warm, loving embrace of your favorite relative, Grandma Martha. However, be sure to not get so carried away with your details that your narrative loses its focus. Every detail you include should help support the main point of your narrative.

6. Present the Details in a Logical Sequence

When you write a narrative, you'll typically want to present the events in chronological order. Use a variety of transitions to help your reader follow your sequence of events. Transitional expressions, such as *first, next, then,* and *after that,* will help keep your readers on track. (See Chapter 3 for more on transitions). Experiment with different transitions to see which ones help your narrative to flow smoothly. You don't want your essay to sound like a checklist, nor do you want to write one long paragraph. Instead, write fully developed paragraphs to get your point across to your audience.

You may even decide to include specific times or dates along the way to help make the flow of ideas clear for the reader. Sometimes it may be appropriate to include a flashback to illuminate an event that occurred before the current action in your story. If you choose the flashback method, be sure to signal the change in sequence with a transition so you don't lose your readers. Also, don't overdo the use of flashbacks. Your audience shouldn't have to read your narrative several times to figure out what happened when.

7. Use Dialogue Effectively

Often in a narrative you can use dialogue to help make your story more realistic. Including the exact words that someone says can sometimes be more effective than you, as the narrator, just summarizing their ideas. For example, it would be much more dramatic to quote your cousin as saying, "Help, I can't swim! Please save me!" rather than simply state that Marisa said she couldn't swim and pleaded for someone to save her. If you do use dialogue, be sure to make the language appropriate for the speakers. For instance, your four-year-old nephew shouldn't sound like a rocket scientist, and your great-grandmother shouldn't sound like a rap star.

8. Include Visual Aids if Appropriate

You may want to include pictures, diagrams, or other visual images to help your reader more fully comprehend the story you are retelling. For instance, if you are recalling an experience you had while white-water rafting, you might include a photograph of yourself on a raft. If you do include images, be sure they don't overshadow your writing. Your goal is to use your words to help the reader envision what happened.

9. End with a Thought-Provoking Conclusion

Your narrative needs to make a point about something that you learned or came to understand as a result of your experience. While the point doesn't have to be earth shattering, there should be some purpose for the story. However, don't make your ending sound mechanical by stating, "The point of this story is..." or "The lesson I learned is...." Instead, wrap up your narrative in a natural way and end with something memorable. For example, if your story is about the horrible calamities you suffered on a primitive camping trip in the wilderness, you might end by stating something such as, "Although I am thrilled to have survived the challenges I faced in the Rocky Mountains, I've decided that my next vacation will be aboard a luxurious cruise ship. Grand Cayman, here I come!"

>> *Career-Based* NARRATIVE

[preview] **SUZANNE CURLEY, OTR/L**, is a senior occupational therapist in the Upper Extremity/Hand Therapy outpatient department at Massachusetts General Hospital. She wrote the following clinical narrative about a patient she treated, Sean, to illustrate why her career as an occupational therapist has been challenging and satisfying. Suzanne states, "My experience treating Sean highlights the holistic approach occupational therapists take with our patients and illustrates many of the reasons I feel privileged to specialize in the field of hand therapy. Sean's evaluation and treatment required specific knowledge of hand anatomy, tissue healing, wound care, biomechanics, and sensorimotor function, but also required creative, client-specific solutions to assist him return to the person he was prior to his unfortunate injury."

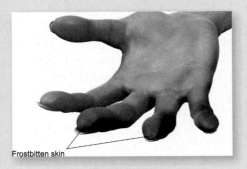
Frostbitten skin

Clinical Narrative **by Suzanne Curley, OTR/L**

When Sean walked in the door of our clinic for his initial evaluation I saw a large, white, bulky dressing on his left hand and surmised from this that he was a burn patient. I immediately began thinking of the various treatment modalities he might need given my knowledge of burn patients.

Then he turned around and I saw the same dressing on his right hand. "Uh oh," I thought, "how is this man able to do anything for himself?" and my thoughts immediately turned from treatment modalities to ways to help this man just get through his day.

It turned out, I was also wrong about his burn injury. This patient had sustained bilateral frostbite injuries one week prior to the day I met him. He was riding his bike to work in 2-degree weather without gloves. When he realized he couldn't feel his hands he went to MGH where he had swollen, erythematous hands with significant blisters throughout and cyanosis at his distal tips. He was hospitalized on the burn unit for two days where he had Silvadene dressings changed twice daily and significant debridement of his wounds once his

blisters broke. When he was discharged home, he was set up with an appointment in the outpatient occupational therapy clinic for one week after his initial injury. This is where I met Sean.

I had not seen many frostbite patients in my experience and certainly none of his significance. However, my role in treating him was clear as it is for all our patients: maximize functional recovery of the affected tissues as well as assist him with as early and safe return back to as normal, independent lifestyle as possible. In essence, help him return to the person he was prior to his injury.

As I assisted Sean with the very basic tasks of removing his coat and taking off his backpack, I immediately began to learn what an accomplished and active person he had been prior to this injury. As he revealed his typical day and week, I realized all the roles and responsibilities he was missing out on since the injury. Sean is a professor of Microbiology at a local medical school and runs a lab doing research of viral materials. In his job, he needs to type long reports as well as perform delicate pipetting to analyze and mix dangerous viral materials. He does all the training for the lab assistants including showing them the precise way to perform the substance analysis. Sean lives with a significant other who has been assisting him with all self-care tasks. He noted that his partner had to return to work so Sean would be alone at home most of the day. In his free time, Sean enjoys cooking, gardening, biking, and other outdoor activities. While Sean was pleasant during this initial assessment, his frustrations and embarrassment over his injury, and his role in causing it, were evident. This was a person who enjoyed much control over his life and work and his new "helplessness" as he called it was affecting every aspect of his life. I hoped I could help him regain some control and bring enjoyment back into his life.

I realized we had much to do during this initial evaluation and I had to prioritize our activities. As I gently removed one of his bulky gauze dressings I noticed his reluctance to look at his hand. I prepared him for what it would likely look like and began explaining how tissues heal so he might have some timeline to consider. Being a planner and a scientist, this interested and distracted him. Underneath this dressing his digits had dusky tips with light bloody exudates along the sides down to the web spaces. His other hand looked similar. In addition, he had significantly increased edema in all eight digits and both thumbs. Further evaluation revealed significantly decreased active and passive ROM and grip/pinch strength as well as impaired sensation and moderate to severe pain while on pain medication. While I documented these impaired client factors and began treatment planning in my mind I was also aware that my primary focus that day for him was to improve his ability to take basic care of himself. I felt we needed to address basic issues such as going to the bathroom, getting a simple bite to eat, turning the key and door handle to get into his home, and doing light hygiene.

I was concerned Sean's frustration with himself and feelings of self-blame would affect his rehabilitation so I decided to put control over his rehab back into his own hands. I asked him about his most important goals. They were consistent with mine but he added doing some light typing in order to be able to take on some work tasks at home and help his colleagues. When he joked that he also thought being able to open a wine bottle was a good goal, I saw that his good humor had returned and felt we'd be able to move forward as a team. I told him I felt all these goals (except the wine opening!) were attainable for him today or in the near future and suggested we begin work on them immediately.

First, I dressed his wounds using xeroform and thin finger stockinette rather than bulky gauze dressings. This immediately allowed him more mobility and

revealed that he had some pressure sense on the pads of his digits. When he noted how much better his fingers felt in these dressings, I suggested that his significant other come to his next appointment so I could show him how to do Sean's dressings at home. Next, I initiated edema management techniques including elevation, use of a compression garment, and active pumping of his digits. Edema limits range of motion and can scar down tendons so I was anxious to manage it quickly. I also instructed him in active range of motion exercises for his digits. I gave him a variety of exercises that encouraged function of the different structures in the hand including the flexor tendons, extensor mechanism, intrinsic muscles, venous/lymphatic system and web spaces. I avoided any passive motion for two reasons. Given his significant amount of edema, I was concerned that aggressive stretches would stretch his collateral ligaments and compress his digital nerves causing further altered sensation. I also wasn't sure how deep or how significant the tissue injury in his digits was and I didn't want to damage any structures. I educated him to watch carefully for signs of blanching or excessive stretching of the dorsal skin. Given his impaired sensation, he might not feel pain or stretching to know if he was overdoing the exercises and causing harm. I also gave him blocking exercises to further increase motion of his interphalyngeal (IP) joints by encouraging some pull of his flexor tendons. These exercises improved his motion while preventing the tendons from adhering to other tissues. The resting splints from his inpatient stay in the hospital still fit so I told him to continue wearing these at night. These splints put his hands in a good resting position to prevent shortening of the soft tissues.

One of my biggest concerns was the darkened tips of his digits as well as the significantly decreased sensation in his tips. I immediately instructed Sean about skin protection to ensure he avoided further injury to his digits. Formal evaluation later that week using the Semmes-Weinstein monofilament test revealed loss of protective sensation on most of his tips. I knew this would make basic self-care such as fasteners difficult to perform let alone trying to perform his delicate work tasks. We would have to take one challenge at a time. I was hopeful the dusky tips were congested blood and not necrotic tissue. In the clinic setting, there was no way to tell. I knew this was of great concern to Sean so I called his surgeon to get his opinion and see if he had noticed any bleeding in the tips when he had done his debridements. His surgeon noted that he had not seen any bleeding and that it was too soon to know if the tissues would survive. He agreed that there was no immediate treatment until the tissue "declared" itself by healing or dying. We decided that we would continue with our plan of care and hoped he wouldn't lose any tissue in his tips. When Sean asked about this potential, I answered his questions honestly given what I knew at the time. He seemed to appreciate my honest answer and this formed the basis for our future relationship.

Next I had Sean attempt several basic self-care tasks. He was unable to hold a utensil in his hand so I put various widths of cylindrical foam on utensils and had him try picking up food from a plate. He required the widest foam but was able to get food into his mouth with this adaptation so this was a big accomplishment. Even with the smaller dressings he lacked the dexterity to do fasteners, particularly his zipper on his pants. He had actually already modified this by adding the twist tie from a loaf of bread to the zipper for him to grasp. This was working fairly well but was still difficult to grip and, as Sean joked, when you're in a hurry, this can be problematic! I suggested he put a silver ring on the zippers of his pants so he just had to hook his finger onto it. This worked quite well. While it could have been awkward discussing delicate hygiene issues so new in our relationship, we found we shared a similar sense of humor that allowed us to be open and frank about issues and brought some fun into a difficult time. Other adaptations included a key turner that allowed him to use a gross grip to turn the key until his fingers were stronger and his tips less sensitive to turn a regular key. He was still significantly limited, and frustrated with his injury, but the ability to do these few basic tasks made him feel a little bit like his old self again.

These were some of the modifications we made during our first session to allow Sean some independence at home and at work. Initially, we compensated for his impairments using adaptive equipment, like the cylindrical foam, to help him resume meaningful activities in his life. Not only does this help him on a practical basis, it improved his self-esteem and encouraged him onward. The self-care activities Sean began to do on the first day also supplemented the range of motion exercises he was given as they are important forms of exercise. Studies show that purposeful activities, such as grasping utensils or typing on a keyboard, motivate patients to perform continued repetitions of motion and reduces their tendency to anticipate pain more than rote exercises or non-purposeful activity. Sean used increasingly smaller grips on his utensils until five weeks later he was able to use a regular utensil. This knowledge was much more satisfying to him than my report to him that his total active motion had improved by 12% on the left and 13% on the right.

There were roadblocks ahead for Sean. Swelling was a significant problem both limiting digit ROM and giving pain to the IP joints of his digits. His tissues were extremely reactive with even small amounts of activity. The third week after his injury Sean had a significant decline in his status when his swelling, pain, and redness increased, ROM decreased, and some functional gains were lost. Initially this was alarming and disheartening for both of us. The swelling looked and felt different from a typical trauma patient. The edema was more diffuse throughout his digits, the color looked sunburned and again was more consistent in color, and it felt softer than usual skin on the outside and almost crunchy to touch deeper down when I did retrograde massage. I wasn't sure if this change in status was due to overexertion despite our judicious level of exercise and activity. I found the changes greater than I had usually seen with injured tissues so I researched and read some articles on frostbite. I read that this hypersensitivity of the injured tissues was common following frostbite due to injury to the skin cells. We modified his home program and were more vigilant about activity levels and soon the tissues calmed down and he made gains again. Eventually, Sean made such improvements in ROM, strength and sensation, and decreases in pain and edema that he was able to hold a regular utensil, grip his bike handlebars, and pipette small test tubes of viral materials.

This last activity was one which we spent weeks working on before he could do it on his own. Once his Semmes-Weinstein test had improved to where he had only minimally diminished light touch sensation and he had adequate ROM and pinch strength, we were ready to focus on this work task. Initially I had Sean practice using large test tubes and water using progressively smaller test tubes and finally the real substances. About 11 weeks after his initial injury he was able to complete a complex test using the smallest test tubes and radioactive materials. He had completed the entire test first using water so he was confident in his abilities. This boosted his confidence and self-esteem enormously. As he returned to these important life roles, I was appreciative that my skills as a hand therapist and creativity as an occupational therapist had combined to find the right solutions for this patient...and I looked forward to the challenge of the next one.

Source: www2.massgeneral.org/pcs/CCPD/Clinical_Recognition_Program/Narrative_Suzann_OT.pdf. This is from the Massachusetts General Hospital Web site: www2.massgeneral.org/pcs/CCPD/Clinical_Recognition_Program/Clin_Rec_Describ_Practice.asp.

1. Suzanne Curley uses the first person point of view throughout the sample report. How does this affect the reader?

2. Identify several examples of dialogue in the narrative. Which examples are most useful to the narrative? Explain your answer.

3. Which specific details from the narrative give you the clearest idea of what happened? Are the details presented in a logical sequence? Explain.

4. This narrative goes beyond the details of the events that Curley observed and includes information about the patient's personal life. Why do you suppose an occupational therapist would want to include that in the narrative? Is it useful information? Why or why not?

5. How do you feel about the ending of the narrative? Does the author accomplish her goal of illustrating why she finds her career as an occupational therapist to be challenging and rewarding? Why or why not?

>> Career-Based NARRATIVE

[preview] **REINALDO IRIZZARY, SR., PH.D.**, wrote the following sample police report narrative so that police officers would have an example to use for their own police report writing. He included a few blank lines where the victim and perpetrator's names would be included in a real police report.

Sample Narrative of a Violent Domestic Incident Police Report by Reinaldo Irizzary, Sr., Ph.D.

On July 10, 2005, at 9:00 PM, I, Officer John Doe, was dispatched to a Violent Domestic call at 125 NW 111 Street Apt. #4A, South point, Miami, Florida. Upon arrival, I met the (victim) White Female, _____ _____ , DOB, 02/07/1960. She was crying and had five large cuts on her right side of her face and was bleeding. I immediately requested rescue and an ID-Unit to respond for photos of the Victim's injuries.

While waiting for rescue, I asked what had happened, if there were any witnesses and how long ago had it occurred. She said that it had just happened, ten minutes before I had arrived. She said her husband White Male, _____ _____ , DOB, 06/19/1955, had come home drunk and because she did not have his food ready began to hit her on her face with his right fist causing many open cuts to her face. She said that there were no witnesses. I immediately requested a description and placed a (BOLO), BE ON THE LOOK OUT to all units in the area.

She described her husband as white male 6' feet tall, weighing about two-hundred pounds with a black mustache, short black hair. He had a two-inch (2") scar on his right cheek of his face. He had on a long sleeve white shirt and faded blue jeans. He was driving a 2006 black four (4)-door Chevy sedan with dark tinted windows with minor damage to the right front passenger door; it had Florida tag #000000. He left the scene west on 111 Street and turned north on 2 Avenue in an unknown direction.

Rescue Unit #25 arrived. Lt. Doe checked and treated the victim, and saw that her injuries needed stitches and more medical attention. He requested if she would go with them to the hospital but she refused. He further advised her to seek medical attention as soon as possible before her injuries became infected. She agreed. ID Unit C-10 also arrived and took ten (10) photos of the victim's injuries.

I advised the victim on the procedure to follow involving a Domestic Victim and to seek a restraining order against her husband for protection. I gave her a Domestic Victims Pamphlet with all the phone numbers she needed to call. I then called and placed her in contact with a Victims Domestic Violent Advocate for further counseling. I then left and canvassed the area for the defendant with negative results.

Detective John Smith, Unit-109 from the Violent Domestic section, was notified of the incident. A copy of the report has been forwarded to him for further investigative follow-up and final disposition of the case.

Source: **http://searchwarp.com/swa220385.htm.**

[QUESTIONS FOR REFLECTION]

Considering Writing Strategies

1. Dr. Irizzary uses the first person point of view throughout the sample report. What effect does this have on the reader?

2. Identify several examples of dialogue in the narrative. Which examples are most useful to the narrative? Explain your answer.

3. Which details give you the clearest idea of what happened? Do you feel the narrative is complete? If not, what additional ideas might be included?

4. This narrative goes beyond the details of the events and includes advice the officer gave to the victim. Why do you suppose a police officer would want to include that in the narrative? Is it useful information? Why or why not?

5. If this woman were sent to the ER, a domestic abuse worker, and a law office, what kinds of narrative writings would personnel in each one of these places need to do for an accurate and detailed medical report, victim file, and legal client profile?

 Activity Career Focus on Narration

Think about your existing or future career. Create a list of instances in which you might be asked to write a narrative. Explain the purpose and audience for these career narratives. Who or what would your quality of writing affect? Be prepared to share your answers.

5.3 > Narrating in the Context of Memories

Of all the resources we have as writers, our memories rank among the best. Without our memories, we would have little understanding of where we have been or where we are going. As human beings, we naturally look back over the past and recall experiences to help us make sense of our lives and our world. Some of our most poignant memories revolve around major life events, such as births and deaths, marriages and divorces, joyous occasions and tragedies. Before writing about your own memory, read one or more of the narratives that follow and answer the questions for reflection. Reading and interpreting the narratives of others can help you write your own narratives for your daily life, school, and career.

[preview] **JOHNNY DEPP** was born in Owensboro, Kentucky, in 1963 and was raised in Miramar, Florida. He left school at the age of 15 with dreams of becoming a rock star, but his garage band, The Kids, did not bring him financial success. He made his film debut in *A Nightmare on Elm Street* (1984) and starred in numerous box office hits, including *Edward Scissorhands* (1990), the *Pirates of the Caribbean* triology, and *Charlie and the Chocolate Factory* (2005). To learn more about Depp, visit one of his fan sites on the Web at **www.johnnydeppweb.com**. In the following interview with Krystal Clark, which originally appeared on the Web site Screencrave.com, Depp recalls some memories

from his childhood, his acting career, and his role as the Mad Hatter in *Alice in Wonderland* (2010). Telling a story to someone else is a great way for writers to organize their details before writing a narrative essay. (You might try relating your own experience later in the "Sharing a Memory" activity on p. 105.)

....

Interview: Johnny Depp for *Alice in Wonderland*

....

After over 25 years in the entertainment business there's nothing Johnny Depp hasn't done. He's played almost every role under the sun and he continues to stun audiences with his character choices. This weekend, he'll star in what seems like his umpteenth Tim Burton production entitled, *Alice in Wonderland*. The actor plays The Mad Hatter, the highly unconventional, and topically crazy confidant of Alice.

When Depp appeared at the *Alice in Wonderland* press conference, his presence was very calming but in the back of your mind you knew there was a major star in the room. For someone who's had his kind of career, he manages to come off as humble, sweet, and oddly funny in a way that only Depp can. He discussed his interest in The Mad Hatter as a tragic character, the evolution of his career, and whether or not he'd star in a motion capture film like *Avatar*. The actor is truly one of a kind and after seeing and hearing him in person, you can tell his degree of success is a natural progression because he's more than just a pretty face.

Depp discussed the first time he read *Alice's Adventures in Wonderland* as a boy and his interpretation of the story. He was particularly drawn to the characters, and to this day he feels like they stick out more than anything else in the story.

I do remember vaguely, maybe when I was roughly 5 years old, reading versions of *Alice in Wonderland*, but the thing is the characters. You always know the characters. Everyone knows the characters, and they're very well defined characters—which I always thought was so fascinating.

Most people who haven't read the book definitely know the characters and reference them. For me, I went back—ironically, it was only maybe a year prior to Tim calling—and I had re-read *Alice in Wonderland* and *Through the Looking Glass*, and what I took away from it was all these very strange, little cryptic nuggets that he'd thrown in there, and I was really intrigued by them and became fascinated by them because they were asking questions that couldn't be answered almost, or were making statements that you couldn't quite understand, like "I'm investigating things that begin with the letter 'M.'" That took me through a whole stratosphere of possibilities, and then doing a little research and discovering that the M is mercury. And then, "Why is a raven like a writing desk?" Those things just became so important to the character. You realize it the more you read the book. If I read the book again today, I'd find a hundred other things that I missed the last time, so it's constantly changing, the book.

Alice in Wonderland isn't the first time Depp has taken on literature from back in the day. He also starred in *Finding Neverland* as J.M. Barrie, the man behind the popular tale of *Peter Pan*. It seems that the actor has an affinity for material from that time period.

I just adore it. From certainly J.M. Barrie and the wonderful characters he created to Lewis Carroll, but even French literature. When you read Baudelaire, or over in the States, Poe, it's like Tim said about Lewis Carroll, you open those books, or you open the *Flowers of Evil*, and you begin to read, and if it were written today, you'd be absolutely stupefied by the work. It's this incredible period where the work is timeless, ageless. So yes, I love all those guys. It's my deep passion, you know, those great 19th century writers.

The actor has collaborated with director Tim Burton for two decades and their professional and personal relationship has steadily grown throughout the years. He talked about how the two creators approach a project and the pressure he always puts on himself to get Tim's roles right.

Each time out of the gate with Tim, the initial thing for me is to obviously come up with a character. But then, there's a certain amount of pressure where I go, "Jesus, will this be the one where I disappoint him?" You know what I mean? So, I try really hard, especially early on, to come up with something that's very different, that he hasn't experienced before and that we haven't experienced together before, and that will stimulate and inspire him to make choices based on that character. I try not to embarrass him, basically.

Being that they have such a trusting relationship, we were interested in knowing the reaction the actor had when the character of The Mad Hatter was brought to him. Depp's no stranger to playing eccentric roles on screen (i.e., Ed Wood, Jack Sparrow), and he attacked this part with the same kind of enthusiasm.

To be honest, he could have said Alice and I would have said yes. [Laughs] I would have done whatever character Tim wanted. But, certainly, the fact that it was the Mad Hatter was a bonus because of the great challenge to try to find this guy and not just be a rubber ball that you heave into an empty room and watch it bounce all over the place, but just to find that part of the character but also a little bit more of the history or gravity to the guy.

The one thing Depp manages to do that's been rarely seen in any interpretation of the Alice story is explore the tragedy of The Mad Hatter. He's essentially insane, sad, and confused about the world around him. The actor constantly plays up that internal conflict throughout the film because of the character's background.

There's the whole Hatter's dilemma, really, which is where the term, "Mad as a Hatter," came from. The amount of mercury that they used in the glue to make the hats and everything was damaging. So, in terms of the Hatter, looking from that perspective as this guy who is literally physically and emotionally damaged goods and a little obtuse, I took that and decided that, as opposed to just this hyper-nutty guy, he should explore all sides of the personality at an extreme level. So he could go, from one second, being very highfalutin with a lot of levity, and then straight into some kind of dangerous potential rage, and then tragedy. It was interesting trying to map it out; it was really interesting.

Since the majority of the characters on his resume could be classified as "off the wall," you might wonder how he keeps them all straight. The actor discussed how he keeps himself in check when doing accents and personas for certain parts.

You definitely have to, I mean, at a certain point, especially if you're dealing with—I've played English a number of times, and used an English accent a number of times, so it becomes a little bit of an obstacle course to go, "Oh, that's teetering into Captain Jackville," or "This one is teetering over into Chocolat or Wonka." You've got to really pay attention to the places you've been. But hopefully, also, that's part of it. That's the great challenge. You may get it wrong. There's a very good possibility that you can fall flat on your face, but again I think that's a healthy thing for an actor.

In Alice in Wonderland, The Mad Hatter has a signature dance called Futterwacking and it's very hard to replicate. It's referred to as his "happy dance," one that he'll only unveil once the evil Red Queen has been defeated. Depp talked about the origin of the dance and how it was created onscreen.

The happy dance was something that Tim was really— he had a very curious vision for the happy dance. And then, I can futterwack with the best of them. We had to treat that like a stunt.

This year, there has been so much talk about Avatar and motion captured performances as compared to real live actors. Depp spoke about whether or not he would get involved in that type of film and wear a blue spandex suit for a particular role in the future.

I don't know. What color is the suit? It's black? Well it matches my eyes. I suppose. I don't care. I mean, I'll put anything on. It doesn't matter to me, obviously. [Laughs] Look at me. [Laughs] No, I don't mind.

Out of all the characters and films he's worked on, the actor divulged which one his own children connect to the most.

It's funny because they've seen it, but they have a difficult time watching it because it's their dad and they make that connection. Edward Scissorhands is, by far, my kiddies' favorite. They connect with the character, and also I think they see their dad feeling that isolation and loneliness. He's a tragic character, so it's hard for them. They bawl when they see that.

Depp has had a successful acting career that's spanned over two decades, with his first major role being Glen in A Nightmare on Elm Street (Yeah, that was him). When he started in the business he had no idea that he would still be acting over 20 years later. His success surprises him more than it does anybody else.

My whole experience on the ride since day one has been pretty surreal in this business and defies logic. I'm still completely shocked that I still get jobs and am still around. But I guess, more than anything, it has been kind of a wonderland. I've been very lucky. I had no idea where anything was going. But you can't—it's almost impossible to predict anything like that.

I had no idea. I felt after I had done *Crybaby* with John Waters and *Edward Scissorhands* with Tim that they were going to cut me off right then. You know what I mean? I felt, at that point, I was on solid ground and I knew where I was going and where I wanted to go. I was sure that they would nix me out of the gig. But, luckily, I'm still here.

Source: Krystal Clark, Screen Crave, **http://screencrave.com/2010-03-05/interview-johnny-depp-for-alice-in-wonderland/**. March 5, 2010.

[QUESTIONS FOR REFLECTION]

Considering Ideas

1. How did Depp's childhood experiences with *Alice in Wonderland* help prepare him for his role as the Mad Hatter? Which characters did he remember most vividly?

2. Depp mentions that he had to be careful not to mix characters from different films. Have you seen Depp in *Alice in Wonderland*? Did any parts of it remind you of his role in other films? Which ones? Explain.

3. Depp says that he is "shocked" that he is able to keep getting roles. What do you think about his perspective? Why do you think he is so humble?

Considering Writing Strategies

1. Instead of writing her exact questions, Clark introduces each segment of Depp's narrative with a little background information and insight into Depp's reply. What effect does this strategy have on the readers? Is it more or less effective than a traditional interview that simply quotes the interviewer's words? Why?

2. Would the narrative parts of the interview have been as good if they had been written in the third person point of view (using the pronoun *he*) instead of the first person point of view (using the pronoun *I*). Why or why not?

3. Which details from the interview are explained the best? Why do those segments stand out in the interview?

Writing Suggestions

1. Do you remember reading a special book when you were a child? Write a narrative essay telling about your reading experience. Comment on the characters and how you envisioned them in your youth. Tell why the book is so memorable and special.

2. Did a specific childhood experience affect your career choice? Write a narrative essay telling about your experience and how it has influenced you to choose a particular career path.

>>READINGS AND REFLECTION

[preview] **AMY TAN** is a Chinese-American author who became famous when her first novel, *The Joy Luck Club* (1993), won multiple awards and was made into a major motion picture. Like millions of other children born in the United States to immigrant parents, Tan grew up speaking one language at home and another in public. In "Mother Tongue" Tan explores this dichotomy. To learn more about Amy Tan and her works, go to her Web site, **amytan.net.** Before reading, consider your own language. Do you always speak the same way around your friends or at work as you do at home? What differences do you notice?

Mother Tongue **by Amy Tan**

I am not a scholar of English or literature. I cannot give you much more than personal opinions on the English language and its variations in this country or others.

I am a writer. And by that definition, I am someone who has always loved language. I am fascinated by language in daily life. I spend a great deal of my time thinking about the power of language—the way it can evoke an emotion, a visual image, a complex idea, or a simple truth. Language is the tool of my trade. And I use them all—all the Englishes I grew up with.

Recently, I was made keenly[1] aware of the different Englishes I do use. I was giving a talk to a large group of people, the same talk I had already given to half a dozen other groups. The nature of the talk was about my writing, my life, and my book, *The Joy Luck Club*. The talk was going along well enough, until I remembered one major difference that made the whole talk sound wrong. My mother was in the room. And it was perhaps the first time she had heard me give a lengthy speech, using the kind of English I have never used with her. I was saying things like, "The intersection of memory upon imagination" and "There is an aspect of my fiction that relates to thus-and-thus'—a speech filled with carefully wrought grammatical phrases, burdened, it suddenly seemed to me, with nominalized[2] forms, past perfect tenses, conditional phrases, all the forms of standard English that I had learned in school and through books, the forms of English I did not use at home with my mother.

Just last week, I was walking down the street with my mother, and I again found myself conscious of the English I was using, the English I do use with her. We were talking about the price of new and used furniture and I heard myself saying this: "Not waste money that way." My husband was with us as well, and he didn't notice any switch in my English. And then I realized why. It's because over the twenty years we've been together I've often used that same kind of English with him, and sometimes he even uses it with me. It has become our language of intimacy, a different sort of English that relates to family talk, the language I grew up with.

So you'll have some idea of what this family talk I heard sounds like, I'll quote what my mother said during a recent conversation which I videotaped and then transcribed[3]. During this conversation, my mother was talking about a political gangster in Shanghai who had the same last name as her family's, Du, and how the gangster in his early years wanted to be adopted by her family, which was rich by comparison. Later, the gangster became more powerful, far richer than my mother's family, and one day showed up at my mother's wedding to pay his respects. Here's what she said in part:

"Du Yusong having business like fruit stand. Like off the street kind. He is Du like Du Zong—but not Tsung-ming Island people. The local people call putong, the river east side, he belong to that side local people. That man want to ask Du Zong father take him in like become own family. Du Zong father wasn't look down on him, but didn't take seriously, until that man big like become a mafia. Now important person, very hard to inviting him. Chinese way, came only to show respect, don't stay for dinner. Respect for making big celebration, he shows up. Mean gives lots of respect. Chinese custom. Chinese social life that way. If too important won't have to stay too long. He come to my wedding. I didn't see, I heard it. I gone to boy's side, they have YMCA dinner. Chinese age I was nineteen."

You should know that my mother's expressive command of English belies how much she actually understands. She reads the *Forbes* report, listens to *Wall Street Week*, converses daily with her stockbroker, reads all of Shirley MacLaine's books with ease—all kinds of things I can't begin to understand. Yet some of my friends tell me they understand 50 percent of what my mother says. Some say they understand 80 to 90 percent. Some say they understand none of it, as if she were speaking pure Chinese. But to me, my mother's English is perfectly clear, perfectly natural. It's my mother tongue. Her language, as I hear it, is vivid, direct, full of observation and imagery. That was the language that helped shape the way I saw things, expressed things, made sense of the world.

Lately, I've been giving more thought to the kind of English my mother speaks. Like others, I have described it to people as "broken" or "fractured" English. But I wince when I say that. It has always bothered me that I can think of no way to describe it other than "broken," as if it were damaged and needed to be fixed, as if it lacked a certain wholeness and soundness. I've heard other terms used, "limited English," for example. But they seem just as bad, as if everything is limited, including people's perceptions of the limited English speaker.

I know this for a fact, because when I was growing up, my mother's "limited" English limited *my* perception of her. I was ashamed of her English. I believed that her English reflected the quality of what she had to say. That is, because she expressed them imperfectly her thoughts were imperfect. And I had plenty of empirical evidence to support me: the fact that people in department stores, at banks, and at restaurants did not take her seriously, did not give her good service, pretended not to understand her, or even acted as if they did not hear her.

---

[1] **Keenly** Sharply.

[2] **Nominalize** To convert a word or phrase to another part of speech.

[3] **Transcribe** To make a written copy of spoken words.

My mother has long realized the limitations of her English as well. When I was fifteen, she used to have me call people on the phone to pretend I was she. In this guise, I was forced to ask for information or even to complain and yell at people who had been rude to her. One time it was a call to her stockbroker in New York. She had cashed out her small portfolio and it just so happened we were going to go to New York the next week, our very first trip outside California. I had to get on the phone and say in an adolescent voice that was not very convincing, "This is Mrs. Tan."

And my mother was standing in the back whispering loudly, "Why he don't send me check, already two weeks late. So mad he lie to me, losing me money."

And then I said in perfect English, "Yes, I'm getting rather concerned. You had agreed to send the check two weeks ago, but it hasn't arrived."

Then she began to talk more loudly. "What he want, I come to New York tell him front of his boss, you cheating me?" And I was trying to calm her down, make her be quiet, while telling the stockbroker, "I can't tolerate any more excuses. If I don't receive the check immediately, I am going to have to speak to your manager when I'm in New York next week." And sure enough, the following week there we were in front of this astonished stockbroker, and I was sitting there red-faced and quiet, and my mother, the real Mrs. Tan, was shouting at his boss in her impeccable broken English.

We used a similar routine just five days ago, for a situation that was far less humorous. My mother had gone to the hospital for an appointment, to find out about a benign brain tumor a CAT scan had revealed a month ago. She said she had spoken very good English, her best English, no mistakes. Still, she said, the hospital did not apologize when they said they had lost the CAT scan and she had come for nothing. She said they did not seem to have any sympathy when she told them she was anxious to know the exact diagnosis, since her husband and son had both died of brain tumors. She said they would not give her any more information until the next time and she would have to make another appointment for that. So she said she would not leave until the doctor called her daughter. She wouldn't budge. And when the doctor finally called her daughter, me, who spoke in perfect English—lo and behold—we had assurances the CAT scan would be found, promises that a conference call on Monday would be held, and apologies for any suffering my mother had gone through for a most regrettable mistake.

I think my mother's English almost had an effect on limiting my possibilities in life as well. Sociologists and linguists[4] probably will tell you that a person's developing language skills are more influenced by peers. But I do think that the language spoken in the family, especially in immigrant families which are more insular, plays a large role in shaping the language of the child. And I believe that it affected my results on achievement tests, IQ tests, and the SAT. While my English skills were never judged as poor, compared to math, English could not be considered my strong suit. In grade school I did moderately well, getting perhaps B's, sometimes B-pluses, in English and scoring perhaps in the sixtieth or seventieth percentile on achievement tests. But those scores were not good enough to override the opinion that my true abilities lay in math and science, because in those areas I achieved A's and scored in the ninetieth percentile or higher.

This was understandable. Math is precise; there is only one correct answer. Whereas, for me at least, the answers on English tests were always a judgment call, a matter of opinion and personal experience. Those tests were constructed around items like fill-in-the-blank sentence completion, such as, "Even though Tom was _____, Mary thought he was _____." And the correct answer always seemed to be the most bland combinations of thoughts, for example, "Even though Tom was shy, Mary thought he was charming," with the grammatical structure "even though" limiting the correct answer to some sort of semantic opposites, so you wouldn't get answers like, "Even though Tom was foolish, Mary thought he was ridiculous." Well, according to my mother, there were very few limitations as to what Tom could have been and what Mary might have thought of him. So I never did well on tests like that.

The same was true with word analogies, pairs of words in which you were supposed to find some sort of logical, semantic relationship—for example, "Sunset is to *nightfall* as _____ is to _____." And here you would be presented with a list of four possible pairs, one of which showed the same kind of relationship: *red* is to *stoplight*, *bus* is to *arrival*, *chills* is to *fever*, *yawn* is to *boring*. Well, I could never think that way. I knew what the tests were asking, but I could not block out of my mind the images already created by the first pair, "*sunset* is to *nightfall*"—and I would see a burst of colors against a darkening sky, the moon rising, the lowering of a curtain of stars. And all the other pairs of words—red, bus, stoplight, boring—just threw up a mass of confusing images, making it impossible for me to sort out something as logical as saying: "A sunset precedes nightfall" is the same as "a chill precedes a fever." The only way I would have gotten that answer right would have been to imagine an associative situation, for example, my being disobedient and staying out past sunset, catching a chill at night, which turns into feverish pneumonia as punishment, which indeed did happen to me.

---

[4] **Linguists** People who study languages.

I have been thinking about all this lately, about my mother's English, about achievement tests. Because lately I've been asked, as a writer, why there are not more Asian Americans represented in American literature. Why are there few Asian Americans enrolled in creative writing programs? Why do so many Chinese students go into engineering! Well, these are broad sociological questions I can't begin to answer. But I have noticed in surveys—in fact, just last week—that Asian students, as a whole, always do significantly better on math achievement tests than in English. And this makes me think that there are other Asian-American students whose English spoken in the home might also be described as "broken" or "limited." And perhaps they also have teachers who are steering them away from writing and into math and science, which is what happened to me.

Fortunately, I happen to be rebellious in nature and enjoy the challenge of disproving assumptions made about me. I became an English major my first year in college, after being enrolled as pre-med. I started writing nonfiction as a freelancer the week after I was told by my former boss that writing was my worst skill and I should hone my talents toward account management.

But it wasn't until 1985 that I finally began to write fiction. And at first I wrote using what I thought to be wittily crafted sentences, sentences that would finally prove I had mastery over the English language. Here's an example from the first draft of a story that later made its way into *The Joy Luck Club*, but without this line: "That was my mental quandary in its nascent state." A terrible line, which I can barely pronounce.

Fortunately, for reasons I won't get into today, I later decided I should envision a reader for the stories I would write. And the reader I decided upon was my mother, because these were stories about mothers. So with this reader in mind—and in fact she did read my early drafts—I began to write stories using all the Englishes I grew up with: the English I spoke to my mother, which for lack of a better term might be described as "simple"; the English she used with me, which for lack of a better term might be described as "broken"; my translation of her Chinese, which could certainly be described as "watered down"; and what I imagined to be her translation of her Chinese if she could speak in perfect English, her internal language, and for that I sought to preserve the essence, but neither an English nor a Chinese structure. I wanted to capture what language ability tests can never reveal: her intent, her passion, her imagery, the rhythms of her speech and the nature of her thoughts.

Apart from what any critic had to say about my writing, I knew I had succeeded where it counted when my mother finished reading my book and gave me her verdict: "So easy to read."

[QUESTIONS FOR REFLECTION]

Considering Ideas

1. When Tan was a child, how did she feel about her mother's language? How has her perception changed as she has aged? What caused this change?

2. Why, even after all the success she has experienced as a writer, does Tan need her mother's approval?

3. Do you feel that standardized tests are equally fair to multilingual speakers? Do they accurately measure someone's potential to succeed? Why or why not?

Considering Writing Strategies

1. What effect does Tan's use of dialogue have on her narrative? Give specific examples to illustrate your point. Would the story work as well without the dialogue? Why or why not?

2. Find examples of transitions that Tan uses to move from one idea to another. How do the transitions affect the flow of ideas in the narrative?

3. Tan uses both past and present verb tenses in her narrative. Does she shift between verb tenses purposely, or are the shifts awkward? Explain your answer using specific examples from the text.

Writing Suggestions

1. Recall a time when you made a conscious choice to vary your language based on your audience. What changes did you make? Why did you alter your speech? Write a narrative telling what happened. Be sure to include specific dialogue of conversations you had to illustrate how you used language differently.

2. When you were a child, did you ever feel embarrassed about something a family member did or said? Write a narrative telling about the situation. What did he or she do to make you feel this way? How did you deal with the situation? Have you changed your mind about what happened now that you're an adult, or do you still feel the same way as you did at the time of the incident?

[preview] **ELWYN BROOKS WHITE,** a native of Mt. Vernon, New York, loved to write even as a young boy. As an adult, E.B. White was an editor and writer for the *New Yorker* and a columnist for *Harper's* magazine. He composed several collections of essays as well as a manual for writing, *Elements of Style,* which became a popular text for college English students. Although he received a gold medal from the National Institute of Arts and Letters and a Pulitzer Prize special citation, perhaps he is best known for his children's books, *Charlotte's Web* and *Stuart Little.* "Once More to the Lake" was originally published in *Harper's* magazine. Before reading, think about your summer vacations as a child. Did you ever go someplace special with your family or friends? What memories does that place hold for you?

Once More to the Lake by E.B. White

One summer, along about 1904, my father rented a camp on a lake in Maine and took us all there for the month of August. We all got ringworm from some kittens and had to rub Pond's[1] Extract on our arms and legs night and morning, and my father rolled over in a canoe with all his clothes on; but outside of that the vacation was a success and from then on none of us ever thought there was any place in the world like that lake in Maine. We returned summer after summer—always on August 1st for one month. I have since become a salt-water man, but sometimes in summer there are days when the restlessness of the tides and the fearful cold of the sea water and the incessant wind which blows across the afternoon and into the evening make me wish for the placidity of a lake in the woods. A few weeks ago this feeling got so strong I bought myself a couple of bass hooks and a spinner and returned to the lake where we used to go, for a week's fishing and to revisit old haunts.

I took along my son, who had never had any fresh water up his nose and who had seen lily pads only from train windows. On the journey over to the lake I began to wonder what it would be like. I wondered how time would have marred this unique, this holy spot—the coves and streams, the hills that the sun set behind, the camps and the paths behind the camps. I was sure that the tarred road would have found it out and I wondered in what other ways it would be desolated. It is strange how much you can remember about places like that once you allow your mind

to return into the grooves which lead back. You remember one thing, and that suddenly reminds you of another thing. I guess I remembered clearest of all the early mornings, when the lake was cool and motionless, remembered how the bedroom smelled of the lumber it was made of and of the wet woods whose scent entered through the screen. The partitions in the camp were thin and did not extend clear to the top of the rooms, and as I was always the first up I would dress softly so as not to wake the others, and sneak out into the sweet outdoors and start out in the canoe, keeping close along the shore in the long shadows of the pines. I remembered being very careful never to rub my paddle against the gunwale for fear of disturbing the stillness of the cathedral.

The lake had never been what you would call a wild lake. There were cottages sprinkled around the shores, and it was in farming country although the shores of the lake were quite heavily wooded. Some of the cottages were owned by nearby farmers, and you would live at the shore and eat your meals at the farmhouse. That's what our family did. But although it wasn't wild, it was a fairly large and undisturbed lake and there were places in it which, to a child at least, seemed infinitely remote and primeval.

I was right about the tar; it led to within half a mile of the shore. But when I got back there, with my boy, and we settled into a camp near a farmhouse and into the kind of summertime I had known, I could tell that it was going to be pretty much the same as it had been before—I knew it, lying in bed the first morning, smelling the bedroom, and hearing the boy sneak quietly out and go off along the shore in a boat. I began to sustain the illusion that he was

---

[1] **Pond's extract** A cream used to heal small cuts and abrasions.

I, and therefore, by simple transposition, that I was my father. This sensation persisted, kept cropping up all the time we were there. It was not an entirely new feeling, but in this setting it grew much stronger. I seemed to be living a dual existence. I would be in the middle of some simple act, I would be picking up a bait box or laying down a table fork, or I would be saying something, and suddenly it would be not I but my father who was saying the words or making the gesture. It gave me a creepy sensation.

We went fishing the first morning. I felt the same damp moss covering the worms in the bait can, and saw the dragonfly alight on the tip of my rod as it hovered a few inches from the surface of the water. It was the arrival of this fly that convinced me beyond any doubt that everything was as it always had been, that the years were a mirage and there had been no years. The small waves were the same, chucking the rowboat under the chin as we fished at anchor, and the boat was the same boat, the same color green and the ribs broken in the same places, and under the floor-boards the same fresh-water leavings and debris—the dead helgramite,[2] the wisps of moss, the rusty discarded fishhook, the dried blood from yesterday's catch. We stared silently at the tips of our rods, at the dragonflies that came and went. I lowered the tip of mine into the water, tentatively, pensively dislodging the fly, which darted two feet away, poised, darted two feet back, and came to rest again a little farther up the rod. There had been no years between the ducking of this dragonfly and the other one—the one that was part of memory. I looked at the boy, who was silently watching his fly, and it was my hands that held his rod, my eyes watching. I felt dizzy and didn't know which rod I was at the end of.

We caught two bass, hauling them in briskly as though they were mackerel, pulling them over the side of the boat in a businesslike manner without any landing net, and stunning them with a blow on the back of the head. When we got back for a swim before lunch, the lake was exactly where we had left it, the same number of inches from the dock, and there was only the merest suggestion of a breeze. This seemed an utterly enchanted sea, this lake you could leave to its own devices for a few hours and come back to, and find that it had not stirred, this constant and trustworthy body of water. In the shallows, the dark, water-soaked sticks and twigs, smooth and old, were undulating in clusters on the bottom against the clean ribbed sand, and the track of the mussel was plain. A school of

---
[2] Helgramite An insect larva used as bait.

minnows swam by, each minnow with its small, individual shadow, doubling the attendance, so clear and sharp in the sunlight. Some of the other campers were in swimming, along the shore, one of them with a cake of soap, and the water felt thin and clear and unsubstantial. Over the years there had been this person with the cake of soap, this cultist, and here he was. There had been no years.

Up to the farmhouse to dinner through the teeming, dusty field, the road under our sneakers was only a two-track road. The middle track was missing, the one with the marks of the hooves and the splotches of dried, flaky manure. There had always been three tracks to choose from in choosing which track to walk in; now the choice was narrowed down to two. For a moment I missed terribly the middle alternative. But the way led past the tennis court, and something about the way it lay there in the sun reassured me; the tape had loosened along the backline, the alleys were green with plantains and other weeds, and the net (installed in June and removed in September) sagged in the dry noon, and the whole place steamed with mid-day heat and hunger and emptiness. There was a choice of pie for dessert, and one was blueberry and one was apple, and the waitresses were the same country girls, there having been no passage of time, only the illusion of it as in a dropped curtain—the waitresses were still fifteen; their hair had been washed, that was the only difference—they had been to the movies and seen the pretty girls with the clean hair.

Summertime, oh summertime, pattern of life indelible, the fade-proof lake, the woods unshatterable, the pasture with the sweet-fern and the juniper forever and ever, summer without end; this was the background, and the life along the shore was the design, the cottages with their innocent and tranquil design, their tiny docks with the flagpole and the American flag floating against the white clouds in the blue sky, the little paths over the roots of the trees leading from camp to camp and the paths leading back to the outhouses and the can of lime for sprinkling, and at the souvenir counters at the store the miniature birch-bark canoes and the post cards that showed things looking a little better than they looked. This was the American family at play, escaping the city heat, wondering whether the newcomers at the camp at the head of the cove were "common" or "nice," wondering whether it was true that the people who drove up for Sunday dinner at the farmhouse were turned away because there wasn't enough chicken.

It seemed to me, as I kept remembering all this, that those times and those summers had been infinitely precious and worth saving. There had been jollity and peace and goodness. The arriving (at the beginning of August) had been so big a business in itself, at the railway station the farm wagon drawn up, the first smell of the pine-laden air, the first glimpse of the smiling farmer, and the great importance of the trunks and your father's enormous authority in such matters, and the feel of the wagon under you for the long ten-mile haul, and at the top of the last long hill catching the first view of the lake after eleven months of not seeing this cherished body of water. The shouts and cries of the other campers when they saw you, and the trunks to be unpacked, to give up their rich burden. (Arriving was less exciting nowadays, when you sneaked up in your car and parked it under a tree near the camp and took out the bags and in five minutes it was all over, no fuss, no loud wonderful fuss about trunks.)

Peace and goodness and jollity. The only thing that was wrong now, really, was the sound of the place, an unfamiliar nervous sound of the outboard motors. This was the note that jarred, the one thing that would sometimes break the illusion and set the years moving. In those other summertimes, all motors were inboard; and when they were at a little distance, the noise they made was a sedative, an ingredient of summer sleep. They were one-cylinder and two-cylinder engines, and some were make-and-break and some were jump-spark, but they all made a sleepy sound across the lake. The one-lungers throbbed and fluttered, and the twin-cylinder ones purred and purred, and that was a quiet sound too. But now the campers all had outboards. In the daytime, in the hot mornings, these motors made a petulant,[3] irritable sound; at night, in the still evening when the afterglow lit the water, they whined about one's ears like mosquitoes. My boy loved our rented outboard, and his great desire was to achieve singlehanded mastery over it, and authority, and he soon learned the trick of choking it a little (but not too much), and the adjustment of the needle valve. Watching him I would remember the things you could do with the old one-cylinder engine with the heavy flywheel, how you could have it eating out of your hand if you got really close to it spiritually. Motor boats in those days didn't have clutches, and you would make a landing by shutting off the motor at the proper time and coasting in with a dead rudder. But there was a way of reversing them, if you learned the trick, by cutting the switch and putting it on again exactly on the final dying revolution of the flywheel, so that it would kick back against compression and begin reversing. Approaching a dock in a strong following breeze, it was difficult to slow up sufficiently by the ordinary coasting method, and if a boy felt he had complete mastery over his motor, he was tempted to keep it running beyond its time and then reverse it a few feet from the dock. It took a cool nerve, because if you threw the switch a twentieth of a second too soon you would catch the flywheel when it still had speed enough to go up past center, and the boat would leap ahead, charging bull-fashion at the dock.

We had a good week at the camp. The bass were biting well and the sun shone endlessly, day after day. We would be tired at night and lie down in the accumulated heat of the little bedrooms after the long hot day and the breeze would stir almost imperceptibly outside and the smell of the swamp drift in through the rusty screens. Sleep would come easily and in the morning the red squirrel would be on the roof, tapping out his gay routine. I kept remembering everything, lying in bed in the mornings—the small steamboat that had a long rounded stern like the lip of a Ubangi, and how quietly she ran on the moonlight sails, when the older boys played their mandolins and the girls sang and we ate doughnuts dipped in sugar, and how sweet the music was on the water in the shining night, and what it had felt like to think about girls then. After breakfast we would go up to the store and the things were in the same place—the minnows in a bottle, the plugs and spinners disarranged and pawed over by the youngsters from the boys' camp, the fig newtons and the Beeman's gum. Outside, the road was tarred and cars stood in front of the store. Inside, all was just as it had always been, except there was more Coca-Cola and not so much Moxie and root beer and birch beer and sarsaparilla[4]. We would walk out with a bottle of pop apiece and sometimes the pop would backfire up our noses and hurt. We explored the streams, quietly, where the turtles slid off the sunny logs and dug their way into the soft bottom; and we lay on the town wharf and fed worms to the tame bass. Everywhere we went I had trouble making out which was I, the one walking at my side, the one walking in my pants.

One afternoon while we were there at that lake a thunderstorm came up. It was like the revival of an old melodrama that I had seen long ago with childish awe. The second-act climax of the drama of the electrical disturbance over a lake in America had not changed in any important respect. This was the big scene, still the big scene. The whole thing was so familiar, the first feeling of oppression and heat and a general air around camp of not wanting to go very far away. In midafternoon (it was all the same) a curious darkening of the sky, and a lull in everything that had made life tick; and then the way the boats suddenly swung the other way at their moorings with the coming of a breeze out of the new quarter, and the premonitory rumble. Then the kettle drum, then the snare, then the bass drum and cymbals, then crackling light against the dark, and the gods grinning and licking their chops in the hills. Afterward the calm, the rain steadily rustling in the calm lake, the return of light and hope and spirits, and the campers running out in the joy and relief to go swimming in the rain, their bright cries perpetuating the deathless joke about how they were getting simply drenched, and the children screaming with delight at the new sensation of bathing in the rain, and the joke about getting drenched linking the generations in a strong indestructible chain. And the comedian who waded in carrying an umbrella.

When the others went swimming my son said he was going in too. He pulled his dripping trunks from the line

---

[3] **Petulant** Insolent or rude in speech or behavior

[4] **Sarsaparilla** A soft drink flavored with the root of a particular plant.

where they had hung all through the shower, and wrung them out. Languidly,[5] and with no thought of going in, I watched him, his hard little body, skinny and bare, saw him wince slightly as he pulled up around his vitals the small, soggy, icy garment. As he buckled the swollen belt suddenly my groin felt the chill of death.

Source: "Once More to the Lake" from *One Man's Meat*, text copyright © 1941 by E.B. White. Copyright renewed. Reprinted with permission of Tilbury House, Publishers, Gardiner, Maine.

---

[5] **Languidly** Lacking in spirit or vitality.

[QUESTIONS FOR REFLECTION]

Considering Ideas

1. What does White compare and contrast in his narrative? Find several specific examples from the story. How do White's comparisons affect the story?

2. What details from the story are most memorable to you? Why did those details catch your attention?

3. How do you relate to White's experiences at the lake? What memories from your own life do you recall?

Considering Writing Strategies

1. What was White's purpose for writing the narrative? What specific details from the story do you feel indicate this purpose?

2. What kind of time sequence does the author use to recall his experiences? Are there any places in the narrative where you become confused about the sequence of events? Why or why not?

3. Does White use a traditional approach to concluding his essay? What effect does the ending have on you?

Why do you think the author chose to leave the readers with those final thoughts?

Writing Suggestions

1. Write a narrative telling about a trip you went on with family or friends. Where did you go? What happened while you were there? Why is this memory significant for you?

2. Write an essay recounting a childhood experience that you would like to relive as an adult. What did you do? If you could go back, would you do everything in the same manner, or would you change some aspect? How would the experience be different as an adult?

> ### ESOL Tip >
>
> Write a narrative about moving from your homeland to a foreign land. From where did you move? How old were you? What was the reason for your move?

>>READINGS AND REFLECTION

[preview] **MAYA ANGELOU,** born Marguerite Johnson in Stamps, Arkansas, has written 12 best-selling books, most of which are autobiographical. She has the distinction of having read her poetry at Bill Clinton's inauguration. In addition to being a highly regarded author, Angelou is an actress, producer, and director. She was nominated for two Grammy Awards for the category of "Best Spoken Word or Non Musical Album." You can learn more about Maya Angelou and her literary works at **mayaangelou.com.** "Momma's Store" is an excerpt from her first and most famous autobiographical novel, *I Know Why the Caged Bird Sings*. In this story Angelou recalls an event that happened in her grandmother's country store. Before reading, think about a favorite place you liked to visit as a child. What is memorable about that place? Did something exciting or scary ever happen to you there?

Momma's Store by Maya Angelou

Weighing the half-pounds of flour, excluding the scoop, and depositing them dust-free into the thin paper sacks held a simple kind of adventure for me. I developed an eye for measuring how full a silver-looking ladle of flour, mash, meal, sugar or corn had to be to push the scale indicator over to eight ounces or one pound. When I was absolutely accurate our appreciative customers used to admire: "Sister Henderson sure got some smart grand-childrens." If I was off in the Store's favor, the eagle-eyed women would say, "Put some more in that sack, child. Don't you try to make your profit offa me."

Then I would quietly but persistently punish myself. For every bad judgment, the fine was no silver-wrapped Kisses, the sweet chocolate drops that I loved more than anything in the world, except Bailey. And maybe canned pineapples. My obsession with pineapples nearly drove me mad. I dreamt of the days when I would be grown and able to buy a whole carton for myself alone.

Although the syrupy golden rings sat in their exotic cans on our shelves year round, we only tasted them during Christmas. Momma used the juice to make almost-black fruitcakes. Then she lined heavy soot-encrusted iron skillets with the pineapples rings for rich upside-down cakes. Bailey and I received one slice each, and I carried mine around for hours, shredding off the fruit until nothing was left except the perfume on my fingers. I'd like to think that my desire for pineapples was so sacred that I wouldn't allow myself to steal a can (which was possible) and eat it alone out in the garden, but I'm certain that I must have weighed the possibility of the scent exposing me and didn't have the nerve to attempt it.

Until I was thirteen and left Arkansas for good, the Store was my favorite place to be. Alone and empty in the mornings, it looked like an unopened present from a stranger. Opening the front doors was pulling the ribbon off the unexpected gift. The light would come in softly (we faced north), easing itself over the shelves of mackerel, salmon, tobacco, thread. It fell flat on the big vat of lard and by noontime during the summer the grease had softened to a thick soup. Whenever I walked into the Store in the afternoon, I sensed that it was tired. I alone could hear the slow pulse of its job half done. But just before bedtime, after numerous people had walked in and out, had argued over their bills, or joked about their neighbors, or just dropped in "to give Sister Henderson a 'Hi y'all,'" the promise of magic mornings returned to the Store and spread itself over the family in washed life waves.

Momma opened boxes of crispy crackers and we sat around the meat block at the rear of the Store. I sliced onions, and Bailey opened two or even three cans of sardines and allowed their juice of oil and fishing boats to ooze down and around the sides. That was supper. In the evening, when we were alone like that, Uncle Willie didn't stutter or shake or give any indication that he had an "affliction." It seemed that the peace of a day's ending was an assurance that the covenant God made with children, Negroes and the crippled was still in effect.

Throwing scoops of corn to the chickens and mixing sour dry mash with leftover food and oily dish water for the hogs were among our evening chores. Bailey and I sloshed down twilight trails to the pig pens, and standing on the first fence rungs we poured down the unappealing concoctions to our grateful hogs. They mashed their tender pink snouts down into the slop, and rooted and grunted their satisfaction. We always grunted a reply only half in jest. We were also grateful that we had concluded the dirtiest of chores and had only gotten the evil-smelling swill on our shoes, stockings, feet and hands. Late one day, as we were attending to the pigs, I heard a horse in the front yard (it really should have been called a driveway, except that there was nothing to drive into it), and ran to find out who had come riding up on a Thursday evening when even Mr. Steward, the quiet, bitter man who owned a riding horse, would be resting by his warm fire until the morning called him out to turn over his field.

The used-to-be sheriff sat rakishly astraddle his horse. His nonchalance was meant to convey his authority and power over even dumb animals. How much more capable he would be with Negroes. It went without saying.

His twang jogged in the brittle air. From the side of the Store, Bailey and I heard him say to Momma, "Annie, tell Willie he better lay low tonight. A crazy nigger messed with a white lady today. Some of the boys'll be coming over here later." Even after the slow drag of years, I remember the sense of fear which filled my mouth with hot, dry air, and made my body light.

The "boys"? Those cement faces and eyes of hate that burned the clothes off you if they happened to see you lounging on the main street downtown on Saturday. Boys? It seemed that youth had never happened to them. Boys? No, rather men who were covered with graves' dust and age without beauty or learning. The ugliness and rottenness of old abominations.

If on Judgment Day I were summoned by St. Peter to give testimony to the used-to-be-sheriff's act of kindness, I would be unable to say anything in his behalf. His confidence that my uncle and every other Black man who heard of the Klan's coming ride would scurry under their houses to hide in chicken droppings was too humiliating to hear. Without waiting for Momma's thanks, he rode out of the yard, sure that things were as they should be and that he was a gentle squire, saving those deserving serfs from the laws of the land, which he condoned.

Immediately, while his horse's hoofs were still loudly thudding the ground, Momma blew out the coal-oil lamps. She had a quiet, hard talk with Uncle Willie and called Bailey and me into the Store.

We were told to take the potatoes and onions out of their bins and knock out the dividing walls that kept them apart. Then with a tedious and fearful slowness Uncle Willie gave me his rubber-tipped cane and bent down to get into the now-enlarged empty bin. It took forever before he lay down flat, and then we covered him with potatoes and onions, layer upon layer, like a casserole. Grandmother

knelt praying in the darkened Store. It was fortunate that the "boys" didn't ride into our yard that evening and insist that Momma open the Store. They would have surely found Uncle Willie and just as surely lynched him. He moaned the whole night through as if he had, in fact, been guilty of some heinous crime. The heavy sounds pushed their way up out of the blanket of vegetables and I pictured his mouth pulling down on the right side and his saliva flowing into the eyes of new potatoes and waiting there like dew drops for the warmth of morning.

[QUESTIONS FOR REFLECTION]

Considering Ideas

1. According to the story, what did Angelou value as a child? Give several specific examples to support your answer.

2. How do you think the young Marguerite's experiences are similar to or different from those of other children her age?

3. How does the narrator feel when the Klan strolls into town and when she and her brother Bailey hide Uncle Willie under a mound of potatoes and onions? Is this type of situation likely to occur today? Why or why not?

Considering Writing Strategies

1. Find examples where Angelou uses nonstandard English and misspelled words. Why does she include these in her narrative, and how do they affect the story? Would the dialogue work as well with perfectly correct grammar? Why or why not?

2. Where does Angelou use sensory details to enhance her narrative? (Find specific examples). What effect do her vivid descriptions have on you as the reader?

3. What tone or mood does the author set at the beginning of the narrative? At what point in the story does the tone change? How is it different? What effect does Angelou achieve by changing the tone partway through the piece?

Writing Suggestions

1. When you were a child, was there a place that you loved to visit, where you felt as if you were in your element? Write a narrative about something that happened in that place. Include a description of the place so your readers can fully comprehend your experience.

2. Have you ever been in a situation where you felt extremely uncomfortable or powerless? Write an essay telling about this experience. What happened? What did you do? Did anyone help you? How did everything turn out in the end?

ESOL Tip >

Has a language barrier ever impeded opportunities you may have had? Write an essay about opportunities you lost because of your language barrier. What happened? What steps have you taken to change your circumstances?

>>READINGS AND REFLECTION

[preview] **PARENTS (OR GUARDIANS)** are responsible for teaching their children and providing them with life lessons. In the following poem, Langston Hughes writes about a mother giving her son advice. He may be recalling an experience he had with his mother. Hughes, who was an early twentieth century writer known especially for his poetry, has captured an endearing moment when a young boy learns about life's challenges. Before reading, think about what kind of advice your mother, or another significant role model, gave you when you were a child. How has the advice affected your life?

Mother to Son by Langston Hughes

Well, son, I'll tell you
Life for me ain't been no crystal stair.
It's had tacks in it,
And splinters,
And boards torn up,
And places with no carpet on the floor—
Bare.
But all the time
I'se been a-climbin' on,
And reachin' landin's,
And turnin' corners,
And sometimes goin' in the dark

Where there ain't been no light.
So boy, don't you turn back.
Don't you set down on the steps
'Cause you find it's kinder hard.
Don't you fall now—
For I'se still goin', honey,
I'se still climbin',
And life for me ain't been no crystal stair.

Source: Langston Hughes. "Mother to Son" from *The Collected Poems of Langston Hughes* by Langston Hughes. Copyright © 1994 by the Estate of Langston Hughes. Used by permission of Alfred A. Knopf, a division of Random House, Inc.

[QUESTIONS FOR REFLECTION]

Considering Ideas

1. What advice is the mother passing along to her son?

2. Why do you think the mother has a need to share this information with her son?

3. What is the theme or overall point of the poem?

Considering Writing Strategies

1. Notice the dialect and missing letters in the poem. Why does Hughes use this style of writing? What effect does he accomplish in doing so?

2. Identify several of the metaphors that Hughes uses in the poem? What do these metaphors represent? How effective are they?

3. What aspects of narration does Hughes incorporate into the poem?

Writing Suggestions

1. Write an essay recalling a time when a parent or other role model gave you some advice. What did he or she say? Why has this memory stuck with you for so long? Was the advice useful to you? Has it changed your life in any way?

2. Write an essay to a younger sibling or child about something you have learned through your experiences. Tell a story to fully illustrate your point.

ESOL Tip >

Is there a particular saying or parable in your home country or culture that has significant meaning to you or that can teach a valuable lesson? Write an essay about this saying or parable. What life lessons can others learn from it?

STUDENT WRITING

Adrenaline Rush
by Claudia Martinez

Skydiving is a wild and amazing experience. Jumping out of an airplane about 15,000 feet in the air and plunging towards the earth at a speed of 160 miles per hour would give anyone an adrenaline rush like no other. The entire skydiving experience takes no more than 30 minutes, but the memory lasts a lifetime. Skydiving is something I would recommend to everyone to try at least once in his or her life. My first and only skydiving experience had my emotions go all the way from fear, to excitement, to relief, making it the most unforgettable day of my life.

Now just because I agreed to jump out of a plane does not mean that I was not scared or nervous. From the mo-

ment I promised my friend, Calixto, that we would go skydiving for our birthdays, I would get that roller coaster feeling in my stomach just thinking about it. Once we arrived at the Sebastian Airport, my fear doubled! I could not believe I was actually there. I almost even backed out when I was filling out the 20-page packet filled with insurance waivers and the words "POSSIBLE DEATH" on every other page I signed. After the paperwork was complete, the instructors prepared my friend and me with the harnesses and goggles, and shortly afterwards we were loading the plane. The plane had a total of 15 people on it. The plane climbed up at such an angle that I had to put my feet firmly on the floor to keep from sliding off the bench on which I was sitting. It seemed like an eternity before we reached the appropriate height, and all I could see through the window was the Atlantic Ocean down below.

After I jumped out of the plane, the excitement I felt falling straight down made me scream at the top of my lungs. There was no way anyone could hear me though because all I could hear was the air rushing up against my body. My instructor and I fell for a minute straight; it was the most awesome feeling in the world. The air hitting my face made my cheeks flap around, and the air coming in my nose was overwhelming. I had difficulty moving my arms towards my face because of the intensity of the wind. When the parachute opened, we were pulled up suddenly. Then we just slowly cruised down to the ground. The view was absolutely gorgeous. I could see some land now and not just the ocean, which made me feel a little more at ease. We glided down for seven minutes, and, surprisingly, landed right where we had taken off.

When I was safe on the ground again, the relief I felt to have survived and enjoyed skydiving is indescribable. I was glad I had the courage to go through with it. My family and fiends seemed to be just as relieved as I was once they saw me again all in one piece after I landed. When the crew took off my equipment, I did not have any particular thoughts in my head. I could not hear much either because of the change in altitude. Everything sounded distant. I was surprised at how different the actual experience was from how I had imagined it. As I walked over to my family and friends, I could see the relief on everyone's faces, especially my parents'. In the end, I think we were all just at ease once my feet were on the ground.

Skydiving is something that I plan on doing again in the near future. I do not think it is something that I will ever get tired of doing because it is a wonderful experience like no other. Although I had never considered doing it before Calixto suggested it, I do not regret it at all. All in all, skydiving is an out of this world experience, and I would recommend that anyone, adventurous or not, should try it.

[QUESTIONS FOR REFLECTION]

1. Identify Claudia's thesis statement. Is it effective? Why or why not?

2. Are the events narrated in a logical sequence? Why or why not?

3. What is the most memorable part of the essay? What makes it memorable?

4. List several transitions used in the essay. Are there enough to keep the essay flowing smoothly? Why or why not?

5. Would you ever want to go skydiving? Why or why not?

STUDENT WRITING

Ireland: A Country of Illumination
by Sally Wilson

Traveling in Europe has always been a wonderful experience for me. I have wandered through the lush green, sloping terrain of Scotland, journeyed within the colorful city streets of England, explored the beautiful yet biting cold areas of rural Estonia, and gorged myself on the whimsical history and illuminating country that is Ireland. The trip that made the deepest impression on me is the trip I took with my sister to our homeland of Ireland; we visited Donegal, Glendalough, and Dublin.

The first place we visited was Donegal, and both of us really appreciated our time there. After an eight-hour airplane ride and a four-hour car ride, my sister and I were plopped into a genuine Irish family home (complete with cows, goats, lambs, and a thatched roof) where many boisterous voices stained with Irish accents clamored for our dazed and dwindling attentions. We were staying within the county lines of Donegal, and after only two weeks, I felt like must have met practically everyone in the county! I respected the families immensely and appreciated how they took my sister and me to a new location every day. One day they took us to a beach, where only the most zealous, extreme surfers would brave the bone chilling ocean water to catch a beautifully proportioned wave. The beach in Donegal was a sight to behold: clear water reflecting the enormous clouds that decorated the sky, the sand, light golden grains mixed with pieces of shiny and colorful shells; the environment was surprisingly virgin in comparison to the molested beaches that I was used to back home, in the United States. I was also lucky enough to explore the historic remains of priories, churches, castles, and other pieces of architecture throughout the country, including a beautiful priory built c. 1508, which was later adapted into a castle, in Rathmullan. Even the local pubs have deep roots in the community, some dating back hundreds of years ago. The pubs in Donegal were filled with the same local people almost every night, and I found it highly enjoyable to sit with a mug of Guinness ale in my hand and my sister at my side, being entertained by their soon-to-be-all-too-familiar stories and songs; it indicated how close their community was, and has been for generations.

After my sister and I said our tearful goodbyes in Donegal, we were off to Glendalough, where we relished another exciting adventure! Glendalough is translated in English as "the glen of two lakes," and is located in the Wicklow Mountains. Glendalough is home to the remains of St. Kevin's Monastery, founded in the latter part of the 6th century. What I found so intriguing was a legendary cave in the mountains called, "St. Kevin's Bed," where St. Kevin was said to have spent seven years in solitude with nothing but prayer and self denial to keep him company. My sister and I got to see the round tower, where St. Kevin's Monastery once stood, but, due to pillaging throughout the ages, not much is left. The last historical site in Glendalough that left an everlasting impression in my mind is an old mining village. A thirty-minute hike through a mountainous forest of pine and oak separates St. Kevin's Monastery from the ruins of an ancient mining village. Boulders, ranging from smaller than my fist to ten times my size, blanket the steep terrain while shells of crudely made rock homes stand firm, mocking the tests of time. The journey and physical exertion from hiking, climbing, and swimming on the trip left me in a state of content euphoria, and I treasure that memory and the connection I felt with my sister while experiencing it.

The last place my sister and I visited in Ireland was the famous city of Dublin, where the experience was different, yet unbelievably wonderful, and a bit more personal than the other parts of the trip because I was without my sister at least half of the time. I say "personal" because during the time I had to myself I created my own experiences, ones I could separate from my sister's with more than just subjective reality. My sister found a job not far from the hostel in which we were staying. While she worked I wandered around the streets of Dublin. I saw Trinity College and its beautiful library/museum that houses "The Book of Kells," which is an historic book that tells a rough story of Celtic beliefs. I also got to stop by numerous shops, pubs, and nightclubs while in Dublin. Good food was hard to come by, but good alcohol was in vast supply!

The articulate mesh of culture, history, geography, romanticism, and beauty that blossoms within Europe manifests itself to me in its diverse people and ancient expressions of art. Although I have traveled to many places, the trip that made the deepest impression on me is the trip I took with my sister to our homeland of Ireland, where we visited Donegal, Glendalough, and Dublin. Ireland showed me that art does not have to be an old painting or piece of architecture—it is all around me, subtly begging to be recognized.

[QUESTIONS FOR REFLECTION]

1. Identify Sally's thesis. What is her overall opinion about her trip to Ireland?

2. How has the student organized her essay? Is this essay structure logical? Why or why not?

3. Which parts of Sally's narrative are especially descriptive? Which specific words help you to visualize her experience?

4. Are any areas unclear? Explain.

5. Do you have a favorite memory of a trip? Where did you go? What did you do?

▶ *Activity* Sharing a Memory

In pairs or small groups, brainstorm a list of events that the members in your group have experienced. These events can be fun, scary, inspirational, exciting, exhilarating, horrifying, and so on. Briefly discuss the list to see which events seem most interesting to the group. Next, each participant will tell a brief story about one incident so the other students have a good idea what happened during the experience. A representative from each group may share a few of the highlights from the stories with the class. This activity may give you ideas for writing a narrative essay.

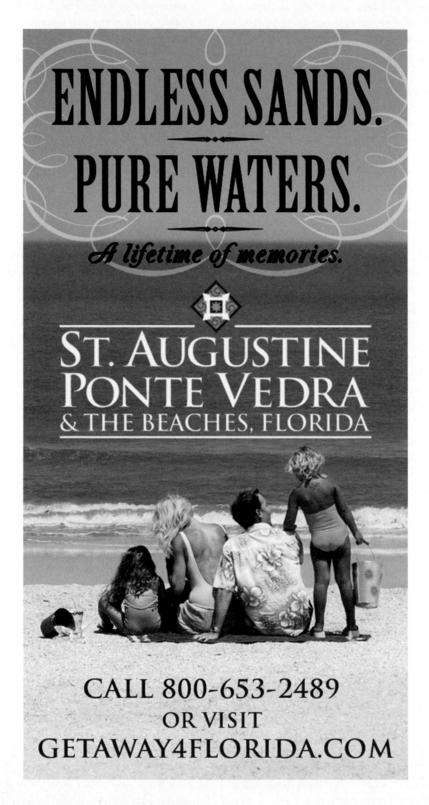

Source: Advertisement from *Arthur Frommer's Budget Travel*, June 2008, p. 134.

This advertisement appeared in *Budget Travel* magazine. Who is the intended audience for the ad? How do the picture and text interact? Why do you suppose the people are facing the other way? Is the advertisement persuasive? Why or why not? What story does it tell?

Writing about an Image

Look at each of the images in this chapter and consider these questions: What experience does the image represent? What story does it tell? What emotions do the people in the image portray? What ideas about your own memories does the image conjure? Write a narrative that relates to one of the images in this chapter. You can tell about the people in the photograph and what they are doing. Imagine what happened before or after the snapshot was taken. What other events might have occurred? Another option is to write about an experience of your own that the image reminds you of. For example, you might write a narrative about a time when you went on a camping trip or visited the beach.

Media Connection for Narration

You might watch, read, and/or listen to one or more of the suggested media to discover additional examples of narratives. Exploring various media may help you to better understand methods for narration. You may also choose to write about one or more of the media suggestions. For example, you might listen to (or watch the music video of) Brad Paisley's song "Letter to Me" and write a letter to yourself in the past, offering advice you have learned as you have gotten older and wiser. Another option is to go to the *This I Believe* Web site and read others' essays before writing about a belief of your own and the life experiences that led you to this belief.

Television	A&E Biography	History Channel	Travel Channel
Film	*Letters to Juliet* (2010)	*Moulin Rouge* (2001)	*The Joy Luck Club* (1993)
Print	*I Know Why the Caged Bird Sings* by Maya Angelou	*Reader's Digest*	*The Color Purple* by Alice Walker
Internet	Adventure Blog **www.adventureblog. org**	This I Believe **thisibelieve.org**	Diaries & Journals **www.worldimage.com/ diaries**
Music	"Letter to Me" by Brad Paisley	*Telling Stories* by Tracy Chapman	*Radio Diaries* (NPR)

Write NOW!

USE ONE OF THE FOLLOWING TOPICS to write an essay recalling a memory. Remember to consider your rhetorical star as well as the steps for writing a narrative as you compose.

1. A memorable childhood experience
2. An entertaining pet story
3. A scary or dangerous event you witnessed or experienced
4. Your best (or worst) vacation
5. A lesson you learned being on a team or in a club
6. Resisting or succumbing to peer pressure
7. Your worst (or best) day on the job
8. An event that led to a significant decision in your life
9. Meeting someone new or losing someone special
10. A day that changed your life forever

FIGURE 5.1
The Rhetorical Star

5.4 > Analyzing the Rhetorical Star for Writing a Narrative

Subject	Have you had an experience that you have been eager to share with others? Maybe you often tell this story to new acquaintances. If so, that may be the perfect story for you to narrate. You'll want to write about a personal experience that has significance for you. Your story could be exciting, humorous, shocking, or terrifying. Maybe you learned something from the experience, or perhaps the experience changed you in some way.
Audience	Who are your readers? What do they need to know about your experience? Will the readers relate to your narrative? What emotions do you want them to experience as they read your narrative? Will they be humored, surprised, or horrified by the details?
Purpose	What are you hoping to accomplish through your narrative? Is your main purpose to inform or entertain the reader? Or are you combining purposes? Are you writing objectively (sticking to just the facts), or are you writing subjectively (including your feelings and opinions)? Keep your purpose in mind as you begin narrating your story.
Strategy	Will you include other writing strategies in addition to narration to tell your story? For example, do you want to use description, process analysis, or cause and effect to enhance your narrative? If you are using other strategies, is narration your main organizational method, or are you using a brief narrative to introduce an essay that uses another strategy?
Design	How long should your narrative be? How many details do you need to include to fully explain your story? What other design elements, such as headings, photographs, or diagrams might help your reader to better understand what happened?

5.5 > Applying the Writing Process for Narrating

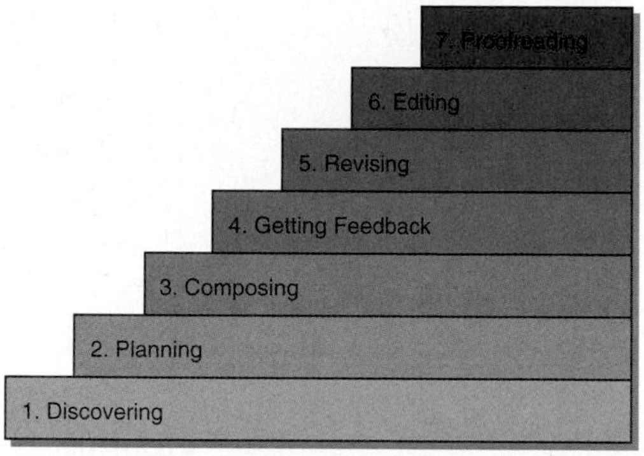

1. **Discovering:** The readings, images, and other media suggestions in this chapter may help you to recall an event that you would like to retell. Look through the chapter and see what comes to mind. Additionally, try listing events from your past that are meaningful to you and might be interesting to others. Explore why those events are meaningful to you. If you don't feel like writing about something from your past, you might try going to a café, watching a sporting event, or attending a concert. Document your experience in your narrative. You can use the journalist's questions to help you generate ideas about your subject.

   After you have come up with some ideas, you might tell one of your stories to a classmate or friend to see if he or she becomes engaged in your narrative.

2. **Planning:** Once you have chosen your topic, try listing everything you can remember about your topic. Also, try numbering the events, creating a cluster, or developing an outline (informal or formal) to help you organize your ideas. Remember to follow a chronological sequence for your narrative.

3. **Composing:** Earlier in this chapter you learned about the nine steps for writing a narrative (see pp. 83–86). These steps are a key part of the writing process:

   1. Begin with an engaging introduction.
   2. Establish the time and place.
   3. Keep a consistent point of view.
   4. Keep a consistent verb tense.
   5. Include plenty of details and sensory appeal.
   6. Present the details in a logical sequence.
   7. Use dialogue effectively.
   8. Include visual aids if appropriate.
   9. End with a thought-provoking conclusion.

   Write a first draft of your narrative using these nine steps. Don't worry too much about grammar and punctuation at this time. Keep focused on retelling the details related to the event. Be sure to keep your overall point in mind as you write.

4. **Getting feedback:** Have at least one classmate or other person read your rough draft and answer the peer review questions that follow. If you have access to a writing tutor or center, get another opinion about your paper as well.

FIGURE 5.2 The Seven Steps of the Writing Process

7. Proofreading
6. Editing
5. Revising
4. Getting Feedback
3. Composing
2. Planning
1. Discovering

FIGURE 5.3 Journalist's Questions

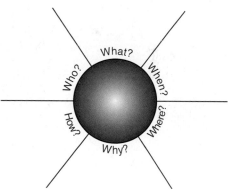

Who? What? When? How? Why? Where?

5. **Revising:** Using all of the feedback available to you, revise your narrative. Make sure that your narrative is full of specific details and that you have used enough transitions for your reader to easily follow the flow of your ideas. Add, delete, and rearrange ideas as necessary.

6. **Editing:** Read your narrative again, this time looking for errors in grammar, punctuation, and mechanics. Pay particular attention to your consistency with verb tenses and the first person point of view, as these areas can be tricky for narrative writing.

7. **Proofreading:** After you have thoroughly edited your essay, read it again. This time, look for typographical errors and any other issues that might interfere with the readers' understanding of your narrative.

>> Peer Review Questions for Narrating

Trade rough drafts with a classmate and answer the following questions about his or her paper. Then, in person or online, discuss your papers and suggestions with your peer. Finally, make the changes you feel would most benefit your paper.

1. Identify the thesis statement. Is its placement appropriate? Why or why not?
2. Are there any additional details that could be included to help you better understand the story? What is missing or unclear?
3. Are the details covered in a logical sequence? If flashbacks are used, are they clear? Why or why not?
4. What part of the narrative is most memorable? Why?
5. Does the narrative include dialogue? If so, does the dialogue flow smoothly and seem appropriate for the speakers?
6. Does the author provide the reader with a sense of completion at the end? If so, how?
7. What kinds of grammatical errors, if any, are evident in the narrative?
8. What final suggestions do you have for the author?

> Writer's Checklist for Writing a Narrative

Use the checklist below to evaluate your own writing and help ensure that your narrative is complete. If you have any "no" answers, go back and work on those areas.

❏ 1. Are my title and introduction enticing?

❏ 2. Is my thesis effective?

❏ 3. Have I included enough details so the reader can visualize my experience?

❏ 4. Are the events presented in a logical sequence?

❏ 5. Have I used transitions to help the sequence of events flow smoothly?

❏ 6. Have I used dialogue to enhance my story?

□ **7.** Have I used a consistent point of view and verb tense?

□ **8.** Is the point of my narrative evident?

□ **9.** Have I ended the story satisfactorily?

□ **10.** Have I proofread thoroughly?

CHAPTER SUMMARY

1. Narrative writing is about retelling a story so that your readers understand what happened during an important event.

2. Narrative writing is an important part of your education, daily life, and career.

3. Interpreting narrative readings and images can help you to prepare to write a narrative.

4. Carefully analyze your rhetorical star before writing a narrative: subject, audience, purpose, strategy, and design.

5. Follow these steps when writing a narrative: begin with an engaging title and introduction; establish the time and place; keep a consistent point of view and verb tense; include plenty of details and sensory appeal; follow a logical sequence; use dialogue effectively; include visual aids if appropriate; and end with a thought-provoking conclusion.

WHAT I KNOW NOW

Use this checklist to determine what you need to work on in order to feel comfortable with your understanding of the material in this chapter. Check off each item as you master it. Review the material for any unchecked items.

□ **1.** I know what a **narrative** writing is.

□ **2.** I can identify several **real-world applications** for writing narratives.

□ **3.** I can **evaluate** narrative readings and images.

□ **4.** I can analyze the **rhetorical star** for writing a narrative.

□ **5.** I understand the **writing process** for writing a narrative.

□ **6.** I can apply the **nine steps** for writing a narrative.

DESCRIBING: MEDIA AND POPULAR CULTURE

LEARNING outcomes

> In this chapter you will learn techniques for the following:

6.1 Identifying real-world applications for writing a description.

6.2 Understanding the steps for writing a description.

6.3 Interpreting images and descriptive readings about media and popular culture.

6.4 Analyzing the rhetorical star for description.

6.5 Applying the steps for writing a description.

> Writing Strategy Focus: Describing

Writing a vivid description can help to evoke an image in the readers' minds. To be good at describing, you need to be a keen observer. While description can be used as a primary method of development for an essay, it is often combined with another writing strategy, such as narration. Whether you are describing people, places, objects, conditions, or events, you'll need to appeal to your readers' senses. Show the readers what you observed by carefully selecting details to accurately portray your observations. In this chapter you'll have an opportunity to interpret images and descriptive readings and to write your own descriptions. You may use descriptive writing in college, in your personal life, and in the workplace.

6.1 > Real-World Applications for Describing

Writing Descriptions in School

College courses will provide you with numerous opportunities for writing descriptions. You might need to describe what you see under a microscope in an anatomy or biology class. If you go on a field trip, your instructor may require that you keep a journal where you describe what you observe while out on the field. In a psychology class, you may need to describe someone's personality traits.

Writing Descriptions in Your Daily Life

Writing descriptions will also be useful in your personal life. If you decide to purchase a home, you'll need to describe the features you desire to a real estate agent. If you have a car accident, you may need to describe what happened to the police or your insurance company. If you sustain an injury, you may need to describe your symptoms to your physician. Additionally, you might need to write a product description for an item you would like to sell on eBay or Craigslist.

Writing Descriptions in Your Career

Being able to write an effective description can be essential on the job. When applying for a job you might describe some of your past achievements. You may need to write a case study or field observation or describe the features of a plan you are proposing. For marketing purposes, you may need to write a description of what products or services your company offers. Here are a few specific applications for writing descriptions in the workplace:

Health care: descriptions of symptoms, X-ray results, or treatment plans.

Law: descriptions of alleged criminals, crimes, and sentences.

Education: descriptions of a child's behavior, a classroom activity, or a lesson plan.

Computer-aided drafting: descriptions of buildings, architectural plans, or concepts for planned neighborhoods.

Business: descriptions of employee duties, business proposals, or marketing plans.

Culinary arts: descriptions of ingredients, menu items, or buffet presentations.

Massage therapy: descriptions of massage techniques, essential materials, or the perfect ambience.

Graduate SPOTLIGHT

Lisa Fournier, President/Owner

Lisa Fournier has a degree in business administration. She is the president and owner of Southern Photo, a retail store that specializes in photo restoration, printing services, custom framing, and photography equipment. Here's what Fournier has to say about the importance of written communication in her field:

"Writing is vital to my career. I have to use a variety of media to get my message across to my customers. I write letters, e-mails, blogs, television and newspaper advertisements, and employee training manuals. I have to understand the power of words to influence my customers as well as my employees. When I write an ad, I have to do much more than just say that Southern Photo provides quality printing. That statement will not motivate the customer to buy prints. Instead I give specific examples to illustrate how my prints are of a higher quality than the local drugstore's prints. I describe what can happen without quality printing, such as 'Aunt Jean turning green' and 'Uncle Fred's cut off head.' I explain that we actually look at the prints and correct the problems before the customer ever sees them so that the photos look natural and will become a treasured keepsake in a photo album.

Additionally, digital technology has caused some people to change their habits. They think that they don't need to print their photos. As a result, I have to remind them that a printed photo can bring back memories and feelings. I write descriptively to evoke the customers' emotions. I recently wrote a blog for my Web site where I described the best birthday gift I ever received, which is a photograph album my two sisters put together especially for me. It contains some of the most embarrassing, memorable, and great pictures of my life. Maybe the customers who read my blog will do the same for someone they love."

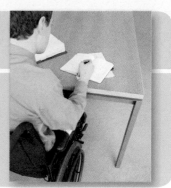

► *Activity* **Real-World Descriptive Writing**

On your own, in pairs, or in small groups, brainstorm uses for writing descriptions at school, in your daily life, and on the job. You may want to choose your career field or the prospective career field(s) of the participants in your group. Be prepared to share your results with your instructor or the class.

6.2 > Steps for Writing a Description

1. Begin by Creating a Dominant Impression

As you begin composing your essay, think about the overall mood or feeling you want your readers to experience. Your thesis statement should portray your dominant impression. Every detail you include should support the dominant impression you are creating. For example, if your dominant impression captures the excitement of New York City, then you probably wouldn't want to mention anything about the elderly woman sitting on a bench reading a trashy novel, oblivious to all that is going on around her. Instead, focus on the details that illustrate what makes New York an exciting city. Keep your dominant impression consistent throughout your entire essay.

2. Use an Objective or a Subjective Approach

Depending on your purpose for writing, you may choose to make your description more objective or subjective. Objective descriptions stick to just the facts and don't include personal opinions or emotions, but subjective descriptions are sometimes more imaginative and do include the writer's interpretations and feelings. For example, a police report describing an incident at a concert might objectively state, "A 16-year-old Caucasian male sustained serious injuries at the arena after the performance ended at 11:55 P.M. last night."

On the other hand, a journalist, who wants to add a little zest to the story by making it more subjective, might write, "Tragedy struck just before midnight last night when an innocent 16-year-old high school boy suffered life-threatening injuries as the panic-stricken, stampeding fans pummeled him on their way out of the overcrowded arena after the heavy metal band finished its wild, head-banging performance." Both accounts of the incident may be accurate, but they serve different purposes and are intended for different audiences. The subjective description, unlike the objective one, is designed to stir the reader's emotions.

3. Appeal to the Senses

When you're writing a description, be sure to include enough sensory details to capture your readers' attention. What do you see, hear, smell, and so on? You'll want your readers to feel as if they are observing firsthand what you are describing.

For example, if you are describing an exciting scene you witnessed from a sidewalk cafe in New York City, let the readers *see* the young man covered in colorful tattoos sporting a purple mohawk and multiple body piercings; enable them to *hear* the honking horns and blasting music; help them to *smell* the delicious aromas emanating from the street vendors' food carts. Be sure to choose precise adjectives for your descriptions. Replace vague words such as *a lot*, *pretty*, and *great* with more precise terms that create stronger imagery for the readers.

4. Include Similes and Metaphors

Often you can enhance your descriptions by using figurative language, such as similes and metaphors. Similes are comparisons that use *like* or *as*. For instance, if you are describing a dragonfly, you might say, "The dragonfly looks like a mini helicopter hovering over the bow of the canoe." Metaphors are more direct comparisons that do not use *like* or *as*. For example, you could say, "The dragonfly is a fragile mini helicopter hovering over the bow of the canoe."

Similes and metaphors can help make your descriptions more vivid for the reader. However, be careful to use original similes and metaphors rather than clichés. You don't want to describe your peer review partner as being "as nervous as a two-tailed cat in a room full of rocking chairs" because that has been said before.

5. Organize Your Description Logically

Use an organizational strategy that makes sense for your topic. If you're describing a panoramic view from a mountain, you might move from left to right. When describing your friend's crazy outfit, you might go from head to toe. If you want to describe your new car, moving from front to back would work well. Choose an organizational pattern that will help your reader to visualize your subject.

6. End with Something Memorable

The conclusion is a good place to remind your reader of the dominant impression you created in the essay. Close with a lasting, vivid image for your readers to envision. Again, stay away from clichés in the conclusion.

▶ *Activity*   Objective and Subjective Descriptions

Observe a person, place, or object. First, write a one-paragraph objective description of your subject. Next, revise your description, making it subjective. How do the paragraphs differ? When might one approach be more effective than the other?

[preview] **THE FOLLOWING** is a description of exercise-induced asthma from **mayoclinic.com**. Have you had trouble breathing? What kinds of symptoms did you experience?

Exercise-Induced Asthma

Description

If you cough, wheeze, or feel out of breath during or after exercise, it may be more than exertion causing your symptoms. You might have exercise-induced asthma. As with asthma triggered by other things, exercise-induced asthma symptoms occur when your airways tighten and produce extra mucus.

Symptoms

Exercise-induced asthma symptoms can include:

- Coughing
- Wheezing
- Shortness of breath
- Chest tightness or pain
- Fatigue during exercise
- Poor athletic performance

Exercise-induced asthma symptoms may start a few minutes after you begin exercising. Some people have symptoms 10 to 15 minutes after finishing a workout. It's possible to have symptoms both during and after exercise.

Feeling a little short of breath or fatigued when you work out is normal, especially if you aren't in great shape. But with exercise-induced asthma, these symptoms can be more severe.

For many people, exercise is just one of a few asthma triggers. Others can include pollen, pet dander and other airborne allergens.

If you have exercise-induced asthma—also called exercise-induced bronchospasm (BRONG-ko-spaz-um)—physical exertion may be the only thing that triggers your symptoms. Or, exercise may be just one of several things that trigger your asthma. But having exercise-induced asthma doesn't mean you shouldn't exercise. Proper treatment and precautions can keep you active—whether you're strolling through the park or competing for Olympic gold.

Source: Mayo Clinic, **www.mayoclinic.com/health/exercise-induced-asthma/DS01040/DSECTION=symptoms.**

[QUESTIONS FOR REFLECTION]

1. What is the primary purpose of the article? Does the article achieve its purpose?

2. Which part of the article uses descriptive words? Does the article include strong sensory appeal? Explain.

3. Compare and contrast the design of this article to the design of a typical college essay. Which type of design is more effective for this type of writing? Why?

4. Why did the writer include headings? Are they useful? Why or why not?

5. What advice does the article give for people who suffer from asthma?

[preview] **MOST OF THE TIME** everything goes smoothly in a junior high school classroom; however, occasionally a student needs help remembering his or her manners. When things go awry, the teacher usually has to describe the problem and the consequences on a discipline form to create a record for the school and the student's parent(s) or guardian(s). A junior high instructor completed the following discipline form when an incident occurred in his classroom. The names have been changed to protect the privacy of the individuals involved. Do you remember attending junior high school? What did some of the children do to get into trouble? How were those children punished?

....

School Discipline Form

....

Description of Infraction:

During today's science class Kenny was loud and unruly. He entered the classroom at the beginning of the period by pushing through the other students who were lined up at the door and then slammed his books down hard on the table. During our opening bell activity, he was turned around in his seat pestering another student to give him a pencil. When asked to turn around, he rudely said, "If I need a dumb pencil, what am I supposed to do?" Finally, during a paired reading activity, Kenny pulled a book out from his partner's hands while she was reading her assigned paragraph and told her to go get another one.

Explanation of Teacher Actions:

After Kenny talked back when he was turned around in his seat, I went to his desk and warned him that he needed to settle down and begin following the classroom procedures or he would need to go to the office. Taking his partner's book away from her was unacceptable and required disciplinary intervention.

Student Explanation:

Kenny did not provide further explanation, nor did he dispute Mr. Williams' account of the events.

Additional Information:

I called and discussed this matter with Kenny's mother on 11/12/2010. Kenny will be serving a 30-minute detention on 11/15/2010, and will write a letter of apology to his reading partner.

[QUESTIONS FOR REFLECTION]

1. Based on the teacher's description, can you envision what happened? Explain.

2. Which words in the description are objective? Which words are subjective?

3. Why did the teacher include dialogue from the student in the description? Is it helpful? Why or why not?

4. What other writing strategy has the teacher used in addition to description? Why did he combine approaches?

5. Was Kenny's punishment fair? Why or why not?

6.3 > Describing in the Context of Media and Popular Culture

Pop culture is all about the way we live, what we do, where we go, how we communicate, what we buy and wear, and what we believe. Various media reflect what is popular in our culture today. The articles and books we read, the movies and television programs we watch, the music and talk shows we listen to, the Web sites we surf, the video games we play, and the advertisements we observe all reveal our popular culture. The media and pop culture offer ample material for descriptive writing. Read one or more of the following descriptive essays. Reading and interpreting professional and student writing samples of descriptive writing can help you to write more descriptively for school, at work, or in your daily life.

[preview] **NEAL GABLER** has written several books, including *Walt Disney: the Triumph of American Imagination* (2006), and has contributed to numerous publications, including the *New York Times* and the *Los Angeles Times*. He also has reviewed movies for PBS on a program called Sneak Previews (originally hosted by Gene Siskel and Robert Ebert) and later became a panelist for Fox News Watch, a weekly media review program. In the following essay, which was originally published in the *Los Angeles Times*, Gabler examines our fascination with urban legends, which are modern stories that become widespread even though they have little or no basis in fact. Before reading, think about an urban myth that you have heard via e-mail or from another person. Was the story plausible? How did you react to it? Were you frightened in some way?

How Urban Myths Reveal Society's Fears by **Neal Gabler**

The story goes like this: During dinner at an opulent wedding reception, the groom rises from the head table and shushes the crowd. Everyone naturally assumes he is about to toast his bride and thank his guests. Instead, he solemnly announces that there has been a change of plan. He and his bride will be taking separate honeymoons and, when they return, the marriage will be annulled. The reason for this sudden turn of events, he says, is taped to the bottom of everyone's plate. The stunned guests quickly flip their dinnerware to discover a photo of the bride *in flagrante*[1] with the best man.

At least that is the story that has been recently making the rounds up and down the Eastern seaboard and as far west as Chicago. Did this really happen? A *Washington Post* reporter who tracked the story was told by one source that it happened at a New Hampshire hotel. But then another source swears it happened in Medford, Massachusetts. Then again another suggests a banquet hall outside Schenectady, New York. Meanwhile, a sophisticated couple in Manhattan has heard it happened at the Pierre.

In short, the whole thing appears to be another urban myth, one of those weird tales that periodically catch the public imagination. Alligators swarming the sewers after people have flushed the baby reptiles down the toilet.

The babysitter who gets threatening phone calls that turn out to be coming from inside the house. The woman who turns out to have a nest of black-widow spiders in her beehive hairdo. The man who falls asleep and awakens to find his kidney has been removed. The rat that gets deep-fried and served by a fast-food outlet. Or, in a variation, the mouse that has somehow drowned in a closed Coca-Cola bottle.

These tales are preposterous, but in a mass society like ours, where stories are usually manufactured by Hollywood, they just may be the most genuine form of folklore we have. Like traditional folklore, they are narratives crafted by the collective consciousness. Like traditional folklore, they give expression to the national mind. And like traditional folklore, they blend the fantastic with the routine, if only to demonstrate, in the words of University of Utah folklorist Jan Harold Brunvand, the nation's leading expert on urban legends, "that the prosaic contemporary scene is capable of producing shocking or amazing occurrences."

Shocking and amazing, yes. But in these stories, anything can happen not because the world is a magical place rich with wonder—as in folktales of yore—but because our world is so utterly terrifying. Here, nothing is reliable and no laws of morality govern. The alligators in the sewers present an image of an urban hell inhabited by beasts—an image that might have come directly from Hades and the River Styx in Greek mythology.

---

[1] **in flagrante** Caught in the act of being unfaithful.

The baby-sitter and the man upstairs exploits fears that we are not even safe in our own homes. The spider in the hairdo says that even on our own persons, dangers lurk. The man who loses his kidney plays to our fears of the night and the real bogymen who prowl them. The mouse in the soda warns us of the perils of an impersonal mass-production society.

As for the wedding reception tale, which one hacker on the Internet has dubbed "Wedding Revenge," it may address the greatest terror of all: that love and commitment are chimerical[2] and even friendship is meaningless. These are timeless issues, but the sudden promulgation[3] of the tale suggests its special relevance in the age of AIDS, when commitment means even more than it used to, and in the age of feminism, when some men are feeling increasingly threatened by women's freedom. Thus, the groom not only suffers betrayal and humiliation; his plight carries the hint of danger and emasculation, too. Surely, a legend for our time.

Of course, folklore and fairy tales have long subsisted on terror, and even the treacly cartoons of Walt Disney are actually, when you parse them, dark and complex expressions of fear—from Snow White racing through the treacherous forest to Pinocchio gobbled by the whale to Dumbo being separated from his mother. But these crystallize the fears of childhood, the fears one must overcome to make the difficult transition to adulthood. Thus, the haunted forest of the fairy tales is a trope for haunted adolescence; the witch or crone, a trope for the spent generation one must vanquish to claim one's place in the world, and the prince who comes to the rescue, a trope for the adult responsibilities that the heroine must now assume.

Though urban legends frequently originate with college students about to enter the real world, they are different from traditional fairy tales because their terrors are not really obstacles on the road to understanding, and they are different from folklore because they cannot even be interpreted as cautionary. In urban legends, obstacles aren't overcome, perhaps can't be overcome, and there is nothing we can do differently to avoid the consequences. The woman, not knowing any better, eats the fried rat. The babysitter is terrorized by the stranger hiding in the house. The black widow bites the woman with the beehive hairdo. The alligators prowl the sewers. The marriage in Wedding Revenge breaks up.

It is not just our fears, then, that these stories exploit. Like so much else in modern life—tabloids, exploitalk programs, real-life crime best sellers—urban legends testify to an overwhelming condition of fear and to a sense of our own impotence within it. That is why there is no accommodation in these stories, no lesson or wisdom imparted. What there is, is the stark impression that our world is anomic.[4] We live in a haunted forest of skyscrapers or of suburban lawns and ranch houses, but there is no one to exorcise the evil and no prince to break the spell.

Given the pressures of modern life, it isn't surprising that we have created myths to express our malaise. But what is surprising is how many people seem committed to these myths. The Post reporter found people insisting they personally knew someone who had attended the doomed wedding reception. Others went further: They maintained they had actually attended the reception—though no such reception ever took place. Yet even those who didn't claim to have been personally involved seemed to feel duty bound to assert the tale's plausibility.

Why this insistence? Perhaps the short answer is that people want to believe in a cosmology of dysfunction because it is the best way of explaining the inexplicable in our lives. A world in which alligators roam sewers and wedding receptions end in shock is at once terrifying and soothing—terrifying because these things happen, soothing because we are absolved of any responsibility for them. It is just the way it is.

But there may be an additional reason why some people seem so willing to suspend their disbelief in the face of logic. This one has less to do with the content of these tales than with their creation. However they start, urban legends rapidly enter a national conversation in which they are embellished, heightened, reconfigured. Everyone can participate—from the people who spread the tale on talk radio to the people who discuss it on the Internet to the people who tell it to their neighbors. In effect, these legends are the product of a giant campfire around which we trade tales of terror.

If this makes each of us a co-creator of the tales, it also provides us with a certain pride of authorship. Like all authors, we don't want to see the spell of our creation broken—especially when we have formed a little community around it. It doesn't matter whether these tales are true or not. What matters is that they plausibly reflect our world, that they have been generated from the grass roots and that we can pass them along.

In a way, then, these tales of powerlessness ultimately assert a kind of authority. Urban legends permit us to become our own Stephen Kings, terrorizing ourselves to confirm one of the few powers we still possess: the power to tell stories about our world.

Source: Neal Gabler, "How Urban Myths Reveal Society's Fears," *Los Angeles Times*, November 12, 1995. Reprinted by permission of the author.

---

[2] **Chimerical** Fanciful or mythical.
[3] **Promulgation** Publication or dissemination.

---

[4] **Anomic** Disoriented or alienated.

Considering Ideas

1. Before reading Gabler's essay, were you familiar with any of the urban legends he mentions? Which ones? What was your initial reaction to them?

2. Why do you think urban myths spread so fast? Why do we find some of them to be fascinating?

3. What fears does Gabler suggest urban myths address? Do you agree or disagree with the author? Why?

Considering Writing Strategies

1. Although Gabler does include descriptions in his essay, what other writing strategies does he employ? Find examples of specific passages where he uses other techniques.

2. What dominant impression is Gabler trying to get across to the reader? How successful is he at making his point? Explain your answer.

3. What specific details caught your attention in the essay? Why are those particular ideas more memorable than others?

Writing Suggestions

1. Have you ever observed (or participated in) something that seems stranger than fiction? Write a descriptive essay about your experience. Make your description vivid by capturing the sensory details and emotions related to the incident.

2. What scares you? Write your own urban myth that addresses one of your fears. Be sure to include enough sensory appeal so that your readers are fully immersed in your creative story.

>> READINGS AND REFLECTION

[preview] **BILL WINE,** a native of San Francisco, California, is an award-winning writer and movie critic. He has achieved three Emmy awards (and eight Emmy nominations) for "Individual Achievement" in the "Writer/Commentary and Review" category. He has contributed numerous articles to a variety of publications, including the *Philadelphia Daily News* and the

New Jersey Monthly. He has also written several plays that have been published and produced. To learn more about Bill Wine, visit his home page, which he calls "The Virtual Vineyard" at **www.calmason.com/personal.htm**. Even in the age of home surround systems and high-definition television, going to the movie theater is still an extremely popular pastime. There's something special about seeing a flick with a captivated audience, but sometimes we are at the mercy of the individuals seated around us. In his essay "Rudeness at the Movies," Wine describes a less than perfect movie-going experience. Before reading, consider your own experiences at the movie theater. Have you experienced rudeness at the movies? What did the other viewers do that annoyed you? Did you do anything about it?

Rudeness at the Movies **by Bill Wine**

Is this actually happening or am I dreaming?

I am at the movies, settling into my seat, eager with anticipation at the prospect of seeing a long-awaited film of obvious quality. The theater is absolutely full for the late show on this weekend evening, as the reviews have been ecstatic for this cinema masterpiece.

Directly in front of me sits a man an inch or two taller than the Jolly Green Giant. His wife, sitting on his left, sports the very latest in fashionable hairdos, a gathering of her locks into a shape that resembles a drawbridge when it's open.

On his right, a woman spritzes herself liberally with perfume that her popcorn-munching husband got her for Valentine's Day, a scent that should be renamed "Essence of Elk."

The row in which I am sitting quickly fills up with members of Cub Scout Troop 432, on an outing to the movies because rain has canceled their overnight hike. One of the boys, demonstrating the competitive spirit for which Scouts are renowned worldwide, announces to the rest of the troop the rules in the Best Sound Made from an Empty Good-n-Plenty's Box contest, about to begin.

Directly behind me, a man and his wife are ushering three other couples into their seats. I hear the woman say to the couple next to her: "You'll love it. You'll just love it. This is our fourth time and we enjoy it more and more each time. Don't we, Harry? Tell them about the pie-fight scene, Harry. Wait'll you see it. It comes just before you find out that the daughter killed her boyfriend. It's great."

The woman has more to say—much more—but she is drowned out at the moment by the wailing of a six-month-old infant in the row behind her. The baby is crying because his mother, who has brought her twins to the theater to save on babysitting costs, can change only one diaper at a time.

Suddenly, the lights dim. The music starts. The credits roll. And I panic.

I plead with everyone around me to let me enjoy the movie. All I ask, I wail, is to be able to see the images and hear the dialogue and not find out in advance what is about to happen. Is that so much to expect for six bucks, I ask, now engulfed by a cloud of self-pity. I begin weeping unashamedly.

Then, as if on cue, the Jolly Green Giant slumps down in his seat, his wife removes her wig, the Elk lady changes her seat, the Scouts drop their candy boxes on the floor, the play-by-play commentator takes out her teeth, and the young mother takes her two bawling babies home.

Of course I am dreaming, I realize, as I gain a certain but shaky consciousness. I notice that I am in a cold sweat. Not because the dream is scary, but from the shock of people being that cooperative.

I realize that I have awakened to protect my system from having to handle a jolt like that. For never—NEVER—would that happen in real life. Not on this planet.

I used to wonder whether I was the only one who feared bad audience behavior more than bad moviemaking. But I know now that I am not. Not by a long shot. The most frequent complaint I have heard in the last few months about the moviegoing experience has had nothing to do with the films themselves.

No. What folks have been complaining about is the audience. Indeed, there seems to be an epidemic of galling inconsiderateness and outrageous rudeness.

It is not that difficult to forgive a person's excessive height, or malodorous perfume, or perhaps even an inadvisable but understandable need to bring very young children to adult movies.

But the talking: that is not easy to forgive. It is inexcusable. Talking—loud, constant, and invariably superfluous—seems to be standard operating procedure on the part of many movie patrons these days.

It is true, I admit, that after a movie critic has seen several hundred movies in the ideal setting of an almost-empty screening room with no one but other politely silent movie critics around him, it does tend to spoil him for the packed-theater experience.

And something is lost viewing a movie in almost total isolation—a fact that movie distributors acknowledge with their reluctance to screen certain audience-pleasing movies for small groups of critics. Especially with comedies, the infectiousness of laughter is an important ingredient of movie-watching pleasure.

But it is a decidedly uphill battle to enjoy a movie—no matter how suspenseful or hilarious or moving—with nonstop gabbers sitting within earshot. And they come in sizes, ages, sexes, colors, and motivations of every kind.

Some chat as if there is no movie playing. Some greet friends as if at a picnic. Some alert those around them to what is going to happen, either because they have seen the film before, or because they are self-proclaimed experts on the predictability of plotting and want to be seen as prescient geniuses.

Some describe in graphic terms exactly what is happening as if they were doing the commentary for a sporting event on radio. ("Ooh, look, he's sitting down. Now he's looking at that green car. A banana—she's eating a banana.") Some audition for film critic Gene Shalit's job by waxing witty as they critique the movie right before your very ears.

And all act as if it is their constitutional or God-given right. As if their admission price allows them to ruin the experience for anyone and everyone else in the building. But why?

Good question. I wish I knew. Maybe rock concerts and ball games—both environments which condone or even encourage hootin' and hollerin'—have conditioned us to voice our approval and disapproval and just about anything else we can spit out of our mouths at the slightest provocation when we are part of an audience.

But my guess lies elsewhere. The villain, I'm afraid, is the tube. We have seen the enemy and it is television.

We have gotten conditioned over the last few decades to spending most of our screen-viewing time in front of a little box in our living rooms and bedrooms. And when we watch that piece of furniture, regardless of what is on it—be it commercial, Super Bowl, soap opera, funeral procession, prime-time sitcom, Shakespeare play—we chat. Boy, do we chat. Because TV viewing tends to be an informal, gregarious, friendly, casually interruptible experience, we talk whenever the spirit moves us. Which is often.

All of this is fine. But we have carried behavior that is perfectly acceptable in the living room right to our neighborhood movie theater. And that *isn't* fine. In fact, it is turning lots of people off to what used to be a truly pleasurable experience: sitting in a jammed movie theater and watching a crowd-pleasing movie. And that's a first-class shame.

Nobody wants Fascist-like ushers, yet that may be where we're headed of necessity. Let's hope not. But something's got to give.

Movies during this Age of Television may or may not be better than ever. About audiences, however, there is no question.

They are worse.

Source: Bill Wine, "Rudeness at the Movies." copyright © 1989. Reprinted by permission of the author.

[QUESTIONS FOR REFLECTION]

Considering Ideas

1. What activities does Bill Wine find to be irritating at the movies? Do those same things bother you, or do you have other pet peeves?

2. Do you feel that Wine is reporting exactly what he has seen while at the movies, or is he exaggerating his examples to make a point? Explain your answer.

3. Why do you think some people behave in the movie theater as they might in their own living room? Do you think those people are aware of the effect they have on others? Why or why not?

Considering Writing Strategies

1. Which parts of the essay seem to have a sarcastic tone? Refer to specific quotes from the essay to support your answer. What effect does his sarcasm have on the reader?

2. Find examples of similes and metaphors in Wine's essay. Which ones do you find to be most interesting or humorous? How do they enhance the essay?

3. Which parts of the essay do you find to be most descriptive? What senses does Wine appeal to? Identify specific examples.

Writing Suggestions

1. Write a description of an event you observed, such as a concert or football game. You might capture what is happening on the stage or field as well as what the spectators are doing. Create an overall impression for the reader, and use as much sensory appeal as is appropriate for your subject. Help your readers to feel as if they are attending the event.

2. Watch a television show or movie and choose one aspect of it to describe. You might write about a character, a scene, or an object that you find to be noteworthy. Use a multitude of adjectives in your description so that your readers can visualize your subject.

>> READINGS AND REFLECTION

[preview] **STEPHEN KING,** born in Portland, Maine, is the master of horror fiction. He became a best-selling author with the publication of his first novel, *Carrie* (1974), which was transformed into a hit movie in 1976. Since then he has written numerous screenplays, short stories, essays, and more than 40 novels, many of which have been made into blockbuster movies. He wrote several popular novels under the pseudonym of Richard Bachman, proving his works would sell even without his famous name. For fun King plays guitar in a charitable band called The Rock Bottom Remainders with Amy Tan, Dave Barry, Matt Groening, and other famous writers. You can visit the band's Web site at  **www.rockbottomremainders.com** and King's home page **www.stephenking.com** for more details. In the following essay, "My Creature from the Black Lagoon," King describes his first moviegoing experience and explores our fascination with the horror genre. Before reading, think about movies you saw as a child. Did any of them truly scare you? Why were you frightened?

My Creature from the Black Lagoon by Stephen King

The first movie I can remember seeing as a kid was *Creature from the Black Lagoon*. It was at the drive-in, and unless it was a second-run job I must have been about seven, because the film, which starred Richard Carlson and Richard Denning, was released in 1954. It was also originally released in 3-D, but I cannot remember wearing the glasses, so perhaps I did see a rerelease.

I remember only one scene clearly from the movie, but it left a lasting impression. The hero (Carlson) and the heroine (Julia Adams, who looked absolutely spectacular in a one-piece white bathing suit) are on an expedition somewhere in the Amazon basin. They make their way up a swampy, narrow waterway and into a wide pond that seems an idyllic South American version of the Garden of Eden.

But the creature is lurking—naturally. It's a scaly, batrachian[1] monster that is remarkably like Lovecraft's half-breed, degenerate aberrations—the crazed and blasphemous results of liaisons between gods and human women (It's difficult to get away from Lovecraft). This monster is slowly and patiently barricading the mouth of the stream with sticks and branches, irrevocably sealing the party of anthropologists in.

I was barely old enough to read at that time, the discovery of my father's box of weird fiction still years away. I have a vague memory of boyfriends in my mom's life during that period—from 1952 until 1958 or so; enough of a memory to be sure she had a social life, not enough to even guess if she had a sex life. There was Norville, who smoked Luckies and kept three fans going in his two-room apartment during the summer; and there was Milt, who drove a Buick and wore gigantic blue shorts in the summertime; and another fellow, very small, who was, I believe, a cook in a French restaurant. So far as I know, my mother came close to marrying none of them. She'd gone that route once. Also, that was a time when a woman, once married, became a shadow figure in the process of decision-making and bread-winning. I think my mom, who could be stubborn, intractable, grimly persevering and nearly impossible to discourage, had gotten a taste for captaining her own life. And so she went out with guys, but none of them became permanent fixtures.

It was Milt we were out with that night, he of the Buick and the large blue shorts. He seemed to genuinely like my brother and me, and to genuinely not mind having us along in the back seat from time to time (it may be that when you have reached the calmer waters of your early forties, the idea of necking at the drive-in no longer appeals so strongly . . . even if you have a Buick as large as a cabin cruiser to do it in). By the time the Creature made his appearance, my brother had slithered down onto the floor of

the back and had fallen asleep. My mother and Milt were talking, perhaps passing a Kool back and forth. They don't matter, at least not in this context; nothing matters except the big black-and-white images up on the screen, where the unspeakable Thing is walling the handsome hero and the sexy heroine into . . . into . . . the Black Lagoon!

I knew, watching, that the Creature had become *my* Creature; I had bought it. Even to a seven-year-old, it was not a terribly convincing Creature. I did not know then it was good old Ricou Browning, the famed underwater stuntman, in a molded latex suit, but I surely knew it was some guy in some kind of a monster suit . . . just as I knew that, later on that night, he would visit me in the black lagoon of my dreams, looking much more realistic. He might be waiting in the closet when we got back; he might be standing slumped in the blackness of the bathroom at the end of the hall, stinking of algae and swamp rot, all ready for a post-midnight snack of small boy. Seven isn't old, but it is old enough to know that you get what you pay for. You own it, you just bought it, it's yours. It is old enough to feel the dowser suddenly come alive, grow heavy, and roll over in your hands, pointing at hidden water.

My reaction to the Creature on that night was perhaps the perfect reaction, the one every writer of horror fiction or director who has worked in the field hopes for when he or she uncaps a pen or a lens: total emotional involvement, pretty much undiluted by any real thinking process—and you understand, don't you, that when it comes to horror movies, the only thought process really necessary to break the mood is for a friend to lean over and whisper, "See the zipper running down his back?"

I think that only people who have worked in the field for some time truly understand how fragile this stuff really is, and what an amazing commitment it imposes on the reader or the viewer of intellect and maturity. When Coleridge spoke of "the suspension of disbelief" in his essay on imaginative poetry, I believe he knew that disbelief is not like a balloon, which may be suspended in air with a minimum of effort; it is like a lead weight, which has to be hoisted with a clean and a jerk and held up by main force. Disbelief isn't light; it's heavy. The difference in sales between Arthur Hailey and H.P. Lovecraft may exist because everyone believes in cars, and banks, but it takes a sophisticated and muscular intellectual act to believe, even for a little while, in Nyarlathotep, the Blind Faceless One, the Howler in the Night. And whenever I run into someone who expresses a feeling along the lines of, "I don't read fantasy or go to any of those movies; none of it's real," I feel a kind of sympathy. They simply can't lift the weight of fantasy. The muscles of the imagination have grown too weak.

In this sense, kids are the perfect audience for horror. The paradox is this: children, who are physically quite

---

[1] **Batrachian** Amphibian or frog-like.

weak, lift the weight of unbelief with ease. They are the jugglers of the invisible world—a perfectly understandable phenomenon when you consider the perspective they must view things from. Children deftly manipulate the logistics of Santa Claus's entry on Christmas Eve (he can get down small chimneys by making himself small, and if there's no chimney there's the letter slot, and if there's no letter slot there's always the crack under the door), the Easter Bunny, God (big guy, sorta old, white beard, throne), Jesus ("How do you think he turned the water into wine?" I asked my son Joe when he—Joe, not Jesus—was five; Joe's idea was that he had something "kinda like magic Kool-Aid, you get what I mean?"), the devil (big guy, red skin, horse feet, tail with an arrow on the end of it, Snidely Whiplash moustache), Ronald McDonald, the Burger King, the Keebler Elves, Dorothy and Toto, the Lone Ranger and Tonto, a thousand more.

Most parents think they understand this openness better than, in many cases, they actually do, and try to keep their children away from anything that smacks too much of horror and terror—"Rated PG (or G in the case of *The Andromeda Strain*), but may be too intense for younger children," the ads for *Jaws* read—believing, I suppose, that to allow their kids to go to a real horror movie would be tantamount to rolling a live hand grenade into a nursery school.

But one of the odd Doppler effects that seems to occur during the selective forgetting that is so much a part of "growing up" is the fact that almost *everything* has a scare potential for the child under eight. Children are literally afraid of their own shadows at the right time and place. There is the story of the four-year-old who refused to go to bed at night without a light on in his closet. His parents at last discovered he was frightened of a creature he had heard his father speak of often; this creature, which had grown large and dreadful in the child's imagination, was the "twi-night double-header."

Seen in this light, even Disney movies are minefields of terror, and the animated cartoons, which will apparently be released and rereleased even unto the end of the world,[2] are usually the worst offenders. There are adults today, who, when questioned, will tell you that the most frightening thing they saw at the movies as children was Bambi's

father shot by the hunter, or Bambi and his mother running before the forest fire. Other Disney memories which are right up there with the batrachian horror inhabiting the Black Lagoon include the marching brooms that have gone totally out of control in *Fantasia* (and for the small child, the real horror inherent in the situation is probably buried in the implied father-son relationship between Mickey Mouse and the old sorcerer; those brooms are making a terrible mess, and when the sorcerer/father gets home, there may be PUNISHMENT. . . . This sequence might well send the child of strict parents into an ecstasy of terror); the night on Bald Mountain from the same film; the witches in *Snow White* and *Sleeping Beauty*, one with her enticingly red poisoned apple (and what small child is not taught early to fear the idea of POISON?), the other with her deadly spinning wheel; this holds all the way up to the relatively innocuous *One Hundred and One Dalmatians* which features the logical granddaughter of those Disney witches from the thirties and forties—the evil Cruella DeVille, with her scrawny, nasty face, her loud voice (grownups sometimes forget how terrified young children are of loud voices, which come from the giants of their world, the adults), and her plan to kill all the dalmatian puppies (read "children," if you're a little person) and turn them into dogskin coats.

Yet it is the parents, of course, who continue to underwrite the Disney procedure of release and rerelease, often discovering goosebumps on their own arms as they rediscover what terrified them as children . . . because what the good horror film (or horror sequence in what may be billed a "comedy" or an "animated cartoon") does above all else is to knock the adult props out from under us and tumble us back down the slide into childhood. And there our own shadow may once again become that of a mean dog, a gaping mouth, or a beckoning dark figure.

Perhaps the supreme realization of this return to childhood comes in David Cronenberg's marvelous horror film *The Brood*, where a disturbed woman is literally producing "children of rage" who go out and murder the members of her family, one by one. About halfway through the film, her father sits dispiritedly on the bed in an upstairs room, drinking and mourning his wife, who has been the first to feel the wrath of the brood. We cut to the bed itself . . . and clawed hands suddenly reach out from beneath it and dig into the carpeting near the doomed father's shoes. And so Cronenberg pushes us down the slide; we are four again, and all of our worst surmises about what might be lurking under the bed have turned out to be true.

---

[2] In one of my favorite Arthur C. Clarke stories, this actually happens. In this vignette, aliens from space land on earth after the Big One has finally gone down. As the story closes, the best brains of this alien culture are trying to figure out the meaning of a film they have found and learned how to play back. The film ends with the words *A Walt Disney Production*. I have moments when I really believe that there would be no better epitaph for the human race, or for a world where the only sentient being absolutely guaranteed of immortality is not Hitler, Charlemagne, Albert Schweitzer, or even Jesus Christ—but is, instead, Richard M. Nixon, whose name is engraved on a plaque placed on the airless surface of the moon. [This note is the author's.]

The irony of all this is that children are better able to deal with fantasy and terror *on its own terms* than their elders are. You'll note I've italicized the phrase "on its own terms." An adult is able to deal with the cataclysmic terror of something like *The Texas Chain Saw Massacre* because he or she understands that it is all make-believe, and that when the take is done the dead people will simply get up and wash off the stage blood. The child is not so able to make this distinction, and *Chainsaw Massacre* is quite rightly rated R. Little kids do not need this scene, any more than they need the one at the end of *The Fury* where John Cassavetes quite literally blows apart. But the point is, if you put a little kid of six in the front row at a screening of *The Texas Chainsaw Massacre* along with an adult who was temporarily unable to distinguish between make-believe and "real things" (as Danny Torrence, the little boy in *The Shining* puts it)—if, for instance, you had given the adult a hit of Yellow Sunshine LSD about two hours before the movie started—my guess is that the kid would have maybe a week's worth of bad dreams. The adult might spend a year or so in a rubber room, writing home with Crayolas.

A certain amount of fantasy and horror in a child's life seems to me a perfectly okay, useful sort of thing. Because of the size of their imaginative capacity, children are able to handle it, and because of their unique position in life, they are able to put such feelings to work. They understand their position very well, too. Even in such a relatively ordered society as our own, they understand that their survival is a matter almost totally out of their hands. Children are "dependents" up until the age of eight or so in every sense of the word; dependent on mother and father (or some reasonable facsimile thereof) not only for food, clothing, and shelter, but dependent on them not to crash the car into a bridge abutment, to meet the school bus on time, to walk them home from Cub Scouts or Brownies, to buy medicines with childproof caps, dependent on them to make sure they don't electrocute themselves while screwing around with the toaster or while trying to play with Barbie's Beauty Salon in the bathtub.

Running directly counter to this necessary dependence is the survival directive built into all of us. The child realizes his or her essential lack of control, and I suspect it is this very realization which makes the child uneasy. It is the same sort of free-floating anxiety that many air travelers feel. They are not afraid because they believe air travel to be unsafe; they are afraid because they have surrendered control, and if something goes wrong all they can do is sit there clutching airsick bags or the in-flight magazine. To surrender control runs counter to the survival directive. Conversely, while a thinking, informed person may understand intellectually that travel by car is much more dangerous than flying, he or she is still apt to feel much more comfortable behind the wheel, because she/he has control . . . or at least an illusion of it.

This hidden hostility and anxiety toward the airline pilots of their lives may be one explanation why, like the Disney pictures which are released during school vacations in perpetuity, the old fairy tales also seem to go on forever. A parent who would raise his or her hands in horror at the thought of taking his/her child to see *Dracula* or *The Changeling* (with its pervasive imagery of the drowning child) would be unlikely to object to the baby sitter reading "Hansel and Gretel" to the child before bedtime. But consider: the tale of Hansel and Gretel begins with deliberate abandonment (oh yes, the stepmother masterminds that one, but she is the symbolic mother all the same, and the father is a spaghetti-brained nurd who goes along with everything she suggests even though he knows it's wrong—thus we can see her as amoral, him as actively evil in the Biblical and Miltonian sense), it progresses to kidnapping (the witch in the candy house), enslavement, illegal detention, and finally justifiable homicide and cremation. Most mothers and fathers would never take their children to see *Survive*, that quickie Mexican exploitation flick about the rugby players who survived the aftermath of a plane crash in the Andes by eating their dead teammates, but these same parents find little to object to in "Hansel and Gretel," where the witch is fattening the children up so she can eat them. We give this stuff to the kids almost instinctively, understanding on a deeper level, perhaps, that such fairy stories are the perfect points of crystallization for those fears and hostilities.

Even anxiety-ridden air travelers have their own fairy tales—all those *Airport* movies, which, like "Hansel and Gretel" and all those Disney cartoons, show every sign of going on forever . . . but which should only be viewed on Thanksgivings, since all of them feature a large cast of turkeys.

My gut reaction to *Creature from the Black Lagoon* on that long-ago night was a kind of terrible, waking swoon. The nightmare was happening right in front of me; every hideous possibility that human flesh is heir to was being played out on that drive-in screen.

Approximately twenty-two years later, I had a chance to see *Creature from the Black Lagoon* again—not on TV, with any kind of dramatic build and mood broken up by adverts for used cars, K-Tel disco anthologies, and Underalls pantyhose, thank God, but intact, uncut . . . and even in 3-D. Guys like me who wear glasses have a hell of a time with 3-D, you know; ask anyone who wears specs how they like those nifty little cardboard glasses they give you when you walk in the door. If 3-D ever comes back in a big way, I'm going to take myself down to the local Pearle Vision Center and invest seventy bucks in a special pair of prescription lenses: one red, one blue. Annoying glasses aside, I should add that I took my son Joe with me—he was then five, about the age I had been myself, that night at the drive-in (and imagine my surprise—my *rueful* surprise—to discover that the movie which had so terrified me on that long-ago night had been rated G by the MPAA . . . just like the Disney pictures).

As a result, I had a chance to experience that weird doubling back in time that I believe most parents only experience at the Disney films with their children, or when reading them the Pooh books or perhaps taking them to the Shrine or the Barnum & Bailey circus. A popular record is apt to create a particular "set" in a listener's mind, precisely because of its brief life of six weeks to three months, and "golden oldies" continue to be played because they are the emotional equivalent of freeze-dried coffee. When the Beach Boys come on the radio singing "Help Me, Rhonda," there is always that wonderful second or two when I can re-experience the wonderful, guilty joy of copping my first feel (and if you do the mental subtraction from my present age of thirty-three, you'll see that I was a little backward in that respect). Movies and books do the same thing, although I would argue that the mental set, its depth and texture, tends to be a little richer, a little more complex, when re-experiencing films and a lot more complex when dealing with books.

With Joe that day I experienced *Creature from the Black Lagoon* from the other end of the telescope, but this particular theory of set identification still applied; in fact, it prevailed. Time and age and experience have all left their marks on me, just as they have on you; time is not a river, as Einstein theorized—it's a big . . . buffalo herd that runs us down and eventually mashes us into the ground, dead and bleeding, with a hearing-aid plugged into one ear and a colostomy bag instead of a .44 clapped on one leg. Twenty-two years later I knew that the Creature was really good old Ricou Browning, the famed underwater stuntman, in a molded latex suit, and the suspension of disbelief, that mental clean-and-jerk, had become a lot harder to accomplish. But I did it, which may mean nothing, or which may mean (I hope!) that the buffalo haven't got me yet. But when that weight of disbelief was finally up there, the old feelings came flooding in, as they flooded in some five years ago when I took Joe and my daughter Naomi to their first movie, a reissue of *Snow White and the Seven Dwarfs*. There is a scene in that film where, after Snow White has taken a bite from the poisoned apple, the dwarfs take her into the forest, weeping copiously. Half the audience of little kids was also in tears; the lower lips of the other half were trembling. The set identification in that case was strong enough so that I was also surprised into tears. I hated myself for being so blatantly manipulated, but manipulated I was, and there I sat, blubbering into my beard over a bunch of cartoon characters. But it wasn't Disney that manipulated me; I did it myself. It was the kid inside who wept, surprised out of dormancy and into schmaltzy tears . . . but at least awake for a while.

During the final two reels of *Creature from the Black Lagoon*, the weight of disbelief is nicely balanced somewhere above my head, and once again director Jack Arnold places the symbols in front of me and produces the old equation of the fairy tales, each symbol as big and as easy to handle as a child's alphabet block. Watching, the child awakes again and knows that this is what dying is like. Dying is when the Creature from the Black Lagoon dams up the exit. Dying is when the monster gets you.

In the end, of course, the hero and heroine, very much alive, not only survive but triumph—as Hansel and Gretel do. As the drive-in floodlights over the screen came on and the projector flashed its GOOD NIGHT, DRIVE SAFELY slide on that big white space (along with the virtuous suggestion that you ATTEND THE CHURCH OF YOUR CHOICE), there was a brief feeling of relief, almost of resurrection. But the feeling that stuck longest was the swooning sensation that good old Richard Carlson and Julia Adams were surely going down for the third time, and the image that remains forever after is of the creature slowly and patiently walling its victims into the Black Lagoon; even now I can see it peering over that growing wall of mud and sticks.

Its eyes. Its ancient eyes.

[QUESTIONS FOR REFLECTION]

Considering Ideas

1. Compare King's most recent viewing of *The Creature from the Black Lagoon* to his first viewing. What similarities and differences do you notice? How does seeing the movie as an adult make him feel?

2. King mentions a number of other movies besides *The Creature from the Black Lagoon*. Why do you think he includes these other movies in his essay? Have you ever seen any of the movies he discusses? What were you thinking, or visualizing, as he mentioned each movie?

3. Why does King think horror movies are so popular in today's culture? What does he feel they do for the viewer? Do you agree or disagree with King's position? Why?

Considering Writing Strategies

1. After reading King's essay, how do you envision his "creature"? Find specific descriptive passages that help you to imagine what it looks like. How realistic is the creature? Does it seem scary to you? Why or why not?

2. Find several examples of similes (comparisons using *like* or *as*) that King uses to help the reader understand his thoughts on horror movies. Are these similes effective? Why or why not?

3. Would you describe King's writing style as being more formal or informal? What specific words give you this impression? How does his style of writing affect you as the reader?

Writing Suggestions

1. Did you have a favorite movie when you were a child? Write an essay describing how you perceived it as a child. Have you seen the movie as an adult? How was your movie-going experience similar to or different from your first viewing?

2. What is your favorite type of movie? Do you prefer horror, drama, comedy, romance, action adventure, or documentary? Write an essay telling why you prefer that particular genre. Be sure to include descriptions of some of the movies that have influenced your preference.

>> READINGS AND REFLECTION

[preview] **FOR MOST OF US**, music plays a significant role in our everyday lives. With the help of modern technology, such as satellite radio and iPods, we can listen to music everywhere we go. Whether we like rock, pop, country, heavy metal, alternative, Latino, new age, dance, punk, jazz, reggae, rhythm and blues, or rap and hip-hop, our musical choices reflect our beliefs, values, and tastes. The rap and hip-hop music of the last few decades has challenged mainstream views and gained popularity. In the following essay, which originally appeared in *Black Collegian Online*, Geoffrey Bennett describes the history of hip-hop and rap music and suggests what might be done to preserve its integrity and cultural richness. Before reading, think about how music has influenced your life. What forms of music do you enjoy listening to? What are your thoughts on hip-hop and rap music?

Hip-Hop: A Roadblock or Pathway to Black Empowerment? by Geoffrey Bennett

In the early 1980s, a highly percussive, cadenced, and repetitive musical form seeped from the inner city streets of the South Bronx to a virtually exclusive African-American audience. Harbingered[1] by originators such as Run DMC, the Sugar Hill Gang, Public Enemy, Afrika Bambaata, and others, the medium was a simple reflection of the daily lives of its creators with topics ranging from the trivial, such as the style of one's new Adidas sneakers, to the significant, like the infuriation spurred by police harassment.

Rap music, as it came to be known, lacked major commercial support in its early stages, and, as a result, it was authentic and unaffected; it was truly "CNN for the streets," as Chuck D once commented. Twenty years later, however, hip-hop culture has since flooded mainstream culture, and rap music is as prevalent in suburban homes as it once was in its native environment, moving from American subculture to the forefront of American attention. "Hip-hop is more powerful than any American cultural movement we've ever had," said rap music impresario Russell Simmons.

Hip-hop is one of the fastest-growing music genres in the United States, accounting for $1.84 billion in sales last year out of a $14.3 billion total for the U.S. recording industry, according to industry statistics. Interestingly, nearly 70 percent of those sales are to white suburban youth, a striking transformation considering rap music's beginnings. Most importantly, perhaps, rap music and its associated hip-hop culture have become a new component of the Black cultural aesthetic. With its rhythmical roots firmly planted in African tradition, hip-hop music is more than just musical expression. For some, it is a way of life, affecting their speech, style of dress, hairstyle, and overall disposition.

Like any other expressive art form, rappers have tested the boundaries of social responsibility, legality, free speech,

---

[1] **Harbingered** Made known.

and old-fashioned "good taste." Labeled as misogynistic,[2] reckless, and even criminal, rappers endured years of public scrutiny with African Americans among some of their most relentless critics. After years of incessant scrutiny, hip-hop mogul Russell Simmons organized a three-day hip-hop music summit for 200 rappers, industry executives, and African-American politicians, the first event of its kind. Sean Combs, LL Cool J, Queen Latifah, Wyclef Jean, Wu-Tang Clan, Chuck D, Jermaine Dupri, KRS-1, Luther Campbell, Ja Rule, and Talib Kweli were just a few of the influential hip-hop artists in attendance at the conference held last June in New York City.

Stars joined forces with some of Black America's intellectual and political elite, including NAACP president Kweisi Mfume; Urban League president Hugh Price; Nation of Islam minister Louis Farrakhan; Martin Luther King, III, leader of the Southern Christian Leadership Council; Georgia Democratic congressional representative Cynthia McKinney; and authors Cornel West and Michael Eric Dyson. The summit ended with musicians and industry executives agreeing to follow voluntary guidelines to advise parents of music's lyrical content while vowing to protect rap artists' freedom of speech by fighting Congressional efforts to censor the music. Minister Louis Farrakhan of the Nation of Islam, one of the political activists who attended the summit, told rappers, "You've now got to accept the responsibility you've never accepted. You are the leaders of the youth of the world."

Today's African-American college students, many of whom as youth were the original fans during rap music's formative years, still remain avid rap music connoisseurs. Rap music, however, has taken a decidedly different direction in recent years. Since rap music is clearly a profitable commercial commodity, rappers consequently perpetuate images and stereotypes that will sell their products, ranging from the excessively violent to the extravagantly wealthy. "Many rappers do not live the type of lives they claim. Those that claim to be affluent often are not, and those that claim to be poor gang-bangers are often millionaires. Fortunately, most college students have the ability to decipher between rap's glamorous images and the realities of life. A problem arises for the younger, impressionable audience, many of whom buy into rap's surface image," said Morehouse College Student Government Association president Christopher J. Graves.

As role models, accepting of the designation or not, rappers have a unique responsibility to be cognizant of their message and their intended audience. Since American pop culture reveres stardom, rappers often garner more attention and respect than they deserve. Consequently, rap music and hip-hop culture have the power to either adversely or positively affect African Americans in specific, and the larger culture in general. While a summit on rap music cannot adequately address all of its dilemmas, a dialogue between interested parties must continue in order to preserve the distinctive art form, while protecting the rich heritage of the African-American cultural aesthetic.

[2] **Misogynistic** Dislike or mistrust of women.

Source: Geoffrey Bennett, "Hip-Hop: A Roadblock or Pathway to Black Empowerment?" Reprinted by permission of the author. Originally appeared in *Black Collegian Online*, 2001.

[QUESTIONS FOR REFLECTION]

Considering Ideas

1. How does Bennett describe the transformation of rap music from the 1980s to the present? What caused this transformation? What is the significance of rap music's changing place in popular culture?

2. The title of Bennett's essay poses two opposing views of hip-hop music. Which view do you think is more accurate: Is it a "roadblock or pathway to black empowerment"? Why?

3. Why do you think rap music is so popular? What effect do you feel it has had on its listeners? Should rap music be censored? Why or why not?

Considering Writing Strategies

1. How has Bennett organized the details in his essay? Is this organization logical? Why or why not?

2. Do you feel the essay is more objective or subjective? How do you know? What particular words does the author use to indicate his approach?

3. Bennett delays his thesis statement until the last paragraph. What is his central point, and why does he wait until the last paragraph to introduce it?

Writing Suggestions

1. Is hip-hop music a "roadblock or pathway to black empowerment"? Write a subjective essay arguing one side of the issue. Include descriptions of specific songs to support your opinion.

2. Choose a particular rap song and write a descriptive essay about the song. What is the tone of the music? What does it sound like or remind you of? How does it make you feel when you hear it? Describe it in such a way that your audience can almost hear it just from reading your words.

[preview] **PEOPLE** from all over the world recognize the Coca-Cola or Coke logo along with other popular American symbols. In the following poem, Martin Espada, who was born in Brooklyn, New York, revisits his roots by describing what it was like for a young boy experiencing Puerto Rico for the first time. Before reading, think about a place you may have visited, in the United States or elsewhere, when you were a child. Did you want to try the foods and beverages of the locals there, or were you more comfortable with sticking to what you were familiar with from home?

Coca-Cola and Coco Frío by Martin Espada

On his first visit to Puerto Rico,
island of family folklore,
the fat boy wandered
from table to table
with his mouth open.
At every table, some great-aunt
would steer him with cool spotted hands
to a glass of Coca-Cola.
One even sang to him, in all the English
she could remember, a Coca-Cola jingle
from the forties. He drank obediently, though
he was bored with this potion, familiar
from soda fountains in Brooklyn.

Then, at a roadside stand off the beach, the fat boy
opened his mouth to coco frío, a coconut
chilled, then scalped by a machete

so that a straw could inhale the clear milk.
The boy tilted the green shell overhead
and drooled coconut milk down his chin;
suddenly, Puerto Rico was not Coca-Cola
or Brooklyn, and neither was he.

For years afterward, the boy marveled at an island
where the people drank Coca-Cola
and sang jingles from World War II
in a language they did not speak,
while so many coconuts in the trees
sagged heavy with milk, swollen
and unsuckled.

Source: Martin Espada, "Coca-Cola and Coco Frio" from *City of Coughing and Dead Radiators* by Martin Espada. Copyright © 1993 by Martin Espada. Used by permission of W. W. Norton & Company Inc.

[QUESTIONS FOR REFLECTION]

Considering Ideas

1. Why did the boy's relatives make such an effort to give him Coca-Cola and sing old jingles to him? Were they successful with what they were hoping to accomplish? Why or why not?

2. Why does the boy prefer coco frío to Coca-Cola? What effect does the exotic beverage have on him?

3. What point is Espada making through the poem? Which lines in the poem help you to identify his point?

Considering Writing Strategies

1. Identify where Espada appeals to the reader's senses. Which words seem to be the most descriptive to you? What effect do those words have on you as you read?

2. What other writing strategies, in addition to description, does Espada incorporate into his poem? How does his combination approach enhance the poem?

3. Does the author use traditional rhythm and rhyme patterns found in some poetry? How would you characterize the style of Espada's poem?

Writing Suggestions

1. Write an essay describing an experience you had as a child away from home. What did you see, hear, smell, taste, and feel? Include as much sensory imagery as you can so that the reader can imagine what it would be like to have that experience.

2. Think about a place you are familiar with that people from somewhere else might find exciting or interesting to experience. Describe the place with as much vivid detail as you can. Help your readers to feel as if they have been there in person.

The Ring
by Danielle Malico

People all over the world spend valuable time and cash to see championship fights. Whether it is for boxing, wrestling, or ultimate fighting, crowds gather in bars and around televisions to support their favorite fighters. Many know what it is like to be a spectator, but few know the fighter's experience. I, on the other hand, have first-hand knowledge of what it is like to be in the ring.

The first sound I hear is the familiar bell that brings me to reality. All around are my friends, family, and people who want to see women brawl. This is far from a quiet event. The onlookers are comparable to screeching howler monkeys with beer and snacks in their hands. My body feels heavy; I am covered in all the necessary places to prevent injury. The guard in my mouth causes excess fluid to run down my chin. The ring smells like rubber and sweat from previous battles. These conditions are not ideal for the average woman, but for me boxing is my place in the world, my sanctuary, my one talent.

I look over at my competition. She is shorter and thicker than I am, and her stance is impeccable. Immediately I realize that this will be a memorable occasion. I can tell everything about my opponent by her reaction to the first punch, whether she backs away or comes in closer. I always test the water with a three-punch combination: a jab, a strong right, and a left hook. With each strike I exhale, making the hits more effective. She moves in closer, mainly because of her height, partially because she is confident. This makes me hesitate, but I know I cannot let this stab of fear affect my performance.

I prance around on my tiptoes, and she follows me like a lost puppy. The first two-minute round consists of she and I doing the well-known first round dance. This is how we figure each other out. Not much damage is done on either end, a couple of simple blows, and soon enough the bell rings signifying our thirty-second break. I stagger over to my corner of the ring. My coach gives me the usual pep talk as I spit my mouth guard into a bowl. He takes a bottle and pours cold water into my mouth, while simultaneously wiping beads of sweat off my head, neck, and chest. He reminds me of a father, very proud of his little girl.

Soon enough, before I am fully rejuvenated, it will be time to go back to the fight for the second round. I am so prepared. Whether I win or lose the fight, I know that I will fight my best and make my coach and myself proud. I will relish in every moment of my time in the boxing ring. There is no other place I would rather be.

[QUESTIONS FOR REFLECTION]

1. When you saw a picture of the author and read the title, what kind of ring did you expect to read about in the essay?

2. Identify several examples of sensory appeal in Malico's essay. What could you see, hear, smell, feel, etc?

3. What comparison does the author make in the essay?

4. Is the description objective or subjective? Explain.

5. What is the point of Malico's essay? How do you know?

▶ *Activity* Sensory Showdown

In pairs or small groups, share a few personal objects, drawings, or photographs that have special meaning or reveal something about yourself. The items should appeal to different senses. Take turns describing the items you chose and explaining why they are significant. As a team, come up with a dominant impression, original similes and/or metaphors, and specific sensory appeal for each item. A representative from each group will share descriptive ideas about a couple of favorite items with the class. This activity may give you ideas for writing a descriptive essay.

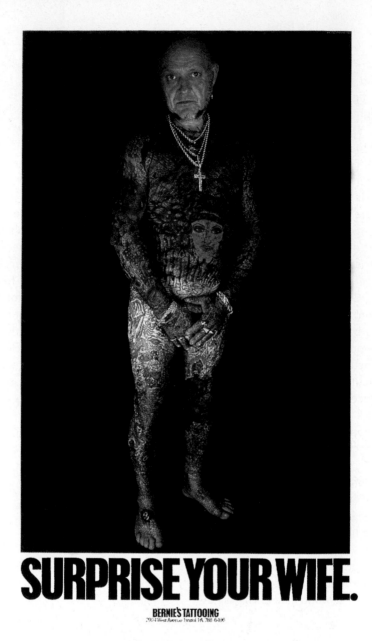

How would you describe this advertisement? Who is the intended audience for the ad? How do the image and text interact? If you were considering getting inked, would you consider Bernie's Tattooing? Why or why not? What does the ad suggest about popular culture? Explain.

Writing about an Image

Look at the images throughout this chapter and consider these questions: How would you describe the image? What aspect of popular culture does the image represent? Is the image mainstream or alternative? Do you personally relate to the image? If so, how? What does the image suggest about pop culture? Write a description that relates to one of the pictures or advertisements above. You may describe what you see in the photograph, or you might describe something that relates to one of the images. For example, you might describe the scene at a concert or café.

Media Connection for Describing

You might watch, read, and/or listen to one or more of the suggested media to discover additional examples of descriptions. Exploring different media may help you to better understand methods for describing. You may also choose to write about one or more of the media suggestions. For example, you might watch a *Star Trek* movie and note descriptions of some of the beings and destinations Captain Kirk and his crew encounter.

Television	*America's Funniest Home Videos*	MTV, VH1, or CMT	QVC
Film	*Across the Universe (2007)*	*Rent (2005)*	*Star Trek (2009)*
Print	*People*	*National Geographic*	*Vanity Fair*
Internet	**eBay.com**	**motherjones.com**	**youtube.com**
Music	"Brown Skin Girl" by Santana	"Lucy in the Sky with Diamonds" by The Beatles	"Topaz" by The B-52's

Write NOW!

USE ONE OF THE FOLLOWING TOPICS to write a descriptive essay. Remember to consider your rhetorical star as well as the steps for writing a description as you compose.

1. A natural setting, such as a beach, mountainside, woods, or lake
2. A work of art, such as a poster, photograph, painting, or sculpture
3. The music of a particular artist or band
4. A shopping mall, parking lot, sports stadium, or other crowded place
5. A ride at a theme park or an exhibit at a zoo or museum
6. The best or worst meal you have ever eaten (or pushed away)
7. A person you love, cherish, or admire
8. A souvenir or artifact from a place you have visited
9. A special photograph of a person, place, pet, or object
10. A restaurant, bakery, or other place that appeals to the senses

FIGURE 6.1
The Rhetorical Star

6.4 > Analyzing the Rhetorical Star for Writing a Description

	Choose a topic that you can observe firsthand or one that you can experience through a picture, television show, or other medium. You might describe an interesting place, an exciting event, a unique person or animal, or an unusual object. Write about something that catches your attention that you would like to capture and share with your readers.
Audience	Who will read your description? What will interest your readers about your subject? What do they already know about it? Are they reading to learn something or be entertained? Think about what kinds of details would be most appealing to your readers.
Purpose	Think about what you are trying to accomplish through your description. Are you using description to inform your reader of something you witnessed? Do you want to describe a scenario so that you can persuade your reader to believe or do something? Perhaps your purpose is to describe some of the graphics in a video game you are evaluating. Keep focused on your purpose as you write your description.
Strategy	Sometimes a description can stand alone, but often it can be combined with other writing strategies. For example, you might include a description of a character in a television show you are evaluating, or you may describe two music groups you are comparing and contrasting. Chose the strategies that will best suit your purpose.
Design	How lengthy should you make your description? How many details do you need to convey your point to your audience? What other design elements, such as a photograph or drawing, might aid your readers? If you decide to include visuals in your description, be sure that they don't overshadow your words.

6.5 > Applying the Writing Process for Describing

1. **Discovering:** The readings, images, and other media suggestions in this chapter may help you find something to describe. Look through the chapter and see what comes to mind. You may try going somewhere scenic, such as a beach, the woods, or a mountainside, to find something beautiful to describe. As you begin to explore your topic, you might make a list of sensory details, freewrite everything that comes to mind about your topic, make a rough sketch of your subject, describe it to someone else, or complete a graphic organizer like the one below.

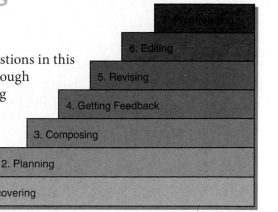

FIGURE 6.2 The Seven Steps of the Writing Process

2. **Planning:** Create a list of adjectives you'd like to include. Decide what order your want to use to present the details. If you are describing a scene, you may want to describe it from left to right, top to bottom, or close to far. You might try creating a cluster or an outline to determine how you want to organize your description.

3. **Composing:** Write a first draft of your description using the six steps outlined earlier in the chapter. (See pp. 115–116 for more details.)

   - Begin by creating a dominant impression.
   - Use an objective or a subjective approach.
   - Appeal to the senses.
   - Include similes and metaphors.
   - Organize your description logically.
   - End with something memorable.

   Don't worry too much about grammar and punctuation at this time. Focus on concrete sensory details. Describe your subject so that your audience's senses are engaged. Be sure to keep your dominant impression in mind as you write.

FIGURE 6.3 Describing

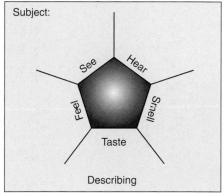

4. **Getting feedback:** Have at least one classmate or other person read your rough draft and answer the peer review questions that follow. If you have access to a writing tutor or center, get another opinion about your paper as well.

5. **Revising:** Using all of the feedback available to you, revise your description. Make sure that your description is full of specific sensory details to help your readers feel as if they are experiencing your subject. Check to see that your essay is unified. In other words, look for any details that don't fit with the dominant impression you are creating for your audience. Also, pay particular attention to using precise diction (word choice). Replace vague words with concrete words. Add, delete, and rearrange ideas as necessary.

6. **Editing:** Read your description again, this time looking for errors in grammar, punctuation, and mechanics. Look carefully for sentence fragments, which are common in rough drafts of descriptive writing. Writing in complete sentences will help you to communicate your ideas more clearly to your audience.

7. **Proofreading:** After you have edited your essay one or more times, read it again. This time, look for typographical errors and any other issues that might interfere with the readers' understanding of your description. Check it again to make sure you have written complete sentences rather than fragments.

>>Peer Review Questions for Describing

Trade rough drafts with a classmate and answer the following questions about his or her paper. Then, in person or online, discuss your papers and suggestions with your peer. Finally, make the changes you feel would most benefit your paper.

1. What is the dominant impression in the essay? Do the ideas in the paper help to support this overall mood or feeling? Why or why not?

2. Which sensory details are most appealing to you? Could any additional sensory details be included to help you better imagine the subject? What is missing or unclear?

3. Are the ideas in the description organized logically? If not which parts could be rearranged?

4. Is the description more objective or subjective? Do you feel the author's approach is appropriate for the subject? Why or why not?

5. Does the description include similes and/or metaphors? How effective are they?

6. What part of the description is most memorable? Why?

7. What kinds of grammatical errors, if any, are evident in the description?

8. What final suggestions do you have for the author?

> Writer's Checklist for Describing

Use the checklist below to evaluate your own writing and help ensure that your explanation of the process is complete. If you have any "no" answers, go back and work on those areas.

❏ 1. Is my dominant impression clear?

❏ 2. Is my description objective or subjective? Is this the best approach for my topic?

❏ 3. Have I included enough sensory details so the reader can imagine what I am describing?

❏ 4. Are the details organized logically?

❏ 5. Have I used similes and/or metaphors to enhance my description?

❏ 6. Are my adjectives precise?

❏ 7. Is my conclusion effective?

❏ 8. Have I proofread thoroughly?

CHAPTER SUMMARY

1. Descriptive writing is about appealing to the senses to evoke images in the minds of the audience.

2. Descriptive writing is an important part of your education, daily life, and career.

3. Interpreting descriptive readings and images can help you to prepare to write a description.

4. Carefully analyze the rhetorical star before writing a description: subject, audience, purpose, strategy, and design.

5. Follow these steps when writing a description: begin by creating a dominant impression; decide whether to use an objective or subjective approach; appeal to the senses; include similes or metaphors; organize your description logically; end with a memorable conclusion.

WHAT I KNOW NOW

Use this checklist to determine what you need to work on in order to feel comfortable with your understanding of the material in this chapter. Check off each item as you master it. Review the material for any unchecked items.

❏ 1. I know what **descriptive writing** is.

❏ 2. I can identify several **real-world applications** for writing descriptions.

❏ 3. I can **interpret** descriptive readings and images.

❏ 4. I can analyze the **rhetorical star** for writing a description.

❏ 5. I understand the **writing process** for writing a description.

❏ 6. I can apply the **six steps** for writing a description.

EXPLAINING A PROCESS:
CULTURES
AND
TRADITIONS

LEARNING outcomes

 In this chapter you will learn techniques for the following:

7.1 Identifying real-world applications for explaining a process in writing.

7.2 Understanding the steps for explaining a process.

7.3 Interpreting images and readings about processes related to cultures and traditions.

7.4 Analyzing the rhetorical star for explaining a process.

7.5 Applying the steps for explaining a process in writing.

> Writing Strategy Focus: Explaining a Process

Process writing is designed to explain how to do something, how something works, what something does, or how something was done. Writing about a process, sometimes called process analysis, involves breaking a procedure into its component steps. Processes can be instructional or informative. If the readers need to be able to perform the process, then the writing is instructional. For example, a step-by-step explanation of how to conduct a business meeting with someone from an Asian country would be instructional. If the readers just want to understand the basic sequence of steps or events, then the writing is informative. A news article explaining what happened during a recent event on campus or in your community would be informative. In that case, the readers would not try to replicate the process. Instead they would just want to understand what took place. You will have opportunities to write about processes in school, in your personal life, and in your career.

7.1 > Real-World Applications for Explaining Processes

Process Writing in School

You will have many opportunities for writing about processes in college. You might need to explain a process, such as mitosis or meiosis, on a biology exam or explain for a history paper what happened during a particular battle. For classes in your major, your instructor may ask you to write step-by-step instructions for performing a particular procedure to demonstrate your understanding of the process.

Process Writing in Your Daily Life

Writing about processes will also be a necessary part of your personal life. You may need to write instructions for someone taking care of your home, pets, or children while you are away. You might want to write out a dessert recipe to share with a friend or family member. Maybe you'll need to explain a step-by-step process to the police or insurance company if you witnessed or experienced an accident or natural disaster.

Process Writing in Your Career

Every career field includes processes that need to be explained or performed. You might need to leave instructions for someone who will be filling in for you when you are on vacation or away at a seminar, or you may need to write an explanation of how to perform your job for the person replacing you because of your promotion. Here are a few specific applications for process writing on the job:

Health care: admitting a patient, drawing blood, dressing a wound, diagnosing an illness, recording medical exam findings, taking an X-ray.

Massage therapy: creating ambience, using Swedish techniques, working with hot stones.

Computers: installing a program, utilizing a new software application, designing a three-dimensional illustration.

Criminal justice: investigating a crime scene, handling evidence, documenting findings in a police report.

Business: opening or closing for the day, keeping the books, tracking inventory, dealing with customer service issues.

Culinary arts: sharpening knives, baking a casserole, cleaning up the kitchen.

Graduate
SPOTLIGHT

Deborah Buza, Caterer

Chef Deborah A. Buza is a caterer who graduated with her culinary arts degree in 2006. She owns her own company, Buza's Catering, and is currently writing a cookbook. Here's what Buza has to say about the importance of writing in her career:

❝ In the catering business, everything relies on possessing good communication skills. I have to be able to explain my menu to potential clients over the phone and in writing in order to get their business. I have to write in clear, complete sentences, or the client will think I am incompetent. Because my parents are from different cultures, Polish and Italian, I enjoy deconstructing recipes from each culture and then combining them to create something totally different. I have to be able to explain how to perform the procedures and techniques that each culture uses during the cooking process. Also, my grandmother always said to put in a pinch of this or a handful of that, but our culture today is much more technical. I have to be precise with the measurements and ingredients. Overall, writing is imperative to my career as a caterer. **❞**

Activity Real-World Process Writing

On your own, in pairs, or in small groups, brainstorm uses for process writing at school, in your daily life, and on the job. You may want to choose your own career field or the prospective career field(s) of the participants in your group. Be prepared to share the results with your instructor or the class.

7.2 > Steps for Writing about a Process

1. Begin with a Clear Title and Introduction

Create an informative title for your process. It can be straightforward, such as "How to Throw the Perfect Themed Party" or catchy, such as "Surviving a Week with the In-Laws." Your introduction should include some kind of attention-getter to engage your readers in the process. For instance, an essay could begin with a question, such as, "Have you ever dreaded having your in-laws come to stay with you for the holidays?" Of course the most important part of your introduction is your thesis statement. State your thesis clearly so readers know what to expect. For example, "If you are trying to throw the best birthday bash ever, then you need to plan a great menu, invite the right people, organize some fun activities, and decorate appropriately."

2. Include a List of Materials

If your reader is going to perform the process you are explaining, you'll need to list all of the materials (ingredients, tools, equipment) necessary to complete the process. Be sure to include specific details and amounts. For example, if you are explaining how to create a costume for a Mardi Gras parade, you would include the types, colors, and quantities of fabrics, sequins, beads, feathers, and makeup that are needed. You would need to mention useful tools for making and assembling the costume, such as scissors, a stapler, and a tape measure. You would also need to include types and quantities for materials needed to hold the costume to-gether, such as staples, glue, elastic, and thread. Try to think of every essential detail.

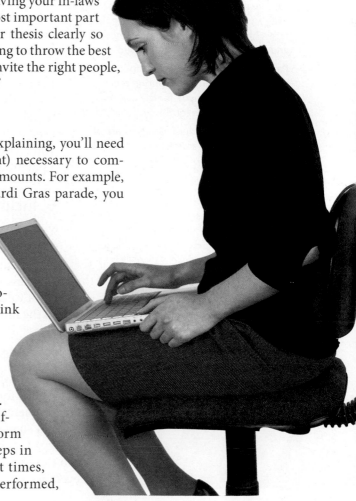

3. Explain Each Step in Chronological Order

As you write your steps, keep in mind whether your main purpose is to instruct or inform the audience. Include every necessary step, even if it seems insignif-icant, to ensure that your reader will be able to perform or understand the process. Make sure to place your steps in chronological order so as not to confuse the reader. At times, you may need to explain why a particular step is performed,

especially if you feel the reader may try to skip it. To help your reader understand the flow of steps in the process, use transitions, such as *first, next, then, after that,* and *meanwhile.* Also, be sure to use a variety of action words (verbs) to guide your reader through the process. For example, if you are instructing your readers on how to bake a traditional Mardi Gras king cake, you might use verbs such as *preheat, combine, decorate,* and *bake.* Finally, be sure you cover everything you promised the reader in the introduction.

4. Define Special Terms

If you are using a term that your reader may not know, then be sure to define the word the first time you mention it. Most of the time, you won't need to include a dictionary definition. Instead, explain the term in your own words based on your own experiences. For example, if you are writing about your family's Kwanzaa traditions, you might define *Kwanzaa* by saying it is a tradition celebrated from December 26 through January 1 in African communities around the world that has origins all the way back to the ancient first fruit harvest ceremonies in Africa. You may include additional details about the significance of the holiday, such as the seven principles of Kwanzaa, in your explanation of your family's customs.

5. Give Helpful Tips and Warnings as Needed

You may find that you need to mention useful tips or safety warnings, especially if the process you are explaining is instructional. Include tips or warnings just before or right along with the step they relate to because many readers won't read all of the instructions before trying to complete the process (even if the directions tell them to do so). For example, if you are explaining how to make the most of an Independence Day celebration, you might need to include a cautionary note about handling fireworks safely. You could use a symbol, such as a skull and crossbones to indicate a potential danger.

6. Include Visual Aids as Needed

You may want to include pictures, diagrams, or other visual images to help your reader more fully comprehend the process you are explaining. For instance, if you are explaining how to make a Japanese origami crane, pictures illustrating each step would be of great value to the reader. You would likely want to include a picture of the finished product as well.

7. End with a Decisive Conclusion

Let the reader know when the process is complete. For example, if you're explaining the steps for making potatoes au gratin, you might mention that the dish is ready when the cheese on top turns golden brown. Finally, end with any additional suggestions you have for the readers. For instance, if you explain the steps for preparing a traditional Mexican dish, you might make a suggestion to serve it with margaritas or mojitos (or nonalcoholic versions of those beverages).

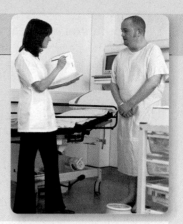

[preview] **WHILE THEY** are in college, most people learn the job knowledge and skills they need to be successful in their careers; however, sometimes they do not get training on how to be polite in the workplace. The following poster is designed by Calvin Sun to hang on a wall in the workplace to provide employees with some tips for being considerate of their colleagues. Have you ever had an annoying co-worker? What did he or she do to get on your nerves?

10 Ways to Improve Your Office Etiquette

By Calvin Sun

We spend one-third of our working lives at the office. The people we work with can affect our productivity and our careers, and vice versa. Practicing office etiquette makes the place and the workday just a bit more bearable.

1 Watch the volume of your voice

Keep your voice at a reasonable level. Other people are trying to work, and your voice may distract them. Besides, do you really want them to overhear what you're saying? If you have something personal or otherwise sensitive to discuss, consider doing it in a private office or conference room.

2 Use speakerphones with care

If you're on hold and waiting for someone to pick up, then yes, a speakerphone can save you time. Just keep the volume as low as possible. On the other hand, if you're planning to have a regular conversation with the other person, do it behind closed doors. Your co-workers in the area will not appreciate your disturbing them with a conference call.

3 Be sensitive about what you bring for lunch

We're supposed to be inclusive and accepting of people from different backgrounds and cultures, I know. And those other people are supposed to behave likewise. Nonetheless, be aware of how others may react to the lunch you bring. If you think about it, any reaction it causes can't be good for you. They'll either hate the smell and complain about you, or they'll love the smell, assassinate you, and eat your lunch. Either way, you lose out. If you have food with a distinctive aroma, consider either eating it outside or in the lunchroom, rather than at your desk. And some foods probably shouldn't be brought in at all, even to the lunchroom, such as <u>stinkytofu</u> or <u>durian</u>.

4 Respect people's privacy

Because you're most likely in a cubicle or other open office area, you inevitably will overhear snippets of conversations other people are having. Maybe you'll hear something about a project you're involved with or a problem you've encountered before, and you believe you have something to contribute. Yes, if you go over and join the conversation, you could save the day or provide valuable insight. However, you might also be viewed as a busybody.

Think carefully before joining that conversation. One consideration might be the amount of desperation you sense in their voices. The more desperate, the more willing they might be to hear from others.

If you do choose to join them, I suggest you go to their office or cubicle, let them see you as you're listening to them. Then, at a break, casually mention that it sounds like there is a problem, and that if you can help, you'd be happy to. This approach is better than rushing over and telling them you overheard their conversation.

5 Fix, or attempt to fix, what you break

How many times have you gone to the photocopier to find that it was either out of toner, out of paper, or experiencing a paper jam? The problem was still around when you arrived because the previous person did nothing about it and simply left the copier in its problem condition.

Don't be that person. If you can clear the paper jam safely and according to procedure, try to do so. Most photocopiers have diagrams to show you how. If you can't fix the jam or the other problem, leave a signed dated note describing the issue and what you are doing to fix it or have it fixed. Those actions could be a call to the maintenance vendor or to an administrative department. Your co-workers will appreciate your efforts, and signing your name to the note demonstrates your willingness to take ownership.

6 Keep the lunchroom clean

Neither the refrigerator nor the microwave should resemble the Queens Botanical Garden. If you spilled something in either place, clean it up. If you forgot to eat something from the refrigerator, and it's starting to mold, throw it out yourself. Don't leave it for someone else.

7 Be punctual for meetings

If you're an attendee, be on time. If you can't make a meeting or you're going to be late, let someone know. Don't arrive late and ask for a recap. Doing so wastes everyone else's time. If you're the one who's running the meeting, start it on time and resume it on time after a break. To do otherwise (for example, to start late to accommodate latecomers) is unfair to those who showed up on time and only encourages more lateness in the future.

8 Be careful about solicitations

Even if your company has no strict prohibition against solicitations (for example, selling candy for a child's sports team fund-raiser), be careful about doing so. Your co-workers may not appreciate being put on the spot. If you do anything at all, the best approach is to display the merchandise in a central location, with a notice about the reason, and an envelope to receive checks or cash.

9 Avoid borrowing or lending

The rich rule over the poor, and the borrower is servant to the lender.

We've heard, in the past few weeks, more than we want to about issues with borrowing and lending. Those issues still apply even at the office level, even between individuals. Any borrowing that occurs can jeopardize a relationship if the repayment is slow, late, less than expected, or nonexistent. No matter how small the amount, the lender may feel resentment. In fact, a small amount might cause resentment precisely because the lender feels embarrassed about asking about repayment.

Avoid borrowing or lending if you can. If you absolutely must borrow, write the lender an IOU with the amount and sign it. Then, pay it back as soon as you can.

10 Don't ask co-workers how to spell

Microsoft Word has a spell checker. Use it. Don't bother your co-workers with such questions. It hampers their productivity and lowers their opinion of you. Some probably won't even want to answer, because doing so makes them feel stupid. When I get such questions, my response is, "Wait a minute while I check the dictionary" or "Wait while I use the Word dictionary."

Source: www.scribd.com/doc/12589359/10-things-for-office-etiquette.

[QUESTIONS FOR REFLECTION]

1. What is the purpose of the poster? Is the poster helpful? Why or why not?

2. Make a list of the action verbs in each heading. Which ones are most effective? Why?

3. Discuss the design of the poster. Is it appealing? Which features are the strongest? Do you think employees would take the time to read it? Why or why not?

4. Which office etiquette tips are the most important? Which are the least important? Why?

5. Have you ever violated any of the tips on the poster? Which ones? How did your co-workers react?

>> *Career-Based* PROCESS WRITING

[preview] **HAVE YOU EVER** given blood for a test at the doctor's office or as a donation to a blood bank? What was the experience like? The following instructions for drawing blood came from ehow.com. As you are reading them, imagine that you are following the steps or that someone is drawing your blood.

How to Draw Blood

There are precise steps that must be followed when a health care worker draws blood. These steps protect the patient, ensure the safety of the phlebotomist or nurse drawing the blood, and lead to a successful blood draw. Learn to draw blood safely and effectively using a Vacutainer and needle with syringe.

Instructions

Step 1: Ask the patient his name and date of birth. Make sure he answers with his full name and full date of birth to ensure his identity. Mark all specimen tubes with his identification and pull on protective gloves to protect yourself from bodily fluids.

Step 2: Set out all of the tubes you need by the order of the draw and have any necessary tools (tourniquet and alcohol swabs) nearby.

Step 3: Draw blood from the most common point—the median cubital vein—which runs on the inner part of the forearm. This is the optimum vein because it's close to the skin surface and there aren't a lot of nerves surrounding it.

Step 4: Prep the chosen location by placing a tourniquet on the upper part of the arm, tight enough to make the vein bulge. Gently pat the vein and look at its size. Find the best angle from which to draw the blood.

Step 5: Insert the needle into the vein with a smooth, fast motion. This technique helps lessen pain.

Step 6: Push the Vacutainer (blood specimen tube) into the holder, keeping the needle steady. The Vacutainer will automatically start filling with the right amount of blood needed for a specific specimen. If using an old-fashioned syringe and needle system, manually pull back on the syringe to start filling the tube with blood.

Step 7: Pull the needle out at the same angle you inserted it once the last specimen is collected. Immediately dispose of the needle in the proper place and apply gauze to the patient's wound, holding it to apply pressure.

Step 8: Mix the specimens thoroughly by gently swishing them around. Confirm that each specimen is labeled correctly.

Source: Ehow.com, **www.ehow.com/how_2079835_draw-blood.html.**

[QUESTIONS FOR REFLECTION]

1. Who is the audience for the instructions? Do the instructions effectively meet the needs of the audience? Why or why not?

2. Which steps are the clearest? Do any steps need further explanation? Explain your answers.

3. Make a list of the major action verbs in each step. Which ones are the most effective? Why?

4. Identify the statements that should be more gender neutral (not just masculine) and revise them.

5. If you have never drawn blood before, would you be able to do so after simply reading these steps? Why or why not?

STUDENT WRITING

How to Feed a Nursing Home Resident
by Marissa Scott

Working in a nursing home with different residents can be difficult at times, especially when it comes to feeding a resident who is in bed. While working in a nursing home, you will encounter people from different cultures, backgrounds, and languages. You will also have to deal with residents who are confused or suffering from dementia. There are a few important steps to remember that can help to simplify the feeding process.

The first step is to greet the resident. You should knock on the door to show the patient respect. Then, as you enter the room, greet the resident and identify yourself. Next, explain to the resident that you are there for a feeding, and obtain his or her consent to continue. At this time if the patient is confused or speaks a different language, try to point or use gestures or pictures to help explain the procedure to him or her. If the resident just does not want to be bothered, you should encourage him or her and be supportive. Keep in mind that the patient may come from a culture or background that causes him

or her to feel embarrassed that another person has to help with feeding. However, if the resident is confused or combative, just leave him or her alone for a few minutes then go back and try it again.

The second step, after the resident agrees to the feeding procedure, is to raise the head of the bed, making sure that the resident is sitting in an upright position. Adjust the bed to where you will be able to sit at the resident's eye level. While doing this, you should make sure the resident is aware that you are moving the bed to a different position; otherwise he or she might become frightened. Once you start adjusting the bed, make sure the patient is conscious of what you are about to do because, as previously stated, you need to respect the cultural background of the resident.

Then, once you have the bed adjusted, make the final preparations for feeding the patient. Be sure resident's hands are clean. Additionally, place the food tray over the bed table at a comfortable position for the resident to see the food on the tray. Next, ask the resident if he or she would like a clothing protector. Some people consider a clothing protector to be too similar to a child's bib and would not like to have one on while eating. You don't want to offend the patient and interrupt the feeding process. Then tell the resident what foods are on the tray and ask what he or she would like to eat first. You shouldn't just choose for the resident. Now you are ready to feed the patient.

Begin feeding the resident with fairly small amounts of food on a fork or spoon. Give the patient time to chew and swallow before offering another bite. Look for cues from the resident to help you determine the pace. After every few bites, you should ask if the patient wants a sip of the drink. During the feeding, you should try to make conversation with the resident to help him or her feel more comfortable. Be sure to speak only English. For example, if another person walks into the room and you hold a conversation with that person in Spanish or another language that the resident does not speak, the resident may become offended, confused, or scared and think he or she is in a foreign country. Continue feeding until the patient says he or she is full or until the tray of food is empty. Then you can remove the tray and make sure the patient, the bed, and the tray are clean.

While working in a nursing home with residents or patients from different cultures and backgrounds, make sure you give them respect during the feeding process because someone could easily get offended and feel like you are not being considerate of his or her feelings. As you greet the patients, get them ready for a meal, and feed them, always keep these steps in mind to help the nursing home residents feel as comfortable as possible.

[QUESTIONS FOR REFLECTION]

1. Which sentence in the introduction explains the process that will be described? Is it clear? Why or why not?

2. Does the order of the steps make sense? Why or why not?

3. Which steps are explained the best? Why?

4. Which transitions seem to work best in the essay? What effect do they have on the explanation of the process?

5. Does Scott identify any special tips that the reader should consider before performing the process? If so, what are they?

7.3 > Process Writing in the Context of Cultures and Traditions

In the readings that follow, you will have an opportunity to examine cultures from different perspectives. The term *culture* refers to the way people in a particular group behave based on their beliefs and values. Groups can have a multitude of cultural orientations. They can be based on social interests, attitudes, hobbies, values, ethnicity, educational goals, work endeavors, or a variety of other characteristics. People from various cultures all around the world have traditions that they like to uphold. Whether these traditions are for sports, holidays, birthdays, entertainment, religious ceremonies, work, or everyday life, they all have specific procedures that the participants or observers follow. For example, fans at a heavy metal concert display completely different behaviors than the audience at a symphony orchestra concert.

As human beings we need to be aware of and sensitive to different cultures and traditions. One reason for this is that we are likely to encounter people from many different cultures in the workplace. Additionally, each work environment has its own culture (beliefs, values, and guidelines). These principles guide the behavior of the employees. How employees dress, communicate, perform their tasks, and interact with their clients, customers, or patients all depends on the culture of the organization. The readings in this chapter relate to a variety of different types of cultures and include some of the processes that go along with those cultures. Reading and interpreting what others have written can help you see the structure and style of a process analysis and learn how to write about processes for school, work, and your daily life.

[preview] THE FOURTH OF JULY is a holiday that many Americans celebrate every year. To some it is a day to remember the nation's independence from England. For others, it's merely an opportunity to get a day off of work or school to have a cookout, hang out with friends and family, and watch a spectacular array of fireworks. In the following essay, Pulitzer Prize-winning humor columnist Dave Barry has some suggestions for celebrating this traditional American holiday. Or does he? If you like Barry's sense of humor, you might want to visit his Web site at **www.DaveBarry.com**. Before reading, think about some Independence Day celebrations you have experienced. Did everything go as planned?

Independence Day **by Dave Barry**

This year, why not hold an old-fashioned Fourth of July Picnic?

Food poisoning is one good reason. After a few hours in the sun, ordinary potato salad can develop bacteria the size of raccoons. But don't let the threat of agonizingly painful death prevent you from celebrating the birth of our nation, just as Americans have been doing ever since that historic first July Fourth when our Founding Fathers—George Washington, Benjamin Franklin, Thomas Jefferson, Bob Dole and Tony Bennett—landed on Plymouth Rock.

Step one in planning your picnic is to decide on a menu. Martha Stewart has loads of innovative suggestions for unique, imaginative and tasty summer meals. So you can forget about her. "If Martha Stewart comes anywhere near my picnic, she's risking a barbecue fork to the eyeball" should be your patriotic motto. Because you're having a traditional Fourth of July picnic, and that means a menu of hot dogs charred into cylinders of industrial-grade carbon, and hamburgers so under-cooked that when people try to eat them, they leap off the plate and frolic on the lawn like otters.

Dad should be in charge of the cooking, because only Dad, being a male of the masculine gender, has the mechanical "know-how" to operate a piece of technology as a complex as a barbecue grill. To be truly traditional, the grill should be constructed of the following materials:

— 4 percent "rust-resistant" steel;
— 58 percent rust;

— 23 percent hardened black grill scunge from food cooked as far back as 1987 (the scunge should never be scraped off, because it is what is actually holding the grill together);
— 15 percent spiders.

If the grill uses charcoal as a fuel, Dad should remember to start lighting the fire early (no later than April 10) because charcoal, in accordance with federal safety regulations, is a mineral that does not burn. The spiders get a huge kick out of watching Dad attempt to ignite it; they emit hearty spider chuckles and slap themselves on all eight knees. This is why many dads prefer the modern gas grill, which ignites at the press of a button and burns with a steady, even flame until you put food on it, at which time it runs out of gas.

While Dad is saying traditional bad words to the barbecue grill, Mom can organize the kids for a fun activity: making old-fashioned ice cream by hand, the way our grandparents' generation did. You'll need a hand-cranked ice-cream maker, which you can pick up at any antique store for $1,875. All you do is put in the ingredients, and start cranking! It makes no difference what specific ingredients you put in, because—I speak from bitter experience here—no matter how long you crank them, they will never, ever turn into ice cream. Scientists laugh at the very concept. "Ice cream is not formed by cranking," they point out. "Ice cream is formed by freezers." Our grandparents' generation wasted millions of man-hours trying to produce ice cream by hand; this is what caused the Great Depression.

When the kids get tired of trying to make ice cream (allow about 25 seconds for this) it's time to play some traditional July Fourth games. One of the most popular is the "sack race." All you need is a bunch of old-fashioned burlap sacks, which you can obtain from the J. Peterman catalog for $227.50 apiece. Call the kids outside, have them line up on the lawn and give each one a sack to climb into; then shout "GO!" and watch the hilarious antics begin as, one by one, the kids sneak back indoors and resume trying to locate pornography on the Internet.

Come nightfall, though, everybody will be drawn back outside by the sound of loud, traditional Fourth of July explosions coming from all around the neighborhood. These are caused by the fact that various dads, after consuming a number of traditionally fermented beverages, have given up on conventional charcoal-lighting products and escalated to gasoline. As the spectacular pyrotechnic show lights up the night sky, you begin to truly appreciate the patriotic meaning of the words to "The Star-Spangled Banner", written by Francis Scott Key to commemorate the fledgling nation's first barbecue:

And the grill parts' red glare;
Flaming spiders in air;
Someone call 911;
There's burning scunge in Dad's hair

After the traditional visit to the hospital emergency room, it's time to gather 'round and watch Uncle Bill set off the fireworks that he purchased from a roadside stand operated by people who spend way more on tattoos than dental hygiene. As Uncle Bill lights the firework fuse and scurries away, everybody is on pins and needles until, suddenly and dramatically, the fuse goes out. So Uncle Bill re-lights the fuse and scurries away again, and the fuse goes out again, and so on, with Uncle Bill scurrying back and forth with his Bic lighter like a deranged Olympic torchbearer until, finally, the fuse burns all the way down, and the firework, emitting a smoke puff the size of a grapefruit, makes a noise—"phut"—like a squirrel passing gas. Wow! What a fitting climax for your traditional old-fashioned July Fourth picnic!

Next year you'll go out for Chinese food.

Source: "Independence Day," from *Dave Barry Is Not Taking This Sitting Down* by Dave Barry, copyright © 2000 by Dave Barry. Used by permission of Crown Publishers, a division of Random House, Inc.

[QUESTIONS FOR REFLECTION]

Considering Ideas

1. Barry mentions the word *traditional* numerous times in this essay? Does he explain a traditional Independence Day celebration? Why or why not?

2. What parts of Barry's essay do you find to be humorous? Why are those parts funny?

3. Have you ever had a Fourth of July Celebration that turned out like Dave's? What happened?

Considering Writing Strategies

1. Satire occurs when what is said conflicts with what is meant. Where does Barry use satire in the essay? What effect does his satirical approach have on the reader?

2. Why does Barry approach this essay from a "how to" standpoint? What elements of process writing does he include in the essay? Why does he use this approach? Is he really suggesting the reader follow his advice?

3. What other writing strategies, in addition to explaining a process, does Barry include in the essay? Identify particular passages that use other forms of writing.

Writing Suggestions

1. Do you celebrate the Fourth of July? If so, what does this holiday mean to you? Why do you celebrate it? Write an essay explaining the significance of Independence Day to you. How do you usually celebrate this holiday?

2. Have you ever had a holiday event or family celebration that didn't turn out as planned? Write an essay explaining what happened. You may choose to use a serious or sarcastic tone. Include plenty of details in your explanation so the reader can visualize your experience.

ESOL Tip >

Write about a significant day the people in your native country celebrate. Why is this day important to you and the people of your country? How do you celebrate?

[preview] **E. BARRIE KAVASCH** is a Cherokee herbologist who has written more than 20 nonfiction books about Native American culture and traditions. Her books provide a wealth of information about American Indian folklore, tribal history, genealogy, rituals, festival celebrations, healing arts, and cuisine. She also ventured into the world of fiction in 2005 with her first novel, *Sacred Cave: A Novel Set in America's Prehistoric Southeast.* The following excerpt is from a chapter called "November" from her book titled *Enduring Harvests: Native American Foods and Festivals for Every Season.* Here she explains the background of an ancient Aztec festival, Los Días de los Muertos (Days of the Dead), that is still celebrated today all around the world, especially by people from American Indian and Mexican cultures. She also includes recipes for making "bread of the dead" and icing to accompany it. Before reading, think about the celebrations you participate in as part of your culture.

Los Días de los Muertos (Days of the Dead) by E. Barrie Kavasch

One of Mexico's most important festivals since pre-Hispanic times, Los Días de Los Muertos (Days of the Dead) are occasions for drawing all levels of society together into shared experiences of death and rebirth. In celebrating death, the ancient Aztecs made continued life possible.

The Aztecs believed that when a person died the soul went to one of thirteen heavens or nine underworlds. *Mictlantec-uhtli,* the Aztec god of death, would be rejoicing, since death was not negative or frightening but simply a step to another stage of life in an eternal cycle. This ancient Aztec belief has evolved today into ceremonies full of nostalgia, gentleness, and loveliness. As their Aztec, Zapotec, or Mixtec ancestors had been accustomed to doing for centuries, contemporary Indians and Mexicans generously share their best offerings with their dead.

This festival is a distinctive blending of pre-Hispanic beliefs and practices with the Spanish Roman Catholic observation of All Saints' Day on November 1 and All Souls' Day on November 2. Though every city and Pueblo in Mexico celebrates, different regions have evolved their own unique customs and traditions, as the dead's annual homecoming takes on special flair and involves almost everybody.

Coincidental with the rituals of the ancient Aztec corn harvests, this is one of the happiest times of the Native American year and also one of the most prosperous times for the artisans who fashion the unique breads, candies, foods, and sculptures for this major festival.

Urban stalls in the town plaza, or *zocalo,* and rural markets are filled with gaily decorated skulls and bones, miniature coffins and tombstones made of marzipan (a sugar-almond paste), amaranth seed skulls with peanut incisors, and *pan de los muertos* (bread of the dead), which are made only at this time of the year. Vendors also display enormous varieties of miniature skeletons of cardboard, wood, paper, and papier-mâché; some have tinfoil eyes and gold grins, some are serape-clad dancers, musicians, or gamblers in hilarious postures.

Mexican women clean their houses, make candles, purchase special sweet treats, and prepare quantities of tortillas, chicken, mole, verdolagas, atole, hot chocolate, and a special bread baked in shapes of twisted bones, round skulls, or little animals. Men and children create beautiful altars on which they place toys, candles, sweet foods, and favorite drinks for their departed loved ones. In Puebla, the fourth largest city in Mexico, tiny shops as well as private homes are lovingly adorned with decorations.

The special foods created for this festival serve many purposes. Families take time to honor and celebrate their dead, and also to mock death itself, and as they later share and eat the choice foods, they symbolically consume death. Together, the sweets and toys shaped like bones and skeletons serve to portray Death as an amusing, mischievous, and friendly figure.

At midnight, the people leave their homes carrying candles, precious food items, drinks, and sometimes musical instruments, as they make processions to the cemetery to arrange flowers and offerings on the graves of their dead, with whom they spend the long night. They know, when the candle flames flutter, that the souls, or alma (essence), are visiting, and eating the soul of the foods. Afterwards, as the new day dawns, the people return to their homes, after their night spent in communion and prayer, around their temporary altars in the cemetery, and enjoy the day resting, feasting, and reflecting.

Octavio Paz observes in his *Labyrinth of Solitude* that "Life extended into death, and vice versa. Death was not the natural end of life but one phase of a natural cycle. Life, death, and resurrection were stages of a cosmic process which repeated itself continuously." The distinction between life and death was not so absolute as it is to us today in our less mature society. Death has been a most popular subject in Mexican art for centuries, and this holiday is increasingly viewed as a reinforcement of cultural identity. Increasingly sophisticated museum exhibitions are devoted to this idea and to the festival, and almost all Mexican restaurants around the globe celebrate *Los Días de los Muertos* with the special breads and candies associated with the holiday.

PAN DE LOS MUERTOS (BREAD OF THE DEAD)

In Oaxaca, the men of Teotitlán del Valle bake a certain kind of bread in great demand just at this time. Baking in constant shifts for three days to fill orders, they make considerable money for their families. In other parts of the country as well, bakers fashion this special bread to look like twisted bones, round skulls, or little animals (animalitos) glistening with white icing. These are placed on the beautiful ofrendas that are sanctuaries of the spirits and the places for rendezvous between the living and the dead

Recipes differ from region to region, as do the shapes, flavors, and decorations, and pan de los muertos can be quite complicated to make. This is a basic version from which your imagination can take flight.

½ cup water
½ cup milk
½ cup butter or light vegetable oil
1 teaspoon salt
½ cup sugar
½ cup honey
2 packages dry yeast
5 to 6 cups sifted flour, divided
½ teaspoon anise seed
½ teaspoon ground allspice
1 teaspoon freshly grated orange peel and zest
4 eggs, well-beaten and light

Heat the water, milk, and butter in a small pan over low heat, just enough to warm them well. Stir in the salt, sugar, and honey and blend well. Cool slightly to a moderate-warm temperature (comfortable to a finger-touch.) Remove from the heat.

Sprinkle the yeast over the top of this warm mixture, and stir it in gently. Set this to rest in a warm place for 15 minutes.

In a large bowl, combine 2 cups of the flour with the anise seed, allspice, and orange peel and zest. Add the warm liquid and beat well by hand or with a mixer. Add the beaten eggs and 1 more cup of flour; beat well. Using a wooden spoon, carefully blend in the remaining 2 to 3 cups of the flour, gradually adding the correct amount to make a soft dough.

Turn the dough out onto a lightly floured breadboard or other clean, lightly floured surface, knead for about 10 minutes. Place the kneaded dough into a greased bowl and cover with a damp towel; rest it in a warm place to rise for about 1 ½ hours or until doubled in size.

Punch down the risen dough and pinch off varying amounts to begin making various shapes. Fashion several round loaves and place them, well spaced, on a lightly greased baking sheet. Roll and twist some small dough strips to be used as "bones" and festive symbols and designs on the round loaves. When the small designs are made, moisten them and press them as decorations onto the round loaves. Let these finished designs rise again for an hour. Preheat oven to 350°.

When breads have risen, place them on baking sheets in the oven and bake for 40 minutes.

Remove baked bread to cooling rack. You may wish to decorate the *pan de los muertos* with the simple icing on the next page.

Makes about 6 loaves.

PAN DE LOS MUERTOS BREAD ICING

½ cup powdered sugar
½ teaspoon orange or vanilla extract
1 to 2 tablespoons milk or water
few drops of food coloring, if you like

Beat all ingredients together until smooth, then drizzle or brush icing over the finished bread.

Makes ½ cup

Source: E. Barry Kavasch, "Días de los Muertos." In E.B. Kavasch *Enduring Harvests: Native American Foods and Festivals for Every Season* (Old Saybrook, CT: The Globe Pequot Press, 1995), pp. 64–68.

Considering Ideas

1. What is the significance of the Días de los Muertos festival? What are the participants hoping to accomplish and why?

2. What are some of the customs associated with the "Days of the Dead" celebrations?

3. Some people who celebrate Los Días de los Muertos like to make the special bread and icing as part of the festivities. What celebrations in other cultures traditionally have special recipes associated with them? Give several specific examples.

Considering Writing Strategies

1. What is Kavasch's purpose for writing this explanation and recipes? Is her goal merely to inform the reader of how to make bread, or does the piece serve a larger purpose?

2. What elements of explaining a process does Kavasch include in her essay and recipes about Los Días de los Muertos?

3. What action verbs does Kavasch use to explain the process of making the "bread of the dead"? Where does she typically place those verbs in her sentences? What is the effect of that placement?

Writing Suggestions

1. What kinds of celebrations do you participate in as part of your culture? Based on your personal experiences, write an essay explaining one of your customs. Include plenty of details so that your reader has an understanding of the significance of the celebration and the festivities associated with it.

2. Does your family have a special holiday recipe that has been passed down through the generations? Write an explanation of how to make the special dish. You may want to begin with an introduction explaining a little history about your family's recipe, such as who in your family usually makes the dish and when it is typically served. Also, be sure to include a list of ingredients with specific amounts along with the detailed procedure so that your reader can follow your instructions to make the recipe.

>> READINGS AND REFLECTION

[preview] **MARLO MORGAN,** a doctor from Kansas City, decided to sell her practice and travel to Australia to provide medical assistance for the people there. When she arrived in Australia, she imagined that she was being taken to a luncheon where she might receive an award. She even prepared a speech just in case. Instead, she found herself an unwilling participant in a 1,400-mile journey across the rugged Outback with a tribe of Aborigines.

In her novel *Mutant Message Down Under*, Dr. Morgan describes some of the experiences she had on this "walkabout," as the Aborigines called it. In the following excerpt, she explains some of the traditions that the Aborigines celebrate and mentions some American traditions that she taught to the people she encountered on her adventure. The "Mutants" she refers to in the story are people who don't share the beliefs and practices of the Aborigines or "Real People." Even though Morgan did not volunteer for this journey, she made some unexpected discoveries about the unique people of Australia and about herself. Before reading, think about an adventure that you have gone on that has had a lasting impact on your life. How has that experience affected you?

During our journey there were two occasions that we celebrated by honoring someone's talent. Everyone is recognized by a special party, but it has nothing to do with age or birthdate—it is in recognition of uniqueness and contribution to life. They believe that the purpose for the passage of time is to allow a person to become better, wiser, to express more and more of one's beingness. So if you are a better person this year than last, and only you know that for certain, then you call for the party. When you say you are ready, everyone honors that.

One of the celebrations we had was for a woman whose talent, or medicine, in life was being a listener. Her name was Secret Keeper. No matter what anyone wanted to talk about, get off their chest, confess, or vent, she was always available. She considered the conversations private, didn't really offer advice, nor did she judge. She held the person's hand or held their head in her lap and just listened. She seemed to have a way of encouraging people to find their own solutions, to follow what their hearts were directing them to do.

I thought of people at home in the United States: the number of young people who seemed to have no sense of direction or purpose, the homeless people who think they have nothing to offer society, the addicted individuals who want to function in some reality other than the one we are in. I wished I could bring them here, to witness how little it takes, sometimes, to be a benefit to your community, and how wonderful it is to know and experience a sense of self-worth.

This woman knew her strong points and so did everyone else. The party consisted of Secret Keeper, sitting slightly elevated, and the rest of us. She had requested that the universe provide bright foods, if that was in order. Sure enough, that evening we found ourselves walking in plants that held berries and grapes.

We had seen a rainfall in the distance some days before, and we found scores of tadpoles in small pools of water. The tadpoles were laid upon the hot rocks and quickly dried into another form of food I had never dreamed possible. Our party menu also included some type of unattractive mud-hopping creature.

At the party we had music. I taught the Real People a Texas line dance, Cotton-Eyed Joe, which we modified to their drumbeat, and before long we were all laughing. Then I explained how Mutants like to dance with partners and asked Regal Black Swan to join me. He learned waltz steps immediately, but we couldn't get the beat just right. I started humming the tune and encouraged them to join me. Before long we had the group humming and waltzing under the Australian sky. I also showed them how to square dance. Ooota did a great job as the caller. That night they decided that perhaps I had already mastered the art of healing in my society and might wish to go into the music field!

It was the closest I ever got to receiving an Aborigine name. They felt I had more than one talent and were discovering that I could love them and their way of looking at life as well as remaining loyal to my own, so they nicknamed me Two Hearts.

At Secret Keeper's party, various people took turns telling what a comfort it was to have her in the community and how valuable her work was for everyone. She glowed humbly and took the praise in a dignified and royal manner.

It was a great night. As I was falling asleep, I said, "Thank you" to the universe for such a remarkable day.

I would not have agreed to come with these people had I been given the choice. I would not order tadpole to eat if it were on a menu; and yet I was remembering how meaningless some of our holidays have become and how wonderful these times were.

Source: M. Morgan, "Happy Unbirthday." In M. Morgan, *Mutant Message Down Under* (Thorndike, ME: Thorndike Press, 1994), pp. 218–21 (large print edition).

[QUESTIONS FOR REFLECTION]

Considering Ideas

1. What Aborigine customs does Morgan explain? Do any of these customs seem unusual to you? Which ones? Why?

2. What is the significance of an "unbirthday" in the Aborigine culture? How does this celebration compare to birthday celebrations in your culture?

3. Based on the last two paragraphs, how does Morgan feel about her "unbirthday" experience with the Aborigines?

Considering Writing Strategies

1. Identify several paragraphs where Morgan explains processes. Is her purpose to be instructional or informative? How effective are her explanations?

2. What other writing strategies, besides process writing, does she use?

3. What is Morgan's tone in this chapter? What specific words indicate this tone?

Writing Suggestions

1. Write an essay explaining the details about one of your favorite holiday celebrations. When and where does the celebration take place? What do you do? Why is this event important to you?

2. Write an essay comparing and contrasting your family's birthday celebration with the Aborigine's "unbirthday" celebration. Does your family recognize birthdays in a special way? Does someone prepare a special meal? Does the birthday boy or girl receive gifts?

>> READINGS AND REFLECTION

[preview] **BEST-SELLING AUTHOR** Esmeralda Santiago was born in San Juan, Puerto Rico, where she spent the first 13 years of her life before immigrating to America with her family. Santiago and her 10 younger siblings resided in New York with their single mother, who struggled to make ends meet. Despite all the challenges she faced, Santiago managed to graduate from Harvard magna cum laude and become an award-winning writer and filmmaker. In the following excerpt from her memoir *When I Was Puerto Rican*, Santiago recalls a special moment she shared with her mother doing a simple chore. You can learn more about Esmeralda Santiago and watch a clip from her documentary *Writing a Life* on her Web site at **www.EsmeraldaSantiago.com**. Before reading, think about your favorite and least favorite chores that you performed as a child. What did you like or dislike about them?

Ironing by Esmeralda Santiago

Because of all the running around she had to do with Raymond, Mami couldn't work a steady job anymore. Still, his medications and doctor visits meant we needed money, so Mami talked our landlord into paying her for cooking a daily *caldero* of rice and beans and a stack of fried chicken pieces or pork chops, which he then sold at the bar. Sometimes she left the house, not in her work clothes but dressed a little better than what she wore around the house. She didn't tell us where she was going on those days, and it was years before I learned that she went to clean other people's houses. One day I came back from school to find a rope stretched across the front room and men's white shirts, lean and crisp, hanging in a row.

"Don't touch them. They're not ours."

"Whose are they?"

"They belong to the laundry down the street."

She spritzed some water from a bottle onto the cuff of a shirt and pressed the iron against it, making the steam rise up to her face.

"How come you're doing their ironing?"

"They were very nice and let me bring the work home instead of do it there." She finished the shirt and put it on a wire hanger alongside the others.

Of all the things in the world Mami had to do, this was her least favorite. She liked cooking, sewing, mopping, even dusting. But she always complained about how much she hated ironing.

"Can I try?"

"Her eyebrows formed a question mark over her round eyes. Her mouth toyed with a smile. This was probably the first time I'd ever volunteered to learn anything useful.

She turned off the iron and looked for one of Papi's old shirts in her clean laundry hamper. "We wouldn't want you burning a customer's shirt," she chuckled. She stretched it on the board.

Quietly she showed me how to set the temperature for linen or cotton, how to wet my finger on my tongue and listen for the sizzle when I touched the flat bottom of the iron, and how to keep the electric cord from touching the hot metal, which could cause a fire. She turned over the bottle of cold water and sprinkled the inside of my wrist.

"This is how little moisture you need to get the steam to rise." She curved my fingers around the handle, pressing the iron against the fabric while with the other hand she pulled the cloth taut.

"Always iron the inside button and hole plackets first, then the inside and outside collar, then the cuffs." We danced around the ironing board, with Mami guiding my hand, pressing down on the iron, and standing away for a minute to see me do as she'd taught. The steam rose from the shirt and filled my head with the clean fresh scent of sun-dried cotton, and bubbles of perspiration flushed along my hair line and dripped down my neck. But I pressed on, absorbed by the tiny squares in the weave, the straight, even stitches that held the seams in place, the way the armhole curved into the shoulder.

"You're doing a good job," Mami murmured, a puzzled expression on her face.

"This is fun," I said, meaning it.

"Fun!" she laughed. "Then from now on you do all the ironing around the house." She said it with a smile, which meant she was teasing. And she never asked me to do it. But after that, whenever I wanted to feel close to Mami, I stacked wrinkled clothes into a basket, and, one by one, ironed them straight, savoring the afternoon when she taught me to do the one thing she most hated.

Source: Esmeralda Santiago. From *When I Was Puerto Rican* by Esmeralda Santiago. Copyright © 1993 by Esmeralda Santiago. Reprinted by permission of Da Capo Press, a member of Perseus Books, LLC.

[QUESTIONS FOR REFLECTION]

Considering Ideas

1. Ironing seems like such a simple, insignificant task. Why is this memory so important to Santiago?

2. What was the author's purpose in writing the story?

3. Where is Santiago's Puerto Rican heritage evident in the story? What specific references does she include?

Considering Writing Strategies

1. Where does Santiago explain the process of ironing in her memoir? What is her purpose in doing so?

2. Find passages where Santiago incorporates dialogue into her memoir. How does this dialogue affect the reader's understanding of the events that take place?

3. What are some examples of transitional words and phrases that Santiago uses to explain the process of ironing? How do these transitions enhance the reader's understanding of the process?

Writing Suggestions

1. Do you remember a family member teaching you something as a child? Write an essay explaining the process and why this process has special meaning for you.

2. Is there a chore or other household activity that you have become particularly good at doing? Write an essay explaining how to complete a task. If it is a task that most people are likely to have performed already, then be sure to include special tips for having better success at accomplishing the task.

>> READINGS AND REFLECTION

[preview] **STOCK CAR RACING** was wildly popular in the United States after World War II. Bill France, Sr., incorporated the National Association for Stock Car Auto Racing (NASCAR) in 1948. Red Baron, the legendary driver from Atlanta, Georgia, won the first NASCAR race on the shores of Daytona Beach, Florida, in his Ford Modified. Since then, watching NASCAR has become a popular American tradition for a growing number of fans. Country singer Keith Bryant pays tribute to three

of the most famous NASCAR families of all time in his song "Traditions Sure Run Deep." He also acknowledges the significance of the fans as he highlights some of the most memorable moments in NASCAR history, including the untimely death of Davey Allison, who met his tragic fate in a 1993 helicopter crash. If you are interested in learning more about NASCAR, you might want to explore the Web site **NASCAR. com.** Before reading, think about sporting events that you like to attend with friends or family. What do you find to be exciting about those events?

We've got a family tradition here
It's been around for 50 years
A long blood line and getting longer
Running harder and racing stronger
Lee Petty drove with pride
When his son Richard pulled along beside
How could he have ever known
That young man would hold the throne?

These traditions sure run deep
From the drivers to the fans in the seats
It's a common thread we all keep
Passed down from father to son
A little slice of America
These traditions sure run deep

Ned Jarrett, now there's a name
What a man for the Hall of Fame
Did it ever enter his mind
He'd be callin' the race when Dale crossed the line?

Allisons what a legacy
Made their place in history
Bet you wonder how high he'd a climbed
If Davey could have had a little more time

These traditions sure run deep
From the drivers to the fans in the seats
It's a common thread we all keep
Passed down from father to son
A little slice of America
These traditions sure run deep

There's a lot of high expectations
For carryin' on the hopes and dreams
To the next generation

These traditions sure run deep
From the drivers to the fans in the seats
It's a common thread we all keep
Passed down from father to son
A little slice of America
These traditions sure run deep
These traditions sure run deep

Source: Keith Bryant, "Traditions Sure Run Deep," *Ridin' with the Legends* CD (Label: Lofton Creek, 2004).

[QUESTIONS FOR REFLECTION]

Considering Ideas

1. Have you ever known a NASCAR fan, or are you one? To what extremes might NASCAR fans go to see their favorite drivers?

2. What traditions does Bryant emphasize through his lyrics?

3. What other traditions might be considered American?

Considering Writing Strategies

1. What is Bryant's purpose for this song? How well does he achieve that purpose?

2. Who is Bryant's intended audience? Was he also considering a secondary audience? Who else might he reach besides his primary audience?

3. Where does Bryant explain a process in the song? How effective is his explanation?

Writing Suggestions

1. Write an essay explaining a family tradition that a parent or other family member has passed along to you. You might explain what this tradition entails and why it holds special meaning for you, or you may give the reader how-to instructions for following your family's tradition.

2. Write an explanation related to your favorite sport or hobby. One option is to write a step-by-step explanation of how to perform a process, such as the steps for effectively blocking a goal in a soccer game. Another option is to explain the process so that your readers will have an understanding of what is involved in the activity, such as what it is like to go skiing or skydiving.

Cooking Oxtails, Jamaican Style!
by Karen Ebanks

Jamaica is a beautiful island located in the Caribbean Sea, south of Cuba and west of the Dominican Republic. It is known for its beautiful beaches, reggae music and slow, relaxed pace and has long been a favorite tourist destination. Jamaica's population is made up of many different races, resulting in a multifaceted culture that is as diverse as its people. Food is one of the most important aspects of Jamaican culture.

Jamaicans love to cook, and many of the island's popular dishes contain meat that is not traditionally eaten in the United States. Some of those meats include goat, cow's feet, tripe and oxtails. All of these dishes are standard fare in a Jamaican home and are also served at various traditional events, such as wedding receptions, celebrations, funeral repast services and the like. Serving a Jamaican dish is a great way to add something different to one's traditional weeknight dinner and by following the instructions listed below for Jamaican oxtails, it should not be too difficult. Jamaican oxtails are especially tasty as many seasonings are used to create this dish and although a few hours are required, it is well worth it.

The following ingredients are necessary to cook this dish:

- 3 lbs. beef oxtail
- 2 green onion stalks, chopped
- 1 cup vinegar
- 4 cloves garlic, chopped
- 3 tsp. salt
- 3 pcs. fresh thyme, chopped
- ¼ tsp. cayenne pepper
- ½ green pepper
- 1 tbsp. onion powder
- 6 pimento berries (also called allspice)
- 1 tbsp. garlic powder
- 2 tbsp. vegetable oil
- 1 tsp. paprika
- 1 can butter beans, drained
- 1 tbsp. browning sauce (optional)
- 2 carrots sliced thinly
- 1 onion, chopped
- water

First, trim the fat from the meat and then wash the pieces in a solution of water and vinegar. Next, season the meat with the dry seasonings (salt, pepper, onion powder, garlic powder and paprika) followed by the browning sauce. If you can, let the meat sit for a few hours or possibly overnight in the refrigerator, which will allow it to season more thoroughly. After that, heat the vegetable oil in a large frying pan and transfer the meat to the pan in order to "brown" it, which means to cook the meat for a short time over medium heat to give it a brown color.

When the meat has browned, transfer the pieces of meat into a pressure cooker pot, along with the remaining seasonings, such as the onions, garlic, thyme, green pepper, and pimento berries. Cooking the meat in a pressure cooker will allow it to cook much faster, as oxtail meat can be somewhat tough and take a long time to become tender. Next, pour 4 ½ cups of water into the pot and cook at high pressure for 20 minutes. High pressure is considered the period in which the pressure regulator on the top of the pressure cooker begins to jiggle gently. Remove the pot from the heat and then allow it to cool completely. Running cold water over the pot lid will help it to cool faster. Only when it is fully cooled should you remove the lid from the pressure cooker.

At this point, taste the oxtails to determine if more seasonings are required. If so, add salt, pepper or other seasonings accordingly. Next, add the carrots and cook for an additional 15 minutes over medium heat, stirring occasionally. Finally, add the butter beans, and after cooking for 5 more minutes, your oxtail dish will be done. This recipe takes about 2 1/2 hours to prepare and serves four people.

Jamaican oxtails make a wonderful, tasty meal that is best served over another popular Jamaican dish called rice and peas. (Of course, it never hurts to serve it with a bit of Jamaican rum as well.) You can find oxtails at any typical Jamaican restaurant here in the U.S. or you can choose to be adventurous and attempt to cook your own. Either way, you will enjoy a delicious Jamaican dish that might make you consider taking a trip to the island itself. Yah Mon!

[QUESTIONS FOR REFLECTION]

1. What does Ebanks accomplish in the first paragraph? The author delays the thesis until the second paragraph. Is this approach effective in this essay? Why or why not?

2. The author chose to list the ingredients in a bulleted list rather than include them in one of the paragraphs. Would the essay be stronger or weaker if she had chosen to put the ingredients in paragraph form? Why?

3. Based on these instructions, would you be able to cook Jamaican oxtails if you had all of the necessary ingredients? Why or why not?

4. What transitions does the author use to help guide the reader? Which ones are the most useful? Why?

5. Which parts of the concluding paragraph leave you with a lasting impression? Why?

STUDENT WRITING

How to Make a Traditional Hawaiian Lei
by Alexander Gehring

Lei making is a very rich and time-honored tradition of Hawaii. Leis were first introduced to the islands from early Polynesian settlers traveling across the Pacific from Tahiti. Traditional leis can be made from just about anything you can find in nature. Flowers, leaves, shells, feathers, and even bone and teeth of various animals can be used. Early Hawaiians constructed and wore leis as a way to beautify and to distinguish themselves from others.

The most significant of all leis is the Maile lei. The Maile lei is known as the "lei of royalty" and is given as a sign of respect and honor. In the past they were used as an offering during times of war. The two opposing chiefs would intertwine the Maile vine, officially establishing peace between the tribes. Today, they are reserved for special and memorable occasions such as weddings, birthdays, graduations, and elections. In a traditional Hawaiian wedding the Kahuna (Hawaiian priest) will use the Maile lei and tie the hands of the bride and groom together signifying their commitment to one another. When students in Hawaii graduate from school, they receive so many leis that sometimes it is hard to see their faces.

The fringed ti leaf lei is one of the oldest and simplest leis to make. To make one, all you need are two large ti leaves. If you are lucky enough to live in an area where ti plants are native, then all you need to do is pick your leaves and wash them. If not, you can order them on the Internet. Ti leaves come in two colors: green and red. Traditionally green leaves are used when making leis, but the choice is yours.

Before making the lei, you need to remove the stiff center vein of the leaf. To do this, make a shallow cut on the backside of the leaf along the vein, being careful not to cut all the way through the leaf. After you have made your cut, strip off the vein with your fingers. Next, tie the two leaves together at the stems using a square knot. Finally, fringe the leaves by making small strips in them. You now have an authentic Hawaiian lei that you can wear or give to a friend.

There are, however, a few unspoken rules to keep in mind when receiving a lei from someone. The giving of a lei is a welcomed celebration and should never be refused. Also, it is considered disrespectful to remove a lei when in the presence of the person who gave it to you. To wear a lei, gently drape it over your shoulders, allowing it to hang down in both the front and back.

Hawaiian leis are a fun part of any celebration. People always appreciate them and greet them with a smile. Leis are universal and can be given at almost any event. The next time you want to make someone feel special, make him or her an authentic Hawaiian lei.

[QUESTIONS FOR REFLECTION]

1. Look back through the essay and identify some of the different writing strategies that Gehring uses to explain how to make a Hawaiian lei. Why does this combination approach work well for this topic?

2. Does the author use any words that are new to you? Do you think he defines them sufficiently? Why or why not?

3. Do you have enough information to actually make a lei? Explain.

4. Are there any parts of the essay that would benefit from having a graphic included? Which parts? What would you include?

5. Which part of the essay is most interesting or memorable? Why?

▶ *Activity* Cultural Exchange

In pairs or small groups, brainstorm to create a list of family traditions and cultural traditions the members in your group have experienced. Next, each participant will explain one of his or her cultural traditions in detail so the other students have a good idea of the significance of that tradition. A representative from each group will then share a few ideas with the class. This activity may give you ideas for a writing assignment.

▶ *Activity* Simple Instructions

In pairs or small groups, write an explanation of a short, easy process that can be performed in a classroom setting. Give your instructions to another student or group to see if they can perform the process. Likewise, you or your group will attempt to perform the instructions from another group. Discuss any areas that were lacking in either set of discussions. How could the instructions be improved? Share your results with the class.

Interpreting an Advertisement

Source: **http://carryabigsticker.com/**.

While most advertisements appear in magazines, newspapers, or billboards, sometimes people use their cars to advertise their views. What do you think about the "Coexist" bumper sticker? What message has the artist conveyed and why? Write a response to this bumper sticker or another one. For example, you might write an essay suggesting ways that people can get along (coexist) better with others.

Writing about an Image

Look at the images throughout this chapter and consider these questions: What cultural tradition does the image represent? What process is being performed? What tone does the image portray? How do the artist's techniques affect the image? What ideas about your own culture and traditions does the image conjure? Choose one of the images in the chapter that depicts a process you are familiar with, and write an essay relating to it. You might respond to the image, tell what is happening in the image, or explain how to perform a process that relates to the image in some way. For example, you might choose to write an essay giving instructions for how to perform a particular soccer kick or move, or you may decide to explain how to play a musical instrument.

Media Connection for Explaining Processes

You might watch, read, and/or listen to one or more of the suggested media to discover additional examples of process analysis. Exploring various media may help you to better understand methods for explaining processes. You may also choose to write about one or more of the media suggestions. For example, you might watch an episode of Anthony Bourdain or Samantha Brown on the Travel Channel and then write an essay explaining the best way to experience the culture and take in the sights in a particular city, such as Paris. Be sure to give credit to the source you use in your essay.

Television	*Hell's Kitchen*	Home and Garden (HGTV)	Travel Channel
Film	*How to Train Your Dragon* (2010)	*How to Lose a Guy in Ten Days* (2003)	*How Stella Got Her Groove Back* (1998)
Print	*The World of Chinese*	*Bon Appétit*	*Hispanic Lifestyle*
Internet	**essortment.com**	**guitarvision.com**	**howstuffworks.com**
Music	"Start a Band" by Brad Paisley	"How to Save a Live" by The Fray	"Godbye Earl" by the Dixie Chicks

USE ONE OF THE FOLLOWING TOPICS to write an informative or instructional essay. Remember to consider your rhetorical star as well as the steps for writing about a process as you compose.

1. How to manage time or stress
2. How to study for an exam or how to pass a class, such as English composition
3. How to achieve success (or failure) in college, on the job, or in life
4. How to perform a process on the job
5. How to make the most of a vacation to a particular location
6. How to construct or assemble a small item
7. How a piece of machinery or equipment works
8. How to plan the perfect wedding or other celebration
9. How to eat right or get in shape
10. How an important event in your life (or in history) occurred

7.4 > Analyzing the Rhetorical Star for Explaining a Process in Writing

Subject	Choose a topic appropriate for a college-level audience. It should be a process you are very familiar with but your readers may not understand or know how to do. Make sure that the process isn't too simple or too complicated.
Audience	Who are your readers? What do they need to know about the process? Do you want your readers to be able to perform the process? Or do you want them to just have an understanding of how something was done or how something works? How much detail do you need to include based on the characteristics and needs of the audience? You are better off giving too much detail than not enough detail if you are not sure how familiar your audience is with the process.
Purpose	Is your main purpose to instruct or inform? An instructional process tells the readers how to make or do something. An informative process tells the readers how something works, how a process was done, or how something was made. What additional goals do you have? Is your explanation meant to entertain the reader? Are you trying to convince your readers that a particular method works better than another? Are you combining purposes? Keep your purpose in mind as you begin writing.
Strategy	Will you include other writing strategies in addition to explaining the process? For example, do you want to use definition, description, or narration to enhance your explanation?
Design	Do you want to explain the process in paragraph form? Or would numbered steps be more effective? How long should your explanation be? What other design elements, such as headings, pictures, or diagrams would help your reader to better understand the process?

Sample Design for Instructions

Below is an explanation for the process of transferring a patient from a bed to a stretcher using the "draw sheet transfer" method. What features are especially helpful to the design? Do you think you could be successful doing a draw sheet transfer using these instructions? Why or why not?

Draw Sheet Transfer

STEP 1

- Loosen the draw sheet on the bed, and form a long roll to grasp.
- Prepare the stretcher by unbuckling the straps, adjusting the height of the stretcher so that it is even with the bed, and lowering the side rails.
- Set the brakes on the stretcher (if so equipped) to the ON position.
- Position the stretcher next to and touching the patient's bed.

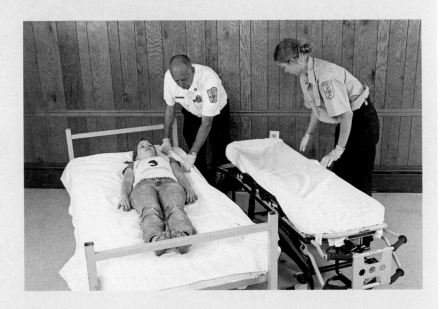

STEP 2

- Both rescuers should stand on the same side of the stretcher and then reach across it to grasp the draw sheet firmly at the patient's head and hips.

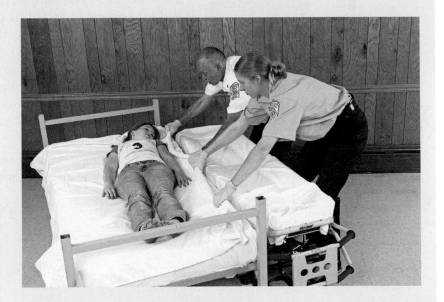

—continued

—*continued from page 161*

STEP 3

 - On a signal from the rescuer at the patient's head, both rescuers gently slide the patient from the bed to the stretcher.

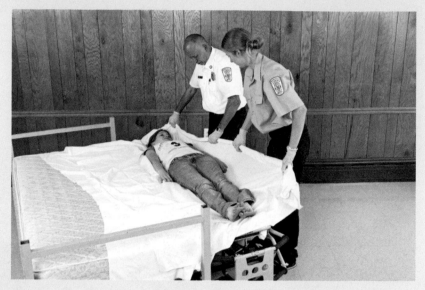

Source: Aehlert, *Emergency Medical Responder*, McGraw-Hill, 2011

7.5 > Applying the Steps for Writing about a Process

FIGURE 7.2 The Seven Steps of the Writing Process

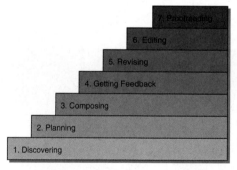

1. **Discovering:** The readings, images, and other media suggestions in this chapter may help you determine what process you would like to explain. Look through the chapter and see what comes to mind. Additionally, try listing processes that you are familiar with performing. Brainstorm tasks that you perform on a regular basis at school, home, or on the job. Try to find one that you already know how to perform and that others might need to learn how to perform. Alternatively, you might choose a machine or other procedure and explain how it works. When you've chosen a topic, you may want to make a rough sketch of the process or procedure to help aid your writing process.

2. **Planning:** Try creating a list or an outline (informal or formal) to help you organize your ideas. Remember to follow a chronological sequence for your process. Go through the process step-by-step in your mind to make sure that your order of ideas is clear and logical.

FIGURE 7.3 Explaining a Process

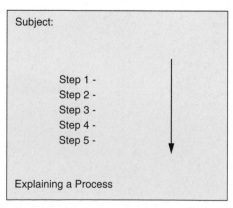

3. **Composing:** Write a first draft of your process analysis. Don't worry too much about grammar and punctuation at this time. Focus on retelling the details related to the event. Be sure to keep your overall point in mind as you write.

Use the seven steps for writing about a process you learned earlier in this chapter (see pp. 141–142). These steps are a key part of the writing process:

1. Begin with a clear title and introduction.
2. Include a list of materials as needed.
3. Explain the steps in chronological order.
4. Define special terms as needed.
5. Give helpful tips and warnings as needed.
6. Include visual aids as needed.
7. End with a decisive conclusion.

4. **Getting Feedback:** Have at least one classmate, or other person, read your rough draft and answer the peer review questions that follow. If you have access to a writing tutor or center, get another opinion about your paper as well. If possible, ask your reviewer to explain which parts are most clear and which steps, if any, need more explanation.

5. **Revising:** Using all of the feedback available to you, revise your process analysis. Make sure that the steps of your process are clear and follow a chronological order. Additionally, check to see that you have kept your audience's needs in mind throughout your explanation of the process. Try going though the process in your head using your explanation to make sure that you haven't left out any important steps or warnings.

6. **Editing:** Read your process analysis again, this time looking for errors in grammar, punctuation, and mechanics. Pay particular attention to your use of chronological order and action verbs because these areas are especially important for writing about processes.

7. **Proofreading:** After you have carefully edited your essay, read it one last time to look for typographical errors and any other issues that might interfere with the readers' understanding of your explanation.

>> Peer Review Questions for Explaining a Process

Trade rough drafts with a classmate and answer the following questions about his or her paper. Then, in person or online, discuss your papers and suggestions with your peer. Finally, make the changes you feel would most benefit your paper.

1. Identify the thesis statement. Does it effectively let you know what process will be explained? Why or why not?
2. Are there any additional materials that need to be included or terms that need to be defined? What are they?
3. Do the steps flow logically and smoothly? Why or why not?
4. Which part do you think is explained best? Why?
5. Do you feel that you fully understand the process the author is explaining? If not, which parts could use more details or clarification?
6. Does the author provide the reader with a sense of completion at the end? If so, how?
7. What kinds of grammatical errors, if any, are evident in the explanation?
8. What final suggestions do you have for the author?

> Writer's Checklist for Explaining a Process

Use the checklist below to evaluate your own writing and help ensure that your explanation of the process is complete. If you have any "no" answers, continue working on those areas.

- ❏ 1. Is my title suitable?
- ❏ 2. Does my thesis statement clearly identify the process I am explaining?
- ❏ 3. Does my introduction give the reader an indication of the points I make in the body of my essay or instructions?
- ❏ 4. If they are necessary, have I identified the materials and quantities effectively?
- ❏ 5. Have I included all of the necessary steps for the reader to understand or perform the process?
- ❏ 6. Are all of my steps in chronological order?
- ❏ 7. Have I used transitions to increase readability?
- ❏ 8. Have I used active verbs to emphasize each step?
- ❏ 9. Have I clearly defined terms that my reader may not understand?
- ❏ 10. Have I indicated when the process is complete?
- ❏ 11. Have I proofread thoroughly?

[CHAPTER SUMMARY]

1. Use the process writing strategy to explain how to do something or describe how something works or was done.

2. Process writing is an important part of your education, daily life, and career.

3. Every culture in the world has traditions and procedures that it follows. Being sensitive to the processes associated with various cultures will help you to be more successful in the workplace.

4. Interpreting readings and images that relate to processes can help you to prepare to write a process analysis essay.

5. Carefully analyze the rhetorical star before explaining a process in writing: Subject, audience, purpose, strategy, and design.

6. Follow these steps when writing about a process: Begin with a clear title and introduction; include a list of materials as needed; explain the steps in chronological order; define special terms as needed; give helpful tips and warnings as needed; include visual aids as needed; end with a decisive conclusion.

[WHAT I KNOW NOW]

Use this checklist to determine what you need to work on to feel comfortable with your understanding of the material in this chapter. Check off each item as you master it. Review the material for any unchecked items.

❏   1. I know what **process writing** is.

❏   2. I can identify several **real-world applications** for process writing.

❏   3. I can evaluate readings and **images** that explain a process.

❏   4. I can **analyze** the rhetorical star for writing about a process.

❏   5. I understand the writing process for **explaining** a process.

❏   6. I can apply the **seven steps** for writing about a process.

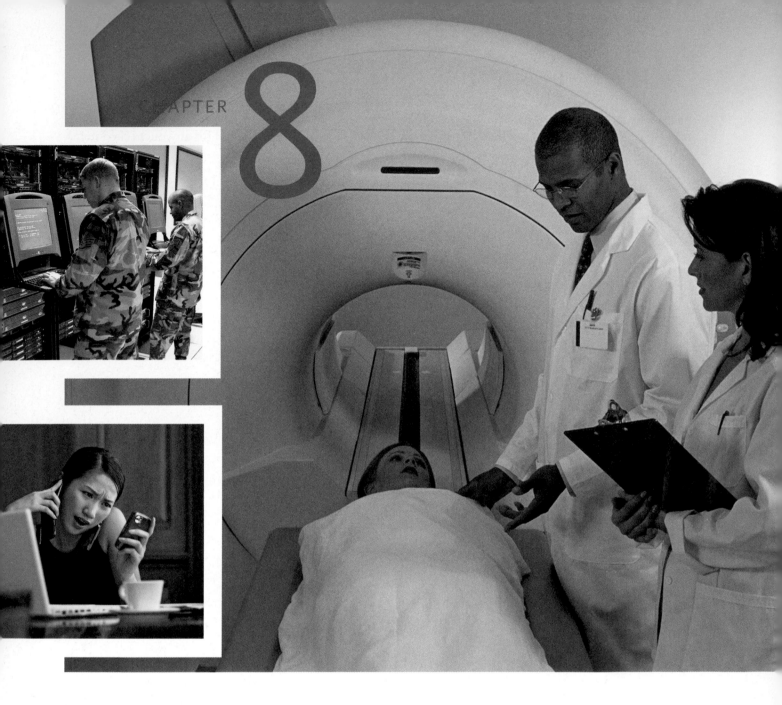

COMPARING AND CONTRASTING: COMPUTERS AND TECHNOLOGY

LEARNING outcomes

> In this chapter you will learn techniques for the following:

8.1 Identifying real-world applications for comparing and contrasting.

8.2 Understanding the steps for comparing and contrasting.

8.3 Interpreting images and readings about computers and technology.

8.4 Analyzing the rhetorical star for comparing and contrasting.

8.5 Applying the steps for writing a comparison and contrast essay.

> Writing Strategy Focus: Comparing and Contrasting

When you compare and contrast subjects, you are looking at similarities and differences between them. People often use comparison and contrast to better understand one subject in terms of another. Furthermore, the comparison and contrast strategy is useful for making decisions. For example, when you decided to enroll in your current college or university, you probably compared it to one or more other schools to determine which one would best fulfill your needs as a student.

When you compare and contrast subjects, you must use specific points, or criteria, for your comparison. When you were comparing schools, you probably considered some of the following criteria to help make your decision: location, programs offered, class size, facilities, accreditation, and so on. Weighing the relevant criteria is essential to the comparison and contrast process. Being able to write an effective comparison and contrast paper will be useful in school, in your daily life, and in your career.

8.1 > Real-World Applications for Comparing and Contrasting

Writing to Compare and Contrast in School

You'll often be asked to identify similarities and differences between two or more subjects in college courses. You might need to compare and contrast characters in a literature class. Your psychology instructor may ask to you compare and contrast two theories or learning styles. In a history class, you may need to compare and contrast significant events, people, or places. Similarly, an instructor in your major course of study may require that you compare and contrast two or more methods for accomplishing a task or performing a skill.

Writing to Compare and Contrast in Your Daily Life

You make comparisons on a daily basis: Deciding what to wear, what to eat, where to go, and what to do all require comparisons. When you decide to make a major purchase, such as an entertainment system, a car, or a home, you'll need to compare the options to see which item best suits your needs and fits within your budget. Additionally, if you need someone to fix your car, babysit your child, or repair your home, then you'll need to compare and contrast your options to make the best possible decision.

Writing to Compare and Contrast in Your Career

Being able to write an effective comparison is also extremely useful in the workplace. When you look for a job you'll need to compare the offers you get based on a number of factors, such as salary, location, benefits, and work environment. You might need to compare and contrast two software packages or pieces of equipment to decide which one would be more effective to use at your place of employment. Or you may need to compare candidates for a position within your organization to decide which one is most qualified for the job. Here are a few specific applications for comparison and contrast writing in your career:

Health care: symptoms, treatments, office procedures, record-keeping methods.

Law: case studies, witnesses' testimonies, legal procedures.

Education: teaching and learning methods, models, and styles.

Computers: hardware, software, applications, designs.

Massage therapy: massage techniques, equipment, and lubricants.

Culinary arts: ingredients, cooking styles, menu designs, knives, cleaning methods.

Business: business models, lending sources, locations, products, and services.

Graduate SPOTLIGHT

Carlos Felix, Software Engineer

Carlos Felix has a degree in computer engineering. He is currently a software engineer for Harris Corporation, which is an information technology and communications company that serves government and commercial markets internationally. Here's what Carlos has to say about the importance of written communication in his career:

❝ Writing is a big part of what I do as a software engineer. Before I start on a development project, I have to make sure that there isn't already a product on the market that accomplishes what we need. I compare and contrast existing hardware and software with what I intend to create and write a report documenting my findings and justifying my plan to upper level management. Then I present a tech memo depicting exactly what I am going to do for the project. I have to assume that the reader may not fully understand the material, so I make sure that my paragraphs are clear and that my writing style isn't too technical. I can't skip anything, or it will cause confusion. **❞**

On your own, in pairs, or in small groups, brainstorm uses for writing comparisons at school, in your daily life, and on the job. You may want to choose your career field or the prospective career field(s) of the participants in your group. Be prepared to share your results with your instructor or class.

8.2 > Steps for Writing about Comparisons and Contrasts

1. Begin by Identifying the Elements You Are Comparing

Somewhere in the first paragraph, mention the items you are comparing. Depending on your subject, you may decide to emphasize similarities, differences, or both. You'll want to make your approach clear in your thesis and introduction. For example, if you are comparing two printers, you might focus on differences and write a thesis like this: Printer X is a better choice for college students than Printer Y because of its superior scanning, copying, and printing capabilities.

2. Use a Block or Point-by-Point Approach

There are two basic patterns for organizing a comparison or contrast essay. When you use the block pattern, you explain your points of comparison for one item, and then you transition into the second item and explain your main points about that one. If you use the point-by-point method, you focus on each point you are making and tell about both items as they relate to that point.

Choose the method that seems to work best for your topic. For example, if you are writing an essay comparing two video game systems, the point-by-point method might work best because you can easily highlight the features of each system. However, if you are writing about how technology has changed the way you spend your leisure time, you might use the block pattern to write about the past first and then the present. Here are two sample outlines to help you see the difference between the block and point-by-point organizational patterns:

Thesis: Printer X is a better choice for college students than Printer Y because of its superior scanning, copying, and printing capabilities.

Block Pattern
- I. Printer X
  - A. Scanning
  - B. Copying
  - C. Printing
- II. Printer Y
  - A. Scanning
  - B. Copying
  - C. Printing

Point-by-Point Pattern
- I. Scanning
  - A. Printer X
  - B. Printer Y

    II. Copying
        A. Printer X
        B. Printer Y
    III. Printing
        A. Printer X
        B. Printer Y

3. Describe Your Subjects Fairly and Accurately

Use vivid descriptions so that your reader can imagine the subjects you are comparing and contrasting. Choose the details that your readers will most need to understand. Also, you'll want to balance your coverage of the subjects you are comparing and contrasting. If you focus mostly on just one of the items, you may have difficulty convincing the readers that your points are valid.

Furthermore, you'll need to ensure that your comparisons are ethical. You don't want to unfairly skew the details and examples you provide about one subject so that you undermine the other. For example, if you are comparing cable and satellite television services, it would be unethical to point out that satellite reception is sometimes interrupted by stormy weather, but neglect to mention that cable reception is also interrupted on occasion for various reasons.

4. Consider Using an Analogy

Often you can enhance your comparisons by using some sort of analogy. Typically, an analogy compares something unfamiliar to something familiar. For example, if you are comparing your experience playing two new video games, you might say that one is as exciting as leaping out of an airplane at 30,000 feet, while the other is about as stimulating as reading all of the ingredients on a cereal box. If you do use an analogy, be careful to avoid clichés. Saying your life is like a roller coaster isn't exactly going to "wow" your readers. You are better off coming up with something fresh and original.

ESOL Tip >

Analogies are especially helpful if your topic is unfamiliar to native readers.

5. Use Transitions to Help Your Writing Flow Smoothly

If you choose the right transitions, your comparison and contrast essay will be more coherent for your audience. When you are emphasizing similarities, transitions such as *also, similarly,* and *both* can be useful. When you focus on differences, you might try transitional devices such as *however, unlike,* and *on the other hand.* (See p. 51 for more details about transitions.) Using transitional expressions can also help you to keep your essay from sounding like a tennis match, where you awkwardly bounce back and forth between the two subjects. Varying your word choice and sentence structure will also help you to avoid the monotony of the tennis ball effect.

6. Conclude Logically

Typically, the conclusion is a good place to restate your main idea and summarize your main points. When writing a comparison, you might also come to a logical conclusion that wasn't obvious from the thesis. For example, if you are comparing two video games or movies, you might determine which one you would recommend. If you include your recommendation in the introduction, your readers might not bother reading your complete comparison.

> ## Activity   Making Analogies

We use analogies in writing to compare something unfamiliar to something familiar.

EXAMPLE In the movie *Forrest Gump*, the title character says, "Life is like a box of chocolates. You never know what you're gonna get."

In pairs, groups, or on your own, come up with an analogy for each of the following subjects. Be careful to avoid clichés. Instead, create original comparisons.

1. Life or happiness
2. A computer, a camera, or another electronic device
3. A joyous occasion, such as a wedding, the birth of a child, or a school graduation
4. A specific messy situation, such as a breakup, job loss, or property foreclosure
5. A specific person or animal from a television show or movie

8.3 > Comparing and Contrasting in the Context of Computers and Technology

We are relying more and more on technological devices for work, school, and entertainment. Most of us use computers, cell phones, and a variety of other gadgets on a daily basis. When we get a break from our hectic schedules, many of us enjoy surfing the Net, watching movies or television, listening to digital music, or playing video games. Additionally, technology has revolutionized the way we communicate with one another. Through e-mail, text messaging, and cell phones, we are able to be in virtually constant contact with our co-workers, classmates, friends, and families. We feel lost when the computer network goes down or our cell phone service is interrupted.

With all of the high-tech products available on the market, we have to make careful decisions about which ones we want to purchase. To do that, we need to compare and contrast the items we are considering to determine which ones have the best design, features, and price to most effectively meet our needs. As you analyze the readings and images in this chapter, consider the following questions: How is the technology portrayed? How does it impact people? Has technology simplified or complicated our lives? What does the future of technology have in store for us? Additionally, seeing how other writers have structured their comparison and contrast essays will help you to organize your own essays.

> ## Grammar Window
> ### ADVERBS
>
> You'll need to choose precise words when you describe items you are comparing or contrasting. In doing so, you may find adverbs to be quite useful. Adverbs modify (or explain) verbs and typically tell how, when, where, or why. Writers commonly use adverbs incorrectly, so you'll want to be careful when writing them. The adverbs are highlighted in the following sentences:
>
> **Incorrect example:** Drive careful when traveling during treacherous weather.
>
> **Correct example:** Drive carefully when traveling during treacherous weather.
>
> **Activity:** Find a paragraph in a magazine, online article, or this textbook. Add at least three adverbs to the paragraph.

[preview] **THE TWO** career-based readings in this section are comparisons of Web browsers. One, written by Jacob Gube, follows the point-by-point pattern, and the other, provided by DOVC, follows the block pattern. Web browsers enable computer users to access and navigate the Internet for school, their personal lives, and their careers. Many college graduates use Web browsers to find job openings, investigate companies they are interested in, and conduct research on the job. Read both comparisons before answering the questions for reflection that follow the second one. What Web browser do you use most often? Did you make a conscious choice to use that browser, or do you simply use the one that came installed on your computer?

Point-by-Point Pattern Performance Comparison of Web Browsers **by Jacob Gube**

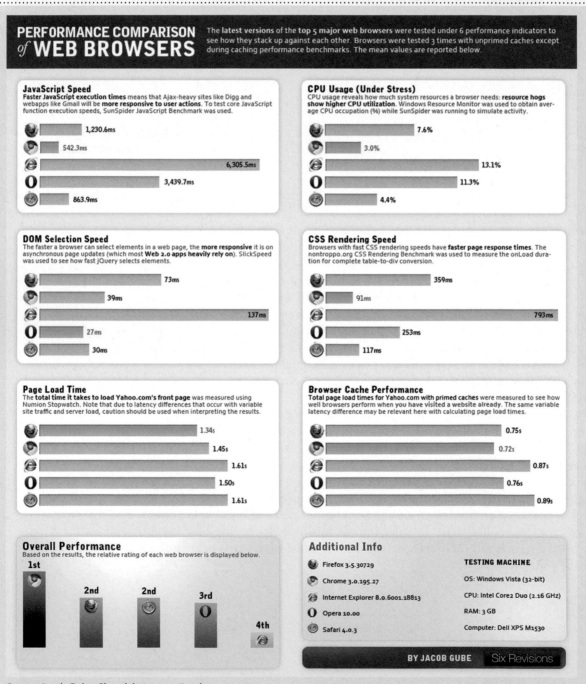

PERFORMANCE COMPARISON *of* **WEB BROWSERS**

The **latest versions** of the **top 5 major web browsers** were tested under 6 performance indicators to see how they stack up against each other. Browsers were tested 3 times with unprimed caches except during caching performance benchmarks. The mean values are reported below.

JavaScript Speed
Faster JavaScript execution times means that Ajax-heavy sites like Digg and webapps like Gmail will be **more responsive to user actions**. To test core JavaScript function execution speeds, SunSpider JavaScript Benchmark was used.

- 1,230.6ms
- 542.3ms
- 6,305.5ms
- 3,439.7ms
- 863.9ms

CPU Usage (Under Stress)
CPU usage reveals how much system resources a browser needs: **resource hogs show higher CPU utilization**. Windows Resource Monitor was used to obtain average CPU occupation (%) while SunSpider was running to simulate activity.

- 7.6%
- 3.0%
- 13.1%
- 11.3%
- 4.4%

DOM Selection Speed
The faster a browser can select elements in a web page, the **more responsive** it is on asynchronous page updates (which most **Web 2.0 apps heavily rely on**). SlickSpeed was used to see how fast jQuery selects elements.

- 73ms
- 39ms
- 137ms
- 27ms
- 30ms

CSS Rendering Speed
Browsers with fast CSS rendering speeds have **faster page response times**. The nontroppo.org CSS Rendering Benchmark was used to measure the onLoad duration for complete table-to-div conversion.

- 359ms
- 91ms
- 793ms
- 253ms
- 117ms

Page Load Time
The **total time it takes to load Yahoo.com's front page** was measured using Numion Stopwatch. Note that due to latency differences that occur with variable site traffic and server load, caution should be used when interpreting the results.

- 1.34s
- 1.45s
- 1.61s
- 1.50s
- 1.61s

Browser Cache Performance
Total page load times for Yahoo.com with primed caches were measured to see how well browsers perform when you have visited a website already. The same variable latency difference may be relevant here with calculating page load times.

- 0.75s
- 0.72s
- 0.87s
- 0.76s
- 0.89s

Overall Performance
Based on the results, the relative rating of each web browser is displayed below.

- 1st
- 2nd
- 2nd
- 3rd
- 4th

Additional Info

- Firefox 3.5.30729
- Chrome 3.0.195.27
- Internet Explorer 8.0.6001.18813
- Opera 10.00
- Safari 4.0.3

TESTING MACHINE

OS: Windows Vista (32-bit)

CPU: Intel Core2 Duo (2.16 GHz)

RAM: 3 GB

Computer: Dell XPS M1530

BY JACOB GUBE   *Six Revisions*

Source: Jacob Gube, **Sixrevisions.com**, October 14, 2009.

With the plethora of web browsers around, web users the world over are scratching their collective heads wondering what exactly is the difference between them. In our ever evolving and increasing online lives, choosing the correct browser to use is becoming increasingly complex. Since the very first web browser was introduced in 1991, the browser has undergone significant changes and improvements. Whilst all browsers fulfill the same function, namely to browse the World Wide Web, they all have something different to offer. So let's explore the world of web browsers.

Internet Explorer

Without a doubt Microsoft's Internet Explorer is the world's most recognized browser and has been around in some version or another since 1995, and whilst figures differ, roughly half of all Internet users use this browser. The latest version is IE8; which features major improvements in speed, security and compatibility. Whereas in the past, IE has been criticized for its frequent and chronic problems, Microsoft's latest version is certainly a vast improvement over its previous versions. Even so, some reviewers are still unimpressed with its performance. In our opinion, it is still unwieldy, clunky and doesn't offer a lot of the useful options and extensions that other browsers offer.

Mozilla Firefox

The poster child for everything a browser should be, Mozilla Firefox has been showered with praise since arriving on the scene in 2004. Mozilla is the second most popular browser after Internet Explorer. Packed full of useful extras, it has been designed specifically for ease of use. Mozilla contains loads of add-ons and extensions that will further enhance and improve your time online. The Firefox browser is recommended for those that want lots of options laid out in a simple-to-use format.

Google Chrome

Following the success of Firefox, Google—the search engine giant—decided to apply the same principles of design that is the hallmark of their search engine to the Chrome browser. It features a super fast, slick interface with a multitude of colorful themes. Simplicity at its finest, Chrome is great for those that need a simple browser without all the confusing clutter that unfortunately is the bane of other browsers. Featuring loads of time saving options such as a homepage with your favorite pages displayed, and an option to search Google with your highlighted selection. In addition, Google has a whole host of extra add-ons that will help you browse better; from next page auto-loading to annoying ad removers.

Apple Safari

The Apple Safari is Apple's default browser. It is the fourth most widely used browser, thanks to the popularity of Apple's computing products. Featuring the classic Apple "skin," its closest comparison is the Google Chrome browser; with many of the same features, it has some enhancements that score some extra points. Like its highly unique Cover Flow that offers a highly visual way of reviewing your site history and bookmarked sites, presenting full-page previews of the websites that look exactly as they did when you last visited them. In addition, if you are using a PC with Windows installed, and the thought of wandering out of familiar territory is as foreign as a trip to the Antarctic, the Safari includes the option to replace the Safari interface with a familiar Windows look. Of course you will still have the same performance of the Safari browser.

Opera

Fast, powerful and efficient is the best way to describe the Opera browser. Despite an intuitive and elegant design, Opera has failed to capture a large segment of the browsing market. But just because it has been overlooked, doesn't mean that it should be ignored. If you prefer a host of great features and usability, and the option to customize pretty much everything, the Opera browser was created for you.

Source: DOVC, "Web Browsers: Chrome, Firefox, Internet Explorer, Safari or Opera?," March 4, 2010.

[QUESTIONS FOR REFLECTION]

1. Does the first article have enough written text to support the visual representations? Explain.

2. Should the second article include visual images to support the written texts? Why or why not?

3. Which comparison do you find to be more useful? Why?

4. The second article is lacking a conclusion. Based on the information in the article, write a concluding paragraph that summarizes the main points and makes a general recommendation.

5. Based on both of these comparisons, are you interested in switching to a different Web browser, or are you going to stay with the one you use now? Explain your choice.

[preview] **MERRILL MARKOE** was born in New York City, but she moved extensively before ending up in San Francisco. Although her master's degree from the University of California at Berkeley is in art, she has made a successful career as a writer. Some of her most notable accomplishments are designing the show *Late Night with David Letterman* and writing for *Newhart, Moonlighting*, and *Sex and the City*. As a freelance writer and columnist, she has published articles for *Rolling Stone, Time, the New York Times, the Los Angles Times*, and more. She has also worked in talk radio and appeared on a variety of television shows, including an episode of the hit television show *Friends*. Markoe has authored several books, including *Walking in Circles Before Lying Down* (2007). To learn more about Merrill Markoe and her works and to see her YouTube videos, please visit her Web site at **www.merrillmarkoe.com**. In the following essay, Markoe compares magazine and Internet personality quizzes and humorously explores the conclusions these quizzes draw. Before reading, consider your own experiences with taking quizzes in magazines or online. Were you surprised with the results? Did you agree with the outcomes?

Who Am I? by Merrill Markoe

Having spent a fair amount of time and money in therapy, debating my every move with a licensed and supposedly caring professional, I was under the impression that I had a pretty good idea of what I was all about. At least until I started taking personality quizzes on the Internet. As any reader of cheesy women's magazines will tell you, this quiz-taking business can be both time-consuming and pointless in terms of gaining meaningful advice. But it can also be as utterly seductive as the horoscope pages. For about a minute and a half, the quiz glistens like a beacon of knowledge before you, offering answers to all the important questions in life. Five minutes later, awash in self-loathing, you can't even remember what it said or why you ever buy that magazine.

As it turns out, the Internet is so full of this kind of self-improvement quiz that it could be argued that the only thing that separates the Net from an average issue of *Cosmopolitan* is that *Cosmo* offers only one quiz at a time. And the Internet seems to have fewer ads for panty liners.

I came to know of this one day when, quite by accident, I encountered a quiz at a handy site called Quiz-Box.com that promised to tell me how "attractive" I was. I guess I needed a little reassurance (with emphasis on the word *little*—if the quiz couldn't see me, how reassuring could it be?). I willingly submitted to seemingly irrelevant questions like "Which city would you like to visit?" (I chose Paris over Tokyo or Beijing because, in the montage in my imagination, I thought I looked more attractive in Paris.) I also selected a peck over a big kiss as my first-date kissing style because a rash of unappealing recent first dates was still fresh in my mind, and this quiz didn't specify whether the guy I was allegedly going on this first date with had any sex appeal.

After my scores were tallied, the quiz passed judgment. It said, in no uncertain terms, that I needed to improve my personality. I also needed to be more optimistic and smile more. I could be attractive if I would try, it sighed, but clearly it didn't think I was trying hard enough.

So there I was, alone my house and suddenly a lot less attractive than I had been a few minutes earlier. I wasn't going to take this lying down. To recoup my losses, like a woman feverishly playing the slot machines, I continued to take more quizzes.

Instantly I was able to wrest myself from the jaws of low self-esteem via the "What kind of personality do you have?" quiz. This time, when asked to answer the question "If you could wish for anything what would it be?" I chose "Become a beauty queen." (After all, my health was already pretty good, my eyes are already pretty nice, and being clever was apparently getting me nowhere.) Much to my delight, the quiz was favorably impressed. "People with your kind of character are few and far between," it informed me. "Everybody likes to be around people with your personality."

Feeling a bit more confident, I was also getting genuinely curious about the possibility of learning something new about myself this way. So I went on taking quizzes. Which is how I came to find out that every single thing I did defined my personality.

There was an egg test that revealed that because I eat fried eggs white-part first, instead of yolk first, I am "logical, smart and inventive...though sometimes too cold and selfish." That I only eat egg whites, period, didn't seem to factor in one way or another.

Next, by picking toilet stall No. 2 out of a drawing of three empty stalls ("The Toilet Test"), I learned I was "an efficient person" yet also " a romantic person" who can be "too hasty making decisions in love." I guess it serves me right for being so cavalier[1] about my toilet-stall selections.

On "The Eating Test," I made the mistake of picking eggs and toast over cereal for breakfast, while also admitting to sometimes skipping lunch entirely because of worry about my weight. Now I had inadvertently shown myself to be "jealous of people who are smarter and better looking" than I am. A harsh evaluation, I felt, for someone "with my kind of character."

So I left QuizBox.com's petty judgments behind and typed "personality quiz" into the Yahoo! search engine. This led me to "The Ultimate Personality Test." Three cups of coffee later (and still in my pajamas at one in the afternoon), I was saddened to learn that I was a "secret agent" who "professionally, likes to work in a cubicle and eat lunch at the desk."

But my mood improved considerably once I clicked on the next test I could find, and my choice of an abstract pattern from an assortment of designs offered me a complete reevaluation. Now, thank heavens, I was "dynamic, active, extroverted" and "willing to accept certain risks and to make a strong commitment in exchange for interesting and varied work."

---

[1] cavalier Arrogant; disdainful.

So which was it? Was I a cubicle worker or a risk taker? Hoping to get off this emotional roller coaster, I wandered over to TheSpark.com, where yet another personality test branded me "an accountant. Reserved. Meticulous. Dependable." And this despite the fact that on the very same page "The Sexy Test" said I was 75 percent sexier than their average quiz taker! Because this puzzling new image of "sexy accountant" didn't provide me with anything excent an idea for a horrible new sitcom, I took a deep, cleansing breath and dived into the elaborate "How Others See You" quiz, where I emerged "extroverted, agreeable but neurotic and not very conscientious." I found this confusing because a quiz at a women's financial site insisted that I was "thorough, meticulous, and calm" only a few minutes later.

By the end of a long day, I also learned that my taste in room decor is "middle class" ("What Class Are You?"), despite the fact that my "plant personality" is "woodland natural." My "workout personality" is "40% inspirational, 30% spontaneous, and 30% analytical (sailing, training for a triathlon, and softball recommended)." And my religious beliefs are Unitarian Universalist, neopagan, or Malayan Buddhist.

Although the Ayurvedic Foundation's site tells me I have a Pitta constitution, meaning I am "hot, sharp, liquid, and oily," an insurance company's longevity quiz says that I will live to be ninety-five.

So there it is: I am extroverted and reserved, passive and active, risk taking and afraid of change. I am also calm, neurotic, and meticulous, dependable and not very conscientious. So what if my workout program of alternating the gym with yoga does not fit my personality? Who cares if I should belong to a religion I have never heard of? All things considered, I have to say that it feels great to really get to know myself at last.

Source: Merrill Markoe, "Who Am I?" First published in ON: *Time Digital* Online Magazine, March 2001. Copyright © 2001 by Merril Markoe. Reprinted with the permission of the Melanie Jackson Agency, LLC.

[QUESTIONS FOR REFLECTION]

Considering Ideas

1. Markoe claims that, with the help of a psychologist, she knew who she was until she began taking Internet quizzes. Is the reader to take this comment seriously? Why or why not?

2. Why do you think the author was so interested in learning about herself through the quizzes? How does she feel about the results?

3. Have you ever taken an online quiz? Did you learn anything about yourself? Did you agree or disagree with the results?

Considering Writing Strategies

1. Do you feel that Markoe's description of Internet quizzes is fair and accurate? Why or why not?

2. What analogy does Markoe make in paragraph five? What effect does her comparison have on you? What did you envision as you read the analogy?

3. How do Markoe's sarcastic remarks affect your understanding of the message she conveys? Use specific examples from the essay to support your answer.

Writing Suggestions

1. Take a few personality quizzes on the Internet. (Go to **google.com** and type in "personality tests.") Write an essay comparing your results with your perception of yourself. How similar or dissimilar are they?

2. Have you ever had an experience where you disagreed with the way a parent, teacher, boss, or peer judged you? Write an essay contrasting the different views and arguing your side.

>> READINGS AND REFLECTION

[preview] **DAVID SEDARIS** is a best-selling author, a radio commentator, and a playwright. He was born in Binghamton, New York; grew up in Raleigh, North Carolina; and currently resides in Paris, France. He is well known for his humor and satire, and he often pokes fun at his Greek Orthodox heritage. One of his recent books, a collection of essays, is titled *When You Are Engulfed in Flames* (2008). You can learn more about David Sedaris at **davidsedaris.net** or **literati.net/sedaris.** In the following essay, which is from his book *Me Talk Pretty One Day* (2000), Sedaris discusses his disdain for computers. Before reading, think about how you feel about technology. Do you embrace the latest and greatest gadgets as soon as they hit the market? Are you a "technophobe"? Or are you somewhere in the middle?

Nutcracker.com by David Sedaris

It was my father's dream that one day the people of the world would be connected to one another through a network of blocky, refrigerator-size computers, much like those he was helping develop at IBM. He envisioned families of the future gathered around their mammoth terminals, ordering groceries and paying their taxes from the comfort of their own homes. A person could compose music, design a doghouse, and . . . something more, something even better. "A person could . . . he could . . . "

When predicting this utopia, he would eventually reach a point where words failed him. His eyes would widen and sparkle at the thought of this indescribable something more. "I mean, my God," he'd say, "just think about it."

My sisters and I preferred not to. I didn't know about them, but I was hoping the people of the world might be united by something more interesting, like drugs or an armed struggle against the undead. Unfortunately, my father's team won, so computers it is. My only regret is that this had to happen during my lifetime.

Somewhere in the back of my mind is a dim memory of standing in some line holding a perforated card. I remember the cheap, slightly clinical feeling it gave me, and recall thinking that the computer would never advance much further than this. Call me naïve, but I seem to have underestimated the universal desire to sit in a hard plas-

tic chair and stare at a screen until your eyes cross. My father saw it coming, but this was a future that took me completely by surprise. There were no computers in my high school, and the first two times I attempted college, people were still counting on their fingers and removing their shoes when the numbers got above ten. I wasn't really aware of computers until the mid-1980s. For some reason, I seemed to know quite a few graphic designers whose homes and offices pleasantly stank of Spray Mount. Their floors were always collaged with stray bits of paper, and trapped flies waved for help from the gummy killing fields of their tabletops. I had always counted on these friends to loan me the adhesive of my choice, but then, seemingly overnight, their Scotch tape and rubber cement were gone, replaced with odorless computers and spongy mouse pads. They had nothing left that I wanted to borrow, and so I dropped them and fell in with a group of typesetters who ultimately betrayed me as well.

Thanks to my complete lack of office skills, I found it fairly easy to avoid direct contact with the new technology. The indirect contact was disturbing enough. I was still living in Chicago when I began to receive creepy Christmas newsletters designed to look like tabloids and annual reports. Word processors made writing fun. They did not, however, make reading fun, a point made painfully evident by such publications as *The Herald Family Tribune* and *Wassup with the Wexlers!*

Friends who had previously expressed no interest in torture began sending letters composed to resemble Chinese take-out menus and the Dead Sea Scrolls. Everybody had a font, and I was told that I should get one, too. The authors of these letters shared an enthusiasm with the sort of people who now arrived at dinner parties hoisting expensive new video cameras and suggesting that, after dessert, we all sit down and replay the evening on TV. We, the regular people of the world, now had access to the means of production, but still I failed to see what all the fuss was about. A dopey letter is still a dopey letter, no matter how you dress it up; and there's a reason regular people don't appear on TV: we're boring.

By the early 1990s I was living in New York and working for a housecleaning company. My job taught me that regardless of their purported virtues, computers are a pain in the ass to keep clean. The pebbled surface is a magnet for grease and dirt, and you can pretty much forget about roaming out the gaps in the keyboard. More than once I accidentally pushed a button and recoiled in terror as the blank screen came to life with exotic tropical fish or swarms of flying toasters. Equally distressing was the way people used the slanted roofs of their terminals to display framed photographs and great populations of plush and plastic creatures, which would fall behind the desk the moment I began cleaning the screen. There was never any place to plug in the vacuum, as every outlet was occupied by some member of the computer family. Cords ran wild, and everyone seemed to own one of those ominous foot-long power strips with the blinking red light that sends the message YOU MUST LEAVE US ALONE. I was more than happy to comply, and the complaints came rolling in.

Due to my general aversion to machines and a few pronounced episodes of screaming, I was labeled a technophobe, a term that ranks fairly low on my scale of fightin' words. The word *phobic* has its place when properly used, but lately it's been declawed by the pompous insistence that most animosity is based upon fear rather than loathing. No credit is given for distinguishing between these two very different emotions. I fear snakes. I hate computers. My hatred is entrenched, and I nourish it daily. I'm comfortable with it, and no community outreach program will change my mind.

I hate computers for getting their own section in the *New York Times* and for lengthening commercials with the mention of a Web site address. Who really wants to find out more about Procter & Gamble? Just buy the toothpaste or laundry detergent, and get on with it. I hate them for creating the word *org* and I hate them for e-mail, which isn't real mail but a variation of the pointless notes people used to pass in class. I hate computers for replacing the card catalog in the New York Public Library and I hate the way they've invaded the movies. I'm not talking about their contribution to the world of

special effects. I have nothing against a well-defined mutant or full-screen alien invasion—that's *good* technology. I'm talking about their actual presence *in* any given movie. They've become like horses in a western—they may not be the main focus, but everybody seems to have one. Each tiresome new thriller includes a scene in which the hero, trapped by some version of the enemy, runs for his desk in a desperate race against time. Music swells and droplets of sweat run down onto the keyboard as he sits at his laptop, frantically pawing for answers. It might be different if he were flagging down a passing car or trying to phone for help, but typing, in and of itself, is not an inherently dramatic activity.

I hate computers for any number of reasons, but I despise them most for what they've done to my friend the typewriter. In a democratic country you'd think there would be room for both of them, but computers won't rest until I'm making my ribbons from torn shirts and brewing Wite-Out in my bathtub. Their goal is to place the IBM Selectric II beside the feather quill and chisel in the museum of antiquated writing implements. They're power hungry, and someone needs to stop them.

When told I'm like the guy still pining for his eight-track tapes, I say, "You have eight-tracks? Where?" In reality I know nothing about them, yet I feel it's important to express some solidarity with others who have had the rug pulled out from beneath them. I don't care if it can count words or rearrange paragraphs at the push of a button, I don't want a computer. Unlike the faint scurry raised by fingers against a plastic computer keyboard, the smack and clatter of a typewriter suggests that you're actually building something. At the end of a miserable day, instead of grieving my virtual nothing, I can always look at my loaded wastepaper basket and tell myself that if I failed, at least I took a few trees down with me.

When forced to leave my house for an extended period of time, I take my typewriter with me, and together we endure the wretchedness of passing through the X-ray scanner. The laptops roll merrily down the belt, while I'm instructed to stand aside and open my bag. To me it seems like a normal enough thing to be carrying, but the typewriter's declining popularity arouses suspicion and I wind up eliciting the sort of reaction one might expect when traveling with a cannon.

"It's a typewriter," I say. "You use it to write angry letters to airport authorities."

The keys are then slapped and pounded, and I'm forced to explain that if you want the words to appear, you first have to plug it in and insert a sheet of paper.

The goons shake their heads and tell me I really should be using a computer. That's their job, to stand around in an ill-fitting uniform and tell you how you should lead your life. I'm told the exact same thing later in the evening when the bellhop knocks on my hotel door. The people whose televisions I can hear have complained about my typing, and he has come to make me stop. To hear him talk, you'd think I'd been playing the kettledrum. In the great scheme of things, the typewriter is not nearly as loud as he makes it out to be, but there's no use arguing with him. "You know," he says, "you really should be using a computer."

You have to wonder where you've gone wrong when twice a day you're offered writing advice from men in funny hats. The harder I'm pressured to use a computer, the harder I resist. One by one, all of my friends have deserted me and fled to the dark side. "How can I write you if you don't have an e-mail address?" they ask. They talk of their B-trees and Disk Doctors and then have the nerve to complain when I discuss bowel obstructions at the dinner table.

Who needs them? I think. I figured I'd always have my family and was devastated when my sister Amy brought home a candy-colored laptop. "I only use it for e-mail," she said. Coming from her, these words made me physically ill. "It's fun," she said. "People send you things. Look at this." She pushed a button, and there, on the screen, was a naked man lying facedown on a carpet. His hair was graying and his hands were cuffed behind his doughy back. A woman entered the room. You couldn't see her face, just her legs and feet, which were big and mean-looking, forced into sharp-toed shoes with high, pencil-thin heels. The man on the carpet shifted position, and when his testicles came into view, the woman reacted as if she had seen an old balding mouse, one that she had been trying to kill for a long time. She stomped on the man's testicles with the toes of her shoes and then she turned around and stomped on them with the heels. She kicked them mercilessly and, just when I thought she'd finished, she got her second wind and started all over again.

I'd never realized that a computer could act so much like a TV set. No one had ever told me that the picture could be so clear, that the cries of pain could be heard so distinctly. This, I thought, was what my father had been envisioning all those years ago when words had failed him, not necessarily this scene, but something equally capable of provoking such wonder.

"Again?" Amy pushed a button and, our faces bathed in the glow of the screen, we watched the future a second time.

Source: David Sedaris, "Nutracker.com" from *Me Talk Pretty One Day* by David Sedaris. Copyright © 2000 by David Sedaris. Used by permission of Little, Brown and Co., Inc.

[QUESTIONS FOR REFLECTION]

Considering Ideas

1. How does the author's view of computers differ from his father's perspective? Why do you think they have such contrasting views?

2. What reasons does Sedaris give for disliking computers? Are they valid reasons? Why or why not?

3. Throughout most of the essay, Sedaris contends that he doesn't like computers, but at the end he seems to change his view. Does he really have a change of heart? Why or why not?

Considering Writing Strategies

1. Identify several of the analogies that Sedaris uses in his essay. Which ones do you find to be most interesting and effective? Why?

2. In addition to comparison and contrast, the author uses several other writing strategies, such as definition, narration, cause and effect, description, and argument. Find specific examples of these strategies and explain how his combination approach affects the essay.

3. Identify several sarcastic passages from the essay. Which ones do you find to be most amusing? Why do those parts stand out?

Writing Suggestions

1. Do you agree or disagree with Sedaris' view of computers? Write an essay comparing or contrasting your view with his. If you disagree with Sedaris, you might argue against some of the points that he made. Consider using humor or satire to add interest to your essay.

2. Do you possess a piece of technology that you feel you couldn't survive without? Maybe you would feel detached from the world without your cell phone, or perhaps you would never arrive at your desired destination without your GPS navigation system. Write a humorous essay where you imagine what life would be like if you could no longer use your most prized electronic gadget.

ESOL Tip >

Compare and contrast the American technology-driven culture with your own culture.

[preview] **DEBORAH TANNEN**, born in Brooklyn, New York, has published more than 20 books and 100 articles. Her best-selling book, *You Just Don't Understand* (1990), has been translated into 29 languages. Her recent books *You're Wearing That?* (2006) and *You Were Always Mom's Favorite!* (2009) have also been quite successful. She has made appearances on numerous radio and television shows, and she has given lectures around the world. She is a university professor in the linguistics department at Georgetown University. You can read more about her and watch some of her interview clips at **www.9.georgetown.edu/faculty/tannend**. Before reading, think about your communication style. Do you prefer to pick up the phone and call a friend? Or would you rather send an e-mail or text message?

Gender Gap in Cyberspace by Deborah Tannen

I was a computer pioneer, but I'm still something of a novice. That paradox is telling.

I was the second person on my block to get a computer. The first was my colleague Ralph. It was 1980. Ralph got a Radio Shack TRS-80; I got a used Apple II+. He helped me get started and went on to become a maven, reading computer magazines, hungering for the new technology he read about, and buying and mastering it as quickly as he could afford. I hung on to old equipment far too long because I dislike giving up what I'm used to, fear making the wrong decision about what to buy and resent the time it takes to install and learn a new system.

My first Apple came with videogames; I gave them away. Playing games on the computer didn't interest me. If I had free time I'd spend it talking on the telephone to friends.

Ralph got hooked. His wife was often annoyed by the hours he spent at his computer and the money he spent upgrading it. My marriage had no such strains—until I discovered e-mail. Then I got hooked. E-mail draws me the same way the phone does: it's a souped-up conversation.

E-mail deepened my friendship with Ralph. Though his office was next to mine, we rarely had extended conversations because he is shy. Face to face he mumbled so, I could barely tell he was speaking. But when we both got on e-mail, I started receiving long, self-revealing messages: we poured our hearts out to each other. A friend discovered that e-mail opened up that kind of communication with her father. He would never talk much on the phone (as her mother would), but they have become close since they both got on line.

Why, I wondered, would some men find it easier to open up on e-mail? It's a combination of the technology (which they enjoy) and the obliqueness of the written word, just as many men will reveal feelings in dribs and drabs while riding in the car or doing something, which they'd never talk about sitting face to face. It's too intense, too bearing-down on them, and once you start you have to keep going. With a computer in between, it's safer.

It was on e-mail, in fact, that I described to Ralph how boys in groups often struggle to get the upper hand whereas girls tend to maintain an appearance of cooperation. And he pointed out that this explained why boys are more likely to be captivated by computers than girls are. Boys are typically motivated by a social structure that says if you don't dominate you will be dominated. Computers, by their nature, balk: you type a perfectly appropriate command and it refuses to do what it should. Many boys and men are incited by their defiance: "I'm going to whip this into line and teach it who's boss! I'll get it to do what I say!" (and if they work hard enough, they always can). Girls and women are more likely to respond, "This thing won't cooperate. Get it away from me!"

Although no one wants to think of herself as "typical"—how much nicer to be sui generis[1]—my relationship to my computer is—gulp—fairly typical for a woman. Most women (with plenty of exceptions) aren't excited by tinkering with the technology, grappling with the challenge of eliminating bugs or getting the biggest and best computer. These dynamics appeal to many

---
[1] **sui generis** Unique.

men's interest in making sure they're on the top side of the inevitable who's-up-who's-down struggle that life is for them. E-mail appeals to my view of life as a contest for connections to others. When I see that I have 15 messages I feel loved.

I once posted a technical question on a computer network for linguists and was flooded with long dispositions, some pages long. I was staggered by the generosity and the expertise, but wondered where these guys found the time—and why all the answers I got were from men.

Like coed classrooms and meetings, discussions on e-mail networks tend to be dominated by male voices, unless they're specifically women-only, like single-sex schools. On line, women don't have to worry about getting the floor (you just send a message when you feel like it), but, according to linguists Susan Herring and Laurel Sutton, who have studied this, they have the usual problems of having their messages ignored or attacked. The anonymity of public networks frees a small number of men to send long, vituperative,[2] sarcastic messages that so many other men either can tolerate or actually enjoy, but turn most women off.

The anonymity of networks leads to another sad part of the e-mail story: there are men who deluge women with questions about their appearance and invitations to sex. On college campuses, as soon as women students log on, they are bombarded by references to sex, like going to work and finding pornographic posters adorning the walls.

---

[2] **vituperative** Harsh and disapproving.

Taking time

Most women want one thing from a computer—to work. This is significant counterevidence to the claim that men want to focus on information while women are interested in rapport. That claim I found was often true in casual conversation, in which there is no particular information to be conveyed. But with computers, it is often women who are more focused on information, because they don't respond to the challenge of getting equipment to submit.

Once I had learned the basics, my interest in computers waned. I use it to write books (though I never mastered having it do bibliographies or tables of contents) and write checks (but not balance my checkbook). Much as I'd like to use it to do more, I begrudge the time it would take to learn.

Ralph's computer expertise costs him a lot of time. Chivalry requires that he rescues novices in need, and he is called upon by damsel novices far more often than knaves. More men would rather study the instruction booklet than ask directions, as it were, from another person. "When I do help men," Ralph wrote (on e-mail, of course), "they want to be more involved. I once installed a hard drive for a guy, and he wanted to be there with me, wielding the screwdriver and giving his own advice where he could." Women, he finds, usually are not interested in what he's doing: they just want him to get the computer to the point where they can do what they want.

Which pretty much explains how I managed to be a pioneer without becoming an expert.

Source: Deborah Tannen, "Gender Gap in Cyberspace," *Newsweek*, May 16, 1994. Copyright © Deborah Tannen. Reprinted with permission.

[QUESTIONS FOR REFLECTION]

Considering Ideas

1. What similarities and differences do the author and Ralph have when it comes to computers?

2. According to Tannen, how are men and women different in their communication styles? Do you agree or disagree with her assertions?

3. Tannen wrote this essay in 1994. Do you think the gender gap in cyberspace is as big today as it was then? Why or why not?

Considering Writing Strategies

1. Does Tannen use the block or point-by-point method for organizing her comparison? Would her essay have been as effective if she had used the other approach? Why or why not?

2. In addition to comparing and contrasting men and women, Tannen uses the cause-and-effect writing strategy to suggest why they are different. Explain the differences that she perceives between men and women as well as some of the causes for these differences.

3. Instead of ending with a fully developed conclusion, Tannen ends with one simple sentence fragment. Why do you think she does this? What effect does this have on the reader?

Writing Suggestions

1. How would you describe yourself as a computer user? Are you an expert or a novice? Do you go online every opportunity you get, or do you just use the computer enough to get by? Write an essay comparing yourself to someone you know in terms of computer usage. Or you might compare how you use a computer now that you're a college student to how you used a computer before you enrolled in school.

2. Do you ever participate in chat rooms or Web logs (blogs)? Go online to some of your favorite places and observe the comments written by men and women. How do they differ? Do the comments coincide with Tannen's observations about men and women, or are they different? Write an essay comparing and contrasting your observations with Tannen's.

[preview] **MARTY WHIDDON** is a traditional country singer from Headland, Alabama. By the time he was 12 years old he was singing, writing songs, and playing guitar. As teenagers, he and his twin brother, John, joined a radio jamboree in Dothan, Alabama. Although Marty continued on with his career in the music business, his brother moved on to become a professional baseball player and signed with the Cleveland Indians. In the following song, Marty pokes fun at the impact that computers have had on his home life. You can find the song on iTunes if you want to listen to it. Before reading, think about how computers have affected you. Has a family member or significant other ever seemed more interested in a computer than in you? How did you feel? Is it hard to compete with a computer for someone's attention?

Computers, Computers by Marty Whiddon

Computers, computers.
They're taking over my life.
My car and my home,
Television, and phone.
My job and now even my wife.
She plays with her computer
All day and all night.
It's something I don't understand.
A woman who'd rather
Enjoy a computer
Than the company of a good-looking man.
Just thinking about it
Blows a fuse in my mind.
Just listen and understand why.
I stammer and stutter
While she's talking to mother
Through Windows, an electronic vice.
She tries to impress me
With the latest technology
And jibberish I ain't never read.
While just being online
Takes up all her time.
She even takes that blamed old computer to bed.

Computers, computers.
They're taking over my life.
I said, "Honey, that's a sin"
The day that she walked in
Carrying a laptop by her side.
Now it's akin to adultery

Carrying on with that Net.
When she ought to be loving me some instead.
I know she ain't lazy.
She's gone computer crazy.
But I'm the one that's going out of my head.
Just thinking about it
Blows a fuse in my mind.
Just listen; I'll tell you why.
Online in the morning.
Internet in the evening.
A CD ROM a blasting all night.
Instead of playing house,
She plays with a mouse.
It beats all I've ever seen in my life.
Shucks, our life ain't the same
Since she bought that blooming thing.
That computer is ruining my life.

Now listen here honey.
If you want to play with some new way out technology,
I can suggest something right off the top of my head.
Turn off that computer and throw it right out the window,
And let's you and me spend more time together instead.
Computers, computers.
They're driving me crazy.
They're taking over my life.
Uh oh, it's too late.
She's done gone off into cyberspace or outer space...

Source: Marty Whiddon, CD *The Best of Marty Whiddon*. Copyright © by Marty Whiddon, 2002. Marc Dean Music.

[**QUESTIONS FOR REFLECTION**]

Considering Ideas

1. Compare and contrast Whiddon's view of computers with his wife's? Why do you think their views are so different?

2. What do you imagine Whiddon's life was like before computers? How does that compare to what he claims his life is like now?

3. Whiddon compares surfing the Net to adultery. Do you think this is a fair comparison? Why or why not?

Considering Writing Strategies

1. Although there is no set pattern, Whiddon uses a fair amount of rhyme in his lyrics. How does the rhyme affect the song?

2. Whiddon switches back and forth between the first and second person points of view. What does he accomplish by doing this?

3. What is the tone or mood of the song? What words indicate this tone?

Writing Suggestions

1. Has someone in your life ever gotten a new gadget, hobby, or other interest that caused you to have to compete for his or her attention? Write an essay comparing how things were before and after the new interest.

2. Think about a new electronic device that you purchased, such as a laptop, iPod, iPad, cell phone, or GPS system. Has the technology been more of a positive or negative influence on your life? Write an essay explaining how this device has affected you. You might compare what it was like before you got the new gadget with what it was like afterward.

>> READINGS AND REFLECTION

[preview] **KURT VONNEGUT, JR.**, a fourth-generation German-American, was born in Indianapolis. Although he is best known for his science fiction short stories and novels, he is also a graphic artist. Vonnegut's writings and illustrations were influenced by the tragedies he experienced when he was a young man. In 1944 he was captured by the German army and was nearly killed during the firebombing of Dresden a few months later. One of his novels, *Slaughterhouse Five*, published in 1969, recounts some of his experiences as a prisoner of war in Germany. You can go to **vonnegut.com** to discover more about Kurt Vonnegut, Jr., and see some of his artwork. The following short story is a work of sci-

ence fiction about a government that uses technology to make everyone "equal." Before reading, think about the possibility of equality. What would it be like if everyone had the same abilities?

Harrison Bergeron by Kurt Vonnegut, Jr.

The year was 2081, and everybody was finally equal. They weren't only equal before God and the law. They were equal in every which way. Nobody was smarter than anybody else. Nobody was better looking than anybody else. Nobody was stronger or quicker than anybody else. All this equality was due to the 211th, 212th, and 213th Amendments to the Constitution, and to the unceasing vigilance of agents of the United States Handicapper General.

Some things about living still weren't quite right, though. April for instance, still drove people crazy by not being springtime. And it was in that clammy month that the H-G men took George and Hazel Bergeron's fourteen-year-old son, Harrison, away.

It was tragic, all right, but George and Hazel couldn't think about it very hard. Hazel had a perfectly average intelligence, which meant she couldn't think about anything except in short bursts. And George, while his intelligence was way above normal, had a little mental handicap radio in his ear. He was required by law to wear it all times. It was tuned to a government transmitter. Every twenty seconds or so, the transmitter would send out some sharp noise to keep people like George from taking unfair advantage of their brains.

George and Hazel were watching television. There were tears on Hazel's cheeks, but she'd forgotten for the moment what they were about.

On the television screen were ballerinas.

A buzzer sounded in George's head. His thoughts fled in panic, like bandits from a burglar alarm.

"That was a real pretty dance, that dance they just did," said Hazel.

"Huh," said George.

"That dance—it was nice," said Hazel.

"Yup," said George. He tried to think a little about the ballerinas. They weren't really very good—no better than anybody else would have been, anyway. They were burdened with sashweights and bags of birdshot, and their faces were masked, so that no one, seeing a free and graceful gesture or a pretty face, would feel like something the cat drug in. George was toying with the vague notion that maybe dancers shouldn't be handicapped. But he didn't get very far with it before another noise in his ear radio scattered his thoughts.

George winced. So did two out of the eight ballerinas.

Hazel saw him wince. Having no mental handicap herself, she had to ask George what the latest sound had been.

"Sounded like somebody hitting a milk bottle with a ball peen hammer," said George.

"I'd think it would be real interesting, hearing all the different sounds," said Hazel a little envious. "All the things they think up."

"Um," said George.

"Only, if I was Handicapper General, you know what I would do?" said Hazel. Hazel, as a matter of fact, bore a strong resemblance to the Handicapper General, a woman named Diana Moon Glampers. "If I was Diana Moon Glampers," said Hazel, "I'd have chimes on Sunday — just chimes. Kind of in honor of religion."

"I could think, if it was just chimes," said George.

"Well—maybe make 'em real loud," said Hazel. "I think I'd make a good Handicapper General."

"Good as anybody else," said George.

"Who knows better than I do what normal is?" said Hazel.

"Right," said George. He began to think glimmeringly about his abnormal son who was now in jail, about Harrison, but a twenty-one-gun salute in his head stopped that.

"Boy!" said Hazel, "that was a doozy, wasn't it?"

It was such a doozy that George was white and trembling, and tears stood on the rims of his red eyes. Two of the eight ballerinas had collapsed to the studio floor, were holding their temples.

"All of a sudden you look so tired," said Hazel. "Why don't you stretch out on the sofa, so's you can rest your handicap bag on the pillows, honeybunch." She was referring to the forty-seven pounds of birdshot in a canvas bag, which was padlocked around George's neck. "Go on and rest the bag for a little while," she said. "I don't care if you're not equal to me for a while."

George weighed the bag with his hands. "I don't mind it," he said. "I don't notice it any more. It's just a part of me."

"You been so tired lately—kind of wore out," said Hazel. "If there was just some way we could make a little hole in the bottom of the bag, and just take out a few of them lead balls. Just a few."

"Two years in prison and two thousand dollars fine for every ball I took out," said George. "I don't call that a bargain."

"If you could just take a few out when you came home from work," said Hazel. "I mean—you don't compete with anybody around here. You just set around."

"If I tried to get away with it," said George, "then other people'd get away with it—and pretty soon we'd be right back to the dark ages again, with everybody competing against everybody else. You wouldn't like that, would you?"

"I'd hate it," said Hazel.

"There you are," said George. "The minute people start cheating on laws, what do you think happens to society?"

If Hazel hadn't been able to come up with an answer to this question, George couldn't have supplied one. A siren was going off in his head.

"Reckon it'd fall all apart," said Hazel.

"What would?" said George blankly.

"Society," said Hazel uncertainly. "Wasn't that what you just said?"

"Who knows?" said George.

The television program was suddenly interrupted for a news bulletin. It wasn't clear at first as to what the bulletin was about, since the announcer, like all announcers, had a serious speech impediment. For about half a minute, and in a state of high excitement, the announcer tried to say, "Ladies and Gentlemen."

He finally gave up, handed the bulletin to a ballerina to read.

"That's all right—" Hazel said of the announcer, "he tried. That's the big thing. He tried to do the best he could with what God gave him. He should get a nice raise for trying so hard."

"Ladies and Gentlemen," said the ballerina, reading the bulletin. She must have been extraordinarily beautiful, because the mask she wore was hideous. And it was easy to see that she was the strongest and most graceful of all the dancers, for her handicap bags were as big as those worn by two-hundred-pound men.

And she had to apologize at once for her voice, which was a very unfair voice for a woman to use. Her voice was a warm, luminous, timeless melody. "Excuse me—" she said, and she began again, making her voice absolutely uncompetitive.

"Harrison Bergeron, age fourteen," she said in a grackle squawk, "has just escaped from jail, where he was held on suspicion of plotting to overthrow the government. He is a genius and an athlete, is under-handicapped, and should be regarded as extremely dangerous."

A police photograph of Harrison Bergeron was flashed on the screen—upside down, then sideways, upside down again, then right side up. The picture showed the full length of Harrison against a background calibrated in feet and inches. He was exactly seven feet tall.

The rest of Harrison's appearance was Halloween and hardware. Nobody had ever born heavier handicaps. He had outgrown hindrances faster than the H-G men could think them up. Instead of a little ear radio for a mental handicap, he wore a tremendous pair of earphones, and spectacles with thick wavy lenses. The spectacles were intended to make him not only half blind, but to give him whanging headaches besides.

Scrap metal was hung all over him. Ordinarily, there was a certain symmetry, a military neatness to the handicaps issued to strong people, but Harrison looked like a walking junkyard. In the race of life, Harrison carried three hundred pounds.

And to offset his good looks, the H-G men required that he wear at all times a red rubber ball for a nose, keep his eyebrows shaved off, and cover his even white teeth with black caps at snaggle-tooth random.

"If you see this boy," said the ballerina, "do not—I repeat, do not—try to reason with him."

There was the shriek of a door being torn from its hinges.

Screams and barking cries of consternation came from the television set. The photograph of Harrison Bergeron on the screen jumped again and again, as though dancing to the tune of an earthquake.

George Bergeron correctly identified the earthquake, and well he might have—for many was the time his own home had danced to the same crashing tune. "My God—"said George, "that must be Harrison!"

The realization was blasted from his mind instantly by the sound of an automobile collision in his head.

Clanking, clownish, and huge, Harrison stood—in the center of the studio. The knob of the uprooted studio door was still in his hand. Ballerinas, technicians, musicians, and announcers cowered on their knees before him, expecting to die.

"I am the Emperor!" cried Harrison. "Do you hear? I am the Emperor! Everybody must do what I say at once!" He stamped his foot and the studio shook.

"Even as I stand here" he bellowed, "crippled, hobbled, sickened—I am a greater ruler than any man who ever lived! Now watch me become what I can become!"

Harrison tore the straps of his handicap harness like wet tissue paper, tore straps guaranteed to support five thousand pounds.

Harrison's scrap-iron handicaps crashed to the floor.

Harrison thrust his thumbs under the bar of the padlock that secured his head harness. The bar snapped like

celery. Harrison smashed his headphones and spectacles against the wall.

He flung away his rubber-ball nose, revealed a man that would have awed Thor, the god of thunder.

"I shall now select my Empress!" he said, looking down on the cowering people. "Let the first woman who dares rise to her feet claim her mate and her throne!"

A moment passed, and then a ballerina arose, swaying like a willow.

Harrison plucked the mental handicap from her ear, snapped off her physical handicaps with marvelous delicacy. Last of all he removed her mask.

She was blindingly beautiful.

"Now—" said Harrison, taking her hand, "shall we show the people the meaning of the word dance? Music!" he commanded.

The musicians scrambled back into their chairs, and Harrison stripped them of their handicaps, too. "Play your best," he told them, "and I'll make you barons and dukes and earls."

The music began. It was normal at first—cheap, silly, false. But Harrison snatched two musicians from their chairs, waved them like batons as he sang the music as he wanted it played. He slammed them back into their chairs.

The music began again and was much improved.

Harrison and his Empress merely listened to the music for a while—listened gravely, as though synchronizing their heartbeats with it.

They shifted their weights to their toes.

Harrison placed his big hands on the girl's tiny waist, letting her sense of weightlessness that would soon be hers.

And then, in an explosion of joy and grace, into the air they sprang!

Not only were the laws of the land abandoned, but the law of gravity and the laws of motion as well.

They reeled, whirled, swiveled, flounced, capered, gamboled, and spun.

They leaped like deer on the moon.

The studio ceiling was thirty feet high, but each leap brought the dancers nearer to it.

It became their obvious intention to kiss the ceiling. They kissed it.

And then, neutraling gravity with love and pure will, they remained suspended in air inches below the ceiling, and they kissed each other for a long, long time.

It was then that Diana Moon Glampers, the Handicapper General, came into the studio with a double-barreled ten-gauge shotgun. She fired twice, and the Emperor and the Empress were dead before they hit the floor.

Diana Moon Glampers loaded the gun again. She aimed it at the musicians and told them they had ten seconds to get their handicaps back on.

It was then that the Bergerons' television tube burned out.

Hazel turned to comment about the blackout to George. But George had gone out into the kitchen for a can of beer.

George came back in with the beer, paused while a handicap signal shook him up. And then he sat down again. "You been crying," he said to Hazel.

"Yup," she said.

"What about?" he said.

"I forget," she said. "Something real sad on television."

"What was it?" he said.

"It's all kind of mixed up in my mind," said Hazel.

"Forget sad things," said George.

"I always do," said Hazel.

"That's rny girl," said George. He winced. There was the sound of a riveting gun in his head.

"Gee—I could tell that one was a doozy," said Hazel.

"You can say that again," said George.

"Gee—" said Hazel, "I could tell that one was a doozy."

[QUESTIONS FOR REFLECTION]

Considering Ideas

1. In Vonnegut's story, the Handicapper General of the United States uses special devices to make everyone equal. Are all of the characters really equal? Why or why not?

2. Describe the Bergeron family and their way of life. How do they feel about their handicaps and their son Harrison?

3. What is wrong with the idea of everyone being equal?

Considering Writing Strategies

1. The author uses a number of comparisons, such as similes and analogies, to make certain concepts more vivid for the reader. Identify several of these comparisons. Which ones seem to be most interesting and effective? Why?

2. Vonnegut presents much of the story through dialogue. What effect does this have on the work? Which comments caught your attention most? Why?

3. What is the tone of the story? What words does Vonnegut use to help you identify the mood of the story?

Writing Suggestions

1. Harrison is a rebel, protesting a government he feels is unjust. Write an essay comparing and contrasting Harrison with another literary figure or with someone real, such as a politician or activist. What do they believe in? What challenges do they face? What do they do to try to accomplish their goals?

2. What do you think the year 2081 will be like? Will we go back to a simpler lifestyle? Will robots do everything for us? Write an essay contrasting today's world with what you imagine for the future. You might consider how you believe technology will affect transportation, lifestyle, education, work, and entertainment.

ESOL TIP >

You may want to compare Harrison to a person from your home country.

STUDENT WRITING

Kindle vs. iPad
by James Ingram, Amanda Laudato, and Daniel Volpe

If you are looking for an electronic book (e-book) reader, two of the choices available to you are the Amazon Kindle DX and the Apple iPad. Both devices cost about the same amount ($489 for the Kindle DX and $499 for the iPad 16 GB), have the same sized screen (9.7" diagonally), allow users to surf the Internet, and, most importantly, provide access to literally millions of books and periodicals. Both the iPad and Kindle offer a reasonably pleasant digital reading experience; however, they vary substantially in terms of their overall capabilities.

First, let's look at the reading capabilities of the Amazon Kindle DX. When you pick it up, it feels very light (at 18.9 ounces) and comfortable in your hands. The DX offers consumers the ability to download a book from virtually anywhere using its free 3G service. Once you have downloaded a book, which takes about one minute, you can read the pages in black and white or listen to the book using the text-to-speech feature. The pages look very similar to those in a paperback book, and turning the pages requires only the touch of a button. If you need to look up a word, the built-in dictionary is right there at your fingertips. Because no light is emitted from the screen, you are able to read the Kindle outside in direct sunlight, and reading the pages for long periods of time will not strain your eyes any more than reading an actual paperback book. Even so, you might decide to move on to another activity.

If you get tired of reading the book or want to further investigate a concept in the book you are reading, you might want to sample some of the other features on your Kindle DX. For example, you can conduct a Google search to get the information you need. Even though scrolling through the dull, black and white Web pages on the Kindle is a bit awkward, it is functional. You may also decide to shop for more books at the Amazon store. Furthermore, you can download documents from your computer and read and store up to 4 GB of books and data on the Kindle. If you run out of storage, you have the option to archive books and periodicals and retrieve them later to make room for more downloads. Finally, the battery life on the Kindle will last an entire week.

Similar to the Kindle DX, the Apple iPad is quite nice to hold, although at 22 ounces it feels slightly heavier than the Kindle. Downloading a book from the iBooks application takes longer than a minute, but not much. To download a book, you need to have Wi-Fi access (or a $629 3G iPad with a $15 per month AT&T plan). When you read a book on the iPad, the full color palette really comes to life, especially in a children's book. However, the backlit screen can strain your eyes after a while, and you can barely see the screen in direct sunlight—so much for reading by the pool or on the beach. The methods for turning pages and looking up words are just as easy on the iPad as they are on the Kindle. Furthermore, like the Kindle, the iPad also has a text-to-speech feature so you can listen instead or read if you like. If you need to take a break from reading, the iPad, unlike the Kindle, offers a number of options.

The major differences between the Kindle and the iPad are most evident when it comes to the other capabilities of the devices besides book reading. On the iPad you can search the Internet in full color using Safari. The touch screen makes navigating Web pages and shopping much easier on the iPad than on the Kindle. On the iPad you have the full range of the Internet, just as you would on a computer. But there's more! An iPad provides you access to hundreds of thousands of Web applications (apps) that are fun and functional. You can read and send e-mail, create and export documents, watch movies and television shows, play games, and listen to music. The apps give the iPad virtually limitless capabilities. Furthermore, you have 16 GB of storage (or more on higher end models) and can archive books and store documents on the Internet to save space on your iPad. While the battery lasts only about ten hours during constant use, that is enough to get most people through an entire day before needing to plug in.

The final verdict comes down to how you want to use your device. If your main goal is to have a reader that most resembles a book, then the Amazon Kindle DX is for you. The free 3G service, easy-on-the-eyes features, and ability to read outside make the DX the clear winner as simply an e-book reader. However, if you are looking for an all around, full-color device that is aesthetically pleasing and more versatile than just an electronic reader, then the Apple iPad is the best choice. The expanded capabilities of the iPad are virtually limitless.

[QUESTIONS FOR REFLECTION]

1. Is the essay organized using the block or point-by-point pattern? Would the essay be more or less effective if the authors had used the other approach? Explain.

2. Which parts of the essay are the most useful? Why?

3. What are some of the similarities and differences between the Kindle and the iPad?

4. Which features are better on the Kindle? Which features are better on the iPad?

5. Based on this comparison, which device would you purchase? Why?

Interpreting an Advertisement

As you can see from the Apple advertisement above, iPad users can open up to 9 windows at a time. How might this feature be useful for making comparisons? What kinds of comparisons would you make if you were using an iPad? Does the advertisement compel you to want to purchase an iPad? Why or why not?

Writing about an Image

Write a comparison or contrast essay that relates to one of the pictures or advertisements in this chapter. You may write about the image itself, or you may choose to write about something the image reminds you of. For example, if you write about the advertisement, you might compare and contrast some of the different ways that you escape from the pressures of work, school, and everyday life.

Media Connection for Comparing and Contrasting

You might watch, read, and/or listen to one or more of the suggested media to discover additional examples of comparison and contrast. Exploring various media may help you to better understand methods for comparing and contrasting. You may also choose to write about one or more of the media suggestions. For example, you might watch the news coverage of a specific topic or event on both FOX and CNN and then compare and contrast the coverage given. Or you may decide to listen to Bucky Covington's song "A Different World" and write an essay explaining what it is like for children today as compared to how it was in the past. Be sure to give credit to any sources you use in your essay.

Television	*The Office*	*The Bachelor*	FOX vs. CNN
Film	*WALL-E* (2008)	*Sliding Doors* (1998)	*The Social Network* (2010)
Print	*Mother Jones*	*Consumer Reports*	*Wired*
Internet	**amazon.com**	**shopper.cnet.com**	**gizmodo.com**
Music	"Nothing Compares 2 U" by Sinead O'Connor	"According to You" by Nicki Bliss	"Online" by Brad Paisley

USE ONE OF THE FOLLOWING TOPICS to write a compare and contrast essay. Remember to consider your rhetorical star as well as the steps for writing a comparison and contrast essay as you compose.

1. Two musicians, actors, comedians, or sports figures
2. Two paintings, photographs, posters, or sculptures
3. Two essays, short stories, songs, poems, plays, movies, or television shows
4. Two pieces of technology, such as computers, smart phones, or MP3 players
5. Two advertisements, commercials, or infomercials
6. Two people, such as parents, siblings, friends, teachers, employers, or health care workers
7. Two buildings, monuments, or other landmarks
8. A Mac vs. a PC
9. A "then and now" comparison of an opinion, attitude, or belief of yours that has changed
10. A "now and then" comparison of a person, place, or thing that has changed over time

8.4 > Analyzing the Rhetorical Star for Writing a Comparison and Contrast Essay

FIGURE 8.1
The Rhetorical Star

Subject	Although you could compare several items, it is usually best to begin with just two items for a comparison and contrast essay as you are developing your skills with this writing strategy. You may choose two items that seem similar but are different, or you may choose two items that seem drastically different but have something in common. Be sure that you can make a worthwhile point through your comparison. While you could compare apples and oranges, think about what the reader will gain from the comparison. If you are analyzing the nutritional value of each fruit and making a recommendation about which one provides the most health benefits, then you might be able to make it work. However, there is no need to simply point out the similarities and differences between apples and oranges without having a specific purpose in mind.
Audience	Who will read your comparison? What will interest your readers about your subject? Do they already know something about the items you are comparing? Are they reading to make a decision, such as whether to buy a PC or a Mac? Or are they just curious about your topic? Think about what kinds of details would be most appropriate for your readers.
Purpose	Think about what you are trying to accomplish through your comparison. You need to have a clear reason for making a comparison. Maybe you want to purchase a new laptop for school, and you've narrowed it down to two brands or models. Or possibly you want to determine which organization would provide you with the best career opportunities. Keep focused on your purpose as you write your comparison.
Strategy	Your main goal may be simply to explore the similarities and/or differences between two people, places, or things. However, you may decide to combine strategies. For example, you might be comparing two cell phones and evaluating which one is the better value or has the most useful features.
Design	How many points do you need to include about each item to make your comparison and contrast clear to the reader? What other design elements, such as photographs or illustrations, might enable your readers to better understand the items you are comparing? Although it wouldn't necessarily be appropriate for a school assignment, if you were creating a brochure for a product you were selling, you might use a chart or bullets to emphasize the similarities and differences between your product and the competition. That way the audience could easily discern why your product is better.

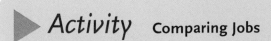 *Activity* **Comparing Jobs**

Research two specific jobs in your career field. Compare them according to several points and determine which one would better suit you. You might use a list or chart to help organize your thoughts. This could be the basis for an essay.

8.5 > Applying the Writing Process for Comparing and Contrasting

1. **Discovering:** You'll want to choose subjects that are worth comparing. In other words, you need to be able to make a valid point for your readers to consider. You might start by brainstorming ideas on paper that could have potential for comparing and contrasting. You could make a list of possible topics and determine which ideas might have value for your audience. You may also want to try a freewriting exercise where you explore the similarities and differences between two people, objects, situations, or events. Finally, the readings, images, and other media suggestions in this chapter may help you to find items to compare or contrast.

2. **Planning:** Once you have decided which subjects to compare, list the similarities and/or differences between the items. Go through the list

FIGURE 8.2   Student Example of a Venn Diagram

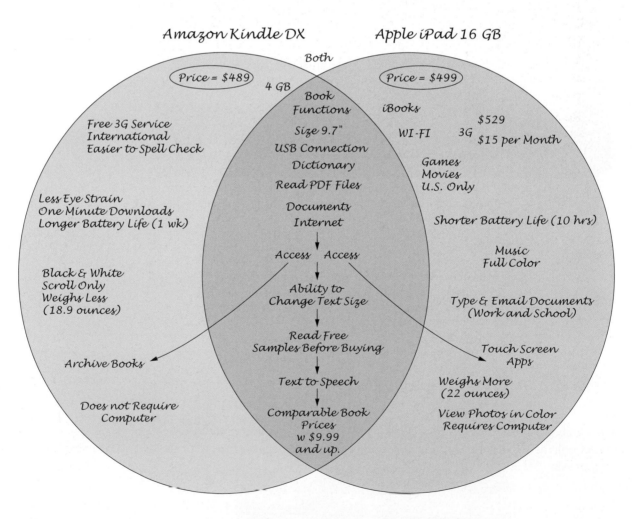

Daniel Volpe
James Ingram
Amanda Laudato

COMPARE & CONTRAST

Amazon Kindle DX   Apple iPad 16 GB

Both

Price = $489   Price = $499

4 GB

Book Functions

Size 9.7"

USB Connection

Dictionary

Read PDF Files

Documents

Internet

Free 3G Service
International
Easier to Spell Check

iBooks

$529

WI-FI   3G $15 per Month

Games
Movies
U.S. Only

Less Eye Strain
One Minute Downloads
Longer Battery Life (1 wk)

Shorter Battery Life (10 hrs)

Access   Access

Ability to
Change Text Size

Black & White
Scroll Only
Weighs Less
(18.9 ounces)

Music
Full Color

Type & Email Documents
(Work and School)

Read Free
Samples Before Buying

Archive Books

Touch Screen
Apps

Text to Speech

Does not Require
Computer

Comparable Book
Prices
w $9.99
and up.

Weighs More
(22 ounces)

View Photos in Color
Requires Computer

and determine which ideas would be most interesting and beneficial to your audience. You might also try making a Venn diagram to help you organize your thoughts. Draw one large circle for each main point, making sure the circles overlap in the middle. The similarities go in the center part that overlaps, and the differences go on the outside areas.

Once you have your main points worked out, you will need to create your thesis. Make sure the thesis states a significant point. Next, decide whether the block or point-by-point pattern will work best for your essay. Then create an outline using the block or point-by-point method. If you change your mind later, you can easily reorganize your essay to follow the other method.

FIGURE 8.3 The Seven Steps of the Writing Process

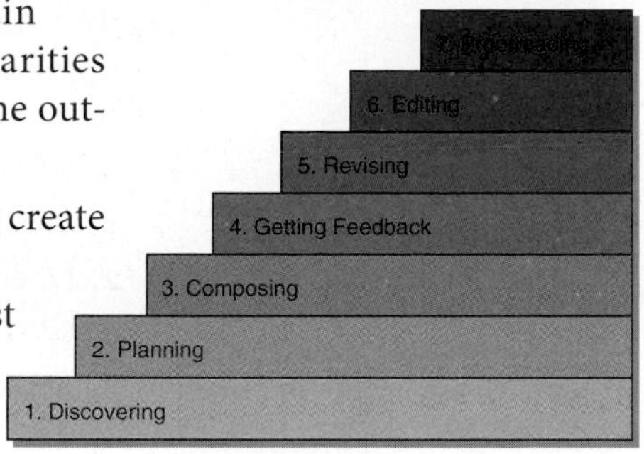

7. Proofreading
6. Editing
5. Revising
4. Getting Feedback
3. Composing
2. Planning
1. Discovering

3. **Composing:** Write a first draft of your comparison or contrast essay using the steps outlined earlier in the chapter on pp. 169–170.

   1. Identify the subjects being compared.

   2. Use the block or point-by-point method.

   3. Describe the subjects fairly and accurately.

   4. Consider using an analogy.

   5. Include transitions.

   6. End with a logical conclusion.

   As usual, don't focus on grammar and punctuation at the composing step. Instead, work on fully developing the details related to each subject you are comparing or contrasting.

4. **Getting feedback:** Have at least one classmate or other person read your rough draft and answer the peer review questions that follow. If you have access to a writing tutor or center, get another opinion about your paper as well. If possible, ask your reviewer(s) if your overall approach (block or point-by-point) works well.

5. **Revising:** Using all of the feedback available to you, revise your comparison and contrast essay. Make sure that you have given fairly equal attention to each subject in your paper and that your points flow smoothly. Add, delete, and rearrange ideas as needed. Additionally, if you have used the block method, you might rearrange it to see if the point-by-point method will work better for your topic. Likewise, if you have used the point-by-point method, you might reorganize it to see if the block method would work better.

6. **Editing:** Read your essay again, this time looking for errors in grammar, punctuation, and mechanics. Pay particular attention to precise diction (word choice) because the way you describe each subject as you compare or contrast will help to give your audience a clear picture of the similarities and differences between them.

7. **Proofreading:** After you have carefully edited your essay, read it one last time. Look for typographical errors and any other issues that might interfere with the readers' understanding of your essay.

Trade rough drafts with a classmate and answer the following questions about his or her paper. Then, in person or online, discuss your papers and suggestions with your peer. Finally, make the changes you feel would most benefit your paper.

1. What elements are being compared in the essay? Are they clearly stated in the thesis?

2. Does the author use the block or point-by-point organizational pattern? Does that pattern seem to be effective? Why or why not?

3. Are the subjects being compared described fairly and accurately, or does the comparison seem to be skewed more in favor of one subject?

4. What analogies, if any, has the author used? How effective are they?

5. What part of the essay is most memorable? Why?

6. Is the conclusion effective? Why or why not?

7. What kinds of grammatical errors, if any, are evident in the essay?

8. What final suggestions do you have for the author?

> Writer's Checklist for Comparison and Contrast

Use the checklist below to evaluate your own writing and help ensure that your comparison and contrast essay is complete. If you have any "no" answers, go back and work on those areas if necessary.

❑ 1. Have I identified the subjects I am comparing and contrasting in my thesis?

❑ 2. Have I organized my ideas logically using the block or point-by-point method?

❑ 3. Have I described the subjects I am comparing and contrasting fairly and accurately?

❑ 4. Have I used analogies to enhance my comparison?

❑ 5. Have I used enough transitions to help my writing flow smoothly?

❑ 6. Is my conclusion effective?

❑ 7. Have I proofread thoroughly?

CHAPTER SUMMARY

1. The comparison and contrast writing strategy focuses on the similarities and differences between subjects.

2. Comparison and contrast writing is an important part of your education, daily life, and career.

3. Interpreting readings and images that reflect comparisons and contrasts can help you to prepare to write your own comparison and contrast essay.

4. Carefully analyze the rhetorical star before writing a comparison and contrast essay: subject, audience, purpose, strategy, and design.

5. Follow these steps to write an effective comparison and contrast essay: identify the subjects being compared; use the block or point-by-point method; describe the subjects fairly and accurately; consider using an analogy; include transitions; end with a logical conclusion.

WHAT I KNOW NOW

Use this checklist to determine what you need to work on in order to feel comfortable with your understanding of the material in this chapter. Check off each item as you master it. Review the material for any unchecked items.

❏ 1. I know what **comparison and contrast** writing is.

❏ 2. I can identify several **real-world applications** for comparison and contrast writing.

❏ 3. I can evaluate readings and **images** that reflect comparisons and contrasts.

❏ 4. I can analyze the **rhetorical star** for comparison and contrast writing.

❏ 5. I understand the **writing process** for comparison and contrast writing.

❏ 6. I can apply the **six steps** for writing about comparisons and contrasts.

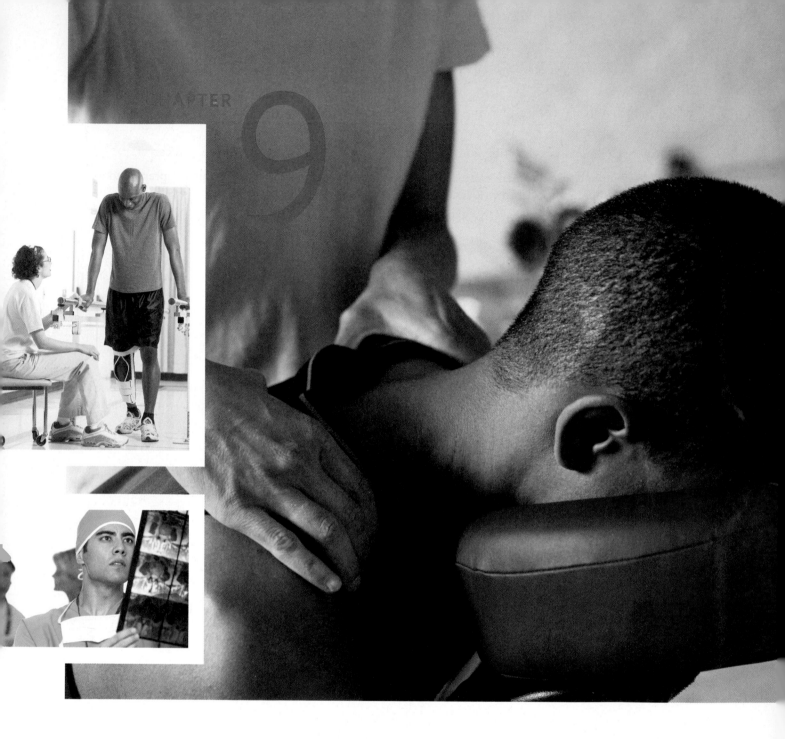

ANALYZING CAUSES AND EFFECTS: HEALTH AND MEDICINE

LEARNING outcomes

> In this chapter you will learn techniques for the following:

9.1 Identifying real-world applications for explaining causes and effects.

9.2 Understanding the steps for writing cause-and-effect analysis.

9.3 Interpreting images and readings about health and medicine.

9.4 Analyzing the rhetorical star for explaining causes and effects.

9.5 Applying the steps for writing a cause-and-effect essay.

> Writing Strategy Focus: Explaining Causes and Effects

Because human beings are so curious, we often wonder why something has occurred. Why do I feel better today than yesterday? Why is my back sore? Why did I lose (or gain) five pounds last month? Why haven't I been sleeping well? Why don't I have the complete health coverage I need? When we ask "why" we are looking for reasons (causes) that have led to a particular result (effect).

Other times we might wonder about the effects of a particular situation or event. What are the effects of that medication, massage, or physical therapy that I received? What will happen if I discontinue my treatment or try something new? Analyzing causes and effects (known as causal analysis) has many applications in your education, personal life, and career.

[**Causal analysis** Analyzing reasons and results

9.1 > Real-World Applications for Explaining Causes and Effects

Writing about Causes and Effects in School

You'll often be asked to identify causes and effects in college courses. Your biology instructor may ask you on a test to discuss the effects of crossbreeding two species of animals. In a history course you might need to write an essay explaining the major causes for a war. A psychology teacher could ask you to research and report on causes for a particular psychological disorder or condition. In a course in your major, your instructor may require you to write a paper analyzing the cause-and-effect relationship of a particular condition, theory, or technique.

Writing about Causes and Effects in Your Daily Life

You probably face cause-and-effect situations regularly in your personal life. For example, you might wonder why you do not have as much time to study as you feel you need, why your paycheck doesn't stretch as far as it used to, or why your relationship doesn't seem to be working out right now. You can search for causes to these problems so that you can implement changes to meet your desired results.

Writing about Causes and Effects in Your Career

Being able to write about causes and effects is essential to your career. Your boss might ask you to write a feasibility study to determine if a new product, service, or procedure is going to meet your needs. You may need to write a report analyzing the possible causes for a work-related problem regarding patients, clients, or customers. Perhaps you'll need to investigate the causes for decreased profits or inefficient methods. Here are some additional ideas for cause-and-effect relationships on the job:

Health care: causes of symptoms or conditions, effects of medications and other treatments.

Law: causes for an accident or dissolution of a marriage, effects of negligence or a violent act.

Education: causes for student achievement or failure, effects of trying a new teaching method or learning tool.

Computers: causes for computer crashes or software freezes, effects of implementing a new software program or network.

Business: causes for business growth or decline, effects of streamlined office procedures or a new marketing strategy.

Culinary arts: causes for following proper safety and sanitation precautions, effects of using high-quality ingredients and cookware.

Massage therapy: causes for creating a peaceful ambience, effects of applying too much or too little pressure.

Graduate SPOTLIGHT

Jamie Wheeler, RN

Jamie Wheeler is a registered nurse (RN) who graduated with her nursing degree in 2007. She currently manages patient care at a subacute rehabilitation center. Here's what Jamie has to say about the importance of written communication in her career:

❝ Effective communication is often the most important link in patient care. In my job as a care plan coordinator, speaking and writing properly are essential to the patients' daily care. I am expected to devise a written plan of care for over 100 patients and keep them current on a daily basis. I must also be able to explain these plans of care in lay terms to both patients and their families. They must understand the reasons for the plans and the effects of not following them exactly. I would not be able to complete any of these tasks without a proper grasp of the English language. Another facet of my job is communicating patient status to doctors, as well as writing and carrying out orders for the patients. Something as simple as a misspelled word or improper grammar could cause a gross error in patient care and medication. In my case, writing clearly and effectively could truly help save someone's life. ❞

On your own, in pairs, or in small groups, brainstorm uses for analyzing causes and effects at school, in your daily life, and on the job. You may want to choose the prospective career field(s) of the participants in your group. Be prepared to share your results.

9.2 > Steps for Writing a Cause or Effect Essay

1. Begin by Identifying the Cause or Effect You Are Analyzing

Start with an attention-getter that relates to your main topic. For instance, if you are writing an essay about the effects of diet and exercise, you might begin by citing statistics, telling a brief story, or asking a question such as this: "Have you ever wished that you had more energy to accomplish all of the tasks you face on a daily basis?"

Next, your thesis statement should give the readers a clear indication of the focus of your essay. For example, a thesis focused on effects might go like this: "Improving your diet and exercise habits can drastically enhance your life." Make sure that you will be able to adequately support your thesis statement in the body of your essay. For instance, you might support the previous thesis statement about health and exercise with details about feeling, performing, and looking better.

2. Explain the Cause-and-Effect Relationship Convincingly

Don't assume that your readers will automatically accept the cause-and-effect relationship you suggest in your essay. You have to illustrate that the connection exists by presenting your ideas logically and fully supporting your thesis. For instance, you might describe a specific example, provide a testimonial from a credible source, explain a similar or hypothetical situation, or use documented research to back up your ideas. Also, your essay will be more convincing if you focus on major causes and effects rather than shifting to remote or minor causes and effects.

3. Organize the Causes and/or Effects Effectively

There are three main patterns for organizing a cause or effect essay. You might focus on the effects of a major cause, the causes for a major effect, or a chain of events that illustrate the cause(s) or effect(s). When you use the major cause pattern, you begin with the cause and then focus on the effects of the cause. Conversely, when you apply the major effect pattern, you start with a major effect, and then examine the causes that led to that effect. At times you may find it appropriate to write a narrative essay to illustrate the chain of events that led to a particular effect. Use the approach that seems to best fit with your rhetorical star.

Here are sample outlines illustrating the three different organizational patterns for a causal analysis essay.

Outline Showing the Effects of a Major Cause

Thesis: Improving your diet and exercise habits can drastically enhance your life.

I. Feel better
    A. More restful sleep
    B. More energy
II. Perform better
    A. Physically
    B. Mentally
III. Look better
    A. Healthier skin
    B. Less body fat
    C. Toned muscles

Outline Showing the Causes for a Major Effect

Thesis: Thousands of people regularly suffer from sleepless nights, not realizing that they might be able to minimize their problem if they identify and address some of the factors that lead to insomnia.

I. Environmental factors
    A. Loud noises
    B. Bright lights
    C. Uncomfortable temperature
II. Physical factors
    A. Illness
    B. Pain
    C. Drug or alcohol use
III. Psychological factors
    A. Stress
    B. Anxiety
    C. Depression
IV. Dietary factors
    A. Too much caffeine
    B. Too many carbohydrates

Causal Chain of Events

Thesis: My mother's breast cancer was the biggest contribution to my decision to become an oncology nurse.

I. Mom diagnosed with breast cancer
    A. Bad news on November 11, 2005
    B. Family felt scared and helpless
II. Attended doctor's appointments with Mom
    A. Observed the medical staff in action
    B. Impressed with medical equipment
III. Mom survived and lives life to the fullest
    A. Mom grateful to medical staff
    B. Inspiration for joining the medical profession

4. Use Sound Logic

Be sure to avoid using logical fallacies in your causal analysis. You don't want to erroneously jump to a conclusion about a cause-and-effect relationship. For example, if someone works out every day for one week without losing weight, that doesn't mean exercise isn't an effective method for weight loss. Other factors could be present, such as diet and the intensity level of the workout.

Additionally, the fact that one event precedes another doesn't mean the first event caused the second one. For instance, if a student always drinks a diet cola and eats a candy bar before passing an exam, that doesn't mean the cola and candy were the cause of the success. A more likely cause would be that the student read the textbook, paid attention in class, and studied the material to achieve a passing test score. Double-check the claims that you make to ensure that you present a cogent cause-and-effect relationship. (See pp. 74–76 for more details about logical fallacies.)

5. Conclude Effectively

As usual, it's a good idea to restate your main idea and summarize your main points in your final paragraph. When writing causal analysis, you'll need to be careful not to overgeneralize in your conclusion. You are probably better off saying that a particular cause *may* lead to several effects than claiming that it *will* absolutely lead to those results. Your thesis will be more plausible if you temper your language in anticipation of potential objections to your claim. Finally, end with a memorable statement that will linger in the minds of the readers.

Grammar Window
PRONOUN AGREEMENT

Sometimes pronoun agreement issues arise when writing about causes or effects. Pronouns need to agree with their antecedents (the nouns to which they refer). If the noun is singular, the pronoun also needs to be singular. Likewise, if the noun is plural, the pronoun needs to be plural as well. Avoid using a pronoun unless it refers to a specific antecedent mentioned previously.

Singular noun/pronoun example: James decided to take the "biggest loser" weight loss challenge at his office, so he has given up cheeseburgers and French fries.

Discussion: *James* is singular, so *he* is the correct singular pronoun.

Plural noun/pronoun example: The school administrators are concerned about the swine flu, so they want to be sure that all students have an opportunity to be vaccinated.

Discussion: *Administrators* is plural, so *they* is the correct plural pronoun.

Faulty pronoun agreement: Each of the blood donors wanted to know their blood type.

Discussion: *Each* is singular and *their* is plural, so the pronouns lack agreement. Ignore the nouns in a prepositional phrase (such as *of the blood donors*) when determining pronoun agreement.

Correction: Each of the blood donors wanted to know his or her blood type.

Activity: Correct the pronoun agreement error in each of the following sentences:

1. Ashley uses hand sanitizer because they want to kill as many germs as possible.

2. Vishnu and Stewart wear lab coats in the lab because he want to stay clean.

3. The student needs to wear shoes in the lab to protect their feet from chemicals and other hazards.

4. Kevin knows not to eat in the microbiology lab because they want to remain healthy.

5. In the medical laboratory, Rose and Tina always place used syringes in the hazardous materials containers because she want to follow the appropriate safety procedures.

[preview] **ALTHOUGH MOST EMPLOYEES** try to be careful on the job, sometimes accidents occur. When that happens, companies usually require that someone write a report detailing the events surrounding the accident and the causes for the accident. The following is a real accident report filed by the Occupational Safety and Health Administration (OSHA) division of the United States Department of Labor. Have you ever experienced or witnessed an accident on the job? What were the causes? What were the effects?

....

Accident Report

....

ACCIDENT SUMMARY No. 69

    Accident Type: Death due to burns
    Weather Conditions: Unknown
    Type of Operation: Excavating for building a road
    Size of Work Crew: 2
    Competent Safety Monitor on Site: No
    Safety and Health Program in Effect: No
    Was the Worksite Inspected Regularly: No
    Training and Education Provided: No
    Employee Job Title: Bulldozer Operator
    Age & Sex: 44-Male
    Experience at this Type of Work: 15 years
    Time on Project: 2 days

BRIEF DESCRIPTION OF ACCIDENT

A bulldozer operator was preparing a road bed by using the machine to lift trees out of the way. A hydraulic line to the right front hydraulic cylinder ruptured, spraying hydraulic fluid onto the engine manifold and into the operator's compartment. Upon contact with the hot manifold, the hydraulic fluid ignited, engulfing the operator in flames. The operator died from the burns he received.

INSPECTION RESULTS

Following an inspection, OSHA issued citations for two serious violations of OSHA standards:

    Frequent and regular inspections of equipment were not made by competent persons designated by the employer in accordance with 29 Code of Federal Regulations (CFR) 1926.20(b)(2). It was determined that the hydraulic hose had been installed backward so that a bend in the fitting connection made contact with the body of the bulldozer, resulting in wear and abrasion of the hose at the connection. This was not discovered during inspection of the machine.

    The employees doing inspections were not instructed to examine the hoses for signs of wear and abrasion as required by 29 CFR 1926.21(b)(2).

ACCIDENT PREVENTION RECOMMENDATIONS

    Train maintenance and operating personnel to recognize potential problems with the operation of the machinery.

    Have competent persons perform periodic inspections of all operating equipment.

    Ensure that the employer initiates and maintains a safety and health program, in accordance with 29 CFR 1926.20(b)(1).

SOURCES OF HELP

OSHA Construction Standards [29 CFR Part 1926], which include all OSHA job safety and health rules and regulations covering construction, may be purchased from the Government Printing Office, phone (202) 512-1800, fax (202) 512-2250, order number 869022-00114-1, $33.

OSHA-funded free consultation services are listed in telephone directories under U.S. Labor Department or under the state government section where states administer their own OSHA programs.

OSHA Safety and Health Training Guidelines for Construction, Volume III (available from the National Technical Information Service, 5285 Port Royal Road, Springfield, VA 22161; phone (703) 487-4650; Order No. PB-239-312/AS, $25) can help construction employers establish a training program.

Courses in construction safety are offered by the OSHA Training Institute, 1555 Times Drive, Des Plaines, IL 60018, 847/297-4810.

OSHA regulations, documents and technical information also are available on CD-ROM, which may be purchased from the Government Printing Office, phone (202) 512-1800 or fax (202) 5122250, order number 729-13-00000-5; cost $79 annually; $28 quarterly. That information also is on the Internet World Wide Web at http://www.osha.gov./

NOTE: The case here described was selected as being representative of fatalities caused by improper work practices. No special emphasis or priority is implied nor is the case necessarily a recent occurrence. The legal aspects of the incident have been resolved, and the case is now closed.

Source: United States Department of Labor (Occupational Safety and Health Administration), **http://www.osha.gov/OshDoc/data_FatalFacts/f-facts69.html**.

1. Discuss the cause-and-effect relationship in the accident report.

2. Review the design of the report, such as the list of details at the beginning and the headings throughout. Is the design effective for this type of report? Why or why not?

3. What could have been done to prevent the accident?

4. Although the details of the settlement are not included in the report, what kind of compensation do you feel the family of the victim should receive? Why?

5. Are you currently employed, or have you ever been? What precautions does your current or former company take to ensure the safety of its employees? What additional measures could the company take to be even more careful?

9.3 > Analyzing Causes and Effects in the Context of Health and Medicine

Although cause-and-effect analysis has applications in virtually every career field, in this chapter you will have an opportunity to examine a few of the cause-and-effect relationships that occur in health and medicine. This theme is useful to explore whether you are going into a health-related field or not. Every human being has to deal with health-related issues at one time or another. Reading and interpreting what others have written can help you see the structure and style of a cause-and-effect analysis and to write your own causal analysis for school, work, and your daily life.

>> READINGS AND REFLECTION

[preview] **SHIRLEY VANDERBILT** is a staff writer for *Body Sense* and *Massage & Bodywork* magazines. She has written numerous articles on massage therapy, reflexology, nutrition, and other health-related issues. In the following essay, Vanderbilt examines the critical role that food plays in our overall health and explains some of the effects of an alternative medicine technique called nutritional cellular cleansing. In her article, Vanderbilt highlights a few of the main points from a book called *The 28-Day Cleansing Program: The Proven Recipe System for Skin and Digestive Repair* by Scott Ohlgren, a holistic health practitioner, and Joann Tomasulo, a whole foods expert. Before reading, consider your own eating habits. How does what you eat affect how you feel?

Food: Your Body's Natural Healer by Shirley Vanderbilt

Your body can heal itself from skin and digestive disorders, as well as a host of other maladies,[1] if you just give it a chance. What does it take?

According to Scott Ohlgren, holistic health practitioner and proponent of nutritional cellular cleansing, it's easy as changing what goes from hand to mouth. What's difficult, he says, is living with the diseased state your diet has created and the rounds of pharmaceuticals that never quire cure what ails you.

If you're filling your body's fuel tank with processed,[2] or even fake foods, the machinery will eventually clog up

[1] **Maladies** Diseases of the body.

[2] **Processed foods** Foods that have been altered from their natural states.

and break down. The symptoms that result, whether a mildly annoying acne or more life-threatening colon condition, are a reaction to this toxic overload and dysfunction. Ohlgren says the first thing you need to look at is your diet. Change to a clean, nutritional intake and you can eliminate the symptoms.

To get started on that path, Ohlgren has published, along with coauthor and whole foods expert Joann Tomasulo, a user-friendly guide for nutritional cellular cleansing—*The 28-Day Cleansing Program* (Genetic Press, 2006).

At the heart of this approach is the principle of cellular regeneration,[3] a process our bodies go through on a continual basis. Cells are constantly renewing themselves, sloughing off used-up matter and regenerating with fresh matter. The materials they use for replacement are derived directly from what you ingest. What have you been giving them to work with lately?

Unwrapping Our Habits

The evolution of our eating habits from a nutrient-rich diet to processed grocery foods has led to a genetic breakdown, Ohlgren says, with each generation influencing the next. It's not likely your body will have the same fortitude and disease resistance as that of your great grandparents, or even your next-door neighbor who comes from different stock. But rather than pointing a finger at someone in the past, he says, we need to focus on personal responsibility in the present. "I am in trouble. I have these conditions. Now what are the steps I need to take in order to strengthen my genetics, my well-being, my immune system?"

Ohlgren suggests we start with "unwrapping our habits of eating." The cleansing foods he recommends are basically what our ancestors ate—foods in a more natural state. Each has an important role in allowing the body to regenerate as nature designed and, in turn, support its innate healing power.

Get With the Program

Ohlgren's first rule of thumb for cellular cleansing is to stop the body's toxic load by eliminating processed food items and replacing them with a variety of grains, beans, vegetables, nuts, and fruits, along with healthy oils, soy products, and, of course, lots of water. To maintain hydration, divide your body weight in half and drink that amount of ounces of pure water every day. Eliminating animal protein is a personal issue, depending on your level of physical activity, but dairy products are out because of their mucus-forming properties.

Next come the three Rs—remineralize, rebacterialize, and reenzymize. Organic vegetables and sea algae grown in mineral-rich environments can provide these essential nutrients. Maintaining a healthy level of friendly bacteria is important to proper digestion and impacts other functions such as immunity and detoxification of harmful substances. Restock your gut-friendly bacteria with fermented cultured foods such as kimchi, sauerkraut, tempeh, and miso, but make sure the products are not pasteurized (a process that kills the bacteria and enzymes you need.) Ohlgren's guidebook offers two hundred recipes, but as he points out, if you don't have time to cook you can still find much of what is needed at your local whole foods deli. Flexibility is the key, and he'll be the first to tell you there's no dogma in this approach.

To complement the diet, Ohlgren encourages including what he calls "physical transformers" such as skin brushing, saunas, alkalinizing baths, and colon hydrotherapy. He also recommends getting a few sessions of cleansing bodywork—deep tissue, Thai massage, and acupuncture, for example—and adding a cardiovascular workout three times a week. These active supplements will support the internal and external cleansing process, aid in lymph system circulation, and revitalize your energy level.

After completing the four-week program, you can go back to eating as you did before, Ohlgren says, but chances are you won't want to. The results of the cleansing program will give you cause to pause and consider the direct relationship between your food choices and your health. "It really comes down to self-empowerment," Ohlgren says. "I want to get people to pay attention to an incredibly powerful action that we do every day and have done since the first day of our life."

---

[3] **Cellular regeneration** The body's ability to restore or replace cells.

Source: S. Vanderbilt, "Food: Your Body's Natural Healer," *Body Sense*, Spring/Summer 2007, pp. 36–37.

....

[QUESTIONS FOR REFLECTION]

Considering Ideas

1. What health issues does the author address in her essay?

2. What suggestions does Vanderbilt offer for helping to resolve those health issues?

3. Have you ever paid attention to how you feel when you vary your diet? What effects have you noticed?

Considering Writing Strategies

1. Does Vanderbilt focus more on causes or effects? Which organizational pattern has she employed?

2. What techniques does the author use to try convince the reader that the cause-and-effect relationship is valid? Is her approach effective? Why or why not?

3. Why does Vanderbilt include headings in her essay? Are they useful? Why or why not?

Writing Suggestions

1. Identify a health issue with which you are familiar. Write an essay explaining the causes or effects that relate to that issue. You might also make suggestions for the reader to follow, as Vanderbilt does in her essay.

2. Have you ever tried a fad diet, such as South Beach or Atkins? Write an essay explaining why you tried it and/or the effects of doing so.

>> READINGS AND REFLECTION

[preview] **BORN IN NEWARK,** New Jersey, Susan Bordo is a professor of philosophy and the Otis A. Singletary Chair in the Humanities at the University of Kentucky. She has written a number of works, including *Twilight Zones: The Hidden Life of Cultural Images from Plato to O. J.* (1997) and her best-known book, *Unbearable Weight: Feminism, Western Culture, and the Body* (2004), which was named a Notable Book by the *New York Times*, was nominated for a Pulitzer Prize, and received a Distinguished Publication Award from the Association for Women in Psychology. To learn more about Susan Bordo and see a photograph of her, go to **www.uky.edu/as/english/faculty/sub.html.** In the following essay, Bordo

looks at how the Western media portray women and how this is affecting various cultures across the globe. Before reading, think about how you feel about your own body image. How does the media affect your self-concept about your appearance?

The Globalization of Eating Disorders **by Susan Bordo**

The young girl stands in front of the mirror. Never fat to begin with, she's been on a no-fat diet for a couple of weeks and has reached her goal weight: 115 lb., at 5'4–exactly what she should weigh, according to her doctor's chart. But in her eyes she still looks dumpy. She can't shake her mind free of the "Lady Marmelade" video from Moulin Rouge. Christina Aguilera, Pink, L'il Kim, and Mya, each one perfect in her own way: every curve smooth and sleek, lean-sexy, nothing to spare. Self-hatred and shame start to burn in the girl, and envy tears at her stomach, enough to make her sick. She'll never look like them, no matter how much weight she loses. Look at that stomach of hers, see how it sticks out? Those thighs–they actually jiggle. Her butt is monstrous. She's fat, gross, a dough girl.

As you read the imaginary scenario above, whom did you picture standing in front of the mirror? If your images of girls with eating and body image problems have

been shaped by *People* magazine and Lifetime movies, she's probably white, North American, and economically secure. A child whose parents have never had to worry about putting food on the family table. A girl with money to spare for fashion magazines and trendy clothing, probably college-bound. If you're familiar with the classic psychological literature on eating disorders, you may also have read that she's an extreme "perfectionist" with a hyper-demanding mother, and that she suffers from "body-image distortion syndrome" and other severe perceptual and cognitive problems that "normal" girls don't share. You probably don't picture her as Black, Asian, or Latina.

Read the description again, but this time imagine twenty-something Tenisha Williamson standing in front of the mirror. Tenisha is black, suffers from anorexia, and feels like a traitor to her race. "From an African-American standpoint," she writes, "we as a people are encouraged to embrace our big, voluptuous bodies. This makes me feel terrible because I don't want a big, voluptuous body! I don't ever want to be fat–ever, and I don't ever want to gain weight. I would rather die from starvation than gain a single pound."[1] Tenisha is no longer an anomaly. Eating and body image problems are now not only crossing racial and class lines, but gender lines. They have also become a global phenomenon.

Fiji is a striking example. Because of their remote location, the Fiji islands did not have access to television until 1995, when a single station was introduced. It broadcasts programs from the United States, Great Britain, and Australia. Until that time, Fiji had no reported cases of eating disorders, and a study conducted by anthropologist Anne Becker showed that most Fijian girls and women, no matter how large, were comfortable with their bodies. In 1998, just three years after the station began broadcasting, 11 percent of girls reported vomiting to control weight, and 62 percent of the girls surveyed reported dieting during the previous months.[2]

Becker was surprised by the change; she had thought that Fijian cultural traditions, which celebrate eating and favor voluptuous bodies, would "withstand" the influence of media images. Becker hadn't yet understood that we live in an empire of images, and that there are no protective borders.

In Central Africa, for example, traditional cultures still celebrate voluptuous women. In some regions, brides are sent to fattening farms, to be plumped and massaged into shape for their wedding night. In a country plagued by AIDS, the skinny body has meant–as it used to among Italian, Jewish, and Black Americans–poverty, sickness, death. "An African girl must have hips," says dress designer Frank Osodi. "We have hips. We have bums. We like flesh in Africa." For years, Nigeria sent its local version of beautiful to the Miss World Competition. The contestants did very poorly. Then a savvy entrepreneur went against local ideals and entered Agbani Darego, a light-skinned, hyper-skinny beauty. (He got his inspiration from M-Net, the South African network seen across Africa on satellite television, which broadcasts mostly American movies and television shows.) Agbani Darego won the Miss World Pageant, the first Black African to do so. Now, Nigerian teenagers fast and exercise, trying to become "lepa"–a popular slang phrase for the thin "it" girls that are all the rage. Said one: "People have realized that slim is beautiful."[3]

How can mere images be so powerful? For one thing, they are never "just pictures," as the fashion magazines continually maintain (disingenuously) in their own defense. They speak to young people not just about how to be beautiful but also about how to become what the dominant culture admires, values, rewards. They tell them how to be cool, "get it together," overcome their shame. To girls who have been abused they may offer a fantasy of control and invulnerability, immunity from pain and hurt. For racial and ethnic groups whose bodies have been deemed "foreign," earthy, and primitive, and considered unattractive by Anglo-Saxon norms, they may cast the lure of being accepted as "normal" by the dominant culture.

In today's world, it is through images–much more than parents, teachers, or clergy–that we are taught how to be. And it is images, too, that teach us how to see, that educate our vision in what's a defect and what is normal, that give us the models against which our own bodies and the bodies of others are measured. Perceptual pedagogy: "How To Interpret Your Body 101." It's become a global requirement.

I was intrigued, for example, when my articles on eating disorders began to be translated, over the past few years, into Japanese and Chinese. Among the members of audiences at my talks, Asian women had been among the most insistent that eating and body image weren't problems for their people, and indeed, my initial research showed that eating disorders were virtually unknown in Asia. But when, this year, a Korean translation of *Unbearable Weight* was published, I felt I needed to revisit the situation. I discovered multiple reports on dramatic increases in eating disorders in China, South Korea, and Japan. "As many Asian countries become Westernized and infused with the Western aesthetic of a tall, thin, lean body, a virtual tsunami of eating disorders has swamped Asian countries," writes Eunice Park in *Asian Week* magazine. Older people can still remember when it was very different. In China, for example, where revolutionary ideals once condemned any focus on appearance and there have been several disastrous famines, "little fatty" was a term of endearment for children. Now, with fast food on every corner, childhood obesity is on the rise, and the cultural meaning of fat and thin has changed. "When I was young," says Li Xiaojing, who manages a fitness center in Beijing, "people admired and were even jealous of fat people since they thought they had a better life. ... But now, most of us see a fat person and think 'He looks awful.'"[4]

Clearly, body insecurity can be exported, imported, and marketed–just like any other profitable commodity. In this respect, what's happened with men and boys is illustrative. Ten years ago men tended, if anything, to see themselves as better looking then they (perhaps) actually

---

[1] From the Colours of Ana website (http://coloursofana.com/ss8.asp). [This and subsequent notes in the selection are the author's.]
[2] Reported in Nancy Snyderman, *The Girl in the Mirror* (New York: Hyperion, 2002), p. 84.
[3] Norimitsu Onishi, "Globalization of Beauty Makes Slimness Trendy," The *New York Times*, Oct. 3, 2002.

[4] Reported in Elizabeth Rosenthal, "Beijing Journal: China's Chic Waistline: Convex to Concave," *The New York Times*, Dec. 9, 1999.

were. And then (as I chronicle in detail in my book *The Male Body*) the menswear manufacturers, the diet industries, and the plastic surgeons "discovered" the male body. And now, young guys are looking in their mirrors, finding themselves soft and ill defined, no matter how muscular they are. Now they are developing the eating and body image disorders that we once thought only girls had. Now they are abusing steroids, measuring their own muscularity against the oiled and perfected images of professional athletes, body-builders, and *Men's Health* models. Now the industries in body-enhancement— cosmetic surgeons, manufacturers of anti-aging creams, spas and salons—are making huge bucks off men, too.

What is to be done? I have no easy answers. But I do know that we need to acknowledge, finally and decisively, that we are dealing here with a cultural problem. If eating disorders were biochemical, as some claim, how can we account for their gradual "spread" across race, gender, and nationality? And with mass media culture increasingly providing the dominant "public education" in our children's lives—and those of children around the globe— how can we blame families? Families matter, of course, and so do racial and ethnic traditions. But families exist in cultural time and space—and so do racial groups. In the empire of images, no one lives in a bubble of self-generated "dysfunction" or permanent immunity. The sooner we recognize that—and start paying attention to the culture around us and what it is teaching our children—the sooner we can begin developing some strategies for change.

Source: Susan Bordo, "The Globalization of Eating Disorders." Copyright © Susan Bordo, Otis A. Singletary Professor of the Humanities, University of Kentucky. Reprinted by permission of the author.

[QUESTIONS FOR REFLECTION]

Considering Ideas

1. According to Bordo, what factors contribute to the body image problem that some people, especially young women, face? Are these reasons feasible? Why or why not?

2. What comparison does the author make in paragraph 10? Is this a valid comparison? Why or why not?

3. In the concluding paragraph, the writer suggests that eating disorders are a cultural problem. Do you agree or disagree with her claim? Explain your answer.

Considering Writing Strategies

1. What type of attention-getter does Bordo use? What purpose does it serve? How effective is the opening of the essay?

2. Does the author focus more on the causes or effects of eating disorders? What specific examples does she use to support her position?

3. Although most of the essay is written from the third person point of view, the author occasionally shifts to the first and second person points of view. Identify passages where these shifts occur. Why does she change points of view in those areas? What effect do the shifts have on the reader?

Writing Suggestions

1. Write an essay focusing on the effects of young Americans' obsession with their appearance. You might consider how having a distorted body image will affect them at school, on the job, and in their personal lives.

2. Have you ever known someone with an eating disorder or other psychological condition, such as panic attacks, schizophrenia, or obsessive compulsive disorder? Write an essay explaining the causes and/or effects of the disorder. Include details about the person you know to provide support for your main points. You may want to use a different name to protect the person's identity. Be sure to cite any resources you use in your paper.

ESOL Tip >

Instead of focusing on American culture, write about how people from your culture perceive body image.

[preview] **MANY PEOPLE** take sleeping pills, without suffering any consequences, other than feeling a little groggy in the morning. However, some people are not so fortunate. For them, the drug becomes a habit or an addiction. In the following essay, Rob Sheffield explores some of the causes and effects related to the use of Ambien, a common sleeping pill. To learn more about the causes and effects of sleeping pill addictions, go to **www.wrongdiagnosis.com/s/sleeping_pill_addiction/intro.htm#whatis**. Before reading, think about your own sleeping habits. Have you used sleep aids to help you get a restful night of sleep? What were the results?

Welcome to the United States of Ambien **by Rob Sheffield**

Ambien has been around since 1993, but only now has it reached its cultural saturation point. Like Ecstasy in 1989 or LSD in 1969, it's the drug that unlocks the fantasy of the moment, which for the owners of 27 million prescriptions means pulling a pillow over their heads. Eminem just did an album about getting hooked on it. Coldplay write their songs on it. It has inspired untold hours of binge-eating and Halo-playing, not to mention years of U.S. foreign policy. ("Everybody here uses Ambien," Colin Powell told a reporter in 2003.) If you stay awake past the 15-minute window when it's supposed to zonk you out, you will end up writing nightmarishly bad poetry and sexting your roommate's exes.

Every night, you can practically smell the Ambien fog settling over a nation of Zolpidem zombies. You can see it in your friends, when they start Twittering in those dangerous late-night hours, when the Ambien has gone down but they haven't fallen asleep yet. You can read it in the after-midnight Facebook status updates along the lines of "Speak to cheese arm steak of united face." It inspires sleep-eating, sleep-driving, sleep-shopping, sleep-blogging. Ambien gives you the hallucinatory urge to indulge your most moronic whims—in other words, it turns you into the pitiful jerk you already are. That's the danger of this drug: The side effect is you.

Insomniacs used to get prescribed sedatives like Tuinal, Valium, Seconal, even Thorazine or lithium, just for their meagerly soporific side effects, which is like sticking your head in the microwave for an earache. But Ambien takes a sharpshooter approach, targeting brain receptors to promote gamma-aminobutyric acid—if other sleep aids were Keith Moon,[1] Ambien was Charlie Watts,[2] getting the job done with ruthless efficiency. So it appeals to casual users who have no idea how to handle its heavy hypnotic effect, which means deep sleep for insomniacs, and cheap laughs for the rest of us.

The Ambien alibi, like Ambien amnesia, is part of the lure. There's something about this moment people are eager not to remember, and the empty Doritos Collisions bags on the floor can always be blamed on the drugs, if not forgotten entirely. No wonder it's become America's drug. It's the drug that turns America into America. So what's in the fridge?

Source: R. Sheffield, "Welcome to the United States of Ambien," *Rolling Stone*, June 11, 2009, p. 91.

---

[1] **Keith Moon** An English drummer for the rock group The Who.
[2] **Charlie Watts** An English drummer for the rock group The Rolling Stones.

[QUESTIONS FOR REFLECTION]

Considering Ideas

1. The author suggests that sleeping pill use is widespread practice. Do you agree or disagree with this concept?

2. What message about sleeping pills is the writer trying to convey to the reader? Is he successful? Why or why not?

3. Have you (or has someone you know) ever tried sleeping pills? Were they helpful? Why or why not?

Considering Writing Strategies

1. Does the essay focus more on causes or effects of sleeping pills?

2. Are the ideas organized clearly? Why or why not?

3. Read the conclusion. Is it an effective way to end the essay? Why or why not?

Writing Suggestions

1. Have you ever written a late night e-mail message or social networking post that you regretted? What prompted (caused) you to write it? What were the consequences (effects)? Write an essay about the experience.

2. Have you (or has someone you know) ever had a bad experience with drugs or alcohol? Write an essay focusing on the effects of the event. You may decide to use the causal chain organizational pattern.

>> READINGS AND REFLECTION

[preview] **BASED IN NEW CITY**, New York, Diane Weber is a freelance writer for *RN* magazine, in which "Finding Their Niche" was originally published. She was formerly the copy chief of *Medical Economics*, a sister publication to *RN*. She has written a number of articles for both publications about nursing, physical therapy, counseling, stress, and a variety of other health-related subjects. You can find more articles about men in the nursing field at **www.minoritynurse.com/features/#men**. In the following article, Weber explores some of the reasons men choose the nursing profession as well as some of the challenges they face because of their gender. Before reading, think about the medical professionals you have come across. What qualities make them good at what they do?

Finding Their Niche: Why Men Choose Nursing by Diane Weber

Ask a man why he became a nurse and he'll probably list familiar reasons: He enjoys helping people, likes the compassionate and caring philosophy of nursing, and wants to make a meaningful contribution to society. He loves to educate patients and interact closely with them. And he'd rather not be on call or deal with the stress that goes along with being a doctor.

But ask him what his family, friends, and acquaintances think of his career choice and he may wince. Stubborn stereotypes fade slowly, despite male-oriented recruitment posters and other marketing efforts designed to dispel them. So nursing remains a predominantly female profession: Only 5.8 percent of the 2.9 million RNs in this country are men, according to the 2004 National Sample Survey of Registered Nurses, the latest conducted by the U.S. Department of Health and Human Services. This translates into 168,181 male nurses, a 14.5 percent increase since 2000, when there were 146,902 male RNs.

How do men who move beyond the gender barrier, like the ones featured here, feel about nursing? In a word, *passionate*. And their stories provide helpful insights for women, as well as other men, in the nursing profession.

A Road with Forks and Bumps

Men who become nurses don't always set out in that direction. "I was accepted into med school and had planned to be a physician, but then found that I like the role of a nurse a lot better," said Jeremiah Jensen, MSN, APRN, who's worked in intensive care, emergency, and telemetry settings. In his chosen role, Jensen explained,

he gets to know patients better, and the work hours allow him time to be with his family.

Like Jensen, Bruce Lovejoy, APRN, MSN, FNP, shifted professional gears. After several years as an EMT, he became an RN and worked on a bone marrow transplantation unit, then as a family NP in a hospital outpatient clinic. Both men have since found a new calling: As instructors for the University of Nebraska Medical Center (UNMC) College of Nursing—Jensen in Kearney, Nebraska, and Lovejoy in Omaha, with the college's department of community-based health—they bring a male perspective to nursing education. And that masculine view, said Chad O'Lynn, RN, CNRN, PhD, an assistant professor for the nursing school at the University of Portland in Oregon, is critical to the future of men in the profession.

"Gender-based barriers occur at the greatest intensity during nursing school," said O'Lynn, co-editor of the 2007 book, *Men in Nursing: History, Challenges and Opportunities.* "Faculty members still push to mold men into feminine-model nurses and discount the great variety in styles of delivering care."

Language geared toward women is one aspect of the problem, acknowledged Carol Bickford, RN-BC, PhD, senior policy fellow for the American Nurses Association. "The ANA has made a strong commitment to remove the 'she' bias from its standards of practice and code of ethics," she said. "Publication materials are also supposed to include both men and women, but I think we miss that mark sometimes."

Another major concern is the lack of enough nursing faculty to educate qualified candidates, which affects men and women alike, said Jim Raper, DSN, CRNP, JD, immediate past president of the American Assembly for Men in Nursing (AAMN), a national advocacy group based in Birmingham, Alabama (**www.aamn.org**).

Still another stumbling block is that many nursing schools don't seriously recruit men, Raper said. "Sure, schools of nursing would like to have more males, but few have done anything tangible to make it happen."

Among nursing schools that have encouraged enrollment by men are those at the University of Pennsylvania in Philadelphia, Excelsior College in Albany, New York, the University of Texas-Austin, and East Carolina University in Greenville, North Carolina. They've all won an annual AAMN "Best School or College of Nursing for Men Award," which recognizes institutions that make a significant effort to recruit and retain men in nursing.

The National League for Nursing (NLN) tracks enrollment in nursing programs and found that from the mid-1980s to the mid-1990s, there was consistent growth in men admitted to basic RN programs (baccalaureate, associate, and diploma), which peaked in 1994 at 13.5 percent, according to Kathy Kaufman, a senior research scientist for public policy for NLN. Enrollment fell to 10.7 percent in 2003, then climbed slightly to 12 percent in 2004–05.

The percentage of graduates from nursing programs mirrors the enrollment figures, with minor fluctuations, Kaufman said. In 2005, the latest year for which data is available, 11.6 percent of graduates from nursing programs were men.

The American Association of Colleges of Nursing, which tracks enrollment trends at the baccalaureate, master's, and doctoral levels, found that the percentage of men enrolled in entry-level BSN programs grew from 8.4 percent in 2002 to 10.2 percent in 2006, according to Robert Rosseter, associate executive director of AACN. Meanwhile, the percentage of men enrolled in master's programs peaked in 2004 and showed a downward trend for the past two years. And while the percentage of men in doctoral programs shows growth over the past 10 years, the actual numbers are low, with only 265 men enrolled in 2006.

Where Men Hit Their Stride

His disappointment over recruitment issues aside, AAMN's Raper has made a home for himself in nursing. During his 28-year career, he has worked in ambulatory care, nursing education, and research capacities, as well as in ORs and EDs—the kinds of fast-paced, technology-driven specialties that attract many men. His current role, as the director of the University of Alabama HIV/AIDS Outpatient and Infectious Disease Clinics in Birmingham, is particularly suitable. "It's a perfect job," he said. "I love it."

Having also been an officer with the U.S. Army Nurse Corps, Raper agreed that the military has a relatively high percentage of men in nursing. In fact, about a third of nurses in the Armed Forces are male. The educational benefits, leadership positions, and potential for travel seem to be big draws.

Wherever and however they serve, all nurses—male and female—are valued assets to health care organizations. But sometimes, a simple matter of gender can improve providers' ability to connect more deeply with patients. For example, Raper recalled teaching a young soldier how to bathe his newborn son and change the baby's diaper. "We connected through his experience as a new father. He told me, 'If you can do this, so can I.'"

The Issues Men Face

Clearly there are gender issues that must be confronted when a man chooses to enter the nursing profession. Some of them have even become topics on the agenda of AAMN's annual conference. Its 2006 schedule included the following sessions: "Socializing Men into Nursing," "Sexual Identity, Ethnicity, and Sex Role Strain in Male Nursing Students," and "How Should I Touch You?"

In 2005, AAMN and several other nursing groups teamed up with a recruitment marketing firm, Bernard Hodes Group, to announce the results of a survey intended to determine the reasons why there were so few men in nursing. Of the 498 male nurses who responded, 73 percent cited negative stereotypes as a barrier to men pursuing a nursing career; 59 percent identified nursing's reputation as a traditionally female profession; and 42 percent reported a lack of male models and mentors.

Still, 83 percent of those surveyed said they would encourage a male friend to become a nurse because of the profession's stability, career options, geographic mobility, and job security. And 80 percent said they would choose nursing again if they had to do it over.

How Male Nurses Are Viewed

Reactions to male nurses vary, depending on the people involved and the situation. Although patients are sometimes surprised to encounter men providing nursing care, often they accept men as well as they do women—but not always.

"A few women have been uncomfortable with me," said UNMC's Jensen. "When personal care issues or activities of daily living are involved, some women—usually older ones—are a little shy. But once I've established that a nurse's aide will do the personal care, I haven't really had problems."

Rodney Gorman, RN, BSN, TNCC, FN, an ICU nurse at Fort Defiance Indian Hospital in Fort Defiance, Arizona, and a flight nurse with the U.S. Air Force Reserve, mentions another common sticking point: "When I walk into a room, patients assume I'm a doctor. People should know that men make good nurses, just like women make good doctors."

UNMC's Bruce Lovejoy said he's often questioned about why he didn't become a physician. "Some people think that becoming a male nurse is just a stepping stone to becoming a doctor," he said. "I always explain that I could have become a doctor if I wanted, but I chose to become a nurse practitioner instead, because of how we approach the problems of health care."

The implication that nurses are less important than physicians grates on male nurses' nerves—as it does on their female counterparts'. Another pet peeve that men and women in nursing share is the sense of disrespect that they sometimes feel from physicians, PAs, and others in the medical profession.

While many female nurses get along just fine with male nurses, the sexes can clash at times simply because their brains process information and approach problem-solving differently. And since feminine relationships and patterns of communication prevail, men can feel left out in the cold, explained UP's O'Lynn. "The 'old-girls' club' in most nursing settings is so entrenched that few of the club's members even acknowledge its existence."

By far, though, men who want to pursue careers in female reproductive health fields, such as labor and delivery, face the most serious resistance—from female nurses as well as patients. That reaction generally baffles male nurses, since male physicians don't necessarily get the same response. The bias against men becomes particularly evident when female patients have been sexually assaulted or abused, noted ANA's Carol Bickford.

The same distrust can arise with female psychiatric patients who may be fearful of men in general, said Sandy Owen, RN, a staff nurse in the psychiatric ED at Westchester Medical Center and a New York State Nurses Association representative. She's worked with several male nurses in her 12 years in emergency psychiatry nursing and found them equal in ability and compassion to women. "Also, sometimes they're used for 'muscle,'" she said—a common occurrence that some men resent.

Jensen acknowledged that he finds it insulting to be seen that way. "I don't like having someone look at me as if I'm here only for physical reasons. I'm here for emotional and other reasons as well. I have the compassion and empathy to care for someone just as well as a female nurse."

UAB's Raper noted that there are other, more subtle examples of gender bias—like when the men's restrooms at nursing conferences are reassigned for women, the majority of attendees. "I don't believe I've ever been discriminated against," Raper said. "However, just as there are patients who prefer not to have a male physician, there are patients who prefer not to have a male nurse. When I encounter those situations, I try to respect the patient's wishes. I have never allowed my pride to overrule the wishes of a patient if I could make reasonable accommodations with another equally qualified female colleague."

He added, "There are plenty of people who have no preference about the gender of their provider, as long as he or she is professional."

Making a Difference

Though the path isn't always easy for men in nursing, by and large they still love the profession and are quick to encourage other men to join their ranks. "If you're an autonomous person who's willing to break with traditional and cultural gender roles without significant regard for what others might say, then you should set your goals high and become a nurse," Raper declared. "The personal and professional rewards can far exceed the investment."

O'Lynn adds: "Don't feel that you have to prove yourself because most people expect nurses to be women. Learn from others but don't force yourself into some supposed mold of the 'ideal nurse.' Instead, accentuate the positive characteristics you bring personally to a clinical situation. Educate others on your unique set of talents and skills, and cherish the talents and skills that others bring as well."

Source: D. Weber, "Finding Their Niche: Why Men Choose Nursing," *RN* 71, no. 2 (2008), pp. 34–39.

[QUESTIONS FOR REFLECTION]

Considering Ideas

1. According to Weber, what are the causes for men choosing nursing as a career field?

2. Why do some people hold the stereotype that nursing is for women? Is this a fair belief? Why or why not?

3. What specific challenges do male nurses face in a predominantly female profession? How can men overcome these challenges?

Considering Writing Strategies

1. The author uses testimonials from various men to support her points. Are these testimonials credible and convincing? Why or why not?

2. Are Weber's headings useful? Why or why not?

3. What overall message is the writer trying to get across to her audience? How effectively does she accomplish this goal? Explain your answer.

Writing Suggestions

1. What kinds of careers tend to be male dominated? Write an essay that focuses on the causes and/or effects of women entering a career field that traditionally has more males than females.

2. What career path are you planning to take? Write an essay explaining the reasons for your choice.

ESOL Tip >

Write an essay about the causes and/or effects of women entering a traditionally male-dominated career field in your native country.

>> READINGS AND REFLECTION

[preview] **BORN IN RUTHERFORD**, New Jersey, William Carlos Williams was a writer as well as a doctor. He earned his M.D. from the University of Pennsylvania. After graduation, he returned to the small town of Rutherford to run his own successful medical practice. In between seeing patients, he wrote poems, novels, essays, and plays. Because of the exact way he uses language and the vivid

pictures he paints through his words, literary scholars consider him to be one of the principal poets from the Imagist period in the early 20th century. In "Spring and All," Williams likens the growth of a plant to the birth of a child, an occasion with which he was quite familiar in his role as a doctor. You can view several different versions of "Spring and All" at **Youtube.com**. Before reading, think about what it must be like to be born, to enter the world "naked, cold, uncertain of all."

Spring and All by William Carlos Williams

By the road to the contagious hospital
under the surge of the blue
mottled clouds driven from the
northeast—a cold wind. Beyond, the
waste of broad, muddy fields
brown with dried weeds, standing and fallen
patches of standing water
the scattering of tall trees
All along the road the reddish
purplish, forked, upstanding, twiggy
stuff of bushes and small trees
with dead, brown leaves under them
leafless vines—

Lifeless in appearance, sluggish
dazed spring approaches—

They enter the new world naked,
cold, uncertain of all

save that they enter. All about them
the cold, familiar wind—

Now the grass, tomorrow
the stiff curl of wildcarrot leaf

One by one objects are defined—
It quickens: clarity, outline of leaf

But now the stark dignity of
entrance—Still, the profound change
has come upon them: rooted they
grip down and begin to awaken

Source: William Carlos Williams, "Spring and All" from *The Collected Poems of William Carlos Williams, 1909-1939*, volume I. Copyright 1938 by New Directions Publishing Corporation.

Considering Ideas

1. Why do you think Williams chose "Spring and All" as the name of his poem?

2. How is the growth of a new plant similar to the birth of a child?

3. What is the effect of being born? What message is the poet sending to the reader?

Considering Writing Strategies

1. Which lines create the most vivid images for the reader? What do you envision?

2. Notice the organization of the poem. Williams begins with the sky and then travels all the way down to the roots of a plant. Is this strategy effective? Why or why not?

3. What is the tone or mood of the poem? Which specific words emphasize this tone?

Writing Suggestions

1. Do you have children or intend to have them some day? Write an essay explaining your reasons for wanting to become a parent or the effects of having become a parent.

2. As an adult, you have learned many of life's lessons. What advice would you offer to a child or teenager about making tough decisions? Write an essay (or letter) to a child offering your insights. Be sure to give reasons for the suggestions you make.

STUDENT WRITING

Get Fit with Wii
by Olivia Covey

For busy students, parents, and professionals, trying to fit in a workout in the middle of a hectic day can be difficult. Luckily, Nintendo Wii has come up with a great way to get fit and lose inches off your waistline in the comfort of your own home. *Wii Fit* is an interactive game designed to help people of all ages and skill levels target specific areas they need to improve by following an individual fitness routine. Exercising with *Wii Fit* will provide you with a fun, convenient, and personalized regimen for getting in shape and losing weight.

Wii Fit has become popular in the health and fitness world is because it has turned the traditional boring fitness routine into a fun and relaxing game for people of all ages. The game is broken down into various stimulating activities that are geared toward different experience levels. One example is an activity called the "hula hoop," which requires the user to balance on the balance board included with the game, while virtually hula hooping. This simple but stimulating activity provides a great aerobic workout. During a workout, the human body releases a hormone called endorphins. Endorphins are neurotransmitters found in the brain that have been linked to psychological feelings of pleasure. The combination of the natural release of these endorphins and the assortment of fun and challenging activities give the user the ultimate workout experience.

With the vast amount of technology available today, some people may find the idea of having a video game help them with fitness to be too difficult. On the contrary, not only is *Wii Fit* easy to use, it is extremely convenient. *Wii Fit* gives flexible options on the intensity of each session. It also provides interactive feedback and step-by-step instructions on how to do each activity, making it simple for anyone to pick up a controller and get moving. With this technology, you can exercise in your own living room anytime you need without having to make a trip to the gym. The convenience of the *Wii Fit* increases the probability of commitment to a fitness regimen, resulting in a healthier, happier person.

Finally, owning a *Wii Fit* system is like having a personal trainer in your home. The system has great features including a program that allows you to input information about specific foods you consume through the day to get an estimated calorie intake number. The *Wii Fit* program then takes this number and matches it with an activity with a corresponding MET level. A MET level simply represents the intensity of an activity. For example, if you are planning to attend a birthday party later in the day, you can add a piece of birthday cake to the calorie calculator. The program then comes up with an estimated calorie number for that cake and matches it with activities to burn those calories right off. *Wii Fit* is also great for targeting specific areas of your body. For instance, if you are particularly concerned with toning mostly your buns and thighs, the *Wii Fit* program can design a series of activities to focus on those specific areas. The *Wii Fit* program then combines and tracks this information on a progress calendar that helps you to see areas that you have accomplished and areas in need of improvement. After working out with the *Wii Fit* system for just a few weeks, you will start to see results.

In closing, exercising with a *Wii Fit* is the most innovative way to get in shape and lose unwanted pounds. It is fun and has a variety of activities to choose from, so you will never get bored doing the same routine over and over again. Furthermore, it is convenient and flexible, providing a variety of activities and instant feedback for everyone from beginners to people who work out regularly. Most importantly, *Wii Fit* is ideal because it is completely personalized. It utilizes a variety of programs to help you set and achieve specific fitness and weight loss goals. With strong willpower and the help of *Wii Fit*, you can achieve your desired workout results.

[QUESTIONS FOR REFLECTION]

1. Identify Covey's thesis statement. Is it effective? Why or why not?

2. According to the author, what are the effects of using Wii Fit? What do you suppose are the causes?

3. What three reasons does the author give for using a Wii Fit program?

4. Are the author's reasons convincing? Why or why not?

5. Have you ever tried using the Wii Fit program? How does your experience compare to the ideas in Covey's essay?

 ## Activity Cause-and-Effect Chart

Sometimes it is challenging to decide whether it would work better to write about the causes or effects for a particular subject. If that's the case, creating a chart can help you to make a choice.

Make a chart of causes and effects for one of the following topics (or the topic about which you are going to write an essay). Draw a line down the center of the page and list causes on the left side and effects on the right side.

Dropping out of school	Enrolling in college
Choosing the right career	Beginning a new job
Good or poor self-concept	Exercising more or less
Peer pressure	Gaining or losing weight
Drug use	Alcohol use or abuse

Be prepared to share a few of the highlights with the class. This activity may give you ideas for writing a cause or effect essay.

Who is the audience for the advertisement? The image and words in the ad suggest that ones fitness depends on purchasing a Wii Fit game and balance board. Is the cause-and-effect relationship logical? Why or why not? Is the advertisement persuasive? Why or why not?

Write a cause-and-effect essay that relates to one of the images in this chapter. You may write about the image itself, or you may choose to write about something the image reminds you of. For example, you might write a creative essay about the photograph of the man on the motorcycle using the causal chain pattern to explain the events that led to his broken arm and leg.

Media Connection for Explaining Causes and Effects

You might watch, read, and/or listen to one or more of the suggested media to discover additional examples of cause/effect analysis. Exploring various media may help you to better understand methods for explaining causes and effects. You may also choose to write about one or more of the media suggestions. For example, you might watch an episode of "Grey's Anatomy" and write an essay explaining the causes or effects for a situation that occurs on the show. Be sure to give credit to any sources you use in your essay.

Television	*The Human Body* on Discovery	*Grey's Anatomy* or *House*	*Nip/Tuck*
Film	*Sicko* (2007)	*Supersize Me* (2004)	*Nova: Dying to be Thin* (2000) (view at **www. pbs.org/wgbh/nova/thin**)
Print	*Fitness*	*Women's Health*	*Men's Health*
Internet	**webmd.com**	**howhealthworks.com**	**freemd.com**
Music	"A Bad Cold" by Hal Shows	"Panic on the Streets of Health Care City" by Thursday	"Alcohol" by Brad Paisley

Write NOW!

USE ONE OF THE FOLLOWING topics to write an essay that emphasizes causes, effects, or both. Remember to consider your rhetorical star as well as the steps for writing a cause-and-effect essay as you compose.

1. A decision you made that changed the direction of your life
2. A person, place, object, or experience that is special to you
3. A contest, sporting event, or hobby you participated in
4. Being on a team or in a club or other organization
5. A mistake that you, a family member, or a friend made
6. Your first job or a new responsibility you accepted
7. Gaining or losing a family member or friend
8. A law, policy, or ruling that affects you or someone you know
9. A fortunate (or unfortunate) experience, event, or diagnosis
10. Peer pressure to do something bad (or good)

9.4 > Analyzing the Rhetorical Star for Writing a Cause-and-Effect Essay

FIGURE 9.1
The Rhetorical Star

FIGURE 9.1
The Rhetorical Star

Subject	Be sure to select a topic that is narrow enough to adequately cover within the parameters of your assignment. If you are writing a longer essay or research paper, then you may be able to cover both causes and effects. However, you will probably want to focus on causes or effects (not both) for a shorter paper. For instance, while you could reasonably focus on the causes or effects of staying fit, you probably wouldn't be able to effectively cover the entire history of fitness in America.
Audience	Who will read your essay? Are you aiming at a particular audience, such as college students, parents, or health care workers? Once you have a specific audience in mind, focus on the details that will be most useful to your readers. Is your audience reading just for information, or do they need to be able to do something as a result of your essay?
Purpose	Think about what you are trying to accomplish as you write your cause or effect essay. Do you want to simply inform the readers about a specific cause-and-effect relationship? Are you writing mainly to persuade your readers that a cause-and-effect relationship exists? Maybe your primary goal is to express your feelings about the serious consequences of a tragic illness or accident that someone you know suffered with a secondary goal of helping others to prevent it from happening to them.
Strategy	Even if your main approach is to explore the causes and/or effects of a particular topic, you may find it useful to combine strategies as well. For example, if you are writing about the effects of your friend's drug use, you might include a description of the behaviors your friend exhibits, compare and contrast your friend's life before the drug use began, or offer instructions for someone needing to seek help to escape a drug addiction.
Design	How should your essay look when you are finished? Do you need to include any photos, illustrations, or graphic organizers to help your reader fully comprehend your ideas? Will other design strategies help your readers to better understand the causes or effects you are explaining?

FIGURE 9.2
The Seven Steps of the Writing Process

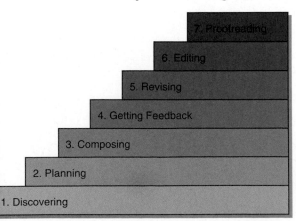

FIGURE 9.2
The Seven Steps of the Writing Process

9.5 > Applying the Writing Process for Explaining Causes and Effects

1. **Discovering:** The readings, images, and other media suggestions in this chapter may help you find a subject for exploring your causal analysis. Look through the chapter and see what comes to mind. Maybe you have some personal experience with a subject worth exploring. Once you have chosen a topic, you might try making a chart of causes and effects to help you determine which you want to cover in your essay.

2. **Planning:** Create a cluster or an outline (informal or formal) to help you organize your ideas. Remember to follow one of the cause-and-effect organizational strategies for your essay: the effects of a major cause, the causes for a major effect, or a chain of events that illustrate the cause(s) or effect(s). (See pp. 197–199 for more details about these organization patterns.)

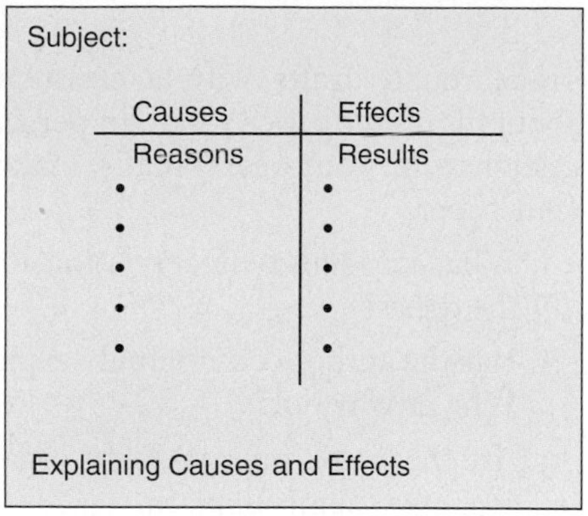

FIGURE 9.3 Explaining Causes and Effects

Subject:

Causes	Effects
Reasons	Results
•	•
•	•
•	•
•	•
•	•

Explaining Causes and Effects

3. **Composing:** Write a first draft of your cause or effect analysis using the steps outlined earlier in the chapter on pp. 197–199. Don't worry too much about grammar and punctuation at this time. Keep focused on the causes or effects you are explaining.

   1. Identify the cause or effect being analyzed.
   2. Explain the cause-and-effect relationship convincingly.
   3. Organize the causes and/or effects effectively.
   4. Use sound logic.
   5. Conclude effectively.

4. **Getting feedback:** Have at least one classmate or other person read your rough draft and answer the peer review questions that follow. If you have access to a writing tutor or center, get another opinion about your paper as well. You'll need to decide which suggestions to accept, reject, or modify.

5. **Revising:** Using all of the feedback available to you, revise your cause or effect essay. Make sure that your causal analysis is logical and that you have fully supported your main points. Add, delete, and rearrange ideas as necessary.

6. **Editing:** Read your cause or effect essay again, this time looking for errors in grammar, punctuation, and mechanics. You might try reading your essay aloud to "listen" to your word choice and sentence structure.

7. **Proofreading:** After you have carefully edited your essay, read it one last time and look for typographical errors and any other issues that might interfere with the readers' understanding of your essay.

Trade rough drafts with a classmate and answer the following questions about his or her paper. Then, in person or online, discuss your papers and suggestions with your peer. Finally, make the changes you feel would most benefit your paper.

1. What cause-and-effect relationship is being analyzed? Is it clearly stated in the thesis?

2. Has the author convincingly explained the cause-and-effect relationship? Why or why not?

3. Are the causes and/or effects organized logically? Is there a better way to organize them? Explain.

4. Has the author included any logical fallacies? Explain?

5. What part of the essay is most memorable? Why?

6. Is the conclusion effective? Why or why not?

7. What kinds of grammatical errors, if any, are evident in the cause or effect essay?

8. What final suggestions do you have for the author?

> Writer's Checklist for Causes and Effects

Use the checklist below to evaluate your own writing and help ensure that your explanation of the process is complete. If you have any "no" answers, go back and work on those areas if necessary.

❏ 1. Have I identified the cause or effect I am analyzing in my thesis?

❏ 2. Have I explained the cause-and-effect relationship convincingly?

❏ 3. Have I organized my causes and/or effects logically?

❏ 4. Have I used sound logic?

❏ 5. Have I concluded my essay effectively?

❏ 6. Have I proofread thoroughly?

[CHAPTER SUMMARY]

1. The cause-and-effect writing strategy focuses on reasons and results.

2. Cause-and-effect writing is an important part of your education, daily life, and career.

3. Interpreting readings and images that reflect causes and effects can help you to prepare to write a cause-and-effect essay.

4. Carefully analyze the rhetorical star before writing a cause or effect essay: subject, audience, purpose, strategy, and design.

5. Follow these steps to write an effective cause-and-effect essay: identify the cause or effect being analyzed; explain the cause-and-effect relationship convincingly; organize the causes and/or effects effectively; use sound logic; conclude effectively.

[WHAT I KNOW NOW]

Use this checklist to determine what you need to work on in order to feel comfortable with your understanding of the material in this chapter. Check off each item as you master it. Review the material for any unchecked items.

❏ **1.** I know what **cause-and-effect writing** is.

❏ **2.** I can identify several **real-world applications** for cause-and-effect writing.

❏ **3.** I can **evaluate readings** and images that reflect causes and effects.

❏ **4.** I can analyze the **rhetorical star** for cause-and-effect writing.

❏ **5.** I understand the **writing process** for cause and effect writing

❏ **6.** I can apply the **five steps** for writing about causes and effects.

PERSUADING:
RELATIONSHIPS

LEARNING outcomes

 In this chapter you will learn techniques for the following:

10.1 Identifying real-world applications for persuading.

10.2 Understanding the steps for writing persuasively.

10.3 Interpreting images and persuasive readings about relationships.

10.4 Analyzing the rhetorical star for persuasive writing.

10.5 Applying the steps for writing a persuasive essay.

> Writing Strategy Focus: Persuasion

Persuasion is all about swaying your audience to see things your way. To compel others to see your point of view about an opinion or belief requires you to be convincing. When you write for the purpose of persuading your audience, you may present a position, defend a belief, attack a point of view, or encourage someone to take action. To do that you will need to support your argument with sound, logical reasons. You may also appeal to your audience's emotions or ethics. The art of persuasion is an important skill to have in school, in your personal life, and in your career.

10.1 > Real-World Applications for Persuading

Writing Persuasively in School

You'll often be asked to write persuasively in your college courses. For example, your political science instructor might ask you to write an argument for or against changing the election procedure. Your literature instructor may require that you write a persuasive essay about a character in a Shakespearean play or Hemingway novel. You might decide to e-mail an instructor requesting an extension for an assignment because of a personal situation you are experiencing. An instructor in your major may ask you to write a report arguing why one theory or procedure works best for a particular situation.

Writing Persuasively in Your Daily Life

Using persuasion in your personal life is a common occurrence. You might write a persuasive letter to your landlord requesting that repairs are made in a timely manner. You may decide to write a letter to the editor of a newspaper or magazine disagreeing with an article you read. Or maybe you'll design a flyer convincing people in your community to donate money or volunteer to help clean up a park or build a playground.

Graduate SPOTLIGHT

Dat Nguyen, Information Technology Administrator

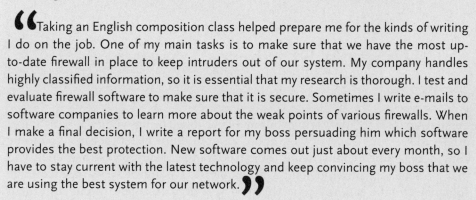

Dat Nguyen graduated from college in 2008 with a degree in information technology. He currently works in the IT department for a large company. Here's what Nguyen has to say about the types of writing he uses in his career:

"Taking an English composition class helped prepare me for the kinds of writing I do on the job. One of my main tasks is to make sure that we have the most up-to-date firewall in place to keep intruders out of our system. My company handles highly classified information, so it is essential that my research is thorough. I test and evaluate firewall software to make sure that it is secure. Sometimes I write e-mails to software companies to learn more about the weak points of various firewalls. When I make a final decision, I write a report for my boss persuading him which software provides the best protection. New software comes out just about every month, so I have to stay current with the latest technology and keep convincing my boss that we are using the best system for our network."

Writing Persuasively in Your Career

Being able to write persuasively is also extremely useful in the workplace. To get the job you desire, you'll need to write a persuasive cover letter and résumé. You might want to persuade your boss to give you a promotion and a raise or some time off for an important out-of-town event you want to attend. You'll also need to convince your clients, patients, or customers, that your organization offers the best product or service in your community. Here are some additional uses for using persuasive strategies in the workplace.

Health care: persuading patients to come in for preventative treatments, to follow prescribed treatments, and to take better care of their bodies.

Law: persuading potential clients that you can help them, presenting opening and closing arguments for a trial, arguing for or against a proposed law or amendment.

Education: persuading the administration to provide more materials, equipment, or books; persuading parents to become more involved in their children's education.

Computers: persuading customers that you can meet their needs so they will purchase hardware, software, or services.

Business administration: persuading clients that your company is reliable and convincing them to purchase products or services.

Massage therapy: persuading clients to use exercise techniques at home and to get more massages to improve their health.

Culinary arts: persuading customers to purchase menu items or catering services and to visit your establishment more often.

Activity Real-World Persuasive Writing

In pairs or small groups, brainstorm uses for writing persuasively at school, in your daily life, and on the job. You may want to choose the prospective career field(s) of the participants in your group. Each group may share its results with the class.

10.2 > Steps for Writing a Persuasive Essay

1. Introduce the Issue You Are Debating

When you are arguing for your perspective on an issue, hold off a bit before stating your thesis because a reader who holds an opinion different from yours may not continue reading your essay. Instead of jumping right in with a claim, begin with an explanation of the situation. Provide your readers with enough information to get a basic understanding of the subject. For example, if you are attempting to persuade the reader that younger siblings are sometimes less responsible than older siblings, you might begin by discussing the psychology of birth order. You may need to do some research to adequately explain the issue if you are not completely familiar with the subject from firsthand experience. As always, cite any outside sources you use in your paper.

After you have introduced the subject, then you may want to pose a question to get your reader to think about the issue. However, keep in mind that a question is not a thesis. A question might hint at where you intend to go with your thesis, but it should not replace your thesis. Here are a few examples of thought-provoking questions:

- Should an employee always outwardly agree with his or her boss?
- Should motorists be allowed to talk on cell phones while driving?
- Should a boy be allowed to join the girls' volleyball team if there is no comparable boys' team?
- Do school uniforms help promote a positive learning environment for children?

2. Make a Claim about Your Subject

Usually, the best place to state your thesis in a persuasive essay is at the end of your first paragraph or the beginning of your second paragraph. Whether you are making an assertion about an issue or demanding that something be done, your claim should definitively state your opinion about the issue. You want to make sure your reader knows exactly where you stand on the issue.

Avoid using phrases such as "I think, "I believe," and "I feel" because that will make you sound tentative and weaken your argument. Keep a third person point of view and make a strong claim. For example, in a paper about stay-at-home fathers, your thesis might be, "Men who serve as the primary caregivers for their children deserve to be treated with the same respect as women who choose that role."

3. Support Your Claim with Evidence that Appeals to Your Audience

To persuade your audience that your claim is valid, you'll need to support it fully. Whether you document personal experience, create your own primary source information, or introduce research based on the findings of others, you can use appeals to convince your audience that your argument is credible. Three types of appeals are used in argument: ethical (from the Greek word *ethos*), emotional (from the Greek word *pathos*), and logical (from the Greek word *logos*). These appeals can be used individually or in combination.

TABLE 10.1

Persuasive Appeals		
Type of Appeal	**Definition**	**Example**
Ethical appeal (ethos)	Persuade the readers by establishing that you are a trustworthy and credible writer. This is sometimes called *character appeal* because you are demonstrating that you are fair in your approach to the issue. Show that you understand the issue, that you are sensitive to it, and that you have considered all sides of it. If you are an expert on the subject, you can mention your profession, experience, or knowledge. Bringing in the opinion of an authority can help you to establish your credibility if you are writing about a topic with which you have little or no firsthand experience. Use an appropriate tone and correct grammar to help maintain your good character.	Now, more than ever before, dual-income families are struggling with how to balance jobs, children, and household tasks. Parents need to work out a fair system for handling these responsibilities. As a counselor, I have helped hundreds of families to deal with these pressures using three simple techniques.
Emotional appeal (pathos)	Persuade the readers by appealing to their emotions. You can use emotionally charged words to stir the reader's feelings. You might try to gain the sympathy or empathy of the audience about a particular cause for which you are arguing. Using vivid descriptions and narratives of emotional events can help you to appeal to your readers' emotions.	Juanita, age 17, is 5 feet tall, weighs just 88 pounds, and suffers from anorexia. She feels fat in comparison to the women on the covers of fashion magazines. The media need to be more responsible with the wafer-thin images of women they display, or more girls are going to fall prey to serious eating disorders.
Logical appeal (logos)	Persuade the readers by appealing to their sense of logic with reasons, facts, statistics, and examples. Citing sources from experts on your subject can help you to convince your audience that your evidence is sound. You can also use inductive and deductive reasoning to logically support your premise. (See Fig. 10.1 and Table 10.3 for more information about induction and deduction.)	While you and your colleagues may not always agree on important issues, both parties may benefit from working together to resolve conflicts that arise. Learning how to compromise on important issues can lead to better communication, a more productive work environment, and greater job satisfaction.

▶ Activity Persuasive Appeals

On your own, in pairs, or in small groups, choose one (or more) of the claims listed below. Make a list of ethical, emotional, and logical appeals that a writer might use to support and/or refute the claim.

- The lottery and other forms of gambling should be illegal in every state.
- Actors and professional athletes are paid too much.
- Beauty pageants are exploitive.
- Cell phones are dangerous.
- We are too dependent on computers.
- Our election process is unfair.
- We should all be concerned about global warming.

A representative from each group may share a few of the highlights with the class.

4. Use Your Supporting Evidence Logically and Ethically

While you do want your argument to be convincing, you don't want to win over your audience by deceiving them. Furthermore, you don't want to mislead them by using logical fallacies or leaving out pertinent information that would shed a different light on your subject. For example, if you are attempting to persuade your readers that the company that employs you is sexist because it doesn't have any women who are in the top positions, then it would be unfair to leave out the fact that one of the key executives is a woman who happens to be temporarily out on maternity leave.

Basically, you will want your argument to seem reasonable to your audience. To do that, you'll need to maintain an appropriate tone and give fair treatment to other positions on the issue. However, you don't want to provide your reader with a completely balanced view of the debate. While it would be unethical to overlook a significant factor that doesn't support your perspective, most of your comments need to support the opinion in your thesis. Otherwise, you will confuse your readers or, even worse, defeat your own argument.

Note: If you use outside sources, you must cite them. See Chapters 13 and 14 for specific details about finding and documenting sources using the MLA and APA formats.

TABLE 10.2

Logical Fallacies			
Logical Fallacies	**Definitions**	**Examples**	**Explanations**
Bandwagon	Implying that an idea must be accurate if it is popular. Join the crowd.	Everyone knows that holistic medicine is better than traditional medicine.	Even if many people believe it, that doesn't provide scientific proof for the argument.
Card stacking	Providing evidence for only one side of a case, deliberately omitting essential information that would change the reader's opinion.	Sunni should get a promotion because she has never missed a day at work.	Supervisors consider many factors when deciding whom to promote. Maybe Sunni often arrives late or does poor work.

—continued

—*Table 10.2 continued*

Logical Fallacies			
Logical Fallacies	**Definitions**	**Examples**	**Explanations**
Character attack or ad hominem	Attacking a person rather than an issue.	Candidate X should not become the next company president because he divorced his wife.	His divorce has nothing to do with whether or not he would make a good company president.
Circular reasoning or begging the question	Attempting to support a position by simply restating it in a different way.	Dr. Brilliant is a good instructor because he teaches his students well.	The idea is merely being repeated without offering any specific evidence as to what makes Dr. Brilliant an effective instructor.
Either/or reasoning	Suggesting there are only two possible solutions to a problem (one right and one wrong) when, in reality, there could be many potential options for resolving the issue.	Either the government needs to subsidize gas costs or our economy is going to collapse.	First of all, does the entire economy depend on the price of gas? Also, there are several ways to cut down on fuel costs other than having the government help to offset the price.
False analogy	Comparing things that are not similar in the most important respects.	The governor scored a touchdown with the new property tax increase proposal.	The governor is not a football player, so the analogy doesn't make sense.
False authority or testimonial	Mentioning an authority figure or celebrity as support for arguing a point.	Eric Zane, who plays Dr. Mark Gnome on *Haye's Anatomy*, recommends taking "Cure it All" pills, so they must be effective.	He is a television character, not a real doctor, so he is not qualified to recommend a specific type of treatment.
False cause or post hoc	Suggesting that because one thing happened after another, the first event caused the second one.	I ate chocolate and my sore throat disappeared.	The sore throat could have gone away for another reason unrelated to the chocolate.
Glittering generality	Using emotionally charged words, such as *love, truth, honor, democracy,* and *justice,* to gain the audience's approval.	If you are truly patriotic, you need to do the honorable thing and vote to increase your property taxes.	The implication is that voting a particular way will determine if someone is (or is not) patriotic and honorable.
Hasty generalization	Drawing a conclusion without having sufficient evidence.	A child comes home from school without homework, so the parent assumes that the teacher did not assign any.	The child may have forgotten to bring home the work or may be intentionally misleading the parent.

Non sequitur	The conclusion does not logically follow the evidence that is provided.	Guns are legal in the United States. No wonder the crime rate is so high.	Many factors contribute to the crime rate in the United States. One can't assume that there is only one cause or that guns are the cause for crime.
Red herring	Diverting the reader's attention away from the main issue by introducing something irrelevant. It comes from the practice of dragging a stinky fish across the ground to distract tracking dogs away from a scent.	The idea of gay marriages is an important issue, but do gay people really want to deal with all of the pressures associated with marriage?	The second part is irrelevant because it has nothing to do with whether gay marriages should be legal or not.
Slippery slope	Suggesting that if one change occurs, then other, unwanted changes will inevitably occur as well. The analogy is that once someone starts sliding down a "slippery slope," then he or she won't be able to stop.	If we allow dogs on the beach, then the next thing you know dogs will be sitting at tables in fine restaurants.	The two events are unrelated, so there's no reason to assume that one event will lead to the other.
Stereotyping	Attaching a trait to people who belong to a particular religious, ethnic, racial, age, or other group.	Old people make terrible drivers, so they shouldn't be allowed to drive.	This is an unfair claim because many senior citizens are fine drivers.
Tradition	If something has always been done a certain way, then it must be the correct way.	Our company has always bought cigars and champagne for our clients during the holidays. We don't need to change to something else.	Just because the tradition is long standing doesn't mean that it's a good one. Some clients may not like cigars, and some might not be able to tolerate alcohol. Another gift might be more appropriate.

5. Organize Your Supporting Evidence Effectively

You can organize the evidence in a persuasive essay in a number of ways. You might begin with your second strongest point, then move to your weaker points, and then end with your strongest point. You may also use *deductive* or *inductive* reasoning in persuasive writing. College writers often organize their essays deductively. They introduce a thesis early in the paper and then support it with specific details, examples, and facts in the body paragraphs. The purpose of deductive reasoning is to apply what is already known. However, you may want to try inductive reasoning, where you give specific details, examples, and facts to lead your readers to a major point. The purpose of inductive reasoning is to discover something new.

Figure 10.1 Deductive and Inductive Reasoning Patterns

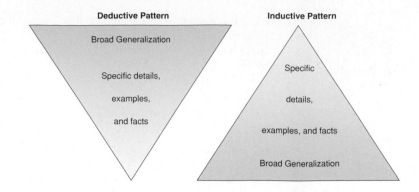

Grammar Window
RUN-ON SENTENCES

When we write to persuade, we may have a lot to say to the readers. If we're not careful, this can lead to run-on sentences. A run-on sentence, also known as a fused sentence, occurs when two complete sentences (independent clauses) run together without a proper punctuation mark or coordinating conjunction.

Run-on sentence: My friend, Leslie, loves watching football on Sunday but her husband, Steve, isn't interested in sports.

Corrected sentence: My friend, Leslie, loves watching football on Sunday, but her husband, Steve, isn't interested in sports.

Discussion: A comma needs to be placed before the coordinating conjunction *but* to avoid the run-on.

Activity: Correct the following run-on sentences by adding a comma or a comma and a coordinating conjunction (*for, and, nor, but, or, yet, so*). In some cases, you could correct a run-on sentence by inserting a period or a semicolon between two complete sentences.

1. Some parents and students feel that school uniforms are beneficial but others find them to be too restrictive.

2. The school is having a meeting tonight so that parents can weigh the pros and cons of school uniforms.

3. Raul likes not having to argue with his daughter about what is appropriate to wear to school he also likes not having to buy a lot of expensive clothes for her.

4. Ai-shi doesn't like wearing a school uniform she feels they are unflattering.

5. Gabriel prefers to wear a uniform to school for he never has to worry about getting picked on for wearing something out of style.

See pp. 397–398 in the Editing Guide for more information on run-on sentences.

TABLE 10.3

Deductive and Inductive Reasoning		
Organizational Strategy	**Definition**	**Example**
Deduction	To organize an argument deductively, begin with a generalization of the most important idea. Then provide more specific details and examples to support the generalization. You can move from a major premise to a minor premise and then draw a plausible conclusion. A classic deductive argument has a conclusion that follows with certainty.	**Topic:** Polygamy **Major premise (claim):** In 1878, the U.S. Supreme Court ruled that polygamy violates criminal law and is not protected by the notion of religious freedom. This ruling has not been overturned. **Minor premise:** While he was living in the United States, Fred married his second wife without divorcing his first wife or nullifying his marriage to her. **Conclusion:** Fred has broken the law.
Induction	To organize an argument inductively, start with the specific details, examples, or observations and then progress to a more general idea. When you use this strategy, you should examine the evidence carefully before drawing a conclusion. An inductive argument has a conclusion that follows with some degree of probability, but not certainty.	**Topic:** Class discussions **Observed evidence:** During my last eight classes at Genius University, the male students have contributed more to class discussions than female students. **Generalization (claim):** Male college students are more talkative than female students.

6. End Your Essay Effectively

There are several ways to conclude a persuasive essay. One method is to use the traditional approach of restating your thesis and summarizing your main points. Other strategies are to suggest the implications of the issue or to encourage your readers to take some sort of action. Whatever you do, be sure to leave your reader feeling satisfied and that you have presented sufficient evidence to support your claim and have made fair judgments about the issue.

[preview] **AFTER YOU GRADUATE** from college, your résumé is one of the most important documents you will ever write. The main goal of your résumé is to persuade a potential employer to invite you to a face-to-face or phone interview. If your résumé doesn't catch the interviewer's eye, then you may never get the chance to explain how great you are in person. Your résumé needs to clearly and concisely convey the message that you are qualified for the job and that you will be a valuable asset to the organization. When you write your résumé, emphasize your best qualifications, organize your strengths logically, and avoid errors in spelling, grammar, punctuation, and mechanics. With the right qualifications and a well-written résumé, you are likely to land the job you desire. The following fictitious résumé illustrates the properties of persuasive writing.

Résumé of Kristin Starr

Kristin Starr

123 Beach View Street
Ft. Lauderdale, FL 33309 kstarr@e-mail.net

954-555-5555 (cell)

Objective:	Position as a medical assistant in a fast-paced physician's office
Education:	Associate of Science in Medical Assisting, June 2010, GPA 3.5 Keiser University, Ft. Lauderdale, Florida
Key Strengths:	• Proficient with EKG, phlebotomy, and radiology • Familiar with electronic health records • Quick to learn office procedures • Adept at multitasking • People oriented/team player • Excellent oral and written communication skills
Certifications:	Registered Medical Assistant, 2010 CPR, 2009
Experience:	Receptionist, Harmony Medical Center Ft. Lauderdale, Florida, August 2007 to present • Manage multiple phone lines • Handle insurance claims • Schedule appointments for multiple physicians • Write office newsletter Intern, Healing Hands Medical Associates Hollywood, Florida, January–May 2010 • Administered injections • Conducted EKGs efficiently • Obtained patients' vital signs • Maintained and filed medical records • Handled multiple phone lines • Scheduled patient appointments
Honors and Activities:	Phi Theta Kappa Honor Society, Secretary 2009 Dean's List, Three Semesters Leadership Distinction Award 2010
Volunteer Work:	Serenity Rehabilitation Center Community Animal Shelter
References:	Available upon request

[QUESTIONS FOR REFLECTION]

1. What are some of Kristin's key strengths?

2. What part of speech is the word that begins each bullet under "experience"? Why?

3. Why did Kristin list her volunteer work on her résumé?

4. Why did she list her education first?

5. If you were an employer with a job opening in this field, would you hire Kristin? Why or why not?

>> Career-Based PERSUASIVE WRITING

[preview] **SARAH HOBAN** is a freelance writer from Chicago. She frequently contributes to *Commercial Investment Real Estate*, the magazine of the CCIM Institute, where the following article first appeared. In the article, Hoban attempts to persuade business owners of the importance of hiring the right employees. She claims that building "professional relationships is an integral part" of the success of a business. Do you agree or disagree with the author's assertion? Read the article and then consider the questions that follow.

Building Business Relationships:
Learn How to Assemble and Maintain Successful Service Provider Networks by **Sarah Hoban**

It's not just the customers who drive your business. Whether you're a solo practitioner or you work for a multistate corporation, you depend on a vast network of people with varying expertise to help get the job done. Establishing, fostering, and burnishing those professional relationships is an integral part of your business's success.

"In any real estate transaction, there are other folks involved—not just the real estate broker," says James V. Cahill, CCIM, vice president and manager of the Staubach Co.'s Bethesda, Md., office. "You have attorneys, accountants, appraisers, construction folks. [Some] are world-class service providers, and [others] are just giving bare-minimum service. It's important that you identify and seek out people in those industries who are going to perform at the same level [as] you."

In other words, it sometimes takes a village to complete transactions. Commercial real estate professionals often depend on related-industry service providers to help deliver strong, consistent client service. Building a well-tooled network of trusted professionals takes patience and persistence. Good people are out there, but it's your job to identify proven performers, make sure they share your goals, and keep the communication lines open so relationships remain positive.

Seek Out Winners

To begin, hone your assessment skills. "You need a genuine interest in other people to find out what kind of character they have," says Tom Hoban, chief executive officer of Coast Real Estate Services in Everett, Wash. "When you ask them to do something for you, and they're paid

for that service, [you have to know] they're giving you the highest level of attention."

For example, Coast assembles a preferred vendors list for its property management portfolio. To be included on the list, vendors "have to first prove themselves in the field," Hoban says. "We generally find quality vendors—from a carpet cleaner all the way up to a structural engineer—by listening to our people. We ask our people to let us know when vendors perform well; those [vendors] who get consistently good remarks will make the list."

Cahill also recommends using independent research and basic experience. "As you're working on projects, you're going to come across service providers, and you're quickly going to be able to determine who is good and who is not so good," he says.

Many related-industry professionals understand this and set their own high service standards. "Consistently delivering" is critical, says Brian Hayes, CCIM, national business development director for Opus North in Rosemont, Ill. "Whether it be a schedule, budget, quality issue, or responsiveness after a deal is completed—all of that is very effective marketing."

Beyond identifying solid performers, you also want to create business opportunities. "You need to seek out people who have the basic understanding of what marketing and business development is all about," Cahill says. "Because if they don't get it—if they don't understand that it's a two-way highway—you're not going to get that return business."

He employs a coaching method: "At some point, very early in the relationship, you have a frank conversation with the other provider and let them know that you're interested in people who can offer the best service to your clients. If you trust them, and they can demonstrate that they're going to perform for your client, you are going to be someone who can help them get in front of new business. But in return, the expectation—and they have to know this—is that when you perform well for their clients, they're going to keep the referrals coming your way."

Building strong reciprocal professional relationships starts with high-end delivery. "You have to be willing to give a lot before you get something in return," Cahill says. "And you're only going to get something in return after you've demonstrated that [the other provider] can trust you and that you're going to provide a level of service that's going to make them look good."

Hoban agrees. "If your word isn't worth anything, over time, these relationships erode. The fundamentals of business start with trust."

Look in the Right Places

While it's easy to spot top-notch performers in action, it sometimes requires a little research to find them initially. Referrals from trusted colleagues are ideal, but sometimes the well runs dry. Then where do you look?

Hoban puts stock in those who belong to credible industry-related professional and trade organizations. "There are meaningful criteria required for people to get into those groups, so that definitely can validate someone," he says. "There's a little more traction there. I can count on that vendor; they're committed to the industry at a level that requires some financial commitment, some time commitment, and even ways to qualify their business." Hoban also networks through his college alumni association, which has been "enormously successful," he says.

However, Cahill urges using some caution. "You have to approach trade organizations the same way you approach service provider relationships," he says. "You have to make sure there's going to be a payoff. The best way to do that is to research organizations that you think are going to offer opportunities and then try them out."

But, "You can't just belong to an organization—you have to be active in it," he adds. "If you get involved on committees, and you're getting to know people and becoming friends, it's less of a business relationship and more of a friendship. That's when those networking organizations start working and become very powerful tools."

Other professionals stress the friendship angle as well. "Turning business relationships into personal relationships has been much more helpful in building my business," says Patrick J. DiCesare, CCIM, of Patrick DiCesare Properties in Greensburg, Pa. He suggests golfing as a good way to break the ice. He treats business contacts and others from their companies to rounds. "When you spend four hours playing golf with somebody, it really

softens the introduction of the relationship and helps promote future business relationships."

Talk the Talk

Perceptive communication skills are vital to sustaining professional relationships. "You need to be informed," Hayes says. "You need to understand how people work; there's a tendency to want to impose your way of doing things onto their way of doing things, and it should be the other way around. You have to work within the context of how they make decisions."

To that end, meet with "all kinds of people on a regular basis ... so that you're always in the mix and aware of what's going on and the realities of those particular situations," he says. "There's no question that you have to talk the language, but you get there by asking questions," Hoban adds. "Most of what I've learned about how people's businesses work is just by asking them, talking to them."

Once you've established solid relationships, you still need to work to keep them strong, and communication is critical. "You need to be touching bases," Cahill says. "Offer [other service providers] opportunities and provide them with information that can help them in their business development activities. Let them know about seminars, invite them to participate in panel discussions, offer to co-author articles that could be used for marketing purposes."

Seminars are especially effective. "They offer you the chance to showcase your area of expertise and are a great opportunity for people who need your services to hear good advice without you coming off as a salesman," he says. When putting together panel discussions, "identify topics of relevance to your prospects and have other panelists who can add to the content. It's a multidimensional approach in which prospects walk away with information that they feel they can use."

DiCesare maintains a steady flow of information to leasing agents in particular (he owns 11 office buildings and shopping centers in the Pittsburgh area), including periodic "leasefaxes" detailing market information. "It keeps that top-of-the-mind awareness for brokers," he says. "I often get comments from brokers saying they appreciate knowing what's on the market."

E-mail makes it easy to stay in touch on a regular basis with quick reminders and greetings. Adrian A. Arriaga Sr., CCIM, principal of AAA Real Estate & Investments in McAllen, Texas, goes a step further. He takes a digital camera to meetings, conferences, and other occasions, photographs participating colleagues, and e-mails the photos after he's returned home. He's gotten a good response from appreciative subjects, he says.

Arriaga also relies on a more traditional form of correspondence: thank-you notes for jobs well done. The pen-to-paper approach stands out, he says. "The art of thank-you notes has been lost. Think about it: When was the last time you got a handwritten note from someone thanking you for something?"

Above all, finding and nurturing good business relationships takes persistence. "You're going to find the right people eventually, but you have to work at it," Cahill says. "They're not going to find you if you're not working at finding them."

Source: Sarah Hoban, "Building Business Relationships," *Commerical Investment Real Estate,* January–February 2004, **www.ciremagazine.com**.

[QUESTIONS FOR REFLECTION]

1. Who is the primary audience for Hoban's article? How do you know?

2. What is the author's claim? Does she state it clearly? Explain.

3. How does Hoban support her claim? Is her support effective? Why or why not?

4. What employee traits are important according to Hoban?

5. Are you the kind of employee Hoban would seek to hire? If not, what skills might you need to develop to become an ideal employee who can help a business to thrive?

10.3 > Persuading in the Context of Relationships

Relationships can be challenging. Disputes between friends, roommates, neighbors, siblings, parents, spouses, partners, and co-workers are quite common. To say that human beings don't always understand each other would be an understatement. People tend to disagree about everything from politics, laws, and finances to values, morality, and religion. A number of factors can contribute to these disagreements, including gender, cultural differences, and experience.

Too often these disputes lead to arguments at home, at school, in the community, or in the workplace. However, instead of arguing over who's right and who's wrong, we can study the issues to gain acceptance, or at least tolerance, of a different perspective. In the following readings, you'll explore a variety of issues. Some are presented as formal arguments while others are designed to give you something to gently debate with classmates and in writing. Reading what others have written can help you write persuasively for school, your personal life, or the workplace.

Opposing Viewpoints on Social Networking Sites

The first two readings in this section reveal opposing viewpoints on the use of social networking sites, such as Facebook. Read both articles before answering the questions for reflection that follow the second one. Consider the following questions before you read the articles: Do you regularly participate on Facebook or another social networking Web site? If so what positive or negative experiences have you had with it? If you don't use an online social network, have you ever considered joining one? What has kept you from joining?

[preview] **LEIGH GOESSL** is a freelance writer for Helium, an online forum where the writers serve as the editors and rate each article published to the Web site. Goessl has a bachelor of science degree in business from Empire State College in New York and is presently working on her MBA. Her primary areas of interest include family, life, technology, music, and, of course, writing.

In the following article, which originally appeared on the Helium Web site, Goessl argues that the use of Facebook can be detrimental to your relationships.

How Facebook Can Harm Your Relationships by Leigh Goessl

Facebook has rapidly soared to become one of the most popular websites across the Net. Every day millions of people across the world log-in to connect with their Facebook friends. These friends may consist of family, friends, long lost relationships, colleagues or new friends. On any given day most people typically see a lot of interaction on their Facebook homepage.

While there are many advantages to being a Facebook member, there are also several drawbacks. It is important to assess the value of Facebook when determining the level of interaction you plan to spend with Facebook.

The drawbacks might be something to consider if you find yourself becoming too involved on Facebook. One of the significant problems that has resulted in society as a result of social networking sites such as Facebook is the impact and harm this interaction has caused to relationships.

All relationships in life pose the risk of being impacted. Here are a few ways Facebook friendships can harm your relationships:

• Marital and Committed Relationships

There are many ways that Facebook can harm committed relationships. Infidelity, addiction, offering too much information and inappropriate interactions are some of the many ways relationships are negatively impacted.

One of the fastest rising factors that is attributed to infidelity is social networking websites. Facebook makes it really easy for people to reconnect and one of the first things many people do is search out their old relationship partners.

Sometimes this is done out of curiosity, but other times it is done with a specific intent to rekindle old flames. Either way, if the person seeking out their old significant others is married, this treads into dangerous territory, especially if the marriage is going through a stressful period or has other issues.

For instance, if a person is frustrated with their significant other, they may turn to the web to look for comradeship, support or an ear to vent to. This can be a very slippery slope, especially if the unhappy partner looks to members of the opposite sex to lean on.

A Facebook addiction is another consideration to look at when assessing how relationships are harmed. One facet of Facebook is that it tends to be overwhelming with so much information being streamed; this is especially true if there are a lot of people listed as friends. Time spent on Facebook is time spent away from the love relationship. A significant other may become jealous or frustrated from the amount of time spent on Facebook.

As part of the Facebook experience, a popular activity is sharing comments, notes, chats or photos with other members. A spouse or significant other may become upset at the types of interaction occurring or the level of personal information streamed onto the site. Often people forget that the web is a public place and comments and photos posted can be embarrassing to a mate.

• Family Relationships

Sometimes people complain, vent or share family problems when they log onto Facebook. This can lead to problematic issues in the family. When private family matters are streamed across Facebook, this can lead to marital strife, problems with children, parents or other extended family. This kind of carelessness can be devastating to family relationships.

Addiction can also impact family relationships. If a parent, child or spouse spends most of their time on Facebook, this means they are less involved with the family. This can result in anger, resentment or major friction.

Either situation can lead to a major argument or rift in the family. A family who likes to keep familial issues private may not be so keen about Facebook.

• Friendships

Facebook can also harm friendships. Insensitive comments can be made, friendships may be ignored in favor of Facebook interaction, and the addiction potential can also factor in. It is always important to consider the feelings of others when making comments or listing photos on Facebook. There is a possibility someone's feelings may get hurt or be embarrassed over something shared, even if strides are made to keep people from seeing things posted.

As mentioned above, Facebook is not private. Sure you can customize and heighten the level of privacy, but it is never really totally private as things can be forwarded or copy/pasted off Facebook pages and e-mailed separated. There is also the interaction of groups that can be joined; these can often be seen by anyone on the Internet depending on the privacy levels set by the group's administrator.

Offline friendships can be harmed if people begin to feel neglected by their friends who are deeply immersed in Facebook. It is a problem when someone knows more about what's going on with their Facebook friends than they do their offline friendships. Additionally people may begin to connect strictly through Facebook instead of picking up a phone or making a visit which can put stress on a friendship.

• Work Relationships

It is pretty common for people to connect with bosses, colleagues and other professional relationships on Facebook.

Facebook is a great networking tool, but one of the side effects is that it blurs personal and professional lives.

Many behaviors people exhibit when off the clock are quite different than the way they act when they are at work. People have to really be careful and not exhibit any levels of unprofessionalism when on Facebook if they are connected to people they work with.

Anything that might be construed as unprofessional can really put a negative impression on a person and lead to problems in their career. Another way work relationships can be harmed is if a person is addicted to Facebook and spends the day interacting on the site. This could cause discord with colleagues and anger bosses when time is frittered away playing instead of working. Facebook is great, but it can damage relationships if you aren't careful. Today's online interaction has begun to really blend with offline relationships and sometimes it is very difficult to maintain both.

In the early Internet days, people used pseudonyms and there wasn't a big problem, but business models such as Facebook are structured to use real names. This has led to people exposing themselves wide open with their online interaction, and unfortunately a negative side effect has been the way it has harmed real-life relationships. If due care isn't taken when on Facebook, people can seriously or permanently harm the people they care about.

Source: Leigh Goessl, Helium, **www.helium.com/items/1731100**.

>> READINGS AND REFLECTION

[preview] **AL RODRICKS**, who is from Enfield, Connecticut, is a staff writer for the Web site ImagineWeMeet.com, an online dating site that allows people to post free personal ads. Although Rodricks' work covers a variety of topics, some of his most interesting articles relate to the online dating scene. For example, in "How to Make Online Dating Successful," he offers useful tips for anyone looking for love on the Internet. The following article originally appeared on the Imagine We Meet site, and presents an opposing viewpoint to the previous article, "How Facebook Can Harm Your Relationships." Where do you stand on the issue? Are social networking sites helpful or harmful to your relationships? Will you agree with Goessl or Rodricks by the time you finish the next article?

The Benefits of Social Networking on YOUR Social Life by Al Rodricks

I remember when the Internet was just starting to get really popular. Many folks feared it would be the end of social interaction. They pictured everyone huddled away in their rooms, typing anonymously to strangers, and giving up any form of human contact whatsoever. Well, as we have seen, this is not the case. In fact, thanks to the advent of social networking, people have been more active than ever before meeting new people, re-connecting with old friends, and learning about different cultures from all over the world. One thing that social networking sites have done is give folks a new and perhaps safer method of online dating.

Social networks, unlike traditional methods of meeting someone, allow you a pretty in-depth method of "checking people out" before actually meeting them. Most social network profiles contain information about the person's interests, work life, family life, and much more. You can even see whom a person is connected to as well, and oftentimes this is how folks meet.

Let's imagine that you just re-connected to an old high school friend. You may not have talked to him or her in years, but thanks to social networking sites, here you are, messaging away to your old buddy! Then let's imagine you start scrolling through the pictures of the people they are connected to online. You see someone who is cute, and you would like to know a little more about him or her. Your friend can give you the scoop, and perhaps even do an online introduction. This process can be much simpler than trying to arrange an in-person date, and MUCH less nerve wracking. Spending a few minutes chatting online with someone is far less intimidating than showing up face to face for a blind date, wouldn't you agree?

In addition, meeting someone through a social network can be a lot like meeting someone through a personal ad, only with a few more "quality checkpoints" installed. Online dating personal ads have been around pretty much since the first power-up of the Internet years ago. The problem is, on a dating profile, it seems that people tend to exaggerate just a bit. I know you are shocked, but it's true. They assume that the only people who will see their ad are others who are "looking for love" as well, and they want to seem as desirable as possible. The same can be true of social networks, of course, but while folks may try to put their best foot forward, the fact that all of their friends will see their profile tends to discourage outright lying.

As far as communicating with those you meet on social networks, the methods are plenty. You can message them right through the platform, chat with them in real time, upload video or audio clips, or perhaps even talk to them live using an interface like Skype, for instance.

It is important to keep in mind that many folks who are members of social networks are not on there exclusively for the purpose of dating. But, if you are looking for true love, spending some time on your favorite social network may just help get you there...

Source: Al Rodricks, "The Benefits of Social Networking on YOUR Social Life," **ImagineWeMeet.com**.

[QUESTIONS FOR REFLECTION]

Compare and contrast the articles by Goessl and Rodricks.

Considering Ideas

1. What is each author's claim?
2. Which article presents a more convincing argument? Why?
3. Based on these articles, as well as your own experiences, what effects, if any, do Facebook and other social networking sites have on relationships? Why?

Considering Writing Strategies

1. In addition to persuasion, what other writing strategies do Goessl and Rodricks use? Give several specific examples from the articles to illustrate your point.
2. Discuss the writing styles of each author. Which author did you connect with more? Why?

3. Which types of appeals (logical, emotional, and/or ethical) does each author use? Give specific examples from the articles.

Writing Suggestions

1. Has a social networking site, such as Facebook, ever enhanced or harmed one of your relationships? Write an essay persuading the readers that the Web site is beneficial or detrimental to relationships. Use your own experience (and possibly other research as well) to support your position. Be sure to cite any sources you use. See Chapters 13 and 14 for more details about citing sources.
2. If you have never used a social networking site, would you consider using one now? Why or why not? Write an essay persuading the readers that using a social networking Web site has positive or negative effects on relationships. Use one of the previous articles (and possibly other research as well) to support your point of view. Be sure to cite any source you use. See Chapters 13 and 14 for more details about citing sources.

[preview] DEBORAH TANNEN, born in Brooklyn, New York, has published more than 20 books and 100 articles. Her best-selling book, *You Just Don't Understand* (1990), has been translated into 29 languages. Her recent books *You're Wearing That?* (2006) and *You Were Always Mom's Favorite!* (2009) have also been quite successful. She has appeared on numerous radio and television shows, and she has given lectures around the world. She is a university professor in the linguistics department at Georgetown University. You can read more about her and watch some of her interview clips at **www9.georgetown.edu/faculty/tannend**. Before reading, think about a friendship or romantic relationship you have had with someone of the opposite sex. What difficulties, if any, did you experience when trying to communicate with one another?

Sex, Lies and Conversation: Why Is It So Hard for Men and Women to Talk to Each Other?
by Deborah Tannen

I was addressing a small gathering in a suburban Virginia living room—a women's group that had invited men to join them. Throughout the evening, one man had been particularly talkative, frequently offering ideas and anecdotes, while his wife sat silently beside him on the couch. Toward the end of the evening, I commented that women frequently complain that their husbands don't talk to them. This man quickly concurred. He gestured toward his wife and said, "She's the talker in our family." The room burst into laughter; the man looked puzzled and hurt. "It's true," he explained. "When I come home from work I have nothing to say. If she didn't keep the conversation going, we'd spend the whole evening in silence."

This episode crystallizes the irony that although American men tend to talk more than women in public situations, they often talk less at home. And this pattern is wreaking havoc with marriage.

The pattern was observed by political scientist Andrew Hacker in the late '70s. Sociologist Catherine Kohler Riessman reports in her new book *Divorce Talk* that most of the women she interviewd—but only a few of the men—gave lack of communication as the reason for their divorces. Given the current divorce rate of nearly 50 percent, that amounts to millions of cases in the United States every year—a virtual epidemic of failed conversation.

In my own research, complaints from women about their husbands most often focused not on tangible inequities such as having giving up the chance for a career to accompany a husband to his, or doing far more than their share of daily life-support work like cleaning, cooking, social arrangements and errands. Instead, they focused on communication: "He doesn't listen to me," "He doesn't talk to me." I found, as Hacker observed years before, that most wives want their husbands to be, first and foremost, conversational partners, but few husbands share this expectation of their wives.

In short, the image that best represents the current crisis is the stereotypical cartoon scene of a man sitting at the breakfast table with a newspaper held up in front of his face, while a woman glares at the back of it, wanting to talk.

Linguistic Battle of the Sexes

How can women and men have such different impressions of communication in marriage? Why the widespread imbalance in their interests and expectations?

In the April [1990] issue of *American Psychologist*, Stanford University's Eleanor Maccoby reports the results of her own and others' research showing that children's development is most influenced by the social structure of peer interactions. Boys and girls tend to play with children of their own gender, and their sex-separate groups have different organizational structures and interactive norms.

I believe these systematic differences in childhood socialization make talk between women and men like cross-cultural communication, heir to all the attraction and pitfalls of that enticing but difficult enterprise. My research on men's and women's conversations uncovered patterns similar to those described for children's groups.

For women, as for girls, intimacy is the fabric of relationships, and talk is the thread from which it is woven. Little girls create and maintain friendships by exchanging secrets; similarly, women regard conversation as the cornerstone of friendship. So a woman expects her husband to be a new and improved version of a best friend. What is important is not the individual subjects that are discussed but the sense of closeness, of a life shared, that emerges when people tell their thoughts, feelings, and impressions.

Bonds between boys can be as intense as girls', but they are based less on talking, more on doing things together. Since they don't assume talk is the cement that binds a relationship, men don't know what kind of talk women want, and they don't miss it when it isn't there.

Boys' groups are larger, more inclusive, and more hierarchical, so boys must struggle to avoid the subordinate position in the group. This may play a role in women's complaints that men don't listen to them. Some men really don't like to listen, because being the listener makes them feel one-down, like a child listening to adults or an employee to a boss.

But often, when women tell men, "You aren't listening," and the men protest, "I am," the men are right. The impression of not listening results from misalignments in the mechanics of conversation. The misalignment beings as soon as a man and a woman take physical positions. This became clear when I studied videotapes made by psychologist Bruce Dorval of children and adults talking to their same-sex best friends. I found that at every age, the girls and women faced each other directly, their eyes anchored on each other's faces. At every age, the boys and men sat at angles to each other and looked elsewhere in the room, periodically glancing at each other. They were obviously attuned to each other, often mirroring each other's movements. But the tendency of men to face away can give women the impression they aren't listening even when they are. A young woman in college was frustrated: Whenever she told her boyfriend she wanted to talk to him, he would lie down on the floor, close his eyes, and put his arm over his face. This signaled to her, "He's taking a nap." But he insisted he was listening extra hard. Normally, he looks around the room, so he is easily distracted. Lying down and covering his eyes helped him concentrate on what she was saying.

Analogous to the physical alignment that women and men take in conversation is their topical alignment. The girls in my study tended to talk at length about one topic, but the boys tended to jump from topic to topic. The

second-grade girls exchanged stories about people they knew. The second-grade boys teased, told jokes, noticed things in the room and talked about finding games to play. The sixth-grade girls talked about problems with a mutual friend. The sixth-grade boys talked about 55 different topics, none of which extended over more than a few turns.

Listening to Body Language

Switching topics is another habit that gives women the impression men aren't listening, especially if they switch to a topic about themselves. But the evidence of the 10th-grade boys in my study indicates otherwise. The 10th-grade boys sprawled across their chairs with bodies parallel and eyes straight ahead, rarely looking at each other. They looked as if they were riding in a car, staring out the windshield. But they were talking about their feelings. One boy was upset because a girl had told him he had a drinking problem, and the other was feeling alienated from all his friends.

Now, when a girl told a friend about a problem, the friend responded by asking probing questions and expressing agreement and understanding. But the boys dismissed each other's problems. Todd assured Richard that his drinking was "no big problem" because "sometimes you're funny when you're off your butt." And when Todd said he felt left out, Richard responded, "Why should you? You know more people than me."

Women perceived such responses as belittling and unsupportive. But the boys seemed satisfied with them. Whereas women reassure each other by implying, "You shouldn't feel bad because I've had similar experiences," men do so by implying, "You shouldn't feel bad because your problems aren't so bad."

There are even simpler reasons for women's impression that men don't listen. Linguist Lynette Hirschman found that women make more listener-noise, such as "mhm," "uhuh," and "yeah," to show "I'm with you." Men, she found, more often give silent attention. Women who expect a stream of listener-noise interpret silent attention as no attention at all.

Women's conversational habits are as frustrating to men as men's are to women. Men who expect silent attention interpret a stream of listener-noise as overreaction or impatience. Also, when women talk to each other in a close, comfortable setting, they often overlap, finish each other's sentences and anticipate what the other is about to say. This practice, which I call "participatory listenership," is often perceived by men as interruption, intrusion and lack of attention.

A parallel difference caused a man to complain about his wife, "She just wants to talk about her own point of view. If I show her another view, she gets mad at me." When most women talk to each other, they assume a conversationalist's job is to express agreement and support. But many men see their conversational duty as pointing out the other side of an argument. This is heard as disloyalty by women, and refusal to offer the requisite support. It is not that women don't want to see other points of view, but that they prefer them phrased as suggestions and inquiries rather than as direct challenges.

In his book *Fighting for Life*, Walter Ong points out that men use "agonistic" or warlike, oppositional formats to do almost anything; thus discussion becomes debate, and conversation a competitive sport. In contrast, women see conversation as a ritual means of establishing rapport. If Jane tells a problem and June says she has a a similar one, they walk away feeling closer to each other. But this attempt at establishing rapport can backfire when used with men. Men take too literally women's ritual "troubles talk," just as women mistake men's ritual challenges for real attack.

The Sounds of Silence

These differences begin to clarify why women and men have such different expectations about communication in marriage. For women, talk creates intimacy. Marriage is an orgy of closeness: you can tell your feelings and thoughts, and still be loved. Their greatest fear is being pushed away. But men live in a hierarchical world, where talk maintains independence and status. They are on guard to protect themselves from being put down and pushed around.

This explains the paradox of the talkative man who said of his silent wife, "She's the talker." In the public setting of a guest lecture, he felt challenged to show his intelligence and display his understanding of the lecture. But at home, where he has nothing to prove and no one to defend against, he is free to remain silent. For his wife, being home means she is free from the worry that something she says might offend something, or spark disagreement, or appear to be showing off; at home she is free to talk.

The communication problems that endanger marriage can't be fixed by mechanical engineering. They require a new conceptual framework about the role of talk in human relationships. Many of the psychological explanations that have become second nature may not be helpful, because they tend to blame either women (for not being assertive enough) or men (for not being in touch with their feelings). A sociolinguistic approach by which male-female conversation is seen as cross-cultural communication allows us to understand the problem and forge solutions without blaming either party.

Once the problem is understood, improvement comes naturally, as it did to the young woman and her boyfriend who seemed to go to sleep when she wanted to talk. Previously, she had accused him of not listening, and he had refused to change his behavior, since that would be admitting fault. But then she learned about and explained to him the differences in women's and men's habitual ways of aligning themselves in conversation. The next time she told him she wanted to talk, he began, as usual, by lying down and covering his eyes. When the familiar negative reaction bubbled up, she reassured herself that he really was listening. But then he sat up and looked at her. Thrilled she asked why. He said, "You like me to look at you when we talk, so I'll try to do it." Once he saw their differences as cross-cultural rather than right and wrong, he independently altered his behavior.

Women who feel abandoned and deprived when their husbands won't listen to or report daily news may be happy to discover their husbands trying to adapt once they understand the place of small talk in women's relationships. But if their husbands don't adapt, the women may still be comforted that for men, this is not a failure of intimacy. Accepting the difference, the wives may look to their friends or family for that kind of talk. And husbands who can't provide it shouldn't feel their wives have made unreasonable demands. Some couples will still decide to divorce, but at least their decisions will be based on realistic expectations.

In these times of resurgent ethnic conflicts, the world desperately needs cross-cultural understanding. Like charity, successful cross-cultural communication should begin at home.

Source: Deborah Tannen, "Sex, Lies, and Conversation: Why Is It So Hard for Men and Women to Talk to Each Other?" Copyright © by Deborah Tannen. Permission granted by International Creative management, Inc.

[QUESTIONS FOR REFLECTION]

Considering Ideas

1. What is the Tannen's overall claim? Where does she most clearly state her thesis?

2. According to the author, how do men and women communicate differently? What kinds of problems can arise in a relationship because of these different communication styles?

3. What can men and women do to try to overcome their communication obstacles?

Considering Writing Strategies

1. How does the author establish herself as an authority figure on the subject? Is her approach convincing? Why or why not?

2. Does Tannen use inductive or deductive reasoning in her essay? What other methods does she use to

3. In the concluding paragraph, the writer compares cross-cultural communication to charity. How effective is this simile?

2. Tannen suggests that once couples understand the types of problems they have communicating, they will be able to improve their relationships. Do you agree or disagree with the author's assertion? Write an essay arguing for or against her claim.

Writing Suggestions

1. In her essay, Tannen draws several conclusions about the different communication styles of men and women. Write an essay arguing for or against her perceptions of the ways in which men and women communicate. Be sure to back up your claim with specific supporting evidence.

support her argument? Identify several specific examples. Which ones seem to be the most effective? Why?

ESOL Tip >

How do men and women communicate in your home country? Is it different from the way in which they communicate in the United States? If so, write a persuasive essay about which communication style works better.

>> READINGS AND REFLECTION

[preview] **M. P. DUNLEAVEY** lives in upstate New York and writes a personal finance column for the *New York Times*. Her first book, *Money Can Buy Happiness* (2007), won the Books for a Better Life Award. She is also the creator for a popular, award-winning series called "Women in Red" on the MSN Money Web site. In the following essay, which originally appeared in the *New York Times*, Dunleavey delves into a world where the traditional roles of a husband and wife are reversed. She uses her personal experience to illustrate what it is like for a woman to support her family while her husband serves as the primary caregiver for their child. Before reading, think about how you would feel if you were in relationship where you played a nontraditional role. What would you like or dislike about the situation? What challenges might you face?

A Breadwinner Rethinks Gender Roles by M. P. Dunleavey

When my son was born last fall, my husband and I had a plan. After a short maternity leave, I would continue to work, and he would quit his job to take care of the baby.

I didn't think of myself as becoming the breadwinner; I had always earned the higher income. The fact that my mate would have a job at home, just not a paying one for now, didn't bother me.

The main hurdle, we assumed, would be figuring out how to afford the shift from two incomes to one. That has turned out to be the least of our problems. The real challenge is navigating the kinds of financial and emotional issues that you can't enter into a calculator or plug into a spreadsheet.

Like so many women raised at the tail end of feminism's first wave, I assumed that my spouse and I would enjoy a relationship based on equality. Equality is an over-worked word, but to me it meant sharing the income, chores, and childcare.

So when my husband asked me the other day, "Did your concept of 'equality' ever include supporting the family?" I had to admit that my answer was no.

I wanted it to be yes. If men could provide for their wives and families, as they have traditionally in many cultures, why shouldn't women feel just fine about assuming that role themselves? Why didn't I?

To put it simply, because we're not there yet, says Kathleen Gerson, a co-author with Jerry A. Jacobs of *The Time Divide: Work, Family and Gender Inequality* (Harvard, 2004). "We are all quite comfortable with the dual-earner household. It's become a cultural template," she said. "But for some reason we hit a roadblock when it comes to single-income households where the single earner is a woman."

Part 2 WRITING STRATEGIES **239**

According to Ms. Gerson's research, the number of households where the wife is the sole earner, from 1970 to 2000, jumped from about 4.1 percent to over 7 percent, and has grown since then. That does not include women who are the primary earners in their families.

A 2003 survey by the Bureau of Labor Statistics indicated that about a third of wives earned more than their husbands. And about 43 percent of household income overall was earned by women, according to a 2003 study by the Families and Work Institute, a group in New York. This data doesn't begin to reveal the uncomfortable situation that breadwinner women are in: How to renegotiate expectations for everything from who manages the money to who does the laundry—when you're C.F.O. of the household.

When I say uncomfortable, I'm trying to be polite. The women I know in these shoes are seething—with uncertainty, resentment, anxiety, and frustration. The patterns that seem "normal" when the husband is the breadwinner don't hold up when women earn most or even all of the income.

That is partly because "men have a sense of esteem, of identity that comes with being the provider," says Barbara Risman, professor of sociology at the University of Chicago. "Women don't get the same identity benefit—there's a sense that one has a double burden."

Take my own situation: I'm supporting the family economically—my husband is supporting us domestically.

While I write, he cooks, cleans, shops, and takes care of our son. It sounds like an idyllic 21st-century twist on the old "Father Knows Best" scenario. Yet I alternate between pride in our arrangement—and terror that I'll be the breadwinner forever.

Does the fact that he's doing so-called women's work have so little value in my eyes—or am I afraid of how others might view a man whose contribution can't be measured in dollars? Am I a Susie homemaker wannabe because I sometimes pray my husband will decide to go to law school and earn a good living?

That sounds petty—especially because, with deepest thanks to my husband, *I'm* earning a good living. But for many frustrated women, financial power hasn't created the balance they were hoping for, and they're still working what the sociologist Arlie Hochschild dubbed "the second shift." As one breadwinner friend of mine put it, quoting an old Enjoli perfume commercial about a woman who "can bring home the bacon/fry it up in a pan": "I didn't think I'd have to serve the bacon and clean the pan, too."

And I didn't think I'd feel so guilty, or derelict in my womanly duties, when my husband is quick to comfort our fussy 4-month-old—or reminds me where we keep the muffin tin. Or that I'd feel so much chest-tightening pressure when I monitor our bills—or remind myself that if I don't sign us up for life insurance, nobody will. Because it's my job.

Source: M. P. Dunleavey, "A Breadwinner Rethinks Gender Roles," *New York Times* (online version), January 27, 2007.

[QUESTIONS FOR REFLECTION]

Considering Ideas

1. What challenges does the author face because she is the primary breadwinner in her home while her husband is a stay-at-home dad?

2. How does Dunleavey reveal these challenges to the reader?

3. The writer claims that women are not yet ready to feel completely comfortable with reversing the traditional gender roles in a family. Do you agree or disagree with her thesis? Why?

Considering Writing Strategies

1. Identify several different kinds of supporting evidence that Dunleavey provides for the audience in her essay. Which support examples seem to be the most effective? Why?

2. Why do you think the author leaves the reader with a sentence fragment at the very end of her essay? What effect does ending with "Because it's my job" have on the reader?

3. Is Dunleavey's argument convincing? Why or why not?

Writing Suggestions

1. In response to Dunleavey's essay, write a persuasive essay assuming the point of view of a man who plays a nontraditional role in the family. You might title your essay "A Caregiver Rethinks Gender Roles." What kinds of challenges might a man encounter if he serves as the primary caregiver for a child instead of bringing home a paycheck?

2. Write an essay arguing for or against the concept of maintaining nontraditional gender roles in a family. What are the advantages or disadvantages of doing so? How does the role reversal affect a couple's relationship?

ESOL Tip >

How are gender roles viewed in your home country? Write an essay arguing for or against the traditional gender roles in your native country.

[preview] **MEDIA CRITIC**, journalist, and novelist Jon Katz began his career as a reporter and editor for the *Philadelphia Inquirer*, the *Boston Globe*, and the *Washington Post*. He also served as an executive producer of the *CBS Morning News*. His media criticism, columns, and reviews have appeared in a variety of publications, including *Rolling Stone*, *New York*, *Wired*, *GQ*, and the *New York Times*. Additionally, Katz has written nearly 20 books, including a series of mystery books about a detective named Kit DeLeeuw, a stay-at-home dad and detective, who uncovers a variety of crimes in Rochambeau, New Jersey. Katz is perhaps best known for his 2007 *New York Times* best seller *Dog Days* and a 2009 title, *Soul of a Dog*. Katz has contributed to several online magazines, including Slate.com. In the following essay, Katz explores the difficulties that a young boy faces as he struggles to grow into manhood, especially if he is a misfit. Before reading, think about what it is like to be a child in a society where bullies are prevalent. What challenges occur?

How Boys Become Men **by Jon Katz**

Two nine-year-old boys, neighbors and friends, were walking home from school. The one in the bright blue windbreaker was laughing and swinging a heavy-looking book bag toward the head of his friend, who kept ducking and stepping back. "What's the matter?" asked the kid with the bag, whooshing it over his head. "You chicken?"

His friend stopped, stood still and braced himself. The bag slammed into the side of his face, the thump audible all the way across the street where I stood watching. The impact knocked him to the ground, where he lay mildly stunned for a second. Then he struggled up, rubbing the side of his head. "See?" he said proudly. "I'm no chicken."

No. A chicken would probably have had the sense to get out of the way. This boy was already well on the road to becoming a man, having learned one of the central ethics of his gender: Experience pain rather than show fear.

Women tend to see men as a giant problem in need of solution. They tell us that we're remote and uncommunicative, that we need to demonstrate less machismo and more commitment, more humanity. But if you don't understand something about boys, you can't understand why men are the way we are, why we find it so difficult to make friends or to acknowledge our fears and problems.

Boys live in a world with its own Code of Conduct, a set of ruthless, unspoken, and unyielding rules:

Don't be a goody-goody.

Never rat. If your parents ask about bruises, shrug.

Never admit fear. Ride the roller coaster, join the fistfight, do what you have to do. Asking for help is for sissies.

Empathy is for nerds. You can help your best buddy, under certain circumstances. Everyone else is on his own.

Never discuss anything of substance with anybody. Grunt, shrug, dump on teachers, laugh at wimps, talk about comic books. Anything else is risky.

Boys are rewarded for throwing hard. Most other activities—reading, befriending girls, or just thinking—are considered weird. And if there's one thing boys don't want to be, it's weird.

More than anything else, boys are supposed to learn how to handle themselves. I remember the bitter fifth-grade conflict I touched off by elbowing aside a bigger boy named Barry and seizing the cafeteria's last carton of chocolate milk. Teased for getting aced out by a wimp, he had to reclaim his place in the pack. Our fistfight, at recess, ended with my knees buckling and my lip bleeding while my friends, sympathetic but out of range, watched resignedly.

When I got home, my mother took one look at my swollen face and screamed. I wouldn't tell her anything, but when my father got home I cracked and confessed, pleading with them to do nothing. Instead, they called Barry's parents, who restricted his television for a week.

The following morning, Barry and six of his pals stepped out from behind a stand of trees. "It's the rat," said Barry.

I bled a little more. Rat was scrawled in crayon across my desk. They were waiting for me after school for a number of afternoons to follow. I tried varying my routes and avoiding bushes and hedges. It usually didn't work.

I was as ashamed for telling as I was frightened. "You did ask for it," said my best friend. Frontier Justice has nothing on Boy Justice.

In panic, I appealed to a cousin who was several years older. He followed me home from school, and when Barry's gang surrounded me, he came barreling toward us. "Stay away from my cousin," he shouted, "or I'll kill you."

After they were gone, however, my cousin could barely stop laughing. "You were afraid of them?" he howled. "They barely came up to my waist."

Men remember receiving little mercy as boys; maybe that's why it's sometimes difficult for them to show any.

"I know lots of men who had happy childhoods, but none who have happy memories of the way other boys treated them," says a friend. "It's a macho marathon from third grade up, when you start butting each other in the stomach."

"The thing is," adds another friend, "you learn early on to hide what you feel. It's never safe to say, 'I'm scared.' My girlfriend asks me why I don't talk more about what I'm feel-

ing. I've gotten better at it, but it will never come naturally."

You don't need to be a shrink to see how the lessons boys learn affect their behavior as men. Men are being asked, more and more, to show sensitivity, but they dread the very word. They struggle to build their increasingly uncertain work lives but will deny they're in trouble. They want love, affection, and support but don't know how to ask for them. They hide their weaknesses and fears from all, even those they care for. They've learned to be wary of intervening when they see others in trouble. They often still balk at being stigmatized as weird.

Some men get shocked into sensitivity—when they lose their jobs, their wives, or their lovers. Others learn it through a strong marriage, or through their own children.

It may be a long while, however, before male culture evolves to the point that boys can learn more from one another than how to hit curve balls. Last month, walking my dog past the playground near my house, I saw three boys encircling a fourth, laughing and pushing him. He was skinny and rumpled, and he looked frightened. One boy knelt behind him while another pushed him from the front, a trick familiar to any former boy. He fell backward.

When the others ran off, he brushed the dirt off his elbows and walked toward the swings. His eyes were moist and he was struggling for control.

"Hi," I said through the chain-link fence. "How ya doing?"

"Fine," he said quickly, kicking his legs out and beginning his swing.

Source: Jon Katz, "How Boys Become Men." From *The Compact Reader*. Originally appeared in *Glamour* in January 1993.

[QUESTIONS FOR REFLECTION]

Considering Ideas

1. According to Katz, what kinds of challenges do boys face as they are trying to grow up and become men? Do you agree or disagree with the notion that boys often mistreat each other?

2. The writer claims, "Women tend to see men as a giant problem in need of solution." Do you agree or disagree with this assertion? Why?

3. According to the author, what are some ways in which men can learn to become sensitive? Is Katz correct in his analysis? Why or why not?

Considering Writing Strategies

1. Identify examples of logical, emotional, and/or ethical appeals that the author uses to persuade his readers. Which ones seem to be most effective? Why?

2. Why does Katz conclude his essay with an anecdote about a boy who has just been harassed by other boys on the playground? What does this ending suggest to the reader?

3. How persuasive is this essay? Do you agree with the author's notion that boys have to "experience pain rather than show fear" in order to follow the rules of their gender and that understanding this principle will help women to better understand men? Why or why not?

Writing Suggestions

1. What were the rules that governed how boys or girls were expected to behave where you were raised? Write a persuasive essay explaining what these guidelines were.

2. Write a persuasive essay titled "How Girls Become Women." In your essay, identify some of the challenges that girls face and suggest how these obstacles influence them as they grow into adulthood.

[preview] **NOEL PERRIN**, born in New York City, was a writer, teacher, and environmentalist. He earned a bachelor's degree from Williams College in Massachusetts and master's degrees from Duke University in North Carolina and Cambridge University in England. After graduation, he became an English instructor at Dartmouth College in New Hampshire and later rose to the position of chairman of the English Department. While living on his 85-acre farm in Vermont, Perrin wrote a series of books highlighting some of his experiences with rural life, the last of which is called *Last Person Rural*.

In the following essay, Perrin scrutinizes the traditional definitions of what it means to be masculine or feminine in the American culture. Before reading, think about your own masculinity or femininity. What traits do you have that people might consider to be masculine or feminine?

Androgynous Man by Noel Perrin

The summer I was 16, I took a train from New York to Steamboat Springs, Colo., where I was going to be assistant horse wrangler at a camp. The trip took three days, and since I was much too shy to talk to strangers, I had quite a lot of time for reading. I read all of "Gone With the Wind." I read all the interesting articles in a couple of magazines I had, and then I went back and read all the dull stuff. I also took all the quizzes, a thing of which magazines were even fuller then than now.

The one that held my undivided attention was called "How Masculine/Feminine Are You?" It consisted of a large number of inkblots. The reader was supposed to decide which of four objects each blot most resembled. The choices might be a cloud, a steam engine, a caterpillar and a sofa.

When I finished the test, I was shocked to find that I was barely masculine at all. On a scale of 1 to 10, I was about 1.2. Me, the horse wrangler? (And not just wrangler, either. That summer, I had to skin a couple of horses that died—the camp owner wanted the hides.)

The results of that test were so terrifying to me that for the first time in my life I did a piece of original analysis. Having unlimited time on the train, I looked at the "masculine" answers over and over, trying to find what it was that distinguished real men from people like me— and eventually I discovered two very simple patterns. It was "masculine" to think the blots looked like man-made objects, and "feminine" to think they looked like natural objects. It was masculine to think they looked like things capable of causing harm, and feminine to think of innocent things.

Even at 16, I had the sense to see that the compilers of the test were using rather limited criteria—maleness and femaleness are both more complicated than that—and I breathed a huge sigh of relief. I wasn't necessarily a wimp, after all.

That the test did reveal something other than the superficiality of its makers I realized only many years later. What it revealed was that there is a large class of men and women both, to which I belong, who are essentially androgynous. That doesn't mean we're gay, or low in the appropriate hormones, or uncomfortable performing the jobs traditionally assigned our sexes. (A few years after that summer, I was leading troops in combat and, unfashionable as it now is to admit this, having a very good time. War is exciting. What a pity the 20th century went and spoiled it with high-tech weapons.)

What it does mean to be spiritually androgynous is a kind of freedom. Men who are all male, or he-men, or 100 percent red-blooded Americans, have a little biological set that causes them to be attracted to physical power, and probably also to dominance. Maybe even to watching football. I don't say this to criticize them. Completely masculine men are quite often wonderful people: good husbands, good (though sometimes overwhelming) fathers, good members of society. Furthermore, they are often so unself-consciously at ease in the world that other men seek to imitate them. They just aren't as free as us androgynes. They pretty nearly have to be what they are; we have a range of choices open.

The sad part is that many of us never discover that. Men who are not 100 percent red-blooded Americans—say, those who are only 75 percent red-blooded—often fail to notice their freedom. They are too busy trying to copy the he-men ever to realize that men, like women, come in a wide variety of acceptable types. Why this frantic imitation? My answer is mere speculation, but not casual. I have speculated on this for a long time.

Partly they're just envious of the he-man's unconscious ease. Mostly they're terrified of finding that there may be something wrong with them deep down, some weakness at the heart. To avoid discovering that, they spend their lives acting out the role that the he-man naturally lives. Sad.

One thing that men owe to the women's movement is that this kind of failure is less common than it used to be. In releasing themselves from the single ideal of the dependent woman, women have more or less incidentally released a lot of men from the single ideal of the dominant male. The one mistake the feminists have made, I think, is in supposing that *all* men need this release, or that the world would be a better place if all men achieved it. It wouldn't. It would just be duller.

So far I have been pretty vague about just what the freedom of the androgynous man is. Obviously it varies with the case. In the case I know best, my own, I can be quite specific. It has freed me most as a parent. I am, among other things, a fairly good natural mother. I like the nurturing role. It makes me feel good to see a child eat—and it turns me to mush to see a 4-year-old holding a glass with both small hands, in order to drink. I even enjoyed sewing patches on the knees of my daughter Amy's Dr. Dentons when she was at the crawling stage. All that pleasure I would have lost if I had made myself stick to the notion of the paternal role that I started with.

Or take a smaller and rather ridiculous example. I feel free to kiss cats. Until recently it never occurred to me that I would want to, though my daughters have been doing it all their lives. But my elder daughter is now 22, and in London. Of course, I get to look after her cat while she is gone. He's a big, handsome farm cat named Petrushka, very unsentimental, though used from kittenhood to being kissed on the top of the head by Elizabeth. I've gotten very fond of him (he's the adventurous kind of cat who likes to climb hills with you), and one night I simply felt like kissing him on the top of the head, and did. Why did no one tell me sooner how silky cat fur is?

Then there's my relation to cars. I am completely unembarrassed by my inability to diagnose even minor problems in whatever object I happen to be driving, and don't have to make some insider's remark to mechanics to try to establish that I, too, am a "Man With His Machine."

The same ease extends to household maintenance. I do it, of course. Service people are expensive. But for the last decade my house has functioned better than it used to because I've had the aid of a volume called "Home Repairs Any Woman Can Do," which is pitched just right for people at my technical level. As a youth, I'd as soon have touched such a book as I would have become a transvestite. Even though common sense says there is really nothing sexual whatsoever about fixing sinks.

Or take public emotion. All my life I have easily been moved by certain kinds of voices. The actress Siobhan McKenna's, to take a notable case. Give her an emotional scene in a play, and within 10 words my eyes are full of tears. In boyhood, my great dread was that someone might notice. I struggled manfully, you might say, to suppress this weakness. Now, of course, I don't see it as a weakness at all, but as a kind of fulfillment. I even suspect that the true he-men feel the same way, or one kind of them does, at least, and it's only the poor imitators who have to struggle to repress themselves.

Let me come back to the inkblots, with their assumption that masculine equates with machinery and science, and feminine with art and nature. I have no idea whether the right pronoun for God is He, She or It. But this I'm pretty sure of. If God could somehow be induced to take that test, God would not come out macho, and not feminismo, either, but right in the middle. Fellow androgynes, it's a nice thought.

Source: "Androgynous Man" by Noel Perrin © 1984. Reprinted by permission.

[QUESTIONS FOR REFLECTION]

Considering Ideas

1. How would the author define the term *androgynous*?
2. What kinds of appeals does the author use to support his main point? How do men and women perceive these behaviors in the 21st century?
3. Why does the writer believe that men have more freedom to display behaviors that were traditionally thought to be feminine? Is he accurate in this claim? Why or why not?

Considering Writing Strategies

1. What point is Perrin arguing through his essay?
2. What kinds of support does the author provide to support his main point? Is his supporting evidence effective? Why or why not?
3. Is Perrin's essay persuasive? Why or why not?

Writing Suggestions

1. Write a persuasive essay looking at the subject from the perspective of a woman. What behaviors do some women display that are considered to be more masculine than feminine? How do others perceive these behaviors? Should women feel free to exhibit behaviors that are thought to be traditionally masculine? Why or why not? Emphasize several different examples to support your thesis.

2. Write an essay arguing against the labeling of men or women as being strictly masculine or feminine. What dangers arise from narrowly defining gender roles? What challenges do stereotypical roles pose for children as they are learning about their own gender roles in society?

>> READINGS AND REFLECTION

[preview] BORN IN Philadelphia, Anna Quindlen is a Pulitzer Prize-winning journalist and best-selling author. She graduated from Barnard College in New York and now serves on its Board of Trustees. She has written numerous novels, nonfiction books, and children's books. Three of her novels have been made into movies: *One True Thing*, *Black and Blue*, and *Blessings*. One of her nonfiction books, *Good Dog Stay*, is about her beloved black Labrador retriever, Beau. Quindlen has been a reporter for the *New York Post*

and a columnist for the *New York Times*. She currently writes a bi-weekly column, "My Turn," for *Newsweek*. You can learn more about Quindlen and her works by visiting her Web site at **www.randomhouse.com/rhpg/annaquindlen**. In the following essay, Quindlen argues for the legalization of gay marriage. Before reading, think about your definition of what a marriage entails. Why do people choose to get married, and what rights are afforded to them for doing so?

Evan's Two Moms by Anna Quindlen

Evan has two moms. This is no big thing. Evan has always had two moms—in his school file, on his emergency forms, with his friends. "Ooooh, Evan, you're lucky," they sometimes say. "You have two moms." It sounds like a sitcom, but until last week it was emotional truth without legal bulwark.[1] That was when a judge in New York approved the adoption of a six-year-old boy by his biological mother's lesbian partner. Evan, Evan's mom, Evan's other mom. A kid, a psychologist, a pediatrician. A family.

The matter of Evan's two moms is one in a series of events over the last year that lead to certain conclusions. A Minnesota appeals court granted guardianship of a woman left a quadriplegic in a car accident to her lesbian lover, the culmination of a seven-year battle in which the injured woman's parents did everything pos-

sible to negate the partnership between the two. A lawyer in Georgia had her job offer withdrawn after the state attorney general found out that she had her lesbian lover were planning a marriage ceremony; she's brought suit. The computer company Lotus announced that gay partners of employees would be eligible for the same benefits as spouses.

Add to these public events the private struggles, the couples who go from lawyer to lawyer to approximate legal protections their straight counterparts take for granted, the AIDS survivors who find themselves shut out of their partners' dying days by biological family members and shut out of their apartments by leases with a single name on the dotted line, and one solution is obvious.

Gay marriage is a radical notion for straight people and a conservative notion for gay ones. After years of being sledgehammered by society, some gay men and lesbian women are deeply suspicious of participating in

---

[1] **Bulwark** Protection.

an institution that seems to have "straight world" written all over it.

But the rads of twenty years ago, straight and gay alike, have other things on their minds today. Family is one, and the linchpin[2] of family has commonly been a loving commitment between two adults. When same-sex couples set out to make that commitment, they discover that they are at a disadvantage: No joint tax returns. No health insurance coverage for an uninsured partner. No survivor's benefits from Social Security. None of the automatic rights, privileges, and responsibilities society attaches to a marriage contract. In Madison, Wisconsin, a couple who applied at the Y with their kids for a family membership were turned down because both were women. It's one of those small things that can make you feel small.

Some took marriage statutes that refer to "two persons" at their word and applied for a license. The results were court decisions that quoted the Bible and embraced circular argument: marriage is by definition the union of a man and a woman because that is how we've defined it.

No religion should be forced to marry anyone in violation of its tenets, although ironically it is now only in religious ceremonies that gay people can marry, performed by clergy who find the blessing of two who love each other no sin. But there is no secular[3] reason that we should take a patchwork approach of corporate, governmental, and legal steps to guarantee what can be done simply, economically, conclusively, and inclusively with the words "I do."

"Fran and I chose to get married for the same reasons that any two people do," said the lawyer who was fired in Georgia. "We fell in love; we wanted to spend our lives together." Pretty simple.

Consider the case of *Loving v. Virginia,* aptly named. At the time, sixteen states had laws that barred interracial marriage, relying on natural law, that amorphous[4] grab bag for justifying prejudice. Sounding a little like God throwing Adam and Eve out of paradise, the trial judge suspended the one-year sentence of Richard Loving, who was white, and his wife, Mildred, who was black, provided they got out of the State of Virginia.

In 1967 the Supreme Court found such laws to be unconstitutional. Only twenty-five years ago and it was a crime for a black woman to marry a white man. Perhaps twenty-five years from now we will find it just as incredible that two people of the same sex were not entitled to legally commit themselves to each other. Love and commitment are rare enough; it seems absurd to thwart them in any guise.

Source: Anna Quindlen, "Evans Two Moms" from *Thinking Out Loud: On the Personal, the Political, and Public and the Private.* Copyright © 1993 by Anna Quindlen. Reprinted with the permission of Random House, Inc.

---

[2] **Linchpin** Something that holds the parts of a structure together.

[3] **Secular** Not sacred or religious.

---

[4] **Amorphous** Having no particular shape.

[QUESTIONS FOR REFLECTION]

Considering Ideas

1. Why does Quindlen believe that not allowing gay and lesbian couples to marry is unjust? Do you agree or disagree with her claim? Why?

2. What rights are afforded to married couples that are not given to gay and lesbian couples? Give several examples from the essay.

3. How would Quindlen define marriage? Do you agree or disagree with her definition? Why?

Considering Writing Strategies

1. Why does Quindlen begin her argument with an anecdote about Evan? What effect does this have on the reader?

2. What specific techniques does the writer use to support her argument? How effective are these methods?

3. Quindlen compares previous laws about interracial marriages with current laws about gay marriages. Why does she make this comparison? How effective is it?

Writing Suggestions

1. Write a persuasive essay that defines a happy marriage as you see it. You might include examples of couples you know to support your definition. What qualities need to exist for a marriage to be successful?

2. Do you feel that gay and lesbian partners should be allowed to marry? Write an essay arguing for or against same-sex marriages.

[preview] **HENRY ROLLINS**, who was born in Washington, D.C., is a singer, songwriter, actor, comedian, and novelist. He was the lead singer for the punk band Black Flag before starting his own group, called Rollins Band. In 1994 he won a Grammy for Best Spoken Word Album, *Get in the Van*. He has hosted his own television and radio talk shows and appeared on numerous television shows, including *The Tonight Show with Jay Leno* and *Saturday Night Live*. He has been in dozens of films, such as *Johnny Mnemonic* (1995), *The Alibi* (2006), and *Sounds Like a Revolution* (2010). Rollins has authored a variety of books, including the *Black Coffee Blues* trilogy, which is based on his travel journals. To learn more about Henry Rollins, check out his Web site at **henryrollins.com** or watch him on **youtube.com**. In the lyrics that follow, Rollins addresses an unfair stereotype about men. Before reading, think about a romantic relationship you have had. Have you ever expected your partner to make a mistake because someone you dated before him or her did something wrong?

Wrong Man **by Henry Rollins**

You say we're all the same
You don't even know my name
Sometime somewhere some man hurt you
I'm one of them so I get stuck with the blame
You think you know about me
You don't know a damn thing about me
I'm not all men, just one man, I'm not all men
There's one subject that everyone enjoys
I heard the boys talk to the boys
I heard the girls talk to the girls
It's all the same noise, neither one's worse
I didn't always tell the truth
But then again, neither did you
I'm not all men
I'm just one man
I'm not that man
I'm not all men
Get away and leave me well alone
Take your damage and take it back on home
I'm not the blame for your misery
Take your threats away from me
Take that damage and leave me all alone
I won't try to patronize you

And tell you that I know exactly what you've been through
You know it just might be
That you have no problem with me
I'm not a rapist in waiting
I'm not the one you should be hating
You take your fear and you pull it inside
It builds up and rage starts to rise
You turn it loose and your anger is blind
And you see me as the enemy
That's not the way it ought to be
You generalize and tell me lies
Like all I want's between your thighs
All the things that I put you through
And all the things that I might do
Don't wonder when I run away
When you tell me it's my time to pay
For all the tears and all the pain
For all the terrible things I never did

Source: "Wrong Man" © 1994, Henry Rollins, 2.13.61, Inc., All Rights Reserved.

Considering Ideas

1. Who is the "you" in Rollins' song? How do you know?
2. What are some of the challenges that men and women sometimes face during the dating game?
3. What specific problem does the lyricist address through his song?

Considering Writing Strategies

1. Discuss the title of the song. What is Rollins' main point? Do you agree or disagree with his perspective? Why?
2. What is the tone, or mood, of the song? Which words indicate that overall feeling?
3. What effect do the rhyming words have on the song?

Writing Suggestions

1. Write a persuasive essay that deals with observations you have made about men or women based on relationships you have had. Be careful to not stereotype men or women in your essay.
2. Choose a television commercial that stereotypes men or women. Write an essay arguing why the portrayal of men or women in the commercial is unfair.

ESOL Tip >

You might choose a commercial from your home country for writing suggestion 2.

STUDENT WRITING

Mursing
by Thomas James "TJ" Pinkerton

Not many people are used to seeing a male nurse or "murse" walk into their room in the hospital due to the fact that there are not many males in the nursing profession. However, nursing is a great profession for men get into, and men can make significant contributions to the nursing field. The physical strength of being a man and the power of male camaraderie are both factors in making nursing a logical career choice for men.

One reason for men to get into the nursing field is the physical requirements of a nursing position. For instance, a nurse might have to move patients who cannot move themselves. One example of this would be if a patient needed to use the restroom but could not find the strength to get out of bed. A male nurse would have the strength to lift most patients off of a bed without needing to call for additional help. Furthermore, during a patient's hospital stay, he or she will often need to be moved from one room to another for testing. In that case a nurse needs to be able to lift the patient out of bed, place him or her into a wheelchair, push the wheelchair to the test site, lift the patient out of the wheelchair, and place him or her on one of the numerous machines used for testing. When the testing is complete, the nurse must repeat this whole process in reverse to return the patient to his or her room. Most men are strong enough to accomplish these tasks on their own, without calling for backup.

Another reason why men may want to consider getting into the nursing field is the rapport they can build with male patients. Of course many of the patients in a hospital are going to be male, and some of them are going to be more comfortable if the nurse attending to them is male also. Some male patients, especially those from an older generation or from a male-dominated culture, are not used to taking orders or advice from women. If that is the case, it is best to assign the patient a male nurse simply as a way to comfort the patient. Another reason why some male patients may prefer a male nurse is that they may be embarrassed about why they are in the hospital, especially if it is for a male-related problem. While the preference for a male nurse may be discriminatory toward women, the hospital is not the place to fix this type of ailment. Getting the patient healthy enough to return should always be the first goal of the hospital, and the comfort of the patient while in the care of the hospital should be a close second. No matter how silly the reason of the patient's request for a male nurse is, his or her needs should be met.

Overall, many career fields, including nursing, that have traditionally been reserved mainly for women are opening their doors to men. While in the past it may have seemed a little awkward for a man to pursue a career as a nurse, today the need for men in the nursing field is evident. Men can provide beneficial services for the nursing industry such as physical strength and male companionship for male patients.

1. Identify Pinkerton's claim (thesis). Is it stated clearly?

2. According to the author, why do some men prefer a male nurse? Do you agree with this point? Why or why not?

3. Which types of appeals (logical, emotional, or ethical) does TJ use in his essay to support his claim? Are they effective? Why or why not?

4. Is Pinkerton's argument convincing? Why or why not?

5. Do you think men should be a part of the nursing field? Why or why not?

 Activity **The Great Debate**

On your own, in pairs, or in small groups, choose one (or more) of the claims listed below. Make a list of ideas that argue for and against the claim. Determine which side seems to have the best support. If possible, share your list with another classmate or other group and discuss your lists. Where do you agree? Where do you disagree? Avoid getting into a heated debate. The point is to discuss different perspectives rather than draw a conclusion about which side is "right."

- The lottery and other forms of gambling should be illegal in every state.
- Actors and professional athletes are paid too much.
- Beauty pageants are exploitive.

- Cell phones are dangerous.
- We are too dependent on computers.
- Our election process is unfair.
- We should all be concerned about global warming.

A representative from each group may share a few of the highlights with the class. This activity may give you ideas for writing a persuasive essay.

> Persuasion and Marketing

One of the most noticeable forms of persuasion is marketing. Virtually every type of organization—whether it sells a product or provides a service—needs to promote itself to increase revenues. As with other types of persuasion, advertisements need to appeal to the audience using logic, emotions, and/or ethics.

Advertising messages are everywhere:

- "Have your surgery at Healthy Hospital, the number one facility in the region."
- "Ace Accounting Associates will provide you with the most accurate audit or tax return."
- "Come to Crazy Carl's Computers for all of your computer networking needs."
- "Dustin's Divine Delicacies is the most exquisite eatery in the East."
- "Support your local friendly fire department or sheriff's office with a donation."
- "Do your part to reduce the carbon footprint; buy a hybrid car from Gregg's Green Garage."

 Activity **Appeals Used in Advertising**

On your own or in pairs or groups, identify the types of appeals used in the fictitious advertising messages listed above. Now, write six one-sentence ads of your own using a variety of appeals. If possible, have another student or group determine which types of appeals you have used in your ads.

Interpreting an Advertisement

Who is the target audience for the Gap advertisement? How do you know? What ideas does the text suggest in addition to explaining the product being promoted? Is the ad persuasive? Why or why not?

Who is the audience for the Carlsberg advertisement? What effect do the images and text suggest that drinking Carlsberg has on friendships among men and women? Do you agree? Why or why not? Is the ad persuasive? Why or why not?

Who is the specific audience for this advertisement? How do you know? Do you think the target audience would want to purchase beauty products from Mac? Why or why not? Is the ad persuasive? Why or why not?

Who is the audience for the Sketchers advertisement? What comparison does the ad make? According to the ad, what effect does wearing Sketchers shoes have on a woman's life? Is the ad persuasive? Why or why not?

Who is the audience for the Body Shop ad above? What assumptions does Body Shop make about love and relation-ships in general? Are these assumptions accurate? Why or why not? What does the ad suggest about relationships between men and women? Is the ad persuasive? Why or why not?

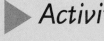 *Activity*   **Writing an Advertisement**

Create an advertisement for a fictitious product on your own, in pairs, or in groups. Include text and images to help convince your audience to purchase your product.

Note: You'll find an extended group project called "Sales Pitch" as well as suggestions for preparing and presenting group presentations in Chapter 15 on pp. 391–393.

Writing about an Image

Write a persuasive essay about one of the images in this chapter. Make a claim about the image itself, or you may choose to write about something that relates to it. For example, you might write an essay about the Carlsberg advertisement, arguing how beer companies glamorize the use of their products. Or you may choose to write about the Body Shop ad and discuss the ways advertisers use sex appeal to market their products.

Media Connection for Persuading

You might watch, read, and/or listen to one or more of the suggested media to discover additional examples of persuasion in the context of relationships. Exploring various media may help you to better understand methods for persuading. For example, you might listen to (or watch the video of) Taylor Swift's song, "Love Story," and write an essay arguing for or against parents telling their children whom they can date. Another option is to watch the 2010 movie *Date Night* and write a persuasive piece about the pros or cons of settling into a long-term relationship.

Television	*Dr. Phil*	*One Tree Hil*	*The Jerry Springer Show*
Film	*The Lottery Ticket* (2010)	*The Blind Side* (2009)	*Date Night* (2010)
Print	*O* (The Oprah Magazine)	*Super Charm*	*Psychology Today*
Internet	**www.createhealthy relationships.com**	**www.forbes.com**	**www.savemymarriage. com**
Music	"Crazy Love " by Michael Bublé	"Love Story" by Taylor Swift	"Daughters" by John Mayer

Write NOW!

USE ONE OF THE FOLLOWING TOPICS to write a persuasive essay. Remember to analyze your rhetorical star as well as the steps for writing a persuasive essay as you compose.

1. Division of labor for household chores, earning an income, and/or raising children
2. Environmental issue, such as going green, recycling, or avoiding pesticides
3. Laws about smoking cigarettes in public places
4. Health care issue, such as benefits, mandatory vaccinations, or alternative medicines
5. Animal testing for research
6. Cell phone usage while driving
7. Helmet laws for bicyclists and/or motorcyclists
8. The legal drinking age
9. Gun control laws
10. The death penalty

10.4 > Analyzing the Rhetorical Star for Writing Persuasively

FIGURE 10.2
The Rhetorical Star

Subject	Choose a debatable topic as the focus for your essay. You should have strong feelings about the issue or controversy. You might want to write about a subject that is currently in the news or one that you have experienced on a personal level. For example, you might write about a law or policy that seems unfair or insufficient. Be sure that your topic is neither too narrow nor too broad for the length of your assignment.
Audience	Who will read your persuasive essay? How much does your audience know about the issue you are addressing? What audience characteristics can you appeal to in your argument? Are you aiming at readers who are personally involved with the issue, or are they just interested in learning more about it? How do your readers feel about the issue? Are they likely to be supportive of your position, hostile toward your stance, or unsure of their own perspective on the issue? Include details that will appeal to your specific audience. For instance, you might write an article for your campus newspaper in an attempt to persuade your readers that more students should take leadership roles in school organizations, such as student government or honorary fraternities, because they will gain leadership skills and strengthen their résumés. In that case your primary audience would be college students.
Purpose	Think about what you are trying to accomplish through your persuasive essay. Are you trying to convince the readers to change their minds about a controversial issue? Do you want the audience to take some sort of action? Maybe you just want the readers to understand your position, even if they have a different stance. Keep your purpose in mind as you carefully craft your argument.

—continued

—continued

Strategy	Even if your primary goal is to persuade your reader, you may also employ other writing strategies. For example, if you are writing an essay persuading the readers that depression should be taken more seriously, then you might define what depression is, describe the symptoms that occur, give a brief narrative or anecdote of someone who suffers from it, and then argue why people need to pay more attention to it and suggest where to go for help.
Design	How many points do you need to make about your subject to fully support your argument? Also, what other design details, such as a photographs or charts, might enhance your persuasive document? Do you want to include headings to help your reader clearly identify your main points? Will including a list of bulleted examples add credibility to your claim? Design your document to be as persuasive as possible.

10.5 > Applying the Writing Process for Persuading

1. **Discovering:** The readings, images, and other media suggestions in this chapter may help you find a subject about which you have a strong opinion. Look through the chapter and see what comes to mind. List debatable subjects you would like to explore further. Additionally, keep your ears open for hot topics at school or work; you may hear a conversation that sparks your interest. You might also read through an online newspaper or magazine to find a controversial issue. Remember to keep track of any sources you use in case you need to cite them in your paper. Once you have decided on a topic, make a list of ideas that support your argument as well as a list of ideas from the opposing point of view.

2. **Planning:** As you plan your draft, list the main points you would like to use to support your persuasive essay. Number your supporting points from most to least persuasive. Then reorder the ideas by putting the second most important supporting point first and the most persuasive supporting point last. This will help your paper be more convincing to the reader. Then create a cluster, an outline (informal or formal), or a graphic organizer (such as the one on the next page), to help you visualize the order of your ideas.

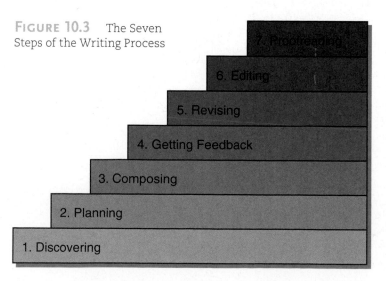

FIGURE 10.3 The Seven Steps of the Writing Process

3. **Composing:** Write a first draft of your persuasive essay. Don't worry too much about grammar and punctuation at this time. Be sure to use the steps outlined on pp. 223–228:

   1. Introduce the subject you are debating.

   2. State a claim about your subject. (This is your thesis).

   3. Support your claim with evidence that appeals to your audience.

4. Use supporting evidence ethically and logically.

5. Organize supporting evidence effectively.

6. End with a logical conclusion.

4. **Getting feedback:** Have at least one classmate or other person read your rough draft and answer the peer review questions that follow. If you have access to a writing tutor or center, get another opinion about your paper as well.

5. **Revising:** Using all of the feedback available to you, revise your persuasive essay. Make sure that your main point is the strongest support for your claim or thesis. Add, delete, and rearrange ideas as necessary.

6. **Editing:** Read your persuasive essay again, this time looking for errors in grammar, punctuation, and mechanics. Make sure you use enough transitions to help your reader follow the logic you present as you work to persuade your audience.

7. **Proofreading:** After you have carefully edited your essay, read it one last time and look for typographical errors and any other issues that might interfere with the readers' understanding of your essay.

FIGURE 10.4 Sample Graphic Organizer

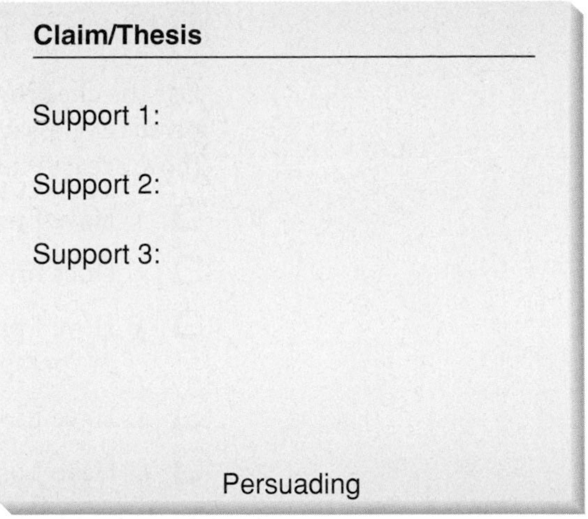

Claim/Thesis

Support 1:

Support 2:

Support 3:

Persuading

>> Peer Review Questions for Persuading

Trade rough drafts with a classmate and answer the following questions about his or her paper. Then, in person or online, discuss your papers and suggestions with your peer. Finally, make the changes you feel would most benefit your paper.

1. Has the author introduced the issue clearly and effectively? What is the issue?

2. Is the author's claim (thesis) clear? What is the author's overall opinion?

3. Identify examples of ethical, emotional, and/or logical appeals that the author has used. Which appeals are most effective? Which appeals could be more effective?

4. Is the supporting evidence presented ethically and logically? Why or why not?

5. Is the essay organized deductively or inductively? Is this organizational pattern clear and effective? Why or why not?

6. What part of the essay is most memorable? Why?

7. Is the conclusion effective? Why or why not?

8. What kinds of grammatical errors, if any, are evident in the essay?

9. What final suggestions do you have for the author?

> Writer's Checklist for Persuading

Use the checklist below to evaluate your own writing and help ensure that your persuasive essay is effective. If you have any "no" answers, go back and work on those areas if necessary.

❑ 1. Have I introduced the issue clearly and effectively?

❑ 2. Does my claim (thesis) clearly state my opinion about the issue?

❑ 3. Have I provided ample supporting evidence to persuade the reader that my perspective is valid?

❑ 4. Have I used my supporting evidence ethically and logically?

❑ 5. Have I organized my supporting evidence effectively?

❑ 6. Is my conclusion sufficient?

❑ 7. Have I proofread thoroughly?

[CHAPTER SUMMARY]

1. Use the persuasive writing strategy to prove a point.

2. Persuasive writing is an important part of your education, daily life, and career.

3. Carefully analyze the rhetorical star before writing a persuasive essay: subject, audience, purpose, strategy, and design.

4. Interpreting persuasive readings and images can help you to prepare to write a persuasive essay.

5. Follow these steps when writing an effective persuasive essay: introduce the subject; state a claim; give supporting evidence; include ethical, emotional, and/or logical appeals; use supporting evidence ethically and logically; organize supporting evidence effectively; end with a logical conclusion.

[WHAT I KNOW NOW]

Use this checklist to determine what you need to work on in order to feel comfortable with your understanding of the material in this chapter. Check off each item as you master it. Review the material for any unchecked items.

❑ 1. I know what **persuasive writing** is.

❑ 2. I can identify several **real-world applications** for persuasive writing.

❑ 3. I can **evaluate** persuasive readings and images.

❑ 4. I can analyze the **rhetorical star** for persuasive writing.

❑ 5. I understand the **writing process** for persuasive writing.

❑ 6. I can apply the **six steps** for persuasive writing.

EVALUATING:
FILM AND THE ARTS

LEARNING outcomes

> In this chapter you will learn techniques for the following:

11.1 Identifying real-world applications for evaluating.

11.2 Understanding the steps for writing an evaluation.

11.3 Interpreting images and evaluating readings about film and the arts.

11.4 Analyzing the rhetorical star for evaluating.

11.5 Applying the steps for writing an evaluative essay.

> Writing Strategy Focus: Evaluating

When you evaluate a subject, you make an overall judgment about it. An effective evaluation needs to be based on several specific criteria. To make an evaluation convincing, you need to support it with specific details and examples. You probably make informal evaluations quite often. For example, if you turn on the television and catch the beginning of a new situation comedy, you'll probably decide within a few minutes whether you like the show or not. Your evaluative criteria might include the premise of the story line, the quality of the acting, and the use of humor. In this chapter, you'll learn how to structure formal written evaluations that are useful at school, in your daily life, and in your career.

11.1 > Real-World Applications for Evaluating

Evaluative Writing for School

You'll often be asked to evaluate subjects in your college courses. If you work in collaborative groups, you may be asked to evaluate the experience or your teammates. You might need to evaluate two different programs of study to determine which one will provide you with the most satisfying career in the long run. In a course in your major, you may need to evaluate a method or procedure for accuracy or effectiveness. Near the end of the term you will likely evaluate the course, your textbook, and your instructor.

Evaluative Writing in Your Daily Life

You evaluate various subjects on a daily basis. If you eat at a restaurant, you are likely to evaluate the meal, service, and overall dining experience. When you see a movie you probably judge whether it was worth your time and money or if you were satisfied with the characters, plot, or ending. As a consumer you make judgments every time you purchase something. Was it worth the price? Did you receive the service or product that you were promised? In elections, you evaluate each candidate and decide who you feel will do the best job in the position.

Evaluative Writing in Your Career

Having strong evaluation skills is extremely useful in the workplace. You may need to write a self-evaluation to get a raise or a promotion. When you are offered several positions, you will need to evaluate which one is the best fit for your needs. Once you are on the job, you will likely need to use your evaluation skills regularly. Which vendor can provide you with the best products and services? What plan will have the most positive results? What is the most efficient and cost-effective way for you to reach your goals?

Health care: evaluations of patients, equipment, and procedures.

Occupational therapy: evaluations of a patient's mobility, life skills, and needs.

Law: evaluations of cases, clients, crime scenes, and who is at fault in an accident.

Education: evaluations of students, faculty, classrooms, lessons, and programs.

Computers: evaluations of hardware, software, personnel, and procedures.

Culinary arts: evaluations of cooking techniques, meals, and ingredients.

Business: evaluations of business plans, facilities, employees, products, and services.

Graduate SPOTLIGHT

Tawana Campbell, Occupational Therapy Assistant

Tawana Campbell earned a degree in occupational therapy assisting in 2008. She currently works as an occupational therapy assistant for a pediatric outpatient facility. Here's what Tawana has to say about the importance of writing in her career:

❝I take careful notes about each session I have with a patient and write a case study. I document everything that happens because the philosophy where I work is, 'If it isn't written down, it didn't happen.' When I meet with a patient, I write out an evaluation of his or her condition and needs, and I determine ways to get effective treatment. Written proof of my evaluation is necessary to persuade the insurance company that special adaptive equipment, such as a wheelchair, splint, or orthotic insert, is necessary.

Because I work with children, I have to be very creative with how I go about treatment. For example, one child had a deficiency in communication skills, so I showed him a movie and asked him to retell the plot. Another child was having problems with sensorimotor skills, so I taught her to dance using her favorite songs from *High School Musical*. Also, I frequently use arts and crafts with children because something as simple as gluing a bead on a piece of construction paper is a useful task. These techniques work great for helping me to establish a good rapport with the children and evaluate their progress. They think we are just playing, but they are really working to overcome the challenges that they face. **❞**

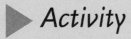

Activity Real-World Evaluative Writing

In pairs or small groups, brainstorm uses for writing evaluations at school, in your daily life, and on the job. You may want to choose the prospective career field(s) of the participants in your group. Each group may share its results with the class.

11.2 > Steps for Writing an Evaluative Essay

1. Describe the Subject You Are Evaluating

You'll need to provide your readers with enough information to understand your subject. For example, if you are evaluating a movie, you might want to explain the premise of the film. That might include what type of film it is (documentary, comedy, action adventure, and so on) as well as where and when the events take place. You may also decide to briefly introduce the main characters and actors. Be careful to avoid merely summarizing the plot of the movie. In fact, if you do that, then your readers won't want to see the movie you are evaluating. If you are evaluating a piece of artwork, you will probably want to include a picture of the work along with your review. Include just enough details for your readers to be able to grasp your meaning.

2. Make a Claim about the Subject You Are Evaluating

Your thesis should state your overall opinion of the subject you are evaluating. Is the movie a great piece of cinema or a ridiculous waste of time? Does the painting leave you awed and inspired or completely unmoved? Keep in mind that an evaluation must do more than simply express your overall like or dislike for your subject. You'll need to be able to back up your claim in the body of your essay. Your reader should have a strong sense of your attitude toward the subject right from the beginning of your essay.

3. Choose Several Criteria for Your Evaluation

For your evaluation to seem valid to your readers, you'll need to base your overall opinion on several specific criteria. If you are evaluating a movie, you might consider ideas that fit with the type of movie you are reviewing. For example, for an action adventure, you might consider the special effects, sound track, and intensity level. If you're evaluating a play, you might judge the actors, costumes, dialogue, and stage props.

4. Make a Judgment about Each Criterion

The majority of your essay should focus on your evaluative criteria, and your topic sentences should each make a claim about one criterion. For example, if you are evaluating a documentary, one of your topic sentences might go like this: Another reason the Imax film *Deep Sea 3D* (2006) is worth seeing is that the narrators, Johnny Depp and Kate Winslet, add insightful comments to the film in a captivating way.

5. Support Your Judgments with Specific Evidence

Once you've determined the opinion you will state about each criterion, you'll need to support your judgments with specific details. These details should help you back up the overall claim in your introduction as well. For example, if you are recommending *Dark Knight* to your readers, then your support material will come from the movie. If one of your judgments is that the acting is superbly chilling, you might support it with specific details about what Christian Bale (Bruce Wayne/Batman), Heath Ledger (the Joker), and Morgan Freeman (Lucius Fox) do to produce chilling results for the audience.

Grammar Window
PRESENT TENSE VERBS

Use present tense verbs when writing about a creative work, even if the author, musician, filmmaker, or artist who created it is deceased. The work lives on even if the creator does not.

Incorrect past tense verbs: Through his song "Imagine," John Lennon *inspired* his fans to envision a peaceful world where everyone *shared*.

Corrected present tense verbs: Through his song "Imagine," John Lennon *inspires* his fans to envision a peaceful world where everyone *shares*.

Discussion: Lennon's song still inspires his fans, even though he was assassinated in 1980. Therefore, present tense verbs are more appropriate than past tense verbs.

Activity: Revise the following sentences, changing the past tense verbs to present tense verbs.

1. Michael Jackson's video *Thriller* was the most popular video of all time.

2. *ET*, *Jaws*, and *Indiana Jones* were all Steven Spielberg movies with corresponding amusement park attractions in Orlando, Florida.

3. Viewers could look at "The Thinker," a famous statue by Rodin, for hours, wondering what was going on in his mind.

4. William Faulkner's novel *As I Lay Dying* was much more humorous than the title implied.

5. The 2008 movie version of the musical *Mamma Mia!* was absolutely hilarious.

6. Be Fair with Your Judgments

You want your evaluation to seem reasonable to your audience. For example, if you dislike a television show that you are reviewing, you might acknowledge that it has one redeeming quality. For example, if your overall claim about the television show "My Big Fat Redneck Wedding" is that it is condescending to the viewers, you might show that you are open-minded by mentioning that there are some funny lines in the show. However, you don't want to provide your reader with a completely balanced view of your subject. If you merely tell what you liked and didn't like about the subject, then your reader might be confused about your overall opinion. The majority of your comments need to support the opinion in your thesis.

7. End with a Final Claim about Your Subject

In addition to restating your thesis and summarizing your main points, you might also make a broader judgment that wasn't stated in the thesis. For example, you might end your movie review with a star rating or other general comment so your readers will know for sure how you feel about the movie. For instance, if you give the movie four and a half out of five stars, then your readers will know for sure how strong your recommendation is.

[preview] **PERFORMANCE EVALUATIONS** are common in the workplace. Employers often use employee evaluations to determine raises and promotions. Your employer may ask you to complete a self-evaluation in addition to the one your supervisor completes. Furthermore, as you advance in your career, you may need to evaluate employees you supervise. When writing an employee evaluation, be sure to include specific details to support the judgments you make. Also, be objective and accurate when writing an evaluation.

Sample Employee Evaluation Form

Name: John Smith
Date of Hire: January 5, 2009
Supervisor: Jill Johnson

Dept. Customer Service
Date of Review: September 1, 2010
Date of Last Review April 6, 2009

Rating System

1 = Unsatisfactory
3 = Satisfactory
5 = Significantly Exceeds Expectations

2 = Needs Improvement
4 = Exceeds Expectations

---

1. Quality of employee's work   4

Comments John does very good work for the company. His attention to detail and ability to provide quality support for his projects and coworkers meet expectations.

2. Exercise of good judgment   5

Comments John has shown exceptional judgment, particularly in regards to prioritizing key accounts and customers.

3. Attendance   3

Comments While John has not missed an excessive number of days, his absences and shorter days are higher than we would normally like to see. John needs to plan ahead a bit better so that his absences can be anticipated and kept to a minimum.

4. Employee involvement/participation in team effort   5

Comments John is an exceptional team player. He strives to work collaboratively with coworkers and his projects often utilize input from multiple departments. He spearheade an initiative to better utilize company-wide resources.

5. Attention to company policies and procedures   4

Comments John always maintains strict adherence to company guidelines and is quick to verify any new idea or procedure. He does occasionally require a reminder when procedures change, but is quick to learn new workflows.

6. Interpersonal relationships and communication with co-workers   5

Comments One of John's key strengths is his ability to work well with others. He is a natural leader and communicates with others clearly.

7. Taking initiative to achieve goals and complete assignments   4

Comments John has good ideas and innovations, but they tend to be at the direction of others. Some of his biggest successes were the implementation of others' ideas. I would like to see John suggest more projects. I know from meetings that he has excellent vision, but is often hesitant to share it with others.

8. Responsiveness to changing work requirement   4

Comments There were two instances this year in which John used outdated forms and, in one case, an outdated workflow. He was quick to rectify the situation, but he should pay closer attention to interoffice memos and trainings.

9. Work ethic   5

   Comments *John has an excellent work ethic. He is attentive to project details and deadlines. His ability to meet or exceed date expectations has helped his projects run successfully.*

10. Overall performance rating   4.3

   Comments *John has expressed an interest in continued career growth within the company and he is on track for promotion and greater responsibility. I encourage him to double-check details and be a bit more consistent in minor areas of performance. Overall, John's performance has exceeded expectations for the year.*

Areas of Strength:

John works very well with others and strives for the best possible outcomes for everything he takes on. His professionalism and willingness to work towards innovation are excellent. He communicates effectively and collaborates with others.

Areas of Improvement:

I would like to see John take on more responsibility this year. He has natural leadership skills and tends to bring the best out in others. I would encourage him to continue doing this in a more strategic way. By his next review I would like to see him initiate and complete a project on his own.

Employee's Comments:

I think the assessment of my performance is a good reflection of my skills and areas of improvement. During my review I discussed strategies for taking on leadership roles and being a more consistent presence in the overall process. I am committed to my continued communication with all members of my team. I also discussed plans to launch monthly employee information sharing sessions that will help with consistency.

Date: *September 1, 2010*

_____

Employee's Signature

[QUESTIONS FOR REFLECTION]

1. What are John's strengths?

2. What are his weaknesses?

3. Which comments need more explanation? What is missing?

4. Based on this evaluation, would you give John a raise? Why or why not?

5. Using this same form, how would you rate yourself as an employee? How would you rate your boss?

11.3 > Evaluating in the Context of Film and the Arts

What would the world be like without film and the arts? Today we have easy access to more types of fine arts than ever before. Through film, television, the Internet, and other media, we can watch a Broadway play, visit the Louvre museum in Paris, take in a hip-hop concert, or listen to an author read her own poetry aloud without ever leaving the comfort of our own homes. We can use the arts to explore ourselves and our beliefs, learn about the world and other cultures, and escape from reality. With so many options available, how do we decide what is worth our precious time? How do we evaluate the arts when personal preference plays a big part in our perceptions of artistic expressions?

We have to base our judgments on clear criteria and specific supporting evidence. The skills you use to evaluate film and the arts will translate to a variety of other areas in your life. Read and discuss one or more of the following evaluations. Doing so will help you to write your own evaluations.

>> READINGS AND REFLECTION

[preview] **LINDA PASTAN** is an award-winning poet who was born in the Bronx, New York, and now resides in Potomac, Maryland. She was the poet laureate of Maryland from 1991 to 1995. Ten volumes of her poetry have been published, including *Queen of a Rainy Country: Poems* in 2006. Pastan, who is an avid sports fan, is among approximately 15 poets, including Langston Hughes, Emily Dickinson, and William Carlos Williams, who have their own baseball cards. To read more of Linda Pastan's poetry, visit **www.american-poems.com/poets/linda-pastan**. In the following poem, Pastan suggests how her family members might evaluate her. Before reading, consider your own family members or friends. What kinds of grades might they give you? How would you rate them?

Marks by Linda Pastan

My husband gives me an A
for last night's supper,
an incomplete for my ironing,
a B plus in bed.
My son says I am average,
an average mother, but if
I put my mind to it
I could improve.

My daughter believes
in Pass/Fail and tells me
I pass. Wait 'til they learn
I'm dropping out.

Source: Linda Pastan, "Marks," from *The Five Stages of Grief* by Linda Pastan. Copyright © 1978 by Linda Pastan. Used by permission of W. W. Norton & Company, Inc.

[QUESTIONS FOR REFLECTION]

Considering Ideas

1. How does the speaker in the poem feel about being evaluated by her family members? Do you ever feel as if your family members or friends are evaluating you? What is your reaction to their comments?

2. What point is Pastan trying to make through her poem?

3. Do you think she is really planning to drop out? Why or why not?

Considering Writing Strategies

1. What is the tone of Pastan's poem? How does she achieve that tone?

2. Why do you think Pastan uses a school analogy to describe her relationship with her family? How effective is her approach?

3. Why do you think the author does not include any rhythm or rhyme in her poem? What effect does this strategy have on the reader?

Writing Suggestions

1. Take a look at yourself as a friend, family member, co-worker, or boss might perceive you. Write an essay evaluating yourself based on the qualities that person would find important.

2. Think about some of your better qualities. Are you hardworking? Do you have specific skills that an employer would desire? Write an evaluation of yourself that emphasizes some of your positive characteristics. You might use these ideas later for a scholarship application or résumé.

[preview] **SIMON BENLOW** is clearly a fan of *The Simpsons*. However, in the following review, Benlow accomplishes more than merely suggesting what he likes about the cartoon. He also comments on what *The Simpsons* reveals about American entertainment and society as a whole. Visit **www. thesimpsons.com** to view full episodes and to learn more about the characters, show information, and specific episodes. You can also check out the star rating for each episode and participate in a variety of interactive activities and discussions. Before reading the following essay, think about cartoons you have watched or read over the years. Do they just provide entertainment, or is there some truth to them? What do they say about society?

Revealing the Ugly Cartoonish Truth: *The Simpsons* by Simon Benlow

It's not often that a television sitcom does more than tickle our most simplistic pleasures. The vast majority of sitcoms, past and present, fill twenty-two minutes (or is it nineteen?) with cliché moralism, empty characters, and adolescent dialog. Every fall we can look forward to a new parade of bad jokes and simpleton plots—created primarily to allow American viewers to gawk at the latest celebrity hairstyles and tight shirts.

However, amidst and exhausting list of here-and-then-gone "real-life" sitcoms, *The Simpsons* has managed to create a new class of television. It has stretched what can (and should) be expected in prime-time entertainment. It goes where most sitcoms, most American entertainment, will not. It satirizes everything (and nearly anything) mainstream America cherishes. From SUVs to friendly fast-food chains, the familiar elements of everyday life are revealed as ridiculous creations of a culture blind to its own vices. Certainly, it takes shots at big targets: nuclear power, organized labor, corporate fraud, slick politicians, organized religion, hyper-consumerism, hyper-consumption, and even television programming (often slamming its own network, FOX). But these are more than easy targets; these are the entities that seem to run amuck consistently, the institutions that maintain their status despite repeated failings, the bullies of our culture that always seem in need of a punch to their maniacal eye sockets.

In "Homer's Odyssey," an episode from the first season, the show does its usual deconstruction of everyday life. The episode reveals some ugly truth: Beneath the daily façade, there lurks an entire set of systems barely working, hardly accomplishing anything beyond their own survival. In the first scene, in front of Springfield Elementary, the children wait for the tardy, pot-smoking bus driver, Otto (who loves to "get blotto"). Once they get settled, they drive in circles through town. They pass by the toxic waste dump where happy workers casually pour mysterious fluid into the river; they pass the prison where they are greeted by hosts of prisoners (who were set free during the children's last field trip). They pass the Springfield tire yard (which becomes the Springfield tire fire in later episodes), and finally arrive at the nuclear power plant. At the gate, several signs announce "employees only," but the guard is sucking on a beverage and watching Krusty the Clown on television, so the children pass through unnoticed.

In the power plant, we see the gross fumblings and even grosser cover-ups of an unchecked system. While Joe Fission, a cartoon icon, feeds the children pro-nuclear propaganda, Homer flummoxes his job and wreaks havoc in the plant. Homer is the poster boy of incompetence—yet he's granted a typical place in the ill-defined bureaucracy of power: Is he the "supervising technician" or the "technical supervisor"? No one knows. Through the episode, Homer is fired and then, for no good reason, hired back. The status quo prevails; three-eyed fish swim happily in the lake and the town continues to live on the brink of nuclear disaster.

In the animated town of Springfield, nothing is worthy of the praise it wants. Schools are not great institutions of learning; they are poorly funded bureaucracies run by flawed and desperate individuals. Government is not "of the people"; it is a mob of self-perpetuating boozers and womanizers. Business is not ethical or productive; it is a race to monopolize and swindle everyone in sight. These are the hard truths that *The Simpsons* offers us. Of course, we get these truths thrown at us in sanctimonious movies and bad morning talk shows, but *The Simpsons* manages to reveal these ideas without romanticizing its own characters or actors.

The Simpsons throws at us what we all might be thinking had we not been programmed to dismiss it. We all might briefly consider the lies the nuclear power industry feeds us, the laziness and self-righteousness of city governments, or the emptiness and humiliation of most jobs, but we've been trained out of being appalled. We've become distracted by our own lives, and the constant barrage of material goodness, so we allow our own institutions to bully us, to humiliate us, to dismiss our general welfare entirely. But *The Simpsons* reminds us of the slipshod work and flagrant thievery going on just outside our own television sets.

Some may argue that *The Simpsons* is just a show; it can't possibly have that much meaning. However, one thing we've learned in America is that our entertainment has more significance than history, literature, philosophy, and politics. Mainstream society gets its values, its slogans, its hairstyles, even its dialects from entertainment. We are, as the world knows, an over-entertained nation.

The average American citizen reads very little (maybe a few books per year), but fills thousands of hours being massaged by the television. As the last thirty years proves undoubtedly, Americans can change their minds at the drop of a hat (about almost anything) if the television set prompts us to do so. When television maintains such influence, it is significant and meaningful when the television itself plays with, pokes at, and parodies that influence.

In a swirling array of giddy and capricious entertainment, *The Simpsons* is far more real than any "real-life" sitcom hopes to be (or wants to be). In its relentless pursuit to overturn our romantic notions of ourselves and our lovely creations, it is probably more real than the audience it attracts (and certainly more real than those whom it doesn't). In fact, if we take the show as seriously as it deserves, we might even see the broad strokes of its irony: that *we* are the cartoons, drawn and colored by the ridiculous institutions that constitute our society. However, as soon as we go that far, Homer belches, Bart moons a head of state, and Grandpa soils himself; *The Simpsons* won't allow anything, including itself, to be taken too seriously.

Source: Simon Benlow, "Revealing the Ugly Cartoonish Truth: *The Simpsons*" from J. Mauk and J. Metz, *The Composition of Everyday Life: A Guide to Writing* (Boston: Thomson Wadsworth, 2004), pp. 376–77.

[QUESTIONS FOR REFLECTION]

Considering Ideas

1. What does Benlow suggest by the title of the essay? What is the "truth" about *The Simpsons* as he sees it? Do you agree or disagree with his notion?

2. *The Simpsons* pokes fun at a lot of things that are wrong with Springfield. Think about the community where you grew up. How similar or dissimilar was your hometown to Springfield? Based on the examples in the essay, what situations seem to be exaggerated on the show?

3. Benlow's asserts that "*we* are the cartoons, drawn and colored by the ridiculous institutions that constitute our society." What does he mean by this claim? Do you agree or disagree with him? Why?

Considering Writing Strategies

1. What does Benlow accomplish with the introductory paragraph? Why does he delay his thesis until the second paragraph? What effect does this strategy have on the readers?

2. Which supporting details from the essay stand out most? How do those details help to support his main idea?

3. Benlow combines the evaluation and argument strategies in his essay. Why does he use both approaches? How effective is this combination?

Writing Suggestions

1. Watch an episode of *The Simpsons* or another animated situation comedy. Write an essay evaluating the show. Be sure to base your evaluation on several specific criteria and to support your ideas with specific examples from the show. You might argue a point about the significance of the show (or lack thereof) in your review.

2. Watch a full-length animated movie. Write an essay evaluating the movie. You might consider some of the following questions: What is the point (theme) of the movie? Is it merely a form of entertainment, or does it reveal something more serious about society? Is the film strictly for children, or does it reach adults on another level? Be sure to back up your judgments with specific details and examples from the film.

[preview] CRAIG OUTHIER is a movie critic who writes reviews for the *Orange County Register* and the *East Valley Tribune*. The essay that follows was originally published in *Get Out*, an entertainment guide in Arizona's *East Valley Tribune*. In this movie review, Outhier reviews *Harry Potter and the Prisoner of Azkaban* based on J. K. Rowling's book of the same title. To see reviews of movies, music, and arts by Outhier and other critics, go to **www.getoutaz. com**. You may also want to check out **www.jkrowling.com** to learn more about the books and characters. Before reading, consider the qualities that make a good movie. What elements are required for a movie to earn a high rating for you?

Potter Power **by Craig Outhier**

In addition to his new Adam's apple, pubescent boy wizard Harry Potter (Daniel Radcliffe) comes equipped with a veritable arsenal of supernatural goodies in *Harry Potter and the Prisoner of Azkaban*, including time travel, omniscient maps, and a majestic horse-bird hybrid that he rides like Funny Cide[1] over the cloud tops.

Unfortunately, Harry's most pressing need goes unmet—specifically, a good family-practice attorney.

As always, this Harry Potter installment—the third in a series based on J. K. Rowling's phenomenally successful children's books—is built around Harry's quest for the truth regarding his dead parents, murdered many years ago by the sinister Lord Voldemort. Just as predictably, Harry is stymied by a tight-lipped adult faculty that inexplicably refuses to surrender its secrets.

Ultimately, this familiar cycle of conceal and reveal grows tiresome. Two hours in, you wish Harry would hire Alan Dershowitz,[2] cite the Freedom of Information Act, and take those cage stiffs at Hogwarts to court. Anything to give this floundering series a little buoyancy.

Granted, there's more psychological texture here than in previous "Potter" offerings, due chiefly to the fact that it was directed by Alfonso Cuaron, who also helmed (sarcasm alert!) that other acclaimed kids' movie, *Y Tu Mamá También*.

Assuming command of the franchise from the competent but monotonic Chris Columbus,[3] Cuaron brings with him a moodier, more baroque visual palette to com-

plement the story's portentous themes. It's like the difference between Mother Goose and Brothers Grimm. Trained and educated in Mexico, Cuaron is a filmmaker who revels in details, one who can harness the sensuous energy from the image of say, a shriveled sunflower and use it to perfume the next scene.

To be sure, something rotten is afoot at Hogwarts, the school for neophyte wizards and witches where Harry—along with pals Ron (Rupert Grint) and Hermione (Emma Watson)—is entering his third year. Now permanently cut off from his abusive, non-magical relatives (in retaliation for an insult against his parents, he turns his uncle's insufferable sister into a human balloon), Harry finds himself facing a more terrifying menace: Sirius Black, the dangerous fugitive wizard who betrayed his parents and orchestrated their death. Played by "Sid and Nancy" nutcase Gary Oldman—who is far too under-used in this movie—Black has escaped from prison and is at large, purportedly hell-bent on killing Harry, too.

Per tradition, Harry is forced to don his invisibility cloak and skulk around to wrest bits of information away from his secretive guardians, but does find an ally in Professor Lupin (David Thewlis from "The Island of Dr. Moreau"), his Defense Against the Dark Arts teacher. Once close to Harry's parents, Lupin confides in Harry his fondness for the deceased Potters and admits that Harry's father was a bit of a rakehell in his youth.

According to fans in the know, this genealogical detail comes to bloom in later "Potter" volumes; explaining, for instance, why Professor Snape (Alan Rickman) harbors such a blistering hatred of young Harry.

---

[1] Winner of the Kentucky Derby and the Preakness Stakes in 2003.
[2] American lawyer and jurist (b.1938).
[3] Director of *Harry Potter and the Sorcerer's Stone* (2001) and *Harry Potter and the Chamber of Secrets* (2002).

However, in the here and now, more questions are posed than answered, including the central mystery of why Harry's parents were murdered in the first place. In the first two movies, the vagaries were tolerable. Now, in the third installment, typically the termination point for most sagas, they have officially been downgraded to tedious.

Of course, the elusiveness of the "Potter" stories is by design—Rowling clearly designed Hogwarts to reflect the adult world through a child's eyes; nurturing yet threatening, scholarly yet enigmatic, rife with horrible, wonderful secrets and half-understood rules. Even Dumbledore, the kindly headmaster played by Michael Gambon (*Gosford Park*), stepping in for the late Richard Harris, seems only conveniently interested in Harry's well-being. Harry's new teacher, the tea leaf–reading Professor Trelawney (Emma Thompson), is a near-sighted gypsy who fills his head with paranoid thoughts of death and doom.

All of which is fine for the rank-and-file "Harry" faithful, who are invested enough in the characters—i.e., "Will Ron ever hook up with Hermione?"—that they can tolerate the ineffectual, snails-clip plot resolution.

The rest of us must find our delights in the movie's bodacious special effects (more seamless than before, including the Quidditch scene), lush production design and generous imagination. It appears that as long as Harry is given neat, audience-pleasing things to ride, eat and incant, he'll stay out of court.

Source: Craig Outhier, "Potter Power," *Get Out Magazine*, June 3, 2004. Reprinted by permission.

[QUESTIONS FOR REFLECTION]

Considering Ideas

1. What is Outhier's overall opinion of *Harry Potter and the Prisoner of Azkaban*? If you have seen the movie, do you agree or disagree with his position? Why?

2. What evaluative criteria does the author use in his review? Does he fully support the judgments he makes? Explain your answer with examples from the essay.

3. Outhier notes that this particular Harry Potter movie asks more questions than it answers. Was the film designed to do that intentionally? Why would the producers use that approach?

Considering Writing Strategies

1. As part of his evaluation of *Harry Potter and the Prisoner of Azkaban*, Outhier compares this movie to the earlier Harry Potter movies. Why does he use this technique? It is it effective? Why or why not?

2. Typically, the purpose of writing a movie review is to steer the audience toward, or away from, a specific movie. Was the author trying to accomplish that task? Why or why not?

3. Even though Outhier identifies positive and negative aspects of the film in the body of the essay, he only focuses on good qualities about the film in the concluding paragraph. Why does he stray from the traditional approach to concluding an essay by restating the thesis and summarizing the main points? What final impression of the movie does this leave for the reader to ponder?

Writing Suggestions

1. Write a review of one of the Harry Potter movies, such as *Harry Potter and the Deathly Hallows: Part I*. Select several criteria for your evaluation, such as the characters, acting, setting, musical score, special effects, and dialogue. Use specific details and examples from the movie to support the judgments you make about each criterion.

2. For a longer project, read one of the Harry Potter books and write an evaluative essay comparing it to the movie based on the book. You might consider some of the following questions as you write your essay: Which medium is more captivating for the audience? Which version is more satisfying? Would you recommend either one to your readers? Why or why not?

ESOL Tip >

As an alternative writing suggestion, write a review of a movie or book that is famous in your native country. Be sure to translate the title in English for your instructor.

[preview] **VINCENT POMARÈDE** is a curator in the paintings department of the Louvre in Paris. He has co-authored several books about famous artists and works, including *1001 Paintings of the Louvre* and *Andre Giroux: A Master of French Nineteenth-century Landscape*. In the following essay, Pomarède provides the reader with some useful biographical details about the artist, Leonardo da Vinci, and suggests why the *Mona Lisa* is such a successful painting. You can go to **www.louvre.fr/llv/commun/home.jsp?bmlocale=en** to virtually visit the Louvre Museum. Before reading, think about why the *Mona Lisa* is so famous. What is it about the painting that has fascinated viewers for centuries?

The Faces of the *Mona Lisa* by Vincent Pomarède

What is the mysterious connection that is established over time between a work of art and its public? What are the factors, profound motivations, and secret techniques which can explain that the Winged Victory of Samothrace, the Venus de Milo, or The Angelus of Jean-François Millet have become universal objects of admiration and contemplation, of adoration almost, to the extent that all modern mediums, from end of the year calendars to advertising, have used them and even sometimes excessively so? The study of the unequalled success over three centuries of Leonardo da Vinci's *Mona Lisa* will perhaps enable a better understanding of the numerous and complex motivations which make visitors of a museum only remember a single work from amongst thousands of others. Indeed, the *Mona Lisa* is beyond doubt the best known painting in the world, today completely identified with the Louvre Museum and even with the general notion of art. If we were able to penetrate the origins of its creation, its aesthetic qualities, and its history following the death of its creator, we would perhaps be able to identify some rules explaining a work of art's success.

It is possible to identify four areas of research which are closely connected to the *Mona Lisa's* unequalled success with its public: the marginal, whimsical, and brilliant personality of its creator, Leonardo da Vinci (1452–1519); the perfection of his pictorial technique; the mysteries, which are moreover still unresolved, surrounding the identity of the model who posed for the work; the developments in its history, which are as surprising and numerous as a detective story.

Was Leonardo da Vinci a Painter, Engineer, Inventor, or Philosopher?

Born in 1452 in a small Toscan village called Vinci, which gave him its name, Leonardo da Vinci was the illegitimate son of the village's lawyer and one of his servants, Catarina Vacca. Statements concerning his appearance and personality differ particularly as legend grew up very early on in his biographical accounts. He is sometimes described as a prodigiously strong colossus, capable of bending a horseshoe in his hands, and often as a young adolescent, effeminate and dreamy. He is sometimes presented to us as a man who loved physical exercise and violent sports, sometimes as an adolescent playing the lyre and singing with perfection. His artistic gifts must, however, have already appeared during his childhood, because in 1469, at the age of 17, he had already spent three years in the studio of the Florentine painter and sculptor Andrea Verrocchio (1435–1488). In this famous artist's studio, in the company of other important painters such as Sandro Botticelli or Perugino, he spent 13 years learning the technique of painting and the secrets of the execution of a picture. He also began to study the subjects which were then considered indispensable for an artist: mathematics, perspective, geometry, and all the sciences of observation and study of the natural environment. He also began to study architecture and sculpture.

After completing his training, he began his career as a painter with portraits and religious paintings, receiving commissions from the leading citizens or monasteries of Florence. But, from this period onwards, it is very difficult (and this continues throughout his career) to know with certitude whether he considered himself as a painter, multidisciplinary artist, or engineer. The limits between the professions had not then been fixed as they are today and a man of talent could move with ease from one function to another. Leonardo then came under the protection of the most influential person in Florence, Lorenzo di Medici, named the Magnificent, a politician and exceptionally rich patron of the arts, who brought him many clients and whom, in 1482, sent him to Milan to serve the Duke Sforza. He wrote at the time an astonishing letter to the Duke of Milan, reading like a curriculum vitae, in which he revealed his ambitions as engineer, inventor, and also soldier: "I can build very light bridges, solid, robust, easily transportable, to pursue and sometimes flee from the enemy [...] I also have the means to make bombardments, very practical and easy to transport, which throw stones almost like a storm, terrorizing the enemy with their smoke [...] In peace time, I believe that I am also able to give complete satisfaction to anyone, whether in architecture, the building of public and private buildings, or in conveying water from one place to another."

Later, he placed his engineering talents at the service of the cities of Pisa and Venice, the sovereigns of Mantua, the Este family, and, of course, the King of France, François I, who invited him to come and work in the Loire valley, where the monarch then resided. This unusual quality of being able to tackle any subject with talent (during his lifetime he was to be better known as a hydraulic engineer than as a painter!) astonished all his contemporaries, as did also the insatiable curiosity with which he ceaselessly studied natural phenomena: "Where does urine come from? Where does milk come from? How does food spread through the veins? Where does drunkenness come from? And vomiting? And gravel and stone? [...] Where do tears come from?" he confided to the pages of his notebooks in a continual quest for answers to every imaginable kind of question. His perfect knowledge of anatomy, the effects of light and the most complex chemical combinations obviously guided his career as painter and, from his first masterpieces, the Virgin on the Rocks (Paris, Louvre Museum), begun in 1483, the Last Supper (Milan, Convent of Santa Maria del Gracia), which he painted in 1493, or the Battle of Anghiari (missing) for which he obtained a commission in 1503 after a hard struggle with Michelangelo, he showed to what an extent his scientific and technological knowledge enriched the creation of his paintings.

Even though his technical experimentations in painting were not always successful—the Last Supper and the Battle of Anghiari were ruined by badly mastered pictorial innovations, which attracted him the contempt and jeering of certain professionals—Leonardo da Vinci was famous for the unequalled level of perfection of his portraits and some of his religious paintings, such as Saint Anne, the Virgin and the Infant Jesus (Paris, Louvre Museum).

The Perfect Technique of the *Mona Lisa*

Indeed, the search for perfection is a true obsession with Leonardo da Vinci: "Tell me, tell me, has one ever finished anything?" he groaned in his notebooks, in which he frequently insisted upon his desire to equal the perfection of divine creation in his own artistic creations.

Painted on a thin backing of poplar wood, which is now extremely fragile (this is why it is today preserved behind a glass case) the *Mona Lisa* is an exemplary creation, thanks to the subtle effects of light on flesh and the panache of the landscape in the painting's background. The modeling of the face is astonishingly realistic. Leonardo executed the painting with patience and virtuosity: after preparing the wooden panel with several layers of coating, he first of all drew his motif directly onto the picture, before painting it in oil, adding very weak turpentine, which enabled him to paint on innumerable layers of transparent color, known as glaze, and to endlessly remodel the face. The glaze, skillfully worked, heightens the effects of light and shade on the face, constituting what Leonardo himself called "sfumato." This technique enables the perfect imitation of flesh, due to refined treatment of the human figure plunged into half-obscurity or "chiaroscuro," and enabled Leonardo to satisfy his preoccupation with realism.

During his lifetime, Leonardo was indeed above all famous for his evident talent for imitating nature to perfection and when his first biographer, the painter Vasari, described the *Mona Lisa,* he above all insisted on the work's realism: "Its limpid eyes had the sparkle of life: ringed by reddish and livid hues, they were bordered by lashes whose execution required the greatest delicacy. The eyelashes, in places thicker or more sparse according to the arrangement of the pores, could not be truer. The nose, with its ravishing delicate, pink nostrils, was life itself. [...] In the hollow of the throat, the attentive spectator can catch the beating of the veins." Through "sfumato" Leonardo could attain one of his primary artistic objectives, that of interesting himself mainly in his model's personality: "The good painter has essentially two things to represent: the individual and the state of his mind," said Leonardo. To paint the soul rather than the body was in fact the ultimate aim of his work and the "sfumato," lighting the portrait through "chiaroscuro," accentuated the work's mysteries: "to plunge things into light is to plunge them into the infinite."

It is here important to recall to what extent the question of the model's realism is connected to its identity. To this day, we still do not know whether Leonardo da Vinci faithfully represented an existing model, whether he idealized a portrait of a woman of his circle, or if he entirely imagined a type of universal woman.

The Mystery of the Model's Identity

Every kind of possibility, including the most far-fetched, has been envisaged concerning the model's identity: Isabelle of Este, who reigned at Mantua during Leonardo da Vinci's stay there (we know a drawing by him showing her); a mistress of Giuliano di Medici's or of Leonardo himself; perhaps an ideal woman; and even an adolescent boy dressed as a woman, or possibly a self-portrait.

The first statement concerning the model for the *Mona Lisa* dates from the last years of Leonardo's life and talks of a portrait "of a certain Florentine lady done from life at the request of the magnificent Giuliano di Medici." We know that Leonardo da Vinci took the portrait to France, during his stay at the court of François I (and no doubt he was still working on it), but he had begun it during his stay in Florence between 1503 and 1506. It therefore appears likely that the model, whoever it was, could have been Florentine. A later second statement by Vasari described the portrait of *Mona Lisa,* the wife of a Florentine gentleman, Francesco del Giocondo. This latter, a rich bourgeois holding a position of political authority in his city, really existed, but we know little about the life of his wife, Lisa Gherardini, born in 1479. We do know that she had married del Giocondo in 1495 but we in fact have no proof that she could have been the mistress of a Medici. A later anonymous statement creates a certain confusion, linking the *Mona Lisa* to a portrait of Francesco del Giocondo—the origin of the risky idea that it is the portrait of a man. Lastly, a later text, dated 1625, refers to a "half-figure portrait of a certain Gioconda," which permanently gave the painting its French title.

Even today, we possess no final proof of the identity of the woman shown by Leonardo. Indeed, it is astonishing to consider that we now remember more the universal aspects of the picture (the evident idealization of the portrait, the painter's imaginative rendering of the landscape, the balance of the model's posture), more than the reference to a personality who really existed. Even if he painted a woman's face with realism, it is clear that Leonardo lastingly freed himself from any obligations to accuracy to search for an abstract description of the human figure.

The Detective Story of the History of the *Mona Lisa*

These intrinsic qualities in Leonardo's work, which had already impressed art lovers and professionals, would not have sufficed to give the *Mona Lisa* its worldwide success if its history had not also been exceptional.

Acquired by François I, either directly from Leonardo da Vinci, during his stay in France, or upon his death from his heirs, the painting remained in the royal collections from the beginning of the sixteenth century to the creation of the Central Arts Museum at the Louvre in 1793. We know that it was kept at Versailles under the reign of Louis XIV and that it was in the Tuileries during the First Empire. Since the Restoration, the *Mona Lisa* has always remained in the Louvre Museum, a key piece of the national collections. Studied by historians and painters, who copied it frequently, the *Mona Lisa* became world famous after its theft in 1911. On August 21, 1911, a slightly mad Italian painter, Vincenzo Peruggia, stole it to return it to its country of origin. After a long police enquiry, during which everyone was suspected, including the Cubist painters and the poet Guillaume Apollinaire, who had one day shouted that "the Louvre should be burnt," the *Mona Lisa* was rediscovered in Italy almost two years later and rehung in the Louvre, treated with the honors accorded to a head of state, after having occupied, throughout this period, the front pages of the world's newspapers.

Since then, the painting has truly become a cult object, considered as sacred to an excessive degree.

The two journeys which she made during the twentieth century, in 1963 to the United States and in 1974 to Japan, were unprecedented successes, the work being welcomed by the crowds like a film star. These two journeys moreover played a major role in building its notoriety, as did the theft of 1911, and the Japanese and American publics have ever since worshipped the work which spent a few weeks in their countries and in front of which hundreds of thousands of visitors filed.

An exceptional artist and faultless technique, combined with the mysteries of its model and its history, were therefore at the origin of the extraordinary craze for the *Mona Lisa* which no other work of art has up until now known. Perhaps too the fact that the painting shows a human figure, that is to say neither a religious or profane scene, subjects that always date and are forgotten as soon as their fashions fade, nor a landscape or still life, subjects sometimes too intellectual, surely explains the crowds' passion. Indeed, the portrait genre, which is accessible for the public, has always been popular and did not Leonardo himself already seem to predict the portrait's success when he wrote: "Can you not see that amongst human beauties, it is a beautiful face that stops passers by, and not the rich ornaments ...," thereby insisting on the mysteries of the look that is exchanged between the visitor and the strange, smiling face.

Source: Vincent Pomarède, "The Faces of the *Mona Lisa*" (No date). Masterpiece Paintings Gallery. Red Hare Communications. **www.masterpiece-paintings-gallery.com/about-mona-lisa.htm**

[QUESTIONS FOR REFLECTION]

Considering Ideas

1. Why does Pomarède include biographical details about Leonardo da Vinci before he gives his review of the *Mona Lisa*? Is this information useful in helping the reader to better understand the painting? Why or why not?

2. What criteria does the author use to evaluate the *Mona Lisa*? Do these criteria seem reasonable for evaluating a work of art? Why or why not?

3. What reasons does Pomarède give for the timeless success of the *Mona Lisa*? Do you feel that people will continue to appreciate this painting, or that viewers will eventually lose interest? Why?

Considering Writing Strategies

1. How effective are Pomarède's headings? As the reader, do you find these headings to be useful? Why or why not?

2. Why does the author use "we" in his first person essay? Who makes up the "we" in his essay? Is he referring to himself and other professionals in the art world, or is he including the reader along with himself? What effect does this writing technique have on the reader?

3. In addition to reviewing the painting, Pomarède also seems to be arguing that this is not just *a* successful painting, but *the* most successful painting of all time. How effective is his argument? Does he fully support

it? Why or why not? If not, what other work of art do you feel is more significant than the *Mona Lisa*?

Writing Suggestions

1. Write a review of a classic work of art or a more contemporary piece that you feel has merit. What is significant about the work? Why is it so popular? Do you feel it will be popular for many years to come, or is it just a passing trend?

2. Find a current example of popular art, such as a CD cover, video game cover, or movie poster that you find appealing (or unappealing). Write an essay evaluating why you feel it is appropriate (or inappropriate). Judge the image using several criteria. You might consider how well it fits with the media it is intended to support. Does it make you want to buy the product or see the movie? Or is it a turnoff? You'll need to include a copy of the image with your essay so your readers can judge it for themselves.

>> READINGS AND REFLECTION

[preview] **ANN POWERS**, who was born in Seattle, has been the chief pop music critic for the *Los Angeles Times* since 2006. She has also been a rock music critic for the *New York Times*, the *Village Voice*, and *Blender* magazine. Additionally, she wrote the 2000 book *Weird Like Us: My Bohemian America* and co-authored *Tori Amos: Piece by Piece* with Amos in 2005. In the following essay, Powers evaluates the Black Eyed Peas' 2009 album, *The E.N.D.*, which stands for "energy never dies." Will.i.am, Apl.de.ap, Taboo, and Fergie make up the Black Eyed Peas, a band that has gained international fame. Go to **www.blackeyedpeas.com** to learn more about the group. If possible, watch the videos for "I Gotta Feeling" or "Boom Boom Pow" on YouTube before reading the following review. Also, think of some of your favorite albums. What criteria do you use to evaluate music?

Album Review: Black Eyed Peas' The E.N.D. **by Ann Powers**

The Los Angeles-based quartet Black Eyed Peas is possibly the greatest bubble gum group of the Extreme Ice Fruit Explosion era. Following in the path forged by the Monkees, the Archies, and the Spice Girls, the Peas present themselves as a cast of zany characters whose music is, on one level, like a child's game, and on another, as calculatedly smart and seductive as test-marketed pop gets.

The titles of the Peas' biggest hits tell the story: the giggle-inducing pun of "Don't Phunk With My Heart," the cheerily crude anatomical gesture of "My Humps," and now the Imax-ready sound effects burst of the chart-topping "Boom Boom Pow." Crass, good-hearted, funny, unfailingly loud scavengers of every shiny thing lying on pop's cross-cultural dance floor, the Peas present themselves as juvenile, but there's a lot going on behind the mugging.

The E.N.D., the group's fifth studio album and the third since the singer Stacy Ferguson (better known as Fergie) joined and took it from the earnest hip-hop underground to the glamorous, necessarily compromised pop mainstream, is more accomplished and more confounding than any of the foursome's previous efforts. It's likely to dominate radio and the Internet this summer, its sharp flavors simultaneously driving listeners nuts and drawing them back.

Will.i.am., the Peas' lead rapper and main idea man, has said that he doesn't envision *The E.N.D.* (The acronym is for "The Energy Never Dies," a nod to quantum physics that's further explained by a robotically voiced introduction to the opening track) as a regular album. Instead, it's a template, designed to be constantly reworked through remixes, both in the recording studio and by DJs on the dance floor. Indeed, this collection has none of the attributes that make listeners love albums: no narrative arc, no ebb and flow, no break from the in-your-face beats and high-fructose hooks.

As a plunge into the users' manual of post-disco dance pop, *The E.N.D.* is quite charming, if predictably goofy. Working with club-savvy collaborators including MSTRKRFT, David Guetta, and Keith Harris, Will takes on electro, deep house, dancehall, and dance-punk, to name just a few trends.

Ever true to their defining characteristic, the Peas have no shame. Fergie puts on ill-fitting dreadlocks for the faux-Jamaican "Electric City" and goes hilariously punk in "Now Generation," a rant about social media that sounds something like Bob Dylan's "Subterranean Homesick Blues" rewritten on a Sidekick. "Ring-a-Ling" is a strangely innocent celebration of drunken bootycalling; "One Tribe" follows a bouncing-ball beat as Will suggests that world peace might come from an amnesia epidemic.

As always, Fergie's performances provide the most interest throughout the album. More than the rappers Taboo and Apl.de.ap, whose spotlight turns are always competent but downplayed, or Will, who clings to an Everyman persona that belies his role as the group's Wizard of Oz, Fergie embraces the essential cartoonishness of being a Pea.

Whether she's being weepy in "Meet Me Halfway" or superbad in "Imma Be," she takes her part to its logical end. Her obviousness once seemed to reflect a lack of skill, but by now it's clear that it's a strategy. As a means of grabbing attention from a hopelessly distracted audience, it works.

Most of *The E.N.D.* doesn't ask too much from those fans. Its more substantive musical and thematic statements are interrupted by many others showing the Peas' deep, deep commitment to a good party. There's "Rock That Body," "Party All the Time," "Rockin' to the Beat," and "Out of My Head," and those are just the ones with telegraphic titles.

This filler, still waiting to be magically morphed by remixes, doesn't add a lot to the experience of listening to *The E.N.D.* all the way through. Yet a strange kind of bliss does arise after being pummeled by nearly 70 minutes' worth of booms, baps, and pows.

And sometimes in the midst of it, the Peas do let in some human sweetness and light. Consider "I Gotta Feeling," whose recently leaked video features brazen images of leggy women kissing, partygoers guzzling booze, and Fergie in a thong and a bra.

And yet the song itself works on a less blatant level. Produced by French house music veteran Guetta with Frederic Riesterer, it's reminiscent of the Five Stairsteps' soul classic "Ooh Child," emulating that song's use of a repetitive, warm vocal line to signify a good mood coming on. That sunlight-colored hook is interrupted by silly raps; by the time Will and his mates are shouting "Mazel Tov!" it's impossible to begrudge the high.

Yes, the song says, this is a sloppy party. But it's one where you're welcome. So come on in.

Source: Ann Powers, "Album Review: Black Eyed Peas' 'The E.N.D.,'" *Los Angeles Times*, June 2, 2009. http://latimesblogs.latimes.com/music_blog/2009/06/album-review-black-eyed-peas-the-end.html.

[QUESTIONS FOR REFLECTION]

Considering Ideas

1. Powers compares the Black Eyed Peas to a number of other artists. Does this help the reader to understand her assessment of the Peas? Why or why not?

2. She includes several lines from the lyrics in her essay. How does this affect you as the reader? Are you familiar with any of them? Could you hear the music in your head as you read them?

3. What is Powers' overall evaluation of The Black Eyed Peas album? Is her claim convincing? Why or why not?

Considering Writing Strategies

1. How effective is Powers' initial description of the group? Which words in her description catch your attention most? Why?

2. What criteria does she use to evaluate the album? Are these criteria appropriate for the subject? Why or why not?

3. Does she include enough supporting details for the reader to have a good concept of what the album is like? Why or why not?

Writing Suggestions

1. Write a review of a new CD by one of your favorite music artists or groups. You might want to compare it with a previous CD by the same group to give your audience a clearer understanding of what the new CD is like. Be sure to base your evaluation on specific criteria and include specific supporting examples to back up your judgments.

2. Find a review of a concert or other performance that you have attended. Write an essay agreeing or disagreeing with the author's evaluation. Support your view with specific details from the performance.

>> READINGS AND REFLECTION

[preview] **HAL SHOWS** was influenced by his viewing of the movie *Lawrence of Arabia* when he wrote the poem "Empire Burlesque," which appears in his book called *Parasol: Poems 1977–2007.* The title of the poem comes from an old Bob Dylan album from the 1980s. Shows grew up in and around the beach towns of North Florida, a fact manifest in many of the poems in *Parasol.* He spent much of the 1970s living in Florence, Italy, where he worked as a waiter, a salesman of gold and silver, a teacher of English, and a translator. These years gave him the chance to explore Europe from Edinburgh to the Peloponnese. A graduate of the writing programs at Florida State University and Goddard College, he has translated the work of Cavalcanti, Leopardi, Rilke, Ungaretti, Pasolini, and other foreign poets, and written extensively on literature and popular culture. Since the early 1980s he has been writing, performing, and recording music that defies genre but is actually only rock and roll. He owns and operates Witching Stick Studio, near Tallahassee, Florida, where he lives with his family. You can listen to Shows' albums, *Lifeboat* and *Native Dancer,* on iTunes. Before reading the poem, think about what it would be like to take a long trip to a foreign country. Have you ever experienced a long journey or seen a movie about one? What was it like?

Empire Burlesque **by Hal Shows**

"Every scene must service the plot," and so on.
But I was thinking of a fine, ghostwritten film
subtle as any of the tales my grandmother told.
Maybe it made the papers; here is its gist:
a west-ender heads east, with a vast wardrobe.
After the disastrously comic lateness of the train
he arrives in colonial pomp but is unreceived.
He feels like a lost bag in the empty station.

What makes the movie is the fact he finds a home.
Half-starved, always hauling his half-digested
European baggage around, he shreds himself.
Skins later he's given away his tailored clothes,
has grown sane and lustrous in the long dusk,
and all the explosive natives take him to heart.

Source: H. Shows, "Empire Burlesque," *Parasol: Poems 1977-2007* (Beckington, UK: Luniver Press, 2007), p. 53.

Considering Ideas

1. In the first line, Shows states, "Every scene must service the plot." Do you agree with this criterion for evaluating movies or other narrative works? Why or why not?

2. A burlesque is a kind of satire or parody, usually presented on stage. In what sense does this poem present a "burlesque" of "empire"?

3. The author suggests that the traveler "has grown sane" after he has "given away his tailored clothes." What do you think he means by this line?

Considering Writing Strategies

1. What effect does the poet achieve by omitting the film's title, or any title, in "Empire Burlesque"?

2. What effect does the simile at the end of the first stanza have on you as the reader? Have you ever felt like a "lost bag" before? What happened?

3. What vivid images does Shows include in his poem? Which parts created a visual image for you as you were reading? What did you envision?

Writing Suggestions

1. Watch the 1962 movie *Lawrence of Arabia* and write a review of it. Base your review on specific criteria, and back up your claims with specific details from the film. You might also compare it to other adventure movies that were produced later.

2. Write a review of a poem that has special meaning to you. You might focus on the ideas in the poem as well as the author's techniques. Be sure to support your opinions with specific examples from the poem.

STUDENT WRITING

Adventures in Crime
by Amanda Archer

The Incredibles, a Pixar Animated Studios production released in 2004, is an action adventure movie filled with excitement. Although *The Incredibles* may be great fun for a family's movie and popcorn Friday night, its PG rating is perhaps not strong enough. The film opens with the local super heroes revealing their previous thoughts and feelings of their work in candid interviews. As the story progresses the audience learns that these characters have been forced into a protection program that keeps what seemed like good deeds at bay. This introduces the characters to average working class lives where the Parr family has been relocated with middle-class employment; however, underneath their average suburban life they are super heroes, or "supers" as they call themselves. The Parr family members struggle with normal everyday challenges and conceal their above average abilities from the public's eyes. The film portrays many positive values that a mature audience can glean. However, be warned that there are plenty of adult situations and undertones. Furthermore, many good deeds are accomplished with violence that will amuse adults but can negatively influence younger viewers.

The Incredibles can have educational value for the right age group; adults can interpret the characters' comments and understand what messages lie underneath. The Parr family goes through events that help them cope with their skills and find constructive outlets that help them lead as normal a life as possible. Mr. and Mrs. Parr revive their struggling marriage, and family members discover new abilities, which they use to promote teamwork and strengthen their family ties. This movie can remind viewers that it is possible to teach children morals and values through events that the family encounters. Robert Parr, who is Mr. Incredible, tries to keep his gifted wife Helen, known as Elastigirl, and their children in a recreational vehicle to keep them safe while he attempts to destroy an enemy. He tells them that he cannot let them join him because he is afraid of losing them and would not know what to do without them. Helen tells him that she will not let him fight alone and she explains that together as a family they can accomplish more. Through events that arise, each character is able to learn about the special abilities he or she possesses and use these abilities as a cooperative team. This demonstrates the value of providing support for family members.

From the beginning of the movie, the adult content can be overwhelming for younger viewers. The humor and sexual innuendos are definitely created to amuse and entertain an older age group. For example, in one of the opening scenes, Mr. Incredible and Elastigirl are up on a rooftop trying to determine who will receive the credit for defeating a criminal when Elastigirl makes a remark to Mr. Incredible that he needs to be more "flexible." While her comment may seem harmless, her tone of voice has a strong sexual connotation. Additionally, the language and actions of the adult characters are constantly geared towards adults and the ability to see through what is said and read into the stereotyping of each character they meet.

Furthermore, the numerous acts of violence are impossible to miss. The super heroes are seemingly regular people who have taken it upon themselves to interject for the greater good where they see fit. This involves participating in a vast selection of violent situations. For example, as Mr. Incredible wraps up his first good deed in the movie, to assist an elderly woman retrieve her cat from a tree, he jumps into his car and is shocked to find a child in his passenger seat. The child exclaims that he is Mr. Incredible's biggest fan and aspires to be his sidekick, Incrediboy. Mr. Parr, who dislikes the annoying boy, ejects the child from the seat, sending him into the air and over the top of the vehicle before crashing onto the ground. This scene reinforces the acceptable use of violence for amusement. Towards the end of the film, Elastagirl tries to sneak into a facility wherein she gets her body stuck in a electronic door and then uses her body as a weapon to knock out several guards and stuff them into a panel in the wall. The continual use of violence toward children as well as "bad guys" is entertaining but not beneficial for young, impressionable viewers. Young children sometimes mimic the super heroes they see on television, but these role models do not set a good example.

Overall, *The Incredibles* portrays several positive family values that audience members sometimes forget. However, the rating of this movie should be TV-PG13 so that people are aware that young children should not view it without parental supervision. The humor is enjoyable for viewers who can understand the adult content and undertones throughout the script. As a result, I would highly recommend renting this movie for viewing after young children have gone to bed for the night. So sit back, pop some popcorn, and enjoy the comic stereotyping of characters and the super heroes' zany reactions to the situations that occur.

[**QUESTIONS FOR REFLECTION**]

1. What is Archer's overall claim about the movie?
2. Is her description of the premise of the film sufficient? Why or why not?
3. What criteria does she use to evaluate the film?
4. Are her judgments fully supported? Explain.
5. What is your reaction to Archer's review? Would you watch the movie? Would you show it to a child under the age of 13? Why or why not?

▶ *Activity*   **Artistic Evaluation**

In pairs or small groups, choose a work of art to review. You might consider using a painting, photograph, sculpture, song, poem, comic strip, or other work that you can evaluate in a reasonably short amount of time. Work together to choose criteria for your evaluation, make a judgment about each criterion, and present an overall opinion of your subject. Your group members may share your results with the class. If possible, provide your audience with a visual image or copy of the poem or song as appropriate. This activity may give you ideas for writing an evaluative essay.

The advertisement depicts "The Battle for Middle Earth" video game. What effect does the artwork have on you? Is it intriguing or repulsive? What kind of audience might be interested in the game? If you are a gamer, would you consider buying this game based on the advertisement? Why or why not?

Writing about an Image

Starry Night Over the Rhone by Vincent van Gogh

Write an essay evaluating one of the images in this chapter. You might start by describing the photograph or painting. Rather than merely focusing on likes and dislikes, evaluate your subject using several criteria that make sense for your subject. You might consider whether the subject has value as a work of art and why it is worthy of being called art. For example, you might listen to Josh Groban's song "Vincent," look at Vincent van Gogh's painting *Starry Night Over the Rhone*, and write your own evaluation of the painting based on specific criteria, such as use of color, shading, and composition.

Media Connection for Evaluating

You might watch read, and/or listen to one or more of the suggested media to discover additional examples of evaluation. Exploring various media may help you to better understand methods of evaluating. You may choose to write about one or more of the media suggestions. For example you might watch an episode of *American Idol* and evaluate one of the contestants for musical ability, showmanship, and rapport with the audience. Be sure to give credit to any sources you use in your essay.

Television	*American Idol*	*Dancing with the Stars*	*At the Movies*
Film	*The Producers* (2005)	*The Simpsons Movie* (2007)	*The Thomas Crown Affair* (1999)
Print	*Consumer Reports*	*Car & Driver*	*Rolling Stone*
Internet	**metacritic.com**	**nybooks.com**	**rottentomatoes.com**
Music	"Performance Evaluation" by Cocoa Tea	"Vincent (Starry, Starry Night)" by Josh Groban	"Mona Lisa" by Grant-Lee Phillips

Write NOW!

USE ONE OF THE FOLLOWING TOPICS to write an evaluative essay. Remember to consider your rhetorical star as well as the steps for writing an evaluative essay as you compose.

1. A book, short story, play, poem, or Web site
2. A movie, documentary, or television show
3. A song, music video, or album
4. A performance, such as a concert, musical, play, opera, or ballet
5. A work of art, such as a painting, sculpture, or photograph
6. A college course or teacher
7. A job, boss, or co-worker
8. A parent, friend, or significant other
9. A weekend trip or vacation
10. The dining experience at a particular restaurant

11.4 > Analyzing the Rhetorical Star for Writing an Evaluation

FIGURE 11.1
The Rhetorical Star

Subject	Choose a topic that interests you to evaluate. You might write a review related to film and the arts, such as a movie, television show, book, song, or piece of art. You may choose to evaluate something school related, such as a class or textbook. Another option is to write an evaluation of a work-related subject, such as your boss or work environment. Be sure to select a topic that you feel qualified to evaluate.
Audience	Who will read your evaluation? What will interest your readers about your subject? Are you offering your readers advice about what to watch, read, or listen to? Do you intend for your audience to do something based on your evaluation, or do you just want your readers to understand your position? Think about what kinds of details would be most appropriate to share with your audience.
Purpose	Think about what you are trying to accomplish through your evaluation. If you saw a movie or show that you loved, you might write a review convincing others to view it. Maybe your goal is to simply inform others about a fantastic Web site that is educational or entertaining. On the other hand, you might want to persuade your audience to take a particular class or go to a specific concert or play.
Strategy	Even if your primary goal is to evaluate your subject, you may decide to use additional writing strategies as well. For example, if you are evaluating a new movie, you might compare and contrast it with an older version of the movie or with a similar movie. If you are evaluating a problem, you may come up with possible solutions for the problem and argue that a particular solution is the most effective.
Design	How many criteria do you need to use about your subject to fully support your evaluation? Also, what other design details, such as photographs or charts, might enhance your evaluation? Will you use some kind of symbol or rating system to make your evaluative criteria clear for the reader?

11.5 > Applying the Writing Process for Evaluating

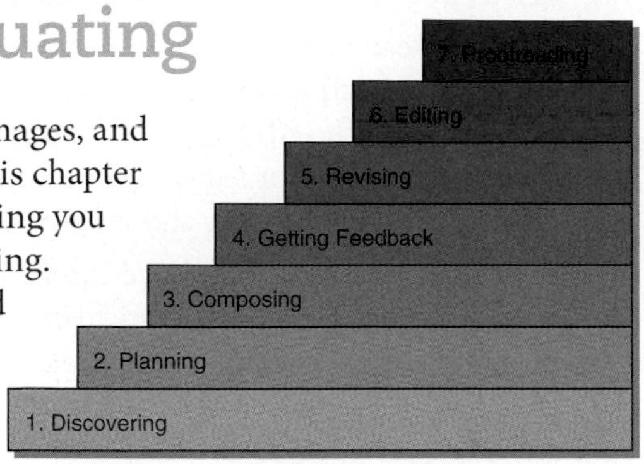

1. **Discovering:** The readings, images, and other media suggestions in this chapter may introduce you to something you would like to evaluate in writing. Look through the chapter and see what comes to mind. Additionally, you might turn on the television and choose a show or movie to evaluate. If you choose that option, you'll want to record the show, if possible, so that you can watch it more than once if necessary. You could also look through an art book or online art museum to find a suitable topic for your evaluation. Once you have chosen a topic, you might make a list of criteria to consider for your evaluation. You could even create a checklist or graphic organizer, like the one that follows, to help you analyze your subject.

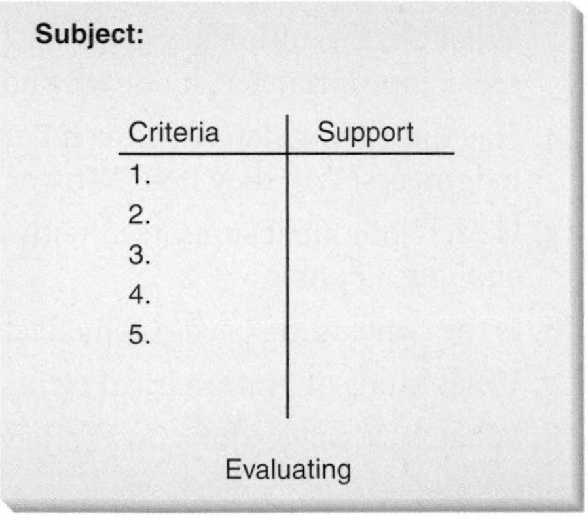

FIGURE 11.2   The Seven Steps of the Writing Process

7. Proofreading
6. Editing
5. Revising
4. Getting Feedback
3. Composing
2. Planning
1. Discovering

2. **Planning:** Decide which criteria you want to use for your evaluation. Create a cluster or an outline (informal or formal) to help you organize your ideas. Because evaluative writing needs to be persuasive, you might save your strongest point for last. Doing so will make your most convincing criterion be more memorable for your audience.

FIGURE 11.3   Sample Graphic Organizer

Subject:

Criteria	Support
1.	
2.	
3.	
4.	
5.	

Evaluating

3. **Composing:** Write a first draft of your evaluation. Remember to focus each body paragraph on one main criterion that supports your overall opinion about your subject. Don't worry too much about grammar and punctuation at this time. Use the steps outlined earlier in the chapter on pp. 261–262:

   1. Describe the subject being evaluated.

   2. Make a claim about the subject.

   3. Use several specific criteria for the evaluation.

   4. Make a fair judgment about each criterion.

   5. Support each judgment with specific evidence.

   6. End with a final claim about your subject.

4. **Getting feedback:** Have at least one classmate or other person read your rough draft and answer the peer review questions that follow. If you have access to a writing tutor or center, get another opinion about your paper as well.

5. **Revising:** Using all of the feedback available to you, revise your evaluation. Make sure that your evaluation is based on specific criteria and that you have fully supported each judgment that you make. Additionally,

make sure that your essay is unified. In other words, every judgment you make needs to help support the opinion in your thesis (your claim). Add, delete, and rearrange ideas as necessary.

6. **Editing:** Read your evaluation again, this time looking for errors in grammar, punctuation, and mechanics. Pay particular attention to your consistency with verb tenses. Generally it is best to use the present verb tense when discussing your subject. For example, write that the artist, filmmaker, or author "captivates" the audience rather than "captivated" the audience.

7. **Proofreading:** After you have carefully edited your essay, read it one last time. Look for typographical errors and any other issues that might interfere with the readers' understanding of your evaluation.

>> Peer Review Questions for Evaluating

Trade rough drafts with a classmate and answer the following questions about his or her paper. Then, in person or online, discuss your papers and suggestions with your peer. Finally, make the changes you feel would most benefit your paper.

1. Has the author described the subject being evaluated clearly and effectively without giving away too much?

2. Is the author's claim (thesis) clear? What is the author's overall opinion about the subject?

3. What are the author's criteria for evaluating the subject? Do these criteria seem appropriate? Why or why not?

4. Has the author stated a clear judgment about each criterion? What are the judgments? Are they fair? Why or why not?

5. Is each judgment supported with specific details and examples? Is there enough support?

6. Is the concluding paragraph effective? Why or why not?

7. What kinds of grammatical errors, if any, are evident in the evaluation?

8. What final suggestions do you have for the author?

> Writer's Checklist for Evaluating

Use the checklist below to evaluate your own writing and help ensure that your evaluation is effective. If you have any "no" answers, go back and work on those areas if necessary.

❏ 1. Have I included a clear description of the subject I am evaluating?

❏ 2. Does my thesis clearly state my opinion of the subject I am evaluating?

❏ 3. Have I used effective criteria to evaluate my subject?

❏ 4. Have I made a clear and fair judgment about each evaluative criterion?

❏ 5. Have I supported each judgment with specific details and examples?

❏ 6. Have I ended with an effective conclusion?

❏ 7. Have I proofread thoroughly?

[CHAPTER SUMMARY]

1. Use the evaluation writing strategy to make a judgment about one or more subjects.

2. Evaluative writing is an important part of your education, daily life, and career.

3. Carefully analyze the rhetorical star before writing an evaluation: subject, audience, purpose, strategy, and design.

4. Interpreting evaluative readings and images can help you to prepare to write an evaluation.

5. Follow these steps to write an effective evaluation essay: describe the subject being evaluated; make a claim about the subject; use several specific criteria for the evaluation; make a fair judgment about each criterion; support each judgment with specific evidence; end with a final claim about the subject you are evaluating.

[WHAT I KNOW NOW]

Use this checklist to determine what you need to work on in order to feel comfortable with your understanding of the material in this chapter. Check off each item as you master it. Review the material for any unchecked items.

❏ 1. I know what **evaluative** writing is.

❏ 2. I can identify several **real-world applications** for writing evaluations.

❏ 3. I can evaluate **readings and images** about film and the arts.

❏ 4. I can **analyze** the rhetorical star for writing an evaluation.

❏ 5. I understand the **writing process** for writing an evaluation.

❏ 6. I can apply the **six steps** for writing an evaluation.

SOLVING A PROBLEM: CRIME AND JUSTICE

LEARNING outcomes

  In this chapter you will learn techniques for the following:

12.1 Identifying real-world applications for solving a problem.

12.2 Understanding the steps for writing about a solution to a problem.

12.3 Responding to and analyzing images and readings about crime and justice.

12.4 Analyzing the rhetorical star for solving a problem.

12.5 Applying the steps for solving a problem in writing.

> Writing Strategy Focus: Solving a Problem

You don't have to look far to find problems that need to be solved. Instead of just complaining about a problem, you can attempt to do something about it. What can you do to help mitigate a problem? One way to initiate change is to write about the problem and offer one or more solutions. If you don't know the answer to a problem, then you can investigate to see what you can learn about the situation. You might conduct research to find an answer to the problem. As always, you'll need to document any sources that you use for your paper.

12.1 > Real-World Applications for Solving a Problem

Writing to Solve a Problem in School

You may be asked to write problem-solving papers in your college courses. In an environmental science course, your instructor may ask you to propose solutions for reducing our dependency on gasoline. Your sociology instructor might assign a paper requiring you propose a solution for a social issue, such as juvenile delinquency or domestic violence. In a course in your major, you may need to write about solutions for improving the public's awareness of an important issue, such as breast cancer, computer piracy, or identity theft.

Writing to Solve a Problem in Your Daily Life

Proposing solutions to problems is also important in your personal life. You might need to come up with a solution for managing your time if you are working and going to school full-time. If you and your significant other have difficulty in deciding who is responsible for certain tasks at home, then you might solve the problem by writing a proposal for an equitable way to divide the chores. If you are having trouble making your finances stretch as far as they need to, then you might solve the problem by drafting a proposed budget for covering all expenses.

Writing to Solve a Problem in Your Career

Being able to write an effective proposal is extremely useful in the workplace. You could suggest solutions for the upper-level administration to improve working conditions and morale. Your employer may assign you to write a proposal for solutions for cutting expenses, increasing profits, and saving jobs. Furthermore, you might need to write a problem-solving report proposing to implement a new program or procedure in your office. Here are some additional ideas for problem-solving writing on the job:

Health care: proposals for purchasing new equipment, implementing a new clinical procedure, or providing better health care coverage.

Law: proposals for reducing crime, improving security, or changing crime scene investigation procedures.

Business: proposals for increasing productivity, personnel, and profits.

Education: proposals for increasing student retention or raising funds for a field trip or a new computer lab.

Computers: proposals for updating software, strengthening network connectivity, or upgrading hardware.

Massage therapy: proposals for gaining more clients, improving the equipment, or creating a more appealing ambience.

Culinary arts: proposals for increasing the customer base, changing the menu, or improving sanitation.

In pairs or small groups, brainstorm uses for problem-solving writing at school, in your daily life, and on the job. You may want to choose the prospective career field(s) of the participants in your group. Each group may share its results with the class.

12.2 > Steps for Writing a Proposal to Solve a Problem

1. Identify a Problem and Demonstrate That It Exists

Solutions to problems are often intended to be persuasive, so you might delay your claim a little bit so that your reader will be more likely to believe that there is a problem that needs to be addressed. First, you'll need to explain what the problem is and prove that it is real. Provide details, examples, a brief narrative, or statistics to convince your audience that there really is a problem. For example, if you are writing about the vandalism in your apartment complex, you might begin by describing specific incidences that have occurred. Maybe Mr. Montana in apartment 27B discovered graffiti on his front door last week, and Ms. Lively in apartment 35C found broken beer bottles and rotten eggs all over her back porch yesterday.

2. Appeal to Your Audience

Make the problem relevant to the audience so that they will care about the situation. For instance, if your audience is other tenants in the complex, then you could point out that they could be targeted next if they don't help to solve the problem. If your audience consists of leaders in the community, then you might suggest that if they ignore the vandalism, then the crimes may escalate into something more serious or become more widespread.

3. State Your Claim

Your thesis might serve to claim that a problem exists and that something needs to be done about it. Another option is to claim that a particular solution is the way to solve the problem. For example, your claim might be that your apartment complex needs to implement a better security system because of all the crime that has been occurring lately.

4. Propose a Solution to the Problem

You might focus on one main solution, several potential solutions, or a combination of solutions. For example, one way to help prevent vandalism from occurring in your apartment complex is to hire more security. Another possible solution is to organize a neighborhood watch program. A third solution might be to set up surveillance cameras in an attempt to discourage vandals and catch anyone who

causes trouble. You can weigh the pros and cons of each solution and then propose the best one.

By considering alternative solutions, you can show the readers that you have carefully considered a variety of options. You can refute all options except for the one you feel would best solve the problem. For instance, although hiring additional security guards might be effective, maybe that solution would be too expensive. Additionally, even though setting up a neighborhood watch system sounds like a good idea, maybe that wouldn't work well for your neighborhood because the vandalism happens during the day when most of the residents are at work. Finally, you might argue that setting up surveillance cameras is the best solution because it is fairly cost effective, and visible cameras would deter potential vandals from causing trouble. If an incident occurs, the apartment supervisor could easily review a video recording and provide it to the police for prosecution purposes.

5. Organize Your Solution(s) Effectively

You have several options for organizing your paper. The chart below outlines two possibilities. Option A takes an inductive approach, where you state your proposal up front and then support it. On the other hand, Option B uses the deductive method, where you explain the problem and possible solutions before proposing a final solution. You may apply these options in various ways.

TABLE 12.1

Organizational Patterns for Solving a Problem	
Option A	**Option B**
Introduction and claim (thesis)	Introduction and explanation of problem
Explanation of problem	Solution one—evaluate pros and cons
Support for proposed solution	Solution two—evaluate pros and cons
Conclusion	Solution three—evaluate pros and cons
	Conclusion and final recommendation

6. Persuade Your Audience That Your Solution Is Feasible and Worthwhile

Once you have made your claim about the best solution for solving the problem, you'll need to persuade your reader that your solution is valid. Illustrate how the proposal will work or suggest what could happen if nothing is done about the problem. If it is appropriate for your subject and assignment, you may be able to use personal knowledge and experience to support your essay.

If your problem-solving essay needs more depth than what you can provide on your own, then you may need to conduct research to back up your ideas. Citing specific statistics, details, and examples will help to make your paper more credible for the readers. For example, if your solution is to install security cameras in your apartment building, then you might include statistics about the effectiveness of using security cameras from a reliable source. If you do use outside sources, you'll need to document them appropriately. Be sure to avoid logical fallacies (see pp. 74–76) in your reasoning.

7. End with a Call to Action

You might conclude your essay by summarizing the problem and solution(s). You may also want to encourage your readers to take action to help solve the problem. Your call to action can take several forms. You might ask the readers to write a letter, get involved, or donate money to help solve the problem.

You might even suggest what the consequences might be if nothing is done to alleviate the problem. However, avoid making idle threats or exaggerating the possible implications of inaction. If your main purpose for writing the essay is to make the readers aware of the problem, rather than offer a specific solution, then you might task your readers with working to find a solution, as Alex Koppelman does in his essay (see pp. 292–294).

>> *Career-Based* PROBLEM-SOLVING WRITING

[preview] **HAVE YOU EVER** had trouble finding a parking spot? Have you been tempted to park somewhere that you know you shouldn't? The following article, which appears on a Web site called *UncivilServants* sponsored by Transportation Alternatives, addresses the issue of illegal parking by government employees. How would you feel if you received a ticket with a hefty fine, but somone with a government parking sticker didn't—even though you both parked illegally?

....

Above the Law: Government Parking Abuse in NYC

....

The Problem

Many government agencies and offices issue parking permits to select employees. Typically placed on a vehicle's dashboard, permits allow government employees to park their vehicles in designated areas. The permits are not meant to allow government employees to block fire hydrants, avoid paying parking meters, park on sidewalks or anywhere else they want. Yet, this is exactly what parking permits are used for. Only in the rarest of circumstances does the NYPD enforce against illegally parked government employees.

Thanks to a lack of enforcement and an unchecked proliferation of government-issued parking permits—legitimate and fraudulent—the widespread abuse of parking permits has persisted for decades and has grown significantly worse in recent years. By default, the ability to abuse a parking permit has become a closely held entitlement, a perk of holding certain government jobs.

Though it may not be explicit policy, the NYPD's traffic enforcement division essentially operates under the premise that citywide there is a "no hit" policy on vehicles with permits in the window. Permit abusers talk of the NYPD extending a "courtesy" to agencies to break the law; business owners and Business Improvement Districts relay accounts of local enforcement officers repeatedly refusing to give tickets to permit holders while ticketing non-permit holders parked in their midst.

While Mayor Bloomberg has vowed to reduce the number of permits on the street, the problem persists. Transportation Alternatives estimates that over 150,000 drivers have access to free parking in the form of valid government-issued parking permits (including the more than 30,000 NYPD "Self-Enforcement Zone" permits and 75,000 teacher permits). Thousands more illicitly enjoy the same privileges by photocopying permits, or by minting their own. In part because of this parking privilege, census data clearly show that government workers drive to work at two times the rate of private sector workers.

The Price

Unfortunately, when drivers with permits cannot find a legal spot, they often park in illegal spaces at the curbside and important metered spaces, hurting businesses that rely on parking turnover and sharply cutting into city revenues that would be generated by meters. Even more egregiously, many government workers endanger public safety by parking in front of fire hydrants, on sidewalks, in crosswalks, in intersections, and in bus stops.

In addition, illegal permit parking generates unnecessary traffic in several ways:

1. Due to their parking privileges, many commuters who could be taking transit opt to drive instead.

2. Because they super-saturate the curb, illegal parkers cause other vehicles to troll to find ever-elusive curbside space.

3. When vehicles cannot find a spot, they double park, compounding traffic problems by blocking lanes and forcing erratic maneuvers.

4. Illegal permit parking degrades the quality of the air that New Yorkers breathe, which contributes to increased risk of health problems like asthma, diabetes, heart disease, and cancer.

5. Illegal permit parking erodes the trust of government and law enforcement in the communities that are overrun by vehicles.

Recommendations

While the recently announced $400,000 Department of Transportation study of parking and permit abuse in downtown Manhattan is a positive step toward better understanding parking patterns, the Mayor need not wait for another study to begin upholding the law and reducing the numbers of permits in circulation. The Mayor and the NYPD should immediately implement the following recommendations that would ameliorate the problem overnight:

- Enforce the law.
- Take inventory of permits and reduce the total.
- Educate government workers to eliminate the "culture of entitlement."
- Update parking signage to reflect the community's needs.

Source: Transportation Alternatives, **http://nyc.uncivilservants.org/ the_problem**.

[QUESTIONS FOR REFLECTION]

1. Who is the primary audience for the report? How do you know? Who else might the author be addressing as well?

2. What is the major problem? Is it explained in a convincing way? Why or why not?

3. What are some of the side effects of the major problem?

4. What solutions does the writer propose? Which solution or solutions do you feel would work best to solve the problem? Why?

5. What additional material might the author include to strengthen the report? Explain.

>> *Career-Based* PROBLEM-SOLVING WRITING

[preview] **HAVE YOU EVER** wanted to write a letter of complaint to your boss or someone in a position to solve a problem that you were dealing with on the job? Sometimes work-related issues can be touchy, so you have to be careful what you write. PRWeb, a company that helps businesses with marketing, pro-

ductivity, and other issues, posts useful items to its Web site for business owners and employees to use for solving problems. The following sample letter appears on a PRWeb Web site called Life 123: Answers at the Speed of Life. Have you ever been inconvenienced by broken office equipment or a malfunctioning toilet? Here's one way to handle the situation.

Toilet Troubles

Business Sample Letter

Dear [Supervisor's name],

This letter is to request action to repair the second toilet in the women's bathroom. It has been at least three months since the toilet broke, and there has been no action to fix it, despite several informal requests to you for repairs. Because there are 15 women who work here, it presents a true inconvenience.

It should be a priority for this company to think about the effects of limited bathroom space. With only one toilet, most of us are forced to wait longer than normal to use the bathroom, cutting into our work time and causing us to take longer breaks than usual. I'm sure the company doesn't want the lack of such a simple repair to eat into our productivity.

I anticipate that the repairs will proceed without delay, but I'm prepared to send a letter on to corporate headquarters after two weeks if no further steps have been taken. The women of this company enjoy their work and appreciate everything that management does to meet their needs. Thank you in advance.

Sincerely,
Michelle Larson

Source: www.life123.com/career-money/business-correspondences/complaint-letters/employee-complaint-letter-sample.shtml.

[QUESTIONS FOR REFLECTION]

1. What is the problem? Is Larson's description of the problem convincing? Why or why not?

2. What reasons does the author give to persuade her supervisor to solve the problem? Are they good reasons? Why or why not?

3. Describe the tone (friendly, serious, sarcastic, etc.) of the letter. Is the tone appropriate for the situation? Why or why not?

4. Do you think the letter will bring about the desired results? Why or why not?

5. Does the threat of taking further action add more weight to the proposed solution? Why or why not?

12.3 > Solving a Problem in the Context of Crime and Justice

If you pay any attention to the news media, you are constantly reminded of problems related to crime and injustice in our society. When you go online, listen to the radio, watch television, or read a newspaper or magazine, you'll often come across stories about criminal activity, such as murders, domestic violence, drug trafficking, and home invasions. You'll also be exposed to reports of injustices, such as people being treated unfairly because of their race, gender, beliefs, or values. As you're discussing the readings and images in this chapter, think about what is right or fair as you work toward proposing solutions to problems. In the words of Dr. Martin Luther King Jr., "Injustice anywhere is a threat to justice everywhere."

[preview] **ALEX KOPPELMAN** was born in Baltimore, Maryland, and is a graduate of the University of Pennsylvania. He is a contributing editor at *SMITH* magazine and a staff writer for Salon.com, where he runs a political blog called War Room. Previously, Koppelman served as a media critic for an interactive online magazine called *DragonFire*, and he has written columns for *New York Magazine, Slate,* the *Washington Post,* and the *Baltimore Sun.* Additionally, Koppelman has appeared as a commentator on Fox News, CNN Headline News, MSNBC, and CourtTV. In the following article, which was originally published in 2006 on Salon.com, Koppelman examines problems related to privacy issues for students who have gotten into trouble with school officials and law-enforcement agents for posting comments on social networking Web sites. Before reading, think about the pictures and comments that some people post on MySpace, Facebook, and other social networking sites. Should school administrators, law enforcement agents, or employers have the authority to take action against individuals for material they have posted online?

MySpace or OurSpace? by Alex Koppelman

In October, seventeen-year-old Dimitri Arethas posted a doctored photo on his MySpace page depicting his public high school's black vice principal as RoboCop. Arethas said he found the photo, which had a racial slur scrawled on it, on another student's Web site, and that he posted it to his own MySpace page thinking it was funny. Arethas, of Charlotte, North Carolina, claims he didn't mean the post to be racist and says that most of his fellow students thought the post was funny too.

But one anonymous student didn't, and brought it to the attention of school administrators. As a result, Arethas says principal Joel Ritchie, who did not respond to a request for comment, suspended Arethas for ten days.

Arethas, who says he apologized and removed the photo when he was initially confronted, was incensed by the suspension, and contacted his local paper, the *Charlotte Observer*, and the American Civil Liberties Union. With the help of ACLU lawyers, Arethas was able to convince the school to end the suspension. He returned after two days.

"Maybe what I did was wrong, morally," Arethas said in a recent e-mail, "but I had every right to express myself. I just chose to do it as a picture, instead of rambling down the hallways yelling, 'Man! This school sucks.'"

Arethas isn't the only student to be disciplined for what he posted to his MySpace profile. The past few years have seen an explosion in the number of schools taking to the Web to find out what students are saying and doing. And punishment has followed, from a Pennsylvania school that suspended one student for creating a parody MySpace profile of his principal to a California school that suspended twenty students simply for viewing one student's MySpace profile, which contained threats against another student. And some public

school systems, like Illinois' Community High School District 128, are even taking steps to monitor everything their students say on sites like MySpace. According to the *Chicago Tribune*, under new guidelines, students who participate in extracurricular activities will need to sign a pledge in which they agree that the school can discipline them if it finds evidence that they have posted any "illegal or inappropriate" material online. Even some police are beginning to patrol MySpace, seeing the site as an effective tool for catching teenage criminals.

All of this new scrutiny poses a vital question for MySpace, which claims 76 million users and is now the largest of all the Web's social-networking sites: What will happen to the site if and when users no longer feel safe expressing themselves there? And in an age where teenagers are accustomed to living their lives online, what will happen when they learn that what they thought was private is, in fact, public, and not without consequence?

"I never thought [this] would happen," Arethas says of his suspension. "I figured only my friends would see my profile page."

Most large online social-networking services have undergone similar challenges as they've grown, with users feeling safe in the widely held though mistaken perception that what they posted was private, or at least that it would only be seen by a select group of people. Other sites have also, like MySpace, dealt with users who have preyed on other more gullible ones, as with the recent high-profile arrests of men who used MySpace to lure young girls. But few sites have grown as large, and as quickly, as MySpace, which was acquired in July 2005 by Rupert Murdoch's News Corporation for $580 million. And few have specialized so effectively in encouraging kids to get comfortable and open up.

As with all forms of electronic media, people still have a hard time wrapping their minds around the fact that little online is truly private. A sampling of MySpace's offerings reveals the evidence: posts explore almost every aspect of users' personal lives, from typical teenage angst about acne and unrequited crushes to more incriminating fare—sexually suggestive images and photos of drinking and drug use—as well as professions of love, anger, and every emotion in between.

"MySpace has encouraged its users to be aware that what they post on their MySpace profile is available for the public to see," says MySpace spokesman Matthew Grossman, adding that "part of why MySpace has been so successful is because people can share their feelings." While Grossman stresses that MySpace does not spy on its users, or share their information, the site will work with law enforcement "if they [law enforcement] go through the proper legal channels," such as a subpoena or warrant. The site's privacy statement makes that caveat explicit. But many users haven't heeded those warnings. They do so now at their peril, because more and more, they are being watched.

"We patrol the Internet like we patrol the streets," officer James McNamee, a member of the Barrington, Illinois, police department's Special Crimes Unit, says. "We'll go in on a MySpace or a Xanga, we'll pick out our area, and we'll just start surfing it, checking it, seeing what's going on."

McNamee says the fact that police have only recently realized what a powerful tool social-networking sites can be for investigative purposes may be what makes MySpace users feel the site is their own private realm.

"We're still playing catch-up," McNamee says. "I wouldn't say we're super far behind, but we're learning as we go and I think that's the reason some [teens] feel like, 'Oh, this is an invasion of our privacy.' Well, no, it's not, it's just that we were behind on learning that we should have been paying attention to this, and now we're paying attention."

McNamee says they've found pictures of graffiti, with the artists standing next to it, "smiling, all happy about their activity," they've found evidence of drug dealing —"where they could hook up, who was dealing drugs . . . photos of their money . . . photos of their drugs"—they've even found a "We Hate Barrington Police Department" blog. ("We don't care," McNamee says of the blog. "It's kind of funny to us; we'll let them vent that way.")

The question of what public-school students have the right to say, and where they have the right to say it, remains murky, with little in the way of definitive jurisprudence to guide schools and courts. Indeed, just about the only thing experts on the topic seem to agree on is that no one really knows what the law is.

"There have been some court decisions, and in all honesty they've been a little bit confused," says Mark Goodman, the executive director of the Student Press Law Center. "And it really isn't just Internet-based speech, but actually any kind of expression by students outside of school. There really have been relatively few cases going to court on this issue, so it's understandable [to a certain extent] why there would be some confusion surrounding it." Goodman, for his part, believes that the law is on the students' side.

> In a public school, I believe the law's pretty clear that the school does not have the authority to punish students for expression they engage in outside of school. There are really important fundamental reasons for that. At the very least, it's a major usurpation of parental authority. Outside of school, parents have the authority to discipline their children . . . I think the problem is a lot of people simply presume that the Internet in effect becomes school expression, and I simply don't believe it does. I think there are legally important distinctions, and very good policy reasons why the school shouldn't have that authority.

Marc Rotenberg, who teaches information privacy law at the Georgetown University Law Center and is the executive director of the Electronic Privacy Information Center, believes the issue is not so clear-cut.

"The key point is whatever is publicly accessible," Rotenberg says. "If a student writes an article in the town paper that defames one of the teachers, the fact that it didn't happen in a school publication really is irrelevant. The school will still act on that information if it's public and available to the community. . . . The courts have not, particularly in the last few years, been sympathetic to student privacy claims, and I don't think there's any reason to think it would be otherwise when the conduct is posted to publicly available Web sites. . . . The critical point here is that yes, I think students should have the freedom to express their views, and I don't think there should be any type of prior restraint on publication, whether it's in print or online media. But that doesn't mean what you say may not have some repercussions."

There are no such questions about whether the police have a right to patrol MySpace.

"If it is a public forum that is accessible to others, then presumably the police are welcome to participate, as they would be welcome to enter a shopping mall or something like that," Rotenberg says.

Kurt Opsahl, a staff lawyer with the Electronic Frontier Foundation, a nonprofit organization whose mission is to defend Internet free speech, agrees.

"You have of course a constitutional right not to incriminate yourself, but you have to exercise that right by not incriminating yourself," Opsahl says. "If you post a photo of yourself engaged in apparently illegal activity with text confirming what you're doing, that can be used against you. Anything you say can and will be used against you, as they say in the Miranda warnings."

But according to James McNamee, MySpace's younger users, or at least the ones he sees in his virtual patrols, haven't yet caught on to that.

"Some people criticize MySpace, and there's no reason to criticize it," he says. "It's a social-networking Internet site that's doing a great function, in my view. The problem is young people aren't sure how to handle it yet. They're not understanding that it's the World Wide Web, they don't get that concept. They think only their friends are looking at it."

Eight MySpace users in Wilkes-Barre, Pennsylvania, learned the hard way that the people visiting their MySpace profiles were not just friends. Wilkes-Barre police, stumped by a rash of graffiti in the downtown area, turned to MySpace to seek suspects.

"The police dug very deep to find me," says one of those arrested in the case, who asked to remain anonymous because of ongoing legal proceedings, and who would communicate only through MySpace. "I didn't have my name, phone number, or any info on me online. I've never used my real name, I've never had my own Internet connection (always another person's name), and I never had my address or name at all posted or registered online."

That user, who denies any involvement in the graffiti, says he was aware of the public nature of the site—"I always think that people are looking," he says — but that some of his friends were not, and that he thinks the police overstepped their bounds.

"I feel that police shouldn't lie and disguise their identity to gain friendship with people they can't see, or ever meet without [informants]."

Dimitri Arethas also feels his rights were violated. "A home page is basically as private as it gets," he told the *Observer* at the time of his suspension.

When asked recently if he still felt that way, his answer was much the same.

"Private like exclusive to only your friends? No, not that kind of private," he said. "[But] someone has to per-

sonally seek out your name and find you in order to view your MySpace, which is what stirs me up. That's where I got some sense of privacy. I could have never imagined someone printing out my profile page and then turning it in."

Mark Goodman worries about the lessons students like Arethas will learn as more face consequences for what they post to sites like MySpace.

What I would hate to see happen, and I think it has happened in some communities at least, is students deciding they can't publish unpopular or controversial viewpoints on their MySpace page or an independent Web site because they're afraid school officials will punish them for it. That, I think, is very disturbing, and those are the young people who, as adults, are going to believe the government should be regulating what the public says. It has very troubling implications for their appreciation of the First Amendment in the world outside of school.

Arethas says that he has become more cautious about what he posts. "Gotta play the political game now," he says. He took his MySpace profile down for a week after the incident, but decided to put it back up—without the offending photo —when he realized, he says, that he "could pretty much get away with it," and that he "had won the case" by being reinstated to school. He still believes the school was wrong to suspend him.

Goodman thinks, though, that few students would act as Arethas did. He points to a study on high school students' attitudes toward the First Amendment, conducted by researchers at the University of Connecticut. Released early last year, the study found that 49 percent of students thought that newspapers should need government approval for their stories, 75 percent didn't realize flag-burning was legal, and more than a third thought the First Amendment went too far. Half believed the government could censor the Internet.

"I think the point of it, ultimately, is how can we expect anything different [than the survey results]," Goodman says. "A direct result of these actions is young people's dismissiveness of the fundamental values of free expression that we as a nation supposedly hold dear." The MySpace user arrested in the Wilkes-Barre case agrees.

I think that MySpace is the epitome of free speech, and censorship, all rolled in one. And I think that America with[out] free speech is not free at all. Just think about the people that have been censored. Go to another country, like Denmark and there is no censorship at all, and the kids growing up there don't look at it as dirty, just as life. When we make things illegal, or "dirty to look at" we create the feeling that it's bad.

Source: Alex Koppelman, "MySpace or OurSpace?" Posted on **www.Salon.com**, June 8, 2006. An online version remains in the Salon archives. Reprinted with permission.

[QUESTIONS FOR REFLECTION]

Considering Ideas

1. What problem does Koppelman identify in his article? Do you feel this is a genuine concern? Why or why not?

2. Should people who post comments on MySpace or Facebook expect their information to be confidential? Why or why not?

3. Should law enforcement, school officials, or employers have the authority to punish someone for what they post online under any circumstances? Explain.

Considering Writing Strategies

1. The author looks at the issue of privacy from two sides: that of the student and that of the law enforcement. Does he give more weight to a particular side, or is his essay balanced? Explain.

2. What kinds of supporting evidence does the writer give for each side of the argument? Give specific examples from the essay. Is the evidence convincing? Why or why not?

3. What is his purpose for writing the article? Has he accomplished that purpose? Why or why not? Why does Koppelman avoid proposing a solution to the problem?

Writing Suggestions

1. Write an essay proposing a solution for the issue that Koppelman addresses in his article. Is the solution to consider material posted online as private and off-limits to school and law enforcement officials? Is the solution to hold everyone accountable for the comments and materials they post online? Is there a compromise between the different points of view? Take a stand on the issue and convince your readers your proposed solution will work. You may want to include additional research in your essay. If you do so, be sure to cite your sources.

2. If you have your own MySpace or Facebook page, think about what you have posted there. Have you included anything that would embarrass you if your classmates, instructors, or employers read it? Write an essay urging college students to be careful about what they post online. You might create hypothetical scenarios to help support your thesis.

>> READINGS AND REFLECTION

[preview] **WILBERT RIDEAU** is an award-winning journalist who spent 44 years at the Louisiana State Penitentiary for killing a teller while robbing a bank when he was 19 years old. After several appeals and four retrials, Rideau's conviction was reduced from murder to manslaughter, and he was released from prison in 2005. *Life* magazine called him "the most rehabilitated prisoner in America." He has helped to produce several films, including one about his life in prison called *The Farm*, which won Best Documentary at the Sundance Film Festival in 1998 and was nominated for an Academy Award for Documentary Feature. You can find several articles about Rideau and the details of his trials at **nytimes.com**. In the following article, published in *Time*, Rideau examines

issues related to long-term prison sentences and proposes a solution for curbing crime. He was still incarcerated at the time he wrote the essay, which provides the readers with a unique perspective on crime from an actual prisoner. Before reading, think about these questions: What can we do to reduce crime in America? Are prisons the only way to deal with criminals?

....

Why Prisons Don't Work by Wilbert Rideau

....

I was among thirty-one murderers sent to the Louisiana State Penitentiary in 1962 to be executed or imprisoned for life. We weren't much different from those we found here, or those who had preceded us. We were unskilled, impulsive and uneducated misfits, mostly black, who had done dumb, impulsive things—failures, rejects from the larger society. Now a generation has come of age and gone since I've been here, and everything is much the same as I found it. The faces of the prisoners are different, but behind them are the same impulsive, uneducated, unskilled minds that made dumb, impulsive choices that got them into more trouble than they ever thought existed. The vast majority of us are consigned to suffer and die here so politicians can sell the illusion that permanently exiling people to prison will make society safe.

Getting tough has always been a "silver bullet," a quick fix for the crime and violence that society fears. Each year in Louisiana—where excess is a way of life—lawmakers have tried to outdo each other in legislating harsher mandatory penalties and in reducing avenues of release. The only thing to do with criminals, they say, is get tougher. They have. In the process, the purpose of prison began to change. The state boasts one of the highest lockup rates in the country, imposes the most severe penalties in the nation, and vies to execute more criminals per capita than anywhere else. This state is so tough that last year, when prison authorities here wanted to punish an inmate in solitary confinement for an infraction, the most they could inflict on him was to deprive him of his underwear. It was all he had left.

If getting tough resulted in public safety, Louisiana citizens would be the safest in the nation. They're not. Louisiana has the highest murder rate among states. Prison, like the police and the courts, has a minimal impact on crime because it is a response after the fact, a mop-up operation. It doesn't work. The idea of punishing the few to deter the many is counterfeit because potential criminals either think they're not going to get caught or they're so emotionally desperate or psychologically distressed that they don't care about the consequences of their actions. The threatened punishment, regardless of its severity, is never a factor in the equation. But society, like the incorrigible criminal it abhors, is unable to learn from its mistakes.

Prison has a role in public safety, but it is not a cure-all. Its value is limited, and its use should also be limited to what it does best: isolating young criminals long enough to give them a chance to grow up and get a grip on their impulses. It is a traumatic experience, certainly, but it should be only a temporary one, not a way of life. Prisoners kept too long tend to embrace the criminal culture, its distorted values and beliefs; they have little choice—prison is their life. There are some prisoners who cannot be returned to society—serial killers, serial rapists, professional hit men, and the like—but the monsters who need to die in prison are rare exceptions in the criminal landscape.

Crime is a young man's game. Most of the nation's random violence is committed by young urban terrorists. But because of long, mandatory sentences, most prisoners here are much older, having spent fifteen, twenty, thirty, or more years behind bars, long past necessity. Rather than pay for new prisons, society would be well served by releasing some of its older prisoners who pose no threat and using the money to catch young street thugs. Warden John Whitley agrees that many older prisoners here could be freed tomorrow with little or no danger to society. Release, however, is governed by law or by politicians, not by penal professionals. Even murderers, those most feared by society, pose little risk. Historically, for example, the domestic staff at Louisiana's Governor's mansion has been made up of murderers, hand-picked to work among the chief-of-state and his family. Penologists have long known that murder is almost always a once-in-a-lifetime act. The most dangerous criminal is the one who has not yet killed but has a history of escalating offenses. He's the one to watch.

Rehabilitation can work. Everyone changes in time. The trick is to influence the direction that change takes. The problem with prisons is that they don't do more to rehabilitate those confined in them. The convict who enters prison illiterate will probably leave the same way. Most convicts want to be better than they are, but education is not a priority. This prison houses 4,600 men and offers academic training to 240, vocational training to a like number. Perhaps it doesn't matter. About 90 percent of the men here may never leave this prison alive.

The only effective way to curb crime is for society to work to prevent the criminal act in the first place, to come between the perpetrator and crime. Our youngsters must be taught to respect the humanity of others and to handle disputes without violence. It is essential to educate and equip them with the skills to pursue their life ambitions in a meaningful way. As a community, we must address the adverse life circumstances that spawn criminality. These things are not quick, and they're not easy, but they're effective. Politicians think that's too hard a sell. They want to be on record for doing something now, something they can point to at reelection time. So the drumbeat goes on for more police, more prisons, more of the same failed policies.

Ever see a dog chase its tail?

Source: Wilbert Rideau, "Why Prisons Don't Work." First published in *Time*, March 21, 1994. Copyright © 1994. Reprinted with permission of the author.

Considering Ideas

1. Rideau claims that prisons are "not a cure-all" for making the public safe? Do you agree or disagree with his claim? Why?

2. The writer states, "Most convicts want to be better than they are, but education is not a priority." Do you agree with the first part of that statement? Why or why not?

3. What solution does the author propose for dealing with crime? What do you think about his proposal?

Considering Writing Strategies

1. Does Rideau seem credible as a writer? Why or why not?

2. What reasons does Rideau give to support his proposal? Are his reasons convincing? Why or why not? Is his proposal feasible? Why or why not?

3. What does the author mean by his last line, "Ever see a dog chase its tail?" Is this an effective conclusion for the essay? Why or why not?

Writing Suggestions

1. Write a proposal suggesting how to reduce crime in your community.

2. Write a proposal offering one or more methods for rehabilitating prisoners.

>> READINGS AND REFLECTION

[preview] **CLIVE THOMPSON** is a columnist for *Wired* magazine, a contributor to the *New York Times Magazine, Fast Company, Wired* magazine's Web site, as well as other publications. From 2002 to 2003 Thompson was a Knight Science Journalism Fellow at the Michigan Institute of Technology. He runs his own Web site, Collision Detection, where bloggers comment on issues related to science, technology, and culture. To participate in Thompson's Web site, go to **www.collisiondetection.net**. In the following essay, which originally appeared in *Wired* magazine, Thompson explains a new technology that is emerging and ponders the legal implications of this technology. Before reading, think about your innermost private thoughts. Would you want someone to have any idea of what you are thinking?

It's All in Your Head: Why the Next Civil Rights Battle Will Be Over the Mind by Clive Thompson

Strolling down the street in Manhattan, I suddenly hear a woman's voice.

"Who's there? Who's there?" she whispers. I look around but can't figure out where it's coming from. It seems to emanate from inside my skull.

Was I going nuts? Nope. I had simply encountered a new advertising medium: hypersonic sound. It broadcasts audio in a focused beam, so that only a person standing directly in its path hears the message. In this case, the cable channel A&E was using the technology to promote a show about, naturally, the paranormal.

I'm a geek, so my first reaction was, "Cool!" But it also felt creepy.

We think of our brains as the ultimate private sanctuary, a zone where other people can't intrude without our knowledge or permission. But its boundaries are gradually eroding. Hypersonic sound is just a portent of what's coming, one of a host of emerging technologies aimed at tapping into our heads. These tools raise a fascinating, and queasy, new ethical question: Do we have a right to "mental privacy"?

"We're going to be facing this question more and more, and nobody is really ready for it," says Paul Root

Wolpe, a bioethicist and board member of the nonprofit Center for Cognitive Liberty and Ethics. "If the skull is not an absolute domain of privacy, there *are* no privacy domains left." He argues that the big personal liberty issues of the 21st century will all be in our heads—the "civil rights of the mind," he calls it.

It's true that most of this technology is still gestational. But the early experiments are compelling: Some researchers say that fMJR brain scans can detect surprisingly specific mental acts—like whether you're entertaining racial thoughts, doing arithmetic, reading, or recognizing something. Entrepreneurs are already pushing dubious forms of the tech into the marketplace. You can now hire a firm, No Lie MRI, to conduct a "truth verification" scan if you're trying to prove you're on the level. Give it 10 years, ethicists say, and brain tools will be used regularly—sometimes responsibly, often shoddily.

Both situations scare civil libertarians. What happens when the government starts using brain scans in criminal investigations—to figure out if, say, a suspect is lying about a terrorist plot? Will the Fifth Amendment protect you from self-incrimination by your own brain? Think about your workplace, too: Your boss can already demand that you pee in a cup. Should she also be allowed to stick your head in an MRI tube as part of your performance review?

But this isn't just about reading minds; it's also about bombarding them with messages or tweaking their chemistry. Transcranial magnetic stimulation—now used to treat epilepsy—has shown that it can artificially generate states of empathy and euphoria. And you've probably heard of propranolol, a drug that can help erase traumatic memories.

Let's say you've been assaulted and you want to take propranolol to delete the memory. The state needs that memory to prosecute the assailant. Can it prevent you from taking the drug? "To a certain extent, memories are societal properties," says Adam Kolber, a visiting professor at Princeton. "Society has always made claims on your memory, such as subpoenaing you." Or what if you use transcranial stimulation to increase your empathy. Would you be required to disclose that? Could a judge throw you off a jury? Could the Army turn you away?

I'd love to give you answers. But the truth is no one knows. Privacy rights vary from state to state, and it's unclear how, or even if, the protections would apply to mental sanctity. "We really need to articulate a moral code that governs all this," warns Arthur Caplan, a University of Pennsylvania bioethicist.

The good news is that scholars are holding conferences to hash out legal positions. But we'll need a broad public debate about it, too. Civil liberties thrive only when the public demands them—and understands they're at risk. The means we need to stop seeing this stuff as science fiction and start thinking about how we'll react to it. Otherwise, we could all lose our minds.

Source: Clive Thompson, "It's All in Your Head: Why the Next Civil Rights Battle Will Be Over the Mind," *Wired*, April 2008, p. 60.

[QUESTIONS FOR REFLECTION]

Considering Ideas

1. How do you feel about the development of new technology that could potentially allow others to have an inkling of what you are thinking? Should this technology eventually be used for criminal investigations? Why or why not?

2. How would you respond to Thompson's ethical question: "Do we have a right to 'mental privacy'?" Would you hire a firm, such as No Lie MRI, to conduct a "truth verification" scan to prove your innocence if someone falsely accused you of committing a crime? Why or why not?

3. The author delays his proposal until the second to last paragraph; what is his main point?

Considering Writing Strategies

1. What cause-and-effect relationship does Thompson highlight in his proposal? Is this relationship logical? Why or why not?

2. What action is the author asking the readers to take? Is this a reasonable request? Explain your answer.

3. How effective is the last part of the writer's final sentence: "...we could all lose our minds"? Is he expecting the reader to take him seriously? Why or why not?

Writing Suggestions

1. Write a proposal suggesting what might happen if the technology explained in Thompson's article comes into widespread use. You might focus on potential positive outcomes or possible negative outcomes of the technology. For example, you might predict possible effects of using this new technology for criminal investigations.

2. Do you feel that anyone has a right to know what someone is thinking? Is the right to having one's own private thoughts different for a citizen on the street than for a potential criminal? Write a proposal suggesting a fair use for the technology described in Thompson's essay. Who, if anyone, should have the right to know what someone else is thinking?

[preview] **BORN IN HARLEM**, Sekou Sundiata was a poet, playwright, songwriter, performer, educator, and activist who had compassion for the human experience, particularly for African Americans. His artistic performances were infused with music that crossed a wide range of genres, including blues, jazz, funk, and Afro-Caribbean rhythms. He performed throughout the United States and abroad, and was featured on the HBO series, *Def Poetry Jam*, and the PBS poetry series, *The Language of Life*. Before becoming a professor of writing at Eugene Lang College of New School University in New York City, he earned degrees from City College of New York and City University of New York. Tragically, after surviving a kidney transplant and a serious car accident, Sundiata met his untimely death in 2007 at the age of 58 due to heart failure. To learn more about Sundiata and hear some of his music, go to **www.puremusic.com/sekou.html**. You can listen to him read poetry on YouTube.com as well. In the following poem, Sundiata tells about a situation with "the Law." Before reading, think about your own experience. Have you ever been pulled over by a police officer while you were driving? Did you think you had done anything wrong? How did you feel about the incident?

Blink Your Eyes by Sekou Sundiata

I was on my way to see my woman
but the Law said I was on my way
thru a red light red light red light
and if you saw my woman
you could understand,
I was just being a man.
It wasn't about no light
it was about my ride
and if you saw my ride
you could dig that too, you dig?
Sunroof stereo radio black leather
Bucket seats sit low you know,
the body's cool, but the tires are worn.
Ride when the hard time come, ride
When they're gone, in other words
the light was green.

I could wake up in the morning
without a warning
and my world could change:
blink your eyes.
All depends, all depends on the skin,
all depends on the skin you're living in.

Up to the window comes the Law
With his hand on his gun
what's up? what's happening?
I said I guess
that's when I really broke the law.
He said a routine, step out the car

a routine, assume the position.
Put your hands up in the air
you know the routine, like you just don't care.
License and registration.
Deep was the night and the light
from the North Star on the car door, déjà vu
we've been through this before,
why did you stop me?
Somebody had to stop you.
I watch the news, you always lose.
You're unreliable, that's undeniable.
This is serious, you could be dangerous.

I could wake up in the morning
without a warning
and my world could change:
blink your eyes.
All depends, all depends on the skin,
all depends on the skin you're living in
New york City, they got laws
can't no bruthas drive outdoors,
in certain neighborhoods, on particular streets
near and around certain types of people.
They got laws.
All depends, all depends on the skin,
all depends on the skin you're living in.

Source: Sekou Sundiata, "Blink Your Eyes" (1995) from Wayne Stein, Deborah Israel, and Pam Washington *Fresh Takes: Explorations in Reading and Writing* (New York: McGraw-Hill, 2008), pp. 375–76.

Considering Ideas

1. What problem has Sundiata identified in his poem?

2. Do you agree with the poet that the law treats people differently based on the color of their skin? Why or why not?

3. Have you ever felt that you were treated differently (better or worse) than someone else because of your ethnicity? What happened?

Considering Writing Strategies

1. Which lines does Sundiata repeat in his poem? What is the effect of the repetition?

2. What point is the poet making through the following lines? "I watch the news, you always lose. You're unreliable, that's undeniable. This is serious, you could be dangerous." Is his point convincing? Why or why not?

3. What is the significance of the title of the poem? What might be different in the morning? What proposal is Sundiata implying?

Writing Suggestions

1. Write a proposal suggesting how to get people, such as law enforcement officers, to treat others fairly, regardless of their race.

2. What can college students do to help people of different ethnicities get along better together? Write a proposal detailing one or more specific suggestions.

>> READINGS AND REFLECTION

[preview] **BORN IN DAVENPORT**, Iowa, Susan Glaspell was a Pulitzer Prize-winning playwright and best-selling fiction writer. After graduating from Drake University, she worked as a journalist for the *Des Moines Daily News*, and her stories have appeared in several publications, including *Harpers* and *Ladies' Home Journal*. She was the founder and director of the Provincetown Players on Cape Cod, Massachusetts, for which she wrote 11 plays. She also wrote more than 50 short stories and nine novels. Many of her works focus on feminist issues. Visit **www.susanglaspell.org/** to learn more about the author and her works. In the following play, which is her most popular, Glaspell reveals the details of a murder investigation. The mystery, however, is not one of whodunit, but one of motive. Glaspell later transformed the play into a short story called "A Jury of Her Peers." If possible, read this play aloud with classmates or other people. Before reading, think about whether you feel that there is any situation in which it is OK for someone to cover up a crime. Under what circumstances, if any, would that be acceptable?

Trifles by Susan Glaspel

CHARACTERS

GEORGE HENDERSON, *Country Attorney*

HENRY PETERS, *Sheriff*

LEWIS HALE, *A Neighboring Farmer*

MRS. PETERS

MRS. HALE

Scene: *The kitchen in the now abandoned farmhouse of* JOHN WRIGHT, *a gloomy kitchen, and left without having been put in order—unwashed pans under the sink, a loaf of bread outside the bread-box, a dish towel on the table—other signs of incompleted work. At the rear the outer door opens, and the* SHERIFF *comes in, followed by the* COUNTY ATTORNEY *and* HALE. *The* SHERIFF *and*

HALE *are men in middle life, the* COUNTY ATTORNEY *is a young man; all are much bundled up and go at once to the stove. They are followed by the two women—the* SHERIFF's *Wife first; she is a slight wiry woman, a thin nervous face.* MRS. HALE *is larger and would ordinarily be called more comfortable looking, but she is disturbed now and looks fearfully about as she enters. The women have come in slowly, and stand close together near the door.*

COUNTY ATTORNEY [*rubbing his hands*]: This feels good. Come up to the fire, ladies.

MRS. PETERS [*after taking a step forward*]: I'm not—cold.

SHERIFF [*unbuttoning his overcoat and stepping away from the stove as if to mark the beginning of official business*]: Now, Mr. Hale, before we move things about, you explain to Mr. Henderson just what you saw when you came here yesterday morning.

COUNTY ATTORNEY: By the way, has anything been moved? Are things just as you left them yesterday?

SHERIFF [*looking about*]: It's just the same. When it dropped below zero last night, I thought I'd better send Frank out this morning to make a fire for us—no use getting pneumonia with a big case on; but I told him not to touch anything except the stove—and you know Frank.

COUNTY ATTORNEY: Somebody should have been left here yesterday.

SHERIFF: Oh—yesterday. When I had to send Frank to Morris Center for that man who went crazy—I want you to know I had my hands full yesterday, I knew you could get back from Omaha by today and as long as I went over everything here myself—

COUNTY ATTORNEY: Well, Mr. Hale, tell just what happened when you came here yesterday morning.

HALE: Harry and I had started to town with a load of potatoes. We came along the road from my place and as I got here I said, "I'm going to see if I can't get John Wright to go in with me on a party telephone." I spoke to Wright about it once before and he put me off, saying folks talked too much anyway, and all he asked was peace and quiet— I guess you know about how much he talked himself; but I thought maybe if I went to the house and talked about it before his wife, though I said to Harry that I didn't know as what his wife wanted made much difference to John—

COUNTY ATTORNEY: Let's talk about that later, Mr. Hale. I do want to talk about that, but tell now just what happened when you got to the house.

HALE: I didn't hear or see anything; I knocked at the door, and still it was all quiet inside. I knew they must be up, it was past eight o'clock. So I knocked again, and I thought I heard somebody say, "Come in." I wasn't sure, I'm not sure yet, but I opened the door—this door [*indicating the door by which the two women are still standing*], and there in that rocker—[*pointing to it*] sat Mrs. Wright.

[*They all look at the rocker.*]

COUNTY ATTORNEY: What—was she doing?

HALE: She was rockin' back and forth. She had her apron in her hand and was kind of—pleating it.

COUNTY ATTORNEY: And how did she—look?

HALE: Well, she looked queer.

COUNTY ATTORNEY: How do you mean—queer?

HALE: Well, as if she didn't know what she was going to do next. And kind of done up.

COUNTY ATTORNEY: How did she seem to feel about your coming?

HALE: Why, I don't think she minded—one way or other. She didn't pay much attention. I said, "How do, Mrs. Wright, it's cold, ain't it?" And she said, "Is it?"—and went on kind of pleating at her apron. Well, I was surprised; she didn't ask me to come up to the stove, or to set down, but just sat there, not even looking at me, so I said, "I want to see John." And then she—laughed. I guess you would call it a laugh. I thought of Harry and the team outside, so I said a little sharp: "Can't I see John?" "No," she says, kind o' dull like. "Ain't he home?" says I. "Yes," says she, "he's home." "Then why can't I see him?" I asked her, out of patience. "'Cause he's dead," says she. "*Dead?*" says I. She just nodded her head, not getting a bit excited, but rockin' back and forth. "Why—where is he?" says I, not knowing what to say. She just pointed upstairs—like that [*Himself pointing to the room above*]. I got up, with the idea of going up there. I walked from there to here—then I says, "Why, what did he die of?" "He died of a rope round his neck," says she, and just went on pleatin' at her apron. Well, I went out and called Harry. I thought I might—need help. We went upstairs, and there he was lyin'—

COUNTY ATTORNEY: I think I'd rather have you go into that upstairs, where you can point it all out. Just go on now with the rest of the story.

HALE: Well, my first thought was to get that rope off. It looked. . . (*Stops, his face twitches.*). . . but Harry, he went up to him, and he said, "No, he's dead all right, and we'd better not touch anything." So we went back downstairs. She was still sitting that same way. "Has anybody been notified?" I asked." "No," says she, unconcerned. "Who did this, Mrs. Wright?" said Harry. He said it business-like—and she stopped pleatin' of her apron. "I don't know," she says. "You don't *know?*" says Harry. "No," says she. "Weren't you sleepin' in the bed with him?" says Harry. "Yes," says she, "but I was on the inside." "Somebody slipped a rope round his neck and strangled him and you didn't wake up?" says Harry. "I didn't wake up," she said after him. We must 'a looked as if we didn't see how that could be, for after a minute she said, "I sleep sound." Harry was going to ask her more questions but I said maybe we ought to let her tell her story first to the coroner, or the sheriff, so Harry went fast as he could to Rivers' place, where there's a telephone.

COUNTY ATTORNEY: And what did Mrs. Wright do when she knew that you had gone for the coroner?

HALE: She moved from that chair to this over here [*Pointing to a small chair in the corner*] and just sat there with her hands held together and looking down. I got a feeling that I ought to make some conversation, so I said I had come in to see if John wanted to put in a telephone, and at that she started to laugh, and then she stopped and looked at me—scared. [*The* COUNTY ATTORNEY, *who has had his notebook out, makes a note.*] I dunno, maybe it wasn't scared. I wouldn't like to say it was. Soon Harry got back, and then Dr. Lloyd came, and you, Mr. Peters, and so I guess that's all I know that you don't.

COUNTY ATTORNEY [*looking around*]: I guess we'll go upstairs first—and then out to the barn and around there. [*To the* SHERIFF] You're convinced that there was nothing important here—nothing that would point to any motive?

SHERIFF: Nothing here but kitchen things.

[*The* COUNTY ATTORNEY, *after again looking around the kitchen, opens the door of a cupboard closet. He gets up on a chair and looks on a shelf. Pulls his hand away, sticky.*]

COUNTY ATTORNEY: Here's a nice mess.

[*The women draw nearer.*]

MRS. PETERS [*to the other woman*]: Oh, her fruit; it did freeze. (*To the* COUNTY ATTORNEY) She worried about that when it turned so cold. She said the fire'd go out and her jars would break.

SHERIFF: Well, can you beat the women! Held for murder and worryin' about her preserves.

COUNTY ATTORNEY: I guess before we're through she may have something more serious than preserves to worry about.

HALE: Well, women are used to worrying over trifles.

[*The two women move a little closer together.*]

COUNTY ATTORNEY [*with the gallantry of a young politician*]: And yet, for all their worries, what would we do without the ladies? [*The women do not unbend. He goes to the sink, takes a dipperful of water from the pail and pouring it into a basin, washes his hands. Starts to wipe them on the roller towel, turns it for a cleaner place.*] Dirty towels! [*Kicks his foot against the pans under the sink.*] Not much of a housekeeper, would you say, ladies?

MRS. HALE [*stiffly*]: There's a great deal of work to be done on a farm.

COUNTY ATTORNEY: To be sure. And yet [*With a little bow to her*] I know there are some Dickson county farmhouses which do not have such roller towels.

[*He gives it a pull to expose its full length again.*]

MRS. HALE: Those towels get dirty awful quick. Men's hands aren't always as clean as they might be.

COUNTY ATTORNEY: Ah, loyal to your sex, I see. But you and Mrs. Wright were neighbors. I suppose you were friends, too.

MRS. HALE [(*shaking her head*)]: I've not seen much of her of late years. I've not been in this house—it's more than a year.

COUNTY ATTORNEY: And why was that? You didn't like her?

MRS. HALE: I liked her all well enough. Farmers' wives have their hands full, Mr. Henderson. And then—

COUNTY ATTORNEY: Yes—?

MRS. HALE [(*looking about*)]: It never seemed a very cheerful place.

COUNTY ATTORNEY: No—it's not cheerful. I shouldn't say she had the homemaking instinct.

MRS. HALE: Well, I don't know as Wright had, either.

COUNTY ATTORNEY: You mean that they didn't get on very well?

MRS. HALE: No, I don't mean anything. But I don't think a place'd be any cheerfuller for John Wright's being in it.

COUNTY ATTORNEY: I'd like to talk more of that a little later. I want to get the lay of things upstairs now.

[*He goes to the left, where three steps lead to a stair door.*]

SHERIFF: I suppose anything Mrs. Peters does'll be all right. She was to take in some clothes for her, you know, and a few little things. We left in such a hurry yesterday.

COUNTY ATTORNEY: Yes, but I would like to see what you take, Mrs. Peters, and keep an eye out for anything that might be of use to us.

MRS. PETERS: Yes, Mr. Henderson.

[*The women listen to the men's steps on the stairs, then look about the kitchen.*]

MRS. HALE: I'd hate to have men coming into my kitchen, snooping around and criticizing.

[*She arranges the pans under sink which the* COUNTY ATTORNEY *had shoved out of place.*]

MRS. PETERS: Of course it's no more than their duty.

MRS. HALE: Duty's all right, but I guess that deputy sheriff that came out to make the fire might have got a little of this on. [(*Gives the roller towel a pull.*)] Wish I'd thought of that sooner. Seems mean to talk about her for not having things slicked up when she had to come away in such a hurry.

MRS. PETERS [(*Who has gone to a small table in the left rear corner of the room, and lifted one end of a towel that covers a pan*)]: She had bread set.

[*Stands still.*]

MRS. HALE [*eyes fixed on a loaf of bread beside the breadbox, which is on a low shelf at the other side of the room. Moves slowly toward it*]: She was going to put this in there. [*Picks up loaf, then abruptly drops it. In a manner of returning to familiar things.*] It's a shame about her fruit. I wonder if it's all gone. [*Gets up on the chair and looks.*] I think there's some here that's all right, Mrs. Peters. Yes—here; [*Holding it toward the window.*] This is cherries, too. [*Looking again.*] I declare I believe that's the only one. [*Gets down, bottle in her hand. Goes to the sink and wipes it off on the outside.*] She'll feel awful bad after all her hard work in the hot weather. I remember the afternoon I put up my cherries last summer.

[*She puts the bottle on the big kitchen table, center of the room.. With a sigh, is about to sit down in the rocking-chair. Before she is seated realizes what chair it is; with a slow look at it, steps back. The chair, which she has touched, rocks back and forth.*]

MRS. PETERS: Well, I must get those things from the front room closet. [*She goes to the door at the right, but after looking into the other room, steps back.*] You coming with me, Mrs. Hale? You could help me carry them.

[*They go in the other room; reappear, MRS. PETERS carrying a dress and skirt, MRS. HALE following with a pair of shoes.*]

MRS. PETERS: My, it's cold in there.

[*She puts the clothes on the big table, and hurries to the stove.*]

MRS. HALE [*examining the skirt*]: Wright was close. I think maybe that's why she kept so much to herself. She didn't even belong to the Ladies Aid. I suppose she felt she couldn't do her part, and then you don't enjoy things when you feel shabby. She used to wear pretty clothes and be lively, when she was Minnie Foster, one of the town girls singing in the choir. But that—oh, that was thirty years ago. This all you was to take in?

MRS. PETERS: She said she wanted an apron. Funny thing to want, for there isn't much to get you dirty in jail, goodness knows. But I suppose just to make her feel more natural. She said they was in the top drawer in this cupboard. Yes, here. And then her little shawl that always hung behind the door. [*Opens stair door and looks.*] Yes, here it is.

[*Quickly shuts door leading upstairs.*]

MRS. HALE [*abruptly moving toward her*]: Mrs. Peters?

MRS. PETERS: Yes, Mrs. Hale?

MRS. PETERS: Do you think she did it?

MRS. PETERS [*in a frightened voice*]: Oh, I don't know.

MRS. HALE: Well, I don't think she did. Asking for an apron and her little shawl. Worrying about her fruit.

MRS. PETERS [*starts to speak, glances up, where footsteps are heard in the room above. In a low voice*]: Mrs. Peters says it looks bad for her. Mr. Henderson is awful sarcastic in a speech, and he'll make fun of her sayin' she didn't wake up.

MRS. HALE: Well, I guess John Wright didn't wake when they was slipping that rope under his neck.

MRS. PETERS: No, it's strange. It must have been done awful crafty and still. They say it was such a —funny way to kill a man, rigging it all up like that.

MRS. HALE: That's just what Mr. Hale said. There was a gun in the house. He says that's what he can't understand.

MRS. PETERS: Mr. Henderson said coming out that what was needed for the case was a motive; something to show anger or—sudden feeling.

MRS. HALE [who is standing by the table]: Well, I don't see any signs of anger around here. [She puts her hand on the dish towel which lies on the table, stands looking down at table, one half of which is clean, the other half messy.] It's wiped to here. [Makes a move as if to finish work, then turns and looks at loaf of bread outside the breadbox. Drops towel. In that voice of coming back to familiar things.] Wonder how they are finding things upstairs. I hope she had it a little more red-up up there. You know, it seems kind of sneaking. Locking her up in town and then coming out here and trying to get her own house to turn against her!

MRS. PETERS: But Mrs. Hale, the law is the law.

MRS. HALE: I s'pose 'tis. [Unbuttoning her coat.] Better loosen up your things, Mrs. Peters. You won't feel them when you go out.

[MRS. PETERS takes off her fur tippet, goes to hang it on hook at the back of room, stands looking at the under part of the small corner table.]

MRS. PETERS: She was piecing a quilt.

[She brings the large sewing basket and they look at the bright pieces.]

MRS. HALE: It's log cabin pattern. Pretty, isn't it?
I wonder if she was goin' to quilt it or just knot it?

[Footsteps have been heard coming down the stairs. The SHERIFF enters, followed by HALE and the COUNTY ATTORNEY.]

SHERIFF: They wonder if she was going to quilt it or just knot it.

[The men laugh; the women look abashed.]

COUNTY ATTORNEY [rubbing his hands over the stove]: Frank's fire didn't do much up there, did it? Well, let's go out to the barn and get that cleared up.

[The men go outside.]

MRS. HALE [resentfully]: I don't know as there's anything so strange, our takin' up our time with little things while we're waiting for them to get the evidence. [She sits down at the big table, smoothing out a block with decision.] I don't see as it's anything to laugh about.

MRS. PETERS [apologetically]: Of course they've got awful important things on their minds.

[Pulls up a chair and joins MRS. HALE at the table.]

MRS. HALE [examining another block]: Mrs. Peters, look at this one. Here, this is the one she was working on, and look at the sewing! All the rest of it has been so nice and even. And look at this! It's all over the place! Why, it looks as if she didn't know what she was about!

[After she has said this, they look at each other, then start to glance back at the door. After an instant MRS. HALE has pulled at a knot and ripped the sewing.]

MRS. PETERS: Oh, what are you doing, Mrs. Hale?

MRS. HALE [mildly]: Just pulling out a stitch or two that's not sewed very good. [(Threading a needle)]. Bad sewing always made me fidgety.

MRS. PETERS [nervously]: I don't think we ought to touch things.

MRS. HALE: I'll just finish up this end. [Suddenly stopping and leaning forward.] Mrs. Peters?

MRS. PETERS: Yes, Mrs. Hale?

MRS. HALE: What do you suppose she was so nervous about?

MRS. PETERS: Oh—I don't know. I don't know as she was nervous. I sometimes sew awful queer when I'm just tired. [MRS. HALE *starts to say something looks at* MRS. PETERS, *then goes on sewing.*] Well, I must get these things wrapped up. They may be through sooner than we think. [*Putting apron and other things together.*] I wonder where I can find a piece of paper, and string.

MRS. HALE: In that cupboard, maybe.

MRS. PETERS [*looking in cupboard*]: Why, here's a birdcage. [*Holds it up.*] Did she have a bird, Mrs. Hale?

MRS. HALE: Why, I don't know whether she did or not—I've not been here for so long. There was a man around last year selling canaries cheap, but I don't know as she took one; maybe she did. She used to sing real pretty herself.

MRS. PETERS [*glancing around*]: Seems funny to think of a bird here. But she must have had one, or why should she have a cage? I wonder what happened to it?

MRS. HALE: I s'pose maybe the cat got it.

MRS. PETERS: No, she didn't have a cat. She's got that feeling some people have about cats—being afraid of them. My cat got in her room and she was real upset and asked me to take it out.

MRS. HALE: My sister Bessie was like that. Queer, ain't it?

MRS. PETERS [*examining the cage*]: Why, look at this door. It's broke. One hinge is pulled apart.

MRS. HALE [*looking too*]: Looks as if someone must have been rough with it.

MRS. PETERS: Why, yes.

[*She brings the cage forward and puts it on the table.*]

MRS. HALE: I wish if they're going to find any evidence they'd be about it. I don't like this place.

MRS. PETERS: But I'm awful glad you came with me, Mrs. Hale. It would be lonesome for me sitting here alone.

MRS. HALE: It would, wouldn't it? [*Dropping her sewing*]. But I tell you what I do wish, Mrs. Peters. I wish I had come over sometimes *she* was here. I—[*Looking around the room.*]—wish I had.

MRS. PETERS: But of course you were awful busy, Mrs. Hale—your house and your children.

MRS. HALE: I could've come. I stayed away because it weren't cheerful—and that's why I ought to have come. I—I've never liked this place. Maybe because it's down in a hollow, and you don't see the road. I dunno what it is, but it's a lonesome place and always was. I wish I had come over to see Minnie Foster sometimes. I can see now—

[*Shakes her head.*]

MRS. PETERS: Well, you mustn't reproach yourself, Mrs. Hale. Somehow we just don't see how it is with other folks until—something comes up.

MRS. HALE: Not having children makes less work—but it makes a quiet house, and Wright out to work all day, and no company when he did come in. Did you know John Wright, Mrs. Peters?

MRS. PETERS: Not to know him; I've seen him in town. They say he was a good man.

MRS. HALE: Yes—good; he didn't drink, and kept his word as well as most, I guess, and paid his debts. But he was a hard man, Mrs. Peters. Just to pass the time of day with him— [*Shivers.*] Like a raw wind that gets to the bone. [*Pauses, her eyes falling on the cage.*] I should think she would 'a wanted a bird. But what do you suppose went with it?

MRS. PETERS: I don't know, unless it got sick and died.

[*She reaches over and swings the broken door, swings it again. Both women watch it.*]

MRS. HALE: You weren't raised round here, were you? [MRS. PETERS *shakes her head.*] You didn't know—her?

MRS. PETERS: Not till they brought her yesterday.

MRS. HALE: She—come to think of it, she was kind of like a bird herself—real sweet and pretty, but kind of timid and—fluttery. How—she—did—change. [*Silence; then as if struck by a happy thought and relieved to get back to every day things.*] Tell you what, Mrs. Peters, why don't you take the quilt in with you? It might take up her mind.

MRS. PETERS: Why, I think that's a real nice idea, Mrs. Hale. There couldn't possibly be any objection to it, could there? Now, just what would I take? I wonder if her patches are in here—and her things.

[*They look in the sewing basket.*]

MRS. HALE: Here's some red. I expect this has got sewing things in it. [*Brings out a fancy box.*] What a pretty box. Looks like something somebody would give you. Maybe her scissors are in here. [*Opens box. Suddenly puts her hand to her nose.*] Why—[MRS. PETERS *bends nearer, then turns her face away.*] There's something wrapped up in this piece of silk.

MRS. PETERS: Why, this isn't her scissors.

MRS. HALE [*lifting the silk*]: Oh, Mrs. Peters—It's—

[MRS. PETERS *bend closer.*]

MRS. PETERS: It's the bird.

MRS. HALE [*jumping up*]: But, Mrs. Peters—look at it. Its neck! Look at its neck! It's all—other side *to.*

MRS. PETERS: Somebody—wrung—its neck.

[*Their eyes meet. A look of growing comprehension, of horror. Steps are heard outside.* MRS. HALE *slips box under quilt pieces, and sinks into her chair. Enter* SHERIFF *and* COUNTY ATTOR-NEY. MRS. PETERS *rises.*]

COUNTY ATTORNEY [*as one turning from serious thing to little pleasantries*]: Well, ladies have you decided whether she was going to quilt it or knot it?

MRS. PETERS: We think she was going to—knot it.

COUNTY ATTORNEY: Well, that's interesting, I'm sure. [*Seeing the birdcage.*] Has the bird flown?

MRS. HALE [*putting more quilt pieces over the box*]: We think the—cat got it.

COUNTY ATTORNEY [*preoccupied*]: Is there a cat?

[MRS. HALE *glances in a quick covert way at* MRS. PETERS.]

MRS. PETERS: Well, not now. They're superstitious, you know. They leave.

COUNTY ATTORNEY [*to* SHERIFF PETERS, *continuing an interrupted conversation*]: No sign at all of anyone having come from the outside. Their own rope. Now let's go up again and go over it piece by piece. [*They start upstairs.*] It would have to have been someone who knew just the—

[MRS. PETERS *sits down. The two women sit there not looking at one another, but as if peering into something and at the same time holding back. When they talk now it is the manner of feeling their way over strange ground, as if afraid of what they are saying, but as if they can not help saying it.*]

MRS. HALE: She liked the bird. She was going to bury it in that pretty box.

MRS. PETERS [*in a whisper*]: When I was a girl—my kitten—there was a boy took a hatchet, and before my eyes—and before I could get there—[*Covers her face an instant.*] If they hadn't held me back, I would have—[*Catches herself, looks upstairs where steps are heard, falters weakly.*]—hurt him.

MRS. HALE [*with a slow look around her*]: I wonder how it would seem never to have had any children around. [*Pause.*] No, Wright wouldn't like the bird—a thing that sang. She used to sing. He killed that, too.

MRS. PETERS [*moving uneasily*]: We don't know who killed the bird.

MRS. HALE: I knew John Wright.

MRS. PETERS: It was an awful thing was done in this house that night, Mrs. Hale. Killing a man while he slept, slipping a rope around his neck that choked the life out of him.

MRS. HALE: His neck. Choked the life out of him.

[*Her hand goes out and rests on the birdcage.*]

MRS. PETERS [*with rising voice*]: We don't know who killed him. We don't know.

MRS. HALE [*her own feeling not interrupted*]: If there'd been years and years of nothing, then a bird to sing to you, it would be awful—still, after the bird was still.

MRS. PETERS [*something within her speaking*]: I know what stillness is. When we homesteaded in Dakota, and my first baby died—after he was two years old, and me with no other then—

MRS. HALE [*moving*]: How soon do you suppose they'll be through, looking for evidence?

MRS. PETERS: I know what stillness is. [*Pulling herself back*]. The law has got to punish crime, Mrs. Hale.

MRS. HALE [*not as if answering that*]: I wish you'd seen Minnie Foster when she wore a white dress with blue ribbons and stood up there in the choir and sang. [*A look around the room*]. Oh, I wish I'd come over here once in a while! That was a crime! That was a crime! Who's going to punish that?

MRS. PETERS [*looking upstairs*]: We mustn't—take on.

MRS. HALE: I might have known she needed help! I know how things can be—for women. I tell you, it's queer, Mrs. Peters. We live close together and we live far apart. We all go through the same things—it's all just a different kind of the same thing. [*Brushes her eyes; noticing the bottle of fruit, reaches out for it.*] If I was you, I wouldn't tell her her fruit was gone. Tell her it ain't. Tell her it's all right. Take this in to prove it to her. She—she may never know whether it was broke or not.

MRS. PETERS [*takes the bottle, looks about for something to wrap it in; takes petticoat from the clothes brought from the other room, very nervously begins winding this around the bottle. In a false voice*]: My, it's a good thing the men couldn't hear us. Wouldn't they just laugh! Getting all stirred up over a little thing like a—dead canary. As if that could have anything to do with—with— wouldn't they laugh!

[*The men are heard coming down stairs.*]

MRS. HALE [*under her breath*]: Maybe they would—maybe they wouldn't.

COUNTY ATTORNEY: No, Peters, it's all perfectly clear except a reason for doing it. But you know juries when it comes to women. If there was some definite thing. Something to show—something to make a story about—a thing that would connect up with this strange way of doing it—

[*The women's eyes meet for an instant. Enter HALE from outer door.*]

HALE: Well, I've got the team around. Pretty cold out there.

COUNTY ATTORNEY: I'm going to stay here awhile by myself [*To the SHERIFF*]. You can send Frank out for me, can't you? I want to go over everything. I'm not satisfied that we can't do better.

SHERIFF: Do you want to see what Mrs. Peters is going to take in?

[*The* COUNTY ATTORNEY *goes to the table, picks up the apron, laughs.*]

COUNTY ATTORNEY: Oh, I guess they're not very dangerous things the ladies have picked up. [*Moves a few things about, disturbing the quilt pieces which cover the box. Steps back.*] No, Mrs. Peters doesn't need supervising. For that matter, a sheriff's wife is married to the law. Ever think of it that way, Mrs. Peters?

MRS. PETERS: Not—just that way.

SHERIFF [*Chuckling*]: Married to the law. [*Moves toward the other room.*] I just want you to come in here a minute, George. We ought to take a look at these windows.

COUNTY ATTORNEY [*scoffingly*]: Oh, windows!

SHERIFF: We'll be right out, Mr. Hale.

[HALE *goes outside. The* SHERIFF *follows the* COUNTY ATTORNEY *into the other room. Then* MRS. HALE *rises, hands tight together, looking intensely at* MRS. PETERS, *whose eyes make a slow turn, finally meeting* MRS. HALE'*s. A moment* MRS. HALE *holds her, then her own eyes point the way to where the box is concealed. Suddenly* MRS. PETERS *throws back quilt pieces and tries to put the box in the bag she is wearing. It is too big. She opens box, starts to take bird out, cannot touch it, goes to pieces, stands there helpless. Sound of a knob turning in the other room.* MRS. HALE *snatches the box and puts it in the pocket of her big coat. Enter* COUNTY ATTORNEY *and* SHERIFF.]

COUNTY ATTORNEY [*facetiously*]: Well, Henry, at least we found out that she was not going to quilt it. She was going to—what is it you call it, ladies!

MRS. HALE [*her hand against her pocket*]: We call it—knot it, Mr. Henderson.

Curtain

Source: Susan Glaspell, *Trifles*, 1916.

[QUESTIONS FOR REFLECTION]

Considering Ideas

1. How do the men and women differ in their separate investigations of Mr. Wright's murder? Why are their approaches so dissimilar?

2. How had Mrs. Wright changed since she was Minnie Foster 30 years ago? What do you suppose led to that change?

3. What problem do Mrs. Peters and Mrs. Hale face as they uncover the details of the investigation? How do they finally decide to resolve that problem at the end of the play? Do you feel that their resolution is justified? Why or why not?

Considering Writing Strategies

1. What is ironic about the title *Trifles*? Do you prefer this title or "A Jury of Her Peers," the short story version of the play? Why?

2. What analogy does Glaspell draw between the canary and Mrs. Wright? What is the significance of the cage in this analogy?

3. How does the writer appeal to the audience? Has she made you feel compassion for Mrs. Wright? Why or why not?

Writing Suggestions

1. In response to Glaspell's *Trifles*, write a proposal suggesting what Mrs. Peters and Mrs. Hale should do with the evidence they found. You might weigh the pros and cons of several possible solutions before making your final recommendation.

2. Write an essay proposing ways for women, or men, to deal with domestic abuse.

Drinking and Driving
by Brittney Balogh

Every weekend, countless people go to bars with their friends and have a few too many drinks. Even after drinking too much, many of these individuals get into their cars and drive home without giving any thought to the people who are driving around them. These drunk drivers are a menace on the roadways and frequently cause car crashes that can result in serious injury or even death for innocent drivers and passengers. This common practice needs to change. Bar owners should take responsibility to help prevent their patrons from drinking and driving. Three possible solutions to this potentially deadly practice are for bar owners to offer a breath test, facilitate a designated driver system, or provide a ride home for intoxicated customers.

One solution for solving the dangerous problem of drinking and driving is for bar owners to give their customers an opportunity to take a breath test to determine if they register over the legal blood-alcohol ratio limit for driving. Before leaving the bar, customers could blow into one of these little handheld devices, which can be found on eBay for as little as $5.00, to see if they are safe to drive home. The main benefit of using this device is that it would help to cut down on the number of people who leave bars intoxicated. On the downside, the bar would have to purchase protective covers for the machine to prevent customers from sharing germs and diseases with one another through the mouthpiece that the customers breathe into.

A second solution that would help solve the drinking and driving problem is for bar owners to encourage customers to participate in a designated driver system. Each establishment could allow groups of friends to choose a designated driver for the group. The bars could provide each designee with a hand stamp or wristband so that bar tenders would know who is not allowed to purchase alcoholic drinks. Additionally, bar tenders could offer free non-alcoholic drinks to the designated drivers. Getting a free cola product, iced tea, or cup of coffee might be a good incentive for the designated drivers to stay sober. This solution would be very cost effective, and it would reduce the number of drunk drivers out on the road. However, it isn't foolproof. The designated drivers could remove their stamps or wristbands, or they could add their own alcohol to their free drinks.

A third solution for helping to reduce drinking and driving is for bar owners to provide rides home for guests who are clearly intoxicated. Bartenders could take notice of patrons who seem to be drinking too much and encourage them to accept a free ride home. Similar to the first two solutions, this procedure would help to ensure that the drunken customers would not get behind the wheel and cause harm to themselves or others. However, it could be costly for bars to pay for drivers, cars, and the insurance to make this operation work. Also, people may refuse to take the free ride home.

Overall, the best solution for reducing the number of drunk drivers endangering the lives of other drivers and passengers is for bar owners to offer breath tests and a designated driver program for all customers. They might reserve calling a taxi or giving a ride home to drunken customers only if the first two methods fail. Even though bar patrons should be responsible for their own actions, when they drink too much, they can lose the ability to make a good decision about how to get home. Therefore, bar owners should step up and help those who are not able to or chose not to take care of themselves. Doing so will make the roads safer for everyone.

[QUESTIONS FOR REFLECTION]

1. Does Balogh's introduction convince the reader that the problem exists? Explain.
2. What three possible solutions does Balogh propose?
3. What are the pros and cons of each possible solution?
4. Is the author's final solution convincing? Why or why not?
5. What other solutions might help to solve the problem?

▶ *Activity* Proposing Solutions

On your own or in small groups, identify three problems that you have experienced at home, school, or work. Brainstorm several possible solutions for each problem. Weigh the pros and cons of each possible solution, and determine which solution seems to be the most feasible. Be prepared to share your results with the class. This activity may give you ideas for writing a problem-solving essay.

Interpreting an Advertisement

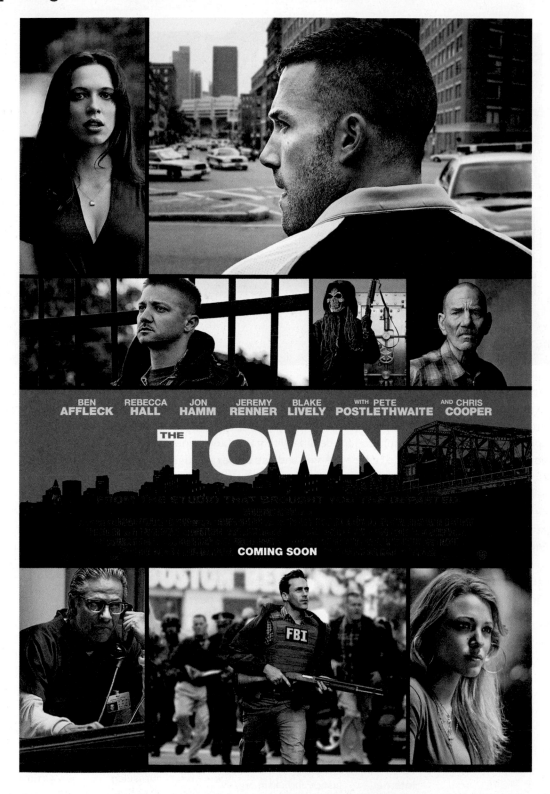

Who might be interested in the advertisement above? How do the images and text interact? What does the ad suggest about investigations of criminal activity? What details catch your eye? Does the movie look appealing? Why or why not? Is the advertisement effective? Why or why not?

Writing about an Image

Write a problem-solving essay related to one of the images in this chapter. What kind of crime has occurred? Could it have been prevented? What should be done about it? You may write about the image itself, or you may choose to write about something that relates to it. For example, you might write an essay about the first image in the chapter, showing a courtroom and gun, proposing a solution for dealing with gangs and guns. Or you may choose to write about the image above, suggesting ways to help reduce the sale and use of illegal drugs in the United States.

Media Connection for Solving a Problem

You might watch, read, and/or listen to one or more of the suggested media to discover additional examples of problem solving. Exploring various media may help you to better understand methods for solving problems. You may also choose to write about one or more of the media suggestions. For example, you might watch the movie *Burn after Reading* and propose alternate solutions for how the characters dealt with the problems they faced. Be sure to give credit to any sources you use in your essay.

Television	CSI, The Closer	Prison Break, Criminal Minds	Law and Order, Boston Legal
Film	Runaway Jury (2003)	High Crimes (2002)	Burn after Reading (2008)
Print	Conflict Resolution Quarterly (magazine)	Criminal Justice (journal)	Crime & Justice (journal)
Internet	www.justicejournalism.org/crimeguide/	www.rider.edu/~suler/psycyber/conflict.html	www.crimeandjustice.org/
Music	"Please Man" by Big & Rich	"I Fought the Law" by Green Day	"Hurricane" by Bob Dylan

Write NOW!

WRITE A PROPOSAL ABOUT A PROBLEM related to one of the following topics. You'll need to narrow the topic to something you can reasonably cover within the scope of your assignment. Remember to consider your rhetorical star as well as the steps for writing a proposal as you compose.

1. Managing time or money
2. Relationships
3. Teenage pregnancy
4. Drug or alcohol abuse
5. Drinking and driving
6. Divorce
7. Plagiarism or cheating on tests
8. Overcrowded prisons
9. Pollution
10. Poverty or homelessness

ESOL Tip >

You may choose to propose a solution to a problem that exists in your culture or native country.

12.4 > Analyzing the Rhetorical Star for Solving a Problem

FIGURE 12.1
The Rhetorical Star

Subject	Identify a problem that you have observed in your community, at home, or at work. The issue can be one you have witnessed or experienced firsthand or one that you have noticed in the media. For example, maybe you have heard that someone has been vandalizing apartments in your complex and want to urge someone to do something about it. Or perhaps you feel your credit card company is taking unfair advantage of you by charging outrageous interest rates and you want to do something about it.
Audience	Who will read your proposal? What will interest your readers about your subject? What do they already know about the problem? Why will they care about it? Are your readers experiencing the problem or contributing to it? Will the problem affect them in some way? Are they in a position to do something about the problem? Think about what kinds of details would be most appropriate to share with your audience. Appeal to the interests and needs of your specific audience and anticipate their potential responses to your proposal. For example, if you are writing about problems in your apartment complex, then your audience could be the landlord, supervisor, other tenants, surrounding community members, security personnel, and/or the police department.
Purpose	Think about what you are trying to accomplish through your proposal. Do you simply want your readers to have a better understanding of the problem and possible solutions for solving it? Do you intend for your audience to do something based on your proposal? Either way, your main goal is to convince your readers that a problem exists and offer a reasonable solution.
Strategy	Even if your primary goal is to propose a solution to a problem, you may decide to use additional writing strategies as well. For example, you might show the causes or effects of not solving the problem, you may compare and contrast what the situation will be like in the future if your solution is implemented or not, or you could decide to evaluate several possible solutions before persuading your reader that one particular solution is the best.
Design	What is the best format for your proposal? Should you write an essay or newspaper article? Would a letter or e-mail be appropriate? Could you post a flyer at work, on campus, or in the community? Also, what other design details might enhance your proposal? Maybe using bullets, headings, photographs, or charts might strengthen your problem-solving essay.

12.5 > Applying the Writing Process for Solving a Problem

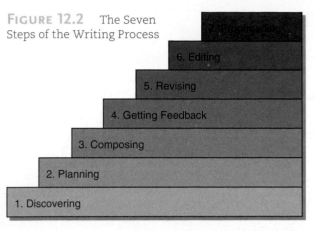

FIGURE 12.2   The Seven Steps of the Writing Process

1. **Discovering:** The readings, images, and other media suggestions in this chapter may help you find a problem to explore. Look through the chapter and see what comes to mind. Additionally, make a list of problems that you have experienced or witnessed that might be meaningful to others. You might try discussing the problem with a classmate or friend to get some ideas for solving the problem.

2. **Planning:** Once you have chosen a topic, you might write out the problem and then make a list of potential solutions. Consider the pros and cons of each solution before choosing which one or ones to include in your essay. Use the graphic organizer below or create a cluster or an outline (informal or formal) to help you arrange your ideas.

3. **Composing:** Using your plan from the previous step, write a first draft of your problem-solving essay. Don't worry too much about grammar and punctuation at this time. Keep focused on explaining the problem and offering viable solutions. Use the steps outlined on pp. 287–289.

   1. Identify a problem and demonstrate that it exists.
   2. Appeal to your audience.
   3. State your claim (thesis).
   4. Propose a solution to the problem.
   5. Organize your solution(s) effectively.
   6. Persuade your readers that your proposal is feasible.
   7. End with a call to action.

4. **Getting feedback:** Have at least one classmate or other person read your rough draft and answer the peer review questions that follow. If you have access to a writing tutor or center, get another opinion about your paper as well.

5. **Revising:** Using all of the feedback available to you, revise your problem-solving essay. Be sure that your overall solution is reasonable and explained clearly. Add, delete, and rearrange ideas as necessary.

6. **Editing:** Read your problem-solving essay again, this time looking for errors in grammar, punctuation, and mechanics. Pay particular attention to your choice of words and tone. Also, keep in mind that there may be other possible solutions that would work, so you don't necessarily want to imply that your solution is the only viable one.

7. **Proofreading:** After you have carefully edited your essay, read it again. This time, look for typographical errors and any other issues that might interfere with the readers' understanding of your problem-solving essay. Make your final corrections.

FIGURE 12.3   Sample Graphic Organizer

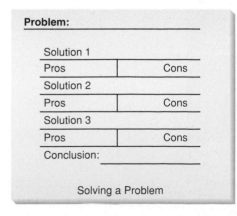

Trade rough drafts with a classmate and answer the following questions about his or her paper. Then, in person or online, discuss your papers and suggestions with your peer. Finally, make the changes you feel would most benefit your paper.

1. Has the author clearly identified a problem? What is it?

2. Has the author demonstrated that a problem exists?

3. How does the author appeal to the audience?

4. What is the author's claim (thesis)? Is it clear?

5. Has the author effectively supported the problem-solving essay? What kind of evidence is included?

6. Is the problem-solving essay organized effectively? Why or why not?

7. What is the strongest part of the essay?

8. Does the conclusion contain a call to action? Is it effective? Why or why not?

9. What kinds of grammatical errors, if any, are evident in the problem-solving essay?

10. What final suggestions do you have for the author?

> Writer's Checklist for Problem Solving

Use the checklist below to evaluate your own writing and to help ensure that your problem-solving essay is effective. If you answer no to any of the questions, go back and work on those areas if necessary.

❏ 1. Have I clearly identified the problem?

❏ 2. Have I demonstrated that the problem exists?

❏ 3. Have I appealed to my audience?

❏ 4. Have I stated a clear claim?

❏ 5. Have I proposed a reasonable solution?

❏ 6. Have I organized my proposal effectively?

❏ 7. Have I supported my solution in a convincing manner?

❏ 8. Have I included a call to action in my conclusion?

❏ 9. Have I proofread thoroughly?

CHAPTER SUMMARY

1. Use the problem-solving strategy to determine a solution to a challenging issue or situation.

2. Problem-solving writing is an important part of your education, daily life, and career.

3. Interpreting readings and images related to problems and solutions can help you to prepare to write a problem-solving essay.

4. Carefully analyze the rhetorical star before writing a problem-solving essay: subject, audience, purpose, strategy, and design.

5. Follow these steps when writing an effective problem-solving essay: identify a problem and demonstrate that it exists; appeal to your audience; state your claim; propose a solution; organize your solution(s) effectively; persuade your readers that your proposed solution is feasible; end with a call to action.

WHAT I KNOW NOW

Use this checklist to determine what you need to work on in order to feel comfortable with your understanding of the material in this chapter. Check off each item as you master it. Review the material for any unchecked items.

❏ 1. I know what **problem-solving** writing is.

❏ 2. I can identify several **real-world applications** for problem-solving writing.

❏ 3. I can **evaluate** readings and images that reflect problems and solutions.

❏ 4. I can analyze the **rhetorical star** for problem-solving writing.

❏ 5. I understand the **writing process** for writing about problems and solutions.

❏ 6. I can apply the **seven steps** for problem-solving writing.

PART 3

Research Guide

Why Research Skills Are Essential

The chapters in Part 3 are geared toward helping you plan, write, document, and present a research paper. In the real world, you often conduct research when you want to know the answer to a question, even if you don't realize that is what you are doing. For example, if you want to know where to go to get your computer fixed without spending a fortune, then you might ask a friend who is a computer science major for suggestions. If you are looking for a job, you may go to **monster.com** or look in the classifieds section of your local newspaper for possible employment opportunities. If you want to know who the lead singer is for a new band, you can go online and conduct a Google search to find out whose voice it is that you keep replaying in your head. All of these activities require research of one type or another.

Being able to write an effective research paper is an essential skill for college, the work world, and your personal life. You need to be able to gather pertinent information and put it together in a meaningful way. You also need to avoid plagiarism throughout the research process. That's why documentation methods are so important.

If you panic when you hear the words *research essay*, you are not alone. The good news is that writing a research paper can be a rewarding and worthwhile experience. The keys to success are choosing the right topic, planning your paper effectively, selecting appropriate sources, and budgeting enough time to revise and complete the paper by the due date. You'll probably spend more time on this assignment than any other you complete for your composition course. Therefore, you'll need to get organized and make the most of your opportunity to learn and write about something new and interesting.

CHAPTER 13

PLANNING AND WRITING A RESEARCH PAPER

13.1 > Discovering a Research Subject

The first step to conducting research is to find a suitable topic. To do that, you must understand the parameters of the assignment. Read the instructions carefully and make sure you know what topics are acceptable and what your instructor expects from you. Ask questions to clarify any uncertainties you have. Your instructor may assign a topic or allow you to choose a topic to explore. If you do have an opportunity to select your own topic, then you will want to make your selection carefully. You'll spend a fair amount of time on your research assignment, so you'll want to choose a topic that is interesting and meaningful to you.

Perhaps you would like to know more about your major field of study so that you can have a clearer understanding of what types of duties you will be expected to perform on the job. Maybe you've always wondered what it would be like to go into outer space or to go scuba diving. Your topic doesn't have to be stuffy or academic. If you choose a subject you genuinely want to learn more about, you'll find the research process can be quite enjoyable. To find an appropriate topic, you can brainstorm ideas, skim through written sources, browse the library, surf the Internet, watch television, listen to the radio, or discuss your assignment with others.

13.2 > Narrowing a Research Subject

After you have selected a topic, you'll want to narrow it so that you can adequately cover it within the parameters of your assignment. For example, if you choose space exploration as your broad topic, then you might focus on how space exploration affects life on Earth. You can narrow that topic even further by focusing on how National Aeronautics and Space Administration (NASA) technology designed for space exploration can be used to improve everyday household items.

Similarly, if you decide to write about a hobby you'd like to try, such as scuba diving, you might narrow your subject by focusing on what you would need to get started. Understanding the specific requirements for the assignment will also help you decide how to narrow your topic. Consider the length of the assignment, the number and type of sources you need to use, and the due date when determining how to focus your topic.

13.3 > Creating a Researchable Question

Developing a researchable question can guide your research process. An effective research question has enough depth to help you develop a thesis, but is narrow enough to fit within the guidelines of your assignment. Think about what you already know about your subject and what you would like to learn. Make sure that you don't already know the answer to the question and that you truly want to know the answer. You can always revise your question after you have begun your preliminary research.

Sample Questions

- **Too broad:** How has NASA affected the average American citizen?
- **Too narrow:** Has NASA affected the average American citizen?
- **Appropriate:** How has NASA's technology designed for space exploration helped to improve everyday household products?
- **Too broad:** What does scuba diving involve?
- **Too narrow:** What is scuba diving?
- **Appropriate:** What is required to begin scuba diving?

13.4 > Writing a Preliminary Thesis Statement

Developing a researchable question can help give you a sense of direction for your research process, but it will not substitute for a clear thesis. As you begin the research process, you'll need to draft a preliminary thesis, sometimes called a working thesis. As with any essay, your research paper needs a thesis that includes your subject and an opinion. Having a working thesis will help you as you begin to select sources. You may decide to refine your original thesis later as you come across new ideas in the sources you find.

Sample Thesis Statements

- NASA has developed a number of high-tech devices for space exploration that have practical applications for everyday household products.
- The most essential requirements for becoming a scuba diver are purchasing (or borrowing) equipment, taking lessons, and getting certified.

13.5 > Locating Library and Internet Sources

To be successful with a research project, it is essential that you find the right resources to use. For most research topics you will benefit from using a variety of sources, including books, periodicals, the Internet, and primary research. Learning how to conduct library and Internet research effectively will save you valuable time. Going to a library on campus or in your community is one of the best ways to gather information about your topic.

If you are not familiar with the library where you will be conducting your research, then you should check to see if the library offers a workshop or tour that shows you how to find useful sources for your subject. If one of those options is not available, then you can ask if there is a brochure or online tutorial that you can use to learn your way around the library. You can also benefit from talking to a librarian. In addition to finding books, periodicals, and films on your subject, your library probably has a variety of other sources, such as specialized databases and reference materials that will help you in the search process. As you learn more about the library, look for the following features:

FIGURE 13.1 Keiser University Card Catalog

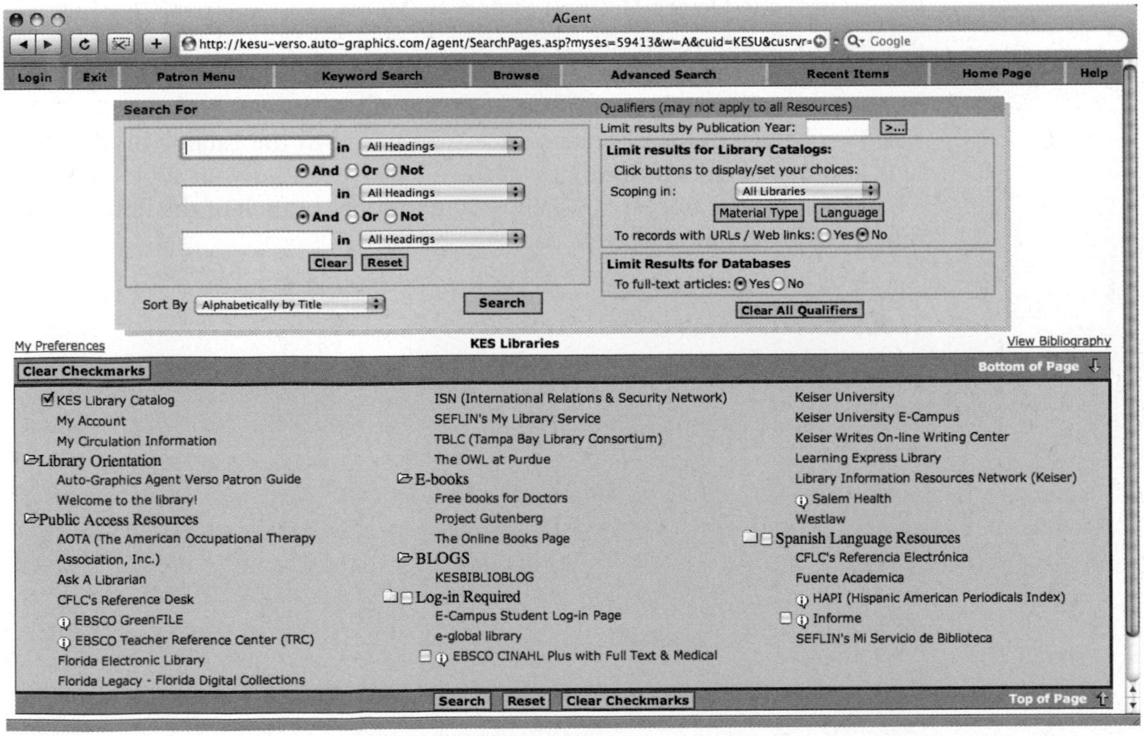

Computerized Card Catalog

More than likely, the library you use will have a computerized card catalog, which is an index of the library's holdings with specific information about each item. You may also be able to determine if the item you need is on the shelf or checked out by another library patron. The card catalog is an excellent place to begin your research. Typically, you can search by title, author, ISBN, or subject.

Type keywords into the catalog to find what you need. Be careful to spell the words correctly, or you may not find anything that matches your subject. Also, you may need to experiment with different keywords until you find exactly what you need. Use the words *and, or,* or *not* (known as Boolean logic) to help narrow your search. (see p. 325 for more on Boolean logic). Print out or jot down important information about the sources that are relevant to your topic, such as the author, title, call number, and date of publication. Having that information will help you locate the source on the shelf.

Stacks

Take the list of potential sources that you found in the card catalog and head to the stacks (shelves of books) to retrieve them. The easiest way to find the sources is to use the call number, located on the spine of the book. Check to see if your library uses the Dewey Decimal System or Library of Congress Classification System to organize materials. Each method organizes the materials in the stacks differently. The Dewey Decimal System divides subjects into 10 numbered categories, and the Library of Congress Classification uses 20 lettered categories. (See below). As you locate sources you found in the catalog on the shelf, look at nearby books to see if any of them are relevant to your topic as well. If a book you need is not on the shelf or is at another branch of the library, ask a reference librarian to help you locate the book.

TABLE 13.1

Dewey Decimal System	
000–099	General Knowledge
100–199	Psychology and Philosophy
200–299	Religions and Mythology
300–399	Social Sciences and Folklore
400–499	Languages and Grammar
500–599	Math and Science
600–699	Medicine and Technology
700–799	Arts and Recreation
800–899	Literature
900–999	Geography and History
Library of Congress Classification	
A	General Works
B	Philosophy, Psychology, Religion
C	Auxiliary Sciences of History
D	World History
E–F	History of the Americas

G	Geography, Anthropology, Recreation
H	Social Sciences
J	Political Sciences
K	Law
L	Education
M	Music
N	Fine Arts
P	Language and Literature
Q	Science
R	Medicine
S	Agriculture
T	Technology
U	Military Science
V	Naval Science
Z	Bibliography, Library Science, Information Resources

Periodicals

In the periodical section of the library, you will find recent issues of magazines, newspapers, and professional journals. Periodicals make good sources for research papers because they contain information that is precise and up-to-date. Magazine and newspaper articles tend to be more general than professional journals. They appeal to the average reader whereas journal articles typically go into more depth and are geared toward an audience that is knowledgeable in a particular field.

Current periodicals and newspapers are typically shelved alphabetically by title. Back issues may be bound and stored in the stacks or another area of the library. Here are a few of the many Web sites you can use to locate additional periodical sources that may not be available in your library:

TABLE 13.2

Online Periodical Sources	
The Internet Public Library	**www.ipl.org**
Newspapers.com	**www.newspapers.com**
CNN Interactive	**www.cnn.com**
CSPAN Online	**www.c-span.org**
Free Management Library	**www.managementhelp.org**

Computerized Databases

Most libraries have computers available for you to use to conduct research. Also, your school may subscribe to a specific database network, such as the Library and Information Resources Network (LIRN). If so, a school librarian or administrator can provide you with a password that will allow you to access the databases from the library, your own home, or anywhere you can find Internet access.

As you locate possible sources for your paper, you can read the abstracts of the articles that look promising. When you find a source that you think will be suitable, you can e-mail yourself the article or print it out. Be sure to use the full text, not just the abstract, for your research paper. Abstracts may be inaccurate and are often not written by the author of the article. Here are a few databases that might provide useful sources on your research topic:

TABLE 13.3

Computer Databases	
Info Trac	eLibrary
ProQuest	eGlobal Library
LexisNexis	

Reference Materials

In the reference area you will find encyclopedias, dictionaries, almanacs, handbooks, periodical indexes, and other sources that might help you with the research process. Typically, reference materials may not be checked out, which makes them always available to library patrons. Be careful to not rely too heavily on reference materials, such as dictionaries and encyclopedias, for your research. You may use these types of references to look up words or find basic information about your subject, but do not use reference books as primary sources.

A number of online reference materials are available as well. Please note, however, that Wikipedia is not a credible source for a research paper. Anyone can add, modify, or delete information that has been posted on a topic; therefore, there is no guarantee that the material you find on Wikipedia is accurate. You can find a wealth of reputable resources by going to the Web site of the American Library Association (ALA) **www.guidetoreference.org/homepage. aspx** and signing up for a free trial membership.

Audiovisual Materials

Many libraries have an area where you can locate nonprint media, such as films, music CDs, slides, and other audiovisual materials. You may find a suitable source for your research paper in this part of the library. For instance, you might find a documentary that relates to your research subject. These materials are often organized by type and shelved alphabetically. However, there is no standard method for classifying audiovisual materials. Ask your librarian for help if you have trouble locating what you need.

Internet Searches

The Internet is a valuable research tool that you can use to supplement the traditional sources for your research paper. You can access a great variety of sources on the World Wide Web by using a Web browser, such as Microsoft Internet Explorer, Safari, Netscape Navigator, or Mozilla Firefox.

The Internet contains massive amounts of information; consequently, finding exactly what you need can be a challenge. Fortunately, you can use a search engine to help you find the Web sites that pertain to your research subject. A search engine serves the same purpose as a card catalog in a library. Using a search engine will help you to sift through the billions of pages on the Internet to find exactly what you need. For example, if you want to find Web sites that include information about NASA and household products, then you might try a Google search.

Note: A search engine is not a source. For example, instead of citing Google you should cite an article you find using Google.

FIGURE 13.2 Google Search

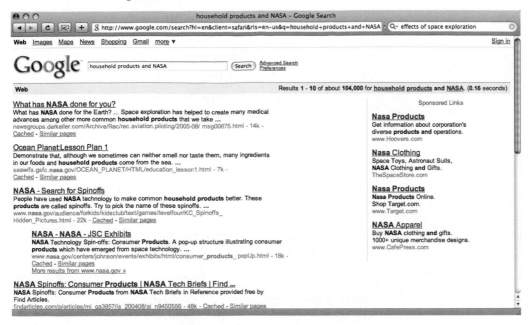

Discussion Groups

In addition to all of the Web sites, periodicals, and reference materials available on the Internet, you can use a search engine to participate in discussion groups on your topic. You might come across some interesting ideas. Keep in mind, however, that anyone can post comments to discussion groups, so you will need to check the accuracy of any information you gather.

Mailing lists: If you sign up for a mailing list on your subject, you will periodically receive updates about your topic via e-mail.

Newsgroups: You can find newsgroups on select subjects by going to **groups. google.com**. These groups are similar to mailing lists except that you will need to find the information online, rather than have it e-mailed to you.

Blogs: Short for Weblog, a blog is a personalized online journal. Businesses, organizations, and individuals can create blogs. Typically, almost anyone interested in the discussion can post a comment to a blog.

Tips for Conducting Internet Searches

1. **Spell your search words correctly.** Otherwise, your search may not yield the results you need.
2. **Use Boolean logic (*and, or, not*) to make your search more precise.**
   - Use the word *and* to tell the search engine to look for sources that contain both terms. Example: "phobias and famous people"
   - Use the word *or* to tell the search engine to look for any of two or more words. Example: "phobias or fears or aversions"
   - Use the word *not* to tell the search engine to exclude one or more words. Example: "phobias not obsessions"
3. **Click on hyperlinks to get more information.** If you see a highlighted word or a special icon, you can usually click on it to learn more information about the term.

TABLE 13.4

Search Engines	
Alltheweb	www.alltheweb.com
Alta Vista	www.altavista.com
Ask	www.ask.com
Excite	www.excite.com
Google	www.google.com
Google Scholar	scholar.google.com
HotBot	www.hotbot.com
Kartoo	www.kartoo.com
Lycos	www.lycos.com
MSN Search	www.msn.com
Open Directory Project	www.dmoz.org
WebCrawler	www.webcrawler.com
Yahoo!	www.yahoo.com
Meta-Search Engines	
Clusty	www.clusty.com
Copernic Agent	www.copernicagent.com
Dogpile	www.dogpile.com
Mamma	www.mamma.com
SurfWax	www.surfwax.com

FIGURE 13.3 Web Page Navigation Arrows

4. **Use the back and forward arrows to navigate Web pages.** For example, if you click on a hyperlink and want to return to the previous page, click the back button (see Figure 13.3). If you keep clicking the back button, you can get all the way back to your original search. This will allow to you go to another source without retyping your search.

5. **Bookmark or print out useful sources.** Keeping track of sources you may want to use in the future will save you time later if you decide to use the source.

Use several of the search engines listed above to locate pertinent information on your research subject (or a subject your instructor gives you). Try using Boolean logic to vary your search. If you want to use several search engines at one time, then you can utilize a meta-search engine. Which search engines seem to yield the most useful results on your subject? Which ones are the least helpful? Print out or bookmark some of the information you locate in case you need it for the next activity.

13.6 > Evaluating Research Sources

You are likely to come across far more information on your subject than you could ever incorporate into your research paper; therefore, you will need to evaluate the print and Web-based sources you locate before choosing which ones are the most appropriate to use. The accuracy and credibility of your paper depend on your use of high-quality sources. Here are some tips for evaluating research sources:

1. **Author and publisher:** Is the author an expert in the field with the appropriate credentials? Is the publisher or Web site reputable? If you have doubts about the reliability of the source, then you may want to investigate by searching for a biography of the author or the history of the publisher or sponsoring organization.

2. **Date**: Check to see when the information was published or posted on the Internet. If you are reporting on a famous study or historical event, then you may find that older sources are appropriate for your research paper. In other cases, you'll need to have the most up-to-date information. New discoveries in science and technology are being made every day. If the information seems too old, then find a more current source.

3. **References:** Has the author documented the sources? Most reputable sources will include a bibliography to back up the information presented. If there is a list of sources, look to see if they seem appropriate. If no sources are cited, be wary of the information unless the author is an expert with the appropriate credentials.

4. **Bias:** Is the information objective and fair, or does the author seem to have an agenda? For example, a Web site sponsored by a drug company

may not be the most reliable source to use to determine if a particular drug is the best treatment for an illness.

5. **Effectiveness:** How useful is the content? Is it relevant to the specific areas you plan to cover in your research paper? Is it presented clearly and logically? Does the material seem accurate?

13.7 > Taking Notes from Research Materials

After you have determined which sources will be the most useful for your research paper, then you'll need to begin reading them and taking notes from them. Taking effective notes from the sources you find is essential to successfully completing a research paper. Whether you use a computer, a research journal, a legal pad, or index cards to keep track of your notes is your personal choice. You might want to make two columns, one side for your notes and the other side for your thoughts on why those ideas are relevant and where they might fit into your paper. Be sure to note exactly where you found the information by labeling it with the author, title, date, and page number or URL. Doing so will help you later as you draft your paper and document your sources.

Plagiarism The use of another's words or ideas without giving appropriate credit.

Any time you use summarized, paraphrased, or quoted material in your paper, you must give credit to the original source(s) to avoid **plagiarism**. Your instructor will let you know what exact system of documentation you need to follow in your final research paper. If you add personal comments to your notes, be sure to include them in brackets [ ] so that you can distinguish your ideas from the concepts presented in your source materials.

Summarizing

When you write a summary, you condense ideas from an article, chapter, or passage and use your own words. Include the main ideas, but not most of the specific details and examples. Read the original work, write the summary from memory, and then go back to the original to make sure your ideas are accurate. Summarizing is useful in helping you manage large amounts of information. The following is a summary of an essay that appears earlier in this textbook.

▶ illustrate a POINT   Summary

Although urban myths are typically Hollywood stories that have no merit, they often catch the attention of the public. They represent our modern-day version of folklore because they combine unreal circumstances with everyday occurrences. People tend to believe urban legends because they tap into the fears that they have. Even though urban legends have been found to be completely false, some people will claim to have witnessed the incredible events that are portrayed through them. People may support these legends because the stories explain the unexplainable. Everyone who shares an urban legend has a hand in shaping it and takes ownership of its creation.

Source: From "How Urban Myths Reveal Society's Fears," Neal Gabler, *Los Angeles Times*, November 12, 1995.

Paraphrasing

When you paraphrase, you restate a sentence or passage from an original work in your own words. Unlike a summary, your goal is not to condense the original. Instead, your aim is to revise the original sentences, keeping every idea. As you paraphrase, change the sentence structure and word choice so that the new sentences are not too similar to the original, even though they express the same ideas. Although it should be used sparingly, paraphrasing is useful when the original sentence or passage is complex or technical.

illustrate a POINT — Paraphrase

>> Original Passage

"Though urban legends frequently originate with college students about to enter the real world, they are different from traditional fairy tales because their terrors are not really obstacles on the road to understanding, and they are different from folklore because they cannot even be interpreted as cautionary. In urban legends, obstacles aren't overcome, perhaps can't be overcome, and there is nothing we can do to avoid the consequences."

Inappropriate Paraphrase

Neal Gabler says that even though urban legends often originate with university students who are about to go into the real world, they are not the same as fairy tales because their terrors are not roadblocks on the way to comprehending, and they are not the same as folklore because they aren't cautionary. In urban legends, roadblocks are not overcome, and we can't avoid the repercussions.

Appropriate Paraphrase

According to Neal Gabler, many urban myths relate to students who are about to graduate from college and join the workforce. However, urban myths should not be confused with fairy tales because they do not provide a warning for the reader, and the results are inevitable.

Discussion

The inappropriate paraphrase follows the original passage too closely and uses exact words from Gabler's essay. Occasionally substituting a word with a synonym does not constitute an acceptable paraphrase. On the other hand, the appropriate paraphrase covers the main ideas presented in Gabler's original passage, but the sentence structure and word choice are unique.

Source: From "How Urban Myths Reveal Society's Fears," Neal Gabler, *Los Angeles Times*, November 12, 1995.

Quoting

When you quote, you take someone else's exact words and put quotation marks around them. Like paraphrasing, quoting should be used sparingly. Only introduce a quote when the original is particularly vivid or expressive or when you want to use an authority figure's exact words to add credibility to your paper. Be sure to carefully copy any quotes you use word for word. If you decide to leave out part of a sentence that you are quoting, then use an ellipsis (…) to show that you have omitted words. However, do not alter the intended meaning of the author. Also, if you find an error (such as a misspelled word) in the sentence or passage you are quoting, include the Latin word *sic* in brackets right after the error to show that the mistake was the original author's, not yours, and that you copied the quote faithfully. (See Chapter 14 for examples of quoted material in the MLA and APA formats.)

 illustrate a POINT   Quotation

According to Gabler, "Though urban legends frequently originate with college students about to enter the real world, they are different from traditional fairy tales because their terrors are not really obstacles on the road to understanding, and they are different from folklore because they cannot even be interpreted as cautionary."

Remember to follow the documentation method that your instructor requires any time you summarize, paraphrase, or quote material from a source. If you don't give appropriate credit to the source, then you are plagiarizing.

Source: From "How Urban Myths Reveal Society's Fears," Neal Gabler, *Los Angeles Times*, November 12, 1995.

▶ *Activity*   Note Taking

Choose a magazine or newspaper article, or use one provided by your instructor.

1. Write a summary of the article. Be sure to include the most important ideas and to put all of the ideas into your own words.

2. Write a paraphrase of two or three sentences in the article. Be sure to include every idea from the original source, but put the ideas into your own words.

3. Write a direct quote from the source. Introduce the author and or title of the work, and use quotation marks around exact wording.

13.8 > Conducting Primary Research

In addition to using the research of others, you can gather firsthand information about your subject. Conducting a survey or personal interview is a credible way to supplement the information you find in the library and other sources. One benefit of conducting field research is that you can tailor it to yield the exact results you need. For example, in addition to using books and magazines about scuba diving, you might send out a survey to several divers, asking for their opinions about the most important things to know before beginning to dive. Similarly, if you are writing about a topic related to your major, then you may choose to interview an instructor in that program or a professional in your chosen field who works in your community.

Surveys

A survey is a questionnaire geared toward gaining information from people who are familiar with the subject you are researching. Surveys are particularly useful for learning about the habits or opinions of a particular group of people. For example, you might use a questionnaire for a college-related topic, such as study skills, school resources, or extracurricular activities. While surveys can be useful, keep in mind that they can be challenging to create, administer, and interpret. Check with your instructor to see if a survey is appropriate for your subject. Here are some tips for designing and conducting a survey if you decide that one will benefit your research paper.

1. **Clarify your purpose.** Make sure you know exactly what kind of information you hope to gain from the survey, and make your purpose known to the respondents. You might include a cover letter or note at the top of the survey explaining why you are conducting the survey and how you will use the information. For example, if you are writing a persuasive research paper about the benefits of being actively involved in student organizations, such as student government or an honorary fraternity, then you might mention to the respondents that you will share the results with the school administration and that more extracurricular activities might become available as a result of their participation in your survey.

2. **Choose your participants carefully.** Decide who will be able to provide the best answers for your survey. Make sure your target audience is very familiar with the subject you are researching. For instance, if you are writing about student organizations, then you might invite some students who are involved in organizations on campus and some who are not. You might separate the responses according to those two criteria in your analysis. Additionally, you'll want to make sure that your audience represents a fair sampling of the student population, so you'll need to include males and females as well as people with different majors and ethnicities in your survey group.

3. **Set clear expectations for the respondents.** Be sure to give a reasonable deadline for the recipients to respond. Allowing them a few days to complete the questionnaire should be enough. Also, make it easy for the participants to respond. If you are polling your class, then you might hand out a survey on campus or send out a survey via e-mail.

4. **Design effective questions.** Make sure that your questions or potential answers don't overlap. You may want to test your questions on a few people before sending them out to more people so that you can modify the survey as needed. To avoid confusion, avoid using too many different kinds of questions. One or two should be sufficient. Choose the type(s) of question(s) that will give you the best results for your subject.

5. **Compile and interpret the results.** Tally the results from the surveys that are returned to you and analyze their significance. Be sure to include information in your report that reflects all of the completed results, not just the ones that support the position you are taking in your paper. Also, you should include the raw data you receive as an appendix to your research paper so that your readers can review the information for themselves. Keep in mind, the results you gather are merely the opinions of the respondents, so you can't necessarily assume that these results will hold true for college students in general, just for the ones you survey.

TABLE 13.5

Sample Survey Questions

- **True/False**

  I belong to an extracurricular student organization.

  _____True

  _____False

- **Rating System**

  Participating in a student organization helps the participants to strengthen their leadership skills.

  _____ 1. Strongly agree

  _____ 2. Agree somewhat

  _____ 3. Neither agree nor disagree

  _____ 4. Disagree somewhat

  _____ 5. Strongly disagree

- **Checklist**

  Check all that apply.

  Belonging to student organizations...

  _____ helps students to strengthen their leadership skills.

  _____ provides students with more scholarship opportunities.

  _____ impresses potential employers on a résumé.

  _____ takes away from valuable study time.

  _____ doesn't have any benefits.

  _____ isn't worth the effort required.

- **Multiple Choice**

  Choose one answer.

  How much time do you spend with extracurricular student organizations each week?

  _____ 0 hours

  _____ 1-2 hours

  _____ 3-4 hours

  _____ 5 or more hours

- **Open-Ended**

  How has belonging to an extracurricular student organization affected you?

Personal Interviews

Sometimes, conducting a personal interview can provide you with additional insights that are not available through the library and online sources. You may find an expert on your subject who can answer specific questions that would be difficult to answer through your research. Here are some suggestions for planning and conducting a personal interview.

1. **Clarify your purpose.** Make sure you know exactly what kind of information you hope to gain from the personal interview, and make your purpose known to the interviewee. Keep your interview focused on the information that will be useful for your paper.

2. **Choose your interviewee carefully.** You may need to make several phone calls before you discover who would be the best person to provide you with the specific information you need for your paper. You

may decide that someone in your community or at your college campus will be able to aid your research process.

3. **Determine how you will conduct the interview.** Whenever possible, a face-to-face interview is ideal. If you are able to schedule a meeting in person, then call ahead to make an appointment. If the interviewee is not available to meet in person, then schedule a phone call or communicate via e-mail.

4. **Prepare your questions.** To ensure that your interview session runs efficiently, have 5 to 10 questions written out. The questions will help guide the interview. If you feel that you will get nervous during the interview, you might test your questions on someone before the real interview. Typically, open-ended questions work best for interviews. For example, if you are researching what it would be like to specialize in pediatric nursing, you might ask a pediatric nurse several questions, including the following:

   - What are the most rewarding aspects of being a pediatric nurse?
   - What challenges do you face on the job?
   - Would you recommend your area of specialty to someone just getting started in the nursing field? Why or why not?

5. **Be courteous to the interviewee.** Show up on time for the interview and dress appropriately. Also, tell the interviewee a little bit about what you are trying to accomplish through the interview. Listen carefully to what the interviewee has to say, and ask additional questions if you need the interviewee to clarify or expand on a point of interest. Be sure to thank the interviewee for taking the time to help you with your research project.

6. **Take thorough notes during the interview.** Even if you have a good memory, you'll need to take copious notes during the discussion. Make sure to document the time and date of the interview as well as the interviewee's name and title. Additionally, write the answers to all of the questions you ask. If you would like to record the conversation, ask the interviewee permission first. Some people may be uncomfortable being recorded. If you are able to record the interview session, then you'll need to go back and transcribe the answers later. Carefully documenting the entire interview will make it easier for you to include ideas from the interview in your research paper.

ESOL Tip >

You may be more comfortable taking your interview notes in your native language and transcribing them into English later.

▶ *Activity* **Conducting Primary Research**

Develop and administer a survey and/or conduct a personal interview to gain information about your research subject. Follow the steps on the previous pages. Keep track of your raw data as well as your interpretation of the information you gain through your primary research.

13.9 > Creating an Outline

After you have gathered all of your research notes, you'll need to organize them into a logical sequence by drafting a preliminary outline. Determine the major points you want to cover in your paper and make sure that all of the points help to support your thesis statement. The outline will serve as the framework for your entire paper. You might begin with a topic outline and then expand it into complete sentences. Stay flexible as you begin drafting your paper. You may find that you can't get to everything on your outline, or that you need to include additional points to fully substantiate your thesis. If your instructor requires that you submit an outline with your final paper, then you'll need to revisit your outline and make any necessary changes to ensure that your final outline reflects the organization of your final research paper.

How Scared Are You?
by Neil Harris

Thesis: Although some people may think phobias sound silly or trivial, they are a frighteningly real phenomenon for those who suffer from them. Fortunately, with proper treatment, many people are able to live a reasonably normal life despite their phobias.

I. Description of phobias
   A. Categories
      1. Panic disorders
      2. Anxiety disorders
   B. Symptoms
II. Types of phobias
   A. Common phobias
   B. Strange phobias
   C. Ironic phobias
III. Treatment for phobias
   A. Relaxation and exercise
   B. Psychotherapy
      1. Changing view of phobia
      2. Exposure or desensitization
   C. Flooding
   D. Medications

13.10 > Composing Your Research Paper

Follow the preliminary outline you constructed, and write a first draft of your research paper. Remember to consider your rhetorical star (subject, audience, purpose, strategy, and design) and follow the steps of the writing process (discovering, planning, composing, getting feedback, revising, editing, and proofreading).

As you compose your essay, you may combine the ideas in your notes from secondary sources as well as any primary research you may have conducted. Even though most of the ideas in your research paper will come from outside sources, you'll want to make sure that your voice is the strongest in the paper. Keep in mind that a research essay is more than merely a string of quotes or series of facts. Choose your angle on the topic, and shape your paper to make it an original work.

A research paper follows the same basic structure as a traditional essay; however, you may need two or more paragraphs to fully develop each supporting point. Also, you must cite sources throughout your paper to indicate exactly where you have used primary or secondary research in your paper. As you synthesize ideas from your sources, be careful to note the author, work, and page number (or the Web site address) so that you know exactly where you obtained the information. Later, you can put it into the specific format that your instructor requires, such as APA or MLA. (See Chapter 14 for documentation methods.)

You'll notice that Neil chose to use numbers to keep track of his sources. Also, he covers his points in a different order in his draft than he does in his outline. Finally, his draft lacks a concluding paragraph. He addressed theses issues in later drafts.

How Scared Are You?
by Neil Harris

When confronted with a phobia, the individual experiences what is in effect a panic attack symptoms include but are not limited to rapid heartbeat, high bloodpressure, dry mouth, nausia, and rapid breathing. "A phobia are is a type of anxiety disorder" 4 grouped into two categories, panic disorder and generalized anxiety disorder (GAD). Panic Disorders is "Recurrent episodes of unprovoked feelings of terror or impending doom" 2 while generalized anxiety disorder is " Exaggerated work about health, safty, money, and other aspects of daily life that lasts 6 months or more. GAD may be a response to a 24 hour news cycle and due times we live in. But panic disorders are a very serious, life activity condition pitobias are grouped into three genres specific, social, and Agoraphobia. Specific phobias entail the individual being paniced by one trigger. This phenomenon will be disgussed later in detail. Social phobias or social anxiety disorder (SAD) is the fear of public situations. Individuals suffering from SAD will avoid public places. Some are worried of being embarrased or caring attention & themselves lastly Agorophobia is a category in and of itself defined as "Fear of having a panic attack in public"5, Agorophobia is typically portrayed as fear to leave safe confines people suffering from this disorder can progress to home confinement but is often observed in lesser degrees.

Many will known personalities deal with phobias, when it vary widely from normal to very strange. Some phobias were much more prominent in the past. Napolean Bonapart, Agustus Caesar, Julius Caesar, and Alexander the great all suffered from allurophobia or fear of cats, others are more recent developments. Verminophobia is the fear of germs. Howard Hughes, Michael Jackson, and Donald Tewmph all are "GERMOPITOBES". Madonna shares her phobia with many dogs, Brontophobia is the fear of thunder. The phobias can seem strange such as David Beckhams fear of disorder Ataxophobia. Anything out of place will drive him crazy. Billy Bob Thorton is terrified of antique furnature, called Panophobia. There is nothing funny about Clowns to Johnny deep and sean who combs who suffer from Clourophobia, the fear of clowns. Famous both former monday night football anouncers John Madden and tony cornheiser will not fly[141]. Their fear of flying is called Aerophobia, Marilyn Monroe suffered from Agorophobia, the fear of open spaces, while uma thurman is claustrophobic, which is the fear of confined spaces. Some people suffer from phobias that clash with their carriers. Rodger moore, who played james bond 007 for years, is afraid of guns or Hoblophobia. The famous vampire novalist Anne Rice, is Achluophobic, she is afraid of the dark[210]. Sheryl crow has one of the more common phobias called Acrophobia, or the fear of heights odd phobias would include Nicole Kidmans Lepidopterophobia or fear of butterflies and christina Ricci's Botanophobia or fear of indoor parts. But, may be phobias are there for a reason. Natalie wood suffered from Hydrophobia or a fear of water, which, sadly she drown in[269]. By far one of the best phobias is Hippopotomonstrosesquipedaliophobia which is the fear of long words. Linguist have their jokes too.[290]

Now you should be ready to get started on the first draft of your research paper. Chapter 14, "Documenting a Research Paper," addresses avoiding plagiarism and documenting your sources.

[CHAPTER SUMMARY]

1. Choose a research topic that is interesting and meaningful to you.

2. Narrow your topic to fit within the parameters of your assignment.

3. Create a researchable question to investigate.

4. Write a preliminary thesis statement to guide your research paper.

5. Locate appropriate library and Internet sources for your paper.

6. Conduct firsthand research through a survey or interview to supplement your library and Internet sources.

7. Evaluate your research sources carefully.

8. Take notes from your sources by summarizing, paraphrasing, and quoting the ideas presented in them.

9. Create an outline to help you organize the ideas you want to include in your paper.

10. Compose a first draft of your research paper.

[WHAT I KNOW NOW]

Use this checklist to determine what you need to work on in order to feel comfortable with your understanding of the material in this chapter. Check off each item as you master it. Review the material for any unchecked items.

❏ 1. I know how to discover and narrow a meaningful **research subject**.

❏ 2. I understand how to create a **researchable question** and write a preliminary thesis.

❏ 3. I understand how to locate and evaluate library and Internet **sources**.

❏ 4. I understand how to conduct **primary research** through a survey or interview.

❏ 5. I know how to take **notes** from research materials.

❏ 6. I know how to create an **outline** for my research paper.

❏ 7. I know how to compose a first **draft** of my research paper.

CHAPTER

14

DOCUMENTING A RESEARCH PAPER

LEARNING outcomes

> In this chapter you will learn techniques for the following:

14.1 Avoiding plagiarism.

14.2 Determining when to cite or not cite a source.

14.3 Applying the MLA format for in-text citations, a works cited page, and a research paper.

14.4 Applying the APA format for in-text citations, a references page, and a research paper.

14.1 > Avoiding Plagiarism

Would you walk into a store, take something off the shelf, and shove it into your backpack because you think no one is looking? That is unethical, right? Stealing someone's words or ideas without properly citing them is just as wrong. Many people cringe when they hear the word *plagiarism*, especially college students and English teachers. To understand how to avoid plagiarism, you need to be sure of exactly what it entails. According to the Merriam-Webster Online Dictionary, there are four definitions for the verb *plagiarize*:

1. To steal and pass off (the ideas or words of another) as one's own

2. To use (another's production) without crediting the source

3. To commit literary theft

4. To present as new and original an idea or product derived from an existing source

All of these definitions represent serious forms of academic dishonesty. The consequences for committing plagiarism at the college level range anywhere from failure of an assignment or the entire course to permanent dismissal from college. This problem goes beyond school. In the workplace, people can be terminated for plagiarism. However, there is no need to panic. If you learn the proper techniques for avoiding plagiarism, then you will have nothing to fear.

Basically, unless you are reporting commonly known facts or your original ideas, you need to document every source that you incorporate into your essay to avoid plagiarism. For example, if you are writing an essay on the effects of television violence on young children, and you want to include some statistics to support your thesis, then you would need to cite your source. Similarly, in a persuasive essay you may want to include a quote from a famous doctor about a new medical treatment for curing the common cold. To cite sources in some types of essays, your instructor may allow you to note the source in your paper with an informal citation, as the following fictitious examples illustrate:

Examples of Informal Citations

- According to psychologist Amy Telly, children who watch television for more than 50 hours per week are more likely to demonstrate violent behaviors at school than children who watch fewer than 25 hours per week.

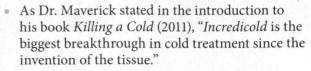

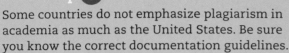

Some countries do not emphasize plagiarism in academia as much as the United States. Be sure you know the correct documentation guidelines.

- As Dr. Maverick stated in the introduction to his book *Killing a Cold* (2011), "*Incredicold* is the biggest breakthrough in cold treatment since the invention of the tissue."

- *Incredicold* is a new product that is taken orally, in gel or pill form, that helps to relieve patients of nearly all of their cold symptoms (www.incredi-cold.com).

Citing sources in the methods shown above is appropriate for some writing situations. Your instructor may ask you to provide a copy of the original source(s) to be sure that you summarized, paraphrased, and/or quoted materials correctly (see Chapter 13 for more on note taking). However, if your primary assignment is to write a formal research paper, then your instructor will probably require that you follow the specific guidelines of the Modern Language Association (MLA) or the American Psychological Association (APA). The rules for each format are extremely precise, so follow the directions very carefully so that you document your papers correctly and avoid plagiarism.

14.2 > Determining When to Cite or Not Cite a Source

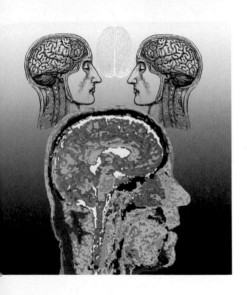

What Doesn't Need to Be Cited?

1. **Common knowledge:** Common knowledge includes widely known facts that can be found in multiple sources. No one *owns* these facts. For example, the fact that George Washington was the first president of the United States is commonly known. Likewise, many people know that Betsy Ross sewed the first American flag.

2. **Your original research:** If you conduct your own research, such as through a survey, then you do not need to document a source. However, you might need to include your raw data in an appendix. Check with your instructor about his or her preference.

3. **Personal experience:** If it is relevant, you may decide to incorporate your own personal experience into your paper. For example, if you are writing a paper about autism and want to include your sibling or child as an example, then you would not need to cite a source for that information. Ask your instructor if using a personal example is appropriate for your paper.

What Does Need to Be Cited?

1. **Direct quotes:** Anytime you use someone else's exact words in your paper, you must enclose the exact wording in quotation marks and give credit to the source.

2. **Facts that aren't common knowledge:** Even if you come across the same idea in several sources, it may not be considered common knowledge. For example, you may find several sources that explain how brain surgery is performed, but your average reader would probably not be familiar with the intricacies of that process. Think about what your audience is likely

to know about your subject. If most people won't know about your subject, then cite your source. If you're not sure, cite it just to be safe.

3. **Opinions:** If you come across an interesting opinion in one of your sources and want to include it in your paper, then you must give credit to the original source. For instance, if you are writing a research paper for an economics course, you might cite an economist whose opinions about the state of the current economy help support your thesis.

4. **Statistics:** Anytime you incorporate statistics into your paper, you must give credit to the originator. For instance, you might decide to include statistics from a reputable source to support your thesis that earning a college degree will lead to a higher-paying job.

5. **Original ideas:** Often writers will create original theories or ideas for their publications. Be sure to give appropriate credit to the author. If you decide to write a paper about the theory of relativity for a science class, then be sure to mention Albert Einstein in addition to citing the sources you used to find the information.

6. **Studies and experiments:** If you are writing a paper for a behavioral or science class, you might want to refer to a professional study or experiment. For example, in a psychology paper on sleep deprivation you might cite a landmark study to illustrate your main idea.

Basically, cite a source in your paper every time you present summarized or paraphrased material that isn't common knowledge or your original idea. If you are not sure whether you need to cite an idea in your paper, then you should be cautious and document the source. You are better off over-citing than under-citing. Also, you can check with your instructor if you are in doubt.

14.3 > MLA Format

Many English and humanities courses use the Modern Language Association (MLA) format. The most up-to-date information about the MLA format is included in the 7th edition of *MLA Handbook for Writers of Research Papers* (2009). You can find more information about the MLA format by going to **www.mla.org**. The MLA style of documentation requires that you cite sources in your text as well as on a *works cited* page at the end of your paper. The following examples will help you to cite sources using the MLA format. You may also want to try using an electronic source, such as **www.noodletools.com**, to help you correctly document your sources.

MLA In-Text Citations

An *in-text citation*, also known as a *parenthetical citation*, shows the reader exactly where you have borrowed ideas from outside sources in your paper. When using the MLA format, you generally need to include the author's last name and page number. Providing this information allows the readers to locate the correct entry on the works cited page so they can find additional information about the subject if desired. You may include the author's last name in the text or in parentheses with the page number. If there is no author, use the title of the work. If there is no page number, such as for a Web site, omit that part. To keep your writing fresh, vary the way in which you introduce sources in your paper. Be sure to include the correct information and make it clear exactly what material comes from a particular source.

One Author

According to Bernsten, people who have popular first names or last names should be cautious that they receive the correct treatment when hospitalized (173).

People who have popular first names or last names should be cautious that they receive the correct treatment when hospitalized (Bernsten 173).

Two Authors

Barber and Takemura recommend that sushi eaters only use small amounts of soy sauce to avoid "drowning" the flavor of the sushi or making it come apart (230).

Sushi eaters should only use small amounts of soy sauce to avoid "drowning" the flavor of the sushi or making it come apart (Barber and Takemura 230).

Three Authors

Ma, Mateer, and Blaivas have observed that even though three-dimensional ultrasound technology can provide amazing images, it is currently not the best tool for making a diagnosis (25).

Even though three-dimensional ultrasound technology can provide amazing images, it is currently not the best tool for making a diagnosis (Ma, Mateer, and Blaivas 25).

Four or More Authors

According to Bishop et al., image editors, such as Macromedia Fireworks or Adobe Photoshop, are useful for enhancing images in a document or Web page (C22).

Image editors, such as Macromedia Fireworks or Adobe Photoshop, are useful for enhancing images in a document or Web page (Bishop et al. C22).

Note: Use the Latin term *et al.*, which means "and others," to show that you have omitted all but the first author. Notice there is no period after *et* but there is one after *al.* Also, this book includes section letters and page numbers.

Multiple Works by the Same Author

Morrison begins her novel *Paradise* with a powerful scenario in a small, racist town: "They shoot the white girl first. With the rest they can take their time" (3).

Morrison depicts the racist attitudes of a small town by catching the reader's attention right from the start: "They shoot the white girl first. With the rest they can take their time" (*Paradise* 3).

Some of the most successful writers begin with a shocking statement to immediately engage their readers, as in the following example: "They shoot the white girl first. With the rest they can take their time" (Morrison, *Paradise* 3).

Note: In addition to the author's name and page number, cite the title of the book to distinguish it from another book by the same author that you are citing in your paper. Place a comma after the author's name.

No Author

According to the book *Getting Yours*, public relations is about getting credit for doing a good job (3).

Basically, public relations is about getting credit for doing a good job (*Getting Yours* 3).

Note: Use the first few of the words of the title in place of an author's name. The entry needs to match the beginning of the corresponding entry on the works cited page.

Corporate Author

Children's Hospital Boston suggests that the parenting process becomes less demanding when a child enters into school (277).

The parenting process becomes less demanding when a child enters into school (Children's Hospital Boston 277).

Indirect Source

According to Budman et al., studies show that children who have Tourette Syndrome may experience "rage" attacks when they see a specialist at a clinic (qtd. in Chowdhury 61).

Note: Use this example if you want to use a quote or information you find in a source that was cited by a different author. Give credit to the original author of the material in your text and the source where you found the quote or information in your parenthetical citation.

Multiple Works

The most common side effect of having a Botox injection is droopy eyelids (*Botox Cosmetic;* Langdon 75).

Note: Use this example when you find the same information in two sources and want to cite both to add credibility to your paper. Cite each work the same way you normally would, and add a semicolon between the works in parentheses. In the above example, the first work is a Web site with no author, and the second is a book.

Long Quote

Glave urges his readers to help do their part to save the planet:

> Do something. Do it now. Dream up your own Eco-Shed, Eco-Car, Eco-Boat, Eco-Garden, Eco-Concrete, Eco-Whatever, and start on it today. Sit right up front and take charge of the process. Stop thinking about what you have to give up, or whom you might tick off, and start thinking about what you'll gain. Each of us must earn our own green belt at our own pace. But believe me, once you begin punching and kicking in that direction, you won't ever look back. (248–249)

Note: For quotes that are longer than four lines, set the entire quote off from the text and begin it on a new line. Indent the quote one inch from the left margin and double space it. Omit the quotation marks and place the final period before the citation.

TABLE 14.1

MLA Works Cited

When using the MLA format, you must include a *works cited* page at the end of the paper to fully document your sources. Literally, this means that you list any *work* you have *cited* in your paper. You may need to look at several examples of works cited entries to find exactly what you need to document your research sources. For example, if you need to cite the fourth edition of a book with three authors, then you would need to look at the sample entries for "Book with Two or Three Authors" and "Book in Edition other than the First." Generally, you will alphabetize the entry according to the authors' last names. If there is no author, begin with the title. Ignore words such as *a* and *the* when alphabetizing an entry by the title on the list of works cited.

Books Here is a list of the basic information you need to include for book sources using the MLA format. List the information in each works cited entry in order, and follow the punctuation guidelines of the examples. You should be able to find all of the information you need on the title and copyright pages of the book. (See Figure 14.1.)

1. **Author:** List the author's last name, followed by a comma and the author's first name and middle name or initial as it appears on the title page of the book. Do not include degrees or titles, such as "PhD" or "Sister," with the author's name. If the book has more than one author, invert only the first author's name and include a comma between authors. If the author is unknown, begin with the title of the book.

2. **Title:** Italicize the complete title of the book. Use title case capitalization, which means that you capitalize every word except articles (words such as *a* and *the*), conjunctions (words such as *but* and *for*) and prepositions (words such as *to, from, for,* and *with*). If there is subtitle, add a colon between them and capitalize the first word after the colon, even if it is an article or preposition. You may need to include additional information after the title, depending on the type of source you are citing. For example, you may be using an edition other than the first or one volume of a multivolume set. See the corresponding examples that follow.

3. **Place of publication:** List the city, followed by a comma, and the two-letter state abbreviation used by the United States Postal Service, followed by a colon. (Go to **www.usps.com** for a complete list.) For major cities that are well known for publishing, such as Boston, Chicago, Los Angeles, London, New York, Paris, or Philadelphia, you may omit the state (or country if the city is not in the United States). If multiple cities are included in the book, list only the first one.

4. **Publisher:** Include a shortened version of the publisher's name. For example, use McGraw instead of McGraw-Hill, U of California P for University of California Press, and Gale rather than Gale Research, Inc. The point is to give the reader enough information to be able to find the publisher if necessary. Eliminate extraneous words such as *books, house,* and *publisher.* If the publisher is named after a person, use only the last name. For instance, W. W. Norton & Company simply becomes Norton.

5. **Date of publication:** List the year, followed by a period.

6. **Publication medium:** Include the word *print* (not italicized) after printed sources. This distinguishes a printed book from an online or electronic book. MLA added this element in the 2008 update to the citation guidelines.

Sample MLA Book Citation

- Author's Last Name, First Name. *Title of Book*. City of Publication: Publisher, Year of Publication. Publication Medium.

Book Example

Russell, Karin L. *Write Now: Read. Think. Research. Persuade. Communicate.* New York: McGraw Hill, 2012. Print.

FIGURE 14.1
Book Title Page

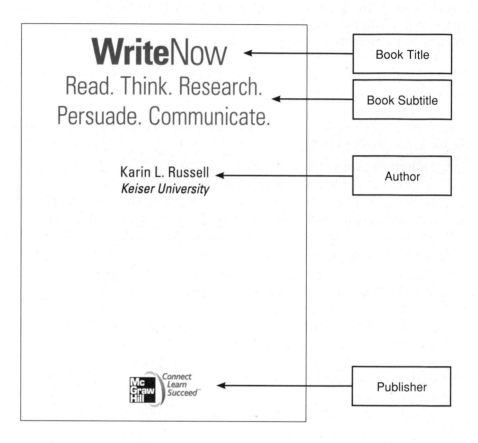

Book with One Author

Bernsten, Karin Janine. *The Patient's Guide to Preventing Medical Errors*. Westport, CT: Praeger, 2004. Print.

Chowdhury, Uttom. *Tics and Tourette Syndrome: A Handbook for Parents and Profesionals*. New York: Kingsley, 2004. Print.

Langdon, Robert. *Understanding Cosmetic Laser Surgery*. Jackson: U P of Mississippi, 2004. Print.

Book with Two Authors

Barber, Kimiko, and Hiroki Takemura. *Sushi: Taste and Technique*. New York: DK, 2002. Print.

Vernberg, F. John, and Winona B. Vernberg. *The Coastal Zone: Past, Present, and Future*. Columbia: U of South Carolina P, 2001. Print.

Note: Invert only the first author's name. The first author was listed on the book as F. John Vernberg.

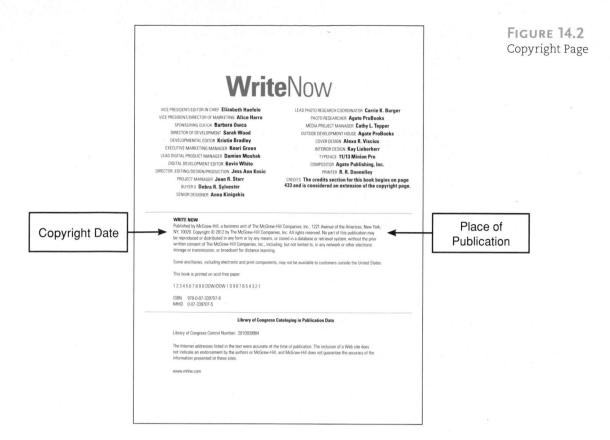

FIGURE 14.2
Copyright Page

Book with Three Authors

Ma, O. John, James R. Mateer, and Michael Blaivas. *Emergency Ultrasound*. 2nd ed. New York: McGraw, 2008. Print.

Book with Four or More Authors

Bishop, Sherry, et al. *The Web Collection*. Boston: Course Technology, 2004. Print.

Wysocki, Anne Frances, et al. *Writing New Media: Theory and Applications for Expanding the Teaching of Composition*. Logan, UT: Utah State UP, 2004. Print.

Note: Use the Latin term *et al.*, which means *and others*, to show that you have omitted all but the first author. Notice there is a period after *al* but not after *et*, in the example.

Book with No Author

Getting Yours: A Publicity and Funding Primer for Nonprofit and Voluntary Organizations. Lincoln, NE: Contact Center, 1991. Print.

Edited Book in a Series

Harris, Nancy, ed. *Space Exploration*. Detroit: Greenhaven, 2005. Print. Exploring Science and Medical Discoveries.

Note: If there are two editors, then use the plural abbreviation for editor, *eds*. The name of the series appears at the end of the entry. If there is an author, begin with the author rather than the editor.

Two or More Books by the Same Author

Morrison, Toni. *Paradise*. New York: Knopf, 1998. Print.

---. *A Mercy*. New York: Knopf, 2008. Print.

Note: Use three hyphens in place of the author's name for the second book (and subsequent books). Alphabetize the books on the works cited page according to the author. Ignore words such as *a* and *the* when alphabetizing the list of works cited. Use the second word instead. Start with the oldest text first, going to the latest.

Book in an Edition other than the First

Baker, Nancy L., and Nancy Huling. *A Research Guide for Undergraduate Students: English and American Literature*. 6th ed. New York: MLA, 2006. Print.

Book by a Corporate Author

Children's Hospital Boston. *The Children's Hospital Guide to Your Child's Health and Development*. Boston: Children's Hospital-Boston, 2001. Print.

Discovery Channel. *North American & Alaskan Cruises*. London: Insight, 2005. Print.

Work in an Anthology

Poe, Edgar Allan. "The Raven." 1845. *The Norton Anthology of American Literature*. Shorter 7th ed. Ed. Nina Baym. New York: Norton, 2008. 675–678. Print.

Note: An anthology is a collection of works selected by one or more editors. Use this example if you are citing an essay, letter, poem, short story, or other work that appears in an edited collection or compilation of works by different authors. "The Raven" was originally published in 1845, and it appears on pages 675–678 in the anthology.

Multivolume Book

LaBlanc, Michael L., ed. *Poetry for Students: Presenting Analysis, Context, and Criticism on Commonly Studied Poetry*. Vol. 10. Detroit: Gale, 2001. Print.

Note: This book has an editor rather than an author.

Dictionary or Encyclopedia Article

"Italy." *The Encyclopedia Americana*. 2006 ed. Print.

Note: Use the word you looked up in the reference book as the title in quotation marks.

Printed Periodicals (Journals, Magazines, Newspapers)

Here is a list of the basic information you need to include for periodical sources using the MLA format. List the information in each works cited entry in order, and follow the punctuation guidelines of the examples. You should be able to find all of the information you need on the cover of the periodical and the article itself. (See Figures 14.3 and 14.4.)

1. **Author:** Include the author's last name, followed by a comma and the author's first name and middle name or initial as it appears on the article. Do not include titles or degrees (such as "PhD" or "Sister") with the author's name. If the book has more than one author, invert only the first author's name and include a comma between authors. If the author is unknown, begin with the title of the article.

2. **Title:** Put the complete title of the article in quotation marks. Use title case capitalization, which means that you capitalize every word except articles (words such as *a* and *the*), conjunctions (words such as *but* and *for*), and prepositions (words such as *to, from, for,* and *with*). If there is a subtitle, add a colon between the title and subtitle. Capitalize the first word after the colon, even if it is an article or preposition.

3. **Publication:** Italicize the title of the periodical using title case capitalization.

4. **Volume and issue numbers:** If the periodical has volume and issue numbers, use only the numerals to cite them, putting a period between them. For example, you would cite an article that appears in volume 10 of issue 3 this way: 10.3.

5. **Date of publication:** Include as much information about the date as you can find on the journal, magazine, or newspaper. If you find the day, month, and year, list the day first, followed by the month, and the year, like this: 21 Apr. 2010. If you find just the month(s) and year, cite it this way: July-Aug. 2010. Follow the date with a colon.

6. **Page number(s):** List the inclusive page numbers of the article, not just the ones you used. If the pages are consecutive, write them this way: 25–31. If the pages are not consecutive, then use a plus sign. For example, if the article starts on page 13 and then skips to page 26, cite it like this: 13+. For a newspaper, also include the section letter before the page number: A4. Follow the page number(s) with a period.

7. **Publication medium:** Include the word *print* after the source for most printed sources. This distinguishes a printed article from an online or CD version. MLA added this element in the 2009 update to the citation guidelines.

Sample MLA Periodical Citation

- Author's Last Name, First Name. "Title of Article." *Name of Periodical* Volume. Issue (Date): Page(s). Medium.

Periodical Example

Taslitz, Andrew E. "Prosecutorial Preconditions to Plea Negotiations: 'Voluntary' Waivers of Constitutional Rights." *Criminal Justice* 23.3 (2008): 14–27. Print.

FIGURE 14.3 Journal Cover

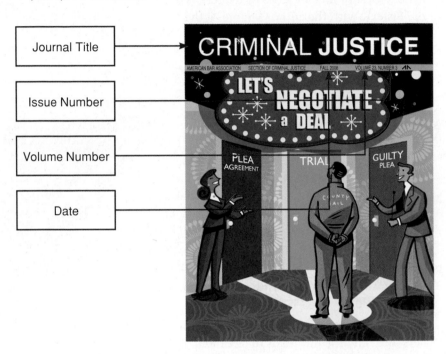

FIGURE 14.4 Journal Article

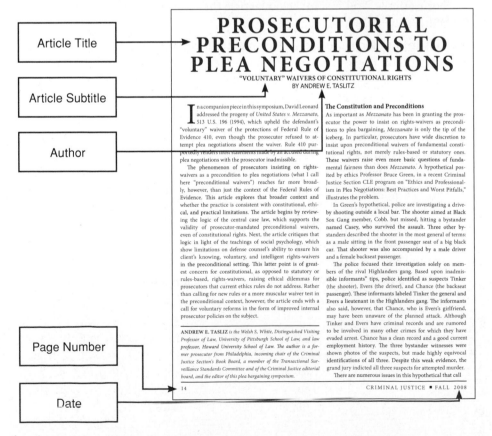

Scholarly Journal Article

Black, Anne C., et al. "Advancement Via Individual Determination: Method Selection in Conclusions about Program Effectiveness." *The Journal of Educational Research* 102.2 (2008): 111–123. Print.

DeVoe, Jennifer E., Carric Tillotson, and Lorraine S. Wallace. "Uninsured Children and Adolescents with Insured Parents." *JAMA* 30.16 (2008): 1904–1913. Print.

Magazine Article

Flaim, Denise. "Nothin' but a Hound Dog." *Dog Fancy* Dec. 2008: 38–41. Print.

Lashinsky, Adam. "Apple: The Genius Behind Steve." *Fortune* 24 Nov. 2008: 71+. Print.

Note: Use the complete date if it appears on the cover. Also, the "+" sign after the page number indicates that the article started on page 71 and continued later in the magazine with interruptions of advertisements and/or other articles.

Newspaper Article

Bearak, Barry. "South Africa is Aiming to Ease Dangers of Digging for Gold." *New York Times* 21 Nov. 2008: A6. Print.

Winslow, Ron. "Cholesterol Drug Cuts Heart Risk in Healthy Patients." *Wall Street Journal* 10 Nov. 2008: B1+. Print.

Note: The section number is included before the page number for newspaper articles.

Letter to the Editor

Pisenti, Dan. Letter. *Wall Street Journal.* 9 Dec. 2008: A16. Print.

Electronic Sources Here is a list of the basic information you need to include for electronic sources using the MLA format. List the information in each works cited entry in order, and follow the punctuation guidelines of the examples. In 2009, MLA changed its recommended method for documenting online sources by taking out the requirement for listing the URL or Web site address. The rationale is that URLs often change, and people are more likely to find the correct Web site using the author's name and/or the article's title.

1. **Author:** Begin with the author's last name, followed by a comma, the author's first name, and a period. If there is no author, include the editor, compiler, narrator, or director of the work. If no name is listed, begin with the title.

2. **Article title:** Italicize the title if it is an independent work, and put it in quotation marks if it is part of a larger work. Use title case capitalization, which means that you capitalize every word except articles (words such as *a* and *the*), conjunctions (words such as *but* and *for*), and prepositions (words such as *to, from, for,* and *with*). If there is a subtitle, add a colon

between the title and subtitle and capitalize the first word after the colon, even if it is an article or preposition.

3. **Web site title:** Italicize the Web site name and use title case capitalization. Omit this part if the title of the work and Web site are the same. Also include the edition or version you accessed if applicable.

4. **Publisher, sponsor, or periodical title:** Include this information even if the publisher or sponsor is the same as the title of the Web site. If the publisher or sponsor information is not available, use *n.p.* instead to indicate that there is no publisher.

5. **Date of publication:** Include the day, month, and year if they are available, like this: 15 Jan. 2009. Use the month and year or just the year if that is all that is available. If there is no publication date, use *n.d.*

6. **Medium of publication:** Use *Web* to show you found the information on the Internet.

7. **Access date:** Include the day, month, and year you accessed the source. This is important because Web sites frequently change.

Sample MLA Electronic Citation

- Author's Last Name, First Name. "Title." *Web Site*. Publisher or Sponsor, Date of Publication. Medium. Access Date.

Electronic Source Example

"Endeavour Crew Returns Home after 'Home Improvement' in Orbit." *NASA*. NASA, n.d. Web. 22 Jan. 2010.

Note: The article was not dated, so *n.d.* replaces the publication date.

FIGURE 14.5 Web Site Article

Web Site Article

"Alleged Sept. 11 Plotters Offer to Confess." National Public Radio. Nat. Public Radio, 8 Dec. 2008. Web. 23 Jan. 2010.

Botox Cosmetic. Allergan. 2008. Web. 23 Jan. 2010.

Online Scholarly Journal Article

Nayar, Pramod K. "New Media, Digitextuality and Public Space."
    Postcolonial Text 4.1 (2008): n. pag. Web. 24 Jan. 2010.

Note: Use *n. pag.* when no page number is available.

Online Magazine Article

Fallows, James. "Be Nice to the Countries that Lend You Money." *TheAtlantic.*
    com. Atlantic Monthly Group, Dec. 2008. Web. 24 Jan. 2010.

Online Newspaper Article

Phillips, Rich. "Ex-FBI Agent Faces 30 Years to Life for Mob Hit." *CNN.com.*
    Cable News Network, 4 Dec. 2008. Web. 24 Jan. 2010.

Online Encyclopedia or Dictionary

"Albuquerque." *Encyclopaedia Britannica Online.* Encyclopaedia Britannica,
    2010. Web. 23 Jan. 2010.

"Carpaccio." *Merriam-Webster Online Dictionary.* Merriam-Webster, 2010.
    Web. 1 Feb. 2010.

Periodical Article from an Online Database

Waterman, K. Krasnow, and Matthew T. Henshon. "What's Next for
    Artificial Intelligence and Robotics?" *Scitech Lawyer* 5.1 (2008): 20–21.
    Proquest. Web. 8 Dec. 2008.

Note: Follow the MLA guidelines for the type of source you are citing, and then
add the database information and your access date to the end of the citation.

E-Mail

Record, Michael. "Using SmartThinking.com." Message to Karin Russell. 20
    Oct. 2010. E-mail.

Other Sources You may decide to use other types of sources in your research
paper. Each type of source has its own unique format. Be sure to give readers
enough information to be able to find the source if they so desire. Many of the
MLA rules from previous examples apply to the following sources.

Advertisement

Apple iPod Touch. Advertisement. *Wired* Nov. 2008: 150. Print.

AT&T. Advertisement. CNN. 6 July 2009. Television.

Personal Interview

Blush, Linda. Personal interview. 6 Jan. 2010.

Hillier, Ashley. Telephone interview. 12 Dec. 2009.

Broadcast Interview

Jackman, Hugh. Interview. *The Oprah Winfrey Show*. ABC.WFTV, Orlando. 10 Nov. 2008. Television.

Note: After the network, include the call letters and city of your local station.

Work of Visual Art

Bonnard, Pierre. *Before Dinner*. 1924. Oil on canvas. Metropolitan Museum of Art, New York.

Simmons, Laurie. *Walking House*. 1989. Photograph. Museum of Mod. Art, New York.

Note: Include the medium and current location of the artwork after the date of its creation.

Music Recording

Keys, Alicia. "Superwoman." *As I Am*. J-Records, 2007. CD.

Note: Begin with the artist or group as appropriate.

Spoken-Word Recording

Gore, Al. *The Assault on Reason*. 2007. Narr. Will Patton. Penguin, 2007. CD.

Note: The first date is the publication for the book, and the second is for the sound recording. They just happen to have the same date in this example. Also, "Narr." refers to the narrator (reader).

Television Broadcast

"Kid Rock." *Storytellers*. VH1. 10 Dec. 2008. Television.

Film

No Country for Old Men. Dir. Joel Coen, and Ethan Coen. Perf. Tommy Lee Jones, Javier Bardem, Josh Brolin, and Kelly MacDonald. 2007. Miramax. 2008. DVD.

Note: Include the original date of release as well as the DVD date.

Brochure or Pamphlet

Abraham Lincoln: A Man of His Time, a Man for All Times. New York: Gilder Lehrman Institute of American History, 2008. Print.

Note: Include an author if there is one.

From Stigma to Status
by Margaret Rowland

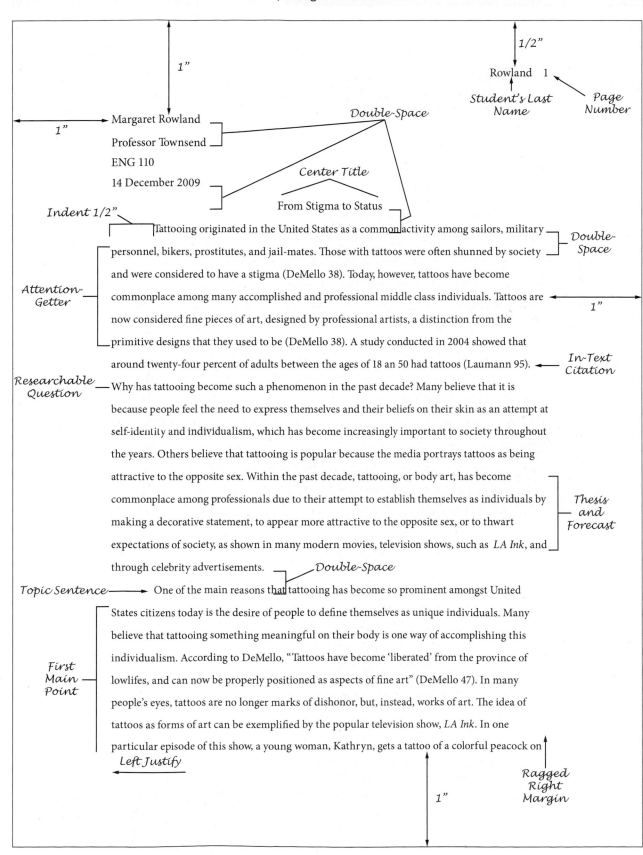

1/2"

Rowland   1

Student's Last Name   *Page Number*

1"

1"

Margaret Rowland

Professor Townsend

ENG 110

14 December 2009

Double-Space

Center Title

From Stigma to Status

Indent 1/2"

Tattooing originated in the United States as a common activity among sailors, military personnel, bikers, prostitutes, and jail-mates. Those with tattoos were often shunned by society and were considered to have a stigma (DeMello 38). Today, however, tattoos have become commonplace among many accomplished and professional middle class individuals. Tattoos are now considered fine pieces of art, designed by professional artists, a distinction from the primitive designs that they used to be (DeMello 38). A study conducted in 2004 showed that around twenty-four percent of adults between the ages of 18 an 50 had tattoos (Laumann 95).

Double-Space

1"

In-Text Citation

Attention-Getter

Researchable Question

Why has tattooing become such a phenomenon in the past decade? Many believe that it is because people feel the need to express themselves and their beliefs on their skin as an attempt at self-identity and individualism, which has become increasingly important to society throughout the years. Others believe that tattooing is popular because the media portrays tattoos as being attractive to the opposite sex. Within the past decade, tattooing, or body art, has become commonplace among professionals due to their attempt to establish themselves as individuals by making a decorative statement, to appear more attractive to the opposite sex, or to thwart expectations of society, as shown in many modern movies, television shows, such as *LA Ink*, and through celebrity advertisements.

Thesis and Forecast

Double-Space

Topic Sentence

One of the main reasons that tattooing has become so prominent amongst United States citizens today is the desire of people to define themselves as unique individuals. Many believe that tattooing something meaningful on their body is one way of accomplishing this individualism. According to DeMello, "Tattoos have become 'liberated' from the province of lowlifes, and can now be properly positioned as aspects of fine art" (DeMello 47). In many people's eyes, tattoos are no longer marks of dishonor, but, instead, works of art. The idea of tattoos as forms of art can be exemplified by the popular television show, *LA Ink*. In one particular episode of this show, a young woman, Kathryn, gets a tattoo of a colorful peacock on

First Main Point

Left Justify

Ragged Right Margin

1"

1/2"

1"

1"

1"

First Main Point Continued

her arm to represent the strength of her mother who had recently been in a coma for two months and completely lost her memory. Kathryn was not a biker or involved in crime, but was an educated, middle-class individual who desired to make a statement about her mother's heartbreaking situation in the form of body art (*LA Ink—Peacock Tattoo*). In DeMello's article, "Not Just for Bikers Anymore," she quotes an individual who was interviewed about his decision to get a tattoo. He responded, "The power of the tattoo is in the ability to express individuality and in its permanence" (DeMello 41). Kathryn, from *LA Ink—Peacock Tattoo*, and this quoted individual share similar beliefs about tattoos and their meanings. Whether they are designed in memory of a loved one or to symbolize an important value or belief of the individual, tattoos are most commonly acquired in the form of unique, decorative statements.

Topic Sentence → Another fundamental motivation for people in this country to get tattoos is the belief that they create sex appeal. A study of college students found that "almost three-fourths of the undergraduate women reported that they 'sometimes' viewed openly visible tattoos as attractive when on a man" (Horne et al. 1011). On the other hand, "58.8 percent of the undergraduate men viewed such visible tattoos as attractive when on a woman" (Home et al. 1011). Therefore, men and women may get tattoos if they feel that it will add to their sex appeal. A large portion of this thinking has derived from the fact that many celebrities have tattoos, and, because celebrities are often seen as sex icons, common people believe that if they get tattoos then they will be appealing to the opposite sex as well (Horne et al. 1011). DeMello states, "Tattooing has moved from being a symbol of the outcast to that of a rock star, model, and postmodern youth, and with this shift in public perception has come a shift in meaning as well, as tattoo moves from stigma to status" (49). The idea that tattoos are sexy is exemplified in many modern movies, including *Wanted*. The most famous scene of this movie depicts Angelina Jolie getting out of a bathtub, completely naked, with large tattoos covering her back, Jolie seductively peers around her shoulder at the camera, an obvious attempt of the director to attract men with her tattoo-covered body (*Wanted*). Since the premier of the movie, this scene has become extremely famous to the public eye. However, Jolie is not the only celebrity to endorse tattoos. Others, including David Beckham, Rihanna, Michael Jordan, and Gisele have been pictured in advertisements that show

Second Main Point

1"

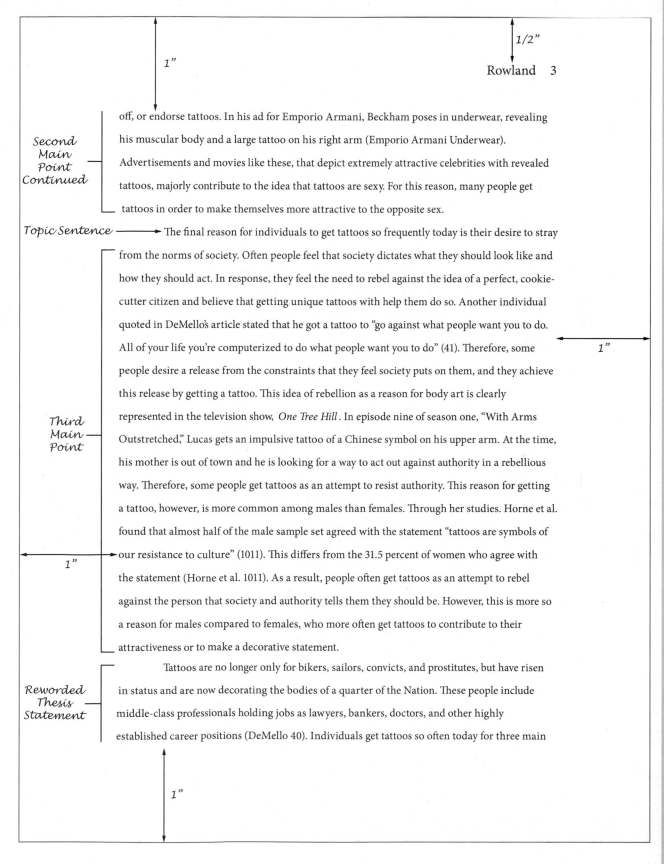

Second Main Point Continued — off, or endorse tattoos. In his ad for Emporio Armani, Beckham poses in underwear, revealing his muscular body and a large tattoo on his right arm (Emporio Armani Underwear). Advertisements and movies like these, that depict extremely attractive celebrities with revealed tattoos, majorly contribute to the idea that tattoos are sexy. For this reason, many people get tattoos in order to make themselves more attractive to the opposite sex.

Topic Sentence — The final reason for individuals to get tattoos so frequently today is their desire to stray from the norms of society. Often people feel that society dictates what they should look like and how they should act. In response, they feel the need to rebel against the idea of a perfect, cookie-cutter citizen and believe that getting unique tattoos with help them do so. Another individual quoted in DeMello's article stated that he got a tattoo to "go against what people want you to do. All of your life you're computerized to do what people want you to do" (41). Therefore, some people desire a release from the constraints that they feel society puts on them, and they achieve this release by getting a tattoo. This idea of rebellion as a reason for body art is clearly represented in the television show, *One Tree Hill*. In episode nine of season one, "With Arms *Third Main Point* — Outstretched," Lucas gets an impulsive tattoo of a Chinese symbol on his upper arm. At the time, his mother is out of town and he is looking for a way to act out against authority in a rebellious way. Therefore, some people get tattoos as an attempt to resist authority. This reason for getting a tattoo, however, is more common among males than females. Through her studies. Horne et al. found that almost half of the male sample set agreed with the statement "tattoos are symbols of our resistance to culture" (1011). This differs from the 31.5 percent of women who agree with the statement (Horne et al. 1011). As a result, people often get tattoos as an attempt to rebel against the person that society and authority tells them they should be. However, this is more so a reason for males compared to females, who more often get tattoos to contribute to their attractiveness or to make a decorative statement.

Reworded Thesis Statement — Tattoos are no longer only for bikers, sailors, convicts, and prostitutes, but have risen in status and are now decorating the bodies of a quarter of the Nation. These people include middle-class professionals holding jobs as lawyers, bankers, doctors, and other highly established career positions (DeMello 40). Individuals get tattoos so often today for three main

MLA Format

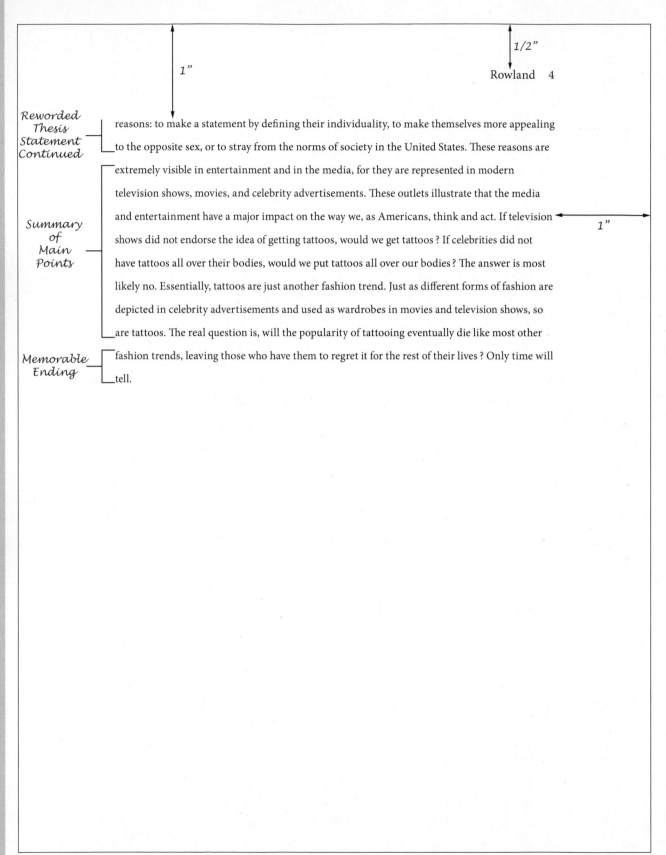

1"

Reworded Thesis Statement Continued — reasons: to make a statement by defining their individuality, to make themselves more appealing to the opposite sex, or to stray from the norms of society in the United States. These reasons are

Summary of Main Points — extremely visible in entertainment and in the media, for they are represented in modern television shows, movies, and celebrity advertisements. These outlets illustrate that the media and entertainment have a major impact on the way we, as Americans, think and act. If television   1" shows did not endorse the idea of getting tattoos, would we get tattoos? If celebrities did not have tattoos all over their bodies, would we put tattoos all over our bodies? The answer is most likely no. Essentially, tattoos are just another fashion trend. Just as different forms of fashion are depicted in celebrity advertisements and used as wardrobes in movies and television shows, so are tattoos. The real question is, will the popularity of tattooing eventually die like most other

Memorable Ending — fashion trends, leaving those who have them to regret it for the rest of their lives? Only time will tell.

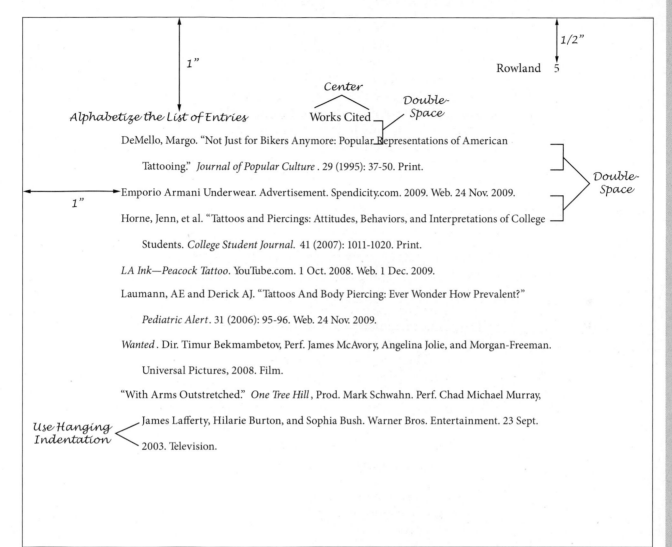

Alphabetize the List of Entries

Center

Works Cited

Double-Space

1"

1/2"

Rowland   5

DeMello, Margo. "Not Just for Bikers Anymore: Popular Representations of American

Tattooing." *Journal of Popular Culture* . 29 (1995): 37-50. Print.

Emporio Armani Underwear. Advertisement. Spendicity.com. 2009. Web. 24 Nov. 2009.

Horne, Jenn, et al. "Tattoos and Piercings: Attitudes, Behaviors, and Interpretations of College

Students. *College Student Journal.* 41 (2007): 1011-1020. Print.

LA Ink—Peacock Tattoo. YouTube.com. 1 Oct. 2008. Web. 1 Dec. 2009.

Laumann, AE and Derick AJ. "Tattoos And Body Piercing: Ever Wonder How Prevalent?"

Pediatric Alert . 31 (2006): 95-96. Web. 24 Nov. 2009.

Wanted . Dir. Timur Bekmambetov, Perf. James McAvory, Angelina Jolie, and Morgan-Freeman.

Universal Pictures, 2008. Film.

"With Arms Outstretched." *One Tree Hill* , Prod. Mark Schwahn. Perf. Chad Michael Murray,

James Lafferty, Hilarie Burton, and Sophia Bush. Warner Bros. Entertainment. 23 Sept.

2003. Television.

Double-Space

Use Hanging Indentation

1"

[QUESTIONS FOR REFLECTION]

1. Based on Rowland's introductory paragraph, what three main points does she promise to cover in the body of her paper? Does she follow through with her promise?

2. What supporting details and examples does she offer for her first main point? Are they sufficient? Why or why not?

3. What supporting details does Rowland offer for her second main point? Which details are the most convincing? Why?

4. Which ideas from the author's third body paragraph are most memorable? Why?

5. What is Rowland's thesis? Do you think she fully supports her thesis in the body of the paper? Why or why not?

14.4 > APA Format

Generally, the American Psychological Association (APA) format is used for courses in the behavioral sciences. Additionally, some colleges have adopted the APA format for use in all subjects. The complete APA guidelines are explained in the 6th edition of the *Publication Manual of the American Psychological Association* (2010). Go to **www.apa.org** for more information about the APA format. The APA style of documentation requires that you cite sources in your text as well as on a reference page at the end of your paper. The following examples will help you to cite sources using the APA format. You may also want to try using an electronic source, such as **www.noodletools.com**, to help you correctly document your sources.

APA In-Text Citations

An *in-text citation*, also known as a *parenthetical citation*, shows the reader exactly where you have borrowed ideas from outside sources in your paper. When using the APA format, you generally need to include the author's last name and date for summarized and paraphrased information. For direct quotes, include the page number in addition to the author's last name and date. Providing this information allows the readers to locate the correct entry on the reference page so they can find additional information about the subject if desired. You may include the author's name in the text or in parentheses with the date. Either way, the date immediately follows the author's name. If there is no author, use the title. To keep your writing fresh, vary the way in which you introduce sources in your paper. Be sure to include the correct information and make it clear exactly what material comes from a particular source.

One Author: First Citation

According to Bernsten (2004), people who have popular first names or last names should be cautious that they receive the correct treatment when hospitalized.

People who have popular first names or last names should be cautious that they receive the correct treatment when hospitalized (Bernsten, 2004).

One Author: Subsequent Citation within the Same Paragraph

Berensten also suggests…

Note: If you cite the source again later in the paper, list the author's name and date again.

Two Authors

Barber and Takemura (2002) recommend that sushi eaters only use small amounts of soy sauce to avoid "drowning" the flavor of the sushi or making it come apart (p. 230).

Sushi eaters should only use small amounts of soy sauce to avoid "drowning" the flavor of the sushi or making it come apart (Barber & Takemura, 2002, p. 230).

Note: Include the page number when you quote any words from the original text. Use an ampersand (&) between the authors' names in parentheses.

Three to Five Authors: First Citation

Ma, Mateer, and Blaivas (2008) have observed that even though three-dimensional ultrasound technology can provide amazing images, it is currently not the best tool for making a diagnosis.

Even though three-dimensional ultrasound technology can provide amazing images, it is currently not the best tool for making a diagnosis (Ma, Mateer & Blaivas, 2008).

Three to Five Authors: Subsequent Citations

Ma et al. (2008) have observed that even though three-dimensional ultrasound technology can provide amazing images, it is currently not the best tool for making a diagnosis.

Even though three-dimensional ultrasound technology can provide amazing images, it is currently not the best tool for making a diagnosis (Ma et al., 2008).

Note: For works with three or more authors, list all of the authors' last names the first time you cite the source. For subsequent citations, use the Latin term *et al.*, which means *and others*, to show that you have omitted all but the first author. Notice there is a period after *al* but not after *et*.

Six or More Authors

Wilson et al. (2010) discovered that…

Note: Even though you list only the first author's name in the in-text citation, you will need to cite up to six authors' names on the reference list. For seven or more authors, use *et al.* for the in-text citation.

Multiple Works by Authors with the Same Last Name

J. E. Rivera (2006) and A. M. Rivera (2010) recommend…

N. D. Goldstein and Hertz (2011) and S. P. Goldstein and Michaels (2007) found…

Note: Include the initials to clearly distinguish the authors with the same last names. Omit the initials for authors with different names.

No Author

According to the book *Getting Yours* (1991), public relations is about getting credit for doing a good job.

Basically, public relations is about getting credit for doing a good job (*Getting Yours*, 1991).

Note: Use the first few words of the title in place of the author's name. The entry needs to match the beginning of the corresponding entry on the reference list.

Anonymous Author

Studies show that… (Anonymous, 2008).

Note: Use this only when the source lists its author as "Anonymous."

Corporate or Group Author

Children's Hospital Boston (2001) suggests that the parenting process becomes less demanding when a child enters into school.

The parenting process becomes less demanding when a child enters into school (Children's Hospital Boston, 2001).

Indirect Source

According to Budman et al. (as cited in Chowdhury, 2004), studies show that children who have Tourette Syndrome may experience "rage" attacks when they see a specialist at a clinic (p. 61).

Note: Use this example if you want to use a quote or information you find in a source by a different author. Give credit to the original author of the material in your text and the source where you found the quote or information in your parenthetical citation.

Multiple Works

The most common side effect of having a Botox injection is droopy eyelids (*Botox Cosmetic*, 2008; Langdon, 2004).

Note: Use this example when you find the same information in two sources and want to cite both to add credibility to your paper. Cite each work the same way you normally would, and add a semicolon between the works in parentheses. In the above example, the first work is a Web site with no author, and the second is a book.

Personal Communication

According to M. Record (personal communication, October 20, 2010) NetTutor and SmarThinking are valuable resources for students to receive constructive feedback on their rough drafts.

Note: Use the above format for personal e-mails, personal interviews, telephone conversations, and other forms of personal communication.

Long Quote

Glave (2008) urges his readers to help do their part to save the planet:

> Do something. Do it now. Dream up your own Eco-Shed, Eco-Car, Eco-Boat, Eco-Garden, Eco-Concrete, Eco-Whatever, and start on it today. Sit right up front and take charge of the process. Stop thinking about what you have to give up, or whom you might tick off, and start thinking about what you'll gain. Each of us must earn our own green belt at our own pace. But believe me, once you begin punching and kicking in that direction, you won't ever look back. (pp. 248–249)

Note: For quotes that are longer than 40 words, set the entire quote off from the text and begin it on a new line. Indent the quote a half inch (about five to seven spaces) from the left margin and double-space it. Omit the quotation marks and place the final period before the citation.

TABLE 14.2

Directory to APA References Examples
Books: Overview, p. 364
Book by One Author, p. 366
Book by Two Authors, p. 366
Book by Three or More Authors, p. 366
Book with No Author, p. 366
Book in an Edition other than the First, p. 366
Book by a Corporate Author, p. 366
Work in an Anthology, p. 367
Multivolume Book, p. 367
Periodicals: Overview, p. 367
Journal Article, p. 369
Magazine Article, p. 369
Newspaper Article, p. 370
Electronic Sources: Overview, p. 370
Web Site Article, p. 371
Online Journal Article with a DOI, p. 371
Online Journal Article without a DOI, p. 371
Online Magazine Article, p. 371
Online Newspaper Article, p. 371
Online Encyclopedia Article, p. 371
Other Sources: Overview, p. 372
Brochure or Pamphlet, p. 372
Motion Picture, p. 372
Music Recording, p. 372
Personal Communications (E-mail, Personal Interview, Phone Conversation), p. 372
Television Episode in a Series, p. 372

APA References

When using the APA format, you must include a list of *references* at the end of the paper to fully document your sources. This means that you list any *work* you have *referenced* (cited) in your paper. You may need to look at several examples of reference entries to find exactly what you need to document your research sources. For example, if you need to cite the fourth edition of a book with three authors, then you would need to look at the sample entries for *Book with Three Five Authors* and *Book in Edition other than the First*. Generally, you will alphabetize the list according to the authors' last names. If there is no author, begin with the title. Ignore words such as *a* and *the* when alphabetizing an entry by the title on the list of works cited.

Books   Here is a list of the basic information you need to include for book sources using the APA format. List the information in each reference entry in order, and follow the punctuation guidelines of the examples. You should be able to find all of the information you need on the title and copyright pages of the book. (See Figures 14.6 and 14.7.)

1. **Author:** List the author's last name, followed by a comma and the author's first initial and middle initial (if you have it). Do not include degrees or titles, such as "PhD" or "Sister," with the author's name. If the book has more than one author, list the additional authors in the same manner as the first author, and include a comma between authors. If the author is unknown, begin with the title of the book.

2. **Date of publication:** List the year in parentheses, followed by a period.

3. **Book title:** Italicize the complete title of the book. Capitalize only the first word of the title and proper nouns. If there is a subtitle, add a colon between the title and subtitle and capitalize the first word after the colon. You may need to include additional information after the title, depending on the type of source you are citing. For example, you may be using an edition other than the first or one volume of a multivolume set. See the corresponding examples that follow.

4. **Place of publication:** List the city, followed by a comma, and the two-letter state abbreviation used by the United States Postal Service, followed by a colon. (Go to **www.usps.com** for a complete list.) If multiple cities are included in the book, list only the first one. For a country other than the United States, list the city followed by the country: London, England.

5. **Publisher:** List the publisher's complete name. If the author and publisher are exactly the same, list the word *Author* (not italicized), where you would normally list the publisher.

Sample APA Book Citation

- Author's Last Name, First Initial. Middle Initial. (Year of Publication).
  Title of book. Place of Publication: Publisher.

Book Example

Russell, K. L. (2012). *Write now: Read. think. research. persuade.
communicate.* New York, NY: McGraw-Hill.

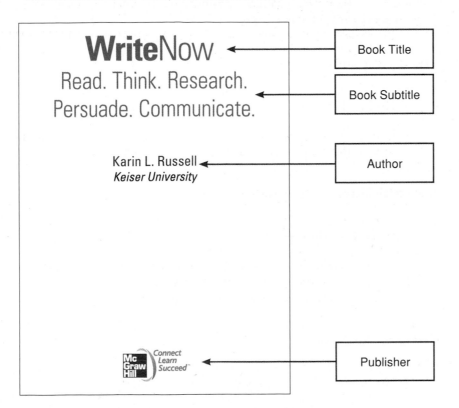

FIGURE 14.6
Book Title Page

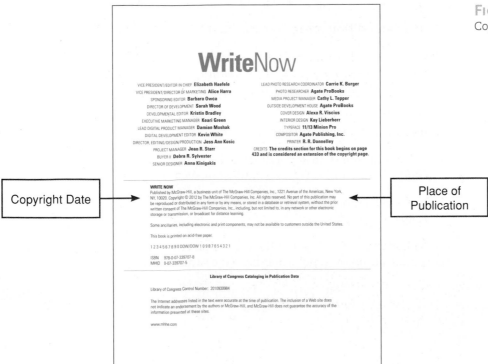

FIGURE 14.7
Copyright Page Page

Book by One Author

Bernsten, K. J. (2004). *The patient's guide to preventing medical errors.* Westport, CT: Praeger.

Chowdhury, U. (2004). *Tics and Tourette syndrome: A handbook for parents and professionals.* New York, NY: Jessica Kingsley Publishers.

Langdon, R. (2004). *Understanding cosmetic laser surgery.* Jackson, MS: University Press of Mississippi.

Book by Two Authors

Barber, K., & Takemura, H. (2002). *Sushi: Taste and technique.* New York, NY: Dorling Kindersley.

Vernberg, F. J., & Vernberg, W. B. (2001). *The coastal zone: Past, present, and future.* Columbia, SC: University of South Carolina Press.

Book with Three or More Authors

Ma, O. J., Mateer, J. R., & Blaivas, M. (2008). *Emergency ultrasound* (2nd ed.). New York, NY: McGraw-Hill.

Note: For books with six or more authors, use the Latin term *et al.*, which means *and others*, to show that you have omitted all but the first author. Notice there is a period after *al* but not after *et*.

Book with No Author

Getting Yours: A Publicity and Funding Primer for Nonprofit and Voluntary Organizations. (1991). Lincoln, NE: Contact Center.

Note: The date goes after the title when there is no author.

Book in an Edition other than the First

Baker, N. L., & Huling, N. (2006). *A research guide for undergraduate students: English and American literature* (6th ed.). New York, NY: Modern Language Association.

Book by a Corporate Author

Children's Hospital Boston. (2001). *The Children's Hospital guide to your child's health and development.* Boston, MA: Author.

Discovery Channel. (2005). *North American & Alaskan Cruises.* London, England: Insight.

Note: Use the word *author* at the end, in place of the publisher, when the corporate author and publisher have the same name.

Work in an Anthology

Poe, E. A. The raven (1845). In N. Baym (Ed.), *The Norton anthology of American literature* (Shorter 7th ed.). (pp. 675–678). New York, NY: W. W. Norton & Company.

Note: An anthology is a collection of works selected by one or more editors. Use this example if you are citing an essay, letter, poem, short story, or other work that appears in an edited collection or compilation of works by different authors. The editor is listed by first initial and last name.

Multivolume Book

LaBlanc, M. L. (Ed.). (2001). *Poetry for students: Presenting analysis, context, and criticism on commonly studied poetry.* (Vol. 10). Detroit, MI: Gale Group.

Note: This book has an editor rather than an author.

Printed Periodicals (Journals, Magazines, Newspapers) Here is a list of the basic information you need to include for periodical sources using the APA format. List the information for each entry on the reference page in order, and follow the punctuation guidelines of the examples. You should be able to find all of the information you need on the cover of the periodical and the article itself.

1. **Author:** List the author's last name, followed by a comma and the author's first initial and middle initial (if you have it). Do not include degrees or titles, such as "PhD" or "Sister," with the author's name. If the source has more than one author, list the additional authors in the same manner as the first author, and include a comma between authors. If the author is unknown, begin with the title of the article.

2. **Date of publication:** Include as much information about the date as you can find on the journal, magazine, or newspaper. If you find the day, month, and year, list the year first, followed by a comma, the month, and the day, like this: (2011, April 21). If you find just the month(s) and year, list it this way: (2010, July-August). Enclose the date in parentheses, followed by a period.

3. **Article title:** List the complete article title, capitalizing only the first word and proper nouns. If there is a subtitle, add a colon between the title and subtitle. Capitalize the first word after the colon.

4. **Publication:** List the complete title of the periodical in italics. Use title case capitalization, which means that you capitalize every word except articles (words such as *a* and *the*), conjunctions (words such as *for* and *but*), and prepositions (words such as *to, from, for,* and *with*). Follow the periodical title with a comma.

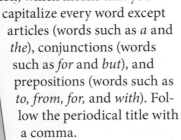

5. **Volume and issue numbers:** If the periodical has a volume number, list it in italics. If the periodical has an issue number, and each issue begins on page one, list the issue number in parentheses, but not italicized, immediately after the volume number. For example, you would cite an article that appears in volume 10 of issue 3 this way: *10*(3). Follow this information with a comma. If the periodical does not have volume and issue numbers, list the year followed by the month or season, like this: (2009, Spring).

6. **Page number(s):** List the inclusive page numbers of the article, not just the ones you used, like this: 25–31. If the page numbers are not continuous, list the specific pages for the article this way for magazines and periodicals, 6, 8, 12–14, and this way for newspaper articles, pp. B1, B4, B6–7. Follow the page number(s) with a period.

Sample APA Periodical Citation

▪ Author's Last Name, First Initial. Middle Initial. (Date of Publication). Title of article. *Name of Periodical*, *Volume*(Issue), Page(s).

Periodical Example

Taslitz, A. E. (2008). Prosecutorial preconditions to plea negotiations: "Voluntary" waivers of Constitutional rights. *Criminal Justice, 23*(3), 14–27.

FIGURE 14.8
Journal Cover

FIGURE 14.9   Journal Article

PROSECUTORIAL PRECONDITIONS TO PLEA NEGOTIATIONS
"VOLUNTARY" WAIVERS OF CONSTITUTIONAL RIGHTS
BY ANDREW E. TASLITZ

Article Title

Article Subtitle

Author

In a companion piece in this symposium, David Leonard addressed the progeny of *United States v. Mezzanato*, 513 U.S. 196 (1994), which upheld the defendant's "voluntary" waiver of the protections of Federal Rule of Evidence 410, even though the prosecutor refused to attempt plea negotiations absent the waiver. Rule 410 purportedly renders most statements made by an accused during plea negotiations with the prosecutor inadmissible.

The phenomenon of prosecutors insisting on rights-waivers as a precondition to plea negotiations (what I call here "preconditional waivers") reaches far more broadly, however, than just the context of the Federal Rules of Evidence. This article explores that broader context and whether the practice is consistent with constitutional, ethical, and practical limitations. The article begins by reviewing the logic of the central case law, which supports the validity of prosecutor-mandated preconditional waivers, even of constitutional rights. Next, the article critiques that logic in light of the teachings of social psychology, which show limitations on defense counsel's ability to ensure his client's knowing, voluntary, and intelligent rights-waivers in the preconditional setting. This latter point is of greatest concern for constitutional, as opposed to statutory or rules-based, rights-waivers, raising ethical dilemmas for prosecutors that current ethics rules do not address. Rather than calling for new rules or a more muscular waiver test in the preconditional context, however, the article ends with a call for voluntary reforms in the form of improved internal prosecutor policies on the subject.

ANDREW E. TASLITZ *is the Welsh S, White, Distinguished Visiting Professor of Law, University of Pittsburgh School of Law, and law professor, Howard University School of Law. The author is a former prosecutor from Philadelphia, incoming chair of the Criminal Justice Section's Book Board, a member of the Transactional Surveillance Standards Committee and of the* Criminal Justice *editorial board, and the editor of this plea bargaining symposium.*

The Constitution and Preconditions

As important as *Mezzanato* has been in granting the prosecutor the power to insist on rights-waivers as preconditions to plea bargaining, *Mezzanato* is only the tip of the iceberg. In particular, prosecutors have wide discretion to insist upon preconditional waivers of fundamental constitutional rights, not merely rules-based or statutory ones. These waivers raise even more basic questions of fundamental fairness than does *Mezzanato*. A hypothetical posited by ethics Professor Bruce Green, in a recent Criminal Justice Section CLE program on "Ethics and Professionalism in Plea Negotiations: Best Practices and Worst Pitfalls," illustrates the problem.

In Green's hypothetical, police are investigating a drive-by shooting outside a local bar. The shooter aimed at Black Sox Gang member, Cobb. but missed, hitting a bystander named Casey, who survived the assault. Three other bystanders described the shooter in the most general of terms: as a male sitting in the front passenger seat of a big black car. That shooter was also accompanied by a male driver and a female backseat passenger.

The police focused their investigation solely on members of the rival Highlanders gang. Based upon inadmissible informants" tips, police identified as suspects Tinker (the shooter), Evers (the driver), and Chance (the backseat passenger). These informants labeled Tinker the general and Evers a lieutenant in the Highlanders gang. The informants also said, however, that Chance, who is Evers's girlfriend, may have been unaware of the planned attack. Although Tinker and Evers have criminal records and are rumored to be involved in many other crimes for which they have evaded arrest. Chance has a clean record and a good current employment history. The three bystander witnesses were shown photos of the suspects, but made highly equivocal identifications of all three. Despite this weak evidence, the grand jury indicted all three suspects for attempted murder.

There are numerous issues in this hypothetical that call

Page Number

Date

14   CRIMINAL JUSTICE ■ FALL 2008

Journal Article

Lleras, C. (2008, December). Race, racial concentration, and the dynamics of educational inequality across urban and suburban schools. *American Educational Research Journal, 45,* 886–912.

Roberts, K. T., Robinson, K. M., Stewart, C., & Wright, J. C. (2008). Integrated mental health practice in a nurse-managed health center. *The American Journal for Nurse Practicioners, 12*(10), 33–34, 37–40, 43–44.

Magazine Article

Flaim, D. (2008, December). Nothin' but a hound dog. *Dog Fancy,* 38–41.

Lemos, R. (2009, January). Use encryption to safeguard your data. *PC World,* 47–48.

Newspaper Article

Bearak, B. (2008, November 21). South Africa is aiming to ease dangers of digging for gold. *New York Times,* p. A6.

Koppel, N., Scheck, J., & Stecklow, S. (2008, December 19). Fast living, bold ambitions drove lawyer's rise and fall. *Wall Street Journal,* pp. A1, A14.

Note: The section number is included before the page number for newspaper articles. Also, for newspaper articles, precede the page numbers with *p.* (for one page) and *pp.* (for multiple pages).

Electronic Sources Here is a list of the basic information you need to include for electronic sources using the APA format. List the information in each reference page entry in order. Note that the various types of electronic sources require different information. Use the examples that follow as a guide. Generally, you will cite electronic sources the same way as print sources, but you will need to add enough electronic retrieval information to help your readers find your source.

1. **Author:** List the author's last name, followed by a comma and the author's first initial and middle initial (if you have it). Do not include degrees or titles, such as "PhD" or "Sister," with the author's name. If the source has more than one author, list the additional authors in the same manner as the first author, and include a comma and an ampersand (&) between the authors' names. If there is no author, include the editor, compiler, narrator, or director of the work. If no name is listed, begin with the title.

2. **Date of publication:** List all of the available information you have about the date. If you find the day month and year, list the year first, followed by a comma, the month, and the day, like this: (2011, April 21). If you find just the month(s) and year, list it this way: (2010, July-August). Enclose the date in parentheses, followed by a period. If the publication date is not available, list *n.d.* in parentheses, like this: (n.d)

3. **Article title:** List the complete article title, capitalizing only the first word and proper nouns. If there is a subtitle, add a colon between the title and subtitle. Capitalize the first word after the colon.

4. **Periodical information:** For online periodicals, list the title of the periodical (in italics) followed by volume (in italics) and issue number (in parentheses). Follow the same guidelines as you would for print periodical sources.

5. **DOI:** Some online journals contain a digital object identifier (DOI), which is a set of numbers and letters that is unique to a particular digital source. If the source you wish to document has a DOI, the publisher will display it on the front page of the article. Unlike a URL, which can change, a DOI is a permanent identifier.

6. **URL:** Only list the URL if a digital object identifier (DOI) is not available. Include the entire URL for Internet sources. Be careful to copy the URL very carefully so that your readers can access the information if desired. Do not include a period after the URL. Remove the blue font and underline.

Electronic Source Example

- Endeavour crew returns home after "home improvement" in orbit. (n.d.). Retrieved from www.nasa.gov

FIGURE 14.10
Web Site Article

Web Site Article

Alleged Sept. 11 plotters offer to confess. (2008, December 8). Retrieved from www.npr.org/templates/story/story.php?storyId=97948707

Note: Include an author if there is one, and list the date immediately after the author.

Online Journal Article with a DOI

Anderson, C. B., Hughes, S. O., & Fuemmeler, B. F. (2009). Parent-child attitude congruence on type and intensity of physical activity: Testing multiple mediators of sedentary behavior in older children. *Health Psychology*, 28, 428–438. doi: 10.1037/a0014522

Online Journal Article without a DOI

Nayar, P. K. (2008). New media, digitextuality and public space, *Postcolonial Text, 4*(1). Retrieved from http://journals.sfu.ca/pocol/index. php/pct/ article/view/786/521

Note: The URL is included because there is no DOI.

Online Magazine Article

Fallows, J. (2008, December). Be nice to the countries that lend you money. *The Atlantic*. Retrieved from www.theatlantic.com

Online Newspaper Article

Couwels, J. (2008, December 22). New Army technology could save soldiers' lives. *CNN*. Retrieved from www.cnn.com/

Online Encyclopedia Article

Robotics. (2008). *The Columbia encyclopedia* (6th ed.). Retrieved from www.encyclopedia.com

Other Sources You may decide to use other types of sources in your research paper. Each type of source has its own unique format. Be sure to give your readers enough information to be able to find the source if they so desire. Many of the APA rules from previous examples apply to the following sources.

Brochure or Pamphlet by a Corporate Author

Gilder Lehrman Institute of American History. (2008). *Abraham Lincoln: A man of his time, a man for all times* [Brochure]. New York, NY: Author.

Note: List *author* in place of the publisher if they are the same.

Motion Picture

Curling, C. (Producer), Meurer, J. (Producer), & Hoffman, M. (Director). (2010). *The last station.* [Motion picture]. United States: Sony Picture Classics.

Music Recording

Swift, T. (2008). Love story. On *Fearless* [CD]. Nashville: Big Machine Records.

Note: The in-text citation for this source would look like this: "Love Story" (Swift, 2008, track 3).

Personal Communications (E-mail, Personal Interview, Phone Conversation)

Cite personal communications in the body of your paper, but not on your reference page. For example, A. Hillier (personal communication, December 12, 2009) suggests that…

Television Episode in a Series

Meyer, G., et al. (Writer). (2008). All about Lisa [Television series episode]. In M. Groening, & J. L. Brooks (Executive producers) *The Simpsons.* Beverly Hills, CA: Fox Broadcasting.

From Stigma to Status
by Margaret Rowland

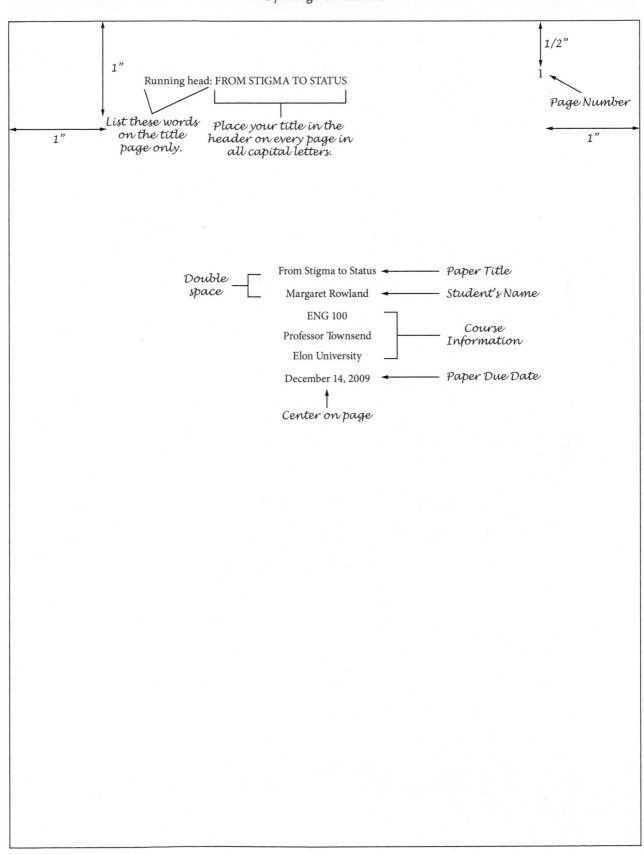

Running head: FROM STIGMA TO STATUS

1/2"

1

Page Number

1"

1"

List these words on the title page only.

Place your title in the header on every page in all capital letters.

1"

Double space

From Stigma to Status ← *Paper Title*

Margaret Rowland ← *Student's Name*

ENG 100

Professor Townsend

Elon University

Course Information

December 14, 2009 ← *Paper Due Date*

Center on page

APA Format

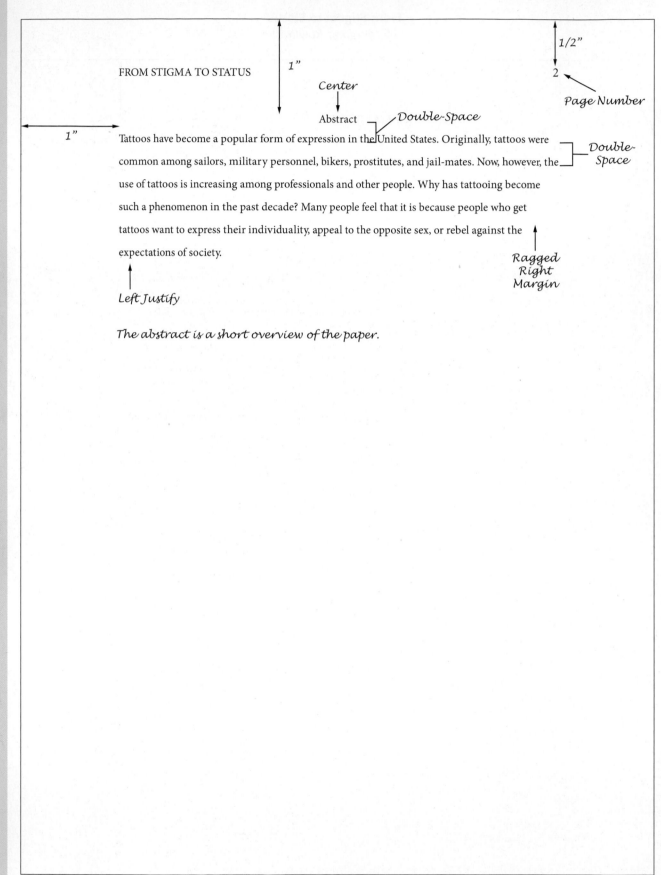

FROM STIGMA TO STATUS   *1"*   *1/2"*

Center   2

                                   Page Number

1"   Abstract   *Double-Space*

Tattoos have become a popular form of expression in the United States. Originally, tattoos were *Double-Space*

common among sailors, military personnel, bikers, prostitutes, and jail-mates. Now, however, the

use of tattoos is increasing among professionals and other people. Why has tattooing become

such a phenomenon in the past decade? Many people feel that it is because people who get

tattoos want to express their individuality, appeal to the opposite sex, or rebel against the

expectations of society.

Ragged Right Margin

Left Justify

The abstract is a short overview of the paper.

APA Format

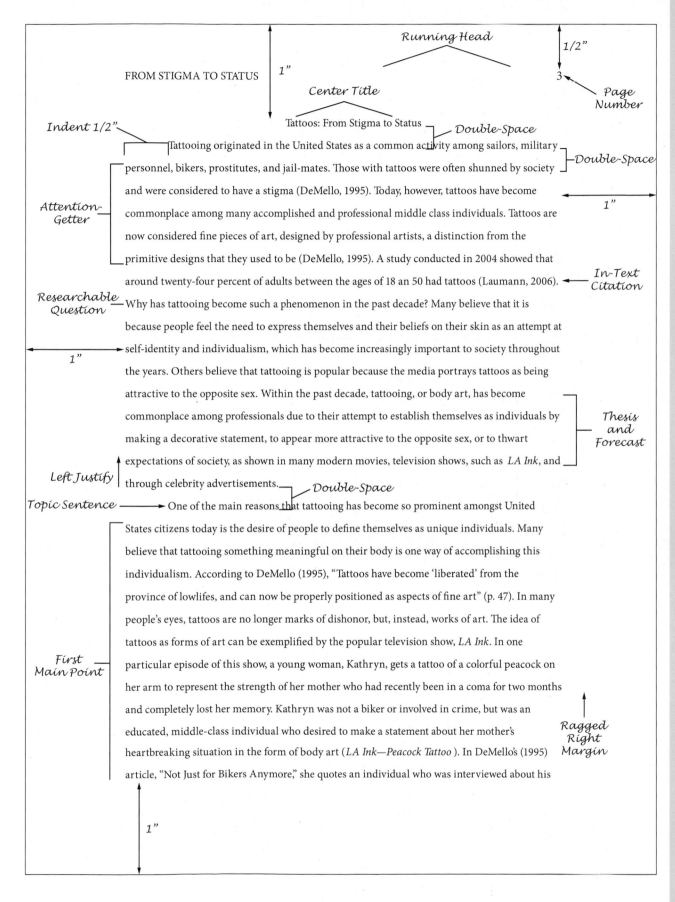

Running Head

FROM STIGMA TO STATUS   1"   1/2"

3

Page Number

Center Title

Tattoos: From Stigma to Status   Double-Space

Indent 1/2"

Attention-Getter

Tattooing originated in the United States as a common activity among sailors, military personnel, bikers, prostitutes, and jail-mates. Those with tattoos were often shunned by society and were considered to have a stigma (DeMello, 1995). Today, however, tattoos have become commonplace among many accomplished and professional middle class individuals. Tattoos are now considered fine pieces of art, designed by professional artists, a distinction from the primitive designs that they used to be (DeMello, 1995). A study conducted in 2004 showed that around twenty-four percent of adults between the ages of 18 an 50 had tattoos (Laumann, 2006).

Double-Space

1"

In-Text Citation

Researchable Question

Why has tattooing become such a phenomenon in the past decade? Many believe that it is because people feel the need to express themselves and their beliefs on their skin as an attempt at self-identity and individualism, which has become increasingly important to society throughout the years. Others believe that tattooing is popular because the media portrays tattoos as being attractive to the opposite sex. Within the past decade, tattooing, or body art, has become commonplace among professionals due to their attempt to establish themselves as individuals by making a decorative statement, to appear more attractive to the opposite sex, or to thwart expectations of society, as shown in many modern movies, television shows, such as *LA Ink*, and through celebrity advertisements.

1"

Thesis and Forecast

Left Justify

Topic Sentence

Double-Space

One of the main reasons that tattooing has become so prominent amongst United States citizens today is the desire of people to define themselves as unique individuals. Many believe that tattooing something meaningful on their body is one way of accomplishing this individualism. According to DeMello (1995), "Tattoos have become 'liberated' from the province of lowlifes, and can now be properly positioned as aspects of fine art" (p. 47). In many people's eyes, tattoos are no longer marks of dishonor, but, instead, works of art. The idea of tattoos as forms of art can be exemplified by the popular television show, *LA Ink*. In one particular episode of this show, a young woman, Kathryn, gets a tattoo of a colorful peacock on her arm to represent the strength of her mother who had recently been in a coma for two months and completely lost her memory. Kathryn was not a biker or involved in crime, but was an educated, middle-class individual who desired to make a statement about her mother's heartbreaking situation in the form of body art (*LA Ink—Peacock Tattoo*). In DeMello's (1995) article, "Not Just for Bikers Anymore," she quotes an individual who was interviewed about his

First Main Point

Ragged Right Margin

1"

4

First Main Point Continued

decision to get a tattoo. He responded, "The power of the tattoo is in the ability to express individuality and in its permanence" (p. 41). Kathryn, from *LA Ink—Peacock Tattoo*, and this quoted individual share similar beliefs about tattoos and their meanings. Whether they are designed in memory of a loved one or to symbolize an important value or belief of the individual, tattoos are most commonly acquired in the form of unique, decorative statements.

Second Main Point

Another fundamental motivation for people in this country to get tattoos is the belief that they create sex appeal. A study of college students found that "almost three-fourths of the undergraduate women reported that they 'sometimes' viewed openly visible tattoos as attractive when on a man" (Horne, Knox, Zusman, & Zusman, 2007, p. 1011). On the other hand, "58.8 percent of the undergraduate men viewed such visible tattoos as attractive when on a woman" (Horne, Knox, Zusman, & Zusman, 2007, p. 1011). Therefore, men and women may get tattoos if they feel that it will add to their sex appeal. A large portion of this thinking has derived from the fact that many celebrities have tattoos, and, because celebrities are often seen as sex icons, common people believe that if they get tattoos then they will be appealing to the opposite sex as well (Horne, Knox, Zusman, & Zusman, 2007, p. 1011). DeMello (1995) states, "Tattooing has moved from being a symbol of the outcast to that of a rock star, model, and postmodern youth, and with this shift in public perception has come a shift in meaning as well, as tattoo moves from stigma to status" (p. 49). The idea that tattoos are sexy is exemplified in many modern movies, including *Wanted*. The most famous scene of this movie depicts Angelina Jolie getting out of a bathtub, completely naked, with large tattoos covering her back. Jolie seductively peers around her shoulder at the camera, an obvious attempt of the director to attract men with her tattoo-covered body (Silvestri, & Bekmambetov, 2008). Since the premier of the movie, this scene has become extremely famous to the public eye. However, Jolie is not the only celebrity to endorse tattoos. Others, including David Beckham, Rihanna, Michael Jordan, and Gisele have been pictured in advertisements that show off, or endorse tattoos. In his ad for Emporio Armani, Beckham poses in underwear, revealing his muscular body and a large tattoo on his right arm (Emporio Armani Underwear, 2009). Advertisements and movies like these, that depict extremely attractive celebrities with revealed tattoos, majorly contribute to the idea that tattoos are sexy. For this reason, many people get tattoos in order to make themselves more attractive to the opposite sex.

Topic Sentence ——→ The final reason for individuals to get tattoos so frequently today is their desire to stray from the norms of society. Often people feel that society dictates what they should look like and how they should act. In response, they feel the need to rebel against the idea of a perfect, cookie-cutter citizen and believe that getting unique tattoos with help them do so. Another individual quoted in DeMello's (1995) article stated that he got a tattoo to "go against what people want you to do. All of your life you're computerized to do what people want you to do" (p. 41). Therefore, some people desire a release from the constraints that they feel society puts on them, and they achieve this release by getting a tattoo. This idea of rebellion as a reason for body art is clearly represented in the television show, *One Tree Hilt*. In episode nine of season one, "With Arms Outstretched," Lucas gets an impulsive tattoo of a Chinese symbol on his upper arm. At the time, his mother is out of town and he is looking for a way to act out against authority in a rebellious way (Schwan & Prange, 2003). Therefore, some people get tattoos as an attempt to resist authority. This reason for getting a tattoo, however, is more common among males than females. Horne, Knox, Zusman, and Zusman (2007) found that almost half of the male sample set agreed with the statement "tattoos are symbols of our resistance to culture" (p. 1011). This differs from the 31.5 percent of women who agree with the statement (Horne, Knox, Zusman, & Zusman, 2007). As a result, people often get tattoos as an attempt to rebel against the person that society and authority tells them they should be. However, this is more so a reason for males compared to females, who more often get tattoos to contribute to their attractiveness or to make a decorative statement.

Third Main Point

Tattoos are no longer only for bikers, sailors, convicts, and prostitutes, but have risen in status and are now decorating the bodies of a quarter of the Nation. These people include middle-class professionals holding jobs as lawyers, bankers, doctors, and other highly established career positions (DeMello, 1995, p. 40). Individuals get tattoos so often today for three main reasons: to make a statement by defining their individuality, to make themselves more appealing to the opposite sex, or to stray from the norms of society in the United States. These reasons are extremely visible in entertainment and in the media, for they are represented in modern television shows, movies, and celebrity advertisements. These outlets illustrate that the media and entertainment have a major impact on the way we, as Americans, think and act. If television shows did not endorse the idea of getting tattoos, would we get tattoos? If celebrities

Reworded Thesis Statement

Summary of Main Points

1/2"

Summary of Main Points Continued

did not have tattoos all over their bodies, would we put tattoos all over our bodies? The answer is most likely no. Essentially, tattoos are just another fashion trend. Just as different forms of fashion are depicted in celebrity advertisements and used as wardrobes in movies and television shows, so are tattoos. The real question is, will the popularity of tattooing eventually die like most other fashion trends, leaving those who have them to regret it for the rest of their lives? Only time will tell.

1"

Memorable Ending

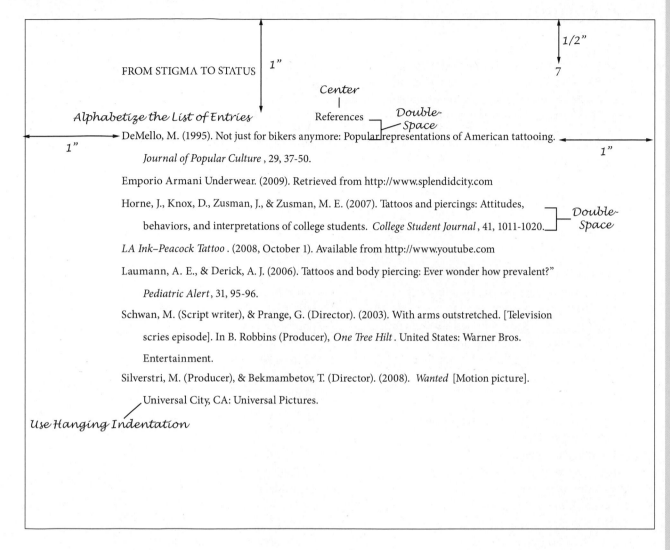

FROM STIGMA TO STATUS   1"

Center

Alphabetize the List of Entries   References   *Double-Space*

DeMello, M. (1995). Not just for bikers anymore: Popular representations of American tattooing.

Journal of Popular Culture , 29, 37-50.

Emporio Armani Underwear. (2009). Retrieved from http://www.splendidcity.com

Horne, J., Knox, D., Zusman, J., & Zusman, M. E. (2007). Tattoos and piercings: Attitudes,

behaviors, and interpretations of college students. *College Student Journal* , 41, 1011-1020.   *Double-Space*

LA Ink–Peacock Tattoo . (2008, October 1). Available from http://www.youtube.com

Laumann, A. E., & Derick, A. J. (2006). Tattoos and body piercing: Ever wonder how prevalent?"

Pediatric Alert , 31, 95-96.

Schwan, M. (Script writer), & Prange, G. (Director). (2003). With arms outstretched. [Television

series episode]. In B. Robbins (Producer), *One Tree Hilt* . United States: Warner Bros.

Entertainment.

Silverstri, M. (Producer), & Bekmambetov, T. (Director). (2008). *Wanted* [Motion picture].

Universal City, CA: Universal Pictures.

Use Hanging Indentation

1/2"

7

1"   1"

[QUESTIONS FOR REFLECTION]

1. Based on the introductory paragraph, what three main points does Rowland promise to cover in the body of her paper? Does she follow through with her promise?

2. What supporting details and examples does she offer for her first main point? Are they sufficient? Why or why not?

3. What supporting details does Rowland offer for her second main point? Which details are the most convincing? Why?

4. Which ideas from the author's third body paragraph are most memorable? Why?

5. What is Rowland's thesis? Do you think she fully supports her thesis in the body of the paper? Why or why not?

Using the six fictitious sources below, create a works cited page in the MLA format or a references page in the APA format. Be sure to follow the exact guidelines of the format you are using. Arrange your entries in alphabetical order.

Tip: You may not need all of the information provided.

Book
Title: all that glitters is gold
Subtitle: earning the big bucks
Author: Showmei Z. Money
Date of publication: 2009
Publisher: Greedy Green Publishing Company, Inc.
Place of publication: Greenville, South Carolina
Medium: Print

Magazine Article
Title: a computer can save your life
Magazine: today's computers
Authors: Joey T. Hacker and Betty Lynn Byte
Date of publication: October 2010
Page numbers: 10, 11, and 16
Medium: Print

Online Magazine Article
Title: justice for juveniles in Jamestown
Magazine: crimesolversareus.com
Author: Jamal J. Jolly
Date of publication: August 19, 2008
Page numbers: None
URL: www.crimesolversareus.com/juvenilesingreenville
DOI: 10.1234/0011-2233.45.6.789
Retrieval Date: January 14, 2010
Medium: Internet

Newspaper Article
Title: stray alligator terrorizes shopping mall
Subtitle: two shoppers injured
Newspaper: trivia tribune
Author: Liza L. Love-Lizzard
Date: July 27, 2009
Page Numbers: 4, 5, and 8
Section number: B
Medium: Print

Scholarly Journal Article
Title: best business practices
Subtitle: earn and keep good customers
Journal: universal business journal
Authors: Kiefer G. Consumer, Mario López Servicio, Fahad Al-Safar
Volume number: 6
Issue number: 3
Date: 2009
Page numbers: 14–15
Medium: Print

Web Site Document
Title: a healthier you
Subtitle: living life to the fullest
Author: Elsie B. Eatwell
Web site: Living Well
Date of publication: April 23, 2007
Retrieval Date: March 25, 2010
Page number: none
URL: www.livingwell.org/ebeatwell/livinglife
Medium: Internet

>> Peer Review Questions for a Research Paper

1. Identify the thesis statement in the introduction. Is it clear and effective? Why or why not?

2. What are the author's main points? Are they fully developed? Explain.

3. What is your favorite part of the research paper?

4. Are any areas confusing? Explain.

5. Does the paper flow well? Which parts, if any, could be smoother?

6. Is the concluding paragraph effective? Why or why not?

7. What kinds of grammatical errors, if any, are evident in the research paper?

8. Are all sources clearly and properly documented in the text and on the works cited or references page? Identify any areas that need attention.

9. What final suggestions do you have for the author?

> Writer's Checklist for a Research Paper

Use the checklist below to evaluate your own writing and help ensure that your research paper is effective. If you answer no to any of the questions, continue work on those areas as needed.

❏ 1. Does my introduction clearly state my thesis and give the reader an indication of the direction my essay will take?

❏ 2. Are my topic sentences and body paragraphs clear and well developed?

❏ 3. Have I fully supported my thesis with ample supporting details and examples?

❏ 4. Have I used a sufficient number and variety of sources in my paper?

❏ 5. Are all of my sources properly cited in the body of my paper according to the MLA or APA format?

❏ 6. Does my conclusion effectively summarize my main points and restate my thesis in different words?

❏ 7. Have I carefully proofread and revised my paper for sentence variety, word choice, grammar, and punctuation?

❏ 8. Does my works cited or references page include every source I cited in the text, and is it in the correct format?

❏ 9. Have I used the correct margins, line spacing, and other format issues required by the format I am using and my instructor?

[CHAPTER SUMMARY]

1. Avoid plagiarism by clearly citing sources you use in a research paper.

2. Follow the specific guidelines of the format your instructor requires you to use, such as MLA or APA.

3. Cite sources within your text and on a works cited page (MLA format) or on a references page (APA format).

4. Use the correct MLA or APA format for your entire research paper.

[WHAT I KNOW NOW]

Use this checklist to determine what you need to work on in order to feel comfortable with your understanding of the material in this chapter. Check off each item as you master it. Review the material for any unchecked items.

❏ 1. I know what **plagiarism** is and understand how to avoid it.

❏ 2. I understand what **sources** I need to cite in a research paper.

❏ 3. I know that I need to cite sources in the body of my paper as well as on a **works cited or references page**.

❏ 4. I know how to use this textbook to cite sources using the **MLA** or **APA** format.

❏ 5. I know how to **format a paper** using the MLA or APA format.

CHAPTER 15

GIVING AN ORAL PRESENTATION

LEARNING outcomes

> In this chapter you will learn techniques for the following:

15.1 Planning and developing the introduction, body, and conclusion of an oral presentation.

15.2 Choosing and preparing visual

aids for an oral presentation.

15.3 Delivering an oral presentation using an outline or note cards.

15.4 Planning and delivering an effective group presentation.

15.1 > Planning an Oral Presentation

Does the idea of giving an oral presentation make you nervous? You're not alone! Some people fear public speaking more than spiders, snakes, or even death. Fortunately, with careful planning and practice, you can become more confident and effective at giving oral presentations. This chapter is not designed to be a complete guide to public speaking. Your school may require that you take a separate speech communications course and read an entire textbook devoted to delivering speeches. This chapter, however, will give you a brief introduction to giving a research paper presentation in your writing class (or another class) in case you haven't taken a speech class yet. If you have already taken a public speaking class, this chapter will serve as a quick refresher.

You'll have many opportunities to give presentations at school, on the job, and in your personal life. Many instructors require students to give presentations based on course material or papers they have written. At work you may need to give a presentation to supervisors, colleagues, clients, customers, or patients. Or, you may need to say a few words to friends or family members at a special occasion or event, such as a wedding or a reunion. Regardless of what type of speaking engagement you may face, you'll benefit from preparing what to say and do ahead of time. Planning a speech is very similar to writing an essay. For both you'll need to have an introduction, a body, and a conclusion.

Developing the Introduction

Similar to your research essay, the introduction of your speech should do three things: capture your audience's attention, state the thesis, and give a forecast of your main points.

1. **Gain the audience's attention.** The fact that you have an audience assembled in front of you doesn't guarantee that they will actually listen to you. Try beginning with a thought-provoking question, a relevant

quote, a brief story or description, a shocking statistic, a surprising statement, or a comparison to help hook your listeners. For example, you might begin a presentation explaining how to budget money with the question, "Have you ever wished you had more money to spend?" Your goal is to entice your listeners to want to hear what you have to say.

2. **State the thesis.** For a presentation based on your research paper, you may choose to use the exact thesis from your paper. Be sure your thesis covers the topic you are addressing as well as your overall opinion about it and that it isn't too wordy for your audience to remember. For example, the thesis might be, "If you effectively plan for your financial future now, you will reap the benefits for a lifetime." Memorize your thesis statement so that you can look right at your audience when you state it.

3. **Give a forecast of the main points.** Provide your listeners with a preview of what they should get from your presentation. For instance, you might say, "There are three steps you can take to reduce your debt and increase your financial status." Being clear about the main points will also help your audience to take notes if they need to. If you are using a research paper as the basis for your presentation, you can go through your paper and determine which points will be most interesting and relevant to the group. You may choose not to include every main point from your paper.

TABLE 15.1

Organizational Strategies	
Narrating	Tell a story about something that happened. Usually you will present the details of the event in chronological order, but occasionally a flashback can be useful. Be sure to cover who, what, where, when, why, and how.
Describing	Use words to paint a picture of an object, scene, or event for your audience using as many senses as are appropriate for your subject: sight, sound, hearing, taste, smell. Include many colorful adjectives to give your listeners a clear impression of your subject.
Explaining a Process	Tell how something works or what something does. You may give step-by-step instructions so your listeners can perform the task or write an explanation so that your audience is able to understand your subject.
Comparing or Contrasting	Show how two people, places, or objects are similar and/or different. Be sure to make a worthwhile point while doing this.
Explaining Causes or Effects	Examine how one event or situation caused another to occur, or determine the effects of an event or situation. Be careful to apply sound logic as you analyze cause and effects.
Persuading	Take a stand about an important or controversial issue, and convince your audience that your position is valid. Use research to support your main idea.
Evaluating	Make a judgment about your subject by determining how well it meets specific criteria that you feel are important for that subject.
Solving a Problem	Explain a problem to your audience and offer several solutions. You may evaluate each possible solution before persuading your listeners that one specific solution is best.

Developing the Body

In the body of your presentation, you want to give the audience what you promised them in your forecast. Although you probably will not want to write out your main points word for word, you will need to decide exactly what you will cover in your presentation. Use an outline or note cards to help you keep track of ideas you want to emphasize in your speech.

1. **Emphasize the main points.** Cover your points in a logical order. Give relevant details and examples to help you support your main ideas. If your presentation is based on a research paper, you do not need to include every example from your paper. Choose the ones your audience will find most interesting and useful. You can use the same strategies you learned about in Chapters 5–12 to organize your speech. Depending on your subject, you may focus on one particular strategy or combine two or more strategies to get your point across to your audience.

2. **Transition smoothly.** Determine your transitions ahead of time so that you don't forget to use them during your presentation. As you move from one point to another, use a transition to signal the change to the listeners. For example, you might use the transitions, *first, second, third,* and *last* to help your audience keep track of your main points.

3. **Cite sources.** If you use words or ideas from an outside source, you need to mention the source to give appropriate credit to the originator of the material. For example, you might say, "According to Suze Orman, a financial expert who has her own television show, people need to spend below their means to get ahead financially." Omitting citations in a speech is just as unethical as leaving them out of a research paper. Work on incorporating your citations smoothly so that they don't interfere with the flow of your presentation.

Suze Orman

Developing the Conclusion

The conclusion of your speech serves the same purpose as the conclusion to an essay. You want to restate your main points and leave your audience with a lasting impression. Keep the conclusion short and interesting.

1. **Restate the thesis.** Remind your listeners of your thesis by restating it using slightly different words than the ones you used in the introduction.

2. **Summarize the main points.** Mention your main points again, but do not restate your specific details and examples. You might say something like, "Remember, the three steps for becoming more financially secure are…"

3. **End with a memorable statement.** Leave your audience with a final vivid thought. You might tell a brief story that relates to your topic or suggest a call to action. Another option is to end with a quote that fits with your overall purpose.

4. **Say thank you.** Saying "thank you" at the end of your presentation is courteous, and it provides a definite signal to your audience that your speech is over. Your listeners will know when it is time to clap and ask questions, if appropriate.

5. **Answer questions.** If you are in a situation where the audience will have an opportunity to ask you questions after your presentation, then you'll need to be prepared. Try to anticipate the types of questions your listeners might have. Have your notes handy in case they might be helpful. It's

all right if you don't know every answer. Be honest and say, "I'm not sure. I didn't research that particular area." Or you might answer, "That's a good question, I'll have to get back to you on that." Don't fake it.

15.2 > Choosing Visual Aids

Visual aids can be a true asset to any presentation. Choose your visual aids carefully. Make sure that each one enhances your speech without overshadowing it. Keep your audience in mind as you decide which visual aids are most appropriate for your presentation.

Objects or Models

Sometimes a three-dimensional object or model can be an effective visual aid. Make sure it is large enough for the audience to see, but not so large that it would be difficult to bring to your presentation. For example, if you were giving a presentation about techniques used in sailing, a sailboat would be too large for the room; however, a 1/18-scale model would be appropriate.

Posters

You may find a poster board to be a useful visual aid for your presentation. You can use it to display photographs, drawings, maps, charts, graphs, timelines, or fairly small three-dimensional items. You may hold up the poster for your audience to see, hang it on the wall, or place it on an easel. Make sure your poster looks neat and professional and that your audience will be able to see it.

Flip Charts or Whiteboards

Writing words or drawing simple figures on a whiteboard or flip chart can be useful during your presentation, especially if you are soliciting responses from your audience. Be sure to write large enough so that everyone can see it. This method is appropriate only for small amounts of information. If the room is equipped with a smart board, use that instead of a whiteboard because the images projected on the wall will be larger and easier to see than what you put on a whiteboard or chalkboard. Face your listeners as much as possible as you are writing or drawing.

Media Presentations

Developing a media presentation using PowerPoint, Keynote, Lotus, Adobe, or another software application can help you to give a smooth speech if you use it correctly. Be careful to include a reasonable number of words on each slide. Write short sentences or phrases on each slide, and elaborate on them during your speech. Avoid making your slides too busy. Combining too many colors and styles may be distracting for your audience.

You may want to incorporate artwork into some of your slides. Choose images that relate to your topic and enhance your presentation. Also, choose transitions that are interesting but not overdone. You don't want to make your audience dizzy with too many spinning or bouncing objects and words. Sound clips, movie clips, and other features can add a little pizzazz to your presentation as well. If you are creating a media presentation for an online class, you'll probably want to design it to play automatically, so that your audience doesn't have to click from slide to slide.

FIGURE 15.1
Inappropriate Slide

Too Much for One Slide

\# This slide has too many details. Because too many ideas have been included, the words are so small that some of the audience members will have trouble seeing them, especially if they are near the back of the room. **Another problem with this slide is that it uses too many different colors and styles.** AVOID MAKING EVERY SENTENCE A DIFFERENT COLOR. USING ONE COLOR OR ALTERNATING BETWEEN TWO WORKS MUCH BETTER. Furthermore, the main points all run together without any bullets or spaces between ideas. This slide would work better if just key ideas were included rather than a complete paragraph. See the next slide for a better example.

FIGURE 15.2
Appropriate Slide

Appropriate Slide

\# Highlight key points.

\# Use short sentences or phrases.

\# Keep colors and styles consistent.

\# Use visuals to paint a picture.

Video Clips

Depending on the type of presentation you are giving, you might find it useful to show a short video clip that relates to your topic. For instance, if your presentation is on scuba diving, you might show a one- or two-minute clip of an underwater coral reef with divers and interesting marine life moving about. Similarly, if the point of your presentation is to give a review of a book you have read, you might show a brief clip of a critical scene from the book that relates to one of your key points. Be sure to have the clip ready so that you can show the right scene on demand. If you are using a videotape or DVD, then pause the scene so that you can just hit the play button when you are ready to show the clip.

Handouts

A handout may serve as an appropriate visual aid for your presentation, especially as a backup in case you have a technical problem with a media presentation. If you decide to create a handout for your audience, consider giving it out after rather than during your presentation. You don't want to unintentionally lose your listeners by diverting their attention elsewhere. Handouts should look professional and be visually appealing. Be sure to proofread them carefully for content and grammar.

15.3 > Delivering an Oral Presentation

1. **Get psyched.** Pump yourself up on the day of the presentation. Focus on positive thoughts. Visualize yourself giving a great presentation. Being a little nervous is fine and even desired because you'll get a boost of adrenaline to keep you going. If your hands are a little shaky or sweaty, it's no big deal. You're probably the only person who will notice. Just before you get up before the audience, take a deep breath and try to relax. Look out at your audience and smile. Look at someone who smiles back as you begin your presentation.

2. **Use an outline or note cards.** You will probably be able to use an outline or 3-by-5-inch note cards to help guide you through the presentation. Avoid writing out your entire speech word for word. Instead, use an outline or note cards to help you keep track of the main points you want to cover. Include any quotes, statistics, and sources you want to mention so that you will give the correct information to your audience. Be careful to not rely on these tools too heavily. Spend more time looking at your listeners than at your notes.

STUDENT OUTLINE

Texting While Driving
by Anita Jitta

Speech Goal: To inform my audience about the dangers of texting while driving.

Introduction

Hook: On November 2, 2009, my husband, Anthony, was driving home when a teenaged girl slammed into him with her car. What was she doing? She was texting while driving. Luckily enough, another driver saw what this girl was doing and decided to wait at the scene of the accident to be a witness when the police arrived. The teenager ended up receiving a citation for reckless driving, but the results could have been much worse, even deadly.

Thesis: Texting while driving is extremely dangerous and can lead to devastating consequences.

Preview: First you will learn what happens when you text while driving. Second, you will learn how people feel about texting while driving. Finally, you will learn about what some famous people are doing to try to prevent drivers from texting while driving.

Body

I. What can happen when someone text messages and drives? According to the Text Free Driving Organization, "57% of American drivers admit to texting behind the wheel."

II. How do people feel about texting and driving? The 2009 AAA survey brought about some interesting responses.

III. Who is against texting and driving, and what do they plan to do about it? President Obama and Oprah Winfrey are trying to change the legislation to help tackle this problem.

Sources

Bruno, Laura. (June 12, 2007). "Stop Text Messaging, Drivers Urged." *USA Today*. Retrieved from **www.usatoday.com**.

Cooney, Michael. (November 4, 2009). "FCC and DOT Team-up, Want High-tech Cure for Distracted Driving." *Networkworld*. Retrieved from **www.infoworld.com**.

Jaimungal, Anthony. (February 10, 2010). Personal interview.

Richtell, Matt. (October 2, 2009) "Texting While Driving Banned for Federal Staff." *The New York Times*, B3.

Schulte, Bret. (February 11, 2008). "Outlawing Text Message While Driving: Legislatures in Several States Respond to Safety Concerns." *US News and World Report*. Retrieved from **www.usnews.com**.

Text Free Driving Organization. (No date). Retrieved from **http://textfreedriving.org**.

Traffic Safety Culture. (September 25, 2009). "Distracted Driving—Time to Start Addressing the Problem." Retrieved from **http://trafficsafetyculture.blogspot.com**.

Note: The sources listed on the above outline are not listed in a particular format. Your instructor may request that you list your sources in the MLA or APA format. If so, please see Chapter 14 for the exact guidelines.

---

3. **Speak clearly and enthusiastically.** If you are excited about your topic, your audience will be too. Vary your pitch and tone to emphasize important words and to keep your listeners interested. Enunciate your words carefully so that your audience can hear each word. Also, make sure your pace is appropriate. Speaking too slowly will give your audience too much time to think about other things. However, if you speak too rapidly, your listeners might not catch everything and get frustrated.

4. **Communicate nonverbally.** In addition to listening to what you have to say, your audience will be paying attention to the nonverbal cues you display. Your clothing, poise, posture, movements, hand gestures, facial expressions, and eye contact all affect the message you are attempting to get across to your audience. You want to communicate an attitude of professionalism and confidence as your give your presentation. If you make a mistake or forget something, don't apologize or stop. Just pick up where you left off and keep going.

5. **Incorporate visual aids.** Decide ahead of time exactly when and how you will show your visual aids to enhance your presentation. Generally, you should display each visual aid only when you are talking about it. As you show each item, hold it up and away from your body so that everyone in your audience can see it. Avoid passing visual aids around the room. You might even walk around the room so everyone can get a closer look. If you are using a PowerPoint or Keynote presentation, talk about each slide as you show it to your audience. Don't read your presentation from the slides. Instead, use the key words on the slide to help you remember what to say.

6. **Have a backup plan.** As you are well aware, things don't always go as they are planned. What happens if the projector doesn't work the day of your presentation? What will you do if the computer freezes? Have a secondary plan. Bring additional materials with you to ensure that you are able to give an effective presentation even if you experience a technological glitch. For example, write out some note cards in case your PowerPoint or Keynote presentation won't work.

7. **Practice your presentation.** Before the big day, practice delivering your presentation several times. If you can, assemble a small audience to simulate the experience as closely as possible. If no one is around, stand in front of a mirror. Explore different methods for using your visual aids, note cards, hand gestures, and so on, to see what feels most comfortable and seems to work best. You may even want to videotape or digitally record your presentation so that you can watch and critique yourself. Make adjustments as needed to smooth out your presentation. Also, time yourself to ensure that your presentation falls with in the time requirements.

ESOL Tip >

Practice your speech for a native English speaker to ensure that you are pronouncing words correctly. For example, some non-native speakers prounce *i's* as *e's*.

> Presenter's Checklist

Use this checklist before you give your presentation to make sure that you are ready. Keep working on any items that don't yet earn a *yes*.

❑ 1. Are my outline and note cards ready?

❑ 2. Are my thesis and main points clear and well organized?

❑ 3. Do I have the right number of details and examples to fully support my main points?

❑ 4. Have I planned how to transition from one point to the next?

❑ 5. Are my visual aids useful and appropriate for the audience?

❑ 6. Do I have a backup plan in case something goes wrong?

❑ 7. Am I ready to give an enthusiastic presentation?

❑ 8. Have I practiced my presentation several times?

Comments:

> Observer's Checklist

Use this checklist to evaluate someone else's oral presentation.

❑ 1. Were the thesis and main points clear?

❑ 2. Was the organization of the presentation effective?

❑ 3. Did the presentation flow well?

❑ 4. Was the speaker enthusiastic?

❑ 5. Were the visual aids useful and handled well?

❑ 6. Did the presenter speak clearly and effectively?

❑ 7. Did the speaker look at the audience?

❑ 8. Were the presenter's posture and movements effective?

❑ 9. What suggestions do I have for the speaker?

❑ 10. What was the best part of the presentation?

Comments:

Activity   Evaluating a Presentation

Go to YouTube.com and find Dr. Martin Luther King's "I Have a Dream" speech. Watch King's speech and evaluate it according to the observer's checklist. Write at least one paragraph explaining what was most memorable or inspiring about his famous speech. You may be asked to share your reaction in groups or with the class.

Note: Another famous speech could be used as an alternative. Additionally, YouTube.com has numerous student speeches to evaluate.

Activity   Oral Research Presentation

Using the ideas from a research paper you have written, plan and deliver an oral presentation.

1. Use your paper to develop an outline or note cards for your presentation.
2. Organize the introduction, body, and conclusion of your presentation.
3. Keep track of your sources so you can cite them as needed.
4. Prepare appropriate visual aids for your presentation.
5. Be ready to answer questions from your listeners.
6. Pay attention to your nonverbal communication and time constraints as you practice delivering your presentation.
7. Relax—this is not a life-or-death situation!
8. Deliver your presentation.

15.4 > Group Presentations

You will have many opportunities to participate in group presentations in school and at work. One of the benefits of working with others is that you gain the perspective of all of the participants. Follow these steps to ensure that your group presentation goes smoothly.

1. **Establish goals.** Everyone in the group needs to understand what the goals are and be willing to help achieve those goals. Keep your overall purpose in mind as well as the effect you want to have on the audience. The goals you develop need to be reasonable. You may want to set benchmarks for accomplishing specific tasks to ensure that you prepare an effective presentation and meet your deadline.

2. **Assign roles.** Each member of the group needs to have a particular role. For example, if your group has five members, then each person might take one of the following roles: leader, note taker, researcher, encourager, and harmonizer. The roles of the group members will vary based on the parameters of the assignment. The group members will also need

to determine who is responsible for each task that needs to be completed before the presentation. While many details can be worked out together, each member may need to work on certain parts of the presentation away from the group.

3. **Participate in group meetings.** If you do not have an opportunity to meet with your group members during class, then you will need to establish meeting times. Find a time that works best for everyone in the group. If face-to-face meetings are impossible or inconvenient, then have virtual meetings via e-mail, teleconferencing, videoconferencing, or online threaded discussions. Everyone needs to cooperate in the meetings and contribute ideas for the presentation.

4. **Organize the group presentation.** Work as a team to organize the introduction, body, and conclusion of the presentation. Decide what each person will say and/or do during the presentation. Listen to everyone's ideas and be open to suggestions. If the group has trouble agreeing on a particular issue, then the group members can go with majority rule or work to come to a consensus. Be willing to compromise for the sake of helping the group to accomplish its goals.

5. **Practice the group presentation.** If you are giving a live presentation, rather than an online presentation, then you will need to practice your presentation before giving it. Have a dress rehearsal complete with visual aids to make sure that everyone and everything is ready. Make sure your presentation flows smoothly and that everyone knows his or her part.

6. **Deliver the group presentation.** On the day of the presentation, everyone should show up prepared to do his or her part. If someone doesn't make it, then the other members need to step in and fulfill that person's duties. The group members need to show enthusiasm, communicate nonverbally, and incorporate visual aids smoothly during the presentation. If someone makes a mistake or forgets something, keep going as if everything is fine.

▶ *Activity*   **Group Presentation: Sales Pitch**

In groups of three to six, invent a realistic or futuristic product or service that you would love to see on the market. For example, maybe you would like to offer a vacation package to Pluto. How will your customers get there? What will they do for fun and relaxation once they arrive? Why is this vacation worth taking? Or maybe you would prefer to present a new product that will wow your audience, such as a robot that will clean your home from top to bottom while you are away or a chocolate bar that helps you to remember important concepts on test day.

Work cooperatively to develop a mini-infomercial to present to your live class or a magazine advertisement to present to your online class. Every member in the group needs to participate in the preparation and presentation of your sales pitch. For this one assignment only, you may invent the supporting details. Use the following guidelines for your sales pitch:

1. Grab your audience's attention with a catchy opening.

2. Describe the product or service and emphasize the benefits it will have to the consumer. You want audience members to be interested in your product or service so that they want to buy it.

3. Create testimonials, statistics, or other data to promote your product or service and convince your audience that your product or service is worth buying.

4. Display appropriate visual aids to enhance your presentation.

5. Let your audience members know how much your product or service costs and what they need to do to get it. Do they need to call a 1-800 number, visit your store, or go online?

6. You might mention any disclaimers or side effects that the product or service may cause the consumer.

Note: Making up the data is appropriate only as an exercise. You should never invent support for a product or service that you are really selling because it is unethical.

[CHAPTER SUMMARY]

1. If you plan carefully, you can become more confident and effective at giving oral presentations.

2. Organize your presentation with a clear introduction, body, and conclusion.

3. Carefully design your visual aids, such as objects, models, posters, flip charts, whiteboards, media presentations, video clips, and handouts, to enhance your presentation.

4. When you deliver an oral presentation, think positive thoughts, use an outline or notes, speak clearly and enthusiastically, communicate nonverbally, and incorporate visual aids smoothly.

5. Always have a backup plan in case your equipment fails during your presentation.

6. Practice, practice, practice your presentation before delivering it.

7. When planning to deliver a group presentation, establish goals, assign roles, work cooperatively, and organize the presentation effectively.

[WHAT I KNOW NOW]

Use this checklist to determine what you need to work on in order to feel comfortable with your understanding of the material in this chapter. Check off each item as you master it. Review the material for any unchecked items.

❏ 1. I know how to plan and develop the **introduction, body, and conclusion** of an oral presentation.

❏ 2. I can choose and **prepare visual aids** for an oral presentation.

❏ 3. I understand how to deliver an oral presentation using an **outline or note cards**.

❏ 4. I can plan and deliver an effective **group presentation**.

PART 4

Editing Guide

While you may not need to worry about your writing style when you send a text message to a friend or write a note to yourself or a loved one, most academic and career-related writing occasions require that you follow the conventions of standard American English. When you write a report for your instructor or boss, a letter to a client or patient, or an e-mail to a coworker, you need to take a few minutes to edit it carefully before you submit it.

Others will judge you on how well you write. If your document is filled with errors, the recipients will question your credibility and the content of your message. As you edit your documents, pay par-ticular attention to your sentence structure, word choice, grammar, punctuation, mechanics, and spelling. Being adept at following the conven-tions of language will help you to communicate your message clearly to your audience and achieve success in your personal, academic, and profes-sional life.

This guide is designed to make it easy for you to find answers to questions you may have about proper sentence structure and diction. It will help you edit your writings for grammar, punctuation, mechanics, and spelling. Activities are included throughout to help with comprehension.

> A. Editing Sentences

Fragments

Most academic and professional writing occasions require that you write in complete sentences. A complete sentence must contain a subject and a verb and express a complete thought. A sentence *fragment* is a group of words that cannot stand on its own because it is lacking one or more of the elements of a complete sentence. Often you can correct a sentence fragment by adding a subject or verb or by connecting it to another sentence.

Fragment: Is fun and relaxing.

Revised: Camping is fun and relaxing.

Discussion: The fragment lacks a subject.

Fragment: Especially on a hot day.

Revised: Going to a lake is refreshing, especially on a hot day.

Discussion: The fragment lacks a verb.

Fragment: While I was driving to school today.

Revised: While I was driving to school today, I saw a red car with yellow flames painted on it.

Discussion: The fragment has a subject and verb, but it does not express a complete thought.

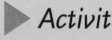 *Activity*   **Editing for Sentence Fragments**

Revise the following sentences to eliminate sentence fragments.

EXAMPLE

Fragment: Many students have strengths and weaknesses in different areas. Especially in subjects such as math and English.

Revised: Many students have strengths and weaknesses in different areas, especially in subjects such as math and English.

1. Many colleges offer tutoring services. For students who need to strengthen their skills in math or English.

2. Because he has good math skills. Hector tutors other college students.

3. He enjoys helping others. And feels good about himself after each tutoring session.

4. Even though Hector is very strong in math. He sometimes needs help with his writing.

5. Hector is grateful that he benefits from the tutoring services. Offered at his college.

Run-Ons and Comma Splices

A *run-on* sentence, also known as a *fused* sentence, occurs when two complete sentences (*independent clauses*) run together without a proper punctuation mark or coordinating conjunction. A comma-spliced sentence occurs when two complete sentences are joined improperly with just a comma.

Run-on sentence: Sara likes to exercise before going to work Enrique prefers to exercise after work.

Comma-spliced sentence: Sara likes to exercise before going to work, Enrique prefers to exercise after work.

To revise a run-on or comma-spliced sentence, try one of these five methods:

1. Separate the sentences.

   Revised: Sara likes to exercise before going to work. Enrique prefers to exercise after work.

2. Combine the sentences using a comma and a *coordinating conjunction*. A coordinating conjunction is a word that joins words or independent clauses that are equal.

   Revised: Sara likes to exercise before going to work, but Enrique prefers to exercise after work.

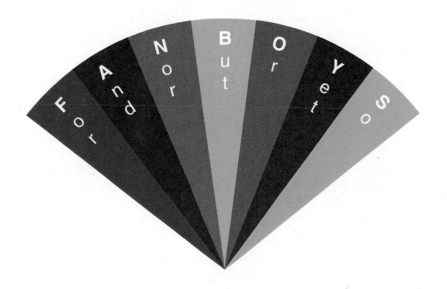

FIGURE 1 The Seven Coordinating Conjunctions (FANBOYS)

3. Combine the sentences using a semicolon. Use this method only if the sentences are fairly short and are similar in content and structure.

   Revised: Sara likes to exercise before going to work; Enrique prefers to exercise after work.

4. Combine the sentences using a semicolon and a *conjunctive adverb*. A conjunctive adverb is an adverb that serves as a transition between two independent clauses.

Common Conjunctive Adverbs			
accordingly	furthermore	meanwhile	similarly
also	hence	moreover	still
anyway	however	namely	then
besides	incidentally	nevertheless	thereafter
certainly	indeed	next	therefore
consequently	instead	nonetheless	thus
finally	likewise	otherwise	undoubtedly

> **Revised:** Sara likes to exercise before going to work; however, Enrique prefers to exercise after work.

5. Combine the sentences by using a *subordinating conjunction*. A subordinating conjunction is a dependent word that helps to show the relationship between the ideas in two independent clauses.

Common Subordinating Conjunctions			
after	as though	if only	until
although	because	now that	what(ever)
as	before	provided (that)	when(ever)
as if	even if	since	where(ever)
as long as	even though	so that	whether
as much as	how	though	which(ever)
as soon as	if	unless	while

Try using subordinating conjunctions in different places in a sentence to emphasize different ideas. If you introduce the first independent clause with a subordinating conjunction, add a comma before the second independent clause. Do not use a comma if you introduce the second independent clause with a subordinating conjunction.

> **Revised**: *Although* Sara likes to exercise before going to work, Enrique prefers to exercise after work.

> **Revised:** Sara likes to exercise before going to work *even though* Enrique prefers to exercise after work.

 Activity   Editing for Run-On and Comma-Spliced Sentences

Revise the following sentences to eliminate run-ons and comma splices. Try different methods to see which one works the best to correct each run-on or comma splice.

1. Watching movies is a popular way for people to unwind movies provide an escape from reality.

2. Some people prefer action adventure movies, others prefer comedies.

3. Action adventure movies are exciting they keep the audience riveted to their seats.

4. Good comedies are hilarious, they can keep the audience laughing from start to finish.

5. It's fun to watch movies in the theater watching them at home can be entertaining too.

Mixed Constructions

If the first part (subject) of a sentence doesn't fit logically with the second part (predicate), the sentence has a *mixed construction*. Using mixed constructions can be confusing for the readers.

Mixed: The best career field for me is becoming a nurse.

Revised: Nursing is the best career field for me.

Discussion: A nurse isn't a career field, but nursing is.

Mixed: The reason I want be a Web designer is because I am good with computers.

Revised: I want to become a Web designer because I am good with computers.

Discussion: Avoid using the construction *the reason...is because.*

Mixed: The fact that I got a new computer is why I'm so excited.

Revised: I'm so excited because I got a new computer.

Discussion: Avoid using the construction *the fact...is why.*

Mixed: The cuisine was prepared by chefs ranging from seafood pasta to chicken burritos.

Revised: The chefs prepared cuisine ranging from seafood pasta to chicken burritos.

Discussion: Did the seafood and chicken really prepare the cuisine?

 Activity   **Editing for Mixed Constructions**

Revise the following sentences to eliminate mixed constructions.

1. The best car I could ever hope for is driving a BMW.

2. The reason I like BMWs is because they are luxurious cars.

3. The fact that my friend Kenny loves his BMW is why I am so interested in getting one.

4. In addition to being fun to drive, I like how fast BMWs are fast.

5. The reason I want to get a used BMW is because new ones are too expensive.

Faulty Parallelism

Ideas in a sentence that have the same level of importance are parallel and, therefore, should be expressed in parallel grammatical constructions. Presenting sentence elements, such as nouns, verbs, and phrases, in parallel terms helps to make sentences flow more smoothly.

Parallel nouns: Laura bought a <u>hotdog</u>, a <u>pretzel</u>, and a <u>soft drink</u> at the concession stand.

Parallel verbs: On the weekends I enjoy <u>bicycling</u>, <u>hiking</u>, and <u>fishing</u>.

Parallel phrases: He drove the car <u>around the tree</u>, <u>across the sidewalk</u>, and <u>into the lake</u>.

Not parallel: Whether she is with a patient, drawing blood, or administering a shot, Kathie is always a professional.

Revised: Whether she is helping a patient, drawing blood, or administering a shot, Kathie is always a professional.

Not parallel: Marcello wrote his résumé, fills out an application, and applied for a job.

Revised: Marcello wrote his résumé, filled out an application, and applied for a job.

 ## *Activity*   Editing for Faulty Parallelism

Revise the following sentences to give them parallel structure.

1. The local hospital offers employees good salaries, flexible hours, and they offer meals that are inexpensive.

2. Employees who work on the top floor go down a hallway, through a lobby, and then they ride an elevator up to get to their station.

3. Employees spend much of their time helping patients, writing charts, and they also develop procedures.

4. Patients are very satisfied with the personnel, treatment, and they are also pleased with the facilities at the hospital.

5. The hospital is raising funds to update the cardiac and pediatric facilities, and it is also raising funds for updating the oncology facilities.

Active and Passive Voice

Many instructors prefer that you use the *active voice* when writing essays. When you write in the active voice, the subject performs the action in the sentence. When you write in the passive voice, the subject receives the action in the sentence.

Passive voice: The award <u>was won</u> by the best writer in the class.

Active voice: The best writer in the class <u>won</u> the award.

Discussion: Placing the subject up front adds emphasis to the subject of the sentence.

Writing in the active voice is more direct and less wordy. However, occasionally you may want to use the passive voice, especially if you do not want to blame someone for causing a problem or if you do not know who performed the action in the sentence.

Active voice: James <u>broke</u> the copy machine.

Passive voice: The copy machine <u>is broken</u>.

Discussion: Is it necessary for everyone to know who broke the machine? If not, the passive voice has a friendlier tone and is more appropriate.

Active voice: Someone <u>hired</u> Veronda immediately after her interview.

Passive voice: Veronda <u>was hired</u> immediately after her interview.

Discussion: If you do not know who hired Veronda, then using the passive voice is appropriate.

 Activity   **Revising for Active or Passive Voice**

Revise the following sentences by changing the passive sentences to the active voice and the active sentence to the passive voice.

1. The job fair was hosted by Star University.
2. The graduates were invited to attend the job fair by the career placement director.
3. Most of the graduates were recruited by well-known employers in the area.
4. Some of the recruits are being given signing bonuses by their new employers.
5. Unfortunately, Susan lost some of the completed job applications.

> B. Editing Words (Diction)

As you edit your documents, pay attention to your choice of words, also known as *diction*. You want to select words that create the most precise and accurate image in the minds of your readers. You also want to choose words that will not offend your readers. Using good diction will help you to communicate your message more clearly to your audience.

Denotation and Connotation

Denotation refers to the dictionary definition of a word; *connotation* refers to the meaning of a word including the attitudes and feelings we associate with the word. For example, a *break-in* and a *home invasion* have similar denotative meanings; however, the term *home invasion* has more negative connotations than a *break-in*. Similarly, while *residence* and *home* have similar definitions, *home* has warmer connotative feelings. Keep in mind that not all readers will have the same connotative meanings for words.

As a writer, you want to be sure to choose words that will suggest the right connotative meaning to your readers. This doesn't mean that emotionally charged words are inappropriate or ineffective. You just want to be sure that you evoke the desired emotions from your readers. For instance, the terms *childish* and *childlike* have similar denotations. However, saying someone is *childish* has more negative connotations than saying someone is *childlike*. If your goal is to illustrate how immature a particular adult is, then *childish* might be the correct term to use.

Activity   Interpreting Connotations

Explain the connotative differences for each set of words.

1. worker, grunt, employee
2. smart, brainy, intelligent
3. artificial, fake, counterfeit
4. educate, train, drill
5. sip, guzzle, slurp

Jargon and Slang

Jargon is the specialized vocabulary that people related to a particular career field, group, or interest use. *Slang* is similar to jargon, except that jargon tends to be formal, and slang tends to be informal and nonstandard. Professionals in the legal, medical, computer, and business fields use vocabulary that is specific to those areas. Likewise, athletes, musicians, surfers, and video gamers use terms that are specific to their interests.

Jargon and slang can be acceptable when writing for other members who share the vocabulary of the field. For example, a professional in the health care field may use medical jargon in an e-mail to a co-worker. As long as the writer and recipient of the message understand the terminology, then effective communication can take place.

However, if your audience might not understand the vocabulary of a particular field, then you are better off using terms that are more generic or standard. For instance, if you write a flyer for patients with instructions for practicing a stretching technique at home, then you'll need to explain the key terms or replace the jargon with more common terms.

Jargon: When Deveney bought a new PC, she nuked her old one.

Revised: When Deveney bought a new personal computer, she deleted her directories without saving her individual files.

Slang: The dude was totally barnwalling on the gnarly wave.

Revised: The surfer was exhibiting poor technique on the treacherous wave.

Activity   Revising for Jargon and Slang

Replace the italicized words with standard terminology.

1. I *totally blew off* my history assignment.
2. Henry *Christmas treed* his psychology test because he didn't bother to study.
3. The new math instructor is a *nut case*.
4. I need to *catch some Z's* before the *mega test* tomorrow.
5. The student who sits next to me in biology class is *da bomb*.

Clichés

A cliché is a worn out expression. While it may have once been original and fresh, by now it has been used so many times that it has lost its impact. Avoid using clichés because they make your writing sound dull and uninspired. Instead, take the time to find a more interesting way to express your ideas.

> **Clichéd:** Employees who *stab their co-workers in the back* rarely find success on the job.

> **Revised:** Employees who *betray their co-workers* rarely find success on the job.

Clichés to Avoid	
above and beyond the call of duty	green with envy
add insult to injury	hard as nails (or as a rock)
back stabber	in my wildest dreams
black as night	last but not least
bright-eyed and bushy-tailed	last straw
busy as a bee (or a beaver)	Life is like a box of chocolates.
cold as ice	like taking candy from a baby
come hell or high water	not the sharpest tool in the shed
cool as a cucumber	older than dirt (or the hills)
cream of the crop	on top of the world
cried like a baby	over the hill
crystal clear	skating on thin ice
Don't burn your bridges.	skeleton in the closet
dumber than a box of rocks	slower than molasses
easy as cake (or pie)	stick out like a sore thumb
dry as a bone	sweet as syrup (or honey)
few and far between	That's the way the cookie crumbles.
first and foremost	too little too late
free as a bird	tried and true

 Activity   **Editing for Clichés**

Write five complete sentences, each including a different cliché. Revise each sentence by replacing the cliché with fresh, original language. Keep the intended meaning of the cliché as you revise.

EXAMPLE
Clichéd: The executive was as *cool as a cucumber* when she delivered her presentation.
Revised: The executive was *calm and poised* when she delivered her presentation.
Note: Pairs or small groups of students may trade sentences to revise.

Biased Language

As you revise your writing, look for biased language that you may have inadvertently used. Biased language reflects an unfair assumption or prejudice about someone without cause. Be sensitive to gender, culture, and age as you choose your words. You don't want to stereotype people or be condescending toward them.

Gender Bias

One way to eliminate bias in your writing is to avoid words that unnecessarily refer to gender, also known as *sexist language*. Sometimes you can do this by making the subject of the sentence plural.

Sexist: A nurse should treat *her* patients with kindness and respect.

Revised: Nurses should treat their patients with kindness and respect.

Discussion: Men and women can be nurses. Unless you are referring to a particular nurse, leave the sentence gender neutral.

Sexist Language	Gender Neutral Language
chairman	chair/chairperson
chicks/girls	women
male nurse	nurse
fireman	firefighter
mankind	humankind/people
mailman	mail carrier
policeman/lady cop	police officer
stewardess/steward	flight attendant
waitress/waiter	server

Cultural Bias

Culturally biased language stereotypes people positively or negatively. Assuming someone has a particular attribute because of his or her culture is unfair and can be offensive. Consequently, you'll want to avoid using culturally stereotypical language in your writing.

Stereotypical: Natsumi is very hardworking because she is Japanese.

Revised: Natsumi is very hardworking.

Age Bias

Identifying someone's relative age can be useful, but you should do it in a dignified way. Avoid using language that is condescending toward people.

Condescending: The old geezer who lives next door invited me to watch the big game with him.

Revised: The elderly man who lives next door invited me to watch the big game with him.

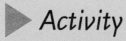 *Activity* **Revising Biased Language**

Identify and revise the biased language in the following sentences.

1. A member of the armed forces should be commended for serving his country.

2. The chick who was hired to replace my boss is intelligent.

3. Because she is Italian, Maria is a great cook.

4. Like most black people, Edward is a terrific basketball player.

5. The punk who lives across the street won an award for his science project.

6. The old hag would like a refund for the defective merchandise.

Wordiness

Including unnecessary words causes strain on the reader and hinders the communication process. Often you can tighten a wordy passage by substituting a single word for a long phrase or by taking out words that are repetitive or don't add meaning to a sentence. You want to be as clear and concise as possible.

Wordy: It seems to be true that much of humankind enjoys having pets, such as felines or canines, around to help alleviate feelings of emptiness or loneliness.

Concise: Many people enjoy having cats and dogs around to keep them company.

Wordy	Concise
at this point in time	now
arrive at a conclusion	conclude
at a later point in time	later
bear a resemblance to	resemble
purple in color	purple
due to the fact that	because
in many cases	often
in the near future	soon
in this day and age	now
on a weekly basis	weekly
persons of the male gender	men
provide aid for	help
small in size	small
without a doubt	certainly

 Activity Revising for Wordiness

Revise the following paragraph to make it more clear and concise. You may eliminate words and phrases and combine sentences as you revise.

There is little doubt that technology has changed the way that people can communicate with other people who are male or female, young or old. Because computers used to be so large in size that they took up an entire room, very few people had access to computers. Additionally, computers used to be extremely expensive; therefore, very few people could afford to own them. Due to the fact that computers have become smaller in size and less expensive, computers are readily available to a wide range of people. Desktop computers and laptop computers are quite common these days. People use them to make phone calls, send text messages, and e-mail other people with whom they want to communicate. Also, in today's day and age, many adults, teenagers, and children have smart phones that they carry around with them in their pockets, purses, backpacks, or briefcases. They can use these phones to call, text message, and e-mail their friends, family members, and co-workers. One can only imagine how computers will continue to affect communication in the near or distant future.

Pronouns

Pronoun/Antecedent Agreement

Pronouns (words that replace nouns) need to agree with their *antecedents* (the nouns they refer to) in number and gender.

Use singular pronouns to refer to singular nouns; use plural pronouns to refer to plural nouns.

Singular: The stethoscope was on the floor because *it* fell off the table.

Singular: Each of the patients received *his or her* lunch at noon.

Plural: The hazardous materials containers were removed because *they* were full.

Note: Some words, such as *everybody, anybody, each,* and *everyone,* seem plural, but they are really singular. Therefore, you will need to use a singular pronoun to refer back to those words.

Nouns and pronouns can be feminine, masculine, or neutral.

Feminine: Carmen was thrilled because *she* got an extra shift at the hospital.

Masculine: John was happy because *he* passed the RN exam.

Neutral: The team completed *its* project ahead of schedule.

Pronoun Reference

A pronoun needs to clearly refer back to a noun (*an antecedent*). Typically, a pronoun will refer back to a preceding noun that matches it in number and gender, if applicable. Sentences need to clearly identify who is doing what to whom.

Unclear: The patient received a call from his brother, but he wasn't happy about it.

Revised: The patient received a call from his brother, but the patient wasn't happy about it.

Discussion: The first sentence does not clarify who is not happy. Is it the patient or the brother?

Unclear: Lucinda had facial plastic surgery six weeks ago, and it already looks better.

Revised: Lucinda had facial plastic surgery six weeks ago, and her face already looks better.

Discussion: The first sentence implies that Lucinda's face looks better, but the pronoun actually refers back to the facial surgery. Saying that the facial plastic surgery looks better does not make sense.

Unclear: It is a nice facility.

Revised: The facility is nice.

Discussion: The word *it* does not refer to anything. Sometimes a sentence can start with the pronoun *it* if the word *it* refers to a noun in a previous sentence.

Example: The new outpatient clinic opened yesterday. It is a nice facility.

Pronoun Case

Pronouns can be subjects, objects, or possessives.

Pronoun Types			
	Subjective	**Objective**	**Possessive**
First person singular	I	me	rny, mine
First person plural	we	us	our, ours
Second person singular	you	you	your, yours
Second person plural	you	you	your, yours
Third person singular	he, she, it who	him, her, it whom	his, her, hers, its whose
Third person plural	they who	them whom	their, theirs whose

Subjective pronouns perform the action in a sentence.

> **Subjective pronoun:** *She* is going to see a nutritionist.

Objective pronouns receive the action in the sentence or are part of a prepositional phrase.

> **Objective pronoun:** The nutritionist gave *her* a diet plan.

> **Objective pronoun:** Between you and *me*, I am having trouble with my diet.

Possessive pronouns show ownership.

> **Possessive pronoun:** The diet plan from the nutritionist is *hers*.

Using the correct type can be tricky at times, especially when a sentence has a compound subject or object, makes a comparison, includes an appositive, or uses *who* or *whom*.

Compound Subjects and Objects

When the subject is compound, eliminate the double subject to figure out which pronoun to use.

> **Single subject:** *I* donated blood.

> **Compound subject:** My mother and *I* donated blood.

> **Single object:** Dr. D'Alessandro gave a list of exercises to *me*.

> **Compound object:** Dr. D'Alessandro gave a list of exercises to Todd and *me*.

Comparisons

Using the correct pronoun when making a comparison is essential to getting the correct message across to your audience. This can be difficult because sometimes words are implied rather than stated.

> **Comparison:** Kristin likes Denny more than *I*.

> **Discussion:** The sentence means that Kristin likes Denny more than I like Denny.

> **Comparison:** Kristin likes Denny more than *me*.

> **Discussion:** The sentence means that Kristin likes Denny more than she likes me.

Appositives An *appositive* is a word or phrase that renames a noun or pronoun. Eliminate the appositive to determine which pronoun to use.

> **Appositive:** We *Floridians* like not having to wear a coat in the winter.
>
> **Discussion:** *Floridians* renames *we*. *We* like not having to wear a coat in winter.

Who and Whom Use *who* as the subject of a sentence. Use *whom* as the object of a sentence.

> **Subjective pronoun:** Dennis wants to know *who* is going to the office party.
>
> **Objective pronoun:** For *whom* did Charlotte buy that gift?
>
> **Tip:** The word *whom* often appears in a prepositional phrase: to whom, for whom, with whom.

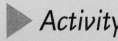

Activity   Problems with Pronouns

Choose the correct pronouns for the following sentences. Look for errors in pronoun/antecedent agreement, pronoun reference, and pronoun case.

1. Each of the participants received (his or her/their) certificate.
2. Patti and (I/me) will ride together to the show.
3. She gave the box of chocolates to Liza and (I/me).
4. (Us/we) college students need to stick together.
5. (Who/Whom) is going to donate money for the charity?

Verbs

Subject-Verb Agreement

Singular and Plural Subjects The subject and verb in a sentence need to match (agree). A singular subject needs to have a singular verb; a plural subject needs to have a plural verb.

> **Singular subject and verb:** The *band is* amazing.
>
> **Singular subject and verb:** The *sound* from the speakers *is shaking* the entire arena.
>
> **Discussion:** The subject in the sentence above is *sound*, so the verb is singular. The word *speakers* is in a prepositional phrase, so it does not affect subject-verb agreement.

> **Plural subject and verb:** The *speakers are* shaking the entire arena.
>
> **Discussion:** In the sentence above, *speakers* is the plural subject of the sentence, so the verb is plural.

Compound Subjects When two or more subjects are combined, the subject is compound. Compound subjects joined by the word *and* are usually plural, so the verb needs to be plural.

> **Compound subject:** *Ashley* and *Jenny are* hosting the event.
>
> **Discussion:** Ashley and Jenny are separate subjects, so the verb is plural.

Sometimes, however, the word *and* appears as part of a singular subject, so the verb needs to be singular.

Singular subject: *Rock and roll is* one of my favorite types of music.

Discussion: Rock and roll is one subject, so the verb is singular.

Compound subjects joined by *or*, *nor*, *either...or*, or *neither...nor* are singular. Therefore, the verb needs to be singular.

Singular subject: *Mark* or *Gregg is* going to advance to the next race.

Singular subject: *Briana is* not going to give up, nor *is Natalie*.

Singular subject: Either *Ellen* or *Margaret is* going to win the contest.

Singular subject: Neither *Edward* nor *Jorge has* bad sportsmanship.

Discussion: The sentences above refer to each person individually, not collectively, so the subjects and verbs are singular.

Collective Nouns Collective nouns have a singular form. However, the verbs that go with them can be singular or plural depending on how writers use them. Below are some examples of collective nouns.

Collective Nouns		
audience	**faculty**	**majority**
band	family	pack
class	group	swarm
choir	herd	team
committee	jury	tribe

When you use a collective noun, consistently treat it as singular or plural in a passage. If you are referring to the collective noun as a single unit, use a singular verb.

Singular collective noun: The *jury is* undecided.

Discussion: The jury, as a whole, is not ready to make a decision.

If you are referring to the collective noun as a group of individuals, use a plural verb.

Plural collective noun: The *faculty have* moved into their new offices.

Discussion: Here, the sentence refers to all of the members of the faculty as individuals with separate offices.

Sometimes you are better off clarifying the collective noun to avoid sounding awkward.

Awkward: The committee were excited about completing the proposal.

Revised: The committee members were excited about completing the proposal.

Indefinite Pronouns *Indefinite pronouns* refer to an unspecific number of subjects. Indefinite pronouns can be singular, plural, or varied (singular or plural depending on the context). You need to determine whether the indefinite pronoun is singular or plural in a particular sentence to make sure that the verb agrees with the subject.

Singular indefinite pronoun: *Everyone is* thrilled about the new policy.

Variable indefinite pronoun (singular): *Most* of the lasagna *is* very cheesy.

Variable indefinite pronoun (plural): *Most* of the employees *are* hardworking.

Plural indefinite pronoun: *Many* of the cupcakes *have* been eaten.

Indefinite Pronouns		
Singular	**Variable (Singular or Plural)**	**Plural**
anybody	all	both
anyone	any	few
anything	more	many
each	most	others
either	none	several
everybody	some	
everything		
neither		
nobody		
no one		
nothing		
somebody		
someone		
something		

Inverted Subject and Verb Determining subject-verb agreement can be tricky if the verb is inverted (comes before the subject). Make sure that the verb agrees with the subject of the sentence, rather than another word that is closer to the verb.

Inverted subject and verb: Sitting in the courtroom *were two suspects.*

Discussion: The subject (*two suspects*) is plural, so the verb (*were*) needs to be plural as well.

Separated Subject and Verb

Separated subject and verb: The *lawyers*, waiting for the judge to arrive, *are* exhausted from the lengthy trial.

Discussion: The plural subject (*lawyers*), needs a plural verb (*are*).

▶ *Activity* **Subject-Verb Agreement**

Identify the subject of each sentence. Choose the verb that agrees with the subject.

1. The music coming from the instruments (is/are) melodic.
2. Lori and Megan (was/were) hoping to attend the concert.
3. Frank, who is one of the guitar players, (is/are) the lead singer.
4. Waiting patiently backstage (is/are) Vicki and Jill.
5. Everyone attending the concert tonight (is/are) going to get a free CD.

Regular Verbs

With regular verbs, you can simply add –d or –ed to the infinitive (base) form of the verb to change the tense. See the examples below.

Regular Verbs		
Infinitive	**Past Tense**	**Past Participle**
arrive	arrived	arrived
earn	earned	earned
graduate	graduated	graduated
receive	received	received
walk	walked	walked

Irregular Verbs

Many verbs in the English language are irregular. The chart includes some of the most common irregular verbs.

Irregular Verbs		
Infinitive	**Past Tense**	**Past Participle**
arise	arose	arisen
be	was, were	been
become	became	become
begin	began	begun
bind	bound	bound
bite	bit	bitten
buy	bought	bought
catch	caught	caught
choose	chose	chosen
come	came	come
dig	dug	dug
drink	drank	drunk
drive	drove	driven
eat	ate	eaten
forbid	forbade	forbidden
freeze	froze	frozen
get	got	gotten
give	gave	given
go	went	gone
grind	ground	ground
grow	grew	grown
have	had	had
hide	hid	hidden
hold	held	held
lay (to put or place)	laid	laid
lay (to recline)	lay	lain
mistake	mistook	mistaken

—continued

pay	paid	paid
proofread	proofread	proofread
ride	rode	ridden
ring	rang	rung
rise	rose	risen
sing	sang	sung
see	saw	seen
seek	sought	sought
set	set	set
speak	spoke	spoken
swear	swore	sworn
think	thought	thought
throw	threw	thrown
wring	wrung	wrung
write	wrote	written

Adjectives and Adverbs

Adjectives and Adverbs

Adjectives and *adverbs* are modifiers, words that describe or *modify* other words. Adjectives are words that modify nouns or pronouns.

> **Adjective:** Scott is *intelligent*.
>
> **Discussion:** The adjective *intelligent* modifies the noun *Scott*.

> **Adjective:** She is *pretty*.
>
> **Discussion:** The adjective *pretty* modifies the pronoun *she*.

Adverbs are words that modify adjectives, verbs, and other adverbs. Adjectives often end in *–ly* and tell *how*.

> **Adverb:** The chili is *especially* good tonight.
>
> **Discussion:** The adverb *especially* modifies the adjective *good*.

> **Adverb:** The chef worked *diligently* on the new recipe.
>
> **Discussion:** The adverb *diligently* modifies the verb *worked*.

> **Adverb:** Julie smiled *very* sweetly.
>
> **Discussion:** The adverb *very* modifies the adverb *sweetly*.

The following adjectives and adverbs often cause problems for writers: good/well; bad/badly; real/really. Remember, adverbs often tell *how*.

Good and Well

> **Adjective:** The sushi is *good*.
>
> **Adverb:** The chef prepared the sushi *well*.

> **Adjective:** Gina feels *good* about the exam.
>
> **Adverb:** Gina performed *well* on the exam.

Bad and Badly

Adjective: The bananas have gone *bad*.
Adverb: Marge used the *badly* bruised bananas for banana bread.

Adjective: The *bad* dog went to obedience school.
Adverb: The dog behaved *badly* in class.

Real and Really

Adjective: These pearls are *real*.
Adverb: Beatrice worked *really* hard to make the necklace.

Adjective: The *real* problem is that we have too many choices.
Adverb: We are *really* confused about all of the choices.
Note: *Real = genuine*

Comparatives and Superlatives

Comparatives are adjectives and adverbs that compare two items. *Superlatives* are adjectives and adverbs that compare three or more items. Usually you can make comparative and superlative forms be adding –*er* and –*est*, *more* and *most*, or *less* and *least*.

Base adjective form: Toby is a *cute* puppy.
Comparative form: Toby is *cuter* than Roofus.
Superlative form: Toby is the *cutest* puppy in the litter.

Avoid doubling comparatives and superlatives.
Incorrect: Cody is the *most sweetest* boy I know.
Revised: Cody is the *sweetest* boy I know.

Comparatives and Superlatives		
Adjective or Adverb	**Comparative Form**	**Superlative Form**
big	bigger	biggest
pretty	prettier	prettiest
good	better	best
expensive	more expensive	most expensive
unusual	more unusual	most unusual
wonderful	more wonderful	most wonderful
desirable	less desirable	least desirable
fascinating	less fascinating	least fascinating
rapidly	less rapidly	least rapidly

Choose the correct word or words for each sentence.

1. Tamika works (good/well) with her group mates.
2. Marco wanted to fire the (bad/badly) employee.
3. William tried (real/really) hard to finish the report on time.
4. John is the (more/most) gifted of the two students.
5. Ava is the (better/more better/best/bestest) swimmer on the team.

Dangling and Misplaced Modifiers

Dangling Modifiers

As you write, you need to make sure that your modifiers clearly describe something specific that is stated in the sentence. Otherwise, you might create a *dangling modifier* and confuse your readers.

> **Dangling modifier:** While driving south on I-95, an iguana ran out in front of Pat's car.
>
> **Question:** Was an iguana really driving the car?
>
> **Revised:** While Pat was driving south on I-95, an iguana ran out in front of Pat's car.
>
> **Discussion:** The revised sentence clearly explains that Pat was driving the car.

> **Dangling modifier:** While talking on a cell phone, Pat's car swerved and missed the iguana.
>
> **Question:** Was the car talking on the cell phone?
>
> **Revised:** While talking on a cell phone, Pat swerved his car and missed the iguana.
>
> **Discussion:** The revised sentence clearly explains that Pat was talking on his cell phone.

Misplaced Modifiers

Misplaced modifiers occur when they appear too far away from the words they describe.

> **Misplaced modifier:** The reckless driver almost angered every other driver on the road.
>
> **Revised:** The reckless driver angered almost every other driver on the road.
>
> **Discussion:** The first sentence suggests that the driver may not have angered any other driver.

> **Misplaced modifier:** Tammy threw the Frisbee for the dog still dressed in her nightgown.
>
> **Revised:** Still dressed in her nightgown, Tammy threw the Frisbee for the dog.
>
> **Discussion:** The first sentence suggests that the dog was wearing a nightgown.

Revise the following sentences to eliminate dangling and misplaced modifiers.

1. The exquisite food was prepared by chefs ranging from lobster bisque to tuna tartar.
2. The jury took a lunch break still undecided about the guilt of suspect.
3. Worried about spreading germs, an antibacterial soap dispenser was installed near every entrance to the hospital.
4. Susan bought a cell phone for her daughter with broken buttons.
5. Getting ready for Sullivan's grand opening, the jewelry was displayed in glass cases.

> D. Editing Punctuation

Commas (,)

Some writers place commas wherever they might pause as they are speaking; however, that approach doesn't always work. Learning the following comma rules will help prevent you from confusing your readers.

Introductory Phrase or Clause

Use a comma to set off introductory material in a sentence.

Example: *After she got to the grocery store*, Diane realized that she had forgotten her purse.

Example: *According to her son*, Diane often forgets things.

Example: *For instance*, one time Diane forgot to bring her running shoes to a marathon in which she was competing.

Nonessential Phrase or Clause

If you can omit a phrase or clause in a sentence without changing the meaning, the phrase or clause is nonessential.

Nonessential: Juanita, *who is my friend's cousin*, loves listening to music.

Discussion: The main point of the sentence is that Juanita loves listening to music. The italicized clause doesn't change that.

Essential: The song *now playing on the radio* is one of Juanita's favorites.

Discussion: The reader wouldn't know which song is Juanita's favorite without the italicized phrase.

Interrupters

Use commas to set off words that interrupt the flow of a sentence. Interrupters can occur at the beginning, middle, or end of a sentence.

Example: *Of course*, Steve may want to choose his own pizza toppings.

Example: We are having tilapia, *one of my favorite foods*, for dinner tonight.

Example: The mayor had a snack attack on Saturday, *according to the local newspaper*.

Items in a Series

Use commas to separate three or more words, phrases, or clauses in a series.

Example: Jamal loaded many items into his backpack, such as *clothes, food,* and *water.*

Example: The dog chased the squirrel *around the tree, over the log,* and *into the house.*

Before Coordinating Conjunctions

Use a comma before a coordinating conjunction (*for, and, nor, but, or, yet, so*) that separates two independent clauses. (See FANBOYS on p. 397.)

Example: I was hoping to bring Aiden to the concert, *but* he wasn't feeling well.

Example: Amanda got elected president of the Student Government Association, *so* she is likely to develop some new leadership skills.

Conjunctive Adverbs

Use commas to set off conjunctive adverbs, such as *however, furthermore,* and *therefore.*

Example: Dave was, *however,* more experienced than James.

Example: *Therefore,* Dave got a promotion.

Adjectives

Use commas to separate adjectives if they modify (describe) the same noun and have equal emphasis.

Example: It is a *hot, sticky* day.

Example: The *cool, refreshing* ocean waves are the perfect remedy for the heat.

Tip: If you can replace the comma with the word *and,* then you need a comma. If not, leave the comma out.

Example: Brad was sitting in the *red lifeguard* booth.

Discussion: You would not say it was a *red and lifeguard* booth, so leave out the comma.

Dialogue

Use commas to separate dialogue from the speaker. You do not need commas to separate indirect quotations.

Example: Ann Marie exclaimed, "I see a shark in the water!"

Example: "It's just a dolphin," replied Brad, "so you have nothing to fear."

Example: Brad told Anne Marie that she had nothing to fear.

Direct Address

Use commas to set off a direct address.

Example: Children, please be quiet.

Example: Please, Harry, I need your advice.

Example: Here, kitty, I have a treat for you.

Titles or Degrees

Use commas to set off a title or degree that comes after a name.

Example: Curtis Counter, C.P.A., does my taxes each year.

Example: Neil Healer, M.D., is a great physician.

Example: One of my favorite teachers was Eric Illuminator, Ph.D.

Addresses and Dates

Use commas to separate items in addresses and dates.

Example: I enjoyed visiting the French Quarter in New Orleans, Louisiana.

Example: He was born on November 30, 2002.

 Activity **Correcting Comma Errors**

Add commas as needed to the following sentences.

1. After Sharon finished her salad she wanted a piece of dark chocolate.
2. Carlos who lives next door bought a new boat last week.
3. Barbara stocked her medicine cabinet with aspirin cough drops and cold medicine.
4. Teresa was looking for a bargain so she shopped at a discount store.
5. Stewart is however a talented singer.
6. Geoff dreaded entering the damp musty cave.
7. Debbie shouted "You're the best friend ever!"
8. Ladies please be seated.
9. I have an appointment with Glen Martin D.D.S. to get my teeth whitened.
10. Lisa visited San Francisco California on August 25 2009.

Semicolons (;) and Colons (:)

Semicolons (;)

Independent Clauses Use a semicolon between two main clauses if the conjunction is left out and if the clauses are closely related in content and style.

Example: Sally likes vanilla caramel ice cream; Gale prefers chocolate ice cream.

Conjunctive Adverbs Use a semicolon before and a comma after a conjunctive adverb that joins two main clauses.

Example: Sally likes vanilla caramel ice cream; however, Gale prefers chocolate ice cream.

Common Conjunctive Adverbs		
accordingly	however	now
also	indeed	otherwise
anyway	instead	similarly
besides	likewise	still
certainly	meanwhile	subsequently
consequently	moreover	then
finally	namely	thereafter
further	nevertheless	therefore
furthermore	next	thus
hence	nonetheless	undoubtedly

Items in a Series with Commas Use semicolons to separate items in a series when commas are present within one or more of the items.

> **Example:** Some of the most exciting cities to visit are London, England; Paris, France; Rome, Italy; and Athens, Greece.

Colons (:)

List of Items Use a colon after a main clause (complete sentence) to introduce a list of items.

> **Correct:** When going on a Caribbean cruise, always pack the following items: a bathing suit, a bottle of suntan lotion, and a book to read.
>
> **Incorrect:** When going on a Caribbean cruise, always pack: a bathing suit, suntan lotion, and a book to read.
>
> **Correct:** When going on a Caribbean cruise, always pack a bathing suit, suntan lotion, and a book to read.
>
> **Discussion:** If what precedes the list is not a complete sentence, then a colon is not needed.

Explanation or Emphasis Use a colon after a main clause when what follows it explains or emphasizes the subject in the main clause.

> **Example:** Maggie is going to school for one reason: to get a better job.

Quotations Use a colon to introduce a quotation after a main clause.

> **Example:** Oscar Wilde, a Victorian playwright, had an interesting view of himself: "I am so clever that sometimes I don't understand a single word of what I am saying."

Salutations Use a colon to follow the salutation of a business letter or formal correspondence.

> **Example:** Dear Ms. Rivera:

▶ *Activity* **Editing for Colons and Semicolons**

Add colons and semicolons to the following sentences as necessary. Note, not every sentence needs a semicolon or colon added.

1. Fred is going hiking Julie is going shopping.
2. Tina wants to get a new job furthermore, she expects higher pay.
3. Pete and Barb have one expectation of vacation relaxation.
4. For the cookout, Rose is going to buy chips, potato salad, and soft drinks.
5. My father always gave me this advice "Never give up on your dreams."

Quotation Marks (" ") and (' ')

Double Quotation Marks

Exact Words Use a set of double quotation marks to enclose the exact words that someone spoke or wrote.

> **Example:** Malcolm X once stated, "Education is our passport to the future, for tomorrow belongs to the people who prepare for it today."

Titles of Short Published Works Use quotation marks to enclose the title of essays, articles, book chapters, poems, and short stories.

> **Example:** "Annabel Lee" is a powerful poem by Edgar Allan Poe.
> *Note:* Do not place quotation marks around your own title, unless it is a published work you are citing in a research-based essay.

Emphasis Use double quotation marks around a word or phrase that introduces a concept that might be unfamiliar to readers or when a word or phrase is used ironically, satirically, or as unfamiliar slang.

> **Example:** The word "textese" refers to the informal language favored by those who send text messages.

Single Quotation Marks

Use a set of single quotation marks to enclose a quote within a quote.

> **Example:** Mirna recalled, "I once heard an instructor say, 'A prepared student is a passing student.'"

> *Note:* The single quotation mark at the end of the quote within a quote goes inside of the double quotation marks.

 Activity **Editing for Quotation Marks**

Add quotation marks to the following sentences as needed.

1. Michael's mother once exclaimed, I brought you into this world, and I can take you out of it.
2. For an extra thirty dollars, explained the dental hygienist, you can have a flavored fluoride treatment.
3. In class we read a student essay called Adrenaline Rush.
4. People assign different meanings to the word love.
5. My friend said, I thought I had received a bad grade on my paper until my instructor exclaimed, Yours was the best in the class!

Ellipses (...)

Omission from a Quote

An *ellipsis* is a series of three dots (periods) used to show that something has been intentionally omitted from a quotation. An ellipsis may occur at the middle or end of a sentence, but not at the beginning. Be careful to not change the intended meaning of the original sentence or passage.

Original Sentence: The future graduates lined up at the ceremony, eagerly anticipating the walk across the stage, the handshake with the school president, and the roar of the crowd when the degrees are conferred.

Example: "The future graduates lined up at the ceremony, eagerly anticipating...the roar of the crowd when the degrees are conferred."

Example: "The future graduates lined up at the ceremony, eagerly anticipating the walk across the stage, the handshake with the school president, and the roar of the crowd...."

Note: Place a period after an ellipsis at the end of a sentence.

Incomplete Thought

Use an ellipsis to indicate an incomplete thought.

Example: This year we are working to pay off the car and the boat. Next year we hope to...well, we will worry about that later.

Apostrophes (')

Possessives

Use an apostrophe to show possession (ownership) for nouns and some indefinite pronouns. (See p. 410 for a list of indefinite pronouns.)

To show possession, add an apostrophe and an *-s* to singular nouns or indefinite pronouns that do not end in *-s*.

Example: The teddy *bear's* eyes are green.

Example: My *sister-in-law's* recipes are delicious.

Example: *Everyone's* paychecks have grown a little this year.

Example: Nicholas received an extra *week's* pay for his unused vacation.

To show possession, add an apostrophe and an *-s* to a singular noun that ends in *-s*.

Example: The *bus's* passengers are all looking out of the windows.

Example: *Carlos's* motorcycle is parked in the garage.

To show possession, add just an apostrophe (but no *-s*) to a plural noun that ends in *-s*.

Example: The *protesters'* signs are insulting to the spectators.

Note: Do not use an apostrophe with a possessive pronoun, such as *its*, *his*, *hers*, *whose*, or *theirs*.

Contractions

Use an apostrophe to indicate where letters are missing in a contraction.

Example: *I've* never seen a sunset that beautiful before.

Common Contractions	
are not	aren't
do not	don't
has not	hasn't
have not	haven't
he will	he'll
I will	I'll
is not	isn't
it is or it has	it's

she will	she'll
should not	shouldn't
that is or that has	that's
we are	we're
we have	we've
we will	we'll
who is or who has	who's
you are	you're

Missing Letters or Numbers

Use an apostrophe to indicate where numbers or letters are missing.

Example: Latrese graduated in the class of *'09*.

Example: The polite country boy said, *"Ma'am,* I am going *fishin'* today."

Note: Apostrophes can be used in a quote to reflect a speaker's dialect.

 Activity **Editing for Apostrophes**

Add or delete apostrophes as needed in the following sentences.

1. The kicker said to the reporter, "Ive been playin football my whole life."
2. The coaches hearts were racing as the football soared toward the goal post.
3. The quarterback couldnt believe he had thrown the pass so far.
4. The fans cheered when the team won it's final game of the season.
5. Bobby Bowden, the Florida State University coach, retired in 09.

Hyphens (-) and Dashes (—)

Hyphens (-)

Adjectives Use a *hyphen* to combine two or more words that serve as a single adjective preceding (but not following) a noun.

Example: Shakespeare is a *well-known* playwright.

Example: The playwright Shakespeare is *well known*.

Example: Simon loves *chocolate-covered* pretzels.

Example: Simon loves pretzels that are *chocolate covered*.

Note: Do not use a hyphen with *–ly* adverbs: quickly eaten dessert.

Compound Numbers Use a *hyphen* with compound numbers.

Example: Judy is *thirty-three* years old.

Example: The *two-year-old* boy was returned safely to his parents.

Example: Trent ate *three-fourths* of the pizza.

Prefixes Use hyphens with the following prefixes: *all-, ex-,* and *self-*.

Example: The spa treatment package is *all-inclusive*.

Example: He and his *ex-wife* get along remarkably well.

Example: The business owner was a real *self-starter*.

Dashes (—)

Create a *dash* with two hyphens. Use a dash to create emphasis; to illustrate a change in direction; or to replace parentheses, semicolons, colons, or commas. Use dashes sparingly, so they do not lose their intended effect of creating interest for your readers.

> **Example:** The storm is drawing near—where are the children?
>
> **Example:** Karen told me—much to my dismay—she is not going to attend Joey's recital.
>
> **Example:** I know why Salvatore did not show up to work today—although I wish I didn't.

 Activity **Editing for Hyphens and Dashes**

Add hyphens and dashes to the following sentences as needed.

1. My father in law is going to help us repair our stone covered walkway.
2. Kevin's exroommate is getting a well deserved letter in the mail.
3. The triplet six year olds each ate one third of their birthday cake.
4. Joy won the lottery how amazing!
5. Holly's landlord that rat has given her only two weeks to move out!

Parentheses ( ) and Brackets [ ]

Parentheses ( )

Use *parentheses* to set off a side comment you want to include in or after a sentence. The comment may be relevant to the main point but is not essential to the reader's understanding of the main point.

> **Example:** My favorite actor (who happens to be from my hometown) is starring in a Broadway play.
>
> **Example:** I'm going to see a Broadway play starring my favorite actor (who happens to be from my hometown).
>
> **Example:** My favorite actor is starring in a Broadway play. (He happens to be from my hometown.)

Note: If the parentheses include a complete sentence, the period goes inside the parentheses.

Use parentheses to set off numbers or letters in a list of items.

> **Example:** Follow these three rules if you are on fire: (1) stop moving, (2) drop to the floor, and (3) roll around to extinguish the flames.

Use parentheses for in-text citations in research papers that follow the guidelines of the Modern Language Association or the American Psychological Association.

> **MLA example:** "Eating dark chocolate makes us feel better" (Rich 65).
>
> **APA example:** "Eating dark chocolate makes us feel better" (Rich, 2011, p. 65).

Brackets [ ]

Use *brackets* to indicate that you have modified or added a letter, word, or group of words to a direct quote.

> **Original:** Eating dark chocolate makes us feel better.
>
> **MLA example:** According to Rich, "[Consuming] dark chocolate makes us feel better" (65).

APA example: According to Rich (2011), "[Consuming] dark chocolate makes us feel better" (p. 65).

Use the word *sic* enclosed in brackets immediate after an error in a direct quote. This lets your readers know you are aware of the error and that you quoted it exactly as it appeared in the original.

Example: According to Dr. Smock, "An elegant black dress is flatering [sic] on most women."

Discussion: The writer used *[sic]* to acknowledge that Dr. Smock misspelled the word *flattering*.

> E. Editing Mechanics

Capitalization

Titles
Capitalize the titles of articles, books, poems, plays, songs, brochures, and so on. Capitalize all main words, but not articles (*a*, *an*, *the*), short prepositions (*to*, *from*, *in*), or conjunctions (*and*, *but*, *or*). Always capitalize the first word of a title as well as the first word after a colon, even if it is an article, a preposition, or a conjunction.

Poem: "Because I Could Not Stop for Death"

Song: "If I Had a Million Dollars"

Book: *The Travel Book: A Journey Through Every Country in the World*

Names
Capitalize the names of specific people, characters, and animals:

Dr. Wigglesworth	Professor Davis	Reverend Calhoun
Judge Crawford	Aunt Mary	Grandpa Chuck
Batman	Snow White	Miss Piggy
Fido	Nellie	Fuzzball

Note: Do not capitalize words that are not part of a proper noun, such as the professor, the judge, and my mom.

Capitalize name brands.

Coca-Cola	Doritos	Godiva

Regions, Locations, Buildings, and Monuments
Capitalize specific regions, but not directions.

Mitch is from the Midwest.   Drive north on I-95.

Capitalize geographical locations, buildings, and monuments.

Austin, Texas	Paris, France	Ocala National Forrest
Pacific Ocean	Lake James	Jetty Park
World Trade Center	Eiffel Tower	Statue of Liberty

Seasons and Events
Capitalize events but not seasons.

The Spring Fling is next week.

My favorite season is summer.

Capitalize historical events, documents, and movements.

Civil War	Declaration of Independence	Renaissance

Language, Ethnic, and Religious References

Capitalize nationalities, languages, and ethnicities.

American	Spanish	Asian
Greek architecture	Hispanic culture	Japanese cuisine

Capitalize religions, religious books, religious followers, religious holidays, and words referring to God.

Christian	Jewish	Muslim
Methodists	Holy Bible	Torah
Easter	Yom Kippur	Buddha
Allah	Jehovah	the Trinity

Courses

Capitalize language courses and complete course names.

French	English 1101	General Biology II

Note: Do not capitalize general subjects: psychology, math, and biology.

 Activity **Editing for Capitalization**

Edit the following sentences for capitalization errors.

1. Terrence loves to visit mount dora every Spring.

2. My sister-in-law amy is looking forward to taking psychology II and calculus.

3. My friend amalie, who is from france, loves to eat yoplait yogurt.

4. The famous dr. oz wrote a book called *you: the owner's manual: an insider's guide to the body that will make you healthier and younger.*

5. One of professor tiffany's favorite songs is called "single ladies."

Abbreviations

Abbreviations in School Papers

Do not use these abbreviations in your papers for school:

&	b/c	co.	dept.	Eng.
Fri.	gov't.	Prof.	thru	w/o

Titles and Degrees

Abbreviate titles that appear before names:

Dr. Goldstein	Ms. Gibson	St. Thomas

Abbreviate titles and degrees that appear after names:

Frieda Walker, Ph.D.	Charles Morse, Jr.	Ed Ellis, D.D.S.

Acronyms

Generally, you should spell out a name before using an abbreviation:

Example: The Children's Home Society (CHS) is a good organization.

Some acronyms are nearly always abbreviated:

Example: The FBI is working with NASA and IBM.

Times and Dates

For exact times, use uppercase or lowercase abbreviations for A.M. (a.m.) and P.M. (p.m.).

Example: The space shuttle is scheduled to launch at 6:51 A.M.

Example: The fundraiser lasts from 7:30 p.m. until 1:00 a.m.

Do not abbreviate days or months in formal writing.

Example: You are invited to attend the Rose Gala on Saturday, August 20.

Place Names

Spell out names of places except in addresses.

Example: Fran visited Rochester, New York, during her vacation.

Example: Mail the payment to 555 Generic Street, Rochester, NY 55555.

Numbers

Spell out numbers for the following situations:

- One or two-word numbers, such as four, thirty-three, six million.
- Numbers beginning a sentence.

  Example: *Two hundred and ten* people participated in the self-defense workshop.

  Example: The self-defense workshop drew *210* participants.

- Numbers forming compound words.

  Example: The *seven-year-old* boy gave *one-half* of his toys to charity.

- Times using *O'clock.*

  Example: I was up writing a paper until *three o'clock* this morning.

Use numerals for these situations.

- Exact times and dates.

  Example: The show starts at 6:30 p.m.

  Example: Graduation will take place on May 23, 2015.

- Numbers with three or more words.

  Example: Jean Luc and Sarah invited 425 guests to their wedding.

  Example: The meeting room will hold 1,250 attendees.

- Addresses.

  Example: Marsden lives at 444 Apple Lane.

- Money and percentages.

  Example: The bake sale raised $695.50.

  Example: According to the survey, 78% of the students voted for the new policy.

- Numbers in a series or list.

  Example: Kara still needs to work on problems 2, 5, 7, and 11.

Activity Editing for Abbreviations and Numbers

Edit the following sentences for errors with abbreviations and numbers.

1. The science dept. just received funding for three hundred and twenty new microscopes.
2. Doctor Snow is hosting a seminar on Thurs., Feb. tenth at 2 o'clock.
3. Sandra is looking forward to her trip to San Francisco, CA on May fifth.
4. Prof. Smith, Doctor of Philosophy is hosting a field trip for 20 students.
5. Jared & Josie are going to the visit the gov't building in Tallahassee, FL at three p.m.

Italics and <u>Underlining</u>

Italics and underlining are equivalent. Use italics when typing on a computer, and use underlining when handwriting.

Emphasis

Italicize or underline words you want to emphasize in your writing.

> **Example:** The word *hate* can be so destructive.

> *Note:* You may use quotation marks for this as well. Be consistent with how you emphasize words in a particular document.

Titles of Longer Works

Italicize or underline titles of books, plays, newspapers, magazines, works of art, CDs, movies, television shows, and Web sites.

> **Example:** I read a book called *The History of Art* that featured Van Gogh's painting *Starry Night*.

Foreign Words

Italicize or underline foreign words that have not become common in the English language.

> **Example:** When Paul spilled his cup of coffee, he said, "*C'est la vie.*"

> **Example:** Marcella is going to eat a burrito with salsa for lunch.

 Activity Editing for Italics and Underlining

Identify words in the following sentences that need to be italicized or underlined.

1. The show American Idol has attracted a lot of attention during the last several years.
2. The word plagiarism is one that scares many novice writers.
3. Brett graduated magna cum laude.
4. I'm hoping to see the Mona Lisa when I'm in France.
5. I read an article about a serial killer in USA Today.

> F. Editing Spelling

Commonly Misspelled Words

While the spell-checker on your computer may help you to identify some misspelled words, you still need to proofread all of your papers before submitting them. Otherwise, you may end up with some spelling errors that could cause your readers to think you are careless.

You may remember a couple of spelling rules from your younger days, such as "use *-i* before *-e* except after *-c*" or "drop the *-y* and add *-ies*." You'll find an extensive list of spelling rules at The Purdue Online Writing Lab: **http://owl. english/purdue.edu/owl.**

Knowing the rules can be useful; however, you have probably already realized that the rules have many exceptions. If you're not sure how to spell a word, look it up in a dictionary or go to **http://dictionary.reference.com.**

You also can study a list of commonly misspelled words, such as the following. Many of the words are irregular or are spelled differently than they sound. Watch out for these words as you edit your writing.

Commonly Misspelled Words			
absence	conscience	harass	occasionally
acceptable	conscientious	height	occurrence
accessible	conscious	hierarchy	pastime
accidentally	consensus	humorous	prejudice
accommodate	convenience	hypocrisy	privilege
accuracy	criticism	ignorance	probably
achievement	criticize	immediately	questionnaire
acquaintance	deceive	incredible	receive
acquire	definitely	intelligence	recommend
a lot	disappoint	interest	reference
amateur	disastrous	jewelry	relevant
analyze	discipline	judgment	restaurant
apparent	efficient	knowledge	rhyme
appearance	eligible	leisure	rhythm
argument	embarrass	license	ridiculous
believe	environment	loneliness	schedule
boundary	exaggerate	maintenance	separate
business	exhilarate	maneuver	sergeant
calendar	existence	medieval	successful
category	experience	memento	tendency
cemetery	familiar	millennium	thorough
changeable	fascinate	miniature	through
collectible	foreign	minuscule	truly
characteristic	gauge	mischievous	vacuum
column	grammar	misspell	villain
committed	grateful	necessary	weird
conceive	guarantee	noticeable	writing

▶ Activity   Editing for Misspelled Words

Identify and revise the misspelled words in the following sentences. Each sentence has two misspelled words.

1. Writers should proofread for grammer and mispelled words.
2. Dave is eligable for a garanteed student loan.
3. Hayley is an amature guitarist who plays with great acuracy.
4. The employee tried to acomodate the customer who had alot of complaints.
5. Raul was greatful for the raise he recieved.

Homonyms

Homonyms are words that sound the same but are spelled differently. Watch out for these homonyms as you edit your writing. If you use the wrong word, you will likely confuse your readers.

Homonyms	Examples
accept—to receive or approve **except**—to take out or exclude	Many local hospitals *accept* interns. Everyone has voted *except* Trisha.
affect—to change or influence **effect**—the result or outcome	His decision *affected* everyone in his family. The counselor had a positive *effect* on her.
allowed—permitted **aloud**—spoken	Monica *allowed* Shannon to borrow her car. Troy read the example *aloud* for the class.
allusion—an indirect reference to **illusion**—a fantasy or deceptive appearance	The rap song makes an *allusion* to a Greek play. Jim created the *illusion* of always studying when he was really reading a magazine.
already—by now **all ready**—fully prepared	Minh has *already* studied for the test. Jessica was *all ready* to give the presentation.
all together—all in one place or time **altogether**—completely	Let's go for a ride *all together*. Susan is *altogether* responsible for her bills.
appraise—to determine the value **apprise**—to tell or notify	The ring *appraised* for $2000. She was *apprised* of the status of her request.
cite—to refer to, to give an example **sight**—vision, something to see **site**—a location	John *cited* Benjamin Franklin in his paper. The Statue of Liberty is an amazing *sight*. The *site* for the new student lounge is perfect.
coarse—rough **course**—path of travel	The exterior paint was very *coarse*. He is on the right *course* to success.
complement—to complete, a counterpart **compliment**—to praise	The curtains *complement* the window. Anna received a *compliment* on her new outfit.
confidant—someone to confide in **confident**—self-assured	Jordan was Edward's best friend and *confidant*. Sue was *confident* she would pass the exam.
conscience—moral right or wrong **conscious**—aware of one's feelings	Bob followed his *conscience* and told the truth. Susan was not *conscious* of her depression.
discreet—confidential or tactful **discrete**—distinct or separate	They were *discreet* about their relationship. They kept their finances *discrete*.

elicit—to bring out **illicit**—illegal	The essay *elicits* feelings of compassion. He was arrested for selling *illicit* drugs.
every day—happening daily **everyday**—ordinary	I ride my scooter to class *every day*. Riding my scooter to class is an *everyday* event.
fair—impartial, evenhanded **fare**—payment	The instructor's policies are *fair*. Trent paid his cab *fare*.
faze—to stun **phase**—part of a sequence	Vicki was *fazed* by the news of her award. Jill started a new *phase* in her life.
its—possessive of *it* **it's**—contraction of *it is*	The dog wagged *its* tail. *It's* time for the show to start.
lead—a heavy metal **led**—past tense of *to lead*	Sidney suffered from *lead* poisoning. The millionaire *led* a good life.
loose—not securely attached **lose**—to fail to win or keep	The door handle was *loose*. Shaquanda didn't want to *lose* her scholarship.
principal—head of school, main **principle**—a general rule or truth	The administration's *principal* goal is student success. You can't go wrong if you follow this *principle*.
stationary—not moving, fixed **stationery**—writing paper	Kevin rode a *stationary* bike in the winter. Tanisha loves to send letters on pretty *stationery*.
than—comparison **then**—at that time or after that	Francesca is taller *than* Maria. First we'll work, and *then* we'll play.
their—possessive form of *them*. **there**—in or at that place **they're**—contraction of *they are*	It is *their* decision to make. Please put the book over *there* on the shelf. I hope *they're* not late for the meeting.
to—toward **too**—excessively or also **two**—the number 2, a couple	I'm going *to* the library. Sasha is *too* hungry to think straight. Amy has *two* papers to write next week.
who's—contraction of *who is* **whose**—possessive of *who*	*Who's* attending the conference in Arizona? *Whose* presentation did you like best?
your—possessive of you **you're**—contraction of you are	*Your* positive attitude will take you far. *You're* likely to get a great job after graduation.

▶ ## Activity **Editing for Homonyms**

Identify and revise the incorrectly used homonyms in the following sentences.

1. Angelica blushed when her boyfriend paid her a complement.
2. Your not going to be able to attend the seminar next week.
3. Terry is more skilled at designing Web pages then Jake is.
4. Bruce was confidant that he would get a promotion soon.
5. Misty was careful to sight her sources in her paper.

A

Amorphous Having no particular shape.   246

Anomic Disoriented or alienated.   120

B

Bulwark Protection.   245

Batrachian Amphibian or frog-like.   124

C

Causal analysis Analyzing reasons and results.   195

Cavalier Arrogant; disdainful.   175

Cellular regeneration The body's ability to restore or replace cells.   202

Charlie Watts An English drummer for the rock group The Rolling Stones.   206

Chimerical Fanciful or mythical.   120

Critical thinking Interpreting ideas and reflecting on them.   63

E

Essay A group of paragraphs related to a particular subject.   53

F

Forecast Helps the reader predict the main points.   55

Freewrite Unstructured writing for a set amount of time.   17

H

Harbingered Made known.   128

Helgramite An insect larva used as bait.   98

I

In flagrante Caught in the act of being unfaithful.   119

K

Keenly Sharply.   94

Keith Moon An English drummer for the rock group The Who.   206

L

Languidly Lacking in spirit or vitality.   100

Linchpin Something that holds the parts of a structure together.   246

Linguists People who study languages.   95

Logical fallacies Occur when someone draws a conclusion not based on sound reasoning.   74

M

Maladies Diseases of the body.   201

Mysogynistic Dislike or mistrust of women.   129

N

Nominalize To convert a word or phrase to another part of speech.   94

P

Petulant Insolent or rude in speech or behavior.   99

Plagiarism The use of another's words or ideas without giving appropriate credit.   328

Pond's extract A cream used to heal small cuts and abrasions.   97

Processed foods Foods that have been altered from their natural states.   201

Promulgation Publication or dissemination.   120

S

Sarsaparilla A soft drink flavored with the root of a particular plant.   99

Secular Not sacred or religious.   246

Sui generis Unique.   179

T

Thesis Identifies the main idea of an essay.   55

Transcribe To make a written copy of spoken words.   94

U

Unity Ensures every idea relates to the overall thesis of the essay.   55

V

Visual literacy The ability to read and interpret a variety of visual texts.   68

Vituperative Harsh and disapproving.   180

TEXT CREDITS

CHAPTER 1 Pages 10–11: J. Weber and P. Christopher, "Be Our Guest. Please," *Business Week*, March 25, 2009, p. 11. Reprinted with permission of *Business Week*.

CHAPTER 3 Pages 56–58: "The Art of Eating Spaghetti" from *Growing Up* by Russell Baker. Copyright © 1982 by Russell Baker. Reprinted by permission of Don Congdon Associates, Inc.

CHAPTER 4 Pages 66-67: "Animating a Blockbuster: Inside Pixar's Creative Magic," by Jonah Lehrer, *Wired*, June 2010. Reprinted with permission of Jonah Lehrer; **p. 69:** "Fish Pedicures: Carp Rid Human Feet of Scaly Skin," Associated Press, July 21, 2008. Reprinted with permission of The YGS Group; **p. 70:** From *Bloomberg Businessweek*, February 1 and 8, 2010, p. 9. Reprinted with permission of *Bloomberg Businessweek*; **p. 73:** http://www.news.nationalgeographic.com/news/2008/09/photogalleries/animal-photos-week10/index.html.

CHAPTER 5 Pages 86-88: From http://www2.massgeneral.org/pcs/CCPD/Clinical_Recognition_Program/Narrative_Suzann_OT.pdf. Reprinted with permission of Suzanne Curley; **pp. 89-90:** "Sample Narrative of a Violent Domestic Incident Policy Report" by Reinaldo Inizarry Sr., PhD, http://searchwarp.com/swa220385.html; **pp. 91-93:** From Screen Crave: http://screencrave.com/2010-03-04/interview-johnny-depp-for-alice-in-wonderland; **pp. 94-96:** "Mother Tongue," by Amy Tan. Copyright © 1989. First appeared in *Threepenny Review*. Reprinted by permission of the author and the Sandra Dijkstra Literary Agency; **pp. 97-100:** "Once More to the Lake" from *One Man's Meat*, text copyright © 1941 by E.B. White. Copyright renewed. Reprinted by permission of Tilbury House, Publishers, Gardiner, ME; **pp. 101-102:** From *I Know Why the Caged Bird Sings* by Maya Angelou, Copyright © 1968 and renewed 1997 by Maya Angelou. Used by permission of Random House, Inc.; **p. 103:** "Mother to Son," from *The Collected Poems of Langston Hughes* by Langston Hughes, edited by Arnold Rampersad with David Roessel, Associate Editor. Copyright © 1994 by the Estate of Langston Hughes. Used by permission of Alfred A. Knopf, a division of Random House, Inc.

CHAPTER 6 Pages 119-120: Neal Gabler, "How Urban Myths Reveal Society's Fears," *Los Angeles Times*, November 12, 1995. Reprinted with permission of Neal Gabler; **pp. 121-123:** Bill Wine, "Rudeness at the Movies," 1989. Reprinted with permission of Bill Wine; **pp. 124-127:** Reprinted with permission. Copyright © Stephen King. All rights reserved. Originally appeared in *Playboy* (1982); **pp. 128-129:** Geoffrey Bennett, "Hip Hop: A Roadblock or Pathway to Black Empowerment?" The Black Collegian Online, 2001. Reprinted with permission of *The Black Collegian Magazine*; **p. 130:** "Coca-Cola and Coco Frio," from *City of Coughing and Dead Radiators* by Martin Espada. Copyright © 1993 by Martin Espada. Used by permission of W. W. Norton & Company, Inc.

CHAPTER 7 Pages 144-145: Reproduced with the permission of Demand Media, Inc., and its eHow service located at www.ehow.com; **pp. 147-148:** "Independence Day," Copyright © 2000 by Dave Barry, from *Dave Barry Is Not Taking This Sitting Down* by Dave Barry. Used by permission of Crown Publishers, a division of Random House, Inc.; **pp.149-150:** E. Barry Kavasch, "Dias de los Muertos," in E. B. Kavasch's *Enduring Harvests: Native American Foods and Festivals for Every Season*, The Globe Pequot Press, pp. 64–68. Reprinted with permission of the author; **p. 152:** "Happy Unbirthday" from *Mutant Message Down Under*, by Marlo Morgan, pp. 218–21. Copyright © 1991, 1994 by Marlo Morgan. Reprinted by permission of HarperCollins Publishers; **pp. 153-154:** From *When I was Puerto Rican* by Esmeralda Santiago. Copyright © 1993 Esmeralda Santiago. Reprinted by permission of Da Capo Press, a member of the Perseus Books Group; **p. 155:** Lyrics from Keith Bryant, *Ridin' with the Legends*, CD 2004, Lofton Creek label. Reprinted with permission of Lofton Creek Records; **pp. 161-162:** "Skill Drill 2-6" from *Emergency Medical Responder: First Responder in Action* by Barbara Aehlert, 2011, p. 66. Reproduced with permission of The McGraw-Hill Companies.

CHAPTER 8 Pages 174-175: Copyright © 2001 by Merrill Markoe. First appeared in *ON: Time Digital Online Magazine*. Reprinted by permission of Melanie Jackson Agency, LLC; **pp. 176-178:** From *Me Talk Pretty One Day* by David Sedaris. Copyright © 2000 by David Sedaris. By permission of Little, Brown and Company and Don Congdon Associates, Inc.; **pp. 179-180:** Deborah Tannen, "Gender Gap in Cyberspace," *Newsweek*, May 16, 1994, pp. 52–53. Copyright Deborah Tannen. Reprinted by permission; **p. 181:** "Computers, Computers" by Marty Whiddon, *Writers & Recording Artist*, Released on Woodrich Record-

Continued on next page

ings Cassettes. Reprinted with permission of Marcus G. "Marty" Whiddon; **pp. 182-185:** "Harrison Bergeron," from *Welcome to the Monkey House* by Kurt Vonnegut Jr. Copyright © 1961 by Kurt Vonnegut Jr. Used by permission of Dell Publishing, a division of Random House, Inc.

CHAPTER 9   Pages 201-202: "Food: Your Body's Natural Healer," by Shirley Vanderbilt, *Body Sense*, Spring/Summer 2007, pp. 36–37. Reprinted with permission of Associated Bodywork & Massage Professionals; **pp. 203-205:** "The Globalization of Eating Disorders" by Susan Bordo, University of Kentucky. Reprinted with permission; **p. 206:** "Welcome to the United States of Ambien," by Rob Sheffield from *Rolling Stone*, June 11, 2009. © Rolling Stone LLC 2009. All Rights Reserved. Reprinted by Permission; **pp. 207-209:** D. Weber, "Finding Their Niche: Why Men Choose Nursing," *RN Magazine* 71, no. 2 (2008): pp. 34–39; **p. 210:** By William Carlos Williams, from *The Collected Poems: Volume I, 1909-1939*. Copyright © 1938 by New Directions Publishing Corp. Reprinted by permission of New Directions Publishing Corp. and Carcanet Press.

CHAPTER 10   Pages 230-232: Reprinted with permission from *Commercial Investment Real Estate, The Magazine of the CCIM Institute* 23, no. 1 (Jan/Feb 2004); **pp. 233-234:** From Leigh Goessl, *Helium*, www.helium.com/items/1731100, May 27, 2010. Reprinted with permission of Leigh Goessl; **pp. 234-235:** Al Rodricks, "The Benefits of Social Networking on YOUR Social Life" from ImagineWeMeet.com. Reprinted with permission; **pp. 236-238:** Deborah Tannen, "Sex, Lies and Conversation," *The Washington Post*, June 24, 1990, p. C3, Copyright Deborah Tannen. Reprinted by permission. This article is adapted from *You Just Don't Understand: Women and Men in Conversation* (New York: Ballantine, 1990). New paperback edition: New York: Quill, 2001; **pp. 239-240:** "Basic Instincts: A Breadwinner Rethinks Gender Roles," The New York Times, January 27, 2007. Reprinted with permission of PARS International; **pp. 241-242:** Jon Katz, "How Boys Become Men," *The Compact Reader*, originally appeared in *Glamour*, January 1993, p. 172; **pp. 243-244:** "The Androgynous Man," by Noel Perrin, 1984, in *Fresh Takes*, 2008, McGraw-Hill, pp. 307–9; **pp. 245-246:** From *Thinking Out Loud* by Anna Quindlen, Copyright © 1993 by Anna Quindlen. Used by permission of Random House, Inc.; **p. 247:** Reprinted with permission of Henry Rollins.

CHAPTER 11   Page 265: "Marks," from *The Five Stages of Grief* by Linda Pastan. Copyright © 1978 by Linda Pastan. Used by permission of W. W. Norton & Company, Inc.; **pp. 266-267:** From J. Mauk and J. Metz, *The Composition of Everyday Life*, 2nd ed., © 2007 Heinle/Arts & Sciences, a part of Cengage Learning, Inc. Reproduced by permission. www.cengage.com/permissions; **pp. 268-269:** Craig Outhier, "Potter Power," from June 3, 2004 issue of *Get Out Magazine*; **pp. 270-272:** V. Pomarède, *The Faces of the Mona Lisa*, Masterpiece Paintings Gallery. Red Hare Communications. Accessed June 26, 2008, from http://www.masterpiece-paintings-gallery.com/about-mona-lisa.htm; **pp. 273-274:** A. Powers, review of *Black Eyed Peas The E.N.D.*, http://latimesblogs.latimes.com/music_blog/2009/06/album-review-black-eyed-peas-the-end.htm. Reprinted with permission of *Los Angeles Times*; **p. 275:** Hal Shows, "Empire Burlesque," *Parasol: Poems 1977-2007*, Luniver Press, p. 53. Reprinted with permission of Hal Shows.

CHAPTER 12   Pages 292-294: Alex Koppelman, "MySpace or OurSpace?" Salon.com, June 8, 2006. This article first appeared in Salon.com, at http://www.Salon.com. An online version remains in the Salon Archives. Reprinted with permission; **p. 296:** Wilbert Rideau, "Why Prisons Don't Work" from *Time*, March 21, 1994. Copyright © 1994 by Wilbert Rideau. Reprinted with the permission of the author c/o The Permissions Company, www.permissionscompany.com; **pp. 297-298:** "It's All in Your Head," by Clive Thompson. First appeared in *Wired*. Copyright © 2010 Clive Thompson. Reprinted with permission; **p. 299:** S. Sundiata, 1995, "Blink Your Eyes," from *The Language of Life: A Festival of Poets* by Bill Moyers, 1995, Doubleday; **pp. 300-309:** Reprinted with permission of Skyhorse Publishing.

CHAPTER 14   Page 350: "Prosecutorial Preconditions to Plea Negotiations" by Andrew E. Talslitz, 2008, Criminal Justice, 23:3. © Copyright 1999 by the American Bar Association. Reprinted with permission. This information or any portion thereof may not be copied or disseminated in any form or by any means or stored in any electronic database or retrieval system without the express written consent of the American Bar Association.

COVER   Thank you to Georgia State University, Atlanta for the cover inspiration and content.

Continued on next page

PHOTO CREDITS, CONTINUED

© The McGraw-Hill Companies, Inc./Rick Brady, photographer; **p. 161 (bottom):** © The McGraw-Hill Companies, Inc./Rick Brady, photographer; **p. 162:** © The McGraw-Hill Companies, Inc./Rick Brady, photographer.

CHAPTER 8 Opener (upper, left): U.S. Air Force photo by Mr. Gerald Sonnenberg; **Opener (middle):** Royalty-Free/Corbis; **Opener (lower, left):** Ken Seet/Corbis; **p. 172:** Jacob Gube, October 14, 2009, Sixrevisions.com. Reprinted with permission.; **p. 174:** © Lars A. Niki; **p. 176:** © Comstock/PunchStock; **p. 179:** moodboard/Corbis; **p. 181:** Ryan McVay/Getty Images; **p. 182:** Ausloeser/Corbis; **p. 187:** Image courtesy of The Advertising Archives.

CHAPTER 9 Opener (upper, left): © Ingram Publishing/AGE Fotostock; **Opener (middle):** Duncan Smith/Getty Images; **Opener (lower, left):** Tetra Images/Corbis; **p. 198 (top):** Whisson/Jordan/Corbis; **p. 198 (bottom):** © Stockbyte/PunchStock; **p. 199:** Chris Hondros/Getty Images; **p. 201:** Nancy R. Cohen/Getty Images; **p. 203:** Duncan Smith/Getty Images; **p. 207:** © Digital Vision/PunchStock; **p. 210:** Stockbyte/PunchStock; **p. 213:** Image courtesy of The Advertising Archives; **p. 214 (top):** Photo: Vivan Zink/ © ABC/ Courtesy Everett Collection; **p. 214 (bottom):** Catherine Cabrol/Kipa/Corbis.

CHAPTER 10 Opener (upper, left): Monalyn Gracia/Corbis; **Opener (middle):** © Sean Justice/Corbis; **Opener (lower, left):** © BananaStock/PunchStock; **p. 223:** McGraw-Hill Companies, Inc./Gary He, photographer; **p. 225:** © Ryan McVay/Getty RF; **p. 232:** Image Source/Getty Images; **p. 234:** Ron Levine/Getty Images; **p. 236:** © Royalty-Free/Corbis; **p. 239:** Don Hammond/Design Pics/Corbis; **p. 241:** Laurence Mouton/Photoalto/PictureQuest; **p. 243:** Chase Swift/Corbis; **p. 245:** © Thinkstock; **p. 247:** Bozi/Corbis; **p. 248:** © JupiterImages/ImageSource; **p. 250 (upper, left):** Image courtesy of The Advertising Archives; **p. 250 (upper, right):** Image courtesy of The Advertising Archives; **p. 250 (lower, left):** Image courtesy of The Advertising Archives; **p. 250 (lower, right):** Image courtesy of The Advertising Archives; **p. 251:** Image courtesy of The Advertising Archives; **p. 252:** Steve Cole/Getty Images.

CHAPTER 11 Opener (upper, left): Lester Lefkowitz/Corbis; **Opener (middle):** © Buena Vista Pictures/Courtesy Everett Collection; **Opener (lower, left):** Lance Manion/Retna Ltd./Corbis; **p. 261:** Blend Images/Getty Images; **p. 262:** © Warner Bros/Courtesy Everett Collection; **p. 265:** Elaine A. Cardella-Tedesco/Getty Images; **p. 266:** © 20th Century Fox/ Courtesy Everett Collection; **p. 268:** © Warner Bros/Courtesy Everett Collection; **p. 270:** Gianni Dagli Orti/Corbis; **p. 273:** Getty Images; **p. 275:** John Springer Collection/Corbis; **p. 276:** © Walt Disney Pictures/Pixar Animation, courtesy Mary Evans/Everett Collection; **p. 278:** Image courtesy of The Advertising Archives; **p. 279:** The Starry Night by Vincent van Gogh.

CHAPTER 12 Opener (upper, left): Brand X Pictures; **Opener (middle):** Guy Cali/Corbis; **Opener (lower, left):** Rubberball Productions; **p. 287:** Tim Graham/Getty Images; **p. 288:** Comstock/JupiterImages; **p. 292:** Myspace.com; **p. 295:** Philip Gould/Corbis; **p. 297:** Royalty-Free/Corbis; **p. 299:** Brand X Pictures; **p. 300:** © Photodisc/Getty Images; **p. 311:** © Warner Bros/Courtesy Everett Collection; **p. 312:** © Mikael Karlsson.

CHAPTER 13 Opener (upper, left): BananaStock/JupiterImages; **Opener (middle):** moodboard/Corbis; **Opener (lower, left):** Tetra Images/Getty Images; **p. 320:** Jack Hollingsworth/Corbis; **p. 322:** BananaStock/JupiterImages; **p. 324:** Photodisc/PunchStock; **p. 326:** Blend Images/Getty Images; **p. 327:** Ryan McVay/Getty Images; **p. 329:** Library of Congress Prints and Photographs Division [LC-USZ62-5513]; **p. 330:** John A. Rizzo/Getty Images; **p. 332:** © Comstock/PunchStock; **p. 334:** Getty Images/Photodisc; **p. 336:** © Stockdisc/ Stockbyte/Getty RF.

PHOTO CREDITS, CONTINUED

CHAPTER 14   **Opener (upper, left):** © BananaStock/Alamy; **Opener (middle):** © Indexstock/Photolibrary; **Opener (lower, left):** © Stockdisc/PunchStock; **p. 340 (top):** Library of Congress, Prints and Photographs Division [LC-USZ62-7265]; **p. 340 (bottom):** © Brand X Pictures/PunchStock; **p. 341:** © Royalty-Free/Corbis; **p. 349:** The McGraw-Hill Companies, Inc./Ken Cavanagh photographer; **p. 350:** Dave Klug; **p. 362:** Science Photo Library RF/Getty Images; **p. 363:** © Goodshoot/PunchStock; **p. 364:** Vince Streano/Corbis; **p. 367:** The McGraw-Hill Companies, Inc./John Flournoy, photographer.

CHAPTER 15   **Opener (upper, left):** Lucas Jackson/Reuters/Corbis; **Opener (middle):** © Justin Sullivan/Getty Images; **Opener (lower, left):** Phil McCarten/Reuters/Corbis; **p. 383:** David P. Hall/Corbis; **p. 384:** © Brand X Pictures/PunchStock; **p. 385 (top):** Axel Koester/Corbis; **p. 385 (bottom):** © PunchStock/Image Source; **p. 386 (top):** Ingram Publishing/SuperStock; **p. 386 (bottom):** © PhotoSpin, Inc./Alamy; **p. 387:** © Comstock Images/Alamy; **p. 388:** Comstock Images/JupiterImages; **p. 389 (top):** PictureNet/Corbis; **p. 389 (bottom):** Digital Vision/Getty Images; **p. 391 (top):** image 100/Corbis; **p. 391 (bottom):** amana productions/Getty Images; **p. 392:** Eyewire/Getty Images.